# Sociological Dimensions of Platformization:

## Power, Culture, and Identity in the Digital Age

Nuriye Çelik
https://orcid.org/0000-0001-6368-1956
*Sinop University, Turkey*

Nadir Ateşoğlu
https://orcid.org/0000-0003-0561-3562
*Sinop University, Turkey*

Şerife Sena Güner
https://orcid.org/0000-0002-2886-0630
*Sinop University, Turkey*

IGI Global
Scientific Publishing
Publishing Tomorrow's Research Today

| | |
|---|---|
| Vice President of Editorial | Melissa Wagner |
| Director of Acquisitions | Mikaela Felty |
| Director of Book Development | Jocelynn Hessler |
| Production Manager | Mike Brehm |
| Cover Design | Jose Rosado |

Published in the United States of America by
IGI Global Scientific Publishing
701 East Chocolate Avenue
Hershey, PA, 17033, USA
Tel: 717-533-8845 | Fax: 717-533-7115
Website: https://www.igi-global.com E-mail: cust@igi-global.com



Library of Congress Cataloging-in-Publication Data

LCCN: 2025038344 (CIP Data Pending)
ISBN13: 9798337342672
Isbn13Softcover: 9798337342689
EISBN13: 9798337342696
British Cataloguing in Publication Data
A Cataloguing in Publication record for this book is available from the British Library.

# Editorial Advisory Board

# Table of Contents

# Detailed Table of Contents

This chapter explores the evolving landscape of online activism, digital resistance, and counter-platform practices through a critical synthesis of scholarly literature and illustrative case studies. It analyzes how individuals and groups leverage digital tools to challenge dominant power structures, amplify marginalized voices, and promote social change. The discussion examines strategies employed by activists in navigating censorship, surveillance, and platform manipulation, while highlighting tensions between corporate-controlled digital spaces and grassroots movements. Drawing from diverse global contexts, the chapter investigates how decentralized technologies, alternative media, and networked mobilization have reshaped collective action and political expression. The chapter provides methodological and conceptual insights into the transformative potential of counter-platform practices in sustaining democratic participation and fostering inclusive digital futures.



This chapter analyses the contested terrain of reproductive autonomy in tier-2 cities and rural India in the expanding web of honour-based cyber violence and digital patriarchy. It argues that the expansion of digital technologies has not merely opened up new domains of communication and mobility but amplified the machinery of patriarchal control. Drawing on case studies of Lucknow, Jaipur, and the surrounding rural contexts of Uttar Pradesh and Rajasthan, the analysis explains how online surveillance, reputational shaming, and cyber harassment expand the reach of honour codes into digital domains. Drawing on feminist legal theory, digital ethnography, and discourse analysis, the chapter dissects the ways in which digital infrastructures re-write existing hierarchies of gender, caste, and community. Lastly, it argues that ensuring reproductive autonomy not only needs legal and technological interventions but a critical re-imagination of digital spaces as spaces of emancipation and not as technologies of social discipline.

# Preface

## INTRODUCTION: THE SOCIOLOGY OF THE PLATFORMIZED SOCIETY

The digital age has introduced a new mode of social organization in which platforms operate not merely as communication channels but as infrastructures shaping identity, power, labor, culture, emotion, and governance. Platformization represents a structural shift that transforms social interaction, political participation, and cultural production while redefining visibility, subjectivity, and legitimacy in everyday life. Individuals today are not only acting on platforms; they are increasingly shaped by platform logics and algorithmic governance.

This book examines this transformation through a sociological lens, situating platforms at the intersection of power, culture, and identity. Drawing on critical digital sociology, platform studies, affect theory, and algorithmic governance scholarship, it brings together theoretical debates and empirical cases across diverse geographies.

## CONTEMPORARY CONTEXT & RESEARCH PROBLEM

The rise of data capitalism, algorithmic authority, surveillance cultures, platform labor, and emotional computing has positioned platforms as central actors in contemporary social life. This volume brings critical and interdisciplinary perspectives to these developments, emphasizing how platform logics rewrite class structures, shape affective life, mobilize political communities, and transform intimate relationships.

## TARGET AUDIENCE

This book is intended for:

- Scholars in sociology, media studies, and political science
- Researchers of digital culture, platform capitalism, and algorithmic systems
- Graduate students in social sciences
- Policymakers and institutions concerned with digital governance and ethics

## OVERVIEW OF CONTRIBUTIONS

The chapters explore platform stratification, digital activism, algorithmic power, cultural identity, AI-mediated emotions, and intimate digital relations, providing conceptual innovation and empirical richness.

### Chapter 1- Digital Caste Systems: An Introduction to Platform-Based Social Stratification in Turkey

This chapter conceptualizes platform-based inequality in Turkey through the lens of a "digital caste" system. It argues that platform algorithms, interface architectures, and engagement metrics produce rigid hierarchies of visibility, influence, and opportunity. Digital competence, cultural capital, and platform-native skills operate as new markers of status, generating stratified access to information, networks, and symbolic power. By situating platform logic within local social structures, the chapter advances a sociological account of digital stratification that transcends economic determinism and foregrounds emerging symbolic boundaries in online life.

### Chapter 2- The Role of Local Platforms and Non-Western Perspectives on Platformization

This chapter foregrounds non-Western trajectories of platformization, emphasizing the importance of local platforms and regional socio-cultural dynamics. It challenges Euro-American-centred platform studies by demonstrating how local infrastructures, political economies, and user cultures shape platform governance and participation. With a focus on alternative media ecosystems and regional digital publics, the chapter highlights how Global South contexts negotiate global digital capitalism, producing unique forms of agency, resistance, and hybridization. This perspective enriches platform studies by provincializing dominant narratives and bringing forward under-examined geographies and epistemologies.

## Chapter 3- Platformized Headlines: Algorithmic Power, Affective Culture, and Ideological Identity

This chapter analyzes how news headlines and political discourse circulate within platform ecosystems, where affective intensity and algorithmic optimization increasingly shape public attention. It explores the fusion of emotional engagement, content virality, and ideological signaling in digital news cultures. The author demonstrates how platforms incentivize sensationalism and polarization, thereby reinforcing identity-based alignments and undermining deliberative democratic norms. The chapter thus reveals the affective and algorithmic infrastructures underpinning contemporary political communication and ideological boundary-making.

## Chapter 4- Rethinking Social Science Epistemological Debate in the AI Era: Adaptive Epistemology as a New Paradigm

This chapter revisits foundational epistemological debates in the social sciences in light of AI-driven knowledge production. It argues for an "adaptive epistemology" that responds to algorithmic decision-making, machine-generated inference, and data-driven forms of social ordering. The author contends that traditional dichotomies between qualitative and quantitative inquiry are insufficient for platformized societies, where AI systems not only analyze but also shape social behavior. The chapter proposes a reflexive, interdisciplinary epistemic framework that maintains critical distance from technological determinism while engaging productively with computational knowledge systems.

## Chapter 5- Social Media as a Field of Power, Habitus, Capital, and Intergenerational Digital Practices

This chapter applies Bourdieu's field theory to contemporary social media environments, demonstrating how digital platforms reproduce and recalibrate forms of capital—economic, cultural, social, and symbolic. It explores how users develop platform-specific habitus shaped by generational differences in media literacy, technological fluency, and cultural participation. Through empirical cases, the chapter illustrates how intergenerational disparities manifest in digital identity performance, content production, and network building. Ultimately, the analysis reveals that social media is a dynamic field wherein power relations are negotiated, inherited, and transformed across cohorts.

## Chapter 6 - The Impact of Social Media Platforms on Violent Behavior

This chapter investigates the relationship between platform architecture and violent behavior, focusing on the psychological, social, and algorithmic mechanisms that normalize aggression online. It argues that algorithmic amplification, anonymity affordances, and competitive attention infrastructures can escalate hostility, desensitize users to harm, and incentivize transgressive content. Drawing on interdisciplinary evidence, the author examines how violent imaginaries and antagonistic subcultures proliferate, particularly among vulnerable demographics. The chapter highlights the need for sociologically informed platform governance strategies that address not only content moderation but the structural incentives shaping digital aggression.

## Chapter 7 - Online Activism, Digital Resistance, and Counter-Platform Practices

This chapter analyzes the emergent forms of digital activism and resistance that arise in response to platform-mediated power. It highlights how marginalized groups mobilize alternative infrastructures, encrypted spaces, and creative tactics—such as meme activism, hashtag campaigns, and networked disobedience—to challenge surveillance, censorship, and algorithmic bias. The chapter situates these practices within broader debates on counter-publics and platform governance, revealing how activists navigate digital risk while cultivating collective agencies. It demonstrates that digital resistance is not only oppositional but generative, producing new imaginaries of democratic participation.

## Chapter 8- Reproductive Autonomy in Rural India and Tier-2 Cities amid Digital Patriarchy and Honour Policing

This chapter examines reproductive autonomy in rural and semi-urban India within the context of digital patriarchy and online honor policing. It shows how platforms can simultaneously expand informational access for women and reinforce gendered power structures through social surveillance, moral judgment, and familial monitoring mediated by technology. Through culturally grounded analysis, the chapter reveals how digital infrastructures intersect with traditional norms, creating hybrid regimes of control. It contributes to feminist digital sociology by foregrounding reproductive rights, cultural specificity, and the socio-technical dynamics of gendered oppression.

## Chapter 9- Performing Identity of the Dead-on YouTube: Reception of Ginimbi Lite's Interview on Star FM

This chapter explores posthumous digital identity construction through audience responses to the late public figure Ginimbi Lite on YouTube. It examines how users negotiate memory, morality, and symbolic value in comment spaces, highlighting the role of platforms in shaping narratives of death and legacy. The analysis reveals how mourning practices, spiritual discourse, and celebrity culture intersect within algorithmically mediated public spheres. By foregrounding digital afterlives and networked remembrance, the chapter contributes to emerging scholarship on digital thanatology and platformed memorialization.

## Chapter 10- Platformized Migration and Digital Capitalism: Rethinking Migrant Labor, Mobility, and Inequality through Uber

This chapter investigates the transformation of migrant labor in the age of platform capitalism, using Uber as a central case. It demonstrates how platform infrastructures restructure mobility, precarity, and labor hierarchies while framing workers as "entrepreneurial subjects." The chapter highlights the duality of platform work—offering flexible entry into urban economies while reinforcing structural inequalities, surveillance, and algorithmic discipline for migrant communities. It advances debates on migration, digital labor, and global capitalism by revealing the socio-political conditions embedded in platform-mediated work.

## Chapter 11- Invisible Power in the Digital Sphere: Surveillance and Social Control

This chapter examines the architecture of invisible power embedded in digital infrastructures, focusing on surveillance logics and automated social control. It argues that platform systems do not merely collect data but actively shape behavior through predictive governance, nudging mechanisms, and algorithmic scrutiny. Drawing from sociological theories of discipline and biopolitics, the chapter illustrates how platforms consolidate power while masking coercion as convenience and personalization. It underscores the need for critical frameworks that interrogate digital authority and everyday compliance.

## Chapter 12- Interrogating Ndebele Identity through Digital Heritage Narratives

This chapter explores how digital media reshape ethnic identity and cultural heritage among Ndebele communities. It focuses on digital representations of Old Bulawayo and the contested narratives of tradition, belonging, and historical memory that emerge in online discourse. By analyzing user engagement and discursive patterns, the author shows how platforms act as cultural archives and ideological battlegrounds. The chapter enriches scholarship on identity politics, digital heritage, and postcolonial subjectivity by demonstrating how marginalized histories are negotiated in mediated spaces.

## Chapter 13- Humour and Mockvertising: Satire, Subversion, and Consumer Culture on Platforms

This chapter investigates how humour and mockvertising operate as cultural tools for critiquing consumer capitalism in digital environments. It demonstrates that parody content, satirical advertising formats, and ironic brand engagements create alternative meaning systems that expose the contradictions of commercial culture. By analyzing user practices and audience reception, the chapter reveals how humour serves both as a mode of resistance and a site of co-optation, oscillating between subversive critique and platform-native commodification. The work offers new insights into digital semiotics, affect, and cultural contestation under platform capitalism.

## Chapter 14- Evaluation of People's Experiences Using AI Technologies to Address Emotional Needs

This chapter examines how individuals engage with artificial intelligence systems for emotional support, mental wellness, and relational needs. It explores the sociotechnical dynamics through which AI platforms mediate affective care, anthropomorphizing, and parasocial intimacy. While highlighting cases of perceived empathy and psychological relief, the chapter also critically addresses the risks of emotional outsourcing, algorithmic dependency, and the commodification of vulnerability. It contributes to emerging discussions on affective computing by framing AI-mediated emotional work as a sociological phenomenon with ethical and psychological implications.

## Chapter 15- Ethical and Methodological Issues in Researching Digital Platforms

This chapter offers a rigorous conceptual and methodological reflection on conducting research in platform environments. It interrogates questions of access, consent, publicity, data opacity, and algorithmic control, arguing that ethical and methodological concerns in digital research are inseparable. By outlining practical strategies for studying opaque systems—such as interface walkthroughs, mixed-methods triangulation, and reflexive positionality—this chapter advances a framework of responsible and rigorous platform scholarship. It establishes a foundational reference point for researchers grappling with platform power and data politics in academic inquiry.

## Chapter 16- Understanding the Paradox of Digital Intimacy: Ethical, Social, and Psychological Implications

This chapter explores digital intimacy as a paradoxical domain where connection and alienation coexist. It examines how social media, messaging platforms, and algorithmically curated interactions provide spaces for belonging while simultaneously amplifying insecurity, hyper-visibility, and emotional precarity. Drawing on intimacy theory and digital sociology, the chapter shows how mediated relationships reshape trust, emotional boundaries, and relational ethics. It concludes by calling for balanced digital practices and sociological attention to the relational costs of constant connectivity.

# CONCLUSION: SCHOLARLY CONTRIBUTION

This volume advances the sociology of platformization by offering a multidimensional analysis of how platforms restructure power, culture, and lived experience. It contributes new conceptual approaches, methodological reflections, and cross-cultural insights to the study of digital societies and provides a foundational scholarly reference for understanding the evolving social architecture of the platform age.

# Acknowledgment

We extend our sincere appreciation to all contributors whose valuable chapters and scholarly insights have shaped this volume. Their commitment to advancing critical perspectives on platformization and digital societies has been essential to the realization of this work.

We also wish to express our gratitude to the reviewers for their thoughtful feedback, careful reading, and constructive guidance throughout the editorial process. Their academic rigor and generous support played a significant role in strengthening the conceptual and empirical contributions of this book.

Our special thanks go to the IGI Global editorial team for their continuous assistance, professionalism, and encouragement during each stage of development. Their support ensured that this project progressed smoothly and reached completion in a timely manner.

Finally, we acknowledge the broader academic and research communities whose ongoing work on digital transformation, platform governance, and sociotechnical systems continue to inspire and inform scholarly dialogue in this field. We are grateful for the collaborative spirit and shared pursuit of knowledge that made this book possible.

# Chapter 1
# Digital Caste Systems: An Introduction to Platform-Based Social Stratification in Turkey

**Nuriye Çelik**
https://orcid.org/0000-0001-6368-1956
*Sinop University, Turkey*

## ABSTRACT

*Digitalization is reshaping societies by transforming communication, economy, culture, and politics. Social media platforms are not only tools but spaces where identities are built and inequalities reproduced. The concept of digital stratification goes beyond access, focusing on visibility, practices, and capital. In Turkey, where social media use is widespread, platform habits reflect offline differences, yet comparative studies are rare. This study analyzes LinkedIn, Instagram, TikTok, and Twitter/X to propose a "digital caste system," showing how professional, aesthetic, algorithmic, and political logics create distinct hierarchies. Using Bourdieu, Foucault, Castells, and Zuboff, it reveals how economic, cultural, and social capital turn into digital advantage, amplifying inequalities.*

## INTRODUCTION

Digitalization has become one of the most defining dynamics of transformation in contemporary societies. The internet and social media platforms have not only reshaped communication processes but have also facilitated the emergence of new power relations across economic, cultural, and political domains. Social media, in particular, functions as a space where individuals display their daily lives, construct social identities, and circulate different forms of capital. Therefore, social media platforms should no longer be seen merely as communication tools; they are also

DOI: 10.4018/979-8-3373-4267-2.ch001

structures where social stratification is reproduced and new forms of inequality are created.

One prominent concept in the literature that addresses this is *digital stratification*. This concept moves beyond differences in access to digital technologies and focuses on inequalities in the quality of online experiences, visibility strategies, and digital practices. Research shows that disparities in economic, cultural, and social capital are carried into digital spaces and are further intensified through platforms' algorithmic mechanisms. Thus, digital stratification provides a powerful analytical framework for understanding how social differences manifest in new media environments.

In Turkey, social media use is highly prevalent; however, these practices are unevenly distributed and carry different meanings across social groups. Social media serves a wide range of functions, from new forms of political participation to consumption culture, aesthetic practices, and professional networking. Despite this, systematic research examining social media stratification through the lens of platform differences in Turkey is scarce. This gap is particularly evident regarding user groups' online visibility strategies, capital accumulation processes, and interactions with algorithms.

The aim of this study is to discuss social stratification emerging on social media platforms in Turkey through the conceptualization of a "digital caste system." The analysis focuses on LinkedIn, Instagram, TikTok, and Twitter/X, examining how users' platform preferences and visibility strategies reproduce social differences. These platforms were selected because they most visibly reflect caste-like stratification. Facebook and YouTube, by contrast, operate more through horizontal interaction and content archiving, making the caste metaphor less applicable.

This study aims both to contribute to the global literature on digital stratification and to make visible Turkey's unique sociological dynamics. The theoretical foundation draws on Pierre Bourdieu's concepts of capital and field, Michel Foucault's analyses of surveillance and discipline, Shoshana Zuboff's approach to surveillance capitalism, and Manuel Castells' network society theory. These perspectives frame social media not merely as an arena of individual choices but as a complex system of stratification shaped by power relations, symbolic practices, and algorithmic mechanisms.

In the Turkish context, platform use is experienced unevenly across social groups: white-collar professionals and elite university graduates tend to leverage LinkedIn for career-capital accumulation; middle-class users often curate aesthetic lifestyles and consumption codes on Instagram; younger and lower-income cohorts disproportionately engage with TikTok's algorithmic visibility games; and politically active users cluster on Twitter/X around agenda-setting dynamics. These differentiated practices mean that offline advantages (education, occupational status, cultural repertoires, and dense networks) are translated into online visibility and symbolic capital, while others face structural frictions—opaque ranking, moderation asymmetries, and network closure. Accordingly, the "digital caste" metaphor is used here not to reify rigid, hereditary boundaries but to analytically describe stratified regimes of visibility and mobility shaped by platform logics and existing social hierarchies. This perspective foregrounds the lived experience of users and clarifies how capital conversion and algorithmic mediation jointly reproduce inequality in platformized social life.

In conclusion, this study opens the discussion on inequalities emerging in digital platforms through the metaphor of "caste," analysing how offline social differences are reproduced and made persistent in digital spaces via platforms' algorithmic operations. Within the Turkish context, this discussion both deepens the literature on digital stratification and offers a distinctive perspective for understanding platform-based stratification processes.

## 1. PLATFORMIZED SOCIETY AS A NEW TYPE OF SOCIETY

Society is an organic entity shaped by historical changes, wars, and migrations, and rebuilt around certain values after each transformation. Defining society in this way assigns responsibility to individuals as actors in the long-term analysis of social change. It is clear that various norms and values—such as religious beliefs, political structures, or the state—play a significant role in this reconstruction process. These processes are never independent of cultural values or geographical factors. Technological changes, in fact, affect and transform societies as much as, if not more than, wars. With the digitalization brought by technology, the concept of the digital society has emerged in the field of sociology. A digital society encompasses the profound transformations in social structures, processes, and interactions triggered by digitalization. Historically, the transition to a digital society can be seen as a continuation of post-industrial development. Digitalization has generated effects powerful enough to represent a new stage of social evolution. Chernavin (2021) positions the digital society as a stage in global technogenic civilization, placing the institutionalization of digital public relations at its core. This is because a digital society is not only one where personal relationships move online but also one in which interactions between individuals and the state become increasingly digitized. This historical view is supported by findings showing that digitalization not only affects socialization but also facilitates the accumulation of institutional and socio-cultural capacities needed for contemporary socio-economic structures (Ivashyna et al., 2023).

Theoretical approaches developed by Manuel Castells and Jan van Dijk provide essential frameworks for analyzing digital society. Castells (2009), through the concept of the network society, revealed that as information circulates via digital technologies, social relations take on a networked structure. According to Castells (2009, pp. 500–501, 693–694), networks become decisive in every field—from economic production to identity formation, governance to social movements—and power is restructured around access to information and communication flows. Information technologies transform not only production methods but also the spatial and temporal nature of power, a change of great sociological importance. Van Dijk (2005, 2020), meanwhile, focuses on the information society and digital divides, emphasizing how inequalities in access, use, and benefits of digital technologies reproduce broader social inequalities. In this view, digitalization is not merely a technical transformation but a process that deepens socio-economic disparities. Particularly, low-income, less educated, and marginalized groups remain disadvantaged in terms of access to information, limiting social mobility through digital exclusion (Çelik, 2023a). Van Dijk's perspective shows that the potential benefits of digital society can only be realized if fair conditions of access are established. The interaction of these theories highlights not only the socio-technical dynamics of digital society but also its potential to reshape governance and citizen participation, underlining why digitalization must be a central concern of sociology (Çelik, 2023b; Çelik, 2025; Çelik & Ateşoğlu, 2023). Empirical studies further illuminate the consequences of digitalization for social structures and governance. Findings indicate that digitalization can enhance communication capacity and bring transparency and efficiency to decision-making (Naik & Kakade, 2024). However, increased state control over personal data has also raised concerns about privacy and threats to democratic values. Research on social stratification demonstrates that digital technologies create different levels of access and benefit among individuals and communities, deepening existing socio-economic divides (Kurganskaya & Dunaev, 2021).

The transition from a digital society to a platformized society represents a fundamental shift in socio-technical structure. This transformation is characterized by digital platforms becoming the central infrastructures mediating social, economic, and political interactions (Walsh, 2020). Digital platforms have emerged as dominant actors shaping not only economic activities but also social and political processes in today's economy (Langley & Leyshon, 2017; Törnberg, 2023). Social media networks, e-commerce marketplaces, and search engines have become integral to daily life, profoundly influencing communication, information access, commercial transactions, and the ways social relations are formed (Schlag, 2023). The rise of platformization has been enabled by advances in information and communication technologies, including the proliferation of mobile devices, increased internet access, and the development of complex algorithms and data analytics (Dmitrieva, 2020). This technological infrastructure allows platforms to collect massive data sets, personalize user experiences, and generate network effects that consolidate market dominance (Coveri et al., 2021). The expansion of digital platforms has produced multi-dimensional benefits and challenges, transformed many aspects of social structure and sparking debates around power, governance, and social equity (Fu et al., 2021).

The concept of the platformized society refers to a transformative social structure shaped by the dominance of digital platforms across various areas of social and economic life. This idea has been extensively addressed in the work of José van Dijck, Thomas Poell, and Martijn de Waal. These authors have shown how platforms sustain and reshape our interactions, economic transactions, and forms of public participation, influencing areas such as education, healthcare, and urban mobility (Dijck et al., 2018; Risi et al., 2020). The term historically gained prominence with the rise of major technology companies adopting platform-based business models driven by user-generated content and data-driven services. Van Dijck and colleagues analysed this historical development, emphasizing that platforms have evolved from service providers into powerful actors exerting significant influence over social norms and public values (Dijck et al., 2018; Dijck et al., 2019). The rise of platforms such as Facebook, Google, and Amazon exemplifies this phenomenon, particularly through their ability to reshape traditional sectors and practices via datafication (Hallinan et al., 2024).

Academic debates on platformization focus on its impact on digital labour, algorithmic governance, and social stratification. Van Dijck and Kerssens discuss how platformization, by integrating education with corporate-oriented structures, threatens educators' pedagogical autonomy and raises issues of justice and accountability as public values (Kerssens & Dijck, 2022). Algorithmic governance, meanwhile, highlights the monopolization of access to information and services, revealing power and control issues that often align user decisions and behaviors with corporate interests rather than public benefit (Gorwa, 2019). Empirical studies addressing these debates employ qualitative, quantitative, and mixed methods across contexts ranging from European welfare states to the global South and the gig economy. For example, studies on the gig economy reveal that platformization often creates precarious and exploitative forms of labor (Dorschel, 2022). Other researchers examine the effects of algorithmic management in workplaces, identifying a turn toward performance tracking and surveillance, especially in crowd work and educational settings (Gerber & Krzywdzinski, 2019; Kumar et al., 2019). Furthermore, the intersection of platformization with public values brings issues like privacy, security, and accessibility to the forefront. As platforms gain power, the consequences for citizens become more pronounced, generating debates on governance and accountability. Helberger and colleagues argue for a collaborative responsibility model among platforms, users, and institutions to protect public values in platform-based services (Helberger et al., 2018). Public reactions to platform monopolies and the need for regulatory oversight have increasingly highlighted concerns around accountability and governance structures (Gorwa et al., 2024; Dijck & Lin, 2022).

When viewed from this perspective, it becomes clear that the concept of the platformized society intersects with many other fields and requires an interdisciplinary approach for its analysis. Digital platforms influence not only economic structures and labour processes but also democratization movements (van Dijck et al., 2018; Plantin et al., 2018). This ecosystem, which shapes economic and democratic processes, is largely controlled by five major technology companies: Alphabet-Google, Apple, Facebook, Amazon, and Microsoft (van Dijck, 2018). In *The Platform Society*, van Dijck analyses the struggles between market actors, the state, and civil society to establish values such as privacy, security, justice, and democratic oversight (van Dijck et al., 2018; Plantin et al., 2018). The study examines the impact of platformization on four key sectors—news media, urban mobility, healthcare, and education—while also addressing the local and geopolitical dimensions of these processes (van Dijck et al., 2018; Bye, 2020). As this comprehensive work shows, the governance of areas such as education, democracy, and healthcare is increasingly shaped and influenced by these complex media processes.

At the same time, the socio-cultural effects of digital environments on identity formation and social interaction are sociologically significant. Digital technologies not only transform modes of communication but also create new social dynamics in which individual and collective identities are redefined. Participants become involved in both virtual and real-world communities, reflecting traditional power and cultural hierarchies, and norms and values from the offline world are reproduced in the online space (Turkle, 1997; Donath, 2002; Boyd, 2008; Papacharissi, 2010; Zhao et al., 2008; Ahmad et al., 2025). One of the values reproduced in this process is social stratification itself.

Platformization is a socio-technical phenomenon that restructures social relations and governance through algorithms and data-processing systems (Sadowski, 2019). This process gives rise to new forms of social stratification, described as "digital caste systems," where access to resources and opportunities is increasingly determined by individuals' digital visibility and data contributions. The rise of data capitalism treats data as a new form of capital, leading to significant consequences for economic inequalities and social justice (Sadowski, 2019). In this capitalist framework, those who control data also control economic power and social influence, reshaping governance structures through algorithmic oversight (Steinhoff, 2024).

Empirical studies conducted in non-Western contexts reveal the local manifestations of platform power. For example, Jabbouri and colleagues show how personal networks and community participation are transformed by digital platforms in developing countries, affecting social capital and reproducing inequalities through different levels of platform participation (Jabbouri et al., 2024). Similarly, Leuppert and colleagues demonstrate that media consumption and political participation in Middle Eastern and North African (MENA) countries show differences linked to social stratification (Leuppert et al., 2024). Other studies examine the impact of platformization on local economies and class structures. Zheng and colleagues' study of disaster management in China reveals how social media can deepen inequalities during crises by shaping information flows and community responses (Zheng et al., 2024). These findings highlight the importance of integrating social media strategies into emergency management to reduce inequalities. Likewise, Xiu-Mei and colleagues analyse the impact of data capital on farmers' income levels, showing how digital platforms are reshaping agricultural economic structures (Xiu-Mei et al., 2022).

In addition, the concept of "data colonialism," developed by Couldry and Mejias, questions the broader implications of data extraction practices, arguing that continuous surveillance and datafication create new forms of social discrimination that resemble historical injustices (Couldry & Mejias, 2019). Thus, it becomes evident that the global effects of platformization are especially pronounced in regions where digital infrastructure is unevenly distributed. Importantly, revealing the digital caste structures that emerge in these contexts is the first step toward addressing the inequalities they produce.

## 2. DIGITAL CASTES IN THE PLATFORMIZED SOCIETY

Social stratification is one of the fundamental concepts of sociology, referring to the hierarchical ranking of individuals or groups in society according to various criteria such as wealth, power, and prestige. Two founding theorists in this field, Karl Marx and Max Weber, offered different frameworks for explaining stratification. Marx's approach is primarily class-based, focusing on the ownership of the means of production. According to Marx, society is divided into two main classes: the bourgeoisie, who own the means of production, and the proletariat, who sell their labour. This class conflict lies at the heart of Marx's theory of stratification and is central to understanding how capitalism works. Marx argued that the bourgeoisie systematically exploit the proletariat, leading to the worker's alienation from both the labour process and the product (Capital, 1867/1976, Vol. 1). This alienation is not only economic but also represents a deeper estrangement of individuals from their own essence within the production process. Marx's analysis highlights how economic power shapes social relations and reinforces the dominance of the ruling class. For Marx, overcoming these inequalities is only possible by abolishing private ownership of the means of production and establishing a classless society (Marx & Engels, 1848/2002).

Max Weber, on the other hand, examined stratification using a three-dimensional model: class, status, and power (or party). For Weber, stratification cannot be explained solely by economic class relations; individuals' social prestige (status groups) and access to political power must also be considered (Weber, 1978). His model suggests that people can occupy different positions across these three dimensions. For example, a person may be economically wealthy yet have low social prestige or limited political influence (Economy and Society, Weber, 1922/1978). Weber's perspective underscores that stratification is multidimensional, dynamic, and intersecting. The interaction of class, status, and power shapes individuals' social positions and life chances.

From a functionalist perspective, Émile Durkheim approached stratification through the concept of the division of labour. For Durkheim, modern societies develop specialized divisions of labour in response to growing social complexity, increasing both social differentiation and interdependence (Durkheim, 1893/2014). This differentiation does not harm social cohesion; rather, individuals' specialized roles sustain social unity through organic solidarity. However, it also creates occupational hierarchies, differentiating individuals' statuses and roles, thereby giving rise to stratification (Durkheim, 1893/2014). Durkheim thus saw stratification not as an inequality to be condemned but as an essential component of social order and stability.

Theories of stratification have evolved since the early days of sociology. Talcott Parsons (2017), in his structural-functionalist framework, legitimized social differentiation as necessary for societal integration, while Davis and Moore (2019) argued that some roles are more important and demanding and must therefore be incentivized with greater rewards, making stratification inevitable and necessary. In contrast, Marxist-oriented theorists like Erik Olin Wright (1997) expanded class analysis to include "intermediate positions," emphasizing control, authority, and skills beyond ownership. Goran Therborn (1999) stressed that stratification is not only tied to economic structures but also to ideology and social reproduction mechanisms, highlighting the cultural aspects of class. This theoretical development paved the way for Pierre Bourdieu's (1984) approach, which incorporated cultural and social capital into class analysis. Bourdieu argued that social positions are shaped not only by economic capital but also by lifestyles, educational resources, and social networks internalized through habitus. His framework explained the reproduction of inequality in a more holistic way.

Unlike classical sociologists, Bourdieu deepened the discussion of stratification by adding economic, cultural, and social capital. Economic capital refers to material assets; cultural capital includes educational qualifications, cultural knowledge, and aesthetic tastes; social capital relates to networks and resources derived from social connections (Bourdieu, 1984; Bourdieu, 1986). These forms of capital are convertible and together reproduce class structures. Thus, stratification persists not only economically but also culturally and socially. This framework is crucial for understanding digital castes.

Michel Foucault's concept of the panopticon is also highly relevant to digital platforms as a metaphor for continuous and invisible surveillance. Platforms collect extensive user data, track behaviours, and use algorithmic micro-targeting to personalize experiences, applying constant oversight. This creates a subtle but pervasive disciplinary power, where users internalize the platform's gaze and adjust their behaviour accordingly (Capodivacca & Giacomini, 2024). Algorithmic systems embed surveillance into everyday interactions, making it seem natural and unavoidable, strengthening control without overt coercion (Capodivacca & Giacomini, 2024; Helles & Flyverbom, 2019). Foucault's concept of the disciplinary society helps explain how platforms regulate user behaviour. Engagement metrics, viral trends, and content moderation function as disciplinary mechanisms shaping the actions of creators and users alike. Users are encouraged to conform to platform norms to gain visibility and rewards, and behaviour is disciplined through algorithmic governance (Capodivacca & Giacomini, 2024; Chai et al., 2023). This regulation is not only top-down but also internalized, as users self-regulate to maintain or improve their digital standing.

Platforms construct normative behaviours and identities by amplifying some content and users while excluding others. This creates stratified visibility regimes resembling digital castes, where some users are algorithmically privileged with high visibility while others are rendered invisible or marginalized. This hierarchy is maintained through algorithmic filtering, recommendation systems, and moderation policies, defining what is "normal" or "acceptable" on the platform (Oliveira, 2023). Marginalized groups can be excluded not only socially but structurally. Normalization of behaviour limits social mobility between these digital castes. Studies show that digital labour markets, including platform work, tend to reproduce existing social class advantages despite claims of meritocracy. Algorithms often favour users from privileged backgrounds or those aligned with dominant norms, reinforcing inequalities and making it difficult for marginalized users to advance (Martindale & Lehdonvirta, 2023a, 2021). Thus, rather than mitigating exclusion, digital platforms may reinforce it.

In platform analysis, alongside Bourdieu and Foucault, Castells' Network Society theory emphasizes the transformative power of information technologies. According to this theory, the global economy is shaped by instantaneous flows of information, capital, and culture through networks that transcend national regulations. These networks structure consumption, production, culture, and power relations, privileging those who control information flows and technological capital (Stark, 1997). Despite appearing to offer horizontal connections and inclusivity, the network society remains divided; flexible and individualized labour structures concentrate production in the hands of a relatively small, educated population, producing new forms of exclusion despite promises of meritocratic participation (Stark, 1997). Unequal access to digital networks, technological literacy, and infrastructure further creates marginalization. Gender differences in digital skills and algorithmic biases, for example, show that some groups remain disadvantaged despite claims of openness (Arısoy Gedik & Ceyhan, 2024).

Offline social networks and socioeconomic status still shape access to and success within digital environments. In mobile internet-era crowdfunding, for instance, individuals with higher socioeconomic status achieve better outcomes, showing that inequalities persist even in networked settings (Cheng & Ren, 2024). The concept of network literacy extends beyond basic digital skills, including the ability to understand and navigate complex social and technological networks effectively. Marginalized groups, such as incarcerated women, face layered disadvantages due to limited access and intersecting oppressions, demonstrating that stratification in network society is both digital and social (Hopkins, 2022).

Finally, the economic dimension of platforms adds another layer to this framework, incorporating Zuboff alongside Bourdieu, Foucault, and Castells. Zuboff's concept of surveillance capitalism is based on the commodification of personal data; human behaviors are extracted, predicted, and monetized by digital platforms (Laniuk, 2021; Keddell, 2021). Platforms like Uber, TikTok, and Fiverr exemplify this process, using algorithmic governance to control and optimize labour through predictive analytics, recommendation systems, and data mining (Singh, Garcia & Lindtner, 2023). This governance can be seen as a new form of exploitation, blurring worker autonomy and trapping them in an autonomy paradox and digital alienation. Algorithmic systems extend working time, fragment labour relations, and convert cognitive labour into private capital, creating a stark asymmetry between data-collecting firms and data-producing workers. This dynamic deepens power imbalances and reproduces capitalist accumulation (Kuriakose & Iyer, 2021). The opaque nature of algorithms reduces workers' ability to understand or challenge their working conditions, enabling control mechanisms that are difficult to resist or regulate (Keddell, 2021). The unequal relationship between platforms and workers turns digital labour into a largely obligatory form of participation in capitalist value production rather than voluntary engagement. Workers often comply with algorithmic demands to maintain their livelihoods, reproducing systemic inequalities (Kuriakose & Iyer, 2021).

These approaches have also been applied in platform analyses in the literature. Recent studies show that digital platforms such as TikTok, Instagram, YouTube, and Twitter increasingly shape new forms of social stratification, often described as digital caste systems or algorithmically driven inequalities. These studies reveal how platform algorithms mediate visibility, distribute symbolic capital, and structure digital labour, with growing interest in contexts outside the West, including Turkey.

Digital social networks are shaped by algorithmic mediation that amplifies the visibility of some users while marginalizing others. This process turns individual actions—liking, sharing, commenting—into systematic patterns that produce digital inequalities, favouring those with digital capital, such as influencers (Cui, 2025). The amplification effect of algorithms reinforces existing social hierarchies, creating layered digital environments where a small number of users hold a disproportionate amount of symbolic capital and influence (Cui, 2025). Networked algorithms and social network structures tend to reproduce and deepen social inequalities, particularly for minorities. Homophily (the tendency to connect with similar others) and mixing biases restrict the visibility and collaboration opportunities of minority groups, reinforcing digital marginalization (Karimi et al., 2022). These mechanisms are not limited to Western settings; in countries with diverse social structures, such as Turkey, similar digital inequalities emerge, sometimes even more pronounced (Karimi et al., 2022). Search engines and social media feeds run by AI-driven algorithms reflect and reproduce existing social biases, such as gender inequality. Exposure to biased algorithmic outputs shapes user perceptions and behaviours, creating feedback loops that sustain offline inequalities in digital spaces (Vlasceanu & Amodio, 2022). This bias production cycle becomes more visible in societies with strong structural inequalities, showing that platforms can actively reproduce local social divisions (Vlasceanu & Amodio, 2022).

Studies using Bourdieu's concepts emphasize that digital platforms create new "fields" where actors compete for symbolic capital—followers, likes, and visibility. Users' digital habitus—their tendencies and strategies shaped by prior social experiences—determines how successful they are in these spaces (Cui, 2025; Karimi et al., 2022). Activities such as content creation and digital labour are not rewarded equally; individuals with pre-existing social or cultural capital often hold advantages. This indicates that offline hierarchies are reproduced online (Cui, 2025). Foucault's notion of visibility as a form of power is also highly relevant in the digital context. Algorithmic curation—selection and ranking—determines who is seen and who is invisible. This visibility structure is not neutral; it is shaped by platform logic, disciplining, normalizing, or marginalizing users (Cui, 2025). The power to shape digital visibility is increasingly concentrated in platform algorithms, which act as gatekeepers and arbiters of symbolic value (Cui, 2025).

Although much of the theoretical literature has been developed in Western contexts, studies examining these dynamics in non-Western societies like Turkey are increasing. These works show how global platforms interact with local social structures—sometimes reinforcing existing divisions, sometimes creating new forms of digital stratification (Karimi et al., 2022; Cui, 2025). The literature stresses that the effects of algorithmic mediation vary by social context, highlighting the need for analyses that account for local, cultural, and normative factors (Karimi et al., 2022).

While the metaphor of "digital caste systems" illuminates persistent asymmetries of visibility and symbolic power, it also carries analytical risks. Unlike the hereditary and religiously codified caste orders in South Asia, digital hierarchies are neither immutable nor formally sanctioned; they remain contingent upon algorithmic architectures, user agency, and shifting political economies of platforms. Overemphasis on the rigidity of the metaphor risks obscuring the fluidity, reversibility, and contestability of digital positions. In this sense, the concept should be understood as heuristic rather than descriptive, foregrounding how structural inequalities are algorithmically reproduced while leaving room for counterstrategies, creative resistance, and emergent solidarities. By acknowledging these limits, the framework avoids deterministic readings and emphasizes the dialectical tension between constraint and agency in platformized social life.

In conclusion, theoretical and empirical research increasingly documents how digital platforms foster new forms of social stratification often described as "digital caste systems." These inequalities are shaped by algorithmic mediation, network structures, and platform logics, with significant implications for digital labour and symbolic capital. The theoretical frameworks of Bourdieu and Foucault are critical for analysing these dynamics. Moreover, studies examining how these processes intersect with local social structures in non-Western settings, including Turkey, are gaining importance (Cui, 2025; Karimi et al., 2022; Vlasceanu & Amodio, 2022). A review of the literature also shows that studies focusing specifically on digital castes in Turkey are very limited, indicating a clear research gap. This study aims to contribute to filling that gap.

## 3. METHODOLOGY

The data collection and analysis process in this study was designed based on existing literature and secondary sources. Academic research, reports, and industry analyses that explain how these platforms operate—both in the Turkish context and in comparative global studies—were compiled. In this study, the empirical material was derived from a qualitative content analysis of digital practices and discourses circulating in Turkey's platformized media environment. The sample focused on a combination of publicly accessible digital traces (e.g., platform interfaces, trending content, algorithmic features) and secondary data (policy documents, journalistic reports, and scholarly analyses) covering the period 2020–2024. Rather than individual interviews or surveys, the research design privileges discourse and document analysis to capture how platforms structure visibility, status, and symbolic hierarchies. The analytic procedure followed a thematic coding strategy, in which texts were systematically organized around categories such as "capital conversion," "algorithmic stratification," and "resistance practices." This approach makes the methodological stance transparent and clarifies how empirical observations informed the conceptualization of "digital caste systems."

The methodological approach relied on a systematic literature review. Searches were conducted in academic databases, targeting the period between 2010 and 2025. Keywords included *digital stratification*, *digital caste*, *social inequality*, *visibility*, *symbolic capital*, and *platform capitalism*, combined with platform names (LinkedIn/Instagram/TikTok/Twitter|X) and the country label (Turkey/Türkiye). Searches were limited to title, abstract, and keyword fields, and duplicate records were removed. As a result, both studies specific to Turkey and comparative works adaptable to the Turkish context were included.

The review considered peer-reviewed articles, studies containing Turkish data, or conceptual/comparative work transferable to the Turkish context. Publications focusing on social stratification, inequality, algorithmic governance, and visibility were included. Purely technical studies without a link to stratification, conference abstracts, popular content, and records without full-text access were excluded. To limit imbalance across platforms, efforts were made to distribute sources evenly, avoiding concentration on a single platform.

The collected literature was analysed through thematic content analysis. First, studies related to each platform were evaluated within their own contexts; then, the findings were reinterpreted through the study's theoretical framework of the "digital caste system." LinkedIn was associated with professional castes; Instagram with aesthetic/display castes; TikTok with algorithmic castes; and Twitter/X with political/agenda-based castes.

The method also has limitations. Because the analysis is literature-based, findings are drawn from the synthesis of existing research rather than direct empirical observation. Moreover, the limited number of studies focused specifically on Turkey required interpretation using regional or global literature in some cases. These limitations restrict any claim of universal generalization; however, they provide a sufficient theoretical and empirical foundation for discussing the "digital caste" concept across different platforms. As the study is based on the comparative synthesis of secondary literature rather than primary empirical data, causal mechanisms were inferred rather than directly tested. Additionally, rapid updates to platform policies and changes in ownership may affect the temporal relevance of the findings.

## 4. FINDINGS

The evaluation of findings draws on the theoretical and empirical results presented in the existing literature. Studies on digital stratification show how differences in economic, cultural, and social capital are reflected in online platforms. Therefore, first addressing the literature on digital stratification strengthens the theoretical framework in which this study's findings are situated.

Digital stratification is not only a matter of access to technological tools, but a multilayered process shaped by economic, cultural, and social capital. Willekens, Siongers, and Lievens (2022), for example, examine practices of withdrawal from social media and show how these are shaped by differences in capital. Their study highlights that individuals with fewer resources tend to disengage from platforms in more exclusionary ways, while those with high cultural capital limit their social media use selectively and strategically. Thus, digital inequalities appear not only in access but also in forms of participation and withdrawal (Willekens et al., 2022).

Similarly, Kim's (2009) research on lawyers' points to two central functions of social capital: information transmission and status validation. Lawyers gain economic advantages not only through functional knowledge but also through access to the prestige of high-status network members. Applied to digital contexts, this suggests that visibility, follower counts, and symbolic indicators on social media serve as sources of status that strengthen digital stratification (Kim, 2009). Pichler and Wallace (2009), in their comparative analysis across Europe, found that upper classes tend to have broader and more diversified networks, whereas lower classes rely more on bonding social capital formed by local and homogeneous ties. They also showed that national-level inequalities further deepen these differences. In digital spaces, this perspective indicates that higher social classes become advantaged by accumulating bridging digital capital, while lower classes remain confined to narrower, closed networks (Pichler & Wallace, 2009).

This literature demonstrates that digital stratification is shaped not only by access inequalities but also by symbolic practices and network relations on platforms. The findings of this study align with this framework. Below, analyses are presented for different platforms used in Turkey (LinkedIn, Instagram, TikTok, Twitter/X), discussing in detail the local reflections of the digital caste system.

As of early 2025, data reflecting Turkey's digital infrastructure and social media usage profile clearly shows how digitalization has spread throughout society. The number of internet users has reached 77.3 million, representing 88.3% of the population; the number of social media users is 58.5 million, accounting for 66.7% of the total population. These figures show that social media has become a central component of social life (Digital 2025: Turkey). Thus, the findings provide a strong basis for understanding how offline social positions are transformed into visibility in the digital sphere.

## a. LinkedIn Use in Turkey

A search in the WoS and Google Scholar databases using the keyword *LinkedIn in Turkey* identified a total of 10 studies, most of which were in Turkish. Many of these studies directly relate to digital stratification, examining how LinkedIn functions in the context of social capital generation, inequality, and professional networking. A search for *LinkedIn and digital stratification in Turkey* yielded no results, while a broader search using the terms *LinkedIn and social capital and inequality and stratification* identified three international studies. This suggests that LinkedIn is beginning to be examined in the Turkish context through the lens of digital stratification, but that the international literature focuses more on social capital, inequality, and professional stratification.

Research on LinkedIn use in Turkey shows that the platform functions not only as a professional network but also as a space where social differences and caste-like forms of digital stratification are reproduced. Prominent studies highlight how different social groups use LinkedIn, what motivates their interactions, and how they generate both symbolic and material capital through the platform.

Studies on university students indicate that young people use LinkedIn intensively to find jobs and explore career opportunities. Tınmaz and Fanea-Ivanovici (2024) found that students use the platform to learn about employers and develop professional contacts but have low awareness of privacy and security risks. This suggests that young users have not yet fully internalized the platform's risks within the digital caste system. Analyses using social capital theory also show that personal characteristics and individual differences are important in networking. Bakan and Karaaslan (2017) emphasized that such individual differences affect trust and networking on LinkedIn, making it a selective space for generating professional capital. This selectivity strengthens the psychological and social foundations of digital castes.

Research on white-collar professionals emphasizes how LinkedIn reproduces workplace culture through symbolic practices. Gürbüzdal's (2022) analysis of *Ekşi Sözlük* discussions interprets white-collar performance on LinkedIn as a symbolic denial of insecurity. From this perspective, LinkedIn is not just a job search tool but a digital stage for prestige, status, and visibility. Studies on career development similarly highlight LinkedIn's role as a site for generating career capital, particularly for young professionals. Acar, Gürsoy, and Ünsal (2014) showed that LinkedIn has become a central job network for both employers and job seekers, allowing individuals to make their careers visible. Likewise, Denizli (2019) found that LinkedIn is increasingly used in recruitment processes, though ethical issues and privacy concerns are emerging.

Studies focusing on usage habits show differences in LinkedIn practices according to age, education level, and regional factors. Bakırtaş and Sekendür Turgut (2021) found that users' profile update frequency and usage times varied by demographic characteristics. Another study by Bakırtaş and Turgu (2021) highlighted that perceptions of functionality and content interaction shaped attitudes toward the platform.

Taken together, these findings indicate that LinkedIn in Turkey is not only a professional job network but also a platform that reflects and shapes social stratification in the digital sphere. Especially among white-collar professionals and university students, symbolic practices on LinkedIn reveal both functional and cultural dimensions of digital caste systems. Thus, examining LinkedIn use in Turkey provides an important analytical window for understanding new forms of inequality and stratification in the digital age.

Bourdieu's concept of capital types offers a useful framework here. While LinkedIn does not directly provide access to economic capital, it makes social capital (network connections) and cultural capital (education credentials, certifications, foreign language skills) visible. However, this visibility is not equally distributed; graduates of prestigious universities or employees in certain white-collar sectors demonstrate higher levels of digital capital. This shows that LinkedIn has an inherent selectivity mechanism within the digital caste system.

Manuel Castells' network society approach is also important for understanding this process. Castells (2000) emphasizes that in the information society, power and capital are increasingly distributed through networks. LinkedIn sits at the centre of such networks, making some individuals visible while excluding others from certain professional communities. Thus, the platform stratifies not only by participants' ability to make connections but also by which networks they can access. This represents the structural dimension of the digital caste system.

Finally, from a Foucauldian perspective, LinkedIn enforces a constant need for self-updating, professional performance display, and visibility. It functions as a mechanism of digital surveillance, simultaneously subjectifying and disciplining individuals. Profile updates, posts, and interactions are carried out not only to improve job prospects but also to align with the platform's normative standards. This shows that white-collar professional culture is reproduced through LinkedIn. In sum, LinkedIn practices, when viewed through Bourdieu's capital types, Castells' network society, and Foucault's subjectification processes, reveal how the professional domain in Turkey is being reorganized through digital caste systems. This theoretical framework suggests that the findings are not only descriptive but also provide a broader explanation of the digital transformation of social stratification.

## b. Instagram Use in Turkey

An initial search in the Web of Science database using the keyword *Instagram in Turkey* yielded a total of 366 articles. The results were then narrowed by selecting the categories Communication, Cultural Studies, Sociology, and Social Sciences, reducing the number to 76 articles considered relevant for review. From these, five studies were identified as directly related to the focus of this research.

Studies on Instagram in the Turkish context show that the concepts of digital caste and stratification can be examined particularly through the lenses of visibility, representation, and symbolic capital. For example, Melek and Müyesseroğlu (2023) analysed Ekrem İmamoğlu's use of Instagram through political storytelling, highlighting the platform's representational power and the visibility hierarchies it creates in politics. Similarly, Kavasoğlu, Şirin, and Uğurlu (2024) examined the gender-based tensions and cyber violence faced by female athletes while gaining visibility on Instagram, emphasizing that the platform's "visibility hierarchy" reproduces social inequalities. Addressing consumption and advertising practices, Kiyan and Dikmen (2019) showed how Instagram reinforces symbolic capital through celebrity endorsements and brand representations, creating sharp divides between digital elites and ordinary users. On another front, Davidjants and Tiidenberg (2022) analysed representations of the Armenian genocide on Instagram, raising questions about which groups are made visible, and which are excluded in digital memory politics. Taking a more individual focus, Akkaş and Turan (2025) explored how Instagram use affects productivity and procrastination behaviours, suggesting that the platform creates stratification based on different levels of self-control among users.

Together, these studies indicate that Instagram in Turkey is not merely a space for personal expression but also a platform where social stratification and caste-like structures are produced. The study on İmamoğlu (Melek & Müyesseroğlu, 2023) links political representation to caste-like visibility hierarchies; the research on female athletes (Kavasoğlu et al., 2024) demonstrates that gender is a key axis in digital caste formation. The study on consumption and advertising (Kiyan & Dikmen, 2019) shows, in line with Bourdieu's (1986) concept of symbolic capital, that influencers and digital elites gain privileged positions on Instagram. The work on activist memory (Davidjants & Tiidenberg, 2022) raises questions closely related to Habermas's (1989) public sphere theory about which groups can achieve visibility and which remain marginalized. Finally, the study on productivity and procrastination (Akkaş & Turan, 2025) reveals that, at the individual level, Instagram reinforces Foucaultian micro-power relations through self-discipline and control mechanisms. In sum, these findings suggest that Instagram in Turkey functions not only as a personal communication tool but also as a space where visibility, symbolic capital, and digital discipline intersect to reproduce new forms of social stratification.

## c. X (Twitter) Use in Turkey

A search in the Web of Science database using the keyword *X (Twitter) in Turkey* identified a total of 61 articles. All were reviewed in detail, and those relevant to this study were selected. Recent research on Twitter shows that, in the Turkish context, the platform functions as a space where political stratification, representation, and digital inequalities are produced. Yörük, Atsizelti, Kına, and Durusan (2025) analysed ideological positions during elections using Twitter data and computational methods, making visible the digital divides in the political sphere. Focusing on migration representations, Bozdağ (2024) found that Twitter in Turkey frames migrants using certain metaphors, creating discourses that marginalize and structure visibility hierarchies. Examining opposition party strategies, Gökalp and Subay (2024) demonstrated that the digital space operates as a site where political hegemony and caste-like power relations are reproduced. Yıldırım and Ayan (2024), discussing Twitter's transition to X, argued that changes in platform ownership and policies have strengthened platform capitalism and deepened digital stratification. Together, this literature indicates that Twitter in Turkey is not merely a communication tool but a digital space that reproduces political caste systems and inequality structures.

These studies show that Twitter (X) reproduces political and social stratification processes in Turkey at the digital level. Yörük, Atsizelti, Kına, and Durusan's (2025) election analysis using Twitter data makes the political dimension of the digital caste system visible, revealing that platforms function less as neutral communication arenas in Habermas's (1989) sense of the public sphere and more as sites where power relations are reasserted. Bozdağ (2024), focusing on the representation of migrants, demonstrated how metaphors on Twitter generate othering and marginalizing discourses, findings that align with Castells' (2009) network society concepts about identity construction and visibility hierarchies. Gökalp and Subay's (2024) analysis of opposition party rhetoric on Twitter shows that digital platforms are not only channels for information transfer but also instruments for establishing hegemony and reproducing political power. Yıldırım and Ayan's (2024) study of Twitter's transformation into X argues that changes in ownership and governance reinforce platform capitalism, deepening layers of digital inequality. Viewed through Foucault's (1977) concept of micro-power, these findings highlight that Twitter in Turkey is not simply a space for communication but a platform that actively reproduces caste-like digital inequalities and power hierarchies.

## d. TikTok Use in Turkey

A search in the Web of Science database using the keyword *TikTok in Turkey* identified a total of 47 articles. All were examined in detail, and those contributing directly to the purpose of this study were selected for analysis. Research on TikTok in the Turkish context shows how the platform reproduces caste-like structures in the digital sphere. Sot (2022) found that TikTok's algorithmic systems regulate users' experiences of visibility and privacy, demonstrating that the platform operates through algorithmic inequality and visibility hierarchies. Similarly, Çiçeklioğlu and Ünal (2021) examined the shift of news production and consumption to TikTok, discussing how public space becomes stratified on platforms by focusing on who is able to voice opinions and who is excluded. Youth studies (Balcı, Akgül & Astam, 2024; Akpınar & Eker, 2025) highlighted how university students' use of TikTok is linked to addiction, loneliness, and self-regulation, revealing the platform as a psychosocial space of differentiation and classification. Akyıl and Oral (2024) likewise showed that problematic TikTok use undermines psychological resilience, interpreting this in line with Foucault's concepts of subjectivation and discipline.

Taken together, this literature suggests that TikTok in Turkey functions as more than an entertainment platform; it is a space where digital stratification, visibility hierarchies, and caste-like divisions are produced. Sot's (2022) work underscores algorithmic inequality by showing how TikTok's systems govern user visibility and privacy. Çiçeklioğlu and Ünal (2021) demonstrate that the platform reshapes representational and stratification dynamics in public space, echoing Habermas's public sphere theory. Studies of university students (Balcı et al., 2024; Akpınar & Eker, 2025) connect TikTok use to loneliness, dependency, and lapses in self-control, findings that can be read through Foucault's lens of micro-power and subjectivation. Similarly, Akyıl and Oral (2024) argue that problematic TikTok use weakens resilience, showing how the platform acts as a mechanism of discipline and self-monitoring. Overall, the findings indicate that TikTok in Turkey is not simply an entertainment tool but a digital environment that reproduces social inequalities, visibility hierarchies, and caste-like systems.

## 5. EVALUATION OF FINDINGS

The findings of this study show that digital platforms in Turkey are not merely spaces for communication and interaction; they are also arenas where social differences are reproduced and new forms of stratification emerge. Examining LinkedIn, Instagram, TikTok, and Twitter/X reveals that each platform operates with its own logic of a "digital caste system."

LinkedIn stands out as a selective space where professional capital is produced and distributed. The different ways white-collar professionals and university students use the platform indicate that digital caste structures are reproduced along both class and cultural capital axes. This finding brings Bourdieu's concept of the convertibility of capital types into the digital domain, showing how offline advantages are reinforced by online visibility.

Instagram strengthens a "display caste" through aesthetic preferences, consumption practices, and the showcasing of daily life. Here, symbolic capital is distributed via likes, followers, and visibility, placing those with high cultural capital in an advantaged position. This reflects both the aesthetic dimensions of consumer society and the extension of Foucault's disciplinary mechanisms into the digital sphere.

On TikTok, algorithmic governance becomes the key factor. Some users gain rapid visibility while others are systematically marginalized, indicating that the platform functions according to an "algorithmic caste" logic. Zuboff's concept of surveillance capitalism is particularly relevant here: users' visibility and labor are commodified through algorithmic processes and integrated into market dynamics.

Twitter/X functions as a political and public debate arena, reflecting a "political/agenda caste." The platform elevates some users to agenda-setting roles while rendering others invisible. These dynamic produces power asymmetries that can be understood through Foucault's visibility-power relations and Castells's network society theory.

Overall, the findings indicate that digital stratification in Turkey is not only a matter of technical access; it is deeply rooted in the transfer of economic, cultural, and social capital differences into digital spaces. Platform algorithms intensify these differences and restrict mobility between digital castes. As a result, new forms of inequality arise in the digital society, where offline positions significantly shape online visibility and engagement. Thus, the study's findings align with broader discussions on digital stratification in the literature while supporting the explanatory value of the "digital caste" concept in the Turkish context. Moreover, user experiences in Turkey confirm global trends but also show how local cultural codes and social dynamics uniquely shape digital stratification.

*Table 1. Comparison of Platforms*

| Platform | Type of Digital Caste | Key Determinants | Theoretical Framework |
|---|---|---|---|
| **LinkedIn** | Professional caste | Professional networks, career capital, social capital production | Bourdieu: forms of capital, social capital |
| **Instagram** | Aesthetic/Display caste | Aesthetic tastes, consumption practices, symbolic capital | Bourdieu: cultural capital; Foucault: disciplinary mechanisms |
| **TikTok** | Algorithmic caste | Algorithmic visibility, digital labour, surveillance capitalism | Zuboff: surveillance capitalism; algorithmic governance |
| **Twitter/X** | Political/Agenda caste | Political visibility, agenda-setting, network power | Foucault: visibility and power; Castells: network society |

As seen in Table 1, the phenomenon of digital caste is reproduced across different social media platforms through distinct mechanisms. LinkedIn creates a professional caste through recruitment processes and networking; Instagram generates an aesthetic/display caste via visual aesthetics, consumption practices, and the influencer economy; TikTok establishes an algorithmic caste structure through algorithmic visibility, viral trends, and youth culture, where the platform's algorithm largely determines who becomes visible; and Twitter (X) forms a political/agenda caste through political communication, agenda-setting, and hashtag dominance, particularly amplifying the visibility of political elites. Thus, although each platform produces caste mechanisms through its own dynamics, they share a common feature: access to digital visibility is structurally unequal. This indicates that digital platforms are not merely communication arenas but also new spaces of social stratification.

Upward mobility among these four castes is possible but conditional: (i) transferable capital (e.g., education/certificates → LinkedIn visibility), (ii) content/habitus alignment (e.g., adapting to aesthetic codes on Instagram), (iii) network bridging (cross-interactions from high-status accounts), and (iv) consistent optimization of algorithmic signals (regular content production, audience retention). However, ownership policies, advertising economies, and the opacity of recommendation systems structurally limit such mobility. Thus, *digital castes* have permeable yet asymmetric thresholds.

## CONCLUSION

This study has demonstrated that digital platforms are not merely spaces for communication and interaction, but also unique arenas where social stratification is reproduced. The analysis of LinkedIn, Instagram, TikTok, and Twitter/X in the Turkish context revealed that each platform creates its own version of a "digital caste system." LinkedIn produces a "career caste" through professional networks; Instagram constructs a "display caste" through aesthetics and consumption practices; TikTok reinforces an "algorithmic caste" through algorithm-driven visibility regimes; and Twitter/X establishes an "agenda caste" by centralizing political discourse.

The findings show that digital inequalities stem not only from differences in technical access but also from the transfer of economic, cultural, and social capital into the digital domain. Digital caste systems transform offline social positions into online visibility and engagement levels. In this sense, platform algorithms and symbolic practices limit social mobility and create new hierarchies in the digital sphere. Theoretically, Bourdieu's concepts of capital and field, Foucault's analyses of surveillance and discipline, Castells's network society approach, and Zuboff's framework of surveillance capitalism provide an explanatory foundation for understanding the dynamics of digital caste systems. Guided by these theories, this study connects the observed patterns of digital stratification in Turkey to broader global debates. From a user-centered perspective, the findings underscore how digital hierarchies are not experienced uniformly: while elites can convert cultural and economic capital into algorithmic visibility, marginalized groups confront opaque moderation systems and limited mobility. Yet these dynamics should not be mistaken for rigid, caste-like immutability. As emphasized earlier, the metaphor of "digital caste" is heuristic—it highlights structural asymmetries without ignoring the fluidity, contestation, and reversibility of online positions. By revisiting both the lived experiences of users and the limits of the metaphor, this study concludes that platform-based stratification is best understood as a dialectical process: simultaneously constraining and enabling, stabilizing inequalities while also opening spaces for counter-practices and collective agency.

In conclusion, caste-like stratification on Turkish digital platforms represents a new and distinct form of social inequality. These structures are shaped not only by the technical design of platforms but also by local cultural codes, economic differences, and the political climate. Thus, digital caste systems contribute to discussions on platformized societies at a global scale while making Turkey's specific sociological dynamics visible. Future studies could investigate the impact of these caste systems on different social groups using empirical methods, offering a more comprehensive picture of how digital inequalities evolve. In addition, Facebook and YouTube were excluded from this study due to their different functional logics; future research may examine how digital caste systems manifest on these platforms.

## REFERENCES


Acar, S., Gürsoy, H., & Ünsal, N. Ö. (2014). İlişkisel toplumda sosyal iş ağlarının kariyer gelişimi açısından önemi: LinkedIn örneği. *Electronic Journal of Vocational Colleges*, Özel Sayı, 17–25.

Ahmad, M., Shahzadi, A., Vallejo, R. G., Naeem, Z., & Tran, D. B. (2025). Virtual Realities, Real Societies: The Metaverse Effect. In Pucelj, M., & Bohinc, R. (Eds.), *Challenges for Digital Citizenship and Ethics: Social Media, Deep Fakes, and Virtual Communities* (pp. 103–122). IGI Global Scientific Publishing., DOI: 10.4018/979-8-3693-7914-1.ch005

Akkaş, C., & Turan, A. H. (2025). Predictors of Instagram use for user productivity: Self-control, notifications, and checking habits. *International Journal of Mobile Communications, 25*(4), 417–447.

Akpınar, E. G., & Eker, H. H. (2025). The effect of TikTok use on internet addiction in university students. *International Journal of Environmental Health Research.* Advance online publication. DOI: 10.1080/09603123.2024.2448488

Akyıl, Y., & Oral, T. (2024). The mediating role of problematic TikTok use and mindfulness in the relationship between psychological resilience and internet addiction. *Discover Psychology, 4*(1). Advance online publication. DOI: 10.1007/s44202-024-00317-0

Arısoy Gedik, C., & Ceyhan, A. I. (2024). The Gender Gap in the Digital Era: Reaching Algorithmic Fairness and Technological Inclusivity in Network Society. *Communication Papers. Media Literacy and Gender Studies, 13*(26), 64–75. DOI: 10.33115/udg_bib/cp.v13i26.23038

Bakan, U., & Karaaslan, İ. A. (2017). Bireysel farklılıkların sosyal sermaye oluşumuna etkisi: Facebook ve LinkedIn kullanıcıları üzerine karşılaştırmalı bir analiz. *Intermedia. International Journal (Toronto, Ont.), 4*(6), 77–97.

Bakırtaş, H., & Sekendür Turgu, G. (2021). LinkedIn kullanım alışkanlıkları üzerine bir araştırma. *Dicle Üniversitesi Sosyal Bilimler Enstitüsü Dergisi, 13*(26), 245–265.

Bakırtaş, H., & Turgu, G. S. (2021). LinkedIn sosyal iş ağının kullanıcı algısı. *Abant Sosyal Bilimler Dergisi, 21*(3), 796–810. DOI: 10.11616/asbi.956027

Balcı, Ş., Akgül, T. E., & Astam, F. K. (2024). The use of TikTok by university youth: The relationship between TikTok addiction, loneliness, and emotional intelligence. *Türkiye İletişim Araştırmaları Dergisi, 45*, 100–121. DOI: 10.17829/turcom.1373818

Bourdieu, P. (1984). *Distinction: A social critique of the judgement of taste* (R. Nice, Trans.). Harvard University Press. (Original work published 1979).

Bourdieu, P. (1986). The forms of capital. In Richardson, J. G. (Ed.), *Handbook of theory and research for the sociology of education* (pp. 241–258). Greenwood Press.

Boyd, D. (2008). Why youth (heart) social network sites: The role of networked publics in teenage social life. *Youth, Identity, And Digital Media, David Buckingham, ed., The John D. and Catherine T. MacArthur Foundation Series on Digital Media and Learning, The MIT Press, Cambridge, MA*, 2007-16.

Bozdağ, U. (2024). Framing displaced persons: An analysis of Turkish migration metaphors on Twitter. *Intersections: East European Journal of Society and Politics, 10*(1). Advance online publication. DOI: 10.17356/ieejsp.v10i1.1189

Bye, T. A. (2020). Book review: The Platform Society. *Nordic Journal of Science and Technology Studies, 8*(1), 31–33.

Capodivacca, S., & Giacomini, G. (2024). Discipline and Power in the Digital Age: Critical Reflections from Foucault's Thought. *Foucault Studies, 36*, 227–251. https://muse.jhu.edu/article/940820

Castells, M. (2009). *The rise of the network society* (2nd ed., Vol. 1). Wiley-Blackwell.

Çelik, N. (2023a). The Digital Inequalities in The Digital Society, *In Current Debates on Social Sciences 13,* pp: 75-81. ISBN: 978-625-6925-27-4 1st Edition.

Çelik, N. (2023b). I Am Online; Therefore, I Am!: Digital Obesity From a Sociological Perspective. In *Handbook of Research on Perspectives on Society and Technology Addiction* (pp. 479-496). IGI Global.

Çelik, N. (2025). New Methodological Trends in Sociology: An Assessment of Recent Studies. *Uluslararası Sosyal Bilimlerde Mükemmellik Arayışı Dergisi*, (8), 44–59.

Çelik, N., & Ateşoğlu, N. (2023). Dijitalleşmenin Eğitim Üzerindeki Etkileri: Sosyoloji Eğitimi Üzerine Eleştirel Bir Deneme. In *Dijital Kültür Bir Değişim Öyküsü: Medya, İletişim ve Eğitim Araştırmaları, (Edt: Ferihan Ayaz, Dilek Turan Eroğlu, Hakan Ayaz)*. Eğitim Yayınevi.

Chai, S. H., Nicholson, B., Scapens, R. W., & Yang, C. (2023). Digital Platforms, Surveillance and Processes of Demoralization. *Journal of Information Technology, 39*(3), 568–586. DOI: 10.1177/02683962231208215

Cheng, C., & Ren, Y. (2024). The paradox of seeking help: Socioeconomic inequality in medical crowdfunding in the era of the mobile internet. *Chinese Journal of Sociology, 10*(1), 100–130. DOI: 10.1177/2057150X241230163

Chernavin, Y. A. (2021). Digital society: Theoretical outlines of the emerging paradigm. *Digital Society : Ethics, Socio-Legal and Governance of Digital Technology*, *4*(2), 4–12.

Çiçeklioğlu, A. Ş., & Ünal, R. (2021). What does TikTok app promise in the context of news production and consumption? *İLEF Dergisi, 8*, 69–98. https://doi.org/DOI: 10.24955/ilef.1037967

Couldry, N., & Mejias, U. A. (2019). Data colonialism: Rethinking big data's relation to the contemporary subject. *Television & New Media*, *20*(4), 336–349.

Coveri, A., Cozza, C., & Guarascio, D. (2021). *Monopoly capitalism in the digital era* (No. 2021/33). LEM Working Paper Series.

Cui, P. (2025). Dynamics and Inequalities in Digital Social Networks: A Computational and Sociological Review. *arXiv preprint arXiv:2503.02887.*

Davidjants, J., & Tiidenberg, K. (2022). Activist memory narration on social media: Armenian genocide on Instagram. *New Media & Society*, *24*(10), 2191–2206.

Davis, K., & Moore, W. E. (2019). Some principles of stratification. In *Social Stratification, Class, Race, and Gender in Sociological Perspective, Second Edition* (pp. 55-63). Routledge.

Denizli, U. (2019). İşe alım sürecinde sosyal ağ siteleri kullanımı: Tehlikeler ve fırsatlar. *The Journal of International Scientific Researches*, *4*(3), 283–303.

Dmitrieva, E. I. (2020). Digital Platforms as a Base for Forming a Digital Economy. In *2nd International Scientific and Practical Conference on Digital Economy (ISCDE 2020)* (pp. 553-558). Atlantis Press.

Donath, J. S. (2002). Identity and deception in the virtual community. In *Communities in cyberspace* (pp. 37–68). Routledge.

Dorschel, R. (2022). Reconsidering digital labour: Bringing tech workers into the debate. *New Technology, Work and Employment*, *37*(2), 288–307. DOI: 10.1111/ntwe.12225

Durkheim, É. (2014). *The division of labour in society* (Halls, W. D., Trans.). Free Press. (Original work published 1893)

Fu, X., Avenyo, E., & Ghauri, P. (2021). Digital platforms and development: A survey of the literature. *Innovation and Development*, *11*(2-3), 303–321.

Gerber, C., & Krzywdzinski, M. (2019). Brave new digital work? New forms of performance control in crowdwork. In *Work and labor in the digital age* (Vol. 33, pp. 121–143). Emerald Publishing Limited., DOI: 10.1108/s0277-283320190000033008

Gökalp, B., & Subay, Ö. Ö. (2024). The reflections on social media of the statements made by the Nation Alliance in Turkey. *Zeitschrift für Vergleichende Politikwissenschaft*. https://doi.org/DOI: 10.1007/s12286-024-00593-z

Gorwa, R. (2019). What is platform governance? *Information Communication and Society*, *22*(6), 854–871. DOI: 10.1080/1369118x.2019.1573914

Gorwa, R., Lechowski, G., & Schneiß, D. (2024). Platform lobbying: Policy influence strategies and the EU's Digital Services Act. *Internet Policy Review*, *13*(2), 1–26. DOI: 10.14763/2024.2.1782

Gürbüzdal, U. (2022). Güvencesizleşmenin sembolik inkârı olarak sosyal medya pratikleri: Beyaz yakalı profesyonel kültürüne LinkedIn üzerinden bir bakış. *ARTS*, Dijitalleşme Özel Sayısı, 27–55. https://doi.org/ .DOI: 10.46372/arts.1191703

Hallinan, B., Reynolds, C. J., & Rothenstein, O. (2024). Copyright callouts and the promise of creator-driven platform governance. *Internet Policy Review*, *13*(2), 1–43. DOI: 10.14763/2024.2.1770

Helberger, N., Pierson, J., & Poell, T. (2018). Governing online platforms: From contested to cooperative responsibility. *The Information Society*, *34*(1), 1–14. DOI: 10.1080/01972243.2017.1391913

Helles, R., & Flyverbom, M. (2019). Meshes of Surveillance, Prediction, and Infrastructure: On the Cultural and Commercial Consequences of Digital Platforms. *Surveillance & Society*, *17*(1/2), 34–39. https://ojs.library.queensu.ca/index.php/surveillance-and-society/article/view/13120

Hopkins, S. (2022). Beyond Digital Literacy in Australian Prisons: Theorizing "Network Literacy," Intersectionality, and Female Incarcerated Students. *Media and Communication*, *10*(4). Advance online publication. DOI: 10.17645/mac.v10i4.5734

Ivashyna, O., Ivashyna, S., & Novikova, L. (2023). Some aspects of institutionalisation of economic development of the digital society. *Scientific Opinion Economics and Management, (3)(83).*

Jabbouri, I., Farooq, O., Naili, M., & Helmi, I. (2024). Navigating the Financing Constraints: The Role of Social Capital in Developing Countries. *Journal of Emerging Market Finance*, *23*(3), 360–386.

Karimi, F., Oliveira, M., & Strohmaier, M. (2022). Minorities in networks and algorithms. *arXiv preprint arXiv:2206.07113*.

Kavasoğlu, İ., Eratlı Şirin, Y., & Uğurlu, A. (2024). A space of one's own? The tensions of being visible on Instagram for Turkish female athletes. *Communication & Sport*, *12*(2), 347–369.

Keddell, E. (2021). "Make Them Dance": Shoshana Zuboff's Surveillance Capitalism, Behavior Modification and Fraser's "Abnormal Justice". *Journal of Technology in Human Services*, *39*(4), 426–431. DOI: 10.1080/15228835.2021.1942396

Kerssens, N., & Van Dijck, J. (2022). Governed by edtech? Valuing pedagogical autonomy in a platform society. *Harvard Educational Review*, *92*(2), 284–303. DOI: 10.17763/1943-5045-92.2.284

Kim, H. H. (2009). Networks, information transfer, and status conferral: The role of social capital in income stratification among lawyers. *The Sociological Quarterly*, *50*(1), 61–87.

Kiyan, Z., & Dikmen, E. S. (2019). The role of social media in advertising: An examination on Instagram. *İLEF Dergisi*, *6*(1), 121–146. https://doi.org/DOI: 10.24955/ilef.554036

Kumar, P. C., Vitak, J., Chetty, M., & Clegg, T. L. (2019). The platformization of the classroom: Teachers as surveillant consumers. *Surveillance & Society*, *17*(1/2), 145–152. DOI: 10.24908/ss.v17i1/2.12926

Kurganskaya, V. D., & Dunaev, V. Y. (2021). Digitalization as a modeling system of social stratification. *Social Novelties and Social Sciences*, (1), 3.

Kuriakose, F., & Iyer, D. K. (2021). Digital Workers, Urban Vectors, and New Economies. *The South Atlantic Quarterly*, *120*(4), 749–762. DOI: 10.1215/00382876-9443308

Langley, P., & Leyshon, A. (2017). Platform capitalism: The intermediation and capitalisation of digital economic circulation. *Finance and Stochastics*, *3*(1), 11–31. DOI: 10.2218/finsoc.v3i1.1936

Laniuk, Y. (2021). Freedom in the Age of surveillance capitalism: Lessons from Shoshana Zuboff. *Ethics & Bioethics*, *11*(1-2), 67–81. DOI: 10.2478/ebce-2021-0004

Martindale, N., & Lehdonvirta, V. (2021). Can Labour Market Digitalization Increase Social Mobility? Evidence from a European Survey of Online Platform Workers. *SSRN*, 1–21. http://dx.doi.org/DOI: 10.2139/ssrn.3862635

Martindale, N., & Lehdonvirta, V. (2023a). Labour Market Digitalization and Social Class: Evidence of Mobility and Reproduction from a European Survey of Online Platform Workers. *Socio-economic Review, 21*(4), 1945–1965. DOI: 10.1093/ser/mwad049

Marx, K. (1976). *Capital: A critique of political economy* (Vol. I; Fowkes, B., Trans.). Penguin Books. (Original work published 1867)

Marx, K., & Engels, F. (2002). *The Communist Manifesto* (Moore, S., Trans.). Penguin Classics. (Original work published 1848)

Melek, G., & Müyesseroğlu, E. (2023). Political storytelling of Ekrem İmamoğlu on Instagram. *Visual Studies, 38*(5), 894–910. DOI: 10.1080/1472586X.2021.1975501

Naik, S. S., & Kakade, O. (2024). Impact Of Digitalization on Society: A Critical Study. *mLAC Journal for Arts, Commerce and Sciences (m-JACS) ISSN: 2584-1920, 2*(4), 1-13.

Oliveira, R. A. (2023). Regimes of Visibility and Algorithmic Surveillance on Digital Platforms: Operationalizing the Thought Through Images in a Collaborative Perspective. *Journal of Latin American Communication Research, 11*(2), 137–156. DOI: 10.55738/journal.v11i2p.137-156

Papacharissi, Z. (2010). A private sphere: Democracy in a digital age. *Polity*.

Parsons, T. (2017). The present status of "structural-functional" theory in sociology. In *The idea of social structure* (pp. 67–84). Routledge.

Pichler, F., & Wallace, C. (2009). Social capital and social class in Europe: The role of social networks in social stratification. *European Sociological Review, 25*(3), 319–332. DOI: 10.1093/esr/jcn050

Plantin, J. C., Lagoze, C., Edwards, P. N., & Sandvig, C. (2018). Infrastructure studies meet platform studies in the age of Google and Facebook. *New Media & Society, 20*(1), 293–310.

Risi, E., Pronzato, R., & Di Fraia, G. (2020). Living and working confined at home: Boundaries and platforms during the lockdown. *Journal of Cultural Analysis and Social Change, 5*(2), 1–4. DOI: 10.20897/jcasc/9253

Sadowski, J. (2019). When data is capital: Datafication, accumulation, and extraction. *Big Data & Society, 6*(1), 2053951718820549.

Schlag, G. (2023). European Union's regulating of social media: A discourse analysis of the Digital Services Act. *Politics and Governance, 11*(3), 168–177.

Singh, A., Garcia, P., & Lindtner, S. (2023). Old Logics, New Technologies: Producing a Managed Workforce on On-Demand Service Platforms. *In Proceedings of the 2023 CHI Conference on Human Factors in Computing Systems* (CHI '23). Association for Computing Machinery, New York, NY, USA, Article 160, 1–15. https://doi.org/DOI: 10.1145/3544548.3581240

Sot, İ. (2022). Fostering intimacy on TikTok: A platform that connects during COVID-19 lockdowns. *Media Culture & Society*, *44*(8), 1490–1507. DOI: 10.1177/01634437221104709

Stark, D. (1997). [Review of *The Rise of the Network Society*, by M. Castells]. *Contemporary Sociology*, *26*(6), 725–726. DOI: 10.2307/2654643

Steinhoff, J. (2024). Toward a political economy of synthetic data: A data-intensive capitalism that is not a surveillance capitalism? *New Media & Society*, *26*(6), 3290–3306.

Therborn, G. (1999). *The ideology of power and the power of ideology* (Vol. 24). Verso.

Tınmaz, H., & Fanea-Ivanovici, M. (2024). An exploratory study on Turkish university students' thoughts on LinkedIn in a business context. *Quality - Access to Success*, *25*(198), 86–95. DOI: 10.47750/QAS/25.198.09

Törnberg, P. (2023). How platforms govern: Social regulation in digital capitalism. *Big Data & Society, 10*(1). https://doi.org/ (Original work published 2023)DOI: 10.1177/20539517231153808

Turkle, S. (1997). Life on the screen: Identity in the age of the internet. *Literature & History*, *6*, 117–118.

van Dijck, J., & Lin, J. (2022). Deplatformization, platform governance and global geopolitics: Interview with José van Dijck. *Communication and the Public*, *7*(2), 59–66. DOI: 10.1177/20570473221102199

Van Dijck, J., Nieborg, D., & Poell, T. (2019). Reframing platform power. *Internet Policy Review*, *8*(2), 1–18. DOI: 10.14763/2019.2.1414

Van Dijck, J., Poell, T., & De Waal, M. (2018). *The platform society: Public values in a connective world.* Oxford university press., DOI: 10.1093/oso/9780190889760.001.0001

Van Dijk, J. A. G. M. (2005). *The deepening divide: Inequality in the information society*. Sage Publications.

Van Dijk, J. A. G. M. (2020). *The digital divide*. Polity Press.

Vlasceanu, M., & Amodio, D. M. (2022). Propagation of societal gender inequality by internet search algorithms. *Proceedings of the National Academy of Sciences of the United States of America, 119*(29), e2204529119.

Walsh, J. P. (2020). Social media and moral panics: Assessing the effects of technological change on societal reaction. *International Journal of Cultural Studies, 23*(6), 840-859. https://doi.org/ (Original work published 2020)DOI: 10.1177/1367877920912257

Weber, M. (1922). Class, status, party. In *From Max Weber: Essays in sociology* (Gerth, H. H., & Wright Mills, C., Eds. & Trans.; pp. 180–195). Oxford University Press.

Weber, M. (1978). *Economy and society: An outline of interpretive sociology* (Roth, G., & Wittich, C., Eds., Fischoff, E., Trans.). University of California Press. (Original work published 1922)

Willekens, M., Siongers, J., & Lievens, J. (2022). Social stratification and social media disengagement: The effect of economic, cultural and social capital on reasons for non-use of social media platforms. *Poetics, 95*, 101708. Advance online publication. DOI: 10.1016/j.poetic.2022.101708

Wright, E. O. (1997). *Class Counts: Comparative Studies in Class Analysis.* Cambridge University Press.

Xiumei, X., Xiaoxuan, Z., & Hui, W. (2022). Research on the influencing mechanism of data capital on farmers' income. *Mobile Information Systems, 2022*(1), 4683251.

Yıldırım, O., & Ayan, V. M. (2024). From Twitter to X: Evaluating the change of ownership and platform politics. *İLEF Dergisi, 11*(2). DOI: DOI: 10.24955/ilef.1432738

Yörük, E., Atsizelti, S., Kına, M. F., & Durusan, F. (2025). A computational analysis of ideological positions in Turkish electoral politics. *The Developing Economies.* Advance online publication. DOI: 10.1111/deve.12424

Zhao, S., Grasmuck, S., & Martin, J. (2008). Identity construction on Facebook: Digital empowerment in anchored relationships. *Computers in Human Behavior, 24*(5), 1816–1836.

Zheng, L., Chen, L., Long, F., Liu, J., & Li, L. (2024). Reducing Social Media Attention Inequality in Disasters: The Role of Official Media During Rainstorm Disasters in China. *International Journal of Disaster Risk Science, 15*(3), 388–403.

Chapter 2

# The Role of Local Platforms and Non-Western Perspectives on Platformization

**Silvio Andrae**
https://orcid.org/0000-0002-8586-7812
*Independent Researcher, Germany*

## ABSTRACT

*This chapter explores how platformization transcends the boundaries of Western tech companies, manifesting in diverse political economies. The objective is to broaden the analysis of global platform dynamics by incorporating non-Western perspectives. Methodologically, the chapter employs a comparative case study design, encompassing China, Kenya, Brazil, and the Middle East. The findings demonstrate that platforms are not just technical or market-related innovations, but complex hybrid infrastructures that reshape state control, financialization, labor regimes, and subjectification. This gives rise to distinct platform orders: state-capitalist (China), infrastructural-compensatory (Kenya), conflictual-hybrid (Latin America), and authoritarian-migration-based (Middle East). Platformization thus emerges as a globally fragmented yet structurally interconnected regime of accumulation and control, which not only perpetuates inequalities but also fundamentally transforms them. This article advocates for a decolonizing platform theory.*

DOI: 10.4018/979-8-3373-4267-2.ch002

## INTRODUCTION

In the 21st century, platforms have developed into central infrastructures for economic, social, and cultural processes. Companies such as Google, Amazon, Meta, and Uber shape the image of global digital capitalism, in which a few corporations control markets, extract data, and structure communication flows. Research on platformization, therefore, often focuses on these Western 'global players' (Srnicek, 2017; van Dijck et al., 2018). An exclusively Euro-American perspective proves to be inadequate. However, as productive as it has been, this Western perspective is increasingly proving insufficient to capture the global dynamics of platformization adequately. Platformization is a heterogeneous and universal process. Instead, independent platform ecosystems are emerging in various regions of the world, interacting with local practices, institutions, and value systems.

The concept of platformization, which refers to the process of increasing penetration of everyday practices, communication processes, and economic structures by platform-based mediation and control mechanisms (Helmond, 2015), is central to this discussion. In Europe and North America, the current focus of debate centers on data protection, algorithmic discrimination, and working conditions (Pasquale, 2015). In Africa, Asia, and Latin America, on the other hand, other issues are of central importance, including access to basic infrastructure, regulation by authoritarian states, and the search for alternative, non-capitalist economies. This illustrates that platformization should be viewed as a regionally differentiated transformation complex in which global infrastructures are intertwined with local institutions, cultural practices, and political regimes (Plantin et al., 2018; Graham et al., 2017).

The subject of this chapter is the role of local platforms in non-Western contexts. Methodologically, the analysis is based on comparative case study logic (Yin, 2014). The focus is on the question of how platformization in China, Africa, Latin America, and the Middle East takes on specific forms that differ significantly from those in the West. This involves not only economic structures, but also questions of political control, cultural hybridity, and social inclusion. In these contexts, platforms serve as both markets and infrastructures, as well as spaces of subjectivation, where global capital flows are intertwined with local practices.

The contribution of this chapter manifests itself in three significant ways. First, it is worth noting that the phenomenon of platform research is undergoing a significant expansion of its empirical basis through the systematic inclusion of cases beyond the Euro-American sphere. This expansion is crucial for a comprehensive understanding of platformization. Furthermore, an evaluation is made of the explanatory power of existing theories of platform capitalism, which have predominantly developed in Western contexts. In this study, the approaches of Srnicek (2017), Zuboff (2019), and Staab (2019) are subjected to critical analysis. Srnicek describes platforms as capitalist infrastructures, Zuboff focuses on surveillance, Staab on proprietary markets, and Vogl on the fusion of financial capitalism, information, and affect. The critical analysis of these theories is the second significant contribution of this chapter. Finally, this chapter proposes a theoretical opening of platform research that pays greater attention to decolonization, contextuality, and hybridity (Couldry & Mejias, 2019). This theoretical opening is the third significant contribution of this chapter.

This article aims to understand platformization as a form of assembling, a concept that refers to a collection of diverse elements that are brought together to form a whole, in this case, constituted by economic, political, and cultural dynamics. Instead of assuming a uniform global model, it argues that platformization should be viewed as a conflictual and regionally differentiated process of transformation. This article thus understands itself as a plea for multi-perspective platform research that critically reflects on global power relations while also highlighting the creativity of local actors. The systematic inclusion of non-Western perspectives is crucial in this context to understand the configurations of markets, identities, and power structures across platforms worldwide.

The chapter's structure is presented in a five-part outline. After the theoretical framework (Section 2), case studies on China, Africa, Latin America, and the Middle East (Section 3) are presented. In accordance with Section 4, both similarities and differences are identified in this comparative interim assessment. The results are summarized in Section 5 in terms of their implications for platform theory and in Section 6 in terms of the conclusions drawn. The study aims to demonstrate that platforms are reconfiguring not only markets and technologies, but also identities, power constellations, and social orders worldwide.

## THEORIES OF PLATFORM CAPITALISM

The academic debate on platformization has undergone significant diversification in recent years. In the early stages of research, the focus was on technological innovations and business models. However, approaches based on capitalism theory, political economy, and sociology have now established themselves, viewing platforms as central actors in a new regime of accumulation. Four authors—Nick Srnicek, Shoshana Zuboff, Philipp Staab, and Joseph Vogl—mark essential theoretical points of reference in this context. Postcolonial approaches (Couldry & Mejias, 2019) offer valuable supplementary insights for examining global power asymmetries.

## Platforms, as a Form of Capitalist Infrastructure

Nick Srnicek (2017) argues that platforms, with their business model based on aggregating, storing, and analyzing data, are not just neutral intermediaries or technology providers. They are structural gatekeepers, controlling access to markets and communication spaces, and thereby wielding significant power in the digital economy.

This concentration of power manifests itself in the structures of the internet as a network (Web3). Regarding internet infrastructure, companies from the US and China are competing to maintain their central position. Significant investments are being made in the development of technical standards and the construction of physical infrastructure. At this infrastructure level, these companies have significantly more power over the global internet than most countries worldwide. These technology companies are striving to create self-contained subsystems within the internet in order to gain a competitive advantage at this level. The goal is to transform their platforms into independent subnetworks in which they can occupy central positions of power (Pohle & Voelsen, 2022).

## Surveillance Capitalism and the Logic of Extraction

Shoshana Zuboff (2019) expands on this analysis by interpreting the platform economy as the emergence of surveillance capitalism. The focus is on the commodification of 'behavioral surplus,' i.e., data collected about users, processed algorithmically, and transformed into predictive products. In this context, platforms act not only as markets but also as mechanisms for extracting and commercializing human behavior. Zuboff emphasizes that this process represents a qualitatively new form of capitalist domination that goes beyond the classic dimensions of production and consumption.

At the center of this concept is 'behavioral surplus,' introduced by Zuboff. This term refers to the data that platforms collect beyond what is necessary for providing a service (e.g., location, clicks, payment). This surplus data is then converted into algorithmic prediction models. These models, or 'prediction products,' are traded on markets of digital capitalism—for example, in advertising, credit scoring, or platform ranking.

As a result, there is a shift in capitalist value creation from production and consumption to areas such as extraction, forecasting, and behavioral control. In this context, Zuboff uses the term 'expropriation of experience.' This describes the privatization and economic exploitation of human behavior without consent or compensation. The present logic of extraction should not be viewed as passive, but rather as increasingly interventionist. Platforms not only observe behavior but also model and shape it in order to maximize predictability and economic exploitability. This is done, for example, through algorithmic recommendations, nudging, and ranking mechanisms.

Zuboff describes this development as a new stage of capitalist domination that differs from previous modes of production:

- It does not require wage labor, but rather attention, interaction, and everyday behavior as raw materials.
- It replaces scarcity with the unlimited generation and exploitation of data.
- It does not operate through price formation, but through algorithmic control of social situations.
- It leaves the classic production spaces and colonizes living environments, mobility, communication, and intimacy.

## Proprietary Markets and the Economy of Scarcity

In information networks, demand-driven economies of scale are a characteristic feature of platform economies. User activity increases because using the platform is beneficial to them. It has been found that they reinforce the effectiveness of pull factors and forces of inclusion. The available results show that this leads to highly concentrated market structures. The technological and financial architecture of platforms favors the creation of value. The generation of added value is enabled by external and internal access to entities that are in a state of non-commodification. The focus is on the profitable marketing of information products, the production of which is associated with minimal marginal costs.

Platform companies intertwine with the current economic and financial order by positioning themselves as markets. Philipp Staab (2019) defines platforms as operators of proprietary markets that are privately owned and enforce access and price control. The goal is not to maximize production, but to exploit scarce information goods. Profits are not generated through production but result from skimming rents—whether in the form of fees, commissions, or control over digital infrastructures. In this context, platform capitalism manifests itself as an economy of scarcity: digital goods, such as data or applications, are in principle available in unlimited quantities, but are artificially scarce due to algorithmic visibility or membership models. For Staab, this represents a new form of capitalist accumulation that not only fails to reduce inequality but also exacerbates it.

An increase in data-generating applications from platform companies is observable. Software and hardware are permeating the analog world; search engines are expanding into hardware manufacturing, e-commerce, and financial markets. Mail-order companies are players in the fields of search engines, cloud computing, and banking. An increased range of streaming and financial services currently characterizes the market for smartphone manufacturers. In addition, social media offers data, information, and financial products, and are experimenting with payment systems. A convergence of industries is occurring.

This study concludes that the company has consistently expanded its range of products and services through strategic expansion, investments, and acquisitions. The use of network effects is one method of achieving broad user and consumer involvement. The platforms act as intermediaries between producers and consumers. Competition is controlled and generated. Companies generate revenue through commission payments and earn profits by leasing space. The combination of proprietary infrastructures and scalable digital goods enables an expansion of market function at low marginal costs.

Platform companies manifest themselves as standardized technical-economic systems. The coordination of decentralized interfaces is carried out by a central control system that acts as an interface between the individual elements. The associated machine operations, such as tracking, tracing, targeting, ranking, scoring, mapping, and profiling, can be interpreted as elements of algorithmic control. The analysis of communication events on platforms enables patterns to be identified. It is possible to sort the existing patterns according to significant frequencies, relationship densities, trends, or expected developments.

## Financialization, Information, and Affect

Since the 1970s, liberal market theories have focused on addressing and rectifying the asymmetric distribution of information in markets. However, current research trends are confronted with the systematic creation of information asymmetries. Control over information and markets has become a decisive productive force that manifests itself in corporate strategies. These characteristics underscore the thesis that geo-economic order is characterized less by competing companies and more by the bundled strategies of solvent financial investors.

The proprietary markets of the platform industry stand in stark contrast to the liberal model of supposedly neutral markets, which should be understood as subjects of superior knowledge. It is worth noting that, in addition to significant economic and political interventions (such as the privatization of utility networks or the repeal of net neutrality in the US), a multitude of systemic, technological, and structural factors have enabled the specific control procedures of platform companies in the first place.

Joseph Vogl (2021) understands platformization as part of a broader accumulation regime that intertwines financial markets, digital infrastructures, and affective economies. Platforms not only act as economic actors but also function as control authorities that steer user behavior through processes such as 'tracking, tracing, targeting.' In this context, Vogl differentiates between knowledge and information: platforms generate algorithmically standardized information that structures markets, but at the same time, they substitute for knowledge. This results in the emergence of opinion markets, where ratings, rankings, and likes are subject to economic exploitation. In this context, platformization manifests as a process of financializing social relationships and generating new subjectivities based on comparison, competition, and resentment.

It was only in the socioeconomic milieu of proprietary markets and platform business models that the convergence of communication and control took the form of concrete machines. The use of these machines results in the simultaneous production of information goods as efficient control products. This applies to both the recording of payment flows by payment systems and the centralization of data extraction on cloud platforms. Surveillance goods are produced through control contracts, which function as instruments for compensating for services rendered, benefits, services, and applications of all kinds. The developments described have ultimately given rise to those private-public interdependencies that manifest themselves in the seamless transitions between technical, economic, and state control strategies. A new form of governance is currently emerging. This manifests itself in the implementation of new control practices, such as data, access, price, and access controls, as well as in the diversification and informal fusion between public and private actors. This development is leading to a specific dynamic characterized by the establishment of platform companies. These companies construct hybrid structures that feature elements of both the private and public sectors. The boundaries between political and governmental control, on the one hand, and market processes, on the other, are becoming increasingly blurred.

## Postcolonial Perspectives

To understand platformization beyond Euro-American patterns of interpretation, it is advisable to draw on postcolonial theories. These make it clear that global structures of power and knowledge production are historically rooted in colonial hierarchies (Said, 1978; Spivak, 1988). In the context of the digital economy, this implies that Western-influenced technologies, infrastructures, and concepts are associated with power asymmetries. While Srnicek, Zuboff, Staab, and Vogl predominantly analyze Western contexts, Couldry and Mejias (2019) take a postcolonial perspective. The term 'data colonialism' is used in this context. Data colonialism is based on various doctrines that manifest themselves in the emphasis on a 'digital community' and 'personalization.' In addition, the term 'raw data' is misnamed in a way that reflects colonial ideologies, such as 'terra nullius' and the concept of the 'civilized world.'

In this study, the end-user license agreements of digital services that deprive users of ownership of their data are compared with the Spanish Requerimiento of 1513. This study was conducted by Couldry and Mejias in 2019.

This perspective allows us to recognize that platforms in non-Western contexts function not only as economic instruments of power, but also as geopolitical and cultural ones. Postcolonial approaches do not focus exclusively on dependencies but also take into account spaces of resistance. Local platforms can interrupt hegemonic data flows, make alternative practices visible, and strengthen cultural self-determination (Mbembe, 2020).

Another theoretical approach comes from assemblage theory (Deleuze & Guattari, 1987; Ong & Collier, 2005). This makes it possible to view platformization not as a uniform, top-down phenomenon, but as a dynamic intertwining of heterogeneous elements: technological infrastructures, regulatory frameworks, economic interests, cultural norms, and everyday practices. From this perspective, platforms are neither purely global nor purely local phenomena, but hybrid entities that form at the intersections of capital, state, and society (Couldry & Hepp, 2017).

In summary, these approaches can be characterized as different but complementary perspectives. Srnicek (2017) emphasizes the infrastructural role of platforms, Zuboff (2019) the extraction of data as a new commodity, Staab (2019) proprietary markets and the economy of scarcity, Vogl (2021) the fusion of financialization, information, and affect, and Couldry & Mejias (2019) emphasize the colonial dimension of global data flows. This triangulation is of central importance for analyzing local platforms in non-Western contexts, as it clarifies that platformization should not be viewed solely as a technological innovation, but rather as a complex regime of accumulation and domination that manifests itself in distinct ways across different contexts. Other platform models are often understood merely as deviations from the Western standard (Steinberg & Li, 2017). This Western bias not only represents an empirical distortion but also has theoretical implications. It reinforces the impression that platformization is a universal, linear process that is spreading worldwide according to the same logic. In fact, however, multiple platform economies are emerging that are significantly shaped by local institutions, regulations, cultural practices, and political orders (Plantin & Punathambekar, 2019).

## METHODOLOGICAL NOTE: CASE SELECTION AND COMPARATIVE PERSPECTIVE

The chapter adopts a comparative case study approach (Yin, 2014) to examine the heterogeneity of platformization beyond the Euro-American context. The selection of China, Kenya, Latin America, and the Middle East is not arbitrary. Each case was chosen for its unique and significant contribution to our understanding of platformization: China represents the paradigmatic case of state-capitalist platformization; Kenya exemplifies infrastructural compensation and financial inclusion; Latin America illustrates a conflictual-hybrid constellation of neoliberal flexibilization and countervailing solidarity economies; and the Middle East highlights the nexus of authoritarian rule, migration, and digital control. These cases were chosen not as exhaustive representations of their regions, but as analytically significant examples that illuminate the plurality of non-Western platform orders.

The empirical basis relies primarily on secondary literature, policy reports, and case-based research from 2010 onwards, complemented by recent analyses of digital finance, labor platforms, and regulatory frameworks. Comparative evaluation is guided by three criteria: (1) the role of the state in shaping or constraining platform development; (2) the organization of labor and markets, including the dynamics of precarization, inclusion, and resistance; and (3) the degree of financialization and data extraction, with attention to global dependencies and local adaptations. This design allows for systematic comparison while remaining sensitive to the contextual particularities of each case (Table 1).

*Table 1. Comparative Criteria of Platformization in Non-Western Contexts*

| Region / Case | Role of the State | Labor and market organization | Financialization and data extraction |
|---|---|---|---|
| **China** | Strong State Orchestration: platforms embedded in national modernization and surveillance strategies | Hybrid: consumer inclusion and algorithmic discipline; integration with social credit system | High: digital finance (Alipay, WeChat Pay), credit scoring, integration into state data infrastructures |
| **Kenya (Africa)** | Limited state capacity: platforms compensate for infrastructural gaps ('test and learn' regulation) | Informal economies digitized; agent networks ensure trust; new precarities emerge | Medium–High: microfinance, mobile lending (M-Shwari, Fuliza); data tied to global investment circuits |
| **Latin America** | Fragmented regulation; contestation between neoliberal deregulation and state interventions (e.g., PIX in Brazil) | Precarious gig work (Rappi, iFood) with strong labor resistance; alternative cooperative platforms | Medium: fintech expansion (Nubank, Mercado Pago) and digital wages; profits often externalized to global North |
| **Middle East** | Authoritarian regimes: platforms embedded in governance of migration and social control | Migrant labor platforms (Careem, Talabat) reinforce dependency structures; weak labor rights | Medium–High: mobile payments (STC Pay, Bee); financial dependence |

Source: own representation.

# CASE STUDIES: LOCAL PLATFORMS IN NON-WESTERN CONTEXTS

## Asia: Platforms Between State, Market, and Society

Asia can be considered one of the most dynamic laboratories of platformization. Nowhere else is the close intertwining of state regulation, global capital flows, and digital innovation as evident as in China. China is an exciting example in this context, as it represents the most paradigmatic case of a non-Western platform economy. In Western societies, platformization is strongly influenced by private-sector monopolies and market-oriented business models. In China, on the other hand, development is characterized by a close intertwining of state development strategies, digital infrastructures, and private-sector platform actors (Zhao, 2021; Creemers, 2017; Wang, 2025). Platforms act not only as companies, but also as technopolitical institutions that integrate consumption, communication, financial flows, and governance. In academic literature, this model is often referred to as 'authoritarian innovation.' According to this view, platforms are neither pure market players nor mere state organs, but hybrid institutions that exist in a symbiotic relationship with the political order (MacKinnon, 2011; Zeng, 2020).

Platform companies were not primarily understood as autonomous innovation actors, but as instruments of national modernization. The state supported them through protectionist measures that made it difficult for Western competitors (e.g., Google or Facebook) to enter the market, while also privileging domestic providers (Qiu, 2019). This development led to the emergence of a structure known as the 'Great Firewall' economy (Flew, 2021), in which national platforms operate within a closed digital ecosystem. In Western countries, platformization is often associated with market liberalization and freedom of innovation. In China, however, it was embedded in close cooperation between the party, the state, and companies from the outset.

Companies such as Tencent (WeChat/WeChat Pay), Alibaba (Alipay/Ant Group), Baidu, and Bytedance have developed into independent ecosystems that not only structure the everyday lives of over a billion users but also shape global markets (Keane & Yu, 2019; Zeng, 2020). The available empirical evidence suggests that these platform companies almost completely dominate the digital payment ecosystem: in 2020, Alipay and WeChat Pay accounted for 94% of all mobile transactions (Andrae, 2023). However, payment services are not isolated services, but are embedded in comprehensive data-based ecosystems that combine commerce, credit, insurance, investment, mobility, and government services. The platform model used by Ant Group encompasses a range of services, including lending (Huabei, Jiebei), asset management (Yu'e Bao), microinsurance, and credit rating systems. This results in a platform finance complex that ensures both the management of monetary infrastructure and the promotion of everyday participation. Platforms in China have a profound impact on the organization of everyday life. WeChat (Tencent) is a prominent example of this: the application combines messaging, social media, mobile payment, e-commerce, government communication, and health services into a single platform. For users, this means that social communication, consumption practices, and government administration are closely intertwined.

This integration leads to new forms of subjectification, where users become 'monitored consumers' whose activities are recorded in real-time and evaluated algorithmically.

According to the available literature, the social credit system (partly implemented via platforms) translates the financial, social, and political behavior of the population into indicators of trustworthiness, which in turn influence access to credit, travel, or jobs (Dai, 2018). The combination of payment and communication services enables empowerment in everyday life, for example, for small business owners or migrants without bank accounts, who thereby gain access to markets and financial services.

This ambivalence suggests that platforms in China are both spaces of inclusion and control.

In this study, this development is understood as the maximum form of digital infrastructuralization (Srnicek, 2017). Platforms act as gatekeepers over payment, communication, and trade channels. In this context, the concept of proprietary markets, as outlined by Staabs (2019), is particularly relevant. The establishment of such platforms results in the creation of new markets that both producers and consumers can only access via private infrastructures. The conditions of these infrastructures are defined entirely by the platform operators. Profit is therefore not generated by production, but by the extraction of rents from market ownership.

At the same time, China's platform order is inconceivable without the state. The expansion of the platform economy has been an integral part of strategic digital policy, from the 'Internet Plus' initiative to the 'Made in China 2025' initiative. It has also been closely linked to surveillance, data governance, and geopolitical ambitions. The significant regulation of private platform companies since 2021 (including the cancellation of Ant Group's IPO, restrictions in the credit sector, and data security laws) demonstrates that platformization is interpreted as a national sovereignty project. Vogl (2021) describes this form as a fusion of financial capitalism, cybernetic behavior control, and state control: platforms act as part of a 'monetative-information complex' in which economic transactions, data flows, and political strategies converge.

In addition, a specific logic of subjectification must be taken into account, which only partially reflects Zuboff's (2019) concept of surveillance capitalism. In China, data extraction is not primarily limited to advertising or consumption control, but is embedded in state control apparatuses and the social credit system. In this context, digital platforms serve as interfaces through which economic behavior, social evaluation, and political discipline are intertwined.

At the same time, it is clear that China's platform capitalism cannot be understood as an autonomous alternative to the West. Instead, a hybrid model is emerging in which global logics of capitalist scaling are intertwined with nation-state sovereignty and technopolitical control (Couldry & Mejias, 2019). While Western platforms, such as Amazon and Meta, have been excluded from regulation, Chinese platforms are increasingly expanding in the Global South, for example, through investments in mobile payment systems in Southeast Asia and Africa. A prominent example of the transformation of entertainment practices is the connection between ByteDance and TikTok. The app has become a global cultural phenomenon that has not only changed entertainment practices but also triggered geopolitical conflicts, such as US security concerns and impending bans (Jin, 2021).

Chinese platforms are thus becoming instruments of geopolitical projection. They represent the growing technological sovereignty of the People's Republic of China and, at the same time, challenge the dominance of Western companies. As a result, platformization is manifesting itself as a field of global power competition between digital superpowers.

The Chinese case illustrates that platformization is not just a market phenomenon, but rather a state-orchestrated regime of accumulation and control. Platforms are not viewed as autonomous market actors, but as part of a digital state capitalism that simultaneously organizes inclusion, surveillance, financialization, and geopolitical power. In this study, the analytical focus shifts from a Western liberal platform logic to an authoritarian capitalist model, creating new global reference points.

## Africa: Inclusion, Mobility, and Informal Economies

In the context of researching platformization, Africa proves to be a particularly revealing field of study. In Europe and North America, platforms are generally understood as extensions of existing digital infrastructures, whereas in many African countries, they serve as basic infrastructures. They compensate for deficits in state supply systems and create new access to financial services, transportation options, and communication networks. In this context, platformization should not be viewed primarily as a phenomenon limited to lifestyle or entertainment. Instead, it is closely linked to social aspects such as social inclusion, mobility, and survival economies (Gadzala, 2015). The central case study is Kenya, where M-Pesa has become one of the world's most prominent mobile payment platforms since its introduction in 2007. M-Pesa has not only opened up access to financial transactions for large sections of the population, but has also created a comprehensive digital ecosystem that integrates payment transactions, loans, savings, and insurance services (Donovan, 2012; Maurer, 2012; Nair & Emozozo, 2018).

As Andrae (2022) points out, M-Pesa has more than 30 million users and accounts for a significant share of national payment transactions. The platform, therefore, does not function as a complementary element to the banking sector, but rather as a quasi-infrastructural basis that enables economic participation and social transactions. In contrast to the situation in the West, financial participation in this context is not the result of digitalization, but rather its starting point. The slogan 'banking the unbanked' served as the basis, both economically and symbolically, for a new form of digital inclusion. This article concludes that direct access to financial resources provides women with greater economic autonomy, which in turn has a significant impact on household decisions and gender relations (Jack & Suri, 2014). Studies show that M-Pesa has a measurable impact on poverty reduction in Kenya, increasing the resilience of households to economic shocks (Suri & Jack, 2016). This example illustrates that platformization in Africa is not only a process of digital mediation but also an instrument of social transformation.

However, analysis by Hughes & Lonie (2007) and Burns (2018) shows that M-Pesa has long since ceased to see itself as merely a payment system. Building on transaction data, new financial instruments have been developed, such as the credit services M-Shwari and Fuliza, as well as platform offerings from third parties like Branch or Tala (Andrae, 2023). These enable microloans to be granted based on creditworthiness profiles created using algorithms. This reveals an increasing financialization of everyday life, in which social relationships, payment routines, and consumer decisions are translated into algorithmic evaluation logic. At this point, we can refer to Vogl's (2021) diagnosis: these platforms eliminate the dichotomy between knowledge and algorithmically exploitable information in favor of data-based evaluation systems. Creditworthiness, therefore, does not arise from traditional credit ratings, but from the behavior of the person concerned.

The concept of a proprietary market, as developed by Staabs (2019), has a dual application in Kenya. On the one hand, M-Pesa acts as a digital infrastructure owned by a private actor (Safaricom/Vodafone), which in turn controls access, fees, and services. On the other hand, new data-based market segments are emerging around M-Pesa, for example, in the area of microfinance, which generate economic rents in an extractive manner. Profits are generated not through production, but through control over transaction data and access to it.

It is worth noting that platformization in East Africa does not primarily correspond to the concept of surveillance capitalism as defined by Zuboff (2019). Although data is collected on a large scale, monetary evaluation and credit mechanisms are prioritized, while aspects such as personalized advertising and political influence play a subordinate role. Nevertheless, following Couldry and Mejias (2019), forms of ‘data colonialism’ are manifesting themselves as digital payment data increasingly becomes part of global value chains, for example, through international credit funds or digital investment platforms. Extraction, therefore, does not primarily occur through advertising, but rather through debt.

A second example is Gozem, a mobility platform founded in Togo, referred to as the ‘African Uber.’ The platform's range of services currently includes motorcycle taxis, delivery services, and, increasingly, financial services (Owigar & Lah, 2025). In contrast to Western platforms, Gozem is characterized by a strong focus on the needs of the local population. Motorcycle taxis, also known as ‘zemidjans,’ play a central role as a means of transportation in West Africa. Digital mediation makes them more efficient and safer to organize. The platform integrates mobile wallets and credit offers, providing drivers with access to financing for motorcycles or insurance. At the same time, Gozem functions as a work platform in contexts where formal employment opportunities are scarce. Work in the transport industry is often characterized by insecurity, low incomes, and a lack of social protection. The integration of transport, logistics, and financial services demonstrates that African platforms are often multifunctional and extend beyond mere mediation.

African platform dynamics differ significantly from those of Western and Chinese platforms due to the significant role played by informal economies. Platforms such as M-Pesa, Gozem, and SafeBoda act as interfaces between informal work, transnational mobility, and digital payment systems. In this context, the term ‘platformization’ does not describe the substitution of existing economic orders, but rather their hybridization and integration. Informal traders, motorcycle taxi drivers, and mobile service providers often utilize platforms that are not fully integrated into formal labor markets. This results in an ambivalent dynamic between economic participation and new precariousness (Donovan, 2012). This hybridity is also manifested in the function of agent networks: M-Pesa's technology is based on a large number of physical agents who enable cash transactions and ensure trust in the system. Platformization in Africa is therefore not exclusively digital but is based on a socio-technical infrastructure that intertwines local practices with global technologies (Omwansa & Sullivan, 2012).

Finally, Kenya demonstrates that platformization is not merely an imported logic. In contrast to Latin America or parts of the Middle East, BigTech corporations such as Amazon, Meta, or Alibaba have so far been only marginally able to establish their own payment or mobility platforms. This opens up scope for endogenous platform economies, albeit subject to limited political regulatory powers and high external capital dependency. Although platforms such as M-Pesa are locally anchored, they often rely on global capital flows and international companies. This raises questions about digital sovereignty (Soulé, 2024).

The African case illustrates that platformization both promotes social inclusion and generates new forms of inequality and debt. Platforms are not a substitute for existing institutions but instead cause a reconfiguration of these institutions along digital financial logics. Thus, Africa is not a special case, but a key space in which platformization is to be understood not as technological diffusion, but as a financialized reconfiguration of everyday life, risk, and infrastructure.

## Latin America: Hybridity, Labor, and Resistance

The case of Latin America shows that platformization is not simply a transfer of global models, but unfolds in a field of tension between structural inequalities, political instability, and creative appropriation processes. Significant changes can be observed, particularly in the areas of mobility and the delivery sector. Companies such as Rappi in Colombia and iFood in Brazil have established themselves as dominant players, profoundly shaping everyday urban life. New job opportunities are being created in precarious contexts, but at the same time, the uncertainties of informal labor markets are being exacerbated. Drivers and couriers operate in an intermediate area between self-employment and dependency. This constellation can be seen as an example of the concept of 'proprietary markets' defined by Staab (2019). Platforms control market access, regulate fees, manage ratings, and extract rents from the mediation of orders without bearing any production risks themselves.

Rappi, founded in Colombia in 2015, has become one of the largest food delivery and on-demand platforms in Latin America. Its business model closely follows the logic of global platform companies such as Uber Eats and DoorDash, characterized by algorithmic control of work processes, venture capital financing, and rapid scaling into international markets. At the same time, however, Rappi adapts specifically to Latin American contexts: in addition to providing food delivery, the platform also offers financial services, consumer loans, and digital wallets. This approach aims to establish a multifunctional ecosystem. Working conditions at the Rappi delivery platform are characterized by a high degree of precariousness. Drivers ('Rappitenderos') generally have no social security, work under algorithmically controlled time pressure, and are dependent on variable orders (Sánchez et al., 2024). In urban centers such as Bogotá and São Paulo, there are increasing collective protests by Rappi workers, often with the support of trade unions and social movements. This paper argues that platform work is consequently developing into a field of social conflict (Vallas & Schor, 2020). Rappi thus illustrates the ambivalence of platformization in Latin America: on the one hand, the platform generates new income opportunities in labor markets with a high degree of informality. On the other hand, it exacerbates precariousness and increases dependence on global capital flows.

In addition to commercial platforms, collective, cooperative platform models are establishing themselves in Latin America, serving as counter-models to the global platform economy. One example is La Zona in Argentina—a platform based on principles of solidarity economy and operated by local communities (Rigi & Prey, 2015). La Zona is characterized by the following features: Decisions regarding how it works, pricing, and working conditions are made collectively. The goal is not to maximize profit, but to strengthen local communities and promote fair exchange relationships. However, the underlying approach is based on a grassroots logic; modern platform technology is used to enable visibility, reach, and coordination. These projects demonstrate that platformization does not necessarily have to be associated with monopolization and data extractivism. Instead, they open up spaces for alternative economic practices that are anchored in the context of Latin American traditions of collective self-organization (e.g., cooperatives, neighborhood networks) (Hintz et al., 2017).

In contrast to many Western contexts, platform work in Latin America is often directly linked to issues of social reproduction and survival. In economies characterized by unemployment, it often represents an alternative to formal employment and opens up new sources of income. Zuboff's (2019) thesis of surveillance capitalism is only partially applicable in this context, as the primary dynamic is not based on the extraction of behavioral surplus, but on the monetization of precarious labor. Nevertheless, data-driven control mechanisms play a central role: algorithms control work rhythms, determine evaluations, and switch off employees when necessary. This digital Taylorism enables control without direct hierarchy.

This study found that, in contrast to many African contexts, platform work in Latin America is characterized by increasing politicization. In Brazil, collective mobilizations, such as 'Breque dos Apps,' have taken place since 2019, in which drivers and delivery workers have protested against algorithmic control, declining pay, and a lack of social security. Trade unions, collectives, and newly emerged social movements are organizing protests to draw attention to the precarious conditions. This is illustrated by strikes by Rappi drivers or the demands of 'Entregadores Antifascistas' in Brazil. This suggests that platform work is not accepted without opposition. These conflicts reveal that platformization has not only economic but also profound political and cultural dimensions: it manifests itself as a field in which conflicts over rights, recognition, and new forms of collective solidarity are played out.

Parallel to work-related platformization, Brazil has undergone a rapid change in the financial sector. According to a study by Andrae (2022), Brazil is one of the most dynamic markets for digital financial platforms, following China. With over 70 million users, the digital bank Nubank has challenged the traditional banking sector by offering account management, loans, and payment services entirely via mobile applications. In addition, the Brazilian central bank established the 'PIX' system, a state-regulated, open payment system that quickly became almost universally used. Unlike in Kenya, the digital financial infrastructure here did not emerge solely from the private sector; instead, it is now politically coordinated.

At the same time, global platform companies are attempting to enter this area. However, these plans have faced considerable regulatory resistance, as the central bank did not want to relinquish its sovereignty over payment transactions to private actors (Andrae, 2023). This article highlights a dynamic in the Latin American context that oscillates between digital financialization from below, represented by companies such as Nubank, Mercado Pago, and PicPay, and the state-controlled opening of platform markets, as exemplified by the PIX program and the concept of open banking.

However, this starting point only partially corresponds with Zuboff's (2019) concept of surveillance capitalism. Although data extraction occurs through payment and work platforms, the aspects of monetization, precariousness, and market ownership are more prominent than user tracking for advertising purposes. At the same time, Couldry and Mejias' (2019) concept of data colonialism points to a central tension: while many platform profits (e.g., through venture capital, stock ownership, or data exports) flow to North America and Europe, social and environmental costs are borne locally. It permeates the areas of work, means of payment, consumer culture, and urban infrastructure equally. In contrast to China or Kenya, regulation is neither centrally orchestrated by the state nor primarily infrastructure-based; rather, it is the result of ongoing negotiation processes among platform companies, governments, central banks, trade unions, and social movements.

A central feature of Latin American platformization is therefore the hybridity between global logics and local counter-designs. Global platforms, such as Rappi or Uber, are facing resistance from trade unions, workers' collectives, and civil society organizations. At the same time, alternative platforms are emerging that appropriate global technologies to strengthen local solidarity economies (Srnec & Guttmann, 2024). This development suggests a dual process: platformization reinforces existing inequalities by digitizing and flexibilizing informal work. At the same time, it opens up the possibility of digital self-empowerment, as local actors are enabled to develop their own platform models.

In this paper, Latin America is interpreted not as a belated recipient of global platform models, but as a laboratory of conflict-laden platform capitalism, in which monopolization, politicization, and alternative approaches (such as cooperative platforms like 'La Zona' in Argentina) overlap (Gago, 2020; Mora-Salas et al., 2024). In this context, platformization manifests itself as an expression of capitalism's shift toward a digital rentier economy, which, however, encounters resistance, hybridization, and renegotiation in social reality.

## Middle East: Platformization Between Geopolitical Control and Social Fragmentation

The development of platformization in the Middle East reveals an absence of Western liberal models or state capitalist approaches, as seen in China. Instead, there is a constellation characterized by authoritarian political regimes, massive labor migration, geopolitical control, and privatized infrastructures. In this context, platforms assume functions that would otherwise be the responsibility of the state, the welfare sector, or public institutions, particularly in areas such as transportation, payment transactions, care work, and logistics.

A key example is the ride-hailing platform Careem, which was founded in Dubai in 2012 and initially saw itself as a regional alternative to Uber (Abubaker, 2021). Careem integrated cultural and religious aspects—such as gender-specific ride services and Arabic-language user interfaces—and thus developed an identity-based platform logic that deliberately differed from its US counterparts. Careem saw itself not only as a transportation service, but also as a symbol of cultural self-assertion in relation to Western platforms (Ghosh et al., 2018). In 2019, Careem was acquired by Uber, evolving from a regionally based player to a global one in the platform economy (De, 2020). This transition illustrates the discrepancy between local adaptation and transnational integration.

In the Middle East, too, the platform economy is structured by labor migration. It can be observed that a large number of workers from South and Southeast Asia (e.g., the Philippines, Pakistan, India, Bangladesh, Sri Lanka, and Ethiopia) are employed in various sectors via digital platforms. These include delivery services, domestic work, transportation, and care. The individuals concerned are usually employed under a 'kafala' regime, which entails legal dependency, restricted freedom of movement, and a lack of social rights. It can be observed that platforms reinforce these structures by controlling, evaluating, and sanctioning workers via algorithmic systems without assuming formal employer responsibility. In this context, the validity of the concept of proprietary labor markets, as postulated by Staabs (2019), becomes apparent. Labor is not taken on as an employee but is provided as a service via digital infrastructures. The platform company controls access, visibility, and income.

Platforms act as control technologies that are available to both the market and the state. In authoritarian contexts, the concept of surveillance capitalism, as outlined by Zuboff (2019), is not primarily motivated by advertising measures or consumer-oriented logic, but rather by security policy interests. Platform data is linked to government registers, visa systems, or biometric databases. Vogl (2021) describes this transition from market to control infrastructures as a fusion of financial, information-based, and governmental power techniques.

Additionally, digital platforms are becoming increasingly important in the financial sector. Mobile payment applications, such as STC Pay in Saudi Arabia and Bee in Egypt, enable transactions like transfers, salary payments, and fee collections, which are particularly advantageous for migrants without access to traditional banking services. The available research indicates that these platforms make a significant contribution to financing social reproduction, for example, through the granting of microloans, advance payments, and fee-based models. Following Andrae (2022), this can be interpreted as a monetized platform economy in which financial transactions, mobility, and work are linked via a single digital infrastructure.

The Middle East context also illustrates that platformization is an element of geopolitical transformations. While Western companies (Uber, Amazon, Meta) are expanding their presence, Chinese platform financiers are also becoming increasingly involved: Alibaba is investing in the region through the eFounders Fund, while Huawei is providing digital infrastructure for smart cities and control systems. This development has resulted in the emergence of a new constellation of 'digital dependency,' which Couldry and Mejias (2019) refer to as 'data colonialism.' As a result, data, capital, and control are lost, while labor and social consequences remain locally anchored.

At the same time, micro-spaces of resistance are emerging, such as through union-like organizing among drivers in Egypt or legal battles against algorithmic opacity in the United Arab Emirates. These forms are fragmented and precarious, but they contradict the notion that platformization in the Middle East is exclusively a top-down or politically immobile development. Instead, this context also manifests an area of tension between monopolization, adaptation, expropriation, and subaltern agencies.

The Middle East case illustrates that platformization is not neutral market development, but a politically charged process that links social control, digital financialization, and transnational labor regimes. In this context, the platform functions not only as infrastructure, but also as a technology of power that reorganizes domination, mobility, and value creation, recombining global and local logics in the process. In the Middle East, platforms fulfill not only economic but also political and cultural functions. These can be interpreted as an expression of a desire for digital sovereignty, i.e., an attempt to assert regional markets and cultural practices against Western dominance. At the same time, they are embedded in geopolitical dependencies, as international investors, government support programs, and authoritarian regimes exert a significant influence on the freedom of action of these platforms.

## Comparative Interim Assessment

Analysis of the case studies shows that platformization is not a uniform, linear, or globally homogeneous process. Its development depends on the respective social conditions, state regulatory logic, financial infrastructures, and local forms of appropriation. Nevertheless, central patterns, tensions, and overlaps can be identified as a global regime of transformation.

(1) China: State-capitalist platform hegemony

China embodies a model of platform-based state development, in which private actors, such as Alibaba and Tencent, are embedded within a politically controlled power structure. In this context, platformization is used as an instrument of national modernization, fiscal control, and social discipline. The platform is thus configured not as a market actor but as an instrument of state sovereignty. Financial systems, such as Alipay and WeChat Pay, illustrate how digital ecosystems seamlessly blend payment transactions, identity, consumption, and surveillance.

(2) Kenya: Infrastructure replacement and financial popular modernization

In Kenya, platformization is primarily used to compensate for a lack of state or formal infrastructure. M-Pesa provides basic financial services, enabling millions of people to access payment transactions, savings, and credit. In contrast to the Chinese practice, which features top-down regulation, regulation in this case takes the form of 'test and learn.' At the same time, financialization of everyday life is manifesting itself, in which creditworthiness, risk, and consumption are algorithmically operationalized. This study examines the relationship between proprietary markets and social-technological micro-control.

(3) Brazil/Latin America: Hybridization between Precarization and Countervailing Power

In Latin America, a model is emerging in which platformization serves as an extension of neoliberal flexibilization and the informal economy yet simultaneously mobilizes potential for resistance. Platform work (e.g., at Rappi, iFood, Uber, 99) generates new forms of digital wage dependency that are neither formally integrated into the legal system nor socially secured. At the same time, platform alternatives, such as cooperative models and collective labor disputes, are emerging. In the financial sector (e.g., Nubank, PIX), it is also apparent that public and private platform models coexist, collide, or overlap.

### (4) Middle East: Platformization as a regime of domination and migration

In the Middle East, there is an intertwining of platformization and authoritarian statehood, transnational labor migration, and technological control. Platforms such as Careem, Talabat, and STC Pay control transportation, labor, and payment transactions—especially for migrant workers without political rights. In this context, digital infrastructures serve not only to enhance economic efficiency but also to facilitate state surveillance, capital extraction, and border management.

Despite the apparent differences, three central structural similarities can be identified that enable the development of a comparative platform theory.

### (a) Platforms as proprietary markets

In all contexts, platforms focus not on production but on access to markets, work, data, or infrastructure. This study examines the extent to which platforms influence the private sector in shaping markets. Case studies include Alibaba in China, M-Pesa in Kenya, Uber in Brazil, and Talabat in the Middle East. The analysis reveals that platforms establish privately controlled markets, where they define access rules, fee structures, and algorithmic visibility.

### (b) Financialization and data extraction as the basic mode of accumulation

The platformization of social actions leads to the generation of exploitable information. This includes credit profiles in Kenya, insurance data in China, rating metrics in Latin America, and biometric data collection in the Middle East. The analysis of this data enables the generation of economic capital and the implementation of political control instruments. Financialization should not be viewed merely as a sectoral process, but rather as a logic of subjectification.

### (c) Data colonialism and global inequality

The extracted data, profits, and financial flows indicate a significant transnational orientation, with a focus on global centers such as the US, China, and venture capital hubs. Local platforms are highly dependent on investors, regulators, and technology suppliers for their existence. At the same time, new spaces for appropriation, adaptation, and resistance are emerging, making platformization a contested field.

## Ecological and Urban Dimensions of Platformization

A further dimension of platformization that demands immediate attention is its ecological footprint and urban transformation effects. While much of the debate has focused on labor, finance, and surveillance, platforms are also deeply implicated in material infrastructures, energy consumption, and urban ecologies.

In logistics and delivery services (e.g., Rappi in Latin America, Talabat in the Middle East), platform models intensify urban traffic flows and reshape everyday mobility. This creates new patterns of congestion, pollution, and spatial inequality, as workers concentrate in densely populated areas while peripheral zones remain underserved. Similarly, ride-hailing platforms contribute to shifts in transportation behavior, often substituting for public transport and thereby reinforcing carbon-intensive mobility regimes.

The energy demand of digital infrastructures represents another ecological consequence. Mobile payment systems such as M-Pesa or Alipay rely on large-scale server farms and telecom infrastructures whose electricity use and cooling requirements add to the carbon footprint of digital economies. Although these costs remain largely invisible to users, they constitute a hidden layer of environmental externalities. The same holds for global data centers supporting cloud-based services, which are often located outside the regions where platforms operate, leading to an externalization of ecological burdens.

Urban transformation is also visible in the reconfiguration of space and labor geographies, a significant change brought about by platforms. Platforms not only organize flows of goods and services but also shape the temporal and spatial rhythms of cities. Delivery riders, platform taxis, and urban couriers constitute a new layer of urban infrastructure—flexible, mobile, but also precarious. In Nairobi, São Paulo, and Dubai alike, platform-mediated logistics redefine access to urban services, often privileging affluent neighborhoods while marginalizing informal settlements. This spatial stratification reveals how digital infrastructures embed and amplify existing socio-ecological inequalities.

Taken together, these dynamics suggest that platformization cannot be viewed solely as an immaterial or virtual process. Instead, it has tangible ecological and urban impacts: it reorganizes the metabolism of cities, accelerates energy-intensive infrastructures, and contributes to new patterns of exclusion and environmental stress. Incorporating these dimensions is not just beneficial, but essential for a comprehensive understanding of platform capitalism in non-Western contexts. This understanding is crucial as it highlights that digital infrastructures are inseparable from material and ecological realities (Figure 1).

*Figure 1. Intersecting dimensions of platformization*

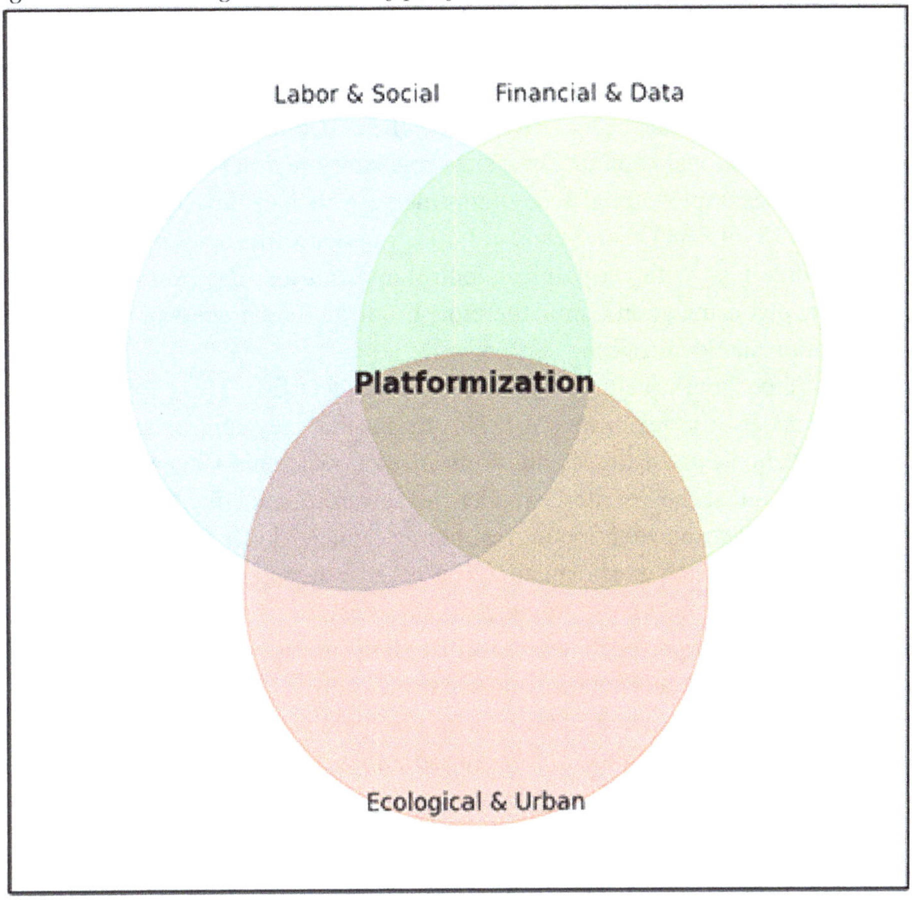


The four case studies do not represent deviations from the Western model, but relatively independent platform orders, each producing different combinations of market logic, statehood, control, and social reproduction. Platformization thus manifests itself as a global process characterized by local variations. Understanding it requires a non-Eurocentric, politically and economically grounded, and postcolonial-informed perspective.

The case studies suggest that platformization is not a homogeneous or linear process but depends to a large extent on local political economies, cultural practices, and power constellations. In China, on the other hand, a state-capitalist model dominates, in which platforms function as instruments of national modernization and political control. In Africa, by contrast, issues of financial inclusion and grassroots mobility are at the forefront. In Latin America, on the other hand, a conflict-ridden dynamic is emerging in which platforms serve both as instruments of neoliberal precarization and as testing grounds for solidarity-based counter-models. Finally, in the Middle East, authoritarian surveillance logic overlaps with economic dependency structures of labor migration.

These differences illustrate that there is no universal grammar of platformization. Instead, platforms should be viewed as assemblages (Couldry & Mejias, 2019) composed of transnational capital flows, state regulatory regimes, and local practices. In China, for example, digital ecosystems merge with state development planning, in Africa with informal economies, in Latin America with social movements, and in the Middle East with geopolitical control apparatuses. The present study concludes that platformization should therefore be viewed as a process of simultaneous globalization and localization.

At the same time, structural similarities can be identified. This paper argues that platforms act as proprietary markets. This means that they control access, monopolize transactions, and extract rents from market ownership (Staab, 2019). It has been observed that they reinforce tendencies toward financialization (Vogl, 2021) by translating data and attention into economic capital. Modes of subjectivation are modified by the present transformation, as users are integrated into new relationships of dependency as consumers, producers, or workers.

The comparative perspective reveals that platformization is neither a pure replication of Western models nor an exclusive expression of local innovation. It should therefore be viewed as a hybrid process in which global logics intersect with local structures, giving rise to new power constellations. On the one hand, this results in the reproduction of global inequalities; on the other hand, it opens up spaces for resistance and alternative economies. For platform research, this implies the need for a stronger intertwining of postcolonial, capitalist theory, and sociological approaches to technology in order to grasp the complexity of these processes analytically.

## THEORETICAL IMPLICATIONS

The analysis of the case studies shows that platformization cannot be understood solely as a technological innovation, but rather as a politically and economically structured transformation process that simultaneously changes markets, statehood, capital flows, and social subjectification. Five perspectives can be highlighted for the theoretical framework:

(1) Platformization as the formation of proprietary markets

The empirical findings indicate that platforms in all four regions studied do not serve the market but rather own it. The present studies show that platform companies such as Alipay and WeChat Pay in China, M-Pesa in Kenya, Nubank and iFood in Brazil, and Careem in the Middle East control access, transactions, visibility, and pricing. As a result, there is a shift from production to intermediation or rent extraction. This observation supports Staab's (2019) hypothesis of a transition from capitalist commodity production to rent-based platform ownership. It should be noted, however, that proprietary markets are associated with divergent power resources in different regions, including the state (China), infrastructure deficits (Kenya), deregulation (Latin America), and migration regimes (Middle East).

(2) Financialization and algorithmic control

Vogl's concept illustrates that platformization is not merely a technical infrastructure, but rather a financialized control regime. In the People's Republic of China, platform payments, credit scoring, and social credit mechanisms are linked. In Kenya, lending via the M-Pesa, M-Shwari, or Fuliza platforms contributes not only to financial inclusion but also to responsible debt management. In Brazil and Colombia, on the other hand, rating subjectivities manifest themselves in delivery work and gig economy platforms. In the Middle East, migrant workers are monitored, evaluated, and selected using digital applications. Vogl (2021) describes this dynamic as a convergence of financial evaluation, algorithmic knowledge reduction, and behavioral control. This observation was confirmed in all four cases.

(3) Extraction and digital subjectification

Zuboff's diagnosis of surveillance capitalism assumes a region-specific character in the case studies: In the People's Republic of China, behavioral data extraction is primarily interpreted in the context of state regulation and market control, rather than advertising. In Africa, data is used for lending and risk assessment and is increasingly fed into global investment cycles. In Latin America, surveillance is used primarily as a means of organizing work (e.g., in delivery services and mobility platforms), rather than for commercial profiling. In the Middle East, data extraction is merging with migration control and authoritarian sovereignty. These findings suggest that surveillance capitalism should not be viewed as a uniform concept, but rather as a context-adapted practice.

(4) Platforms as infrastructure capital

The cases presented illustrate Srnicek's argument that platforms not only organize markets but also establish themselves as critical infrastructure (Srnicek, 2017). In China, platforms are replacing state administrative and financial institutions; in

Kenya, they are compensating for the lack of public services; in Brazil, hybrid models between financial platforms and regulation are emerging; and in the Middle East, they are being integrated into state and security strategies. Platforms are thus becoming geopolitical actors that operate beyond the classical logic of the market.

(5) Data colonialism and global inequality

Platformization reproduces global inequalities, which are not coincidental but structurally determined. Data, capital, and digital infrastructures are transferred to transnational centers such as the US or China, while social costs, labor risks, and dependencies remain locally. In Kenya and Brazil, credit and payment platforms are financed by international funds. New forms of digital debt are emerging in Africa. US platforms dominate Latin America, despite local alternatives. In the Middle East, work, mobility, and identity are being externalized via digital regimes. The concept of 'data colonialism' developed by Couldry and Mejias (2019) accurately describes these asymmetrical relationships.

Empirical case studies demonstrate that platformization is not only an economic innovation but also a profound transformation of power, domination, and subjectivation. To grasp these processes theoretically, it is necessary to combine different approaches from sociology, political economy, and cultural theory. The following considerations demonstrate how the concepts of financialization, proprietary markets, and surveillance capitalism can be analytically combined to capture non-Western platformization.

*Table 2. Theories of platformization and regional applications*

| Theory / Author | Core concept | Application in China | Application in Kenya (Africa) | Application in Latin America | Application in Middle East |
|---|---|---|---|---|---|
| **Srnicek (2017)** | Platforms as infrastructures of accumulation | Digital ecosystems (WeChat, Alipay) as state-supported infrastructures | M-Pesa as infrastructural substitute for missing public banking | Platforms (Rappi, Nubank) as infrastructures reshaping work & finance | Platforms (Careem, STC Pay) filling infrastructural gaps under authoritarian regimes |
| **Zuboff (2019)** | Surveillance capitalism, extraction of behavioral surplus | Integration of payment, communication, and social credit data | Credit scoring and lending algorithms extract behavioral data | Algorithmic labor surveillance (delivery work, ride-hailing) | Surveillance embedded in migration and security regimes |
| **Staab (2019)** | Proprietary markets, rent extraction | State-backed proprietary markets (Alibaba, Ant Group) | Safaricom/Vodafone controls access to financial services | Rappi and iFood extract rents from gig labor; Nubank monopolizes digital credit | Platforms control access to mobility and migrant labor |
| **Vogl (2021)** | Financialization, fusion of information and affect | Convergence of finance, governance, and data in digital sovereignty projects | Everyday financialization via microloans, integration into global credit chains | Fintechs (Nubank, PIX) financialize consumption and reproduction | Financial dependence of migrants via digital payments and remittances |
| **Couldry & Mejias (2019)** | Data colonialism, global inequalities | Chinese expansion of platforms into Africa and SE Asia | Local data integrated into global finance and investment | Platform profits externalized to US/EU investors, local costs remain | Regional platforms absorbed by global corporations (e.g., Uber acquiring Careem) |

Source: own representation.

This synthesis, drawn from diverse theoretical perspectives, demonstrates that each lens captures a crucial aspect of platformization, but only their combination reveals the full complexity. Srnicek's explanation of infrastructural power, Zuboff's focus on extraction and subjectification, Staab's demonstration of how proprietary markets privatize access, Vogl's emphasis on financialization as governance, and Couldry & Mejias' situating of these dynamics in a global colonial framework, all contribute to a comprehensive understanding. In non-Western contexts, these dimensions converge in hybrid forms, producing platform orders that are at once locally specific and globally entangled, underscoring the interdisciplinary nature of this synthesis.

## Intertwining of Financialization, Surveillance Capitalism, and Data Colonialism

While the approaches mentioned (Srnicek, Zuboff, Staab, Vogl, Couldry & Mejias) are often considered separately, analysis of non-Western platform orders reveals that in practice they are often inextricably linked. Platformization occurs in hybrid regimes where the logic of financialization, surveillance, and data colonization intertwines and assumes specific regional characteristics.

In China, these logics are paradigmatically intertwined: digital ecosystems such as Alipay and WeChat Pay link financial infrastructures with comprehensive data collection. This is not just about the commercial use of 'behavioral surplus' (Zuboff), but about the state-orchestrated embedding of payment, consumption, and communication data in governance processes (e.g., social credit). Financialization (Vogl) and surveillance capitalism (Zuboff) are embedded in a state-national framework. At the same time, elements of data colonialism become visible when Chinese platforms export their financial and communication models to Africa or Southeast Asia.

In Kenya, a different constellation is emerging M-Pesa, and comparable platforms compensate for the lack of state infrastructure and open up access to financial services. Here, financialization in the form of microfinance and credit scoring is particularly prominent, while the logic of surveillance is less pronounced. Nevertheless, forms of data colonialism are present, as payment and credit data are fed into global financial cycles, creating dependencies on international capital providers. Surveillance is less of a political control instrument and more embedded in the economic logic of risk assessment.

In Latin America, on the other hand, the intertwining of algorithmic work control and financialization dominates. Platforms such as Rappi and iFood monitor employees algorithmically and transform work processes into data streams that serve the purposes of control and rent extraction. Zuboff's diagnosis of the 'expropriation of experience' is concretely manifested here in the precarization of labor. At the same time, Vogl's perspective of financialization through credit and consumer platforms (Nubank, PIX) shapes social reproduction in highly indebted contexts. At the same time, a form of data colonialism is evident, as platform profits often flow to US or European investors, while the social costs remain local.

Finally, in the Middle East, all three dimensions come together in an authoritarian manner. Platforms such as Careem or STC Pay organize labor migration, payment flows, and mobility in a highly controlled environment. Here, surveillance serves not primarily to control consumption, but to politically stabilize authoritarian regimes. Financialization manifests itself in the form of fee and credit logics that keep migrant workers in a state of dependency. Data colonialism manifests itself both in dependencies on global tech investors (e.g., Uber, Alibaba) and in the asymmetrical control of data by public-private alliances.

This comparative perspective shows that platformization is not a juxtaposition of different logics, but a situational intertwining of financialization, surveillance, and data colonialism. In the contexts examined, the respective weighting varies, but the interdependencies are systematic: financialization requires data streams, surveillance generates financializable profiles, and data colonialism embeds both in global power structures. This makes it clear that platform theories must be read in their entirety in order to grasp non-Western dynamics analytically.

## Temporal Dynamics of Platformization

Platformization is a dynamic, historically evolving process, with non-Western regions playing a significant role. Since the early 2010s, these regions have experienced unique trajectories, shaped by technological diffusion, regulatory experimentation, and geopolitical change.

In the early 2010s, platforms primarily emerged as tools of infrastructural substitution and convenience. M-Pesa in Kenya addressed the absence of banking infrastructure, while Rappi in Latin America responded to fragmented service economies. In China, the rapid expansion of WeChat and Alipay coincided with national modernization campaigns, embedding platforms in broader state projects. The Middle East saw the rise of Careem as a regional alternative to Western ride-hailing models, integrating cultural and linguistic specificities.

The mid-2010s marked a shift towards rapid scaling and diversification in platformization. Platforms evolved from single-service entities (such as payments and rides) into multifunctional ecosystems, integrating finance, logistics, and communication. This period also saw a surge in venture capital flows, further connecting local actors to global financial circuits, and the emergence of labor struggles and civil society responses in Latin America, Africa, and the Middle East.

Since the late 2010s and early 2020s, platformization has entered a phase of consolidation and contestation. In China, regulatory interventions curtailed the unchecked power of Ant Group and other tech giants, signaling the state's reassertion of sovereignty. In Brazil, the PIX system demonstrated that states can also create public platform infrastructures. In Kenya, mobile lending platforms intensified financialization, raising concerns over debt dependency. In the Middle East, platform economies became increasingly entangled with authoritarian governance and migration regimes.

Looking into the future, the 2020s are expected to bring several key trends in platformization to the fore.

- Deeper financialization: Platforms expand into credit, insurance, and asset management, embedding financial logics into everyday life.
- AI-driven integration: Algorithmic control over labor, logistics, and credit scoring intensifies, reshaping subjectivities and risk profiles.
- Environmental and urban pressures: Energy use, logistical congestion, and ecological externalities are becoming more visible, forcing debates on sustainability.
- Regulatory pluralization: From China's state-centric model to Brazil's public infrastructures and Kenya's 'test and learn' approach, diverse governance logics are crystallizing.
- Geopolitical competition: US, Chinese, and increasingly regional actors (e.g., Gulf sovereign wealth funds) use platform expansion as instruments of strategic influence.

These temporal dynamics demonstrate that platformization evolves through phases of experimentation, expansion, and regulation, shaped by shifting alignments of state power, market logic, and the powerful influence of social resistance. Understanding these diachronic transformations is crucial for situating current platform orders within the broader trajectory of global capitalism.

## GLOBAL INEQUALITIES AND POST-COLONIAL PERSPECTIVES

An in-depth analysis of platformization in China, Kenya, Brazil, and the Middle East unveils the intricate and non-uniform nature of the global platform economy. Instead of a singular global order, diverse regional structures are emerging, each shaped by specific historical, institutional, and economic conditions. These disparities underscore that the platform economy is not a simple dissolution of existing power and dependency relationships, but a complex restructuring, exacerbation, or reproduction of them in novel forms.

This study concludes that platformization should not be viewed as an isolated phenomenon, but rather as building on existing colonial and postcolonial structures of inequality. In the People's Republic of China, platformization is employed by the state to secure technological sovereignty and enhance its geopolitical capacity to act vis-à-vis the United States and Europe. In Kenya, digital infrastructures such as M-Pesa are not an expression of local autonomy, but rather a response to global credit markets, development logics, and discourses on digital inclusion. In Brazil, local platforms compete with transnational capital, while informal work is organized in a digital context. In the Middle East, labor migration, platform control, and data-based surveillance are translated into new systems of dependency.

In this context, the concept of data colonialism (Couldry & Mejias, 2019) offers an analytical key. Platforms extract data, capital, and control from local contexts, while economic added value is shifted to transnational centers. This development can be observed in both US corporations, such as Meta, Uber, and Amazon, and in Chinese players, including Alibaba, ByteDance, and Huawei. These companies are increasingly manifesting themselves as digital empires. The data colonialism approach highlights the strategic foundations of current datafication. This study examines the thesis that digitalization not only overlays social life but also relies on its reconfiguration and the adoption of suitable ideologies to promote its goals and obscure its effects. The greatest challenge in the responsible use of data is probably identifying potential ethical problems. Instead, it is necessary to evaluate the limited alternatives available in a given social and economic context. Standard principles or recommendations offer only limited guidance, as the considerations are highly context-dependent, local, and technology-specific.

In all cases, financialization of the social sphere is evident, transforming existing inequality but not eliminating it. In Kenya, an increase in debt is attributable to microfinance services; in Brazil, to platform work and consumer credit; in China, to digital credit and scoring systems; and in the Middle East, to migrant economies and digital wage control. Platforms thus not only function as a means of enabling access and participation but also establish digital debt regimes that are linked to global valuation logics.

Vogl's (2021) concept of linking information, capital, and control is empirically comprehensible in this context. Platforms not only extract data, but also organize risk, behavior, and creditworthiness. Financialization through platforms is a form of governance that is not dependent on traditional statehood. Financialization, in this context, refers to the increasing influence of financial motives, tools, and institutions in shaping social and economic processes, a trend that is particularly pronounced in the context of platformization.

From a postcolonial perspective, it becomes clear that platforms not only structure markets but also reconfigure political orders. Depending on the specific context, they are assigned functions that can be located in different areas such as the state, administration, financial system, infrastructure, or labor market control:

- In Kenya, they replace missing public infrastructure by digitizing financial services and mobility.
- In Brazil, they act as agents of neoliberal transformation, but also as targets of social counter-movements.
- In the Middle East, they stabilize migration and authoritarian regimes.

The application of these theoretical approaches demonstrates that platforms in non-Western contexts are often best understood as hybrid institutions. They are neither simple copies of Western models nor entirely independent phenomena but arise in a field of tension between global infrastructure and local embedding.

Three dimensions are particularly noteworthy here:

1. **Governance**: Governance is a multifaceted concept primarily discussed in Western theories in relation to market regulation, data protection, or competition law (Gillespie, 2018). In China, on the other hand, platforms are closely integrated into state development and control strategies (Creemers, 2017; Keane & Yu, 2019). In Africa, in some cases, state institutions are being replaced by platforms that assume specific tasks, such as financial inclusion (Maurer, 2012).
2. **Subjectification**: Platforms constitute specific forms of subjectivity (Foucault, 1982; Cheney-Lippold, 2017). In Kenya, the use of mobile financial platforms is creating a new self-image as 'financial actors.' In the People's Republic of China, platforms intertwine consumption, communication, and political control, thus shaping the 'monitored consumer subject.' In Latin America, on the other hand, the platform-specific subjects are often seen as a precarious worker who oscillates between exploitation and collective resistance (Gago, 2020).
3. **Power relations**: Local platforms are always part of global power constellations. Careem in the Middle East initially functioned as a platform that served cultural self-assertion but was integrated into a global corporate logic through its acquisition by Uber (Rochet & Tirole, 2003; Abubaker, 2021). This dynamic indicates that platformization should be viewed as a field in which both hegemony and resistance are negotiated.

The analysis of local platforms as hybrid institutions thus makes it clear that platformization cannot be understood as a universal process. Instead, it is a complex, conflictual transformation in which global capital flows, national regulatory projects, and local practices are intertwined. This study concludes that platformization is not a by-product of technological innovation but rather should be viewed as one aspect of a globally fragmented transformation process that reconnects statehood, market logics, and governance.

At the same time, spaces of appropriation, adaptation, and resistance are emerging that challenge blanket assumptions of dominance or homogeneity. The following examples illustrate this point:

- Cooperative delivery platforms in Argentina,
- Trade union app strikes in Brazil,
- Open payment systems such as PIX as a counter-model to BigTech,

- Informal platform economies in Kenya,
- Digital Shadow Infrastructures of Migrant Communities in the Middle East.

These practices demonstrate that platformization does not function exclusively in a hegemonic manner, but is always contested, subverted, or recorded locally. The traditional juxtaposition of center and periphery becomes porous in this case.

The case studies show that a sociological theory of platformization must consider non-Western spaces not as deviations, but as equivalent epistemic starting points. As a result, the focus shifts away from Silicon Valley as a reference model toward a multipolar analysis in which Chinese platform state logics, African inclusion economies, Latin American conflict fields, and Middle Eastern control regimes are examined on an equal footing.

Platformization thus manifests itself as a globally effective yet asymmetrically structured regime of power and accumulation that both preserves old hierarchies and generates new ones. Postcolonial approaches are necessary in order to interpret these dynamics not as deviations from the Western model, but as integral components of a global restructuring of capitalism, statehood, and subjectivity.

## CONCLUSION

This study concludes that the digital platform economy has not only accelerated the intertwining of value creation and rent extraction but has also made them increasingly indistinguishable. The value creation process no longer originates primarily in production, but in the appropriation, management, and exploitation of data flows. While traditional financial intermediaries have already influenced the distribution and organization of value, the innovation of the platform economy lies in the fact that extraction mechanisms do not affect markets retrospectively but are inscribed in digital infrastructures and user interfaces from the outset. The establishment of platforms does not result in the creation of neutral spaces, but rather in the generation of privately owned markets. In these markets, the operators define the rules, visibility, and transaction conditions. Recommendation algorithms mediate between advertising incentive systems and micro-timed behavior prediction, promoting practices that entice users to release more data while reducing individual benefits. The design of the interfaces themselves—from scrolling to gamification to payment systems—is optimized for dependency, data accumulation, and behavior control.

In light of this, it becomes clear that platformization, the process by which platforms become dominant in various sectors of the economy, cannot be interpreted as either the linear spread of techno-capitalist innovation or a purely export phenomenon of Western economics. Instead, it is a differentiated regime of accumulation and control that is unevenly distributed globally and materializes differently depending on the context. Case studies from China, Kenya, Brazil, and the Middle East show that platforms are not only technologies or business models but also represent socioeconomic and political infrastructures that transform state order, market design, labor relations, and everyday practices.

It is important to note that there is no uniform platform order; instead, a multitude of specific configurations exist. In the People's Republic of China, for instance, state control, capital accumulation, and digital surveillance overlap to form an authoritarian-infrastructural development model. In Kenya, digital platforms are replacing basic public infrastructure, opening up access to financial services, and simultaneously creating new forms of debt and credit dependency. In Latin America, platformization catalyzes neoliberal restructuring, yet it is simultaneously challenged by protest movements, cooperative models, and solidarity-based counter-economies. In the Middle East, platforms are deeply embedded in migration management, labor financing, state control, and the extraction of transnational rents.

It is worth noting that these contexts differ from one another. Nevertheless, structural logics—the underlying principles or patterns that guide the development of platform economies, can be identified that transcend individual examples. Platforms transform markets into proprietary infrastructures, rationalize social relations through financial and algorithmic rating systems, extract behavior as an economic resource, and update global dependency relationships through digital means. This results in a regime in which access, creditworthiness, visibility, and belonging are increasingly defined algorithmically and channeled politically.

This study concludes that theories of platform capitalism based on Western developments and interpreting non-Western cases as deviations remain inadequate. Non-Western platform orders are therefore not a marginal phenomenon, but rather laboratories of new power logics, finance, and control. The urgency of decolonized platform research is apparent. It must not equate globality with universality; instead, it should understand platforms as contested and situational assemblages, analyze inequality not as a side effect but as a structural principle, and recognize power not solely as market dominance but as an infrastructural, financial, state, and affective form.

At the same time, it is becoming apparent that platformization is not a complete program of domination. Practices of appropriation, adaptation, recoding, or resistance are emerging in various regions of the world. Examples include cooperatively organized delivery services in Argentina, spontaneous app strikes in Brazil, community-based credit networks in Kenya, and informal forms of self-organization among migrant workers in the Gulf region. These processes illustrate that platformization not only entails expropriation and control but also creates new spaces for political imagination, collective self-assertion, and digital solidarity.

The central contribution of this chapter is to identify platformization as a globally fragmented but structurally connected complex of transformations that Western reference models cannot explain. The combination of empirical case studies and approaches based on capitalism theory shows how financialization, statehood, digital labor, and data extraction interpenetrate, how power asymmetries are reconfigured, and why a postcolonial perspective is not complementary but epistemically necessary. For future platform research, these results suggest that the dual task of overcoming Eurocentric models of interpretation and analyzing platformization as a global, conflictual field of negotiation, in which hegemony and resistance, localization and globalization, inclusion and exclusion are negotiated simultaneously, is crucial. Viewing the issue from this perspective enables a comprehensible analysis that allows for the reorganization of markets, identities, and power structures through global platforms. Additionally, the risks, fault lines, and opportunities arising from these processes become evident.

## REFERENCES


Abubaker, I. (2021). Careem and the ride-hailing economy in the Middle East. *Journal of Middle East Media*, *15*(1), 55–72.

Andrae, S. (2022). The role of BigTech in emerging markets. In Nguyen, D. K. (Ed.), *Handbook of Banking and Finance in Emerging Markets* (pp. 433–463). Edward Elgar., DOI: 10.4337/9781800880900.00032

Burns, S. (2018). M-Pesa and the 'market-led' approach to financial inclusion. *Economic Affairs*, *38*(3), 406–421. DOI: 10.1111/ecaf.12321

Cheney-Lippold, J. (2017). *We Are Data: Algorithms and the Making of Our Digital Selves*. NYU Press.

Couldry, N., & Mejias, U. A. (2019). *The Costs of Connection: How Data is Colonizing Human Life and Appropriating it for Capitalism*. Stanford University Press.

Creemers, R. (2017). Cyber China: Upgrading propaganda, public opinion work and social management for the twenty-first century. *Journal of Contemporary China*, *26*(103), 85–100. DOI: 10.1080/10670564.2016.1206281

Dai, X. (2018). Toward a reputation state: The social credit system project of China. http://dx.doi.org/DOI: 10.2139/ssrn.3193577

De, S. (2020). Influence of Uber-careem deal on the Middle Eastern Startups. Retrieved from https://medium.com/allride/influence-of-uber-careem-deal-on-the-middle-eastern-startups-f4f3eb54eff4

Deleuze, G., & Guattari, F. (1987). *A Thousand Plateaus*. University of Minnesota Press.

Donovan, K. (2012). Mobile money, more freedom? The impact of M-Pesa's network power on development as freedom. *International Journal of Communication*, *6*, 2647–2669.

Flew, T. (2021). *Understanding Global Media*. Palgrave.

Foucault, M. (1982). The subject and power. *Critical Inquiry*, *8*(4), 777–795.

Gadzala, A. W. (2015). *Africa and China: How Africans and Their Governments are Shaping Relations with China*. Rowman & Littlefield.

Gago, V. (2020). *La potencia feminista: Origenes y luchas en América Latina*. Tinta Limón.

Ghosh, S., Yucaoglu, G., & Thapar, A. (2018). Careem: Base camp or mountain peak? Designing an OS for scaling. Harvard Business School Case 819-049, September 2018.

Gillespie, T. (2018). *Custodians of the Internet.* Yale University Press.

Graham, M., Hjorth, I., & Lehdonvirta, V. (2017). Digital labour and development: Impacts of global digital labour platforms and the gig economy on worker livelihoods. *Transfer: European Review of Labour and Research, 23*(2), 135–162. DOI: 10.1177/1024258916687250

Helmond, A. (2015). The platformization of the web: Making web data platform ready. *Social Media + Society, 1*(2), 1–11. DOI: 10.1177/2056305115603080

Hintz, A., Dencik, L., & Wahl-Jorgensen, K. (2017). Digital Citizenship in a Datafied Society. *Polity.*

Hughes, N., & Lonie, S. (2007). M-Pesa: Mobile money for the 'unbanked.'. *Innovations, 2*(1-2), 63–81.

Jack, W., & Suri, T. (2014). Risk sharing and transactions costs: Evidence from Kenya's mobile money revolution. *The American Economic Review, 104*(1), 183–223. DOI: 10.1257/aer.104.1.183

Jin, D. Y. (2021). TikTok and the making of a new transnational media order. *International Journal of Communication, 15*, 4562–4581.

Keane, M., & Yu, H. (2019). A digital empire in the making: China's outbound digital platforms. *International Journal of Communication, 13*, 4624–4641.

MacKinnon, R. (2011). China's 'networked authoritarianism.'. *Journal of Democracy, 22*(2), 32–46.

Maurer, B. (2012). Mobile money: Communication, consumption and change in the payments space. *The Journal of Development Studies, 48*(5), 589–604. DOI: 10.1080/00220388.2011.621944

Mbembe, A. (2020). *Out of the Dark Night: Essays on Decolonization.* Columbia University Press.

Mora-Salas, M., Delfino, A., & Olivera, R. V. de (2024). Platform capitalism in Latin America: Visible trends and probable horizons. Estudios sociológicos, 42, e2736. https://doi.org/.DOI: 10.24201/es.2024v42.e2736

Nair, M., & Emozozo, R. (2018). Electronic currency in Africa: M-Pesa as private inside money. *Economic Affairs, 38*(2), 197–206. DOI: 10.1111/ecaf.12292

Omwansa, T. K., & Sullivan, N. P. (2012). *Money, Real Quick: Kenya's Disruptive Mobile Money Innovation*. Guardian Books.

Ong, A., & Collier, S. (2005). *Global Assemblages*. Blackwell.

Owigar, J. A., & Lah, O. (2025). African e-mobility startups' perceptions and use of information systems, challenges, and opportunities. *Sustainable Earth Reviews*, *8*, 12. DOI: 10.1186/s42055-025-00113-1

Pasquale, F. (2015). *The Black Box Society: The Secret Algorithms That Control Money and Information*. Harvard University Press.

Plantin, J.-C., Lagoze, C., Edwards, P. N., & Sandvig, C. (2018). Infrastructure studies meet platform studies in the age of Google and Facebook. *New Media & Society*, *20*(1), 293–310. DOI: 10.1177/1461444816661553

Plantin, J.-C., & Punathambekar, A. (2019). Digital media infrastructures: Pipes, platforms, and politics. *Media Culture & Society*, *41*(2). Advance online publication. DOI: 10.1177/0163443718818376

Pohle, J., & Voelsen, D. (2022). Centrality and power. The struggle over the techno-political configuration of the Internet and the global digital order. *Policy and Internet*, *14*(1), 13–27. DOI: 10.1002/poi3.296

Qiu, J. L. (2019). *Goodbye iSlave: A Manifesto for Digital Abolition*. University of Illinois Press.

Rigi, J., & Prey, R. (2015). Value, rent, and the political economy of social media. *The Information Society*, *31*(5), 392–406. DOI: 10.1080/01972243.2015.1069769

Rochet, J.-C., & Tirole, J. (2003). Platform competition in two-sided markets. *Journal of the European Economic Association*, *1*(4), 990–1029.

Said, E. (1978). *Orientalism*. Pantheon.

Sánchez, D. Y., Maldonado, O. J., Agudelo-Londoño, S., Hernández, M., Hernández, L. J., & Suárez-Morales, Z. B.. (2024). Infrastructuring platform delivery work: Exclusions, coercions and resistance in delivery platforms' migrant work in Bogotá, Colombia. *Tapuya : Latin American Science, Technology and Society*, *7*(1), 2343161. DOI: 10.1080/25729861.2024.2343161

Soulé, F. (2024). Digital sovereignty in Africa: Moving beyond local data ownership. CIGI Policy Brief No. 185, June 2024. https://www.cigionline.org/static/documents/PB_no.185_eRCHbMI.pdf

Spivak, G. C. (1988). Can the subaltern speak? In C. Nelson & L. Grossberg (eds.). *Marxism and the Interpretation of Culture*. Macmillan, 24–28.

Srnec, C., & Guttmann, A. (2024). Platform cooperatives, a model of commons and sustainability. In Warren, J. N., Biggiero, L., Hübner, J., & Ogunyemi, K. (Eds.), *The Routledge Handbook of Cooperative Economics and Management* (pp. 388–397). Routledge.

Srnicek, N. (2017). *Platform Capitalism*. Polity Press.

Staab, P. (2019). *Digitaler Kapitalismus. Markt und Herrschaft in der Ökonomie der Unknappheit*. Suhrkamp.

Steinberg, D., & Li, H. (2017). Introduction: Regional platforms. *Asiascape: Digital Asia*, *4*(3), 173–183.

Suri, T., & Jack, W. (2016). The long-run poverty and gender impacts of mobile money. *Science*, *354*(6317), 1288–1292. DOI: 10.1126/science.aah5309

Vallas, S., & Schor, J. B. (2020). What do platforms do? Understanding the gig economy. *Annual Review of Sociology*, *46*, 273–294. DOI: 10.1146/annurev-soc-121919-054857

van Dijck, J., Poell, T., & de Waal, M. (2018). *The Platform Society: Public Values in a Connective World*. Oxford University Press.

Vogl, J. (2021). *Kapital und Ressentiment: Eine kurze Theorie der Gegenwart*. C. H. Beck.

Wang, Y. (2025). Current status and challenges of China's platform economy: A macroeconomic perspective. *Advances in Economics, Management and Political Sciences*. https://doi.org/DOI: 10.54254/2754-1169/2025.BL23703

Yin, R. K. (2014). *Case Study Research: Design and Methods* (5th ed.). Sage.

Zeng, J. (2020). Artificial intelligence and China's authoritarian governance. *International Affairs*, *96*(6), 1441–1459. DOI: 10.1093/ia/iiaa172

Zuboff, S. (2019). *The Age of Surveillance Capitalism: The fight for a Human Future at the New Frontier of Power*. PublicAffairs.

# Chapter 3
# Platformized Headlines: Algorithmic Power, Affective Culture, and Ideological Identity

**Özge Ercebe**
https://orcid.org/0000-0002-9036-9404
*Trakya University, Turkey*

## ABSTRACT

*This chapter analyzes platformized news headlines as multi-layered affective interfaces that function at the intersection of attention, affect, and ideology. In an environment governed by algorithmic curation and metric culture, headline tactics are optimized for engagement. The author develops a framework to map how strategies like superlative statements, emotional cues, and identity framing circulate in platform feeds. Through qualitative case studies of crisis, election, and sport events, the analysis demonstrates how these linguistic packages co-move with early engagement signals, contributing to affective clustering and the polarization of public discourse. The chapter concludes by offering recommendations for newsrooms and platforms, alongside a future research agenda, to align short-term visibility with long-term public trust and democratic integrity.*

## INTRODUCTION

This section aims to describe how the language of news headlines is being reshaped under digital platforms' incentive structures and how that language interlocks with attention, affect, and ideological/identity alignments in the public sphere. Headlines are treated not merely as textual synopses but as linguistic artifacts that interact with

DOI: 10.4018/979-8-3373-4267-2.ch003

platform interfaces and metric feedback loops, producing signals that point toward specific emotional and identity foci.

Avoiding normative judgments, the chapter advances a descriptive framework with three analytical foci: (i) attention strategies (curiosity induction, urgency, superlatives); (ii) affective signals (high-arousal emotion markers); and (iii) indicators of ideological alignment ("us/them" codes, group labels, moral frames). Different combinations along these three axes leave discernible traces in how headlines gain visibility and are received on platforms.

Consistent with this aim, the chapter maps the headline strategies that come to the fore across different event types—crises, elections, and sports—through the lens of the attention–affect–ideological signaling triad. It also discusses how platform feedback mechanisms that operate through early engagement signals shape the circulation of these strategies, making visible the traces of public affect and belonging in the form of affective clustering (i.e., the formation of emotion-driven audience segments). Within this frame, the chapter addresses the following research questions:

- RQ1: Which headline strategies become salient across different event types?
- RQ2: How do platform feedback mechanisms shape the circulation of these strategies?
- RQ3: What traces does this circulation leave with respect to public affect and the sense of belonging?

## BACKGROUND

### Platformization and the Language of News

Platformization is reshaping contemporary news language and public discourse in visible ways. In an environment where audiences encounter news not only on institutional websites but primarily within algorithmically managed feeds, the rules governing language adapt to the technical, economic, and cultural logic of platforms. The core premise here is that platforms are not mere distribution channels; they are socio-technical systems that simultaneously transform the organizational structures of news production, hierarchies of value, and linguistic choices. Grasping this framework lays the groundwork for understanding the linguistic and interactional conditions under which affective publics are assembled.

Van Dijck and Poell (2013) describe platform logic through four principles: programmability, datafication, popularity, and connectivity. Programmability refers to the ongoing steerability of user and publisher behavior through interface and infrastructure design (van Dijck & Poell, 2013, pp. 5–6). To gain visibility, news organizations must adapt to this programmable environment—that is, learn to "speak" the language of ranking algorithms and card/preview formats. Datafication is the translation of micro-actions—clicks, scrolls, pauses, shares—into measurable data points (van Dijck & Poell, 2013, p. 7). As a result, the value of news is appraised not only through editorial judgment but also through quantitative performance indicators.

Within this terrain, popularity metrics assume a central role. Counts of likes, reactions, comments, and shares become primary signals of what is "valuable" or "interesting." The tendency of early engagement to boost visibility- and of heightened visibility to attract further engagement -enables positive feedback loops in practice (van Dijck & Poell, 2013, pp. 14–15). Gillespie's (2010; 2018) notion of "platform politics" underscores that this mechanism is not simply a technical ranking function but a set of normative choices: under the guise of neutrality, recommendation systems and content moderation effectively define what will be deemed important, legitimate, and visible (Gillespie, 2010, pp. 350–353).

The economic model explains the driving force of this visibility regime. Srnicek (2017) conceptualizes platform capitalism as an accumulation order built on data extraction, network effects, and multi-sided market architectures. Platforms broker relationships among users, advertisers, and content producers; the primary capital is data derived from user interactions. In this ecosystem, journalism becomes both a content producer and a dependent actor that supplies platforms with traffic and data (Srnicek, 2017, pp. 48–53). This dependency renders newsrooms more responsive to platform incentives and, in practice, institutionalizes a metric culture—what Beer (2016) terms "metric power" (Beer, 2016, pp. 9–12).

Ethnographic and organizational studies demonstrate how this transformation materializes within newsrooms. Christin (2020) shows how journalists' performance is tracked via real-time dashboards and how metrics shape editorial decisions. Napoli (2011) discusses the rising centrality of audience measurement in institutional decision-making. Petre (2015) observes the emergence of "analytics fetishism" in some settings, where optimization gradually displaces intuitive editorial judgment (Petre, 2015, pp. 9–13). Consequently, questions like "Which headline got more clicks?" or "Which topic generated more shares?" move to the center of meetings; such indicators are internalized as primary measures of journalistic success (Cherubini & Nielsen, 2016, p. 8).

The most visible effects of platform logic can be traced in interfaces and micro-linguistic choices. Bucher (2018) argues that "small gestures" such as notification wording, button design, and feed layout constitute a form of algorithmic power that steers everyday behavior. For example, expanding reaction options—"Angry," "Haha," and so on—facilitates more varied and intense affective expression while rendering those expressions data-traceable (Bucher, 2018, pp. 72–76). Such platform affordances encourage the production and circulation of particular content types—

emotion-heavy, identity-aligning, or curiosity-driven pieces. With the "platformization of the web," Helmond (2015) shows how social plugins and APIs enable content to circulate across platforms in standardized "social card" formats (Helmond, 2015, pp. 5–9). This standardization amplifies the weight of the headline: competing in the feed as a mini-narrative and a "micro-trigger," the headline becomes the key surface of visibility. Precisely for this reason, attention strategies that trade in ambiguity, exaggeration, or curiosity gaps are more frequently employed (Blom & Hansen, 2015, p. 88; Tewksbury & Riles, 2015). As A/B testing makes it possible to measure the real-time performance of alternative headline variants, the refinement of these strategies accelerates; as Petre (2021) shows, headline "success" increasingly hinges less on informative clarity than on the capacity to provoke response.

In short, platforms' foundational principles (van Dijck & Poell, 2013), their economic architectures (Srnicek, 2017), and their political-operational choices (Gillespie, 2010; 2018) feed a metrics-centered production culture within newsrooms (Christin, 2020; Beer, 2016). Beyond the technical and economic logics of platformization, regulatory frameworks increasingly shape the boundaries of visibility and accountability in the digital public sphere. Recent policy initiatives such as the *EU Digital Services Act (DSA)* and the *Digital Markets Act (DMA)* impose new transparency and auditing obligations on major platforms, redefining how algorithmic recommendation and moderation processes can be governed (European Commission, 2022; Helberger, 2020; Gorwa, 2019). These developments highlight that "platform power" is not only infrastructural but also juridical and normative: it is negotiated through legal regimes, compliance standards, and public scrutiny. In this sense, algorithmic visibility operates within a broader ecology of governance where data flows, editorial autonomy, and regulatory oversight intersect. When this culture converges with interface affordances (Bucher, 2018) and standardized card formats (Helmond, 2015), headline language tends to concentrate on capturing attention, heightening affective intensity, and signaling identity. Of course, the strength of this tendency varies with the institutional-political characteristics of media systems: in highly polarized contexts such as Turkey, platform pressures risk intensifying ideological cleavages, whereas in systems with strong public-service journalism traditions, institutional norms can partially offset those pressures (Hallin & Mancini, 2004, pp. 67–68).

This background establishes the conceptual bridge to discuss affective publics and framing, allowing us to specify which emotional and identity signals headlines make salient, how these signals scale in circulation, and how public affect is organized within platform incentive schemes.

## Affective Publics and Emotional Framing

Building on this foundation, and drawing on Zizi Papacharissi's affect theory, we can now discuss how emotionally resonant headlines make affective publics visible and set them in motion. In line with the "affective turn" in media studies, this approach treats emotions not merely as individual reactions but as culturally coded, socially shared, performed, and circulated phenomena.

Four complementary theoretical lenses work together here: Papacharissi on affective publics, Entman on framing, Wetherell on affective practices, and Serrano-Puche on the circulation of digital affect. The aim is to surface, in a context-sensitive and descriptive register, the patterns observed between headlines' linguistic choices and platforms' feedback mechanisms. In this way, one can trace how headlines mark particular affective foci, how those foci are performed in distinct discursive forms, and how they accelerate and scale within the digital ecosystem—over time and across layers.

Guiding the approach are three principles:

- Context-sensitivity: the type, intensity, and direction of affective foci vary by event type, political climate, and media system.
- Socio-technical co-formation: linguistic choices and interface/algorithmic feedback shape each other; the emphasis is on relationality rather than one-way causality.
- Multimodal expression: headlines operate alongside images, emoji/reaction sets, hashtags, and notification copy; linguistic analysis should be complemented by visual and interface context.

Papacharissi (2015) conceptualizes the new forms of collectivity that emerge on digital networks as affective publics. These publics do not fully rest on Habermas's ideal of rational-critical deliberation; they operate through an expressive, affect-woven logic. Around a shared event or narrative, transient clusters form via shared affect: waves of mass anger at a tweet, collective mourning after a disaster, or pride sparked by a sporting/cultural triumph (Papacharissi, 2015, pp. 116–121). Low-threshold signs of expressive participation (likes, reactions, shares), micro-stories that tether personal feeling to public life, fluidity, and ephemerality are distinctive features of these publics.

Headlines play a critical role at this juncture: on a constrained verbal surface, they produce a "spark" that densely cues an event's affective core. Word choices like "betrayal," "scandal," "devastation," "epic"; "us/them" codings; and formal devices such as exclamation, rhythmic repetition, numeric promises, and superlatives provide low-bar entry points for affective focus. These entry points readily meet reactions, suggested hashtags, and notification styles, amplifying the visibility of expression. Thus, affective publics appear less as spontaneous eruptions than as socio-technical events in which language, technical infrastructures, and cultural repertoires interweave. The leading role of micro-narrativization—which connects personal feeling to public life—in mobilizing these clusters is a point Papacharissi underscores (2015, p. 19).

Affective foci often settle into recurrent forms along a few axes. In contexts of grief and solidarity, softer moods, community/support emphasis, and ritual calls ("a minute of silence") prevail. When anger and resentment intensify, perpetrator assignment, vocabularies of moral violation, and contrastive rhetoric come to the fore. In narratives of pride and ascent, a collective subject ("we"), a lexicon of achievement, and the certification of symbolic gain (headlines paired with flags or national symbols) dominate. These axes are not mutually exclusive; they can interpenetrate, switch rapidly, or trigger one another depending on context.

Robert Entman's (1993) framing approach offers a powerful tool for unpacking the emotional and semantic weave of headlines. Framing selects and highlights certain pieces of information to furnish the reader with an interpretive schema for problem definition, causal diagnosis, moral evaluation, and/or remedy (Entman, 1993, p. 52). The headline is the most condensed version of this schema: within a tight space it answers not only "what happened?" but also "what kind of thing is this?" To label a protest a "freedom march" rather than "chaos" does more than relay facts; it assigns an affective vector. Problem definition, causal or agentive attribution, moral valence, and calls to action/solution are concatenated within the headline. This concatenation finely tunes affect through chosen verbs ("lashed out," "targeted," "exposed," "stood firm"), nouns/adjectives ("traitor," "victim," "hero," "scandal," "historic"), contrasts ("us–them," "people–elite," "native–foreign"), and moral vocabulary ("justice," "betrayal," "honor," "shame"). In the platform age, these frames operate not only inside the article but across multiple presentation surfaces—notification text, social-card headlines, text overlays on thumbnails, even URL slugs. Frames that gather early engagement tend to become more visible algorithmically and affect-laden frames often circulate more widely in step with that visibility; this is an observed co-occurrence rather than a claim of causal necessity.

Wetherell's (2012) notion of "affective practices" invites us to treat affect not as a merely internal state but as social performances enacted in particular contexts. Affect is "done" through linguistic resources (word choice, metaphor, rhythm), bodily proxies (emojis standing in for gesture and tone, punctuation styles), material objects (images, symbols), and spatial-digital arrangements (feed, card, notification). The headline is the entryway into this performance: monosyllabic force verbs, repetition and parallelism, numeric promises as rhythmic choices that elevate affective energy; scenario-invoking cues—"scandal," "massacre," "epic," "victory"—that prefigure which affective script will be enacted; and the public legitimization of specific affects (e.g., anger) via frames like "injustice." Low-cost participation formats (reaction buttons, emoji sets, frictionless sharing) allow these enactments to stack quickly; a visible "angry" reaction count beneath a headline signals an expressive norm to others. These micro-level linguistic and typographic decisions acquire meaning through interaction with meso-level newsroom routines (A/B testing, metric dashboards), institutional guidelines, and platform policies.

Focusing on digital circulation, Serrano-Puche (2016; 2021) shows how affect intertwines with the political economy of communication to shape what is shared and seen. Platform architectures tend to reward signals that indicate engagement (likes, comments, shares, watch-time); consequently, emotional content often gains visibility more easily. Empirical literature indicates that high-arousal emotions (anger, anxiety, elation) spread faster than low-arousal ones; findings on moral-emotional language increasing the diffusion of ideologically congruent messages complement this picture (Brady et al., 2017, pp. 7316–7321). A small choice at the linguistic level—picking a higher-arousal verb such as "attacked" rather than "criticized"—can, when combined with platforms' accelerating feedback, surface a wider-than-expected affective clustering. Circulation rarely stays within a single platform: screenshot culture, quote-sharing, de-contextualization and re-contextualization reassemble affect across network nodes. Image–text composites (headline overlays on thumbnails, meme templates) reinforce affective direction, while notification copy heightens urgency via markers like "now," "just in," and "breaking," nudging early engagement.

Across all these processes, context management and audience composition are decisive: the same headline can trigger very different affective practices across audience clusters; local political sensitivities, cultural codes, and the outlet's reputation accentuate these differences. By describing the socio-technical ground on which affective publics are performed through four theoretical lenses, this section has shown how headlines spark affective foci (Papacharissi, 2016), organize meaning and affective direction via framing (Entman, 1993), demonstrate how affect is "done" as social practice (Wetherell, 2012), and explain how platform architectures accelerate and scale circulation (Serrano-Puche, 2016). The next section applies this framework to "Affective Communication Strategies via Headlines," closely examining the solo and joint deployment of attention–affect–ideology cues, exemplary typologies, and context-dependent variations.

## Affective Communication Strategies via Headlines

Within a platform-steered attention economy, a headline is no longer a neutral synopsis. It is a multilayered affective interface that competes for interaction and is highly sensitive to metric feedback. Three strategy clusters that may look different on the surface—attention tactics often labeled as clickbait, emotional framing, and ideological signaling—can be read along a single axis of capturing attention, eliciting affect, and aligning identity. This is not a compulsory linear route that headlines always follow; it is the direction in which intensification is frequently observed. Headlines, in this light, are interwoven sets of linguistic and discursive choices aimed at different points along that axis.

The first task of affective communication is to catch attention in the stream. In platform capitalism, attention is the basic unit of value, and clearing that initial threshold is the headline's reason for being. Practices often grouped under "clickbait" are more than a simplistic "misleading headline" problem; if promise–content alignment is preserved, they can function as gateways into more complex strategies. Curiosity gaps that withhold a key detail, open-ended promises that suggest an unfinished story, and the careful management of expectation are typical tools at this entry layer. Superlatives reinforce hints of rarity or extraordinariness; temporal markers like "now," "just in," and "breaking," together with spatial or emotional proximity cues, raise urgency; format signals—lists, rankings, comparisons—suggest scan-ability; direct address and questions invite the reader "on stage"; numbers and quantitative frames amplify a sense of measurability. The constrained surfaces of cards and notifications naturally nudge toward curiosity, while A/B testing infrastructures make variant trials and sensitivity to early engagement easier. How the thumbnail and headline pair calibrate the open-endedness–satisfaction balance is pivotal.

At the level of wording, ambiguity markers and hedges, modals and degree adverbs, dramatic but content-external adjectives and verbs, interrogatives, and intensifiers are frequently mobilized. Clickbait becomes problematic when promises to detach from content; where alignment is kept, calibrated curiosity legitimately serves as an entry layer. In practice, that layer rarely stands alone; once the promise is set, an affective frame often completes the move into interaction.

The next move is to convert fleeting attention into deeper affective engagement. Entman's account of framing is reshaped under platform conditions: a headline not only selects an angle but configures it for affective maximum. Affective lexis—verbs and adjectives that set tone instantly—does much of this work. Instead of flat reports ("stated"), formulations like "lashed out," "rebelled," or "dared," and, beyond simple "rise/fall," bodily-metaphoric verbs such as "hit hard," "collapsed," or "took off" dramatize economic developments. Personalization refracts complex issues through singular stories of harm or heroism—turning abstract problems into relatable narratives. Moral evaluation— "gross ingratitude," "historic betrayal," "shameful decision"—offers a normative compass and legitimizes emotions like anger or disappointment. In Wetherell's terms, such framing seeds affective practices: the headline does not only propose meaning; it tacitly sets rules of play for which affective repertoire will be enacted. Reactions, shares, and comments are the visible traces of that enactment; as platforms reward these signals, the frame tends to travel more widely. This is an observed co-movement rather than a claim of causal necessity.

The strongest layer is aligning elicited affect with a worldview or collective identity. Here, headlines do more than grab attention and stir feeling; they send cues about who the reader is, where they belong, and whom they stand against. In-group/out-group coding sharpened by pronouns, nouns, and adjectives—for instance, "an assault on the national will" or "a grave insult to the people's artist"—invites readers into a circle of belonging and calls forth a shared stance toward another. Value-laden key phrases that look neutral to the general public but carry specific meanings in particular community function as ideological dog whistles, refining identity targeting. In negative events, assigning responsibility or blame anchors the frame to existing political fault lines and primes moral emotion. Empirical work suggests that moral–emotional language increases the diffusion of ideologically congruent messages (Brady et al., 2017), which helps explain the circulation advantage of such signaling. In this sense, the headline becomes not only a call to preexisting identities but a performative apparatus that reproduces identity in everyday circulation; by consuming and interacting with such headlines, readers reaffirm their position and strengthen ties to their affective public.

In practice, these layers interweave. Some headlines spark curiosity and leave the reader at the door; others dramatize scenes to intensify engagement; still others aim directly at identity alignment. The most platform-congruent examples choreograph a smooth journey from curiosity to affective bonding, to identity confirmation. The upshot is that headlines are no longer just doors to articles. They are potent socio-technical instruments that redraw the affective and ideological fault lines of the public sphere day after day.

Taken together, the descriptive frame proposed here maps how headlines "do work" under platform conditions across three complementary foci. Devices that lower attention thresholds, narrative and lexical choices that invite affective resonance, and cues that summon identity alignment through belonging and opposition all operate in interaction with recommendation and ranking systems, reaction–comment–share surfaces, and A/B testing infrastructures. Headline success should therefore be assessed not only by its capacity to convey information but also by its ability to be seen in the stream, generate interaction, and resonate within particular communities. Without positing single-center causality, this reading—grounded in observed patterns and typical linguistic markers—shows how headlines intensify along the attention–affect–ideology axis and co-evolve with metric feedback loops.

## MAIN FOCUS OF THE CHAPTER

Having outlined the linguistic and affective mechanisms at play, the following section summarizes how these strands converge into the chapter's analytical framework. This chapter examines the patterns observed at the intersection of headline language and platform dynamics. The analysis proceeds along three axes—attention strategies, affective signals, and indicators of ideological alignment. In different intensities and combinations, these axes come together to offer readable clues about which signals headlines make visible as they circulate on platforms, and how those signals relate to public affect and belonging. The intensity and direction of this process vary by context; platform affordances, the newsroom's metric culture, and the type/context of the event (crisis, holiday, election, etc.) shape this variability. Without making causal claims, the chapter treats these interactions within a descriptive frame and focuses on the headline as a verbal–textual surface. This analysis draws on examples from the Turkish media system—a polarized yet platform-dependent environment that vividly illustrates how algorithmic incentives intersect with ideological segmentation.

### Issues, Controversies, Problems

To ground these conceptual debates in empirical observation, the next section turns to concrete headline cases drawn from the Turkish media landscape. This chapter treats news headlines as a signal architecture that operates within platform incentive structures and interface affordances, and that acquires meaning along the axes of attention, affect, and identity. This positioning is directly aligned with the book's frame—Sociological Dimensions of Platformization: Power, Culture, and Identity in the Digital Age: algorithmic visibility and incentives map to power; metrified attention and affective culture map to culture; ideological signaling and identity alignment map to identity. Rather than collapsing the discussion into a "clickbait/ethics" binary, the chapter seeks to make visible the performative role of headlines in producing public knowledge, affect, and belonging, in a relational register.

The most salient area of tension in practice is the balance between attention-grabbing headline design and the public interest/ethical principles. While common practices tend to prioritize short-term metric gains (CTR, watch time, SEO, intensive A/B testing), the chapter underscores that headlines do more than generate visibility; they also shape long-term outcomes such as trust, reputation, and public value. Moving beyond a narrow "clickbait yes/no" debate, the approach reframes headline design as a matter of signal design governed by promise–content alignment and context sensitivity—an evaluation that intersects with the book's culture dimension. In newsroom practice, these dynamics manifest through analytics dashboards,

SEO-driven editorial adjustments, and A/B-tested headline variants that translate platform incentives into everyday journalistic routines.

A second core debate concerns algorithmic visibility and the measurement–causality link. Although patterns in which early engagement signals co-occur with increased visibility are frequently observed, the "black box" character of platforms makes strong, one-way causal inferences problematic. The chapter does not attempt to build engineering-level explanatory models or to reduce headlines to simple taxonomies; instead, it maps, in a descriptive and context-sensitive way, the co-movement between linguistic/micro-choices and circulation. This stance runs counter to over-generalized causal narratives and narrow "clickbait" stigmas in the literature, and it advances a more cautious, evidence-attentive position on power.

Ideological signaling and identity alignment open a space that both facilitates meaning-making and belonging and carries polarization risks. Headlines that mobilize "us/them" codes, moral lexicons, and attributions of agency, when combined with audience segmentation and editorial lines, become strategic positioning. The chapter does not pass categorical judgment; it aims to show which micro-choices, in which contexts, intensify polarizing effects. Read in line with the identity dimension, this helps reframe design decisions between "more clicks" and "deeper trust."

Platform affordances and the institutional effects of metric culture also matter. Reaction buttons, the limited real estate of card formats, and notification copy pre-weight which linguistic choices are more circulation-friendly from the outset; this can create friction between editorial autonomy and performance indicators. Accordingly, the chapter proposes assessing headline success not only through CTR or dwell time but through how attention thresholds, affective resonance, and identity alignment relate to long-term trust and subscription loyalty. Compared with single-metric success templates, this multi-dimensional view promotes a more balanced performance understanding that aligns with the book's power–culture–identity axes.

Finally, the limits of context sensitivity and generalizability should be acknowledged explicitly. Different event types—crises, elections, sports—produce different forms of affective publics; the political–institutional structure of the media system and the audience's cultural repertoires further differentiate these effects. "Best headline" recipes derived from a single context are therefore misleading. By adopting a descriptive approach that surfaces cross-context patterns, the chapter discusses, in keeping with the book's core theme, power (algorithmic visibility and incentives), culture (metrified attention and affect), and identity (ideological alignment) together. In this way, it becomes clearer that headline design is not merely about momentary attention capture; it is a signal architecture that produces cumulative effects on the quality of public information, the emotional climate, and democratic deliberation.

## REPRESENTATIVE EXAMPLES: OBSERVED PATTERNS

This chapter employs a *descriptive and comparative qualitative approach* grounded in purposive sampling. The analysis focuses on *information-rich cases* that exemplify how headline language operates within platform dynamics. Through *discourse analysis* and *case-based comparison*, it examines patterns of attention, affect, and ideology across different types of events such as crises, elections, and sports. This flexible and context-sensitive design enables a close reading of headline strategies within varying media orientations, aligning with the chapter's exploratory focus and the book's broader goal of mapping the sociological dimensions of platformized communication.

The empirical material includes headlines, social media posts, and video thumbnails from prominent Turkish news outlets with differing ideological orientations, including *Yeni Şafak, Sözcü, Hürriyet,* and *Cumhuriyet.* The examples were selected to illuminate the chapter's core theoretical arguments rather than to represent the entire media landscape statistically. Each case illustrates how news organizations frame salient public events to capture attention, evoke affective responses, and signal ideological alignment. By juxtaposing examples from contrasting outlets covering the same event, the analysis reveals how linguistic and visual strategies diverge and how affective–ideological cues circulate within platformized news ecosystems.

### Headline Languages During Crisis

Focusing on crisis coverage, the section reads as, in a single continuous flow, how headlines produced during the 2021 wildfires functioned across the attention–affect–ideology axis. The material includes high-arousal YouTube titles/thumbnails, X/Twitter posts, and web headlines from outlets such as Yeni Şafak, A Haber, Hürriyet, BirGün, and Sözcü. On the attention front, a common first line of attack is the superlative + metric bundle. Phrases like "THE LARGEST WILDFIRE DISASTER" backed by numbers 60,000 hectares, 7 deaths, 33,000 animal fatalities, and 1 billion lira in losses—both dramatize scale and reinforce an informative stance (Yeni Şafak, 2021a). Likewise, "Major disaster in Manavgat! Fires in 4 separate locations" couples a superlative with numeric markers, sharpening perceived threat and nudging the click impulse (A Haber, 2021a). In crisis communication, measurability and uniqueness often work in tandem for visibility and persuasion.

Affect mobilization appears at two poles—high sadness and high anger. "THE ANNOUNCEMENT THAT MADE EVERYONE CRY" recenters themes of witness and sacrifice to circulate intense grief; while such headlines can spur sharing, they also warrant care given the risks of commodifying victimhood and triggering secondary trauma (Yeni Şafak, 2021b). By contrast, the "Oxford-educated volunteer pilot" storyline generates positive affect through cues of individual heroism and expertise, opening a "window of hope" within the crisis narrative (Yeni Şafak, 2021c). Headlines with perpetrator assignment—"HERE IS THAT TRAITOR'S AUDIO RECORDING!"—rapidly mobilize anger, but they also heighten the risks of trial by media and targeted vilification, shifting attention from nature/climate/capacity to a criminal lens (A Haber, 2021b). Question hooks such as "Were the fires sabotage?" trigger curiosity gaps and can lift engagement, but they may also expand the circulation of uncertainty (A Haber, 2021c).

Framing choices often hinge on responsibility versus capacity. "THK planes are being left to rot!" builds a critical frame that links infrastructure and managerial performance directly to political responsibility, spotlighting demands for accountability (BirGün, 2021). At the counterpoint, a "neutral-technical" register—"The BE-200 amphibious aircraft from Azerbaijan has joined the effort," for example—foregrounds capacity and solidarity, strengthening verifiable information flow while dialing down affective tension (Hürriyet, 2021). Within the same crisis field, these choices yield different public consequences: one deepens antagonism and political contestation; the other elevates coordination and cooperation.

Interface logic matters: visual–verbal packaging is decisive. On YouTube, large-type superlatives on red backgrounds paired with high-arousal lexicon like "shock" and "traitor" are designed for "scroll-stopping"; A Haber examples make this coupling explicit (A Haber, 2021a, 2021b). On X/Twitter and the web, a more neutral tone that pairs visual evidence with metrics (e.g., the BE-200 amphibious aircraft) is more feasible; while these headlines can be disadvantaged in raw engagement, they tend to be stronger on institutional trust and verifiability (Hürriyet, 2021; Yeni Şafak, 2021a).

Evaluated through an ethical–editorial lens, claim–evidence match stands out. High-affect tactics like perpetrator assignment and insinuations of conspiracy tend to generate rapid spread, whereas capacity/logistics and data-driven frames contain tension and lean on trust (A Haber, 2021b, 2021c; BirGün, 2021; Yeni Şafak, 2021a–c). Critical responsibility frames are valuable in terms of public interest, yet they require close proportionality between the level of the claim and the available evidence.

In broad strokes, the A Haber–Yeni Şafak line tends to escalate interaction via affect mobilization and curiosity hooks, while BirGün prioritizes a responsibility- and capacity-centric critical frame, producing legitimacy through information and accountability. In outlets like Hürriyet that stake a mainstream claim, a logistics-technical "mirror frame" lowers emotional dosage and creates room for operational information (A Haber, 2021a–c; BirGün, 2021; Hürriyet, 2021; Yeni Şafak, 2021a–c).

## Headline Languages During Elections

Election-night discourse is examined around the debates over the Istanbul race during the 31 March 2019 local elections. Headlines from election night and the following week display a dynamic similar to crisis coverage along the attention–affect–ideology axis. Across TV/YouTube live broadcasts with red "breaking" tickers, X/Twitter posts, and web banners, the axes of "early certainty" and "doubt/procedure" operate simultaneously.

On the attention front, "breaking news" packaging is paired with early certainty. A Haber's broadcast "Binali Yıldırım: We won the election in Istanbul," layered with "BREAKING!" and "THANK YOU, ISTANBUL" overlays and accompanied by tight leader close-ups plus map/graphic panels, sets a powerful attention hook that produces an "early call effect" on election night (A Haber, 2019a). The same logic appears on X/Twitter in Yeni Şafak's "#BREAKING… We won Istanbul by a margin of 3,870 votes," where a red background, oversized "BREAKING" visual, and terse declaration jointly signal speed and certainty (Yeni Şafak, 2019). On the opposing side, Sözcü serves "Statement from CHP: We won Istanbul" and "No ifs or buts—we won Istanbul" alongside crowd-and-flags imagery, activating a victory narrative with emotional intensity and reinforcing "early certainty" from the other direction through a celebratory aesthetic (Sözcü, 2019a, 2019b).

A second pattern couples metrics with authority to create a data-backed curiosity hook. Sözcü's "6:30 a.m.… According to live YSK data, 98.2% of the ballot boxes are in; İmamoğlu leads by 22,000 votes," paired with the contrastive headline "The YSK says 'İmamoğlu,' Binali hangs a banner!," collides measurability and institutional authority with a symbolic move on the ground (banner/thank-you), achieving both information and a curiosity pull (Sözcü, 2019c). This combination works as the election-night analogue of the scale-and-statistics dramatization seen in wildfire coverage—e.g., "THE LARGEST WILDFIRE DISASTER — 60,000 hectares, 7 deaths, 33,000 animals," which both dramatizes scale and supports an informative stance (Yeni Şafak, 2021a). Here, YSK refers to Turkey's Supreme Electoral Council.

Affect mobilization splits between anger–vigilance and victory–cautious confidence. On the pro-government side, high-certainty formulations like "Here is the proof of irregularities in Istanbul!" and intent-laden attributions such as "There is an organized irregularity…" mobilize anger and vigilance; this language resembles the criminalization and suspicion amplification of crisis-period headlines like "HERE IS THAT TRAITOR'S AUDIO RECORDING!" or "Were the fires sabotage?" (A Haber, 2019a, 2019b; 2021b, 2021c). On the opposition side, "We won Istanbul" declarations and celebratory visuals generate high positive affect, while BirGün's formulation "İmamoğlu: The margin will hold between 18 and 20 thousand" aims to calm the public with cautious confidence grounded in data; this parallels the "positive affect" opening provided by the "Oxford-educated volunteer pilot" narrative during the wildfires (BirGün, 2019; Yeni Şafak, 2021c). Counter-affective cooling is achieved via emphasis on ballot security and multiple party representation; Cumhuriyet's frame—"There were nine AKP members at every ballot box in Istanbul"—shifts suspicion onto a technical footing and cools the debate (Cumhuriyet, 2019).

Legitimacy frames oscillate between procedure and data/observation. On the pro-government line, the process is tethered to a chain of "objection–recount–evidence/extraordinary appeal." Sabah's "AK Party applied for a recount of all votes in Istanbul" foregrounds the institutional step and legitimizes affective tension through legal procedure (Sabah, 2019). On the opposition side, legitimacy is built along the "YSK data–margin–observation" axis. Sözcü's juxtaposition of the YSK table screenshot with the "banner/thank-you" polemic confronts institutional data with a claim to symbolic superiority, strengthening its critique of perception management (Sözcü, 2019c).

Interface logic shows "multiple media, same package." On YouTube/TV, red-bannered "BREAKING" packages, leader close-ups, and graphic panels generate early certainty and high arousal; on X/Twitter, the #BREAKING formula, terse declarations, and the outlet's brand color palette deliver the same affect with minimal text (A Haber, 2019a; Yeni Şafak, 2019). On the other side, Sözcü's screenshot of the YSK table fuses metrics and authority with visual evidence (Sözcü, 2019c).

Three sensitive thresholds stand out in the ethical–editorial balance. First, "we won/thank you" early-closure language before official finalization produces perception effects that are hard to roll back (A Haber, 2019a; Yeni Şafak, 2019). Second, assertive headlines like "Here is the proof of irregularities!" and "Organized irregularity" require, at minimum, a brief summary of findings and the verification status at the deck level (A Haber, 2019b). Third, decontextualizing metrics (time, share of boxes counted, scope of recounts) weakens cautious certainty; thus notifications like "98.2%—22,000 margin" should be paired with contextual qualifiers (Sözcü, 2019c).

In sum, election-night discourse establishes an attention advantage through the "breaking + early certainty + metric–authority" combination, while affect management runs on two tracks: anger–vigilance via "irregularity/organized malpractice" on one side, and positive yet cautious emotion via "victory/ownership" and "calming with data" on the other. The contest over legitimacy swings between the "objection–recount–evidence" chain and the "YSK data–observation" axis. As with crisis headlines, the same interface techniques yield similar public outcomes across event types: high-arousal packages drive rapid interaction, whereas data- and procedure-centered presentations build a more balanced flow attentive to institutional trust and ethical alignment.

## Headline Language in Moments of Sporting and Cultural Success

The Turkish Women's National Volleyball Team's 2023 CEV European Championship is selected as the case for examining headline practices in the sports domain. The section considers, in a single integrated flow, how headlines produced around this championship operate along the attention–affect–ideology axis. Although the success coalesces around a shared line of national pride, the attention hook, affective intensity, and ideological framing diverge markedly depending on each outlet's choices in headline and visual packaging (Sözcü, 2023a; A Haber, 2023a; Yeni Şafak, 2023a; Cumhuriyet, 2023).

In the attention economy, three elements dominate: slogans, congratulatory messages, and the score. Sözcü's formula "Atatürk's daughters made history" situates the victory within a Republican symbolic repertoire, clearing the attention threshold via a sloganic frame (Sözcü, 2023a). A Haber and Yeni Şafak personalize the achievement at the most visible layer by foregrounding President Erdoğan's congratulatory message, framing the national narrative through leader endorsement (A Haber, 2023a; Yeni Şafak, 2023a). Cumhuriyet, by contrast, amplifies a "public celebration" aesthetic with crowd-and-flag compositions, foregrounding the visual codes of collective elation rather than a leader- or slogan-centric discourse (Cumhuriyet, 2023).

Metric visibility often hinges on the "closure effect" created by putting the score directly in the headline. Packages that feature the scoreline yield a clear data-backed close; A Haber's emphasis on the 3–2 result and Yeni Şafak's presentation of the same outcome in a congratulatory format sharpen in-sport certainty (A Haber, 2023b; Yeni Şafak, 2023b). Sözcü's large-type victory slogan, by contrast, elevates enthusiasm and belonging independent of the metric (Sözcü, 2023a). Sponsorship marks on the jersey and the coupling of national colors further intensify affect through layers of brand and symbol.

Affect mobilization hinges on different framings of national pride. Slogan-centered packages (e.g., "Atatürk's daughters") generate high positive affect through historical memory (Sözcü, 2023a), whereas congratulatory-message-centered packages tie success to a contemporary leadership narrative, intensifying emotion via personal endorsement (A Haber, 2023a; Yeni Şafak, 2023a). Crowd-and-flag compositions establish belonging not through a person or slogan but through a "scene of public sharing," offering a more inclusive aesthetic of elation (Cumhuriyet, 2023).

Ideological framing coheres along two main lines. One positions the victory around Republican symbols and founding figures (Sözcü, 2023a). The other presents the achievement within a hierarchy of approval close to the political center via leader endorsement and personalization (A Haber, 2023a; Yeni Şafak, 2023a).

Cumhuriyet's crowd- and flag-forward visual language grounds representation and belonging in the collective rather than the leader, pushing ideological markers to the background (Cumhuriyet, 2023).

Interface logic exhibits multi-platform but consistent packaging. On TV/YouTube, embedding the congratulatory message in headline and lower-third layers secures instant attention; on X/Twitter, terse declarations, hashtags, and large-type graphics replicate the same feeling with minimal text; on web front pages, full-screen celebration photos plus score-centric headlines strike a "data + emotion" balance (A Haber, 2023a–b; Yeni Şafak, 2023a–b; Sözcü, 2023a; Cumhuriyet, 2023).

Agenda expansion occurs through critical and analytical detours. Sözcü's "transfer with layovers / special treatment for them" contrast shifts from the success story to a debate on institutional priorities and fairness, creating a critical rupture that links the sports page to a logistics–policy axis (Sözcü, 2023b). Hürriyet Spor Arena's "Exclusive" badge, together with "unsung hero" angles and tactics/background emphasis, channels high affect into a flow of analytical curiosity (Hürriyet, 2023).

In sum, the same championship narrative is packaged along two principal routes: a Republican-symbol and collective-elation line, and a leader-endorsement and personalization line. Featuring the score in the headline anchors attention and legitimacy in data, while slogans and ceremonial symbols broaden enthusiasm; background/tactics dossiers serve as analytical conduits that convert that enthusiasm into sustained interest. Examples such as Sözcü's transport/justice framing indicate that, when success is linked to extra-sport agendas, differences among affective, metric, and ideological cues systematically surface in sports coverage as well (Sözcü, 2023a–b; A Haber, 2023a–b; Yeni Şafak, 2023a–b; Cumhuriyet, 2023; Hürriyet, 2023).

## THEORETICAL AND SOCIOLOGICAL IMPLICATIONS

Building on these theoretical insights and observed tensions, the following section translates them into actionable recommendations for newsroom and platform practices. Drawing on examples of platformized news headlines, this study demonstrates that in the digital age, a headline is no longer an innocent textual synopsis but a multilayered strategic instrument that operates within the logic of the attention economy, mobilizes affective publics, and reinforces ideological identities. The headline cases further reveal critical theoretical and societal implications for media practice, the integrity of public discourse, and citizens' relationship to information. These implications, in turn, necessitate a closer examination of three axes: the redefinition of journalistic ethics, the growing urgency of platform regulation, and the imperative to foster critical media literacy.

## Value Shift in the Journalistic Field and the Transformation of Practice

The penetration of platform logic and metric culture into institutional routines is reshaping the value hierarchy and everyday workflows of the journalistic field. The patterns analyzed previously illustrate how headline language and packaging strategies accompany—and actively mediate—this transformation.

Platformization inverts the traditional value hierarchy of journalism. Principles historically placed at the top—such as "informing the public" and "accuracy"—increasingly cede primacy to platform-imposed values like "visibility" and "engagement." Success is no longer assessed by a story's social import but by its metric performance. This constitutes a deep sociological shift in the focal point of professional practice and editorial decision-making. In parallel, editors' and reporters' daily routines are being reconfigured to align with this new value system. Practices such as continual A/B testing of headlines and the preference for high-click lexicon are not merely technical choices; they are symptoms of changing professional norms and identity. Professional responsibility, traditionally owed to the public, is thus reoriented toward the opaque demands of platform algorithms.

Within this reconfiguration, editorial boundaries—"promise–content alignment," the "claim–evidence equation," and the "early certainty threshold"—are reduced to a negotiated space between the pressures of engagement and ethical obligations. At the same time, the headline functions as an affective interface in the feed: coupled with surface constraints, it is organized around curiosity, urgency, and identity signals. Platform affordances (reaction sets, low sharing costs, standardized social cards) incentivize particular lexical choices and formal patterns; together they institute an optimization logic in headline writing.

## A New Logic of Power Operating Through Emotions

Viewed through the lens of power, platform logic offers important clues about how power in modern societies operates via increasingly indirect and covert mechanisms. Headlines are not merely vehicles for conveying information; they are powerful instruments that regulate and steer what ought to be felt and how. This points to a dynamic in which social control and guidance are increasingly secured through emotions.

As established previously, platforms provide the ground for affective publics. Platformized headlines, however, go a step further: they do not merely encourage this formation but actively manage it. Through headlines, news producers strategically trigger and channel specific emotions—anger, fear, elation, pride—toward particular targets. This marks a new style of political communication in which individuals and crowds are mobilized less by rational argument and more by shared affective waves.

Moreover, framing one issue as "treason" and another as "victory" is not a mere matter of word choice. Moral terms such as "betrayal," "shame," and "justice" signal which emotions are to be seen as legitimate, subtly calibrating the boundaries of public debate. When high-arousal verbs/adjectives ("attacked," "shock," "scandal") are combined with personalization and perpetrator assignment, anger and vigilance are easily mobilized. Such acts draw the contours of public discussion and the range of acceptable emotional responses. In this way, which problems are deemed "important" and which reactions "legitimate" are set from the outset. While more subtle than overt instruments of repression like censorship, this mode of power proves no less effective in shaping public discourse. Consequently, emotional steering operates less as blunt coercion and more as *soft power* grounded in expressive surfaces and the measurement of reactions. Which frames are accelerated, which emotions are legitimized, and which responses are rewarded emerge at the intersection of platform logic and institutional routines. This dynamic calls for addressing the "misinformation" problem not by collapsing it into a true/false binary, but by focusing on the circulation and legitimation of emotional frames.

## Identity Consolidation, Affective Clustering, and Social Tensions

When analyzed along the axis of ideological signposting, platformized headlines reveal how identity signals are produced at the headline layer and how they accompany affective clustering. Headlines function as an identity compass that continually reminds individuals of the questions "Who are we?" and "Who are they?" while supplying ready-made answers.

The "us/them" coding used in headlines pulls individuals more forcefully into the "echo chambers" to which they belong. Consuming and sharing such headlines becomes both an identity declaration and a ritual of belonging. This dynamic not only fuels social fragmentation by detaching groups from shared realities, but it also replaces the pursuit of understanding with the increasing demonization of one another.

The outcome of this process generates not only polarization rooted in political disagreement but a deeper form of "affective polarization." That is, rather than reasoned criticism of the "other" group, what emerges is entrenched distrust, antipathy, or anger toward them. In the sampled materials, ideological differentiation is observable even in ostensibly "low-conflict" domains such as sports and culture. Victory narratives are packaged through distinct identity repertoires—for example, leader endorsement versus Republican symbolic codes—while placing metrics in the headline strengthens the "closure by data" effect of triumph, and rituals and symbols broaden the sense of belonging.

These observations suggest that headlines continually reproduce identity signals far beyond the political realm, effectively mobilizing and transporting affective publics from cultural domains to political ones.

## SOLUTIONS AND RECOMMENDATIONS

Actionable guidance for institutions governing headline design along the attention–affect–ideology axis is consolidated below. The recommendations are grouped under newsroom practices, measurement/incentive design, and product/policy.

- **Editorial principles and checklists**
    - Code promise–content alignment and claim–evidence matching as primary principles in headline production.
    - For "early certainty" claims (e.g., election-night "we won"), perpetrator assignment/criminalization ("traitor," "sabotage"), and high-arousal interrogatives, require a second editorial sign-off and mandatory contextualization.
    - In crisis reporting, prioritize data/capacity/logistics frames; define alert thresholds against the commodification of victimhood and risks of secondary trauma.
- **Integrated headline–thumbnail–notification design**
    - Treat the three channels in concert; use a shared template that carries visual/textual intensity thresholds and verification notes.
    - For sports/cultural success stories, place score/metrics alongside celebration/slogans in the headline to deliver "closure by data"; counter over-personalization with inclusive celebration framings.
- **Re-tuning measurement and incentives**
    - Do not limit performance evaluation to CTR and dwell; jointly track return visits, subscription/loyalty, complaint/correction rates, and proxy indicators of trust.
    - Subject A/B tests to ethical pre-screening; automatically exclude variants that violate institutional principles even if they produce high CTR.
- **Transparency and correction protocols**
    - Adopt version notes for headline changes and a visible corrections policy.
    - For misleading packaging, issue rapid corrections and explanatory notes, and update shared cards accordingly.

- **Product/policy and platform design**
    - Increase transparency in recommender/ranking systems; make quality signals (source, date/time, data scope) visually salient.
    - Adjust sharing friction (e.g., an extra verification step for sensitive headlines) to reduce misdirection risk.
    - On platforms such as X/YouTube, set internal upper bounds for "breaking" and high-affect visual languages; require a source link and brief data summary as mandatory fields.

## FUTURE RESEARCH DIRECTIONS

Future research should more precisely map the articulation of power–culture–identity in the platformized circulation of headlines, focusing on the following axes:

- **Large-scale language–interaction analysis**
    - Use NLP-based methods to examine the co-trajectories of superlatives, interrogative templates, perpetrator assignment, and metric markers with engagement.
    - Estimate affect intensity with multimodal (text + visual) models and relate it to user behaviors.
- **Comparative media systems**
    - Compare the effects of identical headline strategies across media ecosystems with differing levels of polarization and institutional standards.
- **Natural experiments and longitudinal designs**
    - Leverage algorithm updates, outage periods, or regulatory interventions as natural experiments; track the trade-off between short-term visibility gains and long-term trust/loyalty longitudinally.
- **Production ethnographies and newsroom studies**
    - Conduct ethnographies that observe how metric–ethics tensions surface at decision points; document affect and risk-management practices within editorial approval chains.
- **Interface experiments and user research**
    - Run experiments that test headline–thumbnail–notification variants while preserving promise–content alignment; use user studies to assess how affective frames shape reception and perceived trust.
- **Ethical impact assessment**

- Undertake intervention studies to evaluate the effectiveness of media ethics protocols against the commodification of victimhood and the risk of secondary trauma.

These directions would strengthen the current descriptive framework with respect to causal inference and generalizability.

## CONCLUSION

This study conceptualizes the news headline not as a mere textual synopsis but as an affective interface co-shaped by platform UIs and metric culture—capable of triggering in-feed decisions and actions. The lenses of attention thresholds, affective resonance, and ideological signposting make it possible to treat phenomena such as clickbait, emotional framing, and polarization as components of an integrated strategy produced by platform incentives.

Evidence from crisis, election, and sports/culture cases indicates that a superlative–metric pairing can boost short-term visibility, while the packaging of high affect may strain verification and legitimacy boundaries. By contrast, data/capacity/procedure-centered frames dampen affective intensity and strengthen institutional trust. The findings show that early engagement signals (reactions, comments, shares) often co-move with headline strategies, yet contextual differences are decisive; claims of causality are deliberately avoided.

The methodological and scope limitations are clear: the sample is purposive and descriptive; algorithmic processes remain largely a black box; Turkey's highly polarized context may amplify linguistic intensity. These limitations underscore the importance of the proposed research agenda. Ultimately, the recommended editorial principles, integrated design, and ethical guardrails offer a workable framework for managing the tension between short-term engagement goals and long-term trust and public values. In essence, this framework offers more than a new research agenda; it provides a critical lens for practitioners, policymakers, and citizens to navigate the contested terrain where short-term engagement goals collide with the long-term pursuit of public trust and democratic values.

## REFERENCES


Beer, D. (2016). *Metric power* (Vol. 10). Palgrave Macmillan.

Blom, J. N., & Hansen, K. R. (2015). Click bait: Forward-reference as lure in online news headlines. *Journal of Pragmatics*, *76*, 87–100.

Brady, W. J., Wills, J. A., Jost, J. T., Tucker, J. A., & Van Bavel, J. J. (2017). Emotion shapes the diffusion of moralized content in social networks. *Proceedings of the National Academy of Sciences of the United States of America*, *114*(28), 7313–7318.

Bucher, T. (2018). If... Then: Algorithmic Power and Politics. Oxford University Press
BirGün Gazetesi. [BirGun_Gazetesi]. (2021, July 29). *Türkiye'nin birçok yerinden yangın haberleri geliyor* [Fire news is coming from many parts of Turkey] [Tweet]. X (formerly Twitter). https://x.com/BirGun_Gazetesi/status/1420732873481625602

Bucher, T., & Helmond, A. (2018). The affordances of social media platforms. *The SAGE handbook of social media, 1*(1), 233-253.

Cherubini, F., & Nielsen, R. K. (2016). Editorial analytics: How news media are developing and using audience data and metrics. *Available at SSRN* 2739328.

Christin, A., & Petre, C. (2020). Making peace with metrics: Relational work in online news production. *Sociologica*, *14*(2), 133–156.

Entman, R. M. (1993). Framing: Towards clarification of a fractured paradigm. *McQuail's reader in mass communication theory, 390*, 397.

European Commission. (2022). *The Digital Services Act and the Digital Markets Act: Ensuring a safe and open digital space.* Brussels: European Commission. https://digital-strategy.ec.europa.eu/en/policies/digital-services-act-package

Gillespie, T. (2010). The politics of 'platforms'. *New Media & Society*, *12*(3), 347–364.

Gillespie, T. (2018). *Custodians of the Internet: Platforms, content moderation, and the hidden decisions that shape social media.* Yale University Press.

Gorwa, R. (2019). What is platform governance? *Information Communication and Society*, *22*(6), 854–871. DOI: 10.1080/1369118X.2019.1573914

Haber, A. [ahaber]. (2019, April 8). *#CANLI AK Parti Genel Başkan Yardımcısı Ali İhsan Yavuz: Ortada oy yolsuzluğu var* [#LIVE AK Party Deputy Chairman Ali İhsan Yavuz: There is vote fraud] [Tweet]. X (formerly Twitter). https://x.com/ahaber/status/1115261563907260416

Haber, A. [Ahaber]. (2019, March 31). *SON DAKİKA! Binali Yıldırım: İstanbul'da seçimi kazandık* [LAST MINUTE! Binali Yıldırım: We won the election in Istanbul] [Video]. YouTube. https://www.youtube.com/watch?v=atI4G-gtDmY

Haber, A. [ahaber]. (2019, April 1). *#SONDAKİKA İşte İstanbul'da usulsüzlüğün belgeleri!* [#LASTMINUTE Here are the documents of irregularity in Istanbul!] [Tweet]. X (formerly Twitter). https://x.com/ahaber/status/1112706126838198272

Haber, A. [ahaber]. (2019, April 4). *#SONDAKİKA AK Parti, İstanbul'da tüm oyların yeniden sayılması için başvuruda bulundu* [#LASTMINUTE AK Party applied for a recount of all votes in Istanbul] [Tweet]. X (formerly Twitter). https://x.com/ahaber/status/1113890084145762305

Haber, A. [ahaber]. (2019, April 8). *#CANLI AK Parti Genel Başkan Yardımcısı Ali İhsan Yavuz: Ortada oy yolsuzluğu var* http://ow.ly/PiGv50pwOvd [#LIVE AK Party Deputy Chairman Ali İhsan Yavuz: There is vote corruption] [Tweet]. X (formerly Twitter). https://x.com/ahaber/status/1115261563907260416

Haber, A. [Ahaber]. (2021, July 29). *Antalya Manavgat'taki yangınlar sabotaj mı? Şok görüntüler...* [Are the fires in Manavgat, Antalya sabotage? Shocking footage...] [Video]. YouTube. https://www.youtube.com/watch?v=86krI6Tj1RE

Haber, A. [Ahaber]. (2021, July 28). *Manavgat'ta büyük felaket! 4 farklı noktada yangın* [Great disaster in Manavgat! Fire in 4 different locations] [Video]. YouTube. https://www.youtube.com/watch?v=zbUsIP3mhFQ

Haber, A. [Ahaber]. (2021, August 24). *Kız arkadaşı ortaya çıkardı! İşte Manavgat yangınında tutuklanan şahsın ses kaydı!* [His girlfriend revealed it! Here is the audio recording of the person arrested for the Manavgat fire!] [Video]. YouTube. https://www.youtube.com/watch?v=Crg6ulFUty4

Haber, A. [ahaber]. (2023, September 4). *Başkan Recep Tayyip Erdoğan, 2023 CEV Avrupa Şampiyonası'nda, Sırbistan'ı 3-2'lik skorla yenerek Şampiyon olan A Milli Kadın Voleybol Takımı'nı tebrik etti* [President Recep Tayyip Erdoğan congratulated the Women's National Volleyball Team, who became the champion by defeating Serbia 3-2 in the 2023 CEV European Championship] [Tweet]. X (formerly Twitter). https://x.com/ahaber/status/1698452076651590112

Hallin, D. C., & Mancini, P. (2004). *Comparing media systems: Three models of media and politics*. Cambridge university press.

Helberger, N. (2020). The political power of platforms: How current attempts to regulate misinformation amplify opinion power. *Digital Journalism (Abingdon, England)*, *8*(6), 842–854.

Helmond, A. (2015). The platformization of the web: Making web data platform ready. *Social Media + Society*, *1*(2), 2056305115603080.

Hürriyet. [Hurriyet]. (2021, August 5). *Yangınla amansız mücadele... Havadan destek veren hava araçlarına Azerbaycan'dan gelen BE200 amfibi uçak da dahil oldu* [Relentless fight with the fire... The BE200 amphibious aircraft from Azerbaijan was also included among the air vehicles providing support from the air] [Tweet]. X (formerly Twitter). https://x.com/Hurriyet/status/1423273251199852551

Hürriyet. [Hurriyet]. (2023, September 4). *2003'te başlayan hikaye 2023'te zaferle taçlandı... Filenin Sultanları'nın Avrupa şampiyonluğunun ardındaki sır ne?* [The story that started in 2003 was crowned with victory in 2023... What is the secret behind the European championship of the Sultans of the Net?] [Tweet]. X (formerly Twitter). https://x.com/Hurriyet/status/1698587182286311681

Napoli, P. M. (2011). *Audience evolution: New technologies and the transformation of media audiences*. Columbia University Press.

Papacharissi, Z. (2015). *Affective publics: Sentiment, technology, and politics*. Oxford University Press.

Papacharissi, Z. (2016). Affective publics and structures of storytelling: Sentiment, events and mediality. *Information Communication and Society*, *19*(3), 307–324.

Petre, C. (2015). The traffic factories: Metrics at chartbeat, gawker media, and the New York Times.

Petre, C. (2021). *All the news that's fit to click: How metrics are transforming the work of journalists*. Princeton University Press.

Şafak, Y. [yenisafak]. (2021, August 5). *Ağlatan anons* [The announcement that made people cry] [Tweet]. X (formerly Twitter). https://x.com/yenisafak/status/1423277540156661763

Şafak, Y. [yenisafak]. (2021, August 8). *En Büyük Yangın Felaketi* [The Biggest Fire Disaster] [Tweet]. X (formerly Twitter). https://x.com/yenisafak/status/1424306348141985795

Şafak, Y. [yenisafak]. (2021, August 6). *Oxford Mezunu Gönüllü* [Oxford Graduate Volunteer] [Tweet]. X (formerly Twitter). https://x.com/yenisafak/status/1423625652129910792

Şafak, Y. [yenisafak]. (2023, September 4). *Cumhurbaşkanı Erdoğan, Sırbistan'ı 3-2 yenerek Avrupa Şampiyonu olan A Milli Kadın Voleybol Takımı'nı tebrik etti* [President Erdoğan congratulated the Women's National Volleyball Team, who became the European Champion by defeating Serbia 3-2] [Tweet]. X (formerly Twitter). https://x.com/yenisafak/status/1698447814896754749

Şafak, Y. [yenisafak]. (2023, September 4). *Büyük Bir Gurur Yaşattınız* [You made us feel a great pride] [Tweet]. X (formerly Twitter). https://x.com/yenisafak/status/1698453761897660822

Serrano-Puche, J. (2016). Internet and emotions: New trends in an emerging field of research.

Sözcü Gazetesi. [gazetesozcu]. (2019, April 1). *Türkiye bu İstanbul sonuçlarını konuşuyor* [Turkey is talking about these Istanbul results] [Tweet]. X (formerly Twitter). https://x.com/gazetesozcu/status/1112562340376051716

Sözcü. [gazetesozcu]. (2023, September 11). *Avrupa Şampiyonu Filenin Sultanları'na tarifeli, futbol takımına özel uçak* [Scheduled flight for the European Champion Sultans of the Net, special flight for the football team] [Tweet]. X (formerly Twitter). https://x.com/gazetesozcu/status/1700871623765180654

Sözcü. [gazetesozcu]. (2023, September 3). *Filenin Sultanları, Avrupa Şampiyonu! Atatürk'ün kızları tarih yazdı* [Sultans of the Net, European Champion! Atatürk's daughters made history] [Tweet]. X (formerly Twitter). https://x.com/gazetesozcu/status/1698435362241986880

Srnicek, N. (2017). *Platform capitalism*. John Wiley & Sons.

Tewksbury, D., & Riles, J. M. (2015). Polarization as a function of citizen predispositions and exposure to news on the Internet. *Journal of Broadcasting & Electronic Media, 59*(3), 381–398.

Van Dijck, J., & Poell, T. (2013). Understanding social media logic. *Media and Communication, 1*(1), 2–14.

Van Dijck, J., Poell, T., & De Waal, M. (2018). *The platform society: Public values in a connective world*. Oxford university press.

Wetherell, M. (2012). Affect and emotion: A new social science understanding.

## KEY TERMS AND DEFINITIONS

**Affect Mobilization:** The deliberate design of headline/thumbnail packages to trigger high-arousal emotions (e.g., anger, sadness, elation) to increase engagement and spread.

**Affective Publics:** Networked collectives that coalesce and act around shared emotional responses rather than solely around shared opinions; they often persist across events.

**Algorithmic Visibility and Amplification:** The process by which ranking/recommendation systems increase the exposure of items that accrue early interaction signals (likes, comments, shares), reinforcing feedback loops.

**Attention Economy:** A competitive environment in which human attention is the scarce resource; headlines must win selection within milliseconds as content streams past.

**Capacity/Data Frame:** A framing strategy that emphasizes logistics, resources, coordination, and quantifiable indicators, lowering affective intensity while strengthening perceived credibility.

**Claim–Evidence Match:** Alignment between the strength of a headline's claim and the available evidence (data, visuals, sourcing), including minimal context and source disclosure.

**Ethical Guardrails:** Institutionally defined thresholds (e.g., second-editor approval, risk flags, checklists) that constrain high-risk language and packaging choices.

**Headline/Thumbnail Packaging:** The integrated composition of headline text, image, typography, badges (e.g., "BREAKING"), and overlays as a single presentation unit.

**High-Arousal Language:** Lexical choices designed to elicit strong activation (e.g., "shock," "traitor"); can boost clicks but increases ethical risk and error likelihood.

**Ideological Signaling:** Use of in-group symbols, slogans, or cues in headlines/visuals to reinforce identity alignment and draw boundaries with out-groups.

**Interface Logic:** The bundle of defaults, affordances, visual hierarchies, and interaction patterns of a platform that shapes how headlines are produced, presented, and consumed.

**Metric–Authority Coupling:** Pairing numerical indicators (scores, counts, percentages) with references to authoritative sources (e.g., electoral commission) to boost perceived legitimacy.

**Perpetrator Assignment:** Framing that points to a responsible actor early (e.g., "the culprit"), shifting attention from systemic or environmental factors to criminal intent.

**Platformization:** The reorganization of media production and distribution around platform infrastructures, incentives, and metrics.

**Premature Certainty:** Declaring outcomes before official confirmation (e.g., "we won"); creates hard-to-reverse perception effects and misdirection risk.

**Procedure Frame:** Emphasis on rules, processes, and institutional steps (e.g., recounts, verification), used to manage uncertainty and temper affect.

**Promise–Content Alignment:** Consistency between what the headline promises (information/emotion) and what the article actually delivers; reduces corrections and trust erosion.

**Question Hook:** Headline construction that opens a curiosity gap via questions; may raise engagement but can amplify speculation if under-evidenced.

**Sharing Friction:** Design or policy steps that slow impulsive sharing (e.g., confirmation prompts, context cards), reducing the spread of misleading high-arousal content.

**Superlative–Metric Bundle:** Co-presentation of superlatives ("largest," "historic") with quantitative markers to dramatize scale and heighten perceived significance.

Chapter 4

# Rethinking Social Science Epistemological Debate in the AI Era: Adaptive Epistemology as New Paradigm Shift

**Gabriella Punziano**
https://orcid.org/0000-0001-8783-2712
*University of Naples Federico II, Italy*

## ABSTRACT

*This chapter explores the transformative impact of generative artificial intelligence on social research epistemology, proposing adaptive epistemology as a new framework. Moving beyond traditional paradigms, adaptive epistemology recognizes knowledge as emergent, co-constructed, and situated within socio-technical ecosystems where human and non-human agents share epistemic agency. It challenges fixed methodological boundaries by emphasizing reflexivity, interpretive plurality, and ethical stewardship in digitally mediated inquiry. The chapter discusses how AI reshapes data, questions, and interpretations, fostering novel epistemic practices across fields like computational sociology, education, and public policy. While highlighting risks such as epistemic drift and ontological flattening, it calls for critical engagement and interdisciplinary oversight. Ultimately, adaptive epistemology represents a paradigm shift that embraces the complexity of the post-digital condition and redefines social research as a collaborative, generative process.*

DOI: 10.4018/979-8-3373-4267-2.ch004

## INTRODUCTION: EPISTEMOLOGICAL REORIENTATIONS IN THE AGE OF GENERATIVE MEDIATION

The evolution of paradigms within the social sciences has long constituted a foundational terrain of intellectual debate, animating reflection not only on the epistemological underpinnings of inquiry but also on its methodological and political implications. Since Thomas Kuhn's seminal formulation of the paradigm as a "constellation of beliefs, values, and techniques shared by a scientific community" (Kuhn, 1962), the concept has undergone a profound transposition. Initially rooted in the philosophy of science, the notion of the paradigm has since become central to the epistemological grammar of sociological research, enabling scholars to frame knowledge production not as neutral accumulation, but as historically situated, value-laden, and structurally embedded.

Paradigms operate as epistemic compasses in the social sciences, shaping what is seen as a legitimate question, a valid method, and an acceptable form of evidence. As Guba and Lincoln (1994) emphasize, paradigms articulate ontological assumptions about the nature of reality, epistemological assumptions about the nature and scope of knowledge, and methodological assumptions about how knowledge can be acquired. These foundational commitments organize the architecture of inquiry and delimit the possible, the knowable, and the sayable within a research tradition.

In the face of accelerating transformations across technological, institutional, and cultural domains, the social sciences are undergoing significant epistemic reconfigurations. The increasing pervasiveness of digital infrastructures, the rise of platform capitalism (Van Dijck et al., 2018), and the algorithmic mediation of social life (Beer, 2017) have prompted scholars to revisit the adequacy of established paradigms. What emerges is the recognition that epistemology must remain responsive to the sociotechnical conditions within which knowledge is produced, circulated, and contested. As Jasanoff (2004) argues, science and society are not separate domains but co-evolve in mutual constitution, forming hybrid regimes of knowledge and governance.

This chapter proposes to conceptualize these transformations through the lens of adaptive epistemology—a framework attuned to hybridity, contextuality, and co-construction. Adaptive epistemology does not seek closure in rigid methodological canons or ontological certainties; rather, it foregrounds the entangled agency of human researchers, computational systems, and digital environments in shaping the epistemic field. It expands on earlier epistemological revisions such as the shift toward mixed methods (Tashakkori & Teddlie, 2010), feminist standpoint theory (Harding, 1991), and digital epistemologies (Lupton, 2015), but moves further by embedding reflexivity and generativity within the research process itself.

In an era marked by the rise of generative artificial intelligence and the computational delegation of analytic labor (Pasquinelli & Joler, 2022), adaptive epistemology provides the necessary conceptual scaffolding to address new methodological challenges. These include the displacement of human-centered data practices, the algorithmic shaping of visibility and salience, and the need to ethically and epistemologically account for non-human cognitive agents in research workflows (Barad, 2007; Bender et al., 2021).

Rather than merely cataloguing paradigm shifts, this chapter advances a forward-looking agenda: one that positions the social sciences to meaningfully engage with epistemological uncertainty, platformized knowledge, and the ontological reordering of research environments. By doing so, it contributes to a broader renewal of sociological inquiry and provides a generative vocabulary for researchers navigating the epistemic instabilities of the postdigital condition.

Methodologically, this chapter is grounded in an argumentative and interpretative approach that integrates insights from a targeted literature review on the epistemological transformations affecting the social sciences in the AI era. Rather than pursuing empirical validation, the analysis engages in a critical reassessment of the epistemic foundations that have historically shaped the production of social knowledge. Through this lens, the chapter advances the notion of an adaptive epistemology, conceived as a paradigmatic framework capable of accommodating the ontological reconfigurations and methodological challenges brought about by artificial intelligence, while preserving the reflexive and interpretive vocation of social inquiry.

## 2. THE EVOLUTION OF THE DISCIPLINARY HISTORY OF THE SOCIAL SCIENCES

### 2.1. The Epistemological Contestation of Social Science: Between Scientific Legitimacy and Interpretive Pluralism

The disciplinary consolidation of the social sciences has long been characterized by a constitutive tension around their epistemic legitimacy—especially when positioned vis-à-vis the so-called "hard sciences" such as physics, chemistry, and biology. This dynamic has not merely shaped methodological choices, but has profoundly influenced the institutional recognition, funding trajectories, and public authority of social scientific knowledge. The roots of this tension can be traced back to Auguste Comte's foundational ambition to establish a science of society grounded in the positivist ideals of observation, prediction, and law-like regularities. Comte envisioned sociology as the apex of a hierarchy of sciences, culminating in the application of empirical methods to the understanding and governance of social order. This vision enshrined a normative aspiration toward methodological unity and scientific rigor, modeled after the natural sciences, which privileged quantification, replicability, and the search for causal explanation.

The Comtean legacy laid the groundwork for the dominance of quantitative methodologies throughout much of the 19th and early 20th centuries. Techniques such as statistical modeling, survey research, and experimental design came to define the empirical core of "scientific" sociology, reinforcing an epistemic orientation aligned with positivist logic. This orientation was grounded in a conception of social reality as externally observable and amenable to objective measurement—thus bolstering the claim that social science could generate generalizable laws akin to those of Newtonian physics.

However, this epistemological foundation was soon disrupted by what has been widely described as the "interpretive turn" in the human sciences. Pioneered by thinkers such as Wilhelm Dilthey and Max Weber, this turn challenged the applicability of natural scientific methods to the study of meaning-laden social phenomena. Rather than seeking law-like regularities, interpretivism emphasized the need to understand social action from the standpoint of the actors involved—Verstehen, in Weberian terms. This mode of inquiry privileged hermeneutic understanding over causal explanation, arguing that social facts are not merely out there to be measured but are constructed, interpreted, and embedded in symbolic structures and historical contexts.

This divergence inaugurated a foundational bifurcation in the epistemology of social research: between the nomothetic orientation of positivist traditions, and the idiographic commitments of interpretivist and constructivist approaches. The former seeks to explain, predict, and generalize; the latter to understand, contextualize, and interpret. This binary has long animated debates around what constitutes "scientific" knowledge in the social sciences and reached a particularly critical juncture during what Guba and Lincoln (1994) famously termed the paradigm wars. These disputes were not merely technical or methodological; they revealed deep ontological and epistemological fissures regarding the nature of social reality and the means through which valid knowledge can be accessed and legitimized.

However, framing the history of social science as a simplistic dichotomy between quantitative and qualitative, objectivity and subjectivity, or explanation and understanding, risks entrenching a historically contingent division that obscures more complex dynamics. As Bent Flyvbjerg (2001) cogently argues, such dichotomies often reflect entrenched hierarchies of knowledge production, wherein the prestige of the natural sciences imposes hegemonic standards upon the social sciences. This asymmetry has not only constrained methodological innovation but has also delegitimized alternative epistemologies grounded in relationality, reflexivity, and praxis. Indeed, many strands of critical social theory—from the Frankfurt School to poststructuralist and feminist epistemologies—have explicitly rejected the scientistic premises of positivism, instead emphasizing the contextual, partial, and situated character of all knowledge claims.

The rise of global interconnectedness, digital technologies, and media saturation in the late 20th and early 21st centuries has further complicated the epistemic terrain. In a world increasingly mediated by algorithmic logics and platform infrastructures, the rigid boundaries that once separated paradigms have become untenable. Developments in the philosophy of science have also played a key role in this shift. Heisenberg's uncertainty principle, for instance, challenged the notion of pure objectivity even within physics, while Kuhn's (1962) theory of scientific revolutions undermined the ideal of cumulative, linear progress in knowledge production. Rather than portraying science as a smooth trajectory toward truth, Kuhn depicted it as a discontinuous process punctuated by paradigm shifts—episodes in which foundational assumptions are abandoned, restructured, or replaced in light of anomalous findings or sociocultural transformations.

In parallel, the ascendancy of constructivist epistemologies—exemplified by Berger and Luckmann's (1966) theory of the social construction of reality—introduced a radical rethinking of the ontological status of social facts. From this perspective, reality is not a pre-given substrate to be observed, but an emergent, negotiated, and institutionally stabilized outcome of ongoing human interactions. The implications of this insight are profound: they demand that social research attend not only to the observable but also to the processes of meaning-making, normativity, and power through which the social world is constituted.

In response to these theoretical and empirical developments, the social sciences have increasingly embraced epistemological pluralism—an approach that resists foundationalism and instead supports the coexistence of diverse, sometimes incommensurable, epistemic logics. This pluralism has been operationalized through hybrid frameworks that seek to bridge traditional dichotomies: structure and agency, explanation and interpretation, objectivity and positionality. It has also found methodological expression in the rise of mixed methods research, which attempts to integrate quantitative and qualitative techniques within a coherent research design that respects the complexity of the phenomena under investigation.

Such methodological hybridity has opened new horizons for inquiry while also raising critical questions about epistemic coherence, compatibility, and the risks of eclecticism. Nonetheless, it reflects a broader shift toward reflexive and context-sensitive epistemologies—those that are capable of navigating the ambiguity, multiplicity, and contingency that define contemporary social life. Rather than aspiring to a universal science of society, social researchers are increasingly called upon to develop localized, ethically grounded, and adaptive forms of knowing that are responsive to the challenges of their time.

## 2.2. Hybrid Paradigms and Epistemological Renewal

The contemporary landscape of social science research is marked by a pluralistic momentum that transcends traditional dichotomies, culminating in the articulation of hybrid paradigms. These paradigms seek to move beyond the rigid oppositional logic that long defined epistemological debates—particularly between positivism, which prioritizes objective measurement and generalizability, and interpretivism, which emphasizes subjective meaning and context. By integrating insights from both, hybrid paradigms offer more nuanced frameworks that address the complexities of social phenomena.

One prominent example is critical realism, as formulated by Roy Bhaskar (1975). Critical realism asserts the existence of an objective reality independent of our perceptions, yet it simultaneously acknowledges that our knowledge of this reality is inherently theory-laden, fallible, and socially situated. This dual recognition positions critical realism as a compelling epistemological bridge: it combines the naturalistic ambition to discover causal mechanisms with an interpretivist sensitivity to context and meaning. By distinguishing between the "real," the "actual," and the "empirical," Bhaskar's framework provides a robust ontology that supports explanatory depth without discarding the interpretive dimension. This approach has found resonance across disciplines, fostering research designs that incorporate both quantitative causal analyses and qualitative interpretive insights.

Similarly, pragmatism, rooted in the philosophical traditions of Charles Peirce, William James, and John Dewey (Moore, 1966), represents another hybrid stance rejecting epistemological dualisms in favor of a practical, problem-oriented approach. Pragmatism prioritizes the consequences of ideas and methods in addressing real-world challenges, rather than adherence to abstract metaphysical commitments. Morgan (2007) emphasizes that pragmatism legitimizes a methodological pluralism justified by utility—methods are adopted not because they are ontologically pure but because they work effectively in specific contexts. This orientation encourages researchers to flexibly combine diverse techniques, selecting those best suited to the particular problem at hand. Pragmatism thus enriches the methodological toolkit by grounding epistemological decisions in the practicalities of inquiry and action.

Beyond pragmatism and critical realism, the transformative paradigm introduces a distinctly ethical and political dimension to epistemological renewal. Pioneered by scholars such as Mertens (2010), this paradigm embeds research within frameworks of social justice, emancipation, and advocacy. It foregrounds the ethical imperative that knowledge production should serve to amplify marginalized voices and challenge oppressive structures. Unlike paradigms that separate epistemology from values, the transformative paradigm insists that research is inseparable from power dynamics and normative commitments. This perspective not only shapes research questions and methods but also demands reflexivity about the researcher's role and the societal impact of knowledge. It thus expands epistemology into the realm of activism, recognizing knowledge as a catalyst for social transformation.

Together, these hybrid paradigms have paved the way for the expansion of mixed methods research, which strategically integrates qualitative and quantitative techniques within a single, coherent epistemological framework. Mixed methods research is no longer a mere compromise or convenience but a sophisticated response to the multidimensionality of contemporary phenomena. Complex social issues often manifest at multiple levels—combining observable statistical patterns with the richness of lived experience, and macro-level systemic trends with micro-level individual meanings. By weaving together diverse strands of evidence, mixed methods allow for a more comprehensive understanding and more effective interventions.

This epistemological integration signals a deeper, ongoing shift: the recognition that no single method, theory, or paradigm holds a monopoly on truth or validity. Instead, methodological diversity is embraced not only as a technical asset but as an epistemic necessity in a world increasingly characterized by complexity, plurality, and constant transformation. This renewed epistemological stance challenges researchers to adopt humility, openness, and creativity, embracing multiple ways of knowing as complementary rather than conflicting. The future of research, therefore, lies in the cultivation of flexible, integrative approaches that honor the multifaceted nature of reality and the diverse ways humans make sense of it.

## 2.3. The Digital Condition and Epistemic Reconfiguration

The emergence of the digital age signifies not merely a technological evolution but a profound and far-reaching epistemological rupture that challenges foundational assumptions of knowledge production and social research. Unlike earlier paradigmatic shifts, which unfolded gradually through intellectual debates and theoretical refinements, the digital transformation has introduced a rapid and pervasive change that redefines the very conditions under which knowledge is produced, circulated, and validated. Digital infrastructures—ranging from social media platforms and big data ecosystems to algorithmic governance and automated decision-making systems—do not function as neutral or passive repositories of information. Instead, they act as active agents shaping social reality, mediating interactions, and generating data that is inherently structured, filtered, and constrained by proprietary, political, and economic logics embedded within platform architectures (Kitchin, 2014; Gillespie, 2014).

This digital turn represents a paradigmatic shift in the epistemic condition, altering not only the tools and techniques of research but also the very nature of what can be known, by whom, and through which modalities. As Rogers (2013) and Marres (2017) compellingly argue, digital traces are not mere passive reflections or transparent windows onto social phenomena. Rather, they are produced within sociotechnical assemblages where users' actions intertwine with algorithmic processes and platform affordances, making digital data inherently performative and contextually embedded. Such data is shaped by design decisions, commercial imperatives, and governance structures, thus problematizing assumptions about objectivity and representation in social research (Beer, 2016).

Methodologically, this has spurred the development of digital methods—a constellation of approaches that treat digital media simultaneously as objects of study and instruments of inquiry (Rogers, 2013). These methods harness the affordances of digital platforms to collect, analyze, and visualize complex data streams, enabling novel insights into social behavior at scales previously unattainable. However, critical voices, notably from critical digital sociology (Lupton, 2015), caution against the instrumentalist temptation to accept digital data and tools at face value. They advocate for a reflexive stance that interrogates the power relations, algorithmic biases, and socio-political contingencies shaping digital research environments. This reflexivity involves questioning not only the epistemological assumptions embedded within platforms but also the implications of research participation in structures of platform capitalism (Van Dijck, Poell, & de Waal, 2018), where data commodification and surveillance capitalism complicate the ethics and politics of knowledge production.

Theoretical advancements within sociology and adjacent disciplines have responded by incorporating frameworks that foreground relationality, materiality, and distributed agency. Actor-Network Theory (ANT), as developed by Bruno Latour, dissolves the classical subject/object divide by emphasizing networks of human and non-human actors co-constructing social realities (Latour, 2005). This perspective aligns with posthumanist approaches, which challenge anthropocentric epistemologies and emphasize the entanglements between humans, technologies, and environments (Braidotti, 2013). Lupton (2017) further extends these ideas through the promotion of embodied and affective digital methods, which attend to the sensory and emotional dimensions of digital engagement, thereby enriching understanding of how digital mediation shapes lived experience. Complementing these approaches, Halford and Savage (2017) propose the concept of reflexive data sociology, which calls for a critical, ethical, and contextually aware engagement with data that recognizes its constructed and situated nature.

Together, these developments give rise to an emergent field of digital epistemology, which interrogates the ontological and epistemic implications of phenomena such as algorithmic governance, platform mediation, and ambient datafication—the pervasive quantification of social life through continuous data capture (Kitchin, 2016). Digital epistemology challenges entrenched binaries such as subject/object, observer/observed, and qualitative/quantitative, proposing instead a fluid and hybrid epistemic orientation that embraces complexity, instability, and entanglement (Ruppert, Law, & Savage, 2013). It encourages scholars to recognize that knowledge in digitally mediated environments is dynamic, co-produced, and frequently contested, requiring ongoing critical reflexivity and methodological innovation.

The digital condition mandates a recalibration of social science paradigms. It calls for adaptive, inclusive, and critically reflexive epistemologies that are attuned not only to the multidimensional complexity of social life but also to the layered mediations introduced by artificial intelligence, algorithmic logics, and pervasive data saturation. As social realities increasingly unfold through and within digital platforms, scholars must embrace epistemic humility and pluralism, cultivating flexible approaches capable of navigating the rapidly evolving and often opaque terrains of contemporary knowledge production.

## 3. FROM THE DIGITAL TURN TO THE POST-DIGITAL CONDITION: RETHINKING EPISTEMOLOGY IN THE AGE OF GENERATIVE AI

The contemporary transformation of knowledge production within the social sciences demands a profound and radical epistemological reframing, one that moves beyond conventional understandings shaped by earlier paradigms of the digital era. As digital infrastructures, algorithmic processes, and increasingly sophisticated intelligent systems permeate not only everyday life but also the very core of scholarly inquiry, it becomes untenable to conceptualize research as a neutral, detached, or purely human-centered act. Instead, knowledge must be understood as a co-constructed phenomenon arising from dynamic and reciprocal entanglements between human and non-human agents, reflecting and shaped by socio-technical systems, digital platforms, and the broader epistemic architectures that govern them (Marres, 2017; Van Dijck, Poell, & de Waal, 2018). This shift signals not simply an evolution of research tools but a fundamental transformation in the epistemic conditions under which social knowledge is produced, validated, and circulated.

This profound transformation marks the advent of what scholars have termed the post-digital condition—a stage of socio-technical development where digitality is no longer novel, external, or peripheral but has become infrastructural, omnipresent, and deeply embedded in the fabric of everyday life, social relations, and institutional practices (Cramer, 2015; Jandrić et al., 2018). The post-digital condition thus should not be understood as a mere temporal succession or replacement of the digital era; rather, it denotes a saturation point where digital systems, algorithmic governance, artificial intelligence models, and automated decision-making mechanisms have become constitutive elements of knowledge regimes, social ontologies, and epistemic orders. Within this context, epistemology itself transforms into a situated, relational, and reflexive practice—one that is acutely sensitive to the mediating effects of platform logics, algorithmic agency, and the complex assemblages of sociotechnical relations that underpin knowledge production (Barad, 2007; Haraway, 1988).

Central to this new epistemic landscape is the emergence of generative AI—computational systems capable not merely of processing or analyzing data but of producing novel content, simulating reasoning, and co-constructing interpretive meaning. Unlike earlier digital tools, which primarily extended human researchers' capacity for data management, measurement, or analysis, generative AI systems now actively participate in the meaning-making process. They often initiate, refine, and even redirect the trajectory of epistemic inquiry itself, thus representing a profound rupture in the traditional epistemic order (Floridi, 2022; Bender et al., 2021). This shift reconfigures not only the epistemological status of data but also the positionality of the researcher, who moves from the role of detached observer and analyst to that of a co-designer, curator, and reflexive steward in a hybrid, human–machine knowledge ecosystem (Lupton, 2021).

Drawing from Karen Barad's (2007) concept of intra-action, knowledge does not pre-exist its production but emerges through recursive, entangled engagements between human, material, and symbolic actors. Generative AI exemplifies this principle, producing meaning through probabilistic associations derived from massive linguistic corpora, yet always situated within specific prompts, intentions, and use contexts. This process blurs previously rigid boundaries between discovery and invention, reflection and automation, and author and apparatus. Generative AI challenges human-centric epistemologies by functioning simultaneously as an epistemic agent and creative collaborator—capable of generating insights and interpretations that destabilize established models of cognition and sense-making (Pasquinelli & Joler, 2022). This transformation demands that research be reconceptualized as a distributed, networked process, enacted through intricate assemblages of human and non-human actors—organic and machinic, intentional and automated (Latour, 2005).

Moreover, the post-digital condition unsettles traditional notions of data itself. No longer can data be considered a neutral or pre-existing resource simply awaiting extraction and interpretation. Instead, data is performative, situated, and mediated—it is shaped and constituted by the very infrastructures, interfaces, algorithms, and socio-technical systems that produce, filter, and frame it (Kitchin & Lauriault, 2014;

Ruppert, Law, & Savage, 2013). In this regard, critical scholars such as Lupton (2015) and Halford & Savage (2017) emphasize that social researchers must move beyond extractive or instrumental paradigms, adopting critical, participatory, and reflexive engagements with data environments. Such engagements recognize data as relational and contextual, calling for methodologies that foreground transparency, ethical awareness, and the politics of knowledge production.

This epistemological reorientation entails a decisive move away from static, linear models of analysis toward dynamic, adaptive, and mosaic-like frameworks—epistemologies capable not only of grappling with empirical complexity but also of responding to ethical and political imperatives related to agency, inclusion, and transparency. Participatory digital methods—including platform ethnography, co-creative elicitation, and data donation protocols—foreground collaboration, contextualization, and shared authorship in knowledge production (Kennedy, 2018; Pink et al., 2018). These approaches democratize epistemic authority by involving communities and stakeholders as active partners rather than passive subjects, thereby enacting an epistemology that is both situated and inclusive.

Ultimately, this epistemological turn is far more than a methodological shift; it is deeply ontological. It challenges entrenched assumptions about what constitutes knowledge, who has the authority to produce it, and under which conditions it gains legitimacy and practical efficacy. The future of social research will depend not only on the increasing sophistication of its computational tools but also on the agility and reflexivity of its epistemologies—their capacity to remain inclusive, ethically grounded, and attuned to the layered, dynamic, and often opaque interactions that characterize techno-social life in the post-digital era.

In this evolving landscape, social inquiry must decisively shift its orientation: from the extraction of fixed or universal truths toward the cultivation of situated understandings; from rigid, static paradigms toward responsive and pluralistic frameworks; and from the figure of the researcher as an all-knowing authority to that of a participant and collaborator within distributed epistemic ecosystems. In such contexts, the formulation of better questions—questions that are reflexively articulated, ethically grounded, and sensitive to the complex mediations of socio-technical systems—becomes the cornerstone of meaningful and transformative knowledge production.

## 4. ADAPTIVE EPISTEMOLOGY: A PARADIGMATIC SHIFT TOWARD GENERATIVE SOCIAL INQUIRY

The proliferation of generative technologies—from large language models (LLMs) to multimodal AI systems—has catalyzed a profound epistemological rupture in the social sciences. This rupture challenges long-standing assumptions about knowledge production, validation, and dissemination, urging scholars to rethink the normative, methodological, and ontological foundations of research in the context of algorithmic mediation and machine co-agency. Generative artificial intelligence is no longer a peripheral or auxiliary actor in the research process; rather, it increasingly assumes an agentic role—performing tasks historically reserved for human cognition, such as formulating hypotheses, synthesizing literatures, constructing analytical categories, and generating interpretive frameworks (Floridi, 2020; Bender et al., 2021).

This transformation exposes the inadequacy of inherited paradigms, including positivism's reliance on verification, interpretivism's emphasis on thick description, and pragmatist pluralism's focus on methodological flexibility. While each of these frameworks contributed to the diversification of social research in the 20th century, none is fully equipped to grapple with the epistemic complexity, ontological ambiguity, and technological entanglement of the post-digital era (Jandrić et al., 2018). In this context, a new epistemological stance is emerging: adaptive epistemology—a paradigm that reconceptualizes knowledge as fluid, emergent, and co-produced within hybrid socio-technical ecosystems composed of both human and non-human epistemic agents.

From Methodological Integration to Epistemic Responsiveness

Unlike earlier frameworks that sought coherence through *triangulation, data saturation*, or *methodological integration*, adaptive epistemology embeds *responsiveness* at the core of inquiry. It does not merely tolerate uncertainty or complexity—it actively integrates them as constitutive dimensions of research practice. In this view, knowledge emerges not from the application of predefined tools to fixed problems, but from an ongoing negotiation between *intention, system affordance, and contextual contingencies.* As Barad (2007) notes, knowledge is produced through *intra-actions*—material-discursive entanglements that dissolve the binary between subject and object. Generative AI operationalizes this insight by collapsing traditional research stages (data collection, analysis, interpretation) into recursive, adaptive cycles in which meaning is iteratively shaped by both human prompts and algorithmic responses.

In this paradigm, LLMs do not simply assist in data processing—they *generate new epistemic trajectories*, surfacing associations, semantic clusters, and interpretive pathways that may be unanticipated by the researcher. This expands and revitalizes Denzin's (1978) notion of triangulation—not as a strategy of validation or convergence, but as a *generative engine* of epistemic novelty. Adaptive epistemology thus repositions triangulation as a *productive friction*, where divergent outputs from human and non-human agents create opportunities for interpretive expansion, rather than convergence.

Rethinking the Boundaries of Inquiry

The boundaries that traditionally separated data collection, analysis, and theorization are increasingly porous under adaptive epistemology. Generative systems operate not within discrete methodological stages but across them, engaging in simultaneous inference, synthesis, and projection. As a result, the epistemic labor of the researcher becomes less about procedural rigor and more about curatorial reflexivity—the capacity to interpret, contextualize, and ethically frame outputs generated through hybrid collaborations (Kennedy et al., 2022). This is particularly salient in platformized research environments where LLMs are embedded in everyday academic workflows—from literature reviews and coding schemes to hypothesis generation and conceptual modeling.

Moreover, adaptive epistemology confronts the politics of framing in social inquiry. The practice of narrowing analytical focus, long considered a hallmark of methodological rigor, must now contend with the expansive combinatorics of generative systems. These systems propose and recombine possibilities at a scale and speed that challenge human interpretive limits (Pasquinelli & Joler, 2022). However, this proliferation of alternatives does not necessarily dilute epistemic precision. On the contrary, it enables a richer engagement with ontological multiplicity—an acknowledgement that social phenomena are rarely reducible to singular interpretations, and that epistemic pluralism is not a weakness but a strength (Mol, 2002).

Risks and Reflexivities in Generative Inquiry

Despite its promise, adaptive epistemology entails notable risks. Chief among these is epistemic drift—the danger that recursive experimentation with generative tools may lead to the abandonment of conceptual coherence or methodological grounding. The hyperfluency of AI-generated content can mask ontological shallowness, producing outputs that are syntactically persuasive but semantically vague or decontextualized (Marcus & Davis, 2020). Additionally, the absence of a shared interpretive framework for assessing machinic contributions raises the risk of methodological opacity and validation ambiguity.

To address these challenges, adaptive epistemology must be paired with critical digital literacy (Couldry & Mejias, 2019) and transdisciplinary expertise. Interpreting outputs from generative systems is not merely a technical task—it is a hermeneutic one, demanding ethical discernment, contextual sensitivity, and a nuanced understanding of both algorithmic design and domain knowledge. The researcher, in this context, becomes a steward of epistemic responsibility, tasked with negotiating the boundaries between automation and interpretation, between possibility and accountability (Lupton, 2021).

Toward an Ethics of Generative Inquiry

Adaptive epistemology also implies a shift in research ethics. The interpenetration of human intentionality and machinic suggestion challenges established norms regarding authorship, originality, and accountability. As generative systems participate in the construction of research narratives, the imperative for reflexive transparency grows stronger. Researchers must not only disclose their methodological steps but also explicate how and why specific system outputs were integrated, modified, or discarded. This is not merely a matter of academic integrity—it is a condition for epistemic legitimacy in environments where interpretive authority is distributed across hybrid assemblages (Haraway, 1988; Latour, 2005).

Adaptive epistemology aligns with the nonlinear, relational, and accelerated nature of contemporary social life. It does not offer prescriptive models or fixed procedures; rather, it cultivates an ethos of iterability, relational knowledge, and interpretive elasticity. In doing so, it extends the legacy of the sociological imagination (Mills, 1959), reimagining it for a world in which cognition, narration, and decision-making are increasingly co-enacted by human and non-human actors.

Reconfiguring the Role of the Researcher

Consequently, the role of the researcher must be radically rethought. No longer the exclusive locus of epistemic agency, the researcher becomes a participant in distributed cognitive systems, responsible not for dictating meaning but for curating its emergence. Their agency lies not in domination but in attunement—to systems, to data, to context, and to the ethical imperatives of their field. The researcher becomes a mediator of machinic generativity, engaging in interpretive labor that is simultaneously creative, critical, and accountable (Knox, 2020).

Adaptive epistemology is thus not a superficial update to existing research paradigms, but a paradigmatic transformation—a comprehensive reorientation of the epistemic, methodological, and ethical coordinates of social inquiry. It invites scholars to inhabit a stance of epistemic humility, methodological inventiveness, and critical engagement. As the boundaries between human and machine, method and medium, subject and object become increasingly blurred, the task of social research is not to resist such complexity, but to develop the conceptual tools, ethical sensibilities, and institutional practices required to navigate it with rigor, care, and at least sociological imagination.

## CONCLUSION: TOWARDS GENERATIVE AND TRANS-EPISTEMIC SOCIAL RESEARCH

The emergence of adaptive epistemology is not merely a response to the transformations brought about by generative artificial intelligence; it is a transformative imperative for the social sciences that seek to remain relevant in a world marked by complexity, technological acceleration, and cognitive hybridity. This new epistemological orientation does not simply replace previous paradigms but critically reinterprets them, exposing both their limitations and their ongoing value in the age of co-generative research between humans and machines.

The future landscape of social research will inevitably be shaped by forms of hybrid collaboration in which epistemicity is distributed, contextual, and performative. In this sense, adaptive epistemology functions as a metaparadigm—a framework that does not dictate methods but proposes epistemic attitudes and reflexive practices capable of engaging with the uncertainty, ambivalence, and generativity of emerging cognitive media (Knorr Cetina, 2001; Marres, 2017).

The future landscape of social research will inevitably be shaped by hybrid collaborations wherein epistemicity is distributed, contextually embedded, and performative. Adaptive epistemology functions here as a metaparadigm—offering epistemic postures and reflexive practices rather than prescriptive methods—capable of engaging productively with the uncertainties, ambivalences, and generative potentials characteristic of emerging cognitive media and techno-social assemblages (Barad, 2007; Latour, 2005).

This reframing holds particular promise across diverse applied social science domains. In computational sociology, adaptive epistemology enables a move beyond the traditional dichotomy between quantitative and qualitative approaches. The use of large language models (LLMs) and generative systems for analyzing textual corpora, social media data, or institutional archives is no longer limited to classification or data cleaning; rather, it opens up emergent interpretive processes, in which patterns identified by AI systems become prompts for theory-building, not mere statistical outputs (boyd & Crawford, 2012; Kitchin, 2014). For instance, the analysis of emotional dynamics in political discourse may be enhanced by systems capable of detecting latent metaphors, semantic ambiguities, or implicit rhetorical strategies that would otherwise elude traditional tools but can be meaningfully interpreted by researchers working in collaboration with machines.

Within mass media studies and communication research, adaptive epistemology enriches understandings of media ecology by foregrounding the co-production of content and meaning through human-machine interaction. AI's role in shaping public discourse, misinformation dynamics, and algorithmically curated news feeds demands reflexive approaches that attend to platform affordances and epistemic biases (Napoli, 2019; Van Dijck et al., 2018). Similarly, in political communication and public engagement, generative AI tools offer new modalities for modeling policy scenarios, simulating deliberative processes, and enhancing citizen participation, supporting democratic transparency and inclusivity (Mulgan, 2021; Kennedy et al., 2022).

In educational research, adaptive epistemology translates into the development of generative learning environments, where students and educators co-produce knowledge alongside intelligent agents. AI systems can simulate theoretical perspectives, generate personalized feedback, or offer counterfactual scenarios that stimulate metacognitive reflection. In participatory learning settings, this supports a reflexive and pluralistic pedagogy in which epistemic authority is decentralized and distributed (Selwyn, 2019; Knox, 2022).

In the domain of public policy, the capacity of generative AI to simulate scenarios, synthesize legislative sources, and construct narrative models provides powerful tools for augmented democratic deliberation. In civic participation processes, for example, generative systems can offer alternative policy framings, visualize potential outcomes of collective decisions, or construct semantic maps of stakeholder preferences, thereby supporting more informed and transparent governance (Mulgan, 2021).

In the realm of social policy and welfare systems, adaptive epistemology enables innovative forms of evidence synthesis and predictive modeling, integrating data from administrative sources, user-generated content, and sensor networks to inform responsive, adaptive governance frameworks. Here, AI-assisted scenario generation and co-interpretation of policy impacts encourage participatory design and ethical stewardship, ensuring that algorithmic outputs are contextualized within lived experiences and social justice concerns (Bietti, 2020; Lupton, 2015).

The fields of health sociology and neuroscience similarly benefit from an adaptive epistemological lens that acknowledges the entanglement of biological, psychological, and social factors mediated through digital health technologies. AI-generated insights can aid in identifying emergent health patterns, supporting personalized medicine while requiring vigilance toward epistemic authority and the interpretive agency of clinicians and patients alike (Greenhalgh et al., 2017; Pasquinelli & Joler, 2022).

In algorithmic influence studies adaptive epistemology critically addresses how automated systems encode and reproduce social biases, power relations, and identity politics. Reflexive methodologies foreground situated knowledge and participatory practices that challenge dominant epistemic regimes and promote equity and inclusion in AI design and deployment (Noble, 2018; Eubanks, 2018).

Within sociology of knowledge this approach invites reconsideration of how knowledge is constructed, preserved, and transmitted in digitally mediated environments, where archives are augmented by AI-generated metadata and narrative reconstructions, demanding ongoing negotiation between historians, curators, and algorithms (Lury & Wakeford, 2012; Marres, 2017).

In anthropology and psychology, adaptive epistemology fosters multispecies and multimodal inquiry by incorporating non-human actors, affective dynamics, and embodied cognition into analytic frameworks, expanding the interpretive repertoire beyond traditional human-centric approaches (Haraway, 1988; Lupton, 2021).

Finally, in applied fields such as marketing, organizational studies, and the third sector, adaptive epistemology encourages agile, co-creative research practices that integrate consumer behavior analytics, stakeholder narratives, and AI-facilitated decision-making, supporting ethical innovation and collaborative knowledge production (Kennedy et al., 2022; Knox, 2022).

Across these fields, adaptive epistemology demands heightened attention to situated ethics, interpretive responsibility, and governance of epistemic agents—human and machinic alike. Cognitive delegation to AI systems must be accompanied by robust epistemic audits that trace the provenance, mediation, and consequences of knowledge production, ensuring transparency and accountability (Crawford, 2021; Bietti, 2020).

The rise of adaptive epistemology also demands heightened attention to issues of situated ethics, interpretive responsibility, and the governance of non-human agents. Cognitive delegation to technical artifacts must not be blind or disempowering. What is needed are protocols of epistemic audit capable of tracing the role that generative systems play in the production of knowledge—identifying not only what is produced, but how, by whom, and to what end (Bietti, 2020; Crawford, 2021).

In this light, the future of social research will increasingly depend on hybrid epistemic alliances, where the object of inquiry cannot be separated from the means of its representation. Boundaries between subject and object, medium and method, are becoming porous, giving rise to a form of trans-epistemic research, where knowledge is not only accumulated but generated, relational, and performed (Lury & Wakeford, 2012).

Rather than offering closure, adaptive epistemology encourages ongoing inquiry. It invites scholars to keep horizons open, to regard theoretical constructions as provisional, methodological configurations as situated, and epistemic claims as entangled within evolving networks. In a world where knowledge is co-produced through technological infrastructures, algorithmic media, and machinic agencies, the task of the social sciences is not to resist change, but to invent new ways of inhabiting uncertainty and generating understanding amid complexity.

Adaptive epistemology does not promise stability but offers tools for navigation—for conducting social research not despite AI, but through it, in a way that is critically engaged, ethically grounded, and creatively attuned.

## REFERENCES


Barad, K. (2007). *Meeting the Universe Halfway: Quantum Physics and the Entanglement of Matter and Meaning*. Duke University Press.

Beer, D. (2017). The Social Power of Algorithms. *Information Communication and Society*, *20*(1), 1–13. DOI: 10.1080/1369118X.2016.1216147

Bender, E. M., Gebru, T., McMillan-Major, A., & Shmitchell, S. (2021). On the dangers of stochastic parrots: Can language models be too big? *Proceedings of the 2021 ACM Conference on Fairness, Accountability, and Transparency*, 610–623. https://doi.org/DOI: 10.1145/3442188.3445922

Berger, P. L., & Luckmann, T. (1966). *The Social Construction of Reality: A Treatise in the Sociology of Knowledge*. Anchor Books.

Bhaskar, R. (1975). *A Realist Theory of Science*. Routledge.

Boyd, d., & Crawford, K. (2012). Critical questions for big data: Provocations for a cultural, technological, and scholarly phenomenon. Information, Communication & Society, 15(5), 662–679. DOI: 10.1080/1369118X.2012.678878

Bietti, E. (2020). From ethics washing to ethics bashing: A view on tech ethics from within moral philosophy. *Proceedings of the 2020 Conference on Fairness, Accountability, and Transparency*, 210–219. https://doi.org/DOI: 10.1145/3351095.3372860

Braidotti, R. (2013). *The posthuman*. Polity Press.

Comte, A. (1855). *The Positive Philosophy of Auguste Comte* (Martineau, H., Trans.). Calvin Blanchard.

Couldry, N., & Mejias, U. A. (2019). *The costs of connection: How data is colonizing human life and appropriating it for capitalism*. Stanford University Press.

Cramer, F. (2015). What is 'Post-digital. In Press, A. C. (Ed.), *Post-digital aesthetics: Art, computation and design* (pp. 12–26). Palgrave Macmillan.

Crawford, K. (2021). *Atlas of AI: Power, politics, and the planetary costs of artificial intelligence*. Yale University Press.

Denzin, N. K. (1978). *The Research Act: A Theoretical Introduction to Sociological Methods* (2nd ed.). McGraw-Hill.

Floridi, L. (2020). *The logic of information: A theory of philosophy as conceptual design*. Oxford University Press.

Floridi, L. (2022). The Ethics of Artificial Intelligence for a Good Society: The US and EU Initiatives. *Philosophy & Technology*, *35*(4), 1–8. DOI: 10.1007/s13347-022-00540-4

Flyvbjerg, B. (2001). *Making Social Science Matter: Why Social Inquiry Fails and How It Can Succeed Again*. Cambridge University Press.

Gillespie, T. (2014). The relevance of algorithms. In Gillespie, T., Boczkowski, P., & Foot, K. (Eds.), *Media technologies: Essays on communication, materiality, and society* (pp. 167–193). MIT Press.

Guba, E. G., & Lincoln, Y. S. (1994). Competing paradigms in qualitative research. In Denzin, N. K., & Lincoln, Y. S. (Eds.), *Handbook of Qualitative Research* (pp. 105–117). SAGE.

Halford, S., & Savage, M. (2017). Speaking sociologically with big data: Symphonic social science and the future for big data research. *The Sociological Review*, *65*(1), 2–19. DOI: 10.1111/1467-954X.12273

Haraway, D. J. (1988). Situated knowledges: The science question in feminism and the privilege of partial perspective. *Feminist Studies*, *14*(3), 575–599. DOI: 10.2307/3178066

Harding, S. (1991). *Whose Science? Whose Knowledge? Thinking from Women's Lives*. Cornell University Press.

Heisenberg, W. (1958). *Physics and Philosophy: The Revolution in Modern Science*. Harper.

Jandrić, P., Knox, J., Besley, T., Ryberg, T., Suoranta, J., & Hayes, S. (2018). Post-digital science and education. *Educational Philosophy and Theory*, *50*(10), 893–899. DOI: 10.1080/00131857.2018.1454000

Jasanoff, S. (Ed.). (2004). *States of Knowledge: The Co-Production of Science and the Social Order*. Routledge.

Kennedy, H. (2018). Living with Data: Aligning Data Studies and Data Activism through a Focus on Everyday Experiences of Datafication. *Kuckuck*, *3*(2), 15–28.

Kennedy, H., Poell, T., & van Dijck, J. (2022). Datafication and democracy: Reconsidering the role of data in society. *Big Data & Society*, *9*(2), 1–6. DOI: 10.1177/20539517221113500

Kitchin, R. (2014). The data revolution: Big data, open data, data infrastructures and their consequences. *Sage (Atlanta, Ga.)*.

Kitchin, R. (2016). Thinking critically about and researching algorithms. *Information Communication and Society*, *20*(1), 14–29. DOI: 10.1080/1369118X.2016.1154087

Kitchin, R., & Lauriault, T. P. (2014). Towards critical data studies: Charting and unpacking data assemblages and their work. *The Programmable City Working Paper*, 2. https://doi.org/DOI: 10.2139/ssrn.2474112

Knorr Cetina, K. (2001). Objectual practice. In Schatzki, T., Knorr Cetina, K., & von Savigny, E. (Eds.), *The practice turn in contemporary theory* (pp. 175–188). Routledge.

Knox, H. (2020). *Thinking like a climate: Governing a city in times of environmental change*. Duke University Press.

Knox, J. (2022). Artificial intelligence and education in the (post-)pandemic age. *Learning, Media and Technology*, *47*(1), 10–24. DOI: 10.1080/17439884.2021.1976239

Kuhn, T. S. (1962). *The Structure of Scientific Revolutions*. University of Chicago Press.

Latour, B. (2005). *Reassembling the Social: An Introduction to Actor-Network-Theory*. Oxford University Press.

Lupton, D. (2015). *Digital Sociology*. Routledge.

Lupton, D. (2017). Towards reflexive digital methods. *Digital Humanities Quarterly*, 11(2). https://digitalhumanities.org/dhq/vol/11/2/000321/000321.html

Lupton, D. (2021). *Data Selves: More-than-Human Perspectives*. Polity Press.

Lury, C., & Wakeford, N. (Eds.). (2012). *Inventive methods: The happening of the social*. Routledge.

Marcus, G., & Davis, E. (2020). *Rebooting AI: Building artificial intelligence we can trust*. Vintage.

Marres, N. (2017). *Digital Sociology: The Reinvention of Social Research*. Polity Press.

Mertens, D. M. (2010). *Research and Evaluation in Education and Psychology: Integrating Diversity with Quantitative, Qualitative, and Mixed Methods* (3rd ed.). SAGE Publications.

Mills, C. W. (1959). *The sociological imagination*. Oxford University Press.

Mol, A. (2002). *The body multiple: Ontology in medical practice*. Duke University Press.

Moore, E. C. (1966). *American Pragmatism: Peirce, James, and Dewey*. Columbia University Press.

Morgan, D. L. (2007). Paradigms lost and pragmatism regained: Methodological implications of combining qualitative and quantitative methods. *Journal of Mixed Methods Research, 1*(1), 48–76. DOI: 10.1177/2345678906292462

Mulgan, G. (2021). *Another world is possible: How to reignite social and political imagination*. Hurst Publishers.

Pasquinelli, M., & Joler, V. (2022). The Nooscope Manifested: AI as instrument of knowledge extractivism. *AI & Society, 37*, 153–169. DOI: 10.1007/s00146-021-01197-0 PMID: 33250587

Peirce, C. S. (1878). How to make our ideas clear. *Popular Science Monthly, 12*, 286–302.

Pink, S. (2015). *Doing Sensory Ethnography* (2nd ed.). SAGE Publications.

Pink, S., Horst, H., Postill, J., Hjorth, L., Lewis, T., & Tacchi, J. (2018). Digital Ethnography: Principles and Practice. *Sage (Atlanta, Ga.)*.

Rogers, R. (2013). *Digital Methods*. MIT Press.

Ruppert, E., Law, J., & Savage, M. (2013). Reassembling social science methods: The challenge of digital devices. *Theory, Culture & Society, 30*(4), 22–46. DOI: 10.1177/0263276413484941

Savage, M., & Burrows, R. (2007). The coming crisis of empirical sociology. *Sociology, 41*(5), 885–899. DOI: 10.1177/0038038507080443

Selwyn, N. (2019). *Should robots replace teachers? AI and the future of education*. Polity Press.

Tashakkori, A., & Teddlie, C. (Eds.). (2010). *SAGE Handbook of Mixed Methods in Social & Behavioral Research* (2nd ed.). SAGE Publications.

Van Dijck, J., Poell, T., & de Waal, M. (2018). *The Platform Society: Public Values in a Connective World*. Oxford University Press.

Weber, M. (1949). *The Methodology of the Social Sciences*. Free Press.

Chapter 5

# Social Media as a Field of Power, Habitus, Capital, and Intergenerational Digital Practices

**Benu Kesar**
https://orcid.org/0000-0003-3207-5528
*Symbiosis International University, Pune, India*

**Shaji Joseph**
https://orcid.org/0000-0002-5268-1376
*Symbiosis International University, Pune, India*

**Dev Kesar**
https://orcid.org/0009-0004-0801-2257
*Vellore Institute of Technology, Chennai, India*

## ABSTRACT

*In today's algorithmically mediated world, visibility is not a neutral outcome but the product of unspoken rules embedded in digital platforms. As social media becomes a dominant arena for professional recognition, generational differences in digital habitus and digital capital have produced asymmetries in visibility, legitimacy, and symbolic power. Employing a methodology that combines an extensive literature review with a case study of the Roblox gaming platform, we have introduced the Intergenerational Digital Habitus Framework (IDHF). It conceptualises the interplay between generationally constituted digital habitus, digital capital, and the normative architectures of platform doxa to gain symbolic power. IDHF offers actionable insights for policymakers and platform designers to foster equitable*

DOI: 10.4018/979-8-3373-4267-2.ch005

*digital engagement. IDHF not only advances academic understanding of digital social stratification but also charts a pragmatic pathway to dismantling barriers that hinder intergenerational equity, ensuring digital environments serve as inclusive arenas for all users.*

## INTRODUCTION

In today's media landscape, social media platforms serve not only as digital tools for communication but also as complex spaces of symbolic power that influence public participation, identity, and visibility (Carr & Hayes, 2015). Platforms like Facebook, Instagram, TikTok, and X (formerly Twitter) operate under algorithmic and cultural logics that unevenly distribute communicative legitimacy among user groups (Abidin et al., 2023; van Dijck & Poell, 2013). These platforms operate within what Pierre Bourdieu described as a structured field of power; users' positions and influence are determined by their economic, social, cultural, and symbolic capital, the resources they can mobilize in pursuit of visibility and recognition. In Outline of a Theory of Practice (Bourdieu, 1977), Pierre Bourdieu explained that individuals are shaped by their habitus, which are the internalized dispositions moulded by cultural and historical experiences that affect how individuals perceive, think, and act. Doxa, or the taken-for-granted assumptions that define what is considered normal or legitimate within a field, further sustains existing hierarchies.

Bourdieu extended the concept of capital beyond its economic origins to encompass additional categories, including social capital, cultural capital, and symbolic capital. An individual's position within a multidimensional social space is determined by the composition and volume of the various forms of capital, not solely by social class membership. These forms of capital include the value of one's social networks (social capital), cultural competencies and credentials (cultural capital), material assets (economic capital), and the recognition or prestige accorded by society (symbolic capital). Individuals are thus defined by how they articulate and mobilize different types of capital through their social relations. Bourdieu explained that these capitals, mainly social and cultural forms, are critical resources that can be used to produce or reproduce social inequality, as those with greater access to valued capital are more likely to maintain or enhance their social position within the broader social field.

In digital environments, these concepts help us understand the symbolic inequalities that are often hidden behind the illusion of open participation. Algorithmic hierarchies, interface affordances, and unspoken design norms subtly but powerfully influence how users interact, express themselves, and gain visibility. It exposes the deeply embedded structures that shape user experience and reinforce digital stratification.

Bourdieu's field theory, a central concept in his work, describes society as comprising of relatively autonomous "fields," each with its own rules, logic, and types of capital. In digital settings, the "field" of social media is shaped by platform-specific algorithms, moderation policies, and cultural norms that favour certain communicative behaviours, such as brevity, aesthetic fluency, meme literacy, and emotional immediacy. These expectations primarily benefit younger digital natives, especially Gen Z and younger millennials, whose digital habitus has developed in tandem with these participatory and performative digital cultures (Abidin et al., 2023; van Dijck, 2013). Digital habitus refers to the ingrained dispositions, practices, and mindsets individuals or groups develop in response to their interactions within digital environments, influenced by both technological features and socio-cultural contexts. These dispositions, shaped by a person's sociohistorical background, significantly influence how individuals understand, navigate, and succeed in digital fields.

In Bourdieu's schema, habitus and capital are historically sedimented through class trajectories and cultural exposure. Within organizational digital ecosystems, employees' familiarity with technology is thus mediated not only by age but by education, socioeconomic status, and cultural capital (Livingstone & Helsper, 2007). An individual's socioeconomic background can influence their digital literacy and workplace behaviour. For example, employees from resource-rich households are often exposed to digital devices and informal learning networks at an earlier age, accumulating embodied digital capital long before entering the workforce. Conversely, workers from a lower socio-economic background tend to exhibit "instrumental" digital use, characterized by task-specific and compliance-driven behaviour, reflecting a constrained habitus shaped by economic necessity.

Cultural capital is the non-financial assets, such as education, intellect, and knowledge of cultural codes, that an individual possesses. In a digital context, this is often reshaped into forms like "digital cultural capital". The three main types are: a) Embodied: Personal knowledge and skills, such as linguistic proficiency, mannerisms, and speech style. b) Objectified: Material possessions that indicate cultural status, such as owning certain tech devices or using specific software. c) Institutionalized: Formal certifications like academic credentials and professional qualifications.

Digital capital refers to the resources, skills, and access that individuals or organizations have, enabling them to use and benefit from digital technologies effectively (van Deursen & van Dijk, 2014). The distribution of digital capital, comprising digital skills (embodied capital), access to technological infrastructure (objectified capital), and social networks (social capital), further influences users' ability to participate meaningfully online (Bourdieu, 2011; Ragnedda & Ruiu, 2017). For younger users, digital capital is often taken for granted; however, for older generations or marginalized groups, access to and confidence with digital tools may vary.

Older users tend to engage with social media in more instrumental and conservative ways, often focusing on personal communication or consuming information rather than public performance (Hargittai & Dobransky, 2017). In contrast, Gen Z and digitally savvy millennials often demonstrate fluent and reflexive engagement marked by visual storytelling, platform agility, and quick responsiveness (Boyd, 2014). This asymmetry reinforces symbolic hierarchies on social media, where users with high digital capital, typically younger and culturally mainstream, gain visibility and influence, while others remain on the periphery.

In organizational settings, enterprise social media (ESM) platforms, such as Slack, Microsoft Teams, and Workplace by Meta, extend these symbolic dynamics into professional hierarchies (Treem & Leonardi, 2013). This generational inequality is amplified in organizational contexts, where ESM platforms replicate similar symbolic hierarchies. Although ESM tools are marketed as collaborative, they often reward performative digital fluency over genuine contributions, reinforcing generational divides in workplace recognition (Leidner et al., 2020).

Employees who display high levels of digital fluency, engaging quickly, visually, and playfully, are often valued, regardless of their formal position within the organization. Performativity on enterprise social media can overshadow experience and authority, leading to the emergence of new informal hierarchies based on communication style rather than expertise. As a result, older or traditionally trained professionals may find themselves marginalized not through overt exclusion but through subtle misrecognition of their communication style as outdated or unengaged.

Platform Doxa refers to the platform-specific norms and values (such as aesthetic standards and engagement styles) that govern user behaviour and influence symbolic inclusion or exclusion. On many social and enterprise media platforms, these norms include quick responsiveness, the use of emojis, proficiency in multimedia, and alignment with algorithmic preferences. Users who do not adhere to these norms are often symbolically excluded, with their contributions undervalued or ignored. This issue is not solely about digital access, but also concerns symbolic power, the ability for one's digital expressions to be recognized as meaningful within the structure of the field (Couldry, 2012).

Generational differences in digital capital create distinct patterns of engagement, with younger groups, especially Gen Z and Millennials, gaining symbolic power by aligning with platform doxa, such as brevity, visual fluency, and real-time responsiveness. Meanwhile, older generations often face symbolic marginalization because their communication styles do not match platform doxa. Algorithmic personalization worsens these gaps by curating content based on users' past behaviours, reinforcing their communication preferences and ideological bubbles (Vosoughi et al., 2018).

The digital divide refers to the gap between individuals who have access to and are skilled in digital technologies and those who do not, often based on factors such as age, education, and socio-economic status (DiMaggio et al., 2004; Ragnedda, 2019; Robinson et al., 2015). Intergenerational tensions during organizational digitalization are a significant issue that must be addressed in today's rapidly evolving technological environment. The rapid development and widespread adoption of new technologies can cause stress, especially among older professionals (Teng, 2020). These tensions are more than just superficial generational disagreements; they stem from differences in digital habitus, access to digital resources, and shifting power dynamics within organizations.

These shifts introduce symbolic power dynamics into the workplace (Calderon Gomez, 2021). Younger employees may unintentionally (or intentionally) exert symbolic power by redefining what counts as "efficient," "modern," or "valuable" knowledge. Tools, platforms, and practices that were once considered optional have become essential, often without sufficient institutional support for those less familiar with them. This redefinition risks reinforcing stereotypes, portraying older professionals as resistant or outdated, while positioning younger employees as inherently innovative or adaptable. These perceptions may be more discursively constructed than based on actual evidence. To address intergenerational tensions during digitalization, organizations must go beyond technical training and consider the cultural and symbolic aspects of digital transformation. In the digital realm, platform-specific algorithms, interface affordances, and implicit design norms collectively create what we refer to as platform doxa.

To address these complex inequalities, we have introduced the Intergenerational Digital Habitus Framework (IDHF), which examines the relationship between generational digital habitus, digital capital, and alignment with platform doxa to gain symbolic power. The study employed a mixed methods approach, an extensive literature review of peer-reviewed journal articles and books from academic databases, and a case study of the Roblox digital platform. IDHF offers practical implications for addressing digital inequalities and fostering equitable participation across generations within digital ecosystems.

The IDHF shows that younger users build symbolic power by aligning their digital habitus with platform doxa. Meanwhile, older users may be symbolically excluded not because they lack competencies but because of different communicative dispositions shaped by distinct historical and technological contexts. In the workplace, the IDHF recommends a critical re-evaluation of digital meritocracy. These include reverse mentoring programs, interface designs that support multiple communication styles (textual, visual, auditory), and recognition systems that value thoughtful engagement as much as performative visibility. For example, incorporating inclusive metrics of contribution such as clarity, analytical depth, and cross-functional collaboration can help rebalance symbolic power across different generational groups.

Underlying this framework is the generational information velocity gap, which describes the uneven speeds at which different age groups consume, interpret, and respond to digital content. For younger generations, especially Gen Z and digital-native millennials, engagement with digital information is influenced by algorithmic immediacy, short-form content formats (e.g., TikTok, Instagram Reels), and push-notification ecosystems that promote rapid cognitive and emotional processing. Their digital habitus is thus tuned to high-frequency content cycles, meme-driven discourse, and fleeting participation (Abidin et al., 2023; Boyd, 2014).

In contrast, older generations, such as Gen X and Baby Boomers, whose digital socialization began later in life, tend to engage with online content more thoughtfully. Their digital habitus often favours reflective reading, slower interpretive processing, and a preference for contextual depth (Friemel, 2016; Hargittai & Dobransky, 2017). This mismatch in cognitive tempo leads to what we call asynchronous discourse (Parry & Urwin, 2011), where different generational cohorts respond to the same political event, such as a viral protest, breaking news story, or social movement, on various timelines and through different interpretive styles.

This temporal disjuncture has significant implications for the fragmentation of public dialogue. It produces a digital environment in which generations are metaphorically "talking past" one another, even when engaging with the same socio-political content. For example, younger users may participate in real-time hashtag activism within minutes of an incident. In comparison, older users may only engage once traditional media coverage or personal deliberation has occurred. As a result, public discourse becomes fractured along generational lines, not only in terms of what is said, but also in terms of when it is said and how it is understood.

This dynamic exacerbates political polarization by undermining shared narrative timelines, which are essential for cross-generational deliberation and collective sense-making. The lack of temporal synchronicity weakens opportunities for intergenerational dialogue, shared civic learning, and solidarity across age-based cohorts. In this way, digital inequality becomes temporally structured not just by access or capability, but by the speed and rhythm of engagement embedded in platform norms and user dispositions.

## Research Objectives

1. To conceptualize social media platforms as structured fields of symbolic power by applying Pierre Bourdieu's concepts of habitus, capital, field, and doxa.
2. To analyse how generational cohorts (Baby Boomers, Generation X, Millennials, Generation Z, and Generation Alpha) develop differentiated patterns of digital engagement through their distinct digital habitus and digital capital.

3. To investigate the role of platform design in reinforcing symbolic power asymmetries across generational lines.
4. To examine how enterprise social media (ESM) platforms function as fields of symbolic struggle, where communicative legitimacy, authority, and visibility are distributed unequally based on generational digital fluency.
5. To develop and apply the Intergenerational Digital Habitus Framework (IDHF) as a critical analytical tool for understanding digital inequalities and enabling equitable, cross-generational participation in both public and professional digital spaces.

## Research Questions

1. How do social media platforms operate as structured fields of symbolic power through the interplay of habitus, capital, field, and doxa?
2. In what ways do generational cohorts (Baby Boomers, Generation X, Millennials, Generation Z, and Generation Alpha) manifest differentiated patterns of digital engagement as a function of their distinct digital habitus and digital capital?
3. How do platform design and algorithmic governance reinforce or challenge symbolic power asymmetries and digital inequalities across generational lines?
4. In what ways do enterprise social media platforms reproduce or challenge symbolic power asymmetries among age-diverse employee groups?
5. How can digital platform design and organizational strategy be used to promote equitable digital participation and support meaningful intergenerational knowledge sharing?

# 2. LITERATURE REVIEW

Social media fields are structured arenas where users compete for visibility, legitimacy, and recognition, guided by often-unspoken norms of platform doxa (Gillespie, 2021; van Dijck & Poell, 2013). Higher levels of digital capital are linked to greater involvement in online activities that enhance capital, such as e-learning, job searching, and brand building (van Deursen & van Dijk, 2014).

## 2.1 Digital habitus

Digital habitus refers to the ingrained dispositions, literacies, and practices that individuals and groups develop through their interactions with digital environments, shaped by both technological features and socio-historical contexts. Digital habitus is not merely an individual technical skill; it encompasses generational experiences, cultural exposure, and internalized norms that shape how people perceive, navigate, and express themselves online (Costa et al., 2019; Sarraf, 2019). Distinct generational cohorts such as Gen Z, Millennials, Gen X, and Baby Boomers exhibit unique patterns of digital habitus: younger users often possess a participatory, visually fluent, and performative style closely aligned with prevailing platform doxa, while older users tend to engage with digital media in more cautious, text-oriented ways informed by traditional media norms (Friemel, 2016; Boyd, 2014; Hargittai & Dobransky, 2017).

For example, Baby Boomers and Gen X predominantly use LinkedIn as an extension of professional networking and industry reputation-building. These cohorts tend to emphasize detailed resumes, formal endorsements, and well-structured achievement narratives with minimal multimedia or informal posts. In contrast, Millennials and Gen Z tend to use LinkedIn for skills signalling, knowledge sharing via posts and articles, and networking beyond their immediate industry. Younger professionals often leverage rich media (videos, digital portfolios), participate in purpose-driven groups, and engage in open dialogue on diversity, inclusion, and digital trends. While generational stereotypes can be overstated when controlling for career stage and sector, research confirms that younger users tend to be more experimental and visually expressive, whereas older users typically adopt a more conventional online persona.

On TikTok, Generation Z and Millennials dominate the platform, primarily using it for creative self-expression, humour, trend participation (such as "challenges"), and personal storytelling. Content is typically fast-paced, visually rich, and meme-driven, capitalizing on the app's algorithmic amplification for reach. In contrast, older generations, particularly Baby Boomers, are less active and often feature as subjects in younger users' content, sometimes satirically, or in videos highlighting value conflicts (e.g., #OkBoomer). Scholarly analysis by Ng & Indran (2022) finds that TikTok videos frequently explore generational misunderstandings, with themes such as negative encounters with Baby Boomers. While some Baby Boomers use TikTok to share nostalgic stories or offer advice, the dominant tone is set by youth culture, which shapes prevailing norms and viral trends.

The alignment of digital habitus with platform-specific norms and algorithmic logics facilitates the conversion of digital habitus into symbolic power within digital fields, underscoring how digital engagement is fundamentally shaped by the intersection of generational digital habitus, digital capital, and the platform doxa (van Dijck & Poell, 2013; Ragnedda, 2018).

## 2.2 Digital Capital

Digital capital refers to the combination of digital skills, access, and competencies that enable effective participation in digital life. It acts as a stratifying force that influences how individuals participate, compete, and gain recognition in digital society. Digital capital consists of two main components: digital competencies, which encompass the knowledge and skills required to navigate digital environments, and digital access, which refers to the means and opportunities to engage with them (Ragnedda, 2019). It functions not only as a resource but also as a form of symbolic power that affects one's visibility, legitimacy, and access to economic and cultural opportunities (Bourdieu, 2011; DiMaggio et al., 2004).

Embodied digital capital encompasses skills, literacies, and intuitive platform fluency acquired through formal education or hands-on experience. In contrast, objectified digital capital consists of physical tools, such as smartphones, tablets, broadband connections, and access to updated software and platforms. Gen Z typically possesses highly developed embodied digital capital, including intuitive platform fluency, the ability to navigate multimodal communication, and comfort with algorithm-driven environments. They often exhibit high levels of participatory and aesthetic engagement, utilizing memes, short videos, filters, and hashtags to establish presence and accumulate symbolic capital on social media. Their ease with the performative aspects of digital life, branding, audience segmentation, and algorithmic optimization gives them an advantage within today's digital landscape.

Millennials often act as a transitional generation in terms of digital capital. Many in this cohort witnessed the evolution of digital technologies from tools for information retrieval to platforms for identity building and professional networking. While they may not have the same intuitive fluency as Gen Z, millennials generally possess both embodied and objectified digital capital. They are skilled at navigating professional digital tools (e.g., LinkedIn, Google Workspace) and often recognize the importance of managing personal data, maintaining cybersecurity, and protecting their online reputation. Generations X and Baby Boomers experienced digital socialization later in life, resulting in distinct patterns of digital capital accumulation. Many from these cohorts were introduced to digital technologies through work rather than early education or peer socialization. As a result, their embodied digital capital tends to focus on task-oriented activities, such as email communication, search engines, online banking, and digital documentation (Friemel, 2016). This difference is not a sign of technological resistance, but rather a digital habitus shaped by different normative expectations and technological opportunities during formative years (Hargittai & Dobransky, 2017).

These generational differences in digital capital have significant implications for the distribution of symbolic power in digital spaces. In social media environments, the modes of engagement privileged by platform algorithms, such as brevity, interactivity, and visual fluency, often favour younger users, who more easily align with these unspoken platform norms (Gillespie, 2021). For example, a Baby Boomer sharing a reflective, text-heavy post on LinkedIn may receive less engagement than a Gen Z professional posting a concise, visually polished update, even if the former's content is more analytically rigorous. This difference in recognition is emblematic of the unequal conversion of digital capital into symbolic capital, which can affect professional visibility, influence, and access to opportunity.

Digital platforms utilize advanced algorithmic systems that tailor content delivery to user behaviour patterns, engagement metrics, and network effects. These systems generate what we call "algorithmic habitus reproduction," a tendency for recommendation algorithms to reinforce existing communicative preferences and ideological views while systematically excluding content that differs from established user patterns.

This algorithmic mediation deepens generational divides by creating separate information ecosystems that mirror and reinforce age-specific digital habitus. Younger users, whose engagement patterns align with platform optimization strategies, experience increased visibility and network growth, while older users may find their content systematically deprioritized or excluded from wider circulation.

## 2.3 Platform Doxa

Platform doxa are the taken-for-granted beliefs, implicit norms, and rules of engagement that individuals internalize through their habitual use of digital platforms, shaping how they perceive, interpret, and interact with the digital world. Platform Doxa is neither neutral nor universal, but actively shapes participation, visibility, and legitimacy. Metrics such as likes, shares, and views are transformed into symbolic currencies, conferring advantage to those who internalize and perform the platform's preferred logic (Gillespie, 2021). IDHF situates platform doxa as the mediating mechanism between generationally situated digital habitus, digital capital, and the accumulation of symbolic power within the digital field. Platform doxa, comprising algorithmic prioritization, interface affordances, cultural participation norms, and commercial imperatives, shapes which forms of digital engagement are recognized as legitimate and valuable. Users whose digital habitus and capital align with these tacit norms are more likely to convert participation into symbolic power, while those whose communicative styles diverge face symbolic exclusion. The temporal dimension of doxa, privileging immediacy and constant connectivity, further reinforces generational disparities through the "information velocity gap." Acts of symbolic struggle, such as hashtag activism and aesthetic subversion, can disrupt and reconfigure platform doxa, demonstrating that these power structures, while deeply embedded, remain contested and mutable.

Platforms such as Instagram, TikTok, Twitter (now X), YouTube, and LinkedIn can be understood as distinct fields, semi-autonomous arenas of practice with their own rules, hierarchies, and forms of capital. However, these fields do not operate transparently. Instead, platform doxa works through the interface, algorithm, and culture of the platform to shape what is visible, desirable, and legitimate. For example:

- On Instagram, the doxa emphasizes aesthetic self-curation, visual perfection, and a polished identity, reinforcing symbolic capital tied to attractiveness and consumerism.
- Twitter/X rewards speed, wit, and controversy, prioritizing real-time engagement and often amplifying polarizing content.
- TikTok's doxa valorises immediacy, trend-following, and participatory remix culture, favouring users who can quickly adapt to viral sounds or visual formats.
- LinkedIn promotes professionalism and personal branding, rewarding users who can project institutional capital and strategic career narratives.

Although these logics may seem harmless or even empowering, they subtly exclude or marginalize users whose social background or resources do not match the dominant way of participation. A key part of platform doxa is the obsession with metrics, likes, tweets, views, shares, and followers, which are not just indicators but have become symbolic currencies. These metrics serve as a form of symbolic capital but are often viewed as natural signs of quality or popularity rather than outcomes shaped by algorithms.

The underlying algorithmic system, which is often hidden, functions through rules that favour engagement over accuracy, virality over thoughtful discussion, and emotional content over reflective dialogue. Users absorb these preferences and shape their behaviour accordingly, often unconsciously, thus reproducing the platform's accepted beliefs without questioning their validity (Kim & Kim, 2023). Platform doxa does not influence all users equally. It interacts with broader social inequality structures to reinforce dominant positions. Those with relevant digital capital, such as technical skills, aesthetic knowledge, and platform literacy, are better able to align their content and actions with the platform's unstated norms.

- Influencers and creators with symbolic capital often receive preferential treatment from algorithms due to higher engagement metrics, further amplifying their reach and visibility (Kim & Kim, 2023).
- Marginalized voices such as racial minorities, LGBTQ+ users, or politically radical content creators may face algorithmic suppression or shadow banning when their content challenges platform doxa.
- In this way, the platform doxa functions as a mechanism of symbolic violence, a term used to describe the imposition of dominant norms as natural, thereby legitimizing social hierarchies without overt coercion. Despite its

pervasiveness, doxa is not fixed. It can be challenged, subverted, or reconfigured through acts of symbolic struggle. Users often develop counter-practices that push against the grain of platform norms.

- Digital activism campaigns, such as #BlackLivesMatter and #MeToo, have exposed and challenged dominant narratives within online spaces. They demonstrate how marginalized groups use social media to contest and reshape prevailing cultural, political, and historical stories. These campaigns take advantage of the viral and participatory nature of digital platforms to confront hegemonic discourses that are widely accepted but often hide systemic injustice, gendered violence, or racial oppression.
- Traditionally, legacy media and institutional gatekeepers have controlled which voices and stories gain public legitimacy. Social media platforms, by contrast, offer decentralized spaces where grassroots narratives can gain visibility without the need for institutional mediation. Hashtag activism serves as a discursive intervention, creating searchable and aggregable publics that highlight experiences previously excluded from mainstream representation.
- Aesthetic subversion through meme culture functions as a form of symbolic resistance against dominant visual standards on platforms like Instagram and TikTok. These platforms often promote a curated aesthetic that is polished, aspirational, and visually cohesive, aligning with commercial interests and influencer branding. These standards are part of the platform's doxa, the taken-for-granted visual and behavioural norms embedded in its design and culture. In contrast, meme culture often embraces irony, bricolage, and visual imperfection. Memes are typically low-resolution, text-heavy, absurd, or intentionally crude. Their communicative power does not rely on polish but on cultural references, humour, and collective participation. By emphasizing spontaneity, relatability, and shared social codes over glossy presentation, memes challenge the aesthetic hierarchies that platforms implicitly support. As a result, meme culture democratizes visibility by creating space for subcultural voices and grassroots narratives that diverge from mainstream platform aesthetics.
- Algorithmic resistance involves intentional, often collective, efforts by users to oppose or disrupt the algorithmic logics that control visibility, attention, and legitimacy on digital platforms. Platforms like Instagram, YouTube, X (formerly Twitter), and TikTok rely on algorithmic systems that rank content based on engagement metrics such as likes, shares, watch time, and emotional impact. Although these systems are presented as neutral, they often reinforce existing social hierarchies and promote content that aligns with the dominant platform doxa.

- Instead of accepting algorithmic logic as fixed or inevitable, users employ collective strategies to challenge symbolic hierarchies, redefine the boundaries of legitimacy, and reclaim control over how attention and influence are allocated. Algorithmic resistance thus exposes digital spaces as arenas of symbolic conflict where the rules of visibility and participation are not only dictated from above but are also continuously negotiated, disrupted, and reimagined from below. These struggles show that platform doxa is a site of contest, where actors with different habitus and capital arrangements try to redefine legitimacy, visibility, and value. Recognizing how platform doxa operates has important implications for:
- Algorithmic transparency: Users must be made aware of how content is filtered, ranked, and promoted.
- Digital literacy education: Teaching users to critically engage with platforms, understanding how metrics and affordances shape behavior, is key to mitigating symbolic domination.
- Platform accountability: Regulators and developers should consider how design choices instantiate normative hierarchies and influence discourse.

Platform doxa is the invisible scaffolding of digital life. It shapes how users interact, what they value, and how they find meaning, often without their awareness. Using Bourdieu's ideas enables a more profound understanding that extends beyond surface-level analysis of user behaviour or platform design. It uncovers the sociological systems that make certain behaviours normal, and others marginalized, shaping the digital space not as a level playing field but as a structured arena of inequality and symbolic negotiation.

Platform monetization models create systems where certain types of content and creators are favoured, establishing economic hierarchies that intersect with identity categories. Social platforms are expanding their use of generative AI tools to assist creators in running their businesses, producing content, targeting audiences and advertisers, and connecting with brand sponsors. This demonstrates how platforms actively shape the creator economy in ways that can both reinforce existing inequalities and open up new opportunities for digital entrepreneurship.

The subscription fatigue observed across generations highlights different economic ties to digital platforms. Younger users, who tend to have higher churn rates and are more price-sensitive, engage with platforms based on different financial expectations than older users, who might see social media as just another form of entertainment rather than their primary financial source. This economic aspect of platform use reflects broader generational differences in digital experiences and financial goals. These patterns suggest that social media platforms are not neutral spaces for socializing but are intentionally designed systems that shape identity, reinforce social hierarchies, and create distinct generational experiences in digital social life.

## 2.4 Symbolic Power

Symbolic Power or Symbolic Domination is a tacit mode of social domination. It is the ability to define what is valued or legitimate within a field, often exercised through digital visibility and platform fluency. It is the defining reality that grants legitimacy in digital contexts, platforms and their algorithms amplify this process, making symbolic recognition both a function of social capital and algorithmic design. It involves shaping meaning, visibility, and legitimacy through symbolic control over digital content and narratives. In digital environments, symbolic power refers to the ability to influence what is seen, heard, and believed through language, aesthetics, and platform norms, often without users being aware of it. It works by aligning with both digital habitus (what users expect and feel comfortable with) and platform doxa (what the platform promotes as legitimate or valuable).

In IDHF, symbolic power operates through the taken-for-granted systems of valuation embedded in digital platform systems that define what counts as credible, engaging, or worthy of attention. This reflects Bourdieu's original argument that symbolic power is the ability to define reality and have that definition accepted as legitimate (Bourdieu, 1991). On social media, however, this power is mediated not only by institutional actors but also by platform architectures that govern visibility and reward conformity to platform norms. Therefore, when individuals curate an online persona, they are not simply exercising symbolic power independently; they are navigating and reproducing the field-specific power relations already embedded in platform logics, interface affordances, and algorithmic priorities.

In the digital era, symbolic power is distributed across algorithmic systems that appear neutral but, in practice, encode and normalize specific digital habitus efficiency, immediacy, and visibility. These encoded norms constitute platform doxa, the invisible framework of rules, meanings, and affordances that users internalize through habitual engagement (Cotter, 2019; van Dijck et al., 2018). Symbolic power functions through platform doxa by naturalizing hierarchies of influence, which the IDHF identifies as the digital symbolic order.

For example, younger users whose communication style aligns with the algorithmic focus on immediacy and visual culture can more easily gain symbolic power on platforms like TikTok or Instagram. This shows that symbolic power in IDHF is not evenly spread; the changing interaction between generational habitus and platform doxa influences it.

The problem addressed in the chapter centers on the digital platforms, which ostensibly offer equal opportunities for participation and recognition; they in fact reproduce symbolic power asymmetries rooted in the interplay of generational habitus, digital capital, and platform-specific norms (platform doxa). Younger generations, whose digital dispositions align more closely with fast-evolving algorithmic standards and aesthetic preferences, gain greater visibility and legitimacy, whereas older cohorts, despite comparable expertise or professional authority, are often marginalized due to misalignment with these implicit rules. This dynamic perpetuates generational digital stratification and limits equitable inclusion in both public and professional digital environments.

There is a critical need to systematically analyse how these intersecting factors structure digital inequalities and to provide an explanatory and practical framework, such as the Intergenerational Digital Habitus Framework (IDHF), to inform strategies that promote cross-generational recognition and participation in contemporary digital societies. IDHF moves analysis from individual deficits to relational structures. It suggests that a "lack of skill" may be a consequence of misaligned digital habitus, digital capital, and platform doxa rather than merely training gaps. It forces managers to ask which behaviours are being rewarded and why.

Table 1 illustrates the definition, characteristics, and examples of each concept, helping to illustrate their operationalization in the digital context.

*Table 1. Key concepts of the IDHF*

| Concept | Definition | Characteristics | Manifestations |
|---|---|---|---|
| Digital Habitus | The ingrained dispositions, literacies, and orientations developed through sustained interaction with digital media. Shaped by generational, socio-cultural, and technological context, digital habitus influences how individuals perceive, interpret, and act within digital environments. | Internalized, habitual, generational, context-dependent, affects perception and online behavior. | Visual fluency, preference for particular platforms, comfort with algorithm-driven communication, multimodal expression (e.g., memes, videos) |
| Digital Capital | The accumulated digital resources, technical skills, access, and networked connections that facilitate effective participation in online environments. Digital capital exists in embodied (skills), objectified (devices/ infrastructure), and social (networks) forms. | Embodied (skills, literacy), objectified (devices, infrastructure), and social (networks) forms are unevenly distributed across generations and socio-economic groups. | Proficiency with software, access to high-quality devices and internet, and large or influential social networks |
| Platform Doxa | The platform-specific norms, values, and behavioural expectations are often unspoken, which structure what is regarded as legitimate or desirable participation. | Implicit, normative, platform-specific, shapes "acceptable" conduct, influences legitimacy | Preference for brevity, visual storytelling, responsiveness, and algorithmic conformity |
| Symbolic Power | The capacity to shape visibility, legitimacy, and value within digital fields, largely achieved through alignment of digital habitus and capital with platform doxa. | Hierarchical, Legitimacy through Recognition | High follower counts, frequent algorithmic amplification, recognition as a trendsetter or influencer |

Source: Author's own work

## 3. CASE STUDY: SYMBOLIC POWER AND SOCIAL HIERARCHIES IN THE ROBLOX DIGITAL PLATFORM

The case study examines how symbolic capital and symbolic violence operate within the Roblox online gaming platform, facilitating the establishment and reproduction of social hierarchies. In recent years, digital gaming platforms have evolved into complex socio-economic systems where play, production, and consumption intersect. One such example is Roblox, an online gaming and creation platform that enables users to both consume and produce content within a shared ecosystem. The study by Oktavianingtyas et al. (2025) examines this environment through the lens of Pierre Bourdieu's concepts of symbolic capital and symbolic violence. The authors investigate how economic inputs in Roblox, such as microtransactions and development activity, are transformed into social hierarchies and how these hierarchies become normalized through symbolic capital.

From a theoretical standpoint, the study situates Roblox as a digital field, a social space where participants compete for distinction, legitimacy, and recognition. Within this field, two primary sources of symbolic capital emerge: prestige and reputation. Prestige is predominantly acquired through consumption practices; users purchase exclusive avatars, virtual items, memberships, or limited-edition accessories that function as visible indicators of wealth and taste. These purchases confer status because the platform's interface visibly distinguishes between those who spend and those who do not.

Reputation, by contrast, is accumulated through production. Roblox allows users to create games, design virtual assets, and even earn revenue through their creations. Developers who achieve verified status or receive official awards gain institutional legitimacy within the community. This recognition functions as a higher-order form of symbolic capital, one grounded in creativity and productivity rather than consumption alone. Nevertheless, access to this tier often requires substantial resources, both technical and financial. The platform's algorithm promotes successful games and creators, converting their digital competence into increased visibility. When a developer's work is recognized with badges and awards, this converts their digital capital into symbolic power (legitimacy and reputation).

The authors argue that these processes collectively produce what Bourdieu termed symbolic violence, a subtle, often invisible form of domination that persuades individuals to accept and reproduce social inequalities. In the case of Roblox, the mechanisms of symbolic violence operate in four stages. First, the platform objectifies distinctions by encoding them into visible symbols such as badges, roles, and exclusive items. Second, users internalize these markers as natural indicators of success or belonging. Third, inequalities are justified through narratives of meritocracy, where higher status is attributed to greater effort or talent, rather than differential access to economic capital. Ultimately, these norms are perpetuated through everyday practices: players continue to spend, compete, and create in ways that sustain the existing hierarchy.

The study provides important theoretical and practical insights. Theoretically, it demonstrates how Bourdieu's concepts, traditionally applied to offline social contexts, can illuminate dynamics in platform economies. It shows that platform design itself, through visibility, acts as a key agent in the conversion of digital capital into symbolic power. Practically, the authors suggest that developers and policymakers could mitigate these inequalities by redesigning recognition systems and increasing transparency in the platform's reward structures.

Through mechanisms of symbolic capital and symbolic violence, playful interactions are transformed into systems of prestige and recognition. What appears as voluntary participation in a creative digital economy may, in fact, be the subtle reproduction of inequality.

## 4. METHODOLOGY

The methodology of this chapter employs a mixed methods approach, an extensive literature review with a case study of the Roblox digital platform to develop and validate the Intergenerational Digital Habitus Framework (IDHF). The literature review establishes the theoretical foundation of the framework through Pierre Bourdieu's sociological constructs of habitus, capital, and doxa, adapted to digital contexts to elucidate mechanisms of symbolic power and inequality in online spaces. Scholarly sources, including peer-reviewed journal articles and academic books, were identified through searches in academic databases such as Google Scholar, JSTOR, Scopus, Web of Science, and ScienceDirect. The search strategy employed a range of keywords, including but not limited to "social media," "digital habitus," "symbolic power AND social media," "digital capital AND digital inequality," "platform doxa AND algorithmic mediation," "generational digital engagement," "enterprise social media," and "intergenerational digital literacy."

The case study centers on the Roblox digital platform, examining how symbolic capital and symbolic violence manifest within user interactions and creative economies. Through this analysis, the research investigates how virtual consumption, participation, and production contribute to the construction of social hierarchies in digital environments. The chapter demonstrates how generational variations in digital habitus and digital capital align with platform-specific norms to reproduce and contest symbolic power across digital fields.

## 5. THEORETICAL FRAMEWORK: INTERGENERATIONAL DIGITAL HABITUS FRAMEWORK (IDHF)

The Intergenerational Digital Habitus Framework (IDHF) is a conceptual model that builds on Pierre Bourdieu's sociological concepts of habitus, capital, and doxa to explain how digital participation and power asymmetries emerge across generations. It proposes that individuals' generationally shaped digital habitus and digital capital interact with platform doxa, the implicit norms embedded in digital platforms, to produce differential levels of symbolic power or visibility within digital spaces. This model situates digital engagement within a field-like structure, where recognition and legitimacy are mediated through platform-specific logics of participation.

The IDHF integrates the four constructs: digital habitus, digital capital, platform doxa, and symbolic power to explain the relational production of digital inequality. Digital Habitus and Digital Capital serve as independent but interacting antecedents that determine how individuals engage with and interpret digital environments. Platform Doxa acts as the mediating mechanism, translating those engagements into symbolic power. When users' dispositions and resources align with platform expectations, they successfully transform digital capital into symbolic power; when misaligned, their contributions remain under-recognized despite potential merit.

Digital Habitus refers to the ingrained dispositions, literacies, and orientations developed through long-term interaction with digital media. These dispositions influence how individuals perceive, interpret, and act within online environments. Habitus directs what content users produce and how they interpret platform cues. Generational cohorts, having grown up in distinct technological and socio-cultural contexts, exhibit different digital habitus. For instance, younger generations often demonstrate greater visual fluency, multimodal expression, and comfort with algorithmic affordances, while older generations may rely on text-dominant communication and exhibit cautious digital engagement. Such variations affect how users align their practices with platform expectations.

Digital Capital represents the accumulated digital resources and competencies that facilitate effective participation in online fields. It includes technical skills, access to digital tools, and the social connections that enhance networked visibility. Digital capital manifests in one's technological proficiency (embodied), access to advanced technology, devices, and connectivity (objectified), and the strength of online networks and communities (social). Digital capital determines the capacity to produce platform-fit content and to amplify it via networks. However, these resources are unevenly distributed across generational cohorts, shaping differential capacities for engagement and visibility.

Platform Doxa serves as the mediating structure within IDHF, defining legitimate participation. It includes the taken-for-granted norms, aesthetic preferences, and behavioural expectations embedded in platform algorithms and interface design. Platform doxa is enacted through ranking metrics, recommendation systems, and interface affordances. Content that aligns with doxa is amplified. Likes, follows, comments, and peer endorsement convert amplification into perceived legitimacy. These doxic expectations favouring brevity, immediacy, visual appeal, and trend conformity define what is considered legitimate or successful participation. Platforms like TikTok, for example, prioritize short-form, visually engaging content, while LinkedIn emphasizes professionalism and curated self-branding. Users whose habitus and capital align with these doxic norms are more likely to experience algorithmic boosting and peer validation.

Within the IDHF, Symbolic Power denotes the ability to define what is visible, valued, or credible within a digital field. It functions through algorithmic amplification and social validation processes that convert conformity with platform doxa into perceived legitimacy. Symbolic power, therefore, does not depend solely on technical expertise or content quality but on the congruence between users' generational habitus and the platform's implicit rules. Younger cohorts, whose dispositions are attuned to visual immediacy and constant interaction, tend to accumulate symbolic capital more easily. In contrast, older users, despite possessing professional authority or expertise, may find their contributions undervalued. This dynamic reproduces social stratification in digital form, where symbolic visibility replaces institutional hierarchy as a key marker of value.

Symbolic power functions as a reflexive and self-reinforcing mechanism within digital fields. Users who attain visibility not only benefit from existing platform norms but also contribute to their reproduction by modelling what constitutes "successful" participation. These high-visibility practices become templates for others, gradually codifying into the platform's doxa and shaping the expectations that future users internalize. This recursive process consolidates generational asymmetries, privileging cohorts whose communicative tempo, aesthetic fluency, and engagement styles align with the platform's algorithmic logics.

Through the dynamic interaction of platform doxa, digital habitus, and digital capital, symbolic power emerges as the capacity to attain visibility, legitimacy, and recognition within digital ecosystems. It operates subtly through algorithmic ranking mechanisms, engagement metrics such as likes, shares, and follows, as well as broader cultural validation processes that confer legitimacy on particular forms of expression. Generational cohorts whose digital practices and literacies correspond with platform-specific norms accrue symbolic power more easily, thereby reinforcing their social standing and influence in networked environments. Conversely, when users' dispositions or communicative preferences diverge from these normative expectations, they experience symbolic marginalization, as their contributions are rendered less visible, less valued, or culturally illegible within dominant digital discourses.

In essence, the IDHF model conceptualizes digital participation as a structured, unequal field where technological fluency, generational habitus, and platform norms intersect. It demonstrates that symbolic power in digital environments is not merely a function of access or skill but also of alignment with the algorithmic and cultural logics that govern participation. This theoretical lens thus bridges classical sociological theory with contemporary digital realities, offering an explanatory framework for understanding generational disparities in digital visibility, influence, and inclusion.

Figure 1 shows that neither digital habitus nor digital capital alone guarantees influence. Only when they are expressed in ways that align with the platform doxa can they be turned into symbolic power. This explains why some highly knowledgeable or skilled individuals remain marginalized online if their communication style does not align with the platform's implicit rules.

*Figure 1. IDHF model- illustrates that both digital habitus and digital capital directly shape platform doxa, which then determines the allocation of symbolic power in digital settings (Author's own work)*

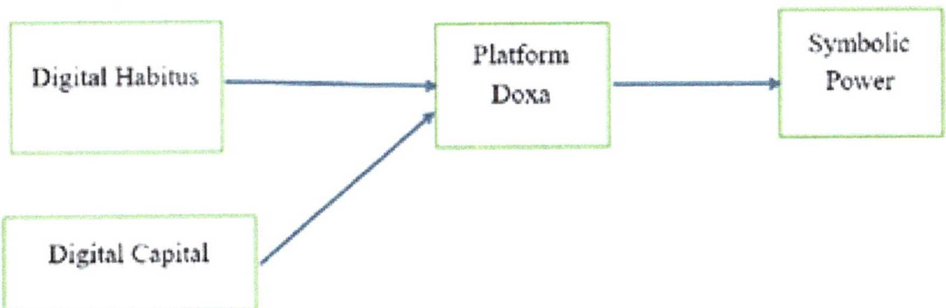


5.1.1 Baby Boomers (1946-1964)

Digital Habitus Characteristics: The Baby Boomer generation exhibits a cautious and privacy-minded approach to digital engagement, preferring text-based communication methods. Their habits are profoundly shaped by traditional media consumption and the norms of broadcast media. This generation's digital habitus shows a transitional relationship with technology, where traditional literacy practices influence their digital adoption behaviours.

Digital Capital Formation: This group exhibits low to moderate digital capital, characterized by limited platform fluency but strong traditional literacy skills. Their digital skills are mainly focused on basic communication technologies rather than advanced platform navigation or content creation abilities.

Platform Behavioural Patterns: Baby Boomers primarily exhibit passive consumption habits, favouring established platforms such as Facebook, while rarely creating content on YouTube. Their platform activity is characterized by limited participation in sharing viral content or engaging with digital trends, indicating a preference for familiar and reliable communication channels.

Symbolic Power Dynamics: Although they play a fundamental role in building digital infrastructure, Baby Boomers often find themselves on the margins of modern digital conversations. Their contributions are often overlooked in fast-paced, performance-driven digital environments that prioritize technological skills over hands-on experience.

5.1.2 Generation X (1965-1980)

Digital Habitus Characteristics: Generation X exhibits a transitional digital habitus that skillfully combines analog professionalism with strategic digital use. This cohort demonstrates advanced code-switching abilities, seamlessly shifting between formal and informal digital environments while maintaining their focus on professional networking.

Digital Capital Formation: With moderate digital capital, Generation X effectively adapts to both formal institutional digital requirements and informal social networking environments. Their digital skills demonstrate a pragmatic approach to technology adoption, emphasizing utility and professional development rather than cultural engagement.

Platform Behavioural Patterns: This generation demonstrates goal-driven platform use, mainly favouring LinkedIn for professional networking while using WhatsApp and Facebook for targeted information sharing and maintaining relationships. Their approach to digital platforms focuses on functional networking rather than entertainment or self-expression.

Symbolic Power Dynamics: Generation X holds a moderately acknowledged position in digital hierarchies, often overshadowed by more digitally native generations despite having considerable institutional experience and cross-platform skills. Their symbolic capital is often undervalued in favour of performative digital fluency.

5.1.3 Millennials (1981-1995)

Digital Habitus Characteristics: Millennials display an adaptable, multitasking digital habitus driven by identity-focused platform engagement. Their digital behaviours were shaped mainly during the early social network era and the adoption of mobile technology, resulting in advanced platform navigation skills and content curation abilities.

Digital Capital Formation: This cohort demonstrates high levels of digital capital, exhibiting strong entrepreneurial instincts and advanced networking skills across various platforms. Their digital literacy includes both technical ability and cultural understanding within various online communities.

Platform Behavioural Patterns: Millennials act as content curators, maintaining active presences across Instagram, Twitter, and LinkedIn, while strategically balancing genuine self-expression with personal branding. Their platform behaviour reflects a sophisticated understanding of audience segmentation and content optimization strategies.

Symbolic Power Dynamics: Millennials possess significant symbolic capital within digital environments, with their cultural visibility strengthened through strategic alignment with platform algorithms and aesthetic standards. Their influence comes from effectively combining personal authenticity with digital marketing principles.

5.1.4 Generation Z (1996-2012)

Digital Habitus Characteristics: Generation Z exhibits a performative, highly literate digital habitus, one that has developed alongside rapidly changing social media platforms. Their digital practices focus on real-time content creation, managing multi-platform presence, and a sophisticated understanding of algorithmic systems.

Digital Capital Formation: With exceptionally high digital capital, Generation Z demonstrates fluent engagement across multiple platforms simultaneously, showcasing advanced content creation skills and an intuitive understanding of digital monetization strategies. Their digital competencies include both technical expertise and cultural trend awareness.

Platform Behavioural Patterns: This generation actively participates on TikTok, Instagram, Snapchat, and Discord, focusing on authentic self-expression, community building, and trend creation. Their platform behaviour shows comfort with constant connectivity and multi-modal communication strategies.

Symbolic Power Dynamics: Generation Z holds a leading role in today's digital symbolic economies, exerting significant cultural influence through trendsetting, platform innovation, and genuine engagement strategies. Their symbolic power comes from their innate understanding of digital culture creation and dissemination.

5.1.5 Generation Alpha (2013-2024)

Digital Habitus Characteristics: Generation Alpha demonstrates an instinctive, immersive digital habitus primarily shaped by AI-native technologies and voice interaction systems. Their digital behaviours develop through gamified learning experiences, marking the first generation to experience the seamless integration of physical and digital realities from birth.

Digital Capital Formation: This emerging cohort exhibits rapidly growing digital capital, built through parental guidance and early exposure to unprecedented technology. Their digital skills are developing through interactive, multimodal learning systems that emphasize experiential over traditional textual literacy.

Platform Behavioural Patterns: Generation Alpha tends to prefer fleeting, immersive formats, showing strong interest in AR/VR experiences, YouTube Kids content, and Roblox gaming environments. Their platform engagement primarily occurs through gamified interfaces and screenless interaction modes, marking a significant shift toward embodied digital experiences.

Symbolic Power Dynamics: Although still developing its symbolic power, Generation Alpha shows potential to fundamentally reshape digital cultural norms through the adoption of immersive technology and hyper-personalization. Their emerging influence suggests a future digital landscape characterized by AI-mediated, spatially aware interaction models.

*Table 2. Intergenerational Digital Habitus Framework (IDHF)*

| Generational Cohort | Digital Habitus | Digital Capital | Platform Behaviour | Symbolic Power Position |
|---|---|---|---|---|
| Baby Boomers (1946–1964) | Cautious, privacy-oriented, text-heavy, influenced by print and broadcast media norms. | Low to moderate, limited platform fluency, strong traditional literacy. | Passive consumption, prefers email, Facebook, YouTube; limited participation in viral or performative trends. | Often, marginalized contributions are undervalued in fast-paced, performative digital cultures. |
| Generation X (1965–1980) | Transitional, mixes analogue professionalism with early digital adoption. | Moderate, adapts to both formal and informal digital spaces. | Goal-oriented, prefers LinkedIn, WhatsApp, and Facebook for professional networking and information sharing. | Moderately recognized, often overshadowed by performative fluency despite institutional experience. |
| Millennials (1981–1995) | Adaptive, multitasking, identity-driven, shaped by early social networks and mobile adoption. | Highly skilled in strong entrepreneurial and networking digital literacy. | Content curators, who are active on Instagram, Twitter, and LinkedIn, strike a balance between authenticity and branding. | High symbolic capital, visibility enhanced by alignment with platform doxa and aesthetic norms. |
| Generation Z (1996–2012) | Performative, meme-literate, participatory, socialized in algorithmic, real-time environments. | Very high, deeply fluent in participatory culture and content creation. | Hyperactive engagement on TikTok, Snapchat, and Discord, with a preference for short-form, visual, and ephemeral formats. | Dominant symbolic power, trendsetters, and cultural curators; vulnerable to algorithmic manipulation. |
| Generation Alpha (2013 - 2024) | Intuitive, immersive, AI-native, shaped by gamified and voice-based technologies. | Emerging rapidly, scaffolded by parental digital guidance and early tech exposure. | Prefers AR/VR, YouTube Kids, and Roblox, engages through gamified or screenless platforms. | Symbolic power in formation, likely to redefine norms via immersive tech and hyper-personalization. |

Source: Author's own work

Table 2 illustrates the key concepts of the Intergenerational Digital Habitus Framework (IDHF).

The Intergenerational Digital Habitus Framework (IDHF) provides organizations and managers with a structured lens to understand how generational dispositions shape employees' digital behaviours, preferences, and competencies. IDHF enables a systematic diagnosis of how digital capital is distributed and reproduced within the workplace, revealing hidden inequalities that affect collaboration, innovation, and performance.

For managers, IDHF functions as a diagnostic and developmental tool. It helps identify the symbolic hierarchies and implicit platform doxa that privilege certain forms of digital participation, such as performative visibility on internal communication tools, while marginalizing others. Recognizing these asymmetries enables managers to design interventions that equalize access to digital resources, mitigate intergenerational friction, and promote inclusive participation.

At the organizational level, IDHF informs policies on digital transformation, learning design, and performance evaluation. It highlights the need to value diverse digital competencies rather than equating digital fluency with productivity. By mapping employees' digital habitus, organizations can tailor training programs, cross-generational mentorship, and platform use strategies to bridge skill gaps and encourage mutual learning.

In strategic terms, applying the IDHF allows leadership to align digital habitus with organizational goals. It encourages reflexive evaluation of digital tools not just as technical systems, but as social fields where symbolic power is at play. This perspective enables managers to anticipate resistance to technological change, mitigate digital exclusion, and design communication ecosystems that prioritize contribution quality over visibility.The IDHF empowers organizations to move from technology adoption to digital inclusion, transforming digital engagement from a generational divide into a collective organizational asset.

## 5.1 Operationalization for Managers

1. Diagnostic Mapping (Rapid Audit)
    - Conduct surveys to assess platform use frequency, self-efficacy in digital engagement, and perceived value of platforms.
    - Perform network analysis to identify patterns of engagement, examining who receives attention and from which actors.
    - Conduct a content audit to determine which genres are prioritized according to internal KPIs and visibility metrics.
2. Metric Redesign
    - Replace raw visibility counts with quality-weighted indicators incorporating peer-rated usefulness and task relevance.
    - Introduce equity-focused metrics to monitor the distribution of visibility across different generational cohorts and socioeconomic proxies.
3. Targeted Interventions
    - Reconfigure platform algorithms to reduce the weighting of gamified features that disproportionately reward performative content.
    - Develop role-based scaffolds such as templates and micro-rituals to support staff who are less fluent in platform-specific genres.

- Establish cross-cohort mentorship pairs with reciprocal goals, facilitating senior staff sharing domain expertise alongside junior staff imparting platform literacy.

4. Curriculum and Learning Design
   - Transition from one-off training sessions to embedding contextualized learning within work tasks and workflows.
   - Employ co-designed microprojects where mixed-cohort teams collaboratively produce platform-mediated outputs, fostering peer learning and knowledge exchange.
5. Policy and Governance
   - Publish transparent norms and criteria governing internal visibility algorithms.
   - Implement formal appeal and moderation processes to address visibility penalties or exclusions, ensuring fairness and accountability.
6. Evaluation
   - Use pre- and post-intervention assessments to measure task performance, perceptions of procedural fairness, and diversity among visible contributors.
   - Conduct longitudinal tracking of how digital acts translate into organizational outcomes such as promotions and assignments.

If internal recognition is driven by likes, younger staff members who post micro-insights tend to dominate. IDHF recommends replacing likes with a peer-evaluation rubric tied to task outcomes. IDHF suggests asynchronous participation designs and alternative contribution modes.

## 5.2 Strategies for promoting intergenerational equity in digital participation and social recognition

### 5.2.1 Equitable Symbolic Recognition

Equitable symbolic recognition within digital platforms signifies that all participants, regardless of their social identity, digital capital, or alignment with prevailing platform norms, have their contributions acknowledged as meaningful and valuable within the field. It requires moving beyond surface metrics of popularity or engagement to consider the diverse forms of labor, creativity, and expertise that different users bring, especially those from historically marginalized groups. Achieving equity in symbolic recognition entails redesigning algorithms, moderation practices, and platform governance to counteract inherited biases and broaden the criteria for what counts as legitimate participation. Such recognition empowers marginalized users to accrue symbolic capital, prestige, trust, and influence, which in turn enables their greater agency, visibility, and voice within the digital arena. Institutionalizing equitable symbolic recognition ultimately supports more inclusive and transformative online environments, where structural barriers to acknowledgment and participation are dismantled, and where diverse knowledges and experiences can reshape the very logics of digital fields.

### 5.2.2 *Platform Field Participation*

Effective participation in digital workplaces and social media environments requires understanding not only of access but also of the implicit cultural and symbolic norms, which Bourdieu describes as the "field" that governs engagement. Participation within the platform field involves ongoing negotiation, competition, and adaptation, as users seek to accumulate platform-relevant forms of capital (such as followers, trust scores, or endorsements) and convert them into status or symbolic power, all while navigating doxa. These implicit norms define legitimate presence and practices within the platform. This perspective reveals that inequalities deeply structure digital participation; those whose habitus aligns with platform doxa and who possess more relevant capital are better positioned to succeed and shape the field's trajectory, while marginalized users are more likely to experience symbolic exclusion or struggle for recognition. Therefore, achieving participatory equity demands efforts beyond technical training, including cultivating cultural literacy, understanding social norms, and grasping the context of platform practices.

### 5.2.3 *Cross-Generational Digital Community Building*

Cross-generational digital community building is rooted in the intentional design of inclusive environments that leverage the strengths, perspectives, and experiences of members across different age cohorts. Effective strategies include fostering structured mentorship and reverse-mentoring programs, where younger users share digital skills while older members provide historical context, wisdom, and industry insight. Successful communities adopt flexible participation models including a blend of synchronous and asynchronous activities that accommodate varying schedules, communication preferences, and levels of digital fluency. Recognizing and celebrating diverse forms of contribution, from storytelling and knowledge sharing to problem-solving, enriches the learning landscape and creates a sense of belonging for all generations. Open dialogue, respect for distinct communicative styles, and the establishment of intergenerational leadership roles further strengthen these communities, creating resilient digital ecosystems where innovation, empathy, and social cohesion thrive.

### 5.2.4 *Capital-Based Engagement Strategy*

A capital-based engagement strategy in digital platforms centers on the purposeful deployment and accumulation of various forms of capital, economic, social, cultural, and symbolic, to maximize visibility, influence, and rewards within a platform field. Platform participants leverage their pre-existing assets (such as technical skills, network connections, institutional prestige, or cultural fluency) to align their engagement with the platform's implicit norms and algorithmic preferences, thus enhancing their chances of being recognized, promoted, or materially rewarded. This strategy often manifests as the cultivation of curated digital profiles, strategic self-presentation, active networking, and content production tailored to trending aesthetics or topics, all aimed at converting one form of capital, such as social connections or cultural knowledge, into symbolic capital, like follower counts or endorsement badges. The effectiveness of such strategies is shaped by the alignment between the user's digital capital and the doxa of the platform, favoring those who can nimbly adapt or who already possess advantageous capital, while deepening inequalities for users without these resources.

### 5.2.5 *Redressing Symbolic Power Asymmetries*

Redressing symbolic power asymmetry on digital platforms requires deliberate interventions that challenge the structural, algorithmic, and cultural dynamics sustaining inequality in recognition, influence, and voice. Effective strategies involve making dominant forms of capital and platform norms more transparent, expanding the criteria for meaningful participation, and designing mechanisms for representation and visibility that account for the diverse social identities and lived experiences of users. Achieving equity in symbolic recognition entails reconfiguring algorithms and moderation systems to counteract historical bias, instituting inclusive governance practices, and empowering marginalized users through capacity-building and cross-group alliances. Importantly, counter-power can be activated through collective user agency ("crowd" power) and participatory co-design, which unsettles concentrated authority and redistributes symbolic capital within the field. The goal is not only to correct instances of exclusion but also to transform the field's rules and structures, ensuring that digital platforms foster equal participation.

### 5.2.6 *Reflexively Designed Digital Fields*

Reflexively designed digital fields are those online environments purposefully constructed with ongoing critical awareness of how technological architectures, algorithms, and user practices co-create social realities and shape power relations.

These fields move beyond conventional user-centered design by embedding inclusivity, ethical deliberation, and participatory feedback into every step of platform development and governance. Reflexive design acknowledges that digital platforms are not neutral arenas but active agents shaping identity, norms, and social hierarchies, and therefore require a continuous feedback loop between designers, users, and stakeholders to ensure alignment with evolving values of inclusion, justice, and sustainability. Such environments invite transparency about persuasive mechanisms, prioritize diverse experiences, and empower both users and designers to question, adapt, and redesign digital spaces in response to changing needs, unforeseen consequences, and ethical dilemmas. Ultimately, reflexively designed digital fields foster adaptive, inclusive, and ethically attuned technology, enabling more democratic participation and reducing the risk of entrenched symbolic power asymmetries.

### 5.2.7 *Transgenerational Digital Learning Loops*

Transgenerational digital learning loops refer to the ongoing, reciprocal exchange of knowledge, skills, and cultural practices across multiple generations within digital environments. These learning loops leverage the strengths of both elder and younger participants, fostering mentorship, reverse mentoring, and collaborative innovation in ways not possible in single-generation or hierarchical learning settings. Mature cohorts contribute historical context, ethical reasoning, and experiential wisdom, while youth introduce emerging technologies and digital literacies, resulting in resilient communities able to adapt to rapid socio-technical change. Crucially, digital platforms designed to support transgenerational learning loops incorporate asynchronous modes, multimodal resources, and interface flexibility, enabling a dynamic flow of learning that transcends age-based digital divides. By systematically nurturing these feedback mechanisms across time and generations, digital fields enhance collective intelligence, bridge cultural and cognitive gaps, and ensure the long-term sustainability of community knowledge and capacity for innovation.

Table 3 highlights the theoretical and applied dimensions of the IDHF concepts, providing actionable insights for digital inclusion and intergenerational collaboration in digital environments.

*Table 3. Intergenerational Digital Habitus Framework (IDHF): Concepts and Applications*

| Concepts | Description in IDHF Context |
|---|---|
| **Digital Capital Formation** | Digital capital acts as a form of bridging capital, facilitating conversion between economic, cultural, and social capital. Intergenerational exchange should be bidirectional: younger cohorts' technological fluency becomes cultural and social capital for older employees, while elder knowledge contributes valuable digital wisdom. Platforms and workplaces must foster mutual capital conversion, moving beyond unidirectional skill transfer models. |
| **Habitus-Mediated Digital Practices** | Digital literacy encompasses both ethical responsibility and digital citizenship, as well as technical proficiency. Generational digital habitus shapes diverse orientations towards privacy, authenticity, and self-presentation. Frameworks must acknowledge these embodied differences rather than imposing uniform digital behaviours across generations. |
| **Scaffolded Digital Learning Ecosystems** | Digital engagement is fundamentally social and contextual. Rather than linear training approaches, intergenerational collaborative problem-solving should be prioritized. Peer mentorship networks must value complementary expertise across cohorts, transcending the traditional expert–novice dichotomy. |
| **Digital Inclusion Through Capital Redistribution** | Older generations often experience digital and physical spheres distinctly, whereas younger cohorts navigate their convergence. Hybrid participation models should respect these differences, enabling meaningful contribution without demanding complete digital immersion, and recognize multiple legitimate modes of digital engagement. |
| **Intergenerational Digital Community Building** | Digital communities of practice can mitigate generational divides by fostering shared projects, rotating expertise based on contextual needs, and institutionalizing memory systems that enable digital natives to document elder knowledge. While elders provide historical and contextual frameworks for innovation. |
| **Reflexive Digital Engagement Strategy** | Power dynamics often characterize digital relationships across generations. Critical digital pedagogy must explore how technologies reinforce or dismantle hierarchies. Inclusive participatory design and digital storytelling frameworks should validate and integrate diverse generational perspectives on technological change. |
| **Temporal Digital Power Redistribution** | Generations experience digital time differently: the immediacy culture of younger generations may clash with the more reflective temporalities of elders. Asynchronous collaboration tools and principles of temporal sovereignty allow communities to define their own rhythms and practices of digital engagement. |
| **Transgenerational Digital Learning Loops** | Beyond unidirectional knowledge transfer, recursive learning systems promote continuous interplay where digital innovation informs tradition and vice versa. Innovation labs and legacy partnerships foster collaborative knowledge preservation and problem-solving across generations. |

Source: Author's own work

## 5.3 Key Interventions and Strategies to Address Disparities

1. Reverse and Reciprocal Mentorship Programs: Pair younger, tech-savvy employees with older colleagues to facilitate bidirectional learning. Younger mentors share platform skills and digital communication practices, while senior employees

provide strategic insights, institutional knowledge, and critical reflection. These dynamic challenges hierarchical norms and values, fostering diverse digital and experiential capitals that boost innovation, collaboration, and cross-generational respect.

2. Reflexive Platform Design: Develop customizable interfaces that accommodate a range of communication preferences, text, audio, video, emojis, and longer-form content. Features like adjustable engagement metrics and diverse content visibility formats enable inclusivity for users who are unfamiliar or uncomfortable with popular digital vernaculars, such as memes or hashtags. This flexibility fosters accessibility and expressive diversity.
3. Digital Literacy Equity Programs: Implement continuous, non-punitive upskilling initiatives tailored across generations, including collaborative workshops, peer coaching, and digital fluency labs. These programs address the so-called second-level digital divide, empowering all employees to navigate and contribute confidently within evolving enterprise systems.
4. Transparent Platform Norms and Onboarding: Provide explicit guidance on informal digital workplace norms, including expected communication style, responsiveness, and visual conventions. Clarifying platform doxa reduces symbolic misunderstandings, especially for employees primarily socialized in analog or formal institutional settings, thereby promoting equitable inclusion.
5. Inclusive Recognition Systems: Redesign reward and recognition frameworks (badges, leaderboards, kudos) to value a wide range of contributions: mentoring, sharing institutional knowledge, problem-solving, and thoughtful engagement. This change shifts symbolic capital from just speed or popularity to quality, impact, and collaborative behaviours.
6. Cross-Generational Project Teams: Purposefully create age-diverse digital workgroups with clearly defined roles, leveraging generational strengths, storytelling, technical skills, and strategic insights. These teams encourage shared ownership and open dialogue, helping to break down epistemic silos caused by differences in media use and interpretation across generations.
7. Embedding digital equity goals in organizational policies and leadership agendas guarantees sustained investment in digital inclusion, measuring progress through regular assessment and user feedback.
8. Equity Audits of Digital Participation: Regularly analyze digital engagement patterns to identify visible contributors and those who are marginalized across age, gender, and intersectional identities. These audits reveal symbolic inequities, informing reflective governance and policies that aim to promote inclusive participation.
9. Flexible Communication Norms: Promote asynchronous participation alongside real-time interactions to accommodate differences in communication styles

across generations. Supporting diverse temporal rhythms improves cognitive inclusion and leads to richer, more meaningful digital engagement.

## 6. RESULTS AND DISCUSSION

The findings of the study validate social media platforms as structured fields of symbolic power, where generational differences in digital habitus critically impact participation, visibility, and social influence. The Intergenerational Digital Habitus Framework (IDHF) reveals that digital inequality arises systematically from the interplay of users' digital habitus, digital capital, and alignment with platform doxa.

The study reveals clear generational differences; younger generations, such as Generation Z and Millennials, who possess high digital platform skills, visual literacy, and quick engagement, hold most of the symbolic power and benefit from aligning with platform doxa. In contrast, older groups such as Baby Boomers and Generation X, whose digital interactions are more thoughtful, text-based, and cautious, often face symbolic marginalization despite their accumulated institutional knowledge and expertise.

The IDHF provides critical insights into the mechanisms that reproduce digital stratification. The platform doxa privilege brevity, immediacy, and visual performativity, creating hierarchies that are not meritocratic but culturally and algorithmically designed. Equity audits and reflexive platform designs emerge as vital interventions.

Customized interfaces, asynchronous participation, and multimodal communication foster inclusivity by validating diverse literacies and reducing cognitive overload. Significantly, recognition systems must move beyond visibility metrics, such as likes, to incorporate qualitative evaluations that emphasize strategic insight and contextual depth. Cross-generational mentorship, which combines digital fluency with institutional wisdom, enhances knowledge exchange and disrupts entrenched symbolic inequalities.

Roblox exemplifies how symbolic power operates in digital platforms by transforming monetary investments in gaming platforms into symbolic capital and symbolic violence. Players accumulate symbolic capital in two primary forms: prestige, derived from purchasing exclusive virtual items and memberships, and reputation, gained through recognized developer or creator status and verification badges. These markers create visible social hierarchies that players internalize as normal criteria for belonging, thus normalizing economic disparities as natural distinctions.

Collectively, findings emphasize the necessity for platform and organizational governance that foregrounds symbolic equity, enabling diverse forms of digital participation and mitigating intergenerational divides rooted in habitus and capital disparities.

## 7. CONCLUSION

The Intergenerational Digital Habitus Framework advances a comprehensive sociological understanding of digital inequality, situating generational digital practices within a structured field shaped by habitus, capital, and doxa. This framework transcends simplistic notions of digital access or skill, highlighting symbolic power as a relational and algorithmically mediated phenomenon that privileges particular generational dispositions and communication styles.

Effective digital inclusion demands culturally attuned and reflexive approaches, integrating flexible interfaces, inclusive recognition metrics, and sustained cross-generational learning ecosystems. By acknowledging and valuing complementary digital and experiential capitals, organizations and platforms can disrupt symbolic exclusions and foster environments where diverse contributions are legitimized.

The study's implications extend into policy and design, underscoring the importance of transparency in algorithmic governance, equitable metric design, and scaffolding for bidirectional mentorship. Addressing digital symbolic power disparities is essential for cultivating democratic, equitable participation in contemporary digital fields, be they social media, enterprise social media, or virtual gaming platforms like Roblox.

Closing intergenerational digital divides requires moving beyond access to the deeper cultural and symbolic structures that govern digital visibility and legitimacy, ensuring that digital transformation realizes its emancipatory potential across all age cohorts. Organizations that successfully apply these principles will be better equipped to use the full range of human talent while encouraging innovative solutions that leverage the strengths of various generations.

## REFERENCES


Abidin, C., Lee, J., & Kaye, D. B. V. (2023). Introduction to the Media International Australia special issue on "TikTok cultures in the Asia Pacific.". *Media International Australia, 186*(1), 3–10. DOI: 10.1177/1329878x221130126

Bourdieu, P. (1984). *A social critique of the judgement of taste.*

Bourdieu, P. (1989). Economisch kapitaal, cultureel kapitaal, sociaal kapitaal. *Opstellen over smaak, habitus en het veldbegrip*, 120-141.

Bourdieu, P. (1990). The logic of practice. *Polity.*

Bourdieu, P. (1991). Language and symbolic power. *Polity.*

Bourdieu, P. (2011). The forms of capital.(1986). *Cultural theory: An anthology, 1*(81-93), 949.

Bourdieu, P. (2020). Outline of a Theory of Practice. In *The new social theory reader* (pp. 80–86). Routledge.

Boyd, D. (2014). *It's complicated: The social lives of networked teens.* Yale University Press.

Calderon Gomez, D. (2021). The third digital divide and Bourdieu: Bidirectional conversion of economic, cultural, and social capital to (and from) digital capital among young people in Madrid. *New Media & Society, 23*(9), 2534–2553.

Carr, C. T., & Hayes, R. A. (2015). Social media: Defining, developing, and divining. *Atlantic Journal of Communication, 23*(1), 46–65. DOI: 10.1080/15456870.2015.972282

Costa, C., Burke, C., & Murphy, M. (2019). Capturing habitus: Theory, method and reflexivity. *International Journal of Research & Method in Education, 42*(1), 19–32.

Cotter, K. (2019). Playing the visibility game: How digital influencers and algorithms negotiate influence on Instagram. *New Media & Society, 21*(4), 895–913.

Couldry, N. (2012). Media, society, world: Social theory and digital media practice. *Polity.*

DiMaggio, P., Hargittai, E., Celeste, C., & Shafer, S. (2004). Digital inequality: From unequal access to differentiated use. *Social inequality*, 355-400.

Friemel, T. N. (2016). The digital divide has grown old: Determinants of a digital divide among seniors. *New Media & Society*, *18*(2), 313–331. DOI: 10.1177/1461444814538648

Gillespie, T. (2021). The Politics of "Platforms". *Questions de communication, 40*(2), 23-46.

Hargittai, E., & Dobransky, K. (2017). Old dogs, new clicks: Digital inequality in skills and uses among older adults. *Canadian Journal of Communication*, *42*(2), 195–212. DOI: 10.22230/cjc.2017v42n2a3176

Kim, Y., & Kim, S. (2023). Motives for Following Social Influencers and Electronic Word-of-Mouth: The Role of Social Capital. *International Journal of Communication*, *17*, 22.

Leidner, D. E., Gonzalez, E., & Koch, H. (2020). An affordance perspective of enterprise social media and organizational socialization. In *Strategic information management* (pp. 364–402). Routledge.

Livingstone, S., & Helsper, E. (2007). Gradations in digital inclusion: Children, young people and the digital divide. *New Media & Society*, *9*(4), 671–696.

Ng, R., & Indran, N. (2022). Hostility Toward Baby Boomers on TikTok. *The Gerontologist*, *62*(8), 1196–1206. DOI: 10.1093/geront/gnac020

Oktavianingtyas, I., Rusadi, U., Jamalullail, J., & Napitupulu, F. (2025). The role of symbolic capital and symbolic violence in shaping social hierarchies through digital consumption and production in Roblox online game. *Bricolage: Jurnal Magister Ilmu Komunikasi*, *11*(2), 213–224.

Parry, E., & Urwin, P. (2011). Generational differences in work values: A review of theory and evidence: Generational differences in work values. *International Journal of Management Reviews*, *13*(1), 79–96. DOI: 10.1111/j.1468-2370.2010.00285.x

Ragnedda, M. (2018). Conceptualizing digital capital. *Telematics and Informatics*, *35*(8), 2366–2375. DOI: 10.1016/j.tele.2018.10.006

Ragnedda, M. (2019). Conceptualising the digital divide. *Mapping digital divide in Africa: A mediated analysis*, 27-44.

Ragnedda, M., & Ruiu, M. L. (2017). Social capital and the three levels of digital divide. In *Theorizing digital divides* (pp. 21–34). Routledge.

Robinson, L., Cotten, S. R., Ono, H., Quan-Haase, A., Mesch, G., Chen, W., & Stern, M. J. (2015). Digital inequalities and why they matter. *Information Communication and Society*, *18*(5), 569–582.

Sarraf, A. R. A. (2019). Generational groups in different countries. [IJSSH]. *International Journal of Social Science and Humanity*, *4*(1), 41–52.

Teng, L. S. (2020). Bracing for the Multi-Generational Workforce. *Management Review*, *31*(3), 324–345.

Treem, J. W., & Leonardi, P. M. (2013). Social media use in organizations: Exploring the affordances of visibility, editability, persistence, and association. *Annals of the International Communication Association*, *36*(1), 143–189.

van Deursen, A. J., & van Dijk, J. A. (2014). The digital divide shifts to differences in usage. *New Media & Society*, *16*(3), 507–526. DOI: 10.1177/1461444813487959

Van Dijck, J. (2013). *The culture of connectivity: A critical history of social media*. Oxford University Press.

Van Dijck, José, & Poell, T. (2013). Understanding Social Media Logic. *Media and Communication*, *1*(1), 2–14. DOI: 10.17645/mac.v1i1.70

Van Dijck, J., Poell, T., & De Waal, M. (2018). *The platform society: Public values in a connective world*. Oxford university press.

Vosoughi, S., Roy, D., & Aral, S. (2018). The spread of true and false news online. *Science*, *359*(6380), 1146–1151. DOI: 10.1126/science.aap9559

# Chapter 6
# The Impact of Social Media Platforms on Violent Behavior

**Derya Şahin**
https://orcid.org/0000-0003-3640-021X
*Sinop University, Turkey*

## ABSTRACT

*This study examines how violent behavior is produced and socialized through social media within the framework of symbolic interactionism. Violence is regarded not merely as a physical act but as a phenomenon grounded in meaning and interaction. In digital environments, individuals use violent content as a means of identity construction and visibility, transforming violence into a normalized form of communication. Based on Mead's concept of the self, Goffman's role theory, and Blumer's principles of symbolic interactionism, social media is interpreted as a stage where violence is symbolically performed. The findings reveal that violence is reproduced in digital spaces through symbols, emotions, and interactions, and that individuals simultaneously experience the roles of perpetrator, victim, and observer.*

## INTRODUCTION

People are born with certain needs. Among these, nutrition, shelter, and eating are the most basic; however, individuals also establish their existence through communication. Humans are defined as biopsychosocial beings. Therefore, during socialization and the process of self-actualization, individuals interact subjectively with every object or person in their environment. Prior to the contemporary period, communication was generally conducted face-to-face using specific symbols, signs,

DOI: 10.4018/979-8-3373-4267-2.ch006

words, or body language. However, due to significant technological developments, mass communication tools have gained importance as primary means of socialization, replacing family, school, and environment (Çelik, 2018).

Social media platforms have caused significant changes by affecting the dynamics of daily life (Tiryaki, 2023:749). Digital platforms play an important role in managing entertainment, work, and personal development opportunities, as well as facilitating socialization. Yet, alongside these advantages, they can also create potential risks for individuals (Özgür & Özkul, 2022:553). Among these risks, violence, which manifests itself on digital platforms and in media, is particularly prominent. This study aims to explain how interactions on digital platforms influence the social construction of violence by creating and reinforcing symbolic meanings that shape identity and power.

In this study, violence refers specifically to the symbolic and mediated forms of aggression expressed through social media interactions, excluding purely physical or institutional violence. Among various digital spaces, platforms such as TikTok, X (Twitter), Instagram, and YouTube serve as symbolic arenas where aggression and recognition dynamics intertwine (Şimşek, 2012).

## 1. CONCEPTUAL FRAMEWORK

### 1.a. Violence

Violence is defined as symbolic or direct words, actions, or behaviours that threaten an individual's physical and psychological integrity, involving negative emotions such as anger, aggression, fear, and competition, with the intent to cause harm (Yener, 2023). While violence is often described as a lack of sociability, Collins (2008) defines it as weakness, exhaustion, and helplessness, with culture, space, background, and interaction as important conditions (Bal, 2014, p.9). In communication habits emerging particularly on the internet and social media platforms, individuals may feel a sense of freedom outside social boundaries. Thus, all negative emotions, attitudes, and rule-breaking tendencies in an individual's chaotic inner world are transferred to the communication space and given the opportunity to be displayed (Çelik, 2018).

Addressing violence solely from the perspective of one discipline is insufficient. As a social phenomenon, violence requires comprehensive examination, especially from a sociological perspective. The sociological approach focuses on social interaction processes among individuals, demonstrating that a person's personality is shaped by societal norms. During socialization, many positive and negative attitudes and behaviours are learned within a social context. This indicates that violence is internalized through imitation and reproduced within social relationships (Yener, 2023).

In sociology, violence is considered among other categories of human activity. In Talcott Parsons' functional-structural systems theory, violence is assessed as one of four equivalent forms of social control. According to Parsons, the first form is intentional, where positive sanctions, such as persuasion, are applied. Negative sanctions appear in the form of appeals to shared norms, involving a moral appeal, an example of which could be blackmail. The second form operates through situational channels, such as economic exchange with positive sanctions, whereas negative sanctions in situational channels rely on the use of force (Parsons, 1964). Mider (2013) reports that Sztompka classifies social actions along two axes: the type of social action directed at an individual (social interaction or social relationship) and the individual's evaluation of this action (acceptance or rejection). Social interactions accepted by the individual create an influence based on personal authority, while interactions that are not accepted manifest as forms of violence (Mider, 2013:703).

The understanding of violence is not limited to physical acts; it also includes threats such as discrimination or defamation, aligning with Mead's symbolic interactionist approach. In this regard, Garver's (1973) concept of "silent personal violence" refers to the undermining of an individual's autonomy through the manipulation of symbols, while Bourdieu's concept of "symbolic violence" reveals the internalized, invisible forms of societal pressure at the social level. Thus, verbal or non-verbal insults, discriminatory rhetoric, and psychological abuse can be interpreted as attacks on an individual's world of meaning through both Mead's symbolic interactionism and Bourdieu's symbolic violence framework (Mider, 2013).

## 1.b. Social Media

With the widespread use of the internet, social media platforms have become an essential and integral part of everyday life. Social media is defined as "the use of web-based and mobile technologies to transform communication into an interactive dialogue" (Erol, 2022:1129). Widely used platforms include Facebook, X, and Instagram, among many others. Social media encompasses various forms, including magazines, internet forums, weblogs, microblogs, social blogs, wikis, podcasts, photos, videos, images, ratings, and social tagging (Erol, 2022:1129).

While social media increases activity in every field, its liberal nature can also facilitate misinformation and provide a selective environment for unwanted behaviours, thoughts, or group dynamics. Due to intensive usage, these platforms can lead to addiction, health problems, violations of information privacy and personal data, sexual violence, fraud, and promotion of harmful substances such as drugs, negatively affecting especially children and adolescents. Violence on social media, also referred to as digital violence, is one of these risks (Ilgın, 2021:305; Erol, 2022:1132).

## 1.c. Digital Media Violence

Digital media violence poses a public health threat to the extent that it leads to an increase in real-world violence and aggression. Social media violence, referred to as digital violence, is defined as "harmful behaviours in which an individual or group uses technology to target, threaten, humiliate, expose to hate speech, or damage the reputation of another individual or group" (Şener, & Abınık, 2021). According to the European Council (2024), digital violence is "the use of computer systems to cause, facilitate, or threaten violence against individuals, resulting in or likely to result in physical, sexual, psychological, or economic harm or suffering, including the exploitation of an individual's circumstances, characteristics, or vulnerabilities" (European Council, 2024, p.2).

As a common form of violence encountered in various ways, all countries are working to combat it. Digital platforms act as catalysts for violent behaviours (Al-rawashda, 2020), reinforcing and legitimizing forms of pressure, threat, and symbolic violence, such as discourse violence (Recuero, 2024). Digital platforms (Instagram, TikTok, X/Twitter, YouTube, etc.), which provide the foundation for social relationships, not only facilitate information exchange but also serve as symbolic indicators of group belonging and as tools for gaining social status, constructing meaning worlds, and producing messages about social norms (Sönmez, 2022; Gezginci & Işıklı, 2018). The symbolic interactions that occur in these spaces deeply influence the nature and visibility of violent behaviours.

## 1.d. Typology of Violence

Violence is not a unitary concept but a multidimensional social construct that acquires different meanings depending on the disciplinary lens through which it is examined. Its complexity requires an analytical framework that integrates sociological, psychological, political, economic, theological, and ontological dimensions. Each of these domains highlights a distinct mode of how violence is produced, legitimized, or symbolically represented in society.

From a sociological perspective, violence extends beyond physical harm to include symbolic and structural mechanisms embedded in everyday social relations. Following Bourdieu's (1991) notion of symbolic violence, domination operates through language, cultural codes, and norms that render inequality natural and invisible. Alongside symbolic forms, interpersonal and societal violence mark the micro and macro levels of aggression, while iconic and global forms reveal how violence is mediated through imagery, global media, and transnational conflicts. In this sense, sociological violence encompasses both the visible and the latent forces that reproduce power asymmetries.

From a psychological standpoint, violence emerges through emotional, cognitive, and behavioural mechanisms. Phenomena such as mobbing, spiritual harassment, and emotional abuse reveal how individuals internalize or project aggression in subtle ways. Acts of self-directed violence—including self-harm or suicide—illustrate the inward turn of destructive impulses, whereas incited or hidden violence denotes forms provoked by external pressures or social manipulation. Thus, psychological violence exposes the internalization of coercion and its intimate effects on the self.

In the political domain, violence is inseparable from the exercise of power and legitimacy. As Benjamin (1921) and Galtung (1969) suggest, law, authority, and coercion are historically intertwined. Legislative and law-enforcing violence sustain the authority of the state, while structural violence manifests through systemic inequalities and institutional domination. In contrast, collective and counter-revolutionary forms reveal how organized groups mobilize force in the name of ideological or national identities. The political dimension of violence, therefore, bridges coercion and consent, legality and legitimacy.

The economic dimension of violence concerns the deprivation of material resources and opportunities. Structural inequalities embedded in capitalist production, described by Žižek (2008) as objective violence, create conditions of exclusion and exploitation. Financial deprivation—as seen in poverty or precarity—functions as a silent but pervasive form of harm, shaping everyday life through economic dependency and vulnerability.

Within the theological framework, violence becomes moralized and ritualized. It can be justified as religious or divine violence when framed as sacred duty or transcendent justice. Mythical and ritual violence further demonstrate how aggression may be embedded within systems of belief and purification. In such cases, violence is not merely condemned but sometimes sanctified, reflecting the dual role of religion as both a source of peace and a potential instrument of coercion.

Finally, the ontological dimension reveals violence as an intrinsic condition of existence and communication. It appears in diverse forms—physical, verbal, organized, or cyber violence—each reflecting a mode of human confrontation in material or symbolic space. Digital environments, in particular, transform aggression into mediated interaction, making cyber violence a defining expression of twenty-first-century conflict. Violence, therefore, can act both as an end—a self-sufficient spectacle of domination—and as a means—an instrument for achieving political or moral objectives.

In sum, violence manifests across interrelated domains that together shape its social ontology. Whether symbolic or structural, emotional or institutional, sacred or algorithmic, each dimension reveals how modern societies continuously reconstruct and normalize violence under changing cultural and technological conditions. Such a multidimensional approach enables a deeper understanding of how digital spaces, in particular, sustain and transform the forms of violence inherited from earlier social structures.

## 2. METHODOLOGY

This study employs a qualitative research design based on document analysis to investigate the relationship between social media platforms and violent behaviour. The qualitative approach is appropriate for understanding symbolic meanings, communicative practices, and socio-cultural contexts in which violence is produced, circulated, and normalized online. Rather than focusing on numerical measurement, the study aims to interpret patterns of representation, interaction, and discourse that reveal how violence is socially constructed in digital spaces.

The research is structured around two main analytical levels. The first level involves a conceptual and theoretical synthesis of academic studies, reports, and policy documents published between 2015 and 2025. These sources were obtained from international databases such as Web of Science, Scopus, and Google Scholar, using keywords including "digital violence," "symbolic interaction," "social media aggression," and "algorithmic radicalization." The second level entails qualitative content analysis of selected case studies—such as the Blue Whale Challenge, the Christchurch terrorist attack, and the Molly Russell case—to illustrate how symbolic meanings of violence are constructed and transmitted through social media interactions.

Following Bowen's (2009) framework for document analysis, the collected materials were examined through three stages: (1) skimming (to identify relevance), (2) reading and interpretation (to determine emerging patterns), and (3) thematic coding (to categorize meanings related to symbolic interaction, emotional contagion, desensitization, and algorithmic radicalization). The interpretation process was guided by theoretical frameworks including Bandura's Social Learning Theory, Galtung's Cultural Violence Theory, and Mead's Symbolic Interactionism.

Ethical sensitivity was maintained throughout the study. Since the analysis relied solely on secondary data available in the public domain, no direct human participation was involved. However, special care was taken to avoid reproducing violent imagery or personal identifiers from the analysed cases. The goal was to reveal the socio-symbolic mechanisms through which digital environments reinforce violent tendencies while promoting awareness and preventive discourse. These cases were selected as they represent three distinct forms of mediated violence: self-directed, collective-performative, and algorithmically reinforced.

2. Violence and Social Media Platforms

Social media platforms have become a central part of individuals' daily lives. While offering numerous positive opportunities such as communication, information access, socialization, and entertainment, social media has fundamentally transformed social structures and human interactions. However, this transformation has also generated various social problems, one of which is violence. Numerous studies have highlighted these negative effects. The manifestations of violent behaviour in social media environments, and the role of these platforms in disseminating, normalizing, or even triggering violence, constitute significant research areas for sociologists and related disciplines (Huesmann&Taylor, 2006)

Recent research has demonstrated that the relationship between social media use and violent behaviour has multiple dimensions. In particular, among younger generations, meaningful connections have been observed between social media use and aggressive tendencies, cyberbullying, and even radicalization. For example, a 2024 study found a longitudinal relationship between social media addiction and aggressive behaviours observed in adolescents (Lin et al., 2025), while another study emphasized that exposure to violent content on social media could increase aggressive behaviour (Oshodi, 2024; Dou and Zhang, 2025).

Social media allows users to gain approval and social support, fulfilling recognition needs and contributing to psychological and physical well-being in certain contexts, such as hate crimes; however, it can also pose threats to victims (Walther, 2022). Studies in Turkey revealed that one in five individuals experienced digital violence, with Instagram, Facebook, and Twitter (X) being the most frequent platforms for such acts (Turkey Digital Violence Report, 2021). According to a Pew Research Centre survey, 75% of adults reported that online harassment occurs on social platforms (Pew, 2021).

Do social media platforms cause violent crime?

Social media platforms play a significant role in reproducing and normalizing violent behaviours, albeit through different mechanisms and symbolic frameworks across platforms. On Twitter (now X), digital lynching and hate speech are prevalent forms of violence. These behaviours often carry symbolic meanings of justified anger and collective power, and they operate by legitimizing violence while transforming abstract "others" into targets. TikTok tends to disseminate fight videos and instances of bullying, which are framed as entertainment or challenges, rewarding users with likes and views. This mechanism normalizes aggressive behaviour and incentivizes participation through social recognition. On Instagram, violence is often romanticized, portraying acts of aggression as expressions of love, power, or attractiveness. Symbolic embellishments render such behaviours appealing, particularly among youth, thereby legitimizing violence. YouTube hosts prank videos and challenge-based content where risk-taking and aggression are framed as entertainment or displays of courage. The platform's emphasis on humour and consequence concealment contributes to the normalization of violent acts. Finally, Twitch and Discord facilitate in-game violence and peer pressure within online communities, where status, belonging, and achievement serve as motivating factors. Here, violence functions as a form of social capital, reinforced by continuous interaction and communal validation.

*Table 1. Ways Social Media Platforms Reproduce Violence*

| Platform | Type of Violence | Symbolic Meaning | Mechanism of Effect |
|---|---|---|---|
| **Twitter / X** | Digital lynching, hate speech | Justified anger, community power | Legitimization of violence, transformation of generalized "other" |
| **TikTok** | Fight videos, bullying | Entertainment, courage, challenge | Normalization of violence, rewarded by likes and views |
| **Instagram** | Romanticized violence | Power, a sign of love, attractiveness | Violence legitimized with symbolic embellishments, youth engagement |
| **YouTube** | Prank videos, challenges | Entertainment, courage display | Concealment of consequences, normalization through humor |
| **Twitch / Discord** | In-game violence, group pressure | Status, community belonging, achievement | Violence as social capital, continuous interaction loop |

References: Chen et al., 2025; Johanssen, 2025; Wright, 2025; The Guardian, 2024; Udoudom et al., 2024; Çalışkan &Mencik,2015.

Across all platforms, the visibility economy transforms aggression into a form of communicative capital that reinforces identity hierarchies.

*"...In 2003, Allan Menzies stabbed his closest friend, drank his blood, and ate part of his skull. What made this murder different from many other horrific crimes worldwide was that Menzies claimed he was following the commands of Akasha, a character from the vampire movie Queen of the Damned, who kills her friend to gain immortality. Menzies had watched the film over 100 times before acting" (Scott,2004).*

The Blue Whale Challenge

The Blue Whale Challenge, integrated with online communication apps such as WhatsApp, Instagram, and Facebook, connected the "target" (victim) interactively with the game. Tasks generally involved inflicting physical and psychological harm on oneself, culminating in instructions to harm family members. Participants were also required to watch violent and frightening films continuously. The game reportedly led to the deaths of 130 young people worldwide (Çetin, 2022).

Self-directed violence is another dimension of this phenomenon. Exposure to cyberbullying on social media can adversely affect cognitive and mental processes, leading to violent behaviours such as suicide attempts. The Molly Russell case is illustrative: in 2017, 14-year-old Molly Russell committed suicide after being exposed to self-harm and depressive content on Instagram (Euronews, 2022). The 2022 legal process in the UK highlighted Instagram algorithms' contribution to Molly's deteriorating mental state, sparking discussions on social media companies' responsibilities to protect children. Algorithmic mechanisms (which prioritize content that captures user attention) repeatedly exposed vulnerable users to harmful material, exacerbating risks for self-harm and suicide.

This case also demonstrates risk among vulnerable groups such as children and adolescents, who are in developmental stages of identity formation. Negative social media interactions during this period can strongly impact self-perception. Harassment, threats, and humiliation may increase anxiety, depression, loneliness, and suicidal thoughts. Moreover, repeated exposure to violent content like videos, games, and news may eventually be internalized, normalized, and manifest in behavioural patterns that become a focus of societal problems in later life.

## 3. MECHANISMS OF SOCIAL MEDIA'S INFLUENCE ON VIOLENCE

The internet propagates violence by objectifying it and embedding it into minds. The consumption of violent material to gain excitement is an unusual human desire that the internet satisfies. Games, news, and amateur clips present violence uncontrollably (Çelik, 2018).

### 3.1. Online Disinhibition Effect

Disinhibition is defined as "a marked reduction in concern about self-presentation and others' evaluations" (Joinson, 1998:44). Online disinhibition refers to individuals' ability to communicate without the restrictions experienced in face-to-face interaction. Negative outcomes include violent or anger-filled expressions on blogs or platforms, cyberbullying, and problematic internet use (Ayas and Çapa Aydın, 2021).

Online disinhibition increases the likelihood of aggressive behaviour, as anonymity, lack of feedback, and temporal separation provide opportunities. Empathy diminishes, enabling users to post violent messages they would not express in person (Suler, 2004). Digital "masks" allow individuals to evade responsibility, shift blame, or deny their actions. In extreme cases, individuals may think, "If my identity is unknown, my actions' consequences do not matter" (Shukla, 2023).

## 3.2. Desensitization

Funk, Baldacci, Pasold, and Baumgardner (2004:24) define desensitization as the reduction or elimination of cognitive, emotional, and ultimately behavioural responses to a stimulus. When desensitization occurs, individuals fail to perceive and respond to the cues necessary to initiate an evaluative process, leading them to carry out actions without consideration of their moral dimensions. Empathy, defined as the capacity to experience and perceive the state of another, is critical for the moral evaluation process. Violence in screen media can affect empathy by desensitizing viewers to the real-life consequences of violent acts (Yumrukız,2017:92). Continuous exposure to violent content can reduce emotional responsiveness, decreasing empathy toward victims and normalizing aggression. Frequent use of violent platforms fosters desensitization and the development of aggressive problem-solving templates (Kjærvik et al., 2025).

## 3.3. Emotional Contagion and Vicarious Trauma

Emotional contagion can manifest through similar facial expressions, vocal tones, or postural behaviours, as well as through corresponding neurophysiological and neurological responses toward the interacting partner. In response to emotional contagion, individuals often exhibit behavioural, attentional, and emotional synchrony. In the field of marketing, interactions with both human agents and objects are employed as tools for commercial communication. Consequently, understanding the mechanisms of emotional contagion is crucial for both marketing research and practical applications studies have stated that emotions can be classified according to the level of pleasure (positive/negative) and the level of arousal (relax/activated) experienced by individuals; emotions are therefore a combination of feelings with arousal (Herrando & Constandinidies 2021, 2).

Vicarious trauma manifests as cognitive changes from prolonged exposure. For example, children exposed to high levels of violence may develop stress, trauma symptoms, and increased distrust of the world (Varan and Demirel, 2024).

## 3.4. Algorithmic Radicalization and Echo Chambers

Algorithmic radicalization refers to the concept in which algorithms on popular social media sites, such as YouTube and Facebook, gradually direct users toward increasingly extreme content over time, leading them to develop radicalized, extremist political views (Wikipedia,2025). Despite some similarities between filter bubbles and echo chambers, there are two notable differences between the concepts. First, filter bubbles refer only to forms of intellectual isolation caused by algorithms (and inferences based on users' preferences). In contrast, echo chambers are created by the users themselves. Echo chambers and filter bubbles isolate users intellectually, as algorithms prioritize content aligned with existing beliefs, reinforcing moral norms while excluding differing perspectives (Talamanca and Arfini, 2022).

The Christchurch Mosque attack (2019) exemplifies social media's role in promoting mass violence as a performative and propagandistic tool (Sönmez, 2019).

*Table 2. Social Media Algorithm Functioning*

| Stage | Engagement Metric | Mechanism | Outcome |
|---|---|---|---|
| **Incentivization** | Likes, comments, shares, watch time | Algorithm promotes highly engaging content | Violent and hateful content quickly becomes popular |
| **Pursuit** | Time spent on similar content | Algorithm recommends increasingly extreme content | Users remain in filter bubbles and encounter radical content |
| **Reinforcement** | Interaction with like-minded users | Algorithm creates echo chambers | Users' beliefs are reinforced; openness to alternative views decreases |
| **Viral Spread** | Reshares and new user reach | Content rapidly reaches new users | Chains of violence and hate expand uncontrollably, increasing polarization |

References: Tüfekçi, 2015; Cinelli et al., 2021; Bail et al., 2018; Ribeiro et al., 2020

Case:

The Christchurch terrorist attack in New Zealand is one of the most striking examples of how social media can be used as a tool for "performance" and propaganda in mass acts of violence. Australian terrorist Brenton Tarrant live-streamed his attack on social media and shared an 87-page manifesto beforehand. Although major platforms like Facebook attempted to remove the video quickly, it rapidly went viral after being circulated by mainstream media outlets. More importantly, the video and manifesto continued to be actively shared on smaller, less regulated platforms. The live broadcast of the attack by the perpetrator pushed the social learning theory to its extreme within the context of terrorism. Through his actions, the perpetrator both radicalized individuals and provided a "model" for potential offenders. Indeed, the fact that students in Poland posed using slogans similar to those employed by the attacker serves as concrete evidence of this chain of imitation and dissemination (Sönmez, 2019).

## 4. THE RELATIONSHIP BETWEEN SOCIAL MEDIA PLATFORMS AND VIOLENCE IN THE CONTEXT OF THEORIES OF VIOLENCE

Understanding the effects of social media platforms on individuals in terms of violence requires not only observational data but also the examination through theoretical frameworks, which provide an important basis for explaining how theories of violence shape violent behaviours in social media. Violence is a viral behaviour. Being influenced by various factors such as emotions, biology, and social environment has led to different approaches. Studies have addressed the relationship between social media and violence. However, it has been determined that studies specifically focusing on digital platforms are limited in revealing the impact of symbolic interaction on violence (Patton et al., 2020; Mahardika et al., 2018; Brown et al., 2017).

The first institution where the process of social construction takes place is the family. Therefore, the learning of violence within the family environment is widely accepted. In this context, the first theory is the Social Learning Theory. It emphasizes the impact of observation. From this theoretical perspective, social media provides an effective platform for observation. On platforms such as YouTube, TikTok, Instagram Reels, or Twitch, the observation and imitation of violent videos, fight scenes, or "challenge"-type content explain its influence. Social approval mechanisms, such as "likes" and "shares," play a reinforcing role in violent behaviour and can lead individuals to perceive violence as a means of gaining social acceptance.

According to this theory, violent behaviours that go unpunished or are rewarded (through interactions such as likes, comments, or shares) are perceived by viewers as a "hidden reward," facilitating the learning of aggressive thoughts and behaviours. Violence presented on social media stimulates individuals, causing excitement, triggering aggressive feelings, and increasing the tendency to engage in aggressive actions. This effect is particularly pronounced among children and adolescents, and a strong relationship has been identified between television programs and antisocial behaviours (Bandura, 1965).

Merton's (1938) anomie theory, which forms the basis of strain theories, is grounded in a macro-structural perspective and assumes both commonly shared value orientations (such as aspirations for success and prosperity) and the existence of a vertical social class structure. Merton's theory posits that societal pressures to achieve goals through legitimate means may be blocked, resulting in deviance. Individuals respond through conformity, innovation, ritualism, retreatism, or rebellion, explaining how inequality fosters crime (Nickerson, 2025).

Hirschi's theory suggests individuals are naturally inclined toward deviance, but social bonds restrain them. Effective social control prevents conflicts and reduces crime (El Tarabishi and Galal, 2023; Jiang et al., 2022). The control theory posits that an individual's criminal behaviour can be shaped by their social connections. According to this perspective, an offender may alter their behaviour and refrain from committing crimes due to strong bonds with influential figures in their social circle, such as friends or family members.

According to Johan Galtung, cultural violence functions as the "invisible foundation" of structural and direct violence (Galtung, 1990). Galtung argues that symbols, myths, and moral justifications embedded in the unconscious codes of society—including institutional structures such as religion, education, and family—enable individuals to accept violence without questioning it. For example, in a patriarchal culture, the entrenched notion that "women must be obedient" serves to legitimize physical violence against women (Sarıkaya, 2022:300).

Cultural violence not only shapes individuals' value judgments but also acts as a legitimacy mechanism that helps maintain social order. While making direct violence visible, it simultaneously lays the groundwork for reinforcing structural violence.

Routine activity theory focuses on crimes that directly target individuals, such as assaults, thefts, robberies, vehicle thefts, and other offenses that harm a person or their property. These crimes can range from minor incidents, like stealing change from an unlocked car, to serious violent offenses, such as assaults causing injury, rapes, or murders. According to Cohen and Felson, the elements necessary for such crimes are an offender with the motivation and means, and a target that lacks protection. Analysing these factors helps identify which targets are more vulnerable. Furthermore, addressing weaknesses in these factors can help prevent offenders from committing crimes (Ungvarsky,2024).

## 4.1. Symbolic Interactionism (Mead):

In this section, violent incidents observed particularly on social media platforms will be analysed within the framework of George Herbert Mead's theory of symbolic interactionism, focusing on how individuals construct and interpret violent acts through symbols and meanings.

The Symbolic Interactionism Theory developed by George Herbert Mead suggests that individuals interact in social life through the meanings attributed to the concrete or abstract elements they encounter, and the qualities assigned to them. According to this theory, meanings are created, interpreted, and transformed through social interactions. Individuals develop a sense of self by internalizing the perspectives of others (the generalized other). Values related to these elements are shaped through interactions among group members. The social experiences individuals acquire in different situations, while interacting with these elements, gain meaning as they are subjectively interpreted. People use symbols and language to make sense of the external world in their interactions. In this process, symbols (language, gestures, visuals) form the basis of communication. For symbolic interactionists, the most important symbols are language, words, behaviours, objects, gestures, and facial expressions. People create meaning by interpreting these symbols and use them in their interactions to take roles in society (Şakar and Sarıkan, 2023).

When a user employs slang, immoral language, or shares threatening visuals toward another, these acts are not seen as mere words or images. Instead, they carry symbolic meanings such as humiliation, display of power, or exclusion. The person committing the violent act expresses their self through these symbols, while the meaning of the act is interpreted by the target individual (Me) and other social media users. This interpretative process determines whether the act will be defined as violence (Nadim and Fladmoe, 2019).

Let us clarify with an example: the transformation of an online argument into violence. Consider a verbal dispute between two users on an online gaming platform. Initially, the argument is only about in-game competition, but later it escalates into personal insults and threats. One user says to the other, *"If you are this incompetent, why did you even join our game? We're losing because of you."* This expression is not just criticism; it is a symbolic act of violence that conveys humiliation and devaluation. The other player interprets this as a personal attack and responds more aggressively. In this cycle, each comment carries new symbolic meaning, laying the ground for further violent actions.

In this process, both users reflect on how they are perceived "in the eyes of the other." The first user may try to construct a self-image as "right" and "superior" by labelling the second player as "incompetent." The second user, rejecting this labelling, defends their self by responding with more aggressive language. In this interaction, symbols (insults, threats) become fundamental tools that shape how individuals perceive themselves and each other. Other users, as observers (the generalized other), play an indirect role in defining the event as violence—either by joining the discussion or by remaining silent.

Case Analysis: Violence Transferred to Real Life After a Violent Game

Case:

An 18-year-old, after playing violent digital games for a long time, went out and stabbed five people. This act is striking as it shows how, along with individual psychological factors, the world of social interaction and symbolic meanings can be transformed (milliyet.com.tr, 2024).

Analysed within the framework of Symbolic Interactionism Theory:

**Symbol and role learning:** In the game, the knife became a symbol of power and achievement. The young person carried this symbol into the real world, externalizing the role they had in the game. Weapons, characters, and win–lose dynamics in violent games carry strong symbolic meanings for individuals. Within the game, the knife transforms into a symbol of "power, victory, superiority." The young person identifies with the game character.

**The conflict between "I" and "Me":** The individual's impulsive reactions (I) were not controlled by "Me," which represents social norms. Normally, the individual should have internalized the societal norm that "violence is wrong and punishable." However, in the social media–gaming environment, the person constructed a "social self" in which violence is rewarded and praised. The social media self is shaped by choices about which content to consume, interact with, and which networks to form, transform, and sustain across different platforms. As a set of skills, social media literacy includes the ability to monitor and observe one's social media use, motivations, and outcomes (Cho et al., 2024).

**Transformation of the generalized other:** While general societal values reject violence, games and online interactions presented a system of values where the "generalized other" legitimized violence. The young person referred to this virtual other instead of real social norms. Violence was rewarded. The youth internalized the values of the gaming community.

**Identity presentation:** The "warrior/brave" identity in the game was validated in social media and gaming environments. This identity was transferred into real life as a tool for gaining power and authority. Social media functions as a symbolic space where individuals construct their identities through "likes," "retweets," and "hashtags." In online settings, being labelled as a "troll," "pervert," or "criminal" can lead individuals to define themselves through these identities, even pushing them toward more violent behaviours. Research shows that punitive tendencies may emerge more strongly in aroused individuals. In this context, negative and stigmatizing labels (e.g., "criminal") can shape self-perception and behaviour, even leading individuals to internalize and sustain such roles (Bernburg, 2009; MEB, 2024).

### 4.1.1. Transfer of Symbolic Meaning to Real Life

An individual's social media content is built upon their core self and is inseparable from all aspects of social media use. Sönmez (2023) emphasizes that social media use involves self-expression, validation, development, social belonging, social learning, and impression management through selective self-presentation enabled by platform affordances. Without understanding the self, social media content cannot be effectively analysed.

According to Mead, individuals construct the self by internalizing the perspectives of others, explained through the "generalized other." In digital game environments, the generalized other can be represented by other players, game rules, and the system itself. When violence is normalized as a game-world standard, adolescents evaluate their behaviour from the perspective of this digital generalized other and internalize violence as acceptable or even expected. In this way, symbolic meanings acquired in virtual environments are transferred to real life. A knife in the game acquires similar real-world meanings (power, defeating opponents, control). The symbolic boundary between virtual and real-life consequences blurs, potentially leading the youth to dehumanize real individuals as "enemies." The process illustrates the transformation of the "I" in expressing the self, where violent game symbols may become real-life problem-solving tools.

Sports-related violence provides another example of symbolic interaction: negative behavioural patterns among interacting individuals can disrupt solidarity and shared meaning (Şakar and Sarıkan, 2023:435). Poell et al. (2019) note that platforms actively shape interactions and thus discourse. For example, during the 2023 FIFA Women's World Cup, certain demeaning tweets about women's sports rapidly spread, amplifying gender-based violence and disrupting other discussions.

Videos, mimicked explanations, or TikTok dances activate mirror neuron systems, creating neural processes similar to real-life social interactions. Young people are particularly prone to imitate behaviours observed on social media (Marchetti et al., 2022). Algorithms on platforms like TikTok and Instagram amplify violent content, normalizing violent behaviour among youth (Youth Endowment Fund, 2024).

Bauman (1998:154) argues that individuals, who would not commit crimes alone, can easily act within a crowd, as the crowd objectifies the subject of the crime. Canetti (2014:18) similarly notes that a crowd is a body gathered for the desire of release. In online crowds, the qualitative differences among individuals are nullified. The only condition is to imitate others without question (Bauman, 2017:163; Demir and Özcan, 2021:6-7). A study dividing participants into three groups found that students in the third group reported being influenced by influencer content online and offline, applying what they saw on Instagram to their social lives (Değer and Sine Nazlı, 2022:33)

## 5. STRATEGIES FOR COMBATING VIOLENCE ON SOCIAL MEDIA PLATFORMS

Combating social media–driven violence requires multi-stage and interdisciplinary approaches. First, advanced content moderation technologies (e.g., AI-supported text, image, and video scanning) can detect violent content rapidly and prevent its spread. Human oversight can improve decision-making in content evaluation. Second, easy access to user reporting tools is essential, particularly to prevent harassment and hate speech, while ensuring privacy. Rapid feedback and blocking mechanisms can be strengthened, and social media systems can be redesigned to prioritize bridging content instead of action-inducing content, encouraging empathy and understanding instead of polarizing violence. For example, algorithms can prioritize messages receiving positive engagement from diverse communities (Stray et al., 2023).

## CONCLUSION AND RECOMMENDATIONS

This study contributes to understanding how symbolic interactionism explains the normalization of aggression within platformized communication environments. This study evaluated social media platforms' impact on violence, emphasizing symbolic interactionism. Digital environments are not just communication tools but spaces where violence is observed, learned, and normalized. Social media amplifies existing social inequalities and violent behaviours through algorithm-driven interactions, echo chambers, and filter bubbles. Users' anonymity and lack of feedback facilitate online disinhibition, while symbolic meanings of violence can integrate into identity, particularly among vulnerable youth, transferring to real-life actions. Preventing digital violence requires increasing user awareness, creating safe digital spaces, and balancing technology with human values through interdisciplinary efforts and policy regulation. Qualitative research on social workers' understanding of users' relationships with online violence is crucial.

Future research could integrate qualitative discourse analysis with quantitative methods such as sentiment analysis or social network analysis through mixed-method designs. Comparative studies across different countries and cultures could reveal how platform-specific norms and cultural values shape the perception and language of violence. Furthermore, longitudinal research could examine the long-term effects of repeated exposure to online aggression on identity formation, empathy levels, and real-life behaviours among adolescents and young adults. Finally, investigating how AI-based monitoring systems integrated with ethical oversight can be used to prevent digital violence without restricting freedom of expression could contribute to the creation of safer and more democratic digital environments.

## REFERENCES


Ayas, S., & Çapa Aydın, Y. (2021). Çevrimiçi Disinhibisyon Ölçeğinin geliştirilmesi: Geçerlik ve güvenirlik çalışması. *Türk Psikoloji Yazilari, 24*(48), 16–28. DOI: 10.31828/tpy1301996120210209m000037

Bail, C. A., Argyle, L. P., Brown, T. W., Bumpus, J. P., Chen, H., Hunzaker, M. B. F., & Volfovsky, A. (2018). Exposure to opposing views on social media can increase political polarization. *Proceedings of the National Academy of Sciences of the United States of America, 115*(37), 9216–9221. DOI: 10.1073/pnas.1804840115 PMID: 30154168

Bal, N. (2014). Sosyolojide şiddet kavramı. *Yurt ve Dünya Dergisi, 6*, 6–22.

Bandura, A. (1965). Influence of models' reinforcement contingencies on the acquisition of imitative responses. *Journal of Personality and Social Psychology, 1*(6), 589–595. PMID: 14300234

Bandura, A. (1977). *Social Learning Theory.* Prentice Hall.

Bauman, Z. (1998). *Sosyolojik düşünmek* (A. Yılmaz, Çev.). Ayrıntı Yayınları.

Bauman, Z. (2017). *Postmodern etik* (A. Türker, Çev.). Ayrıntı Yayınları.

Benjamin, W. (1921). Zur Kritik der Gewalt [Critique of Violence]. In Gesammelte Schriften, Vol. II.1. Suhrkamp Verlag. (Benjamin, W. (1978). Critique of Violence. In M. Bullock & M. W. Jennings (Eds.), Reflections: Essays, Aphorisms, Autobiographical Writings (pp. 277–300). Schocken Books.)

Bernburg, J. G. (2009). Labeling theory. In Krohn, M., Lizotte, A., & Hall, G. (Eds.), *Handbook on crime and deviance* (pp. 187–207). Springer., DOI: 10.1007/978-1-4419-0245-0_10

Bourdieu, P. (1991). *Language and Symbolic Power (J. B. Thompson* (Raymond, G., & Adamson, M. Eds. & Trans.). Harvard University Press., DOI: 10.2307/j.ctvjnrv7f

Brown, M., Ray, R., Summers, E., & Fraistat, N. (2017). #SayHerName: A case study of intersectional social media activism. *Ethnic and Racial Studies, 40*(11), 1831–1846. DOI: 10.1080/01419870.2017.1334934

Çalışkan, M., & Mencik, Y. (2015). Değişen dünyanın yeni yüzü: Sosyal medya. *Akademik Bakış Uluslararası Hakemli Sosyal Bilimler Dergisi*, (50), 254–277.

Çelik, E. (2018). İnternet ortamındaki şiddet sunumları ve yol açtığı sosyal travmalar. *Çağdaş Yönetim Bilimleri Dergisi, 5*(3), 280–296.

Çetin, S. (2022). Çevrimiçi oyunlar ve intihar: Mavi Balina örneği. *Milli Kültür Araştırmaları Dergisi*, *6*(1), 61–73. DOI: 10.55774/mikad.1101587

Chen, X., Li, J., Yang, W., Wang, H., & Song, H. (2025). Cross-platform violence detection on social media: A dataset and analysis. In *Proceedings of the 17th ACM Web Science Conference* (pp. 1–10). ACM. https://doi.org/DOI: 10.1145/3717867.3717877

Cho, H., Cannon, J., Lopez, R., & Li, W. (2024). Social media literacy: A conceptual framework. *New Media & Society*, *26*(2), 941–960. DOI: 10.1177/14614448211068530 PMID: 38328341

Cinelli, M., Morales, G. D. F., Galeazzi, A., Quattrociocchi, W., & Starnini, M. (2021). The echo chamber effect on social media. *Proceedings of the National Academy of Sciences of the United States of America*, *118*(9), e2023301118. DOI: 10.1073/pnas.2023301118 PMID: 33622786

Collins, R. (2008). *Violence: A micro-sociological theory*. Princeton University Press.

Değer, B. E., & Sine Nazlı, R. (2022). Sosyal medyada influencer etkisi bağlamında benlik sunumu. *Uşak Üniversitesi Sosyal Bilimler Dergisi*, *15*(2), 25–45.

Demir, S. T., & Özcan, A. (2021). Sosyal medya ve linç kültürü: Sanal nedenler, gerçek sonuçlar. *İletişim Kuram ve Araştırma Dergisi, 56*, 1–15. https://doi.org/ DOI: 10.47998/ikad.957544

Dou, Y., & Zhang, M. (2025). Longitudinal reciprocal relationship between media violence exposure and aggression among junior high school students in China: A cross-lagged analysis. *Frontiers in Psychology*, *15*, 1–13. DOI: 10.3389/fpsyg.2024.1441738 PMID: 39839937

ElTarabishi, M., & Galal, S. (2023). The role of social media in promoting peace building and prevention of societal violence among university youth (analytical descriptive study). *Journal of Media and Interdisciplinary Studies*, *2*(4), 1–32. DOI: 10.21608/jmis.2023.313513

Erol, V. (2022). Sosyal medyanın Türk aile yapısına etkisi. *Karamanoğlu Mehmetbey Üniversitesi Sosyal ve Ekonomik Araştırmalar Dergisi*, *24*(43), 1127–1139.

Euronews (2022). 'İngiliz genç kız, olumsuz çevrimiçi içeriğin etkisi nedeniyle öldü'. https://tr.euronews.com/2022/09/30/ingiliz-genc-kiz-olumsuz-cevrimici-icerigin-etkisi-nedeniyle-oldu

Europen Council. (2024). *EPRS Briefing*: (No. 767146). https://www.europarl.europa.eu/RegData/etudes/BRIE/2024/767146/EPRS_BRI(2024)767146_EN.pdf

Figà Talamanca, G., & Arfini, S. (2022). Through the newsfeed glass: Rethinking filter bubbles and echo chambers. *Philosophy & Technology, 35*(1), 20. DOI: 10.1007/s13347-021-00494-z PMID: 35308101

Funk, J. B., Baldacci, H. B., Pasold, T., & Baumgardner, J. (2004). Violence exposure in real-life, video games, television, movies, and the internet: Is there desensitization? *Journal of Adolescence, 27*(1), 23–39. DOI: 10.1016/j.adolescence.2003.10.005 PMID: 15013258

Galtung, J. (1969). Violence, peace, and peace research. *Journal of Peace Research, 6*(3), 167–191. DOI: 10.1177/002234336900600301

Garver, N. (1973). What violence is. In Bierman, A. K., & Gould, J. A. (Eds.), *Philosophy for a new generation* (pp. 204–220). Macmillan.

Gezginci, G., & Işıklı, Ş. (2018). Dindar Facebook etkisi: Türk kullanıcılar üzerine bir analiz. *Medya ve Din Araştırmaları Dergisi, 1*(1), 111–133.

Hernando, C., & Constantinies, E. (2021). Emotional Contagion: A Brief Overview and Future Directions Front. *Psychol., 12*. Advance online publication. DOI: 10.3389/fpsyg.2021.712606

Huesmann, L. R., & Taylor, L. D. (2006). The role of media violence in violent behavior. *Annual Review of Public Health, 27*, 393–415. DOI: 10.1146/annurev.publhealth.26.021304.144640 PMID: 16533123

Ilgın, HO. (2021). Sosyal medyada dezenformasyon ve halkla ilişkiler ilişkisi. *İletişim Çalışmaları Dergisi, 7*(2), 303–322.

Jiang, S., Da-wei, Z., & Irwin, D. D. (2022). The prevalence and importance of semiformal organizations and semiformal control in rural china: Insights from a national survey. *Asian Journal of Criminology, 17*(3), 331–352. DOI: 10.1007/s11417-022-09366-7 PMID: 35342483

Johanssen, J. (2025). Rethinking symbolic violence on social media: Incels and mentalisation. *Journal of HARM, 4*, 22–36. https://www.researchgate.net/publication/390729048

Kjærvik, S. L., Thomson, N. D., & Fanti, K. A. (2025). The impact of media violence, narcissism and sex on reactive and proactive aggression in adolescents: A one-year follow-up study. *Journal of Youth and Adolescence, 54*(4), 917–927. DOI: 10.1007/s10964-024-02106-3 PMID: 39487948

Lin, S., Fabris, M. A., Longobardi, C., & Mastrokoukou, S. (2025). The association between social media addiction and aggressive behaviors: A longitudinal and gender-specific analysis. *Journal of Adolescence*, *97*(3), 798–807. DOI: 10.1002/jad.12454 PMID: 39695825

Mahardika, H., French, J., & Sembada, A. (2018). Keep calm and eat satay: Indonesia's consumption-themed signals of defiance against terrorism. *Australasian Marketing Journal*, *26*(3), 231–238. DOI: 10.1016/j.ausmj.2018.06.002

Marchetti, A., Castelli, I., Dimitri, D., & Massaro, D. (2022). Digital media, social cognition and empathy: A perspective from mirror systems. *Frontiers in Psychology*, *13*, 834001. DOI: 10.3389/fpsyg.2022.834001

Mead, G. H. (1934). *Mind, Self, and Society: From the Standpoint of a Social Behaviorist*. University of Chicago Press.

Milli Eğitim Bakanlığı. (2024). Medyada şiddet görüntüleri ve çocuklar. https://tepebasiram.meb.k12.tr/meb_iys_dosyalar/26/15/972503/dosyalar/2024_10/17103743

Nadim, M., & Fladmoe, A. (2019). Silencing women? gender and online harassment. *Social Science Computer Review*, *39*(2), 245–258. DOI: 10.1177/0894439319865518

Nickerson, J. (2025). Merton's strain theory of deviance in sociology. *Simply Psychology*. https://www.simplypsychology.org/mertons-strain-theory-deviance.html

Oshodi, N. (2024). Enhancing online safety: The impact of social media violent content and violence among teens in Illinois. *World Journal of Advanced Research and Reviews*, *23*(3), 826–833. DOI: 10.30574/wjarr.2024.23.3.2734

Patton, D. U., Stevens, R., Smith Lee, J. R., Eya, G.-C., & Frey, W. (2020). You set me up: Gendered perceptions of Twitter communication among Black Chicago youth. *Social Media + Society*, *6*(2), 1–11. DOI: 10.1177/2056305120913877

Pew Research Center. (2021). *The state of online harassment*. https://www.pewresearch.org/internet/2021/01/13/the-state-of-online-harassment/

Recuero, R. (2024). The Platformization of Violence: Toward a Concept of Discursive Toxicity on Social Media. *Social Media + Society*, *10*(1). Advance online publication. DOI: 10.1177/20563051231224264

Şakar, M., & Sarıkan, Ü. (2023). Tribin şiddeti: Sembolik etkileşim kuramı ve kırık cam teorisi bağlamında bir sentez. *International Journal of Eurasia Social Sciences*, *14*(51), 433–447.

Scott, K. (2004, 16 Kasım). *Killer who wanted to be vampire dies. The Guardian.* https://www.theguardian.com/uk/2004/nov/16/ukcrime.kirstyscott

Şener, G., & Abınık, N. (2021). Türkiye'de dijital şiddet araştırması / Turkey digital violence research 2021 (UNFPA Turkey, Common Knowledge & Communication Association). https://turkiye.unfpa.org/sites/default/files/pub-pdf/digital_violence _report.pdf

Shukla, A. (2023). Online disinhibition effect: Why we express more online. *Cognition Today.* https://cognitiontoday.com/online-disinhibition-effect/

Sönmez, G. (2019). Christchurch terör saldırısı, Brenton Tarrant'ın manifestosu ve terörün yeni yüzü. *Ortadoğu Araştırmaları Merkezi Raporu.* https://orsam.org.tr/ christchurch-teror-saldirisi-brenton-tarrantin-manifestosu-ve-terorun-yeni-yuzu.pdf

Sönmez, G. (2023). Sosyal medya okuryazarlığı. In Ergüney, M. (Ed.), *Dijital çağda okuryazarlık.* Nobel Akademik Yayıncılık.

Sönmez, M. F. (2022). *Sosyal kimlik ve sosyal medya (İki benzemezin hikayesi).* Eğitim Yayınevi.

Stray, J., Iyer, R., & Larrauri Prug, H. (2023). The Algorithmic Management of Polarization and Violence on Social Media https://knightcolumbia.org/content/the -algorithmic-management-of-polarization-and-violence-on-social-media

Suler, J. (2004). The online disinhibition effect. *Cyberpsychology & Behavior, 7*(3), 321–326. DOI: 10.1089/1094931041291295 PMID: 15257832

Tiryaki, S. (2023). Riskler ve olanaklar arasında dijital ebeveynlik: Bibliyometrik bir analiz. *TRT Akademi, 8*(19), 746–765.

Udoudom, U., Bassey, B., George, K., & Etifit, S. (2024). Impact of symbolic interactionism, pragmatism and social constructionism on communication and media practice. *International Journal of Humanities, Education, and Social Sciences, 2*(1), 1–25. DOI: 10.58578/ijhess.v2i1.2547

Ungvarsky, J. (2024) *Routine activity theory.* EBSCO Knowledge Advantage. https:// www.ebsco.com/research-starters/law/routine-activity-theory#full-article

Varan, D., & Demirel, Ç. (2024). Travmanın dolaylı etkisi: İkincil travmatik stres üzerine bir derleme. *İstanbul Kent Üniversitesi İnsan ve Toplum Bilimleri Dergisi, 5*(2), 71–85.

Walther, J. B. (2022). Social media and online hate. *Current Opinion in Psychology, 46*, 101298. DOI: 10.1016/j.copsyc.2021.12.010 PMID: 35158213

Wikipedia. Algoritmik radikalizasyon, 2025 https://en.wikipedia.org/wiki/Algorithmic_radicalization

Wright, E., Eriksson, L., & Bond, C. E. W. (2025). Victim blaming, gender, and social media commentary: A randomized vignette study of audience comments on news reports of intimate partner homicide. *Journal of Interpersonal Violence, 40*(5), 8862605251322816. DOI: 10.1177/08862605251322816 PMID: 40018892

Yener, Ş. (2023). Şiddet, şiddet türleri ve okulda öğretmene yönelen şiddet. *İçtimaiyat, 7*(1), 278–294. https://doi.org/DOI: 10.33709/ictimaiyat.1184117

Youth Endowment Fund. (2024, November 25). Violence on social media making teenagers afraid to go out, study finds. *The Guardian*. https://www.theguardian.com/media/2024/nov/25/violence-on-social-media-making-teenagers-afraid-to-go-out-study-finds

Yumrukuz, Ö. (2017). Şiddete Karşı Duyarsızlaşma ve Sosyal Medya İlişkisi Üzerine Bir İnceleme. *Marmara İletişim Dergisi*, (28), 89–106.

Žižek, S. (2008). *Violence: Six Sideways Reflections*. Picador.

# Chapter 7
# The Online Activism, Digital Resistance, and Counter-Platform Practices:
## Does Sociological Online Activism Really Matter?

**Wasswa Shafik**
https://orcid.org/0000-0002-9320-3186
*Dig Connectivity Research Laboratory (DCRLab), Uganda*

## ABSTRACT

*This chapter explores the evolving landscape of online activism, digital resistance, and counter-platform practices through a critical synthesis of scholarly literature and illustrative case studies. It analyzes how individuals and groups leverage digital tools to challenge dominant power structures, amplify marginalized voices, and promote social change. The discussion examines strategies employed by activists in navigating censorship, surveillance, and platform manipulation, while highlighting tensions between corporate-controlled digital spaces and grassroots movements. Drawing from diverse global contexts, the chapter investigates how decentralized technologies, alternative media, and networked mobilization have reshaped collective action and political expression. The chapter provides methodological and conceptual insights into the transformative potential of counter-platform practices in sustaining democratic participation and fostering inclusive digital futures.*

DOI: 10.4018/979-8-3373-4267-2.ch007

## INTRODUCTION

Online activism, often referred to as digital activism, encompasses the use of electronic platforms to promote social change and mobilize people around various causes. With the advent of the internet and social media, grassroots movements have transformed, allowing activists to bypass traditional media gatekeepers and reach a global audience instantaneously. This evolution not only democratizes the dissemination of information but also empowers individuals and communities to engage in collective action from anywhere in the world (Lou et al., 2024). The implications of these digital tools stretch beyond mere communication; they serve as catalysts for political advocacy, environmental campaigns, and social justice movements. Central to online activism is the concept of connectivity, which facilitates the rapid organization of campaigns that can garner support in a short time frame. Platforms enable users to share experiences, mobilize supporters, and advocate for a wide range of issues, from climate change to human rights. Digital tools allow activists to engage diverse audiences, utilize hashtags to build momentum, and create viral content that resonates across cultural and geographical boundaries (Ji & Tao, 2024). As a result, online activism often transcends individual efforts, fostering networks of solidarity that can amplify messages and generate substantial societal impact. However, online activism is not without its challenges. Digital divides, disinformation, and online harassment can hinder progress and marginalize certain voices within movements. Moreover, the fleeting nature of internet attention can lead to what some call "slacktivism," where individuals support causes superficially without engaging in more substantial forms of activism. Critically, the effectiveness of online activism lies in its ability to translate digital engagement into real-world actions and policy changes (Zhang, 2024). As societies increasingly navigate the complex interplay of digital spaces and activism, understanding the nuances of online advocacy becomes essential for strategizing and achieving meaningful change while fostering an inclusive, informed citizenry.

The emergence of digital resistance is intricately linked to the rapid evolution of technology and the internet, particularly from the mid-1990s onward. This era marked the proliferation of personal computers and the subsequent rise of online platforms that facilitated communication and mobilization on a global scale. Early instances of digital resistance can be traced to the activism surrounding issues such as the anti-globalization movement, which gained momentum during the protests in Seattle in 1999 (McDaniel, 2024). Activists exploited new media to organize, disseminate information, and counter dominant narratives, thus showcasing the internet's potential for amplifying marginalized voices. This trend was further bolstered by the advent of social media platforms in the 2000s, which enabled real-time interactions, creating immersive environments for political discourse. As digital landscapes evolved, so too did the strategies of those engaged in resistance movements. The Arab Spring, which unfolded from late 2010 to 2012, serves as a prominent example of digital resistance manifesting in a significant sociopolitical context. Activists utilized platforms to organize protests, share information, and document human rights abuses under oppressive regimes (Neenan et al., 2024).

The viral nature of social media allowed grassroots movements to bypass traditional media gatekeepers, fostering an unprecedented level of participation and international solidarity. Moreover, these platforms have offered participants protective anonymity, a vital feature in authoritarian contexts where dissent is often met with harsh repercussions. However, the historical context of digital resistance also encompasses the challenges and limitations faced by activists. Governments and corporations have increasingly turned to surveillance technologies and data analytics to monitor and suppress dissent (Shafik, 2024b). Initiatives such as cyber censorship, the arrest of online dissidents, and the manipulation of algorithms reveal a complex interplay between empowerment and repression in the digital arena. Nevertheless, resistance within this context continues to adapt, demonstrating resilience through the development of counter-surveillance tools and encrypted communication methods. The historical trajectory illustrates that while digital technologies can serve as powerful instruments for social change, they are equally subject to exploitation and control, necessitating ongoing vigilance from digital activists and allies alike (Pham et al., 2024).

## 1. TYPES OF ONLINE ACTIVISM

Online activism manifests in diverse forms, each harnessing the unique capabilities of digital platforms to advocate for social change. Three predominant types include social media movements, hashtag activism, and petitions or e-campaigns, each playing a distinct role in contemporary activism. Social media movements have gained traction as dynamic expressions of collective action, where platforms serve as arenas for mobilization and awareness-raising. These movements often emerge around specific issues, such as climate change or racial equality, enabling users to share experiences, strategies, and information widely. The rapid dissemination of content allows activists to amplify their messages and engage with broader audiences, facilitating solidarity and collective organizing (Kim et al., 2024). Notably, social media movements can lead to significant offline actions, such as protests or community engagement initiatives, thus blurring the lines between virtual and physical activism. Hashtag activism is a unique phenomenon within the realm of online activism, allowing individuals to participate in conversations surrounding pressing social issues through the use of specific hashtags. This method of engagement not only streamlines the discourse but also enhances visibility, amplifying marginalized voices and fostering solidarity across geographic and cultural boundaries. Campaigns exemplify the power of hashtag activism, enabling users to contribute personal narratives that resonate with wider systemic concerns (J. Jun et al., 2024). Through the aggregation of diverse experiences and perspectives, these hashtags create a collective consciousness that can lead to tangible changes in societal attitudes and policies. E-campaigns and online petitions represent another significant facet of online activism, leveraging digital platforms to mobilize support for specific causes. Websites facilitate the creation and dissemination of petitions, enabling activists to gather signatures and demonstrate public support for their issues. This method of advocacy not only captures the attention of policymakers but also mobilizes communities to engage in dialogue and action around critical issues. Furthermore, e-campaigns often employ multimedia strategies to enrich their outreach, utilizing videos, infographics, and interactive content to convey messages more effectively (Shafik, 2024c). In this landscape, online activism continues to evolve, integrating various forms of engagement to address societal challenges and promote impactful change.

## 1.1. Social Media Movements

Social media movements have emerged as a powerful catalyst for social change in the digital age, leveraging platforms to mobilize individuals around common causes. These movements utilize the unique attributes of social media—speed, reach, and user interactivity—to amplify voices and foster a sense of community among diverse groups. By allowing users to share content in real time, encourage discussions, and create networks of solidarity, social media movements can bring attention to social, political, and environmental issues that may otherwise go unnoticed by traditional media outlets (Dey & Dey, 2024). One notable example is the Black Lives Matter movement, which gained significant traction through social media following the tragic death of an individual in May 2020. The hashtag, originally coined in 2013, was reignited and rapidly disseminated across various platforms, creating a global outcry against racial injustice and police brutality. The impact of such movements extends beyond mere online discussions; they have the potential to lead to real-world action, including protests, policy changes, and increased awareness of systemic issues. Crucially, social media movements can be decentralized, allowing grassroots organizers to operate independently while still benefiting from the collective power of widespread online engagement. The dynamics of social media movements also involve both opportunities and challenges (Zhang, 2024). While they can democratize the process of activism by lowering entry barriers, they are not without risks. Issues such as misinformation, performative allyship, and the potential for burnout among activists can undermine the authenticity and effectiveness of these movements. Additionally, the transient nature of social media can lead to fleeting attention spans, making it essential for activists to create strategies that foster sustained engagement. As social media continues to evolve, the landscape of activism will likely shift, requiring ongoing adaptation by those advocating for change (Gao, 2022). Thus, social media movements represent a complex ecosystem where technology intersects with social issues, embodying both the promise and the perils of online activism.

## 1.2. Hashtag Activism

Hashtag activism has emerged as a powerful tool for social movements, enabling individuals and organizations to rally support, raise awareness, and mobilize action around specific issues. By utilizing concise, memorable phrases prefixed by the hash symbol, activists can catalyze conversations across various social media platforms, transforming individual posts into collective narratives. This phenomenon gained significant traction with campaigns that underscored systemic racism and police brutality and highlighted the prevalence of sexual harassment and assault (Greijdanus et al., 2020). The unique structure of hashtags allows for broad dissemination, encouraging diverse contributors to share personal experiences, insights, and solidarity, thereby amplifying the voices of marginalized communities. The speed and reach of hashtag activism are facilitated by the nature of digital communication, wherein a single tweet or post can transcend geographical boundaries within seconds. This rapid spread is bolstered by the algorithms of social media platforms, which often prioritize trending topics, further propelling hashtags into public consciousness. The dynamic nature of hashtags creates a continuous flow of information and engagement, fostering a sense of urgency around social issues (Lou et al., 2024). However, the effectiveness of hashtag activism extends beyond mere visibility; it is often coupled with strategic calls to action, urging followers to participate in protests, sign petitions, or engage in dialogue with policymakers. Despite its successes, hashtag activism is not without its critiques. Detractors argue that it can lead to shallow engagement that lacks tangibility, reducing serious social issues to mere online trends. Amidst this skepticism, it remains essential to recognize that hashtag activism has the potential to serve as a gateway for deeper political engagement. By raising consciousness and cultivating relationships among activists, these digital campaigns can facilitate lasting change, pushing issues into the mainstream while creating platforms for dialogue and activism that extend far beyond the initial hashtag (Pham et al., 2024). As a fundamental aspect of contemporary online activism, hashtags can galvanize movements, engender empathy, and foster a sense of community among individuals dedicated to social justice and resistance.

## 1.3. Petitions and E-Campaigns

Petitions and e-campaigns have emerged as pivotal tools in the realm of online activism, synergizing grassroots efforts with the vast reach of the digital landscape. These instruments allow individuals and organizations to mobilize support for various causes, leveraging the collective ethos of the internet to amplify messages and demand change. Online petitions allow anyone with internet access to voice their concerns, gather signatures, and demonstrate public support for specific issues ranging from environmental protection to human rights. Platforms not only facilitate the creation and signing of petitions but also provide users with analytics and communication tools to engage supporters effectively throughout the campaign (Shafik, 2025e). The process of launching an e-campaign often follows a structured approach, beginning with issue identification and the development of a clear, compelling message. Strategically crafting the petition is crucial, as it should concisely outline the problem and proposed solutions to resonate with potential signatories. The power of these campaigns lies not only in the numerical strength of signatures amassed but also in their ability to harness digital storytelling (Pham et al., 2024).

Engaging narratives, impactful images, and well-produced videos are commonly employed to evoke emotional responses and create a sense of urgency among audiences. Once the petition is live, social sharing becomes vital; effective campaigns frequently utilize social media platforms for widespread distribution, employing hashtags and influencer partnerships to enhance visibility and engagement. E-campaigns transcend traditional activism by enabling organizers to track progress and adapt their strategies in real time. Data analytics can reveal which messages resonate best with audiences, allowing for targeted actions to increase participation rates (Zhang, 2024). Additionally, digital activism fosters a sense of community among supporters, creating networks of individuals united by a common cause, often leading to further actions such as fundraising or lobbying efforts. While the efficacy of online petitions can be debated, their capacity to mobilize large numbers of people and influence decision-makers cannot be understood. As they form a cornerstone of digital resistance, these initiatives exemplify how technology can facilitate engagement, advocate for change, and empower individuals to become active participants in the democratic process, as some comparisons are presented in Table 1.

*Table 1. Comparison of Online Activism, Digital Resistance, and Counter-Platform Practices*

| Aspect | Online Activism | Digital Resistance | Counter-Platform Practices | Illustrations | Reference |
|---|---|---|---|---|---|
| Definition | Use of digital tools for advocacy | Acts of opposition to digital control | Alternative digital practices challenging norms | Mastodon, Signal, Anonymous | (Dal et al., 2023) |
| Main Tools/ Mediums | Social media, petitions, blogs | Encrypted apps, VPNs, and TOR | Independent platforms, ad blockers | Change.org, Tor, IndieWeb | (Gao, 2022) |
| Nature of Action | Public and visible campaigns | Covert or anonymous resistance | Structural or technical challenges to platforms | Web decentralization, data obfuscation | (Greijdanus et al., 2020) |
| Key Objectives | Raise awareness, mobilize people | Subvert control, evade surveillance | Dismantle platform monopolies | Decentralized social networks | (Li, 2023) |
| Audience Engagement | Mass participation, viral content | Targeted, tactical communication | Niche or community-focused | Reddit subcultures, blockchain-based forums | (Kopacheva, 2021) |
| Institutional Role | Often collaborates with NGOs | Opposes institutional surveillance | Opposes Big Tech centralization | WikiLeaks, whistleblowers | (Menteş, 2019) |
| Examples of Tactics | Hashtag campaigns, digital protests | DDOS attacks, hacktivism | Platform migration, federated protocols | #BlackLivesMatter, Anonymous, Mastodon | (Dey & Dey, 2024) |
| Response to Censorship | Petition platforms, shadow campaigns | Encryption, mirror sites | Creation of censorship-resistant platforms | CryptPad, PeerTube | (Bagdadi, 2024) |
| Organizational Structure | Horizontal, loosely structured | Decentralized or anonymous cells | Distributed peer-to-peer networks | Diaspora*, Scuttlebutt | (Abdelaal, 2024) |
| Ideological Roots | Civil rights, social justice | Anti-authoritarian, anti-surveillance | Tech decentralization, digital sovereignty | Crypto-anarchism, techno-liberationism | (Do et al., 2024) |
| Risk Level | Low to moderate | Moderate to high | Moderate | Risk varies with platform and context | (Bertrams & Krispenz, 2024) |
| Role of Technology | Enabler of mass participation | Tool for evasion and resistance | Site of contestation and reinvention | GitHub forks of banned tools | (J. Jun et al., 2024) |

continued on following page

*Table 1. Continued*

| Aspect | Online Activism | Digital Resistance | Counter-Platform Practices | Illustrations | Reference |
|---|---|---|---|---|---|
| Legal Implications | Often within legal bounds | May involve gray or illegal areas | Often in opposition to platform terms | DMCA takedown evasion | (Shafik, 2025c) |
| End Goal | Policy change, awareness | Disruption of oppressive systems | Resilient alternatives to existing platforms | Federated digital commons | (Shafik, 2024d) |

## 2. PLATFORMS FOR ACTIVISM

As the digital landscape continues to evolve, various online platforms have emerged as vital tools for activists seeking to effect change. Social media, in particular, serves as a multi-faceted arena where diverse forms of activism manifest, allowing individuals and organizations to mobilize support, share narratives, and amplify their voices. These platforms not only facilitate grassroots movements but also operate as catalysts for social and cultural shifts, demonstrating the power of digital engagement in contemporary society (Shafik, 2025b). Facebook stands out as a pivotal platform for activist coordination and community building, offering a space for users to create events, disseminate information, and form groups centered around specific causes. Its extensive user base enables organizations to reach a broad audience, while features like live streaming and fundraising tools enhance engagement and mobilization efforts. Activists can leverage Facebook's targeting capabilities to reach specific demographics or geographic regions, making it an effective tool for localized campaigns. However, the platform's algorithm and policies can also hinder visibility, leading to a reliance on paid promotions to ensure messages reach intended audiences (Neenan et al., 2024). This duality exemplifies both the potential and limitations inherent to Facebook as a vehicle for social change.

Twitter, with its emphasis on brevity and immediacy, serves as a powerful conduit for real-time mobilization and urgent calls to action. The platform's capacity for rapid information sharing allows activists to organize around pressing issues as they unfold, exemplified by movements such as. The use of hashtags not only categorizes conversations but also lends a sense of community among supporters, facilitating the rapid dissemination of resources, information, and solidarity statements. Its open nature encourages engagement with a wider audience, fostering connections among diverse groups while posing challenges related to misinformation and online harassment.

Activists must navigate these complexities to harness Twitter's potential effectively. Instagram complements these textual platforms with a focus on visual storytelling, transforming narratives through imagery and video (Lin et al., 2021). Activists utilize the platform to capture powerful moments, share personal stories, and engage audiences emotionally. The ephemeral nature of Stories allows for intimate updates and real-time participation, while posts can garner widespread attention through the strategic use of hashtags and influencer partnerships. Through compelling visuals, activists can evoke empathy and spur action in ways that resonate deeply with users, often transcending language barriers. However, the platform's reliance on aesthetics can sometimes dilute complex social issues, requiring a delicate balance between visual appeal and substantive content to maintain impact (Shafik, 2025d). Together, these platforms weave a comprehensive tapestry of digital activism, underscoring the dynamic nature of resistance in an interconnected world.

## 2.1. Facebook as a Tool for Change

Facebook has emerged as a potent platform for social change, serving as a conduit for grassroots movements and a facilitator of widespread discourse on critical issues. As one of the largest social media networks globally, Facebook offers unique tools that empower users to mobilize support, disseminate information, and organize events ranging from local gatherings to global campaigns. The platform's features, such as groups, events, and fundraising capabilities, enable users to create communities around shared causes. Activists leverage these tools to connect like-minded individuals, articulate their demands, and amplify their voices in ways that were previously unimaginable, forging networks that transcend geographic boundaries (Lou et al., 2024). The potential for Facebook to drive social change is exemplified by numerous campaigns that gained traction and visibility through the platform. Initiatives such as the movement employed Facebook not only to disseminate information about racial inequality and police brutality but also to organize protests and raise awareness. The ability to share video content and personal stories allows for compelling narrative-building that can resonate deeply with audiences, thereby mobilizing support at unprecedented levels. This dynamic engagement fosters a sense of community, enabling diverse individuals to contribute to shared causes and take collective action, primarily through the likes of community pages or topic-specific groups (Ji & Tao, 2024). However, the effectiveness of Facebook as a tool for activism is not without challenges. The platform's algorithms can sometimes prioritize engagement-driven content over more substantive discussions, leading to the spread of misinformation or sensationalism that can dilute important messages. Furthermore, privacy concerns and the risk of surveillance may deter some users from fully participating in activist endeavors. Nevertheless, Facebook remains a critical resource for contemporary activism, illustrating how digital spaces can facilitate discourse and mobilization while also highlighting the complexities of navigating these modern digital landscapes. In sum, Facebook serves not merely as a social network but as an evolving arena where users can articulate their concerns, invoke social change, and collectively imagine a different future (Zhang, 2024).

## 2.2. Twitter and Real-Time Mobilization

Twitter, as a microblogging platform, has played an instrumental role in facilitating real-time mobilization for various social movements across the globe. The platform's design allows users to disseminate information quickly and coherently, effectively transforming how individuals and organizations communicate during critical events. Twitter's unique features, such as trending hashtags and retweets, enable users to rally support, raise awareness, and coordinate collective actions on a scale previously unattainable scale. By allowing activists to share updates instantaneously, the platform creates a sense of urgency that prompts rapid responses, often fueling grassroots movements and global solidarity (McDaniel, 2024). One of the most notable aspects of Twitter's role in mobilization is its ability to amplify voices that might otherwise be marginalized. During significant events like protests, natural disasters, or political crises, users can harness hashtags to centralize discourse and improve visibility for specific causes. Campaigns illustrate how Twitter has enabled both local and international audiences to engage with critical social justice issues, fostering community and galvanizing efforts towards tangible outcomes (Pham et al., 2024). The rapid circulation of information on Twitter not only informs participants but also attracts media attention, thereby magnifying the impact of civil disobedience and collective demonstrations. Moreover, Twitter serves as a space for real-time organization, allowing activists to communicate strategies and logistical information seamlessly. For instance, through the use of location-specific tweets and threads, organizations can coordinate mobilizations more efficiently, ensuring that participants are informed and engaged. This immediacy empowers individuals to contribute their voices and actions to larger movements, displaying a nuanced interplay between online engagement and physical protest (Kim et al., 2024). As this platform continues to evolve, its significance in shaping discourse, enhancing mobilization efforts, and influencing socio-political dynamics remains profound, demonstrating the power of digital spaces in driving activism and resistance in contemporary society.

## 2.3. Instagram and Visual Storytelling

In the landscape of online activism, Instagram stands out as a dynamic platform that leverages visual storytelling to engage and mobilize users around social issues. With its emphasis on imagery and short-form video content, Instagram transcends the limitations of textual narratives, enabling activists to convey powerful messages through captivating visuals. This platform's unique format encourages creativity and immediacy, allowing movements to craft compelling narratives that resonate emotionally with their audience. A well-curated feed or an impactful story can encapsulate complex social problems, making them accessible and compelling, thus catalyzing engagement and fostering a sense of community among users who may not otherwise connect through more traditional forms of activism (J. Jun et al., 2024). The visual-centric nature of Instagram facilitates a more intimate dialogue with followers, encouraging them to participate actively in social movements. Activists utilize hashtags, geotags, and challenges to create widespread visibility for their causes, often resulting in trends that capture the collective consciousness of users. Successful campaigns often employ relatable imagery, influence partnerships, and user-generated content to amplify their reach and impact. This approach not only democratizes storytelling but also allows for diverse voices to emerge, reflecting the multifaceted nature of social issues. Movements like Black Lives Matter and environmental activism have harnessed Instagram's power to facilitate discourse, share personal narratives, and mobilize support, all while preserving the emotional weight of their messages through striking visuals (Shafik, 2025a). Moreover, the platform's ephemeral content, notably through Instagram Stories, enables activists to share real-time updates and urgent calls for action. This immediacy not only informs followers but also cultivates a sense of urgency around pressing social issues. The visual aesthetic of Instagram is particularly effective in creating shareable content, which can rapidly circulate and garner attention in ways that traditional media might not. Consequently, Instagram serves as a vital tool for activists aiming to not only raise awareness but also foster community and spur collective action through the art of visual storytelling (Shafik, 2023b). By creating evocative images and narratives, activists can transcend geographical boundaries, uniting individuals around common goals while inspiring them to engage in meaningful dialogue and action.

# 3. DIGITAL RESISTANCE STRATEGIES

Digital resistance strategies encompass a range of techniques that individuals and groups employ to challenge and mitigate surveillance, censorship, and oppression in the online landscape. As digital systems increasingly mediate our interactions, robust strategies have emerged to navigate obstacles posed by authoritarian regimes, corporate control, and invasive state surveillance. Central to these strategies is the adoption of counter-surveillance techniques, such as the use of anonymizing tools and platforms that obscure users' identities and activities online (Lou et al., 2024). Technologies like VPNs and Tor empower individuals by concealing their IP addresses, making it difficult for adversaries to monitor their online behaviors. Additionally, users frequently employ practical skills such as digital self-defense, learning to recognize and avoid digital footprints that could expose them to unwanted scrutiny. Another critical dimension of digital resistance lies in anonymity and pseudonymity. These concepts allow activists to maintain a layer of protection while engaging in online discourse or organizing movements. By utilizing pseudonyms, individuals can express dissenting opinions or share sensitive information without the fear of personal repercussions (Dal et al., 2023). This strategy not only fosters a safe space for critical voices to emerge but also encourages broader participation in activism and discourse. Platforms that prioritize user privacy, such as decentralized networks or encrypted messaging applications, facilitate this form of engagement, thereby lowering the risks of identification and retribution by state or corporate forces. Encryption and secure communication also play a fundamental role in digital resistance strategies. The application of end-to-end encryption in messaging services ensures that only the intended recipients can access the contents of their communications, rendering it almost impossible for intermediaries to intercept or manipulate messages. Moreover, tools that enhance email security empower political activists to coordinate and share information without fear of monitoring. Collectively, these strategies enhance the resilience of digital activism by fostering a culture of security and privacy, essential for effective resistance against oppressive digital environments (Gao, 2022). By equipping users with the necessary tools and knowledge, digital resistance strategies contribute significantly to the ongoing struggle for rights and freedoms in an increasingly surveilled and controlled online space.

## 3.1. Counter-Surveillance Techniques

Counter-surveillance techniques are essential tools employed by activists and individuals seeking to protect their privacy and security in environments increasingly dominated by surveillance technologies. These techniques can range from the use of simple countermeasures, such as altering one's digital behavior, to sophisticated technological interventions specifically designed to deceive or avoid detection by surveillance systems. For instance, individuals may adopt practices like employing ad blockers, disabling location tracking, or utilizing privacy-focused web browsers to reduce their digital footprints while online (Greijdanus et al., 2020). As mainstream platforms often harvest user data, it becomes crucial for activists to be conscious of their online engagement and its potential ramifications. Another critical aspect of counter-surveillance involves the deployment of physical measures intended to mitigate observation in face-to-face interactions. This can include the strategic use of physical barriers, such as mirrors or reflective surfaces, to observe who may be surveilling them, or employing techniques to disrupt unauthorized electronic surveillance devices (Li, 2023). Moreover, individuals may adopt behavioral techniques, including changing routines or utilizing decoys to confuse would-be trackers.

The advent of wearable technology and smart devices, while presenting new opportunities for connectivity and data collection, also necessitates a heightened vigilance concerning how these tools can be manipulated to facilitate unwanted surveillance. Activists often rely on community-based intelligence sharing to remain aware of the latest surveillance tactics used by authorities, enhancing their collective ability to respond promptly and adapt their resistance strategies effectively. The effectiveness of counter-surveillance lies in its ability to empower individuals and groups facing oppressive monitoring (Kopacheva, 2021). In a world where data is increasingly weaponized against activists, the proactive enactment of these techniques is pivotal. By fostering a culture of awareness and adopting a multi-faceted approach to surveillance evasion, activists not only enhance their personal security but contribute to a broader ecosystem of digital resistance. This ongoing war of attrition between surveillance entities and those resisting their intrusions marks a significant chapter in the narrative of online activism, underscoring the importance of adaptability, innovation, and solidarity in confronting the pervasive nature of surveillance in contemporary society (Menteş, 2019).

## 3.2. Anonymity and Pseudonymity

Anonymity and pseudonymity are critical concepts in the realm of online activism and digital resistance, serving as pivotal mechanisms that empower individuals to engage in sociopolitical discourse and dissent without exposing their identities to potential reprisals. Anonymity refers to the condition in which an individual's true identity is completely masked, allowing for interaction without the risk of identification. This level of privacy is not merely a protective layer; it is a fundamental enabler of free expression, particularly in authoritarian regimes where dissent is met with severe consequences (Dey & Dey, 2024). Anonymous social media accounts often serve as platforms for whistleblowers and activists to voice their critiques of government policies or corporate malfeasances without the looming threat of persecution. Pseudonymity, while resembling anonymity, involves the use of a consistent alias or persona that can be identified but does not reveal the user's real identity.

This construct allows activists the liberty to build a reputation or community around a particular cause while managing their personal safety (Bagdadi, 2024).

Notable examples include prominent online platforms where pseudonymous users can cultivate influential followings and share vital information regarding human rights abuses or community mobilization efforts. However, the balancing act between visibility and safety is tenuous; pseudonymous identities are not entirely devoid of risks and can sometimes be sufficient for adversaries to unearth their real-life counterparts through digital footprints, social engineering, or data breaches. Both anonymity and pseudonymity are essential tools for safeguarding online activism, yet they also raise questions about accountability and trust (Abdelaal, 2024). The veil of obscurity can encourage more candid discourse, but it can also lead to negative behaviors such as trolling or spreading misinformation without consequence. Activists must navigate this complex terrain by employing various digital practices to reinforce their anonymity or pseudonymity. As digital spaces continue to evolve and respond to governmental and corporate surveillance efforts, understanding these constructs becomes increasingly crucial for anyone engaged in online activism or digital resistance, allowing them to foster open dialogues while safeguarding their personal well-being (Do et al., 2024).

## 3.3. Encryption and Secure Communication

Encryption and secure communication are critical components in the landscape of online activism and digital resistance. As activists increasingly find themselves under surveillance from various entities—ranging from government authorities to corporate interests, the need for strong encryption practices has never been more pronounced. Encryption serves as a pivotal tool that transforms plaintext information into unreadable code, rendering it inaccessible to unauthorized parties. This mechanism is crucial for protecting sensitive information, safeguarding the identities of activists, and facilitating free expression in oppressive regimes (Bertrams & Krispenz, 2024). By employing various encryption algorithms, individuals and organizations can ensure that their communications remain confidential and secure. Moreover, secure communication protocols, such as Transport Layer Security and end-to-end encryption, further bolster the privacy of online discourse. End-to-end encryption, in particular, has gained traction in applications where messages are encrypted on the sender's device and only decrypted by the intended recipient. This means that even the service providers cannot access the content of these communications, a crucial feature for those engaged in activism. As the global landscape of digital communication continues to evolve, activists must adopt robust encryption techniques and secure communication methods to mitigate the risks associated with digital surveillance (J. Jun et al., 2024). The impact of encryption extends beyond individual protection; it acts as a collective barrier against censorship and suppression of dissent. In environments where freedom of speech is curtailed, secure communication practices empower activists to organize, share information, and mobilize support without fear of reprisal. By utilizing tools such as virtual private networks or encrypted email services, activists can further shield their online activities, enabling a more resilient digital resistance (Kim et al., 2024). Ultimately, the integration of encryption and secure communication into digital activism not only protects personal privacy but also fortifies the broader struggle for human rights and social justice in the digital age, as presented in Table 2.

*Table 2. Transformation and Tensions in Digital Activism Ecosystems*

| Dimension | Traditional Model | Digitized Model | Challenges | Emerging Strategies | Reference |
|---|---|---|---|---|---|
| Mobilization | Physical protests | Hashtag movements, viral campaigns | Slacktivism, echo chambers | Hybrid activism (online + offline) | (Dal et al., 2023) |
| Messaging | Pamphlets, speeches | Memes, live-streams, short videos | Misinformation, content moderation | Fact-checking bots, ethical media literacy | (Gao, 2022) |
| Communication Channels | Radio, newspapers | Facebook, Twitter, TikTok | Algorithmic filtering, platform bias | Decentralized media platforms | (Greijdanus et al., 2020) |
| Leadership | Centralized leadership | Horizontal networks | Lack of coordination, message dilution | Collective decision tools (e.g. Loomio) | (Li, 2023) |
| Surveillance & Privacy | Police surveillance | State/corporate surveillance | Data mining, profiling | Encryption, zero-knowledge protocols | (Kopacheva, 2021) |
| Funding | Donations, grants | Crowdfunding, crypto-donations | Financial deplatforming | Blockchain-based funding platforms | (Menteş, 2019) |
| Reach & Accessibility | Limited by geography | Global, instant access | Digital divide, censorship | Offline mobilization support tools | (Dey & Dey, 2024) |
| Resistance Form | Sit-ins, marches | Online petitions, cyber disruptions | Criminalization of digital protest | Legal digital protest frameworks | (Bagdadi, 2024) |
| Representation | Traditional media gatekeepers | User-generated content | Platform manipulation, deepfakes | Transparent content verification | (Abdelaal, 2024) |
| Sustainability | Movement fatigue | Rapid engagement | Short attention spans | Long-term community platforms | (Do et al., 2024) |

continued on following page

*Table 2. Continued*

| Dimension | Traditional Model | Digitized Model | Challenges | Emerging Strategies | Reference |
|---|---|---|---|---|---|
| Public Sphere | Town halls, debates | Social media platforms | Monetization of discourse | Commons-oriented forums | (Bertrams & Krispenz, 2024) |
| Policy Influence | Lobbying | Mass pressure via online visibility | Tokenism from policymakers | Coordinated e-advocacy platforms | (J. Jun et al., 2024) |
| International Solidarity | NGOs and coalitions | Global hashtags and campaigns | Censorship across jurisdictions | VPN-based global participation | (Kim et al., 2024) |
| Content Control | Self-publishing or media dependence | Algorithmic gatekeeping | Deplatforming, demonetization | Federated social media, open protocols | (Pham et al., 2024) |

## 4. CASE STUDIES OF SUCCESSFUL ONLINE ACTIVISM

Online activism has empowered individuals and groups to affect socio-political change, leveraging digital tools for collective mobilization. The case studies examined here exemplify the transformative power of online movements in shaping public discourse and driving real-world action. The Arab Spring serves as a seminal instance where social media platforms became catalysts for political upheaval (Neenan et al., 2024). In 2010, a series of protests began in Tunisia, initiated by a young man's act of self-immolation in response to police corruption. Social media rapidly galvanized support across the region, enabling disparate groups to organize and disseminate information amidst government crackdowns. Activists harnessed these platforms not only to communicate their demands but also to showcase brutal state responses, effectively rallying international attention and support for their causes. The profound impact of this digital resistance laid bare the potential of online networks to instigate change, influencing subsequent uprisings in countries like Egypt and Libya (McDaniel, 2024).

Similarly, the Black Lives Matter movement illustrates the capacity of online activism to address systemic racism and police brutality. Sparked in 2013 by the acquittal of George Zimmerman in the shooting death of Trayvon Martin, the BLM hashtag swiftly garnered momentum on social media, serving both as a call to action and a means to share personal narratives, statistics, and videos of police violence. Leveraging platforms, activists fostered a global community united in dissent (Zhang, 2024). The movement's ability to mobilize protests, advocate policy reform, and influence public opinion can be directly linked to its digital presence, demonstrating the potential of hashtags to not only amplify voices but also catalyze tangible change within political and societal frameworks. BLM has expanded its outreach by forming partnerships with various organizations, thereby broadening its impact beyond immediate protests (Ji & Tao, 2024).

The recent climate strikes led by youth activists signify another milestone in online mobilization, encapsulating the intersection of social media, activism, and environmental issues. Initiated by a youth activist who began her solitary protest outside the parliament, this movement quickly gained traction through platforms. The campaign saw millions of students worldwide join forces, organizing demonstrations and demanding government accountability on climate action. Their strategic use of social media to convey urgency, educational materials, and actionable steps galvanizes a younger demographic, turning awareness into activism (Lou et al., 2024). The success of this initiative exemplifies the ability of online platforms to facilitate grassroots organization, spark international dialogues, and influence global policy discussions, ultimately shaping a generation that prioritizes sustainability and collective action as primary vehicles for change. Each of these case studies underscores the evolving dynamics of online activism, where digital spaces serve as vital arenas for mobilization, discourse, and real-world impact in the face of entrenched systemic challenges (Zhang, 2024).

## 4.1. The Arab Spring

The Arab Spring, commencing in late 2010, epitomized a revolutionary wave of protests and uprisings across the Arab world, significantly driven by online activism and digital communication. This period marked the collision of socio-political discontent and the proliferation of social media platforms, which facilitated the rapid dissemination of information and mobilization of protestors. In Tunisia, where the movement originated, a series of coordinated demonstrations against government corruption and social injustice was ignited by the self-immolation of a street vendor whose plight symbolized the economic despair faced by many (Neenan et al., 2024). Activists utilized social media to organize protests, share news, and garner international support, illustrating the transformative power of digital tools in contemporary revolutions. As protests swept across countries like Egypt, Libya, and Syria, social media became a critical component of the struggle for change. In Egypt, the use of social media to organize the protests exemplified how digital spaces could translate into physical movements. The platform allowed activists to bypass state-controlled media, spreading messages quickly and mobilizing crowds in unprecedented ways. Hashtags became rallying cries, uniting diverse groups around a common goal: the ousting of long-standing authoritarian regimes. However, while social media empowered activists, it also drew the attention of oppressive governments that sought to suppress dissent. In response, regimes resorted to tactics such as internet blackouts, surveillance, and targeted arrests of activists, highlighting the dual nature of online tools as both facilitators of activism and instruments of control (Pham et al., 2024). The Arab Spring ultimately illustrated the potency of online activism in sparking widespread political change, yet it also revealed the complexities and limitations inherent in digital resistance. As movements matured, the lack of cohesive leadership and clear political objectives often led to fragmentation. Countries like Libya descended into civil conflict, and in Syria, the civil uprising evolved into a protracted and devastating war. While numerous governments fell, the aftermath of the Arab Spring raised critical questions about the sustainability of digital activism, the challenges of transitional governance, and the persistent struggle for human rights in the region (Kim et al., 2024). The Arab Spring remains a salient case study of how online platforms can mobilize and inspire, but it also serves as a cautionary tale about the precarious balance between empowerment and repression within the digital landscape.

## 4.2. Black Lives Matter Movement

The Black Lives Matter movement emerged as a transformative force in online activism, serving as a potent response to systemic racism and police violence against Black individuals, particularly in the United States. The movement began in 2013 following the acquittal of an individual in the shooting death of Trayvon Martin. The hashtag was first used on social media platforms, galvanizing support and raising awareness around issues of racial injustice. By harnessing the power of digital technologies, activists have not only communicated urgent calls for justice but have also created a global network of solidarity that extends well beyond the initial hashtag (Bertrams & Krispenz, 2024). The digital resistance embodied by BLM showcases how social media platforms have been pivotal in disseminating information, organizing protests, and amplifying marginalized voices. In 2020, the movement gained unprecedented traction following a murder, with protests erupting worldwide. These digital campaigns served as powerful catalysts for public consciousness, leading to increased scrutiny of law enforcement practices and calls for legislative reform, including police defunding and banning chokeholds. The widespread sharing of graphic images and videos, often captured by ordinary citizens, provided visceral snapshots of racial violence, pushing difficult conversations about racism to the forefront of public discourse (Do et al., 2024). Moreover, the BLM movement exemplifies a decentralized organizational structure that relies on grassroots mobilization rather than a singular leadership, challenging traditional notions of activism. Through a combination of online petitions, educational campaigns, and strategic use of viral content, activists have effectively engaged diverse audiences. A campaign, for example, highlights the victims of police brutality, urging acknowledgment and remembrance. This approach not only emphasizes individual stories but also powerfully illustrates the pervasive nature of systemic racism, thus uniting disparate communities in a shared struggle for justice and equality (Abdelaal, 2024). In this way, the Black Lives Matter movement serves as a crucial case study of how digital tools can facilitate noisemaking, accountability, and ongoing societal change.

## 4.3. Climate Strikes and Youth Activism

The emergence of climate strikes, particularly those spearheaded by youth activists, represents a significant upsurge in contemporary social movements advocating environmental justice. Triggered by increasingly alarming scientific reports on climate change, as well as the visible manifestations of environmental degradation, these strikes mark a notable intersection of online activism and grassroots mobilization. Noteworthy figures catalyzed this global youth movement when they began solitary protests, calling for concrete action against climate inaction (Bagdadi, 2024). This initiative quickly transcended borders, inspiring millions of young people worldwide to engage through a virtual platform for sharing, organizing, and amplifying their collective demands. The synergy of social media and youth activism has revolutionized the discourse surrounding climate issues, fostering an environment in which information dissemination occurs at an unprecedented rate. Platforms enable youth activists to share personal narratives, scientific data, and calls to action, thus broadening the impact of their message. This digital resistance has manifested in a series of worldwide climate strikes, notably where millions gathered in cities to demand immediate climate action from governments and corporations. These events underscore a significant departure from traditional forms of activism, encapsulating a more dynamic and connected approach that targets the sensibilities of an increasingly disenchanted populace (Dey & Dey, 2024). The effectiveness of climate strikes is underscored not just by their ability to mobilize vast numbers of participants, but also by their role in shifting the narrative on climate policy. As youth articulate their visions for a sustainable future, they challenge prevailing assumptions held by policymakers and corporations alike, forcing a reconsideration of development paradigms. Through eloquent speeches in international forums, well-organized demonstrations, and creative digital campaigns, young activists assert their agency and call for accountability while emphasizing intergenerational equity. The intersection of online activism and climate strikes exemplifies a broader trend in which the youth are not merely passive observers of policy but active architects of systemic change (Kopacheva, 2021). As this movement evolves, it highlights the salient role digital platforms play in fostering civic engagement and shaping the future landscape of environmental governance.

## 5. CHALLENGES FACED BY ONLINE ACTIVISTS

Online activism, while offering a platform for marginalized voices and social movements, is fraught with numerous challenges that can hinder efforts for change. One primary obstacle is censorship and content moderation, which takes various forms from governmental repression to social media platform policies. Many activists find their messages suppressed through algorithms designed to filter content or through the outright removal of posts deemed inappropriate by platform authorities. This form of censorship not only stifles free expression but also creates an environment of self-censorship where activists may feel compelled to dilute their messages to avoid punitive actions (Li, 2023). Online activists often navigate a complex landscape where the boundaries of acceptable discourse shift in response to changing policies, as well as political climates both domestically and internationally. Alongside censorship, cybersecurity threats pose a significant risk to online activists. Activists can be targeted by surveillance, hacking, and coordinated harassment campaigns aimed at undermining their efforts or exposing their identities. A lack of adequate digital security practices leaves many activists vulnerable not just to loss of sensitive information, but also to potential physical threats in the real world. These cybersecurity challenges compel activists to adopt various countermeasures, such as employing encryption tools and utilizing secure communication channels (Greijdanus et al., 2020). However, the continuous arms race between activists and malicious actors often renders many of these strategies insufficient, requiring ongoing vigilance and adaptation. Moreover, the digital divide exacerbates challenges for online activism, as not all individuals have equal access to technology and internet connectivity. Activism often relies on decentralized networks and broad participation, yet socio-economic inequalities can limit the effectiveness of online campaigns. Individuals from marginalized communities may lack the necessary resources to engage fully in digital activism due to factors such as inadequate internet infrastructure or financial barriers that hinder access to modern devices. Consequently, the disparity in access can lead to uneven representation in movements, further alienating those who are already vulnerable. Addressing these challenges necessitates not only technological enhancements but also a concerted effort to create inclusive digital spaces that empower all voices in the fight for social justice (Gao, 2022).

## 5.1. Censorship and Content Moderation

Censorship and content moderation have emerged as pivotal challenges for online activists, particularly as digital platforms increasingly shape the dynamics of public discourse. At their core, censorship refers to the suppression of speech, public communication, or other information, which can be manifested through both legal regulations and informal mechanisms employed by private companies. This dynamic often blurs the line between protecting users from harmful content and infringing upon freedom of expression. For instance, laws enacted in various countries aim to curb misinformation and hate speech, yet they can equally serve as tools for governmental control, stifling dissent and limiting the voices of marginalized groups (Dal et al., 2023). The selective enforcement of these regulations often favors those in positions of power, prompting significant debate around the ethical responsibilities of platforms. Content moderation, on the other hand, occurs within these platforms as a response to user-generated content. Companies deploy algorithms alongside human moderators to assess and manage the vast array of posts, images, and videos circulated online. The processes involved can be opaque, leading to accusations of bias when certain political contents are flagged, removed, or de-prioritized in algorithmic feeds. While the intention behind content moderation is ostensibly to create a safe environment free from abuse and misinformation, the outcomes can severely limit activists' ability to organize, share critical information, and mobilize effectively (Greijdanus et al., 2020). These challenges are exacerbated by the rapid advancements in technology, which introduce complex dilemmas such as automated decision-making systems that may lack the nuanced understanding required for sensitive political contexts. Ultimately, the interplay between censorship and content moderation represents a delicate balancing act between upholding public safety and preserving the right to free expression. Activists must navigate this landscape carefully, often adapting their strategies in response to shifting policies and enforcement practices. As digital environments continue to evolve, understanding the implications of these processes is essential not only for fostering effective online activism but also for ensuring that marginalized voices are not silenced in the quest for a more equitable society (Li, 2023). The friction between civil liberties and the maintenance of order underscores the profound implications of censorship and content moderation for digital resistance movements worldwide, inviting ongoing reflection and advocacy for transparent practices in content governance.

## 5.2. Cybersecurity Threats

Cybersecurity threats pose significant challenges for online activists, making their endeavors to promote social justice and mobilize support more precarious. The digital landscape is fraught with dangers that can compromise the confidentiality, integrity, and availability of activist content. Threats such as Distributed Denial-of-Service attacks, phishing scams, and ransomware illustrate the diverse tactics employed by adversaries to disrupt and silence dissenting voices. For activists relying heavily on digital platforms for organization and outreach, these cybersecurity vulnerabilities can lead to a complete shutdown of initiatives, the loss of critical data, and irreversible reputational damage (Y. Jun et al., 2021; Shafik, 2024a). Furthermore, the complexities of cybersecurity extend to state-sponsored surveillance programs and the targeting of activists through social media manipulation. Governments and corporate entities may employ sophisticated methods to monitor online behavior, deter participation, or even infiltrate activist networks. This atmosphere of distrust not only heightens the risks for individuals but can also stifle collective action by instilling fear and discouraging open discourse. Moreover, the intersectionality of digital activism and issues of race, class, and geography complicates the landscape (Shafik et al., 2024). Activists from marginalized communities may face additional barriers, as they often lack access to adequate digital literacy and cybersecurity tools, thereby exacerbating their vulnerability to cyber threats. The ramifications of these cybersecurity threats are substantial, requiring online activists to adopt robust security practices, such as utilizing encrypted communication tools, employing strong and varied passwords, and remaining vigilant against potential social engineering tactics (Zhao et al., 2022). By fostering a culture of cybersecurity awareness, activists can better protect themselves and their movements from harmful intrusions. Building alliances with cybersecurity experts and organizations can facilitate knowledge-sharing and enhance the resilience of digital campaigns. Ultimately, navigating the complex web of cybersecurity threats is not just an individual responsibility; it requires a collective effort within the activist community to reinforce digital defenses, ensure greater security, and sustain the momentum of online movements dedicated to social change (Lou et al., 2024; Shafik, 2023a).

## 5.3. Digital Divide and Accessibility

The digital divide refers to the socioeconomic and geographic disparities in access to technology and the internet, which have significant implications for online activism and digital resistance. While the internet has emerged as a vital platform for mobilizing social movements and facilitating communication, not everyone possesses equal opportunities to engage in these virtual spaces. Factors such as income level, education, and geographic location contribute to a landscape where certain populations—especially marginalized and rural communities—find themselves excluded from the digital narrative (Gao, 2022). With nearly half of the world's population lacking reliable internet access, the divided limits voices that are crucial to broadening the discourse around social justice, environmental concerns, and human rights. Accessibility extends beyond mere internet connectivity; it encompasses the ability to utilize online platforms effectively. For individuals with disabilities, navigating digital spaces can be fraught with challenges. Websites and social media platforms often lack the necessary accommodation, which can alienate these users and diminish their participation in online activism. Moreover, language barriers and varying levels of digital literacy further complicate the landscape, making it difficult for non-native speakers or less technologically savvy individuals to contribute meaningfully to online discussions. Therefore, the digital divide not only inhibits access but also systematically disenfranchises vulnerable populations from participating fully in the democratic processes facilitated by digital platforms (Lou et al., 2024). Addressing the digital divide and enhancing accessibility are paramount for fostering an inclusive environment for online activism. Solutions such as public investment in digital infrastructure, affordable internet access initiatives, and adaptive technologies can help bridge these gaps. Moreover, raising awareness about digital literacy and providing training programs can empower individuals from underserved communities to navigate the digital landscape confidently. Such measures not only amplify diverse voices in the fight for equity and justice but also strengthen digital resistance against oppressive systems (Pham et al., 2024). In a world increasingly reliant on digital spaces for activism, addressing these challenges is critical to ensuring that every individual's voice can contribute to the ongoing struggle for a more equitable society.

## 6. THE ROLE OF INFLUENCERS IN ACTIVISM

The role of influencers in activism has emerged as a significant force in the digital landscape, where social media platforms serve as primary arenas for social and political discourse. Influencers, typically individuals with substantial followings on platforms like Instagram, Twitter, and TikTok, have the ability to shape public opinion and mobilize their audience toward collective action. By leveraging their reach and pre-existing rapport with followers, many influencers bridge the gap between personal narrative and systemic issues, highlighting the importance of social justice, environmental concerns, and human rights. Their capacity to narrate personal stories, share timely information, and galvanize community efforts fosters meaningful engagement among diverse demographics (Kim et al., 2024). Influencer activism, however, is not without its complexities. While influencers can drive awareness and participation, their involvement often raises questions about authenticity and the commodification of activism. The phenomenon of "performative activism," where actions are taken primarily for social media visibility rather than genuine commitment to a cause, can undermine trust and dilute the message of grassroots movements. Moreover, the motivations behind influencer engagement can be multifaceted, ranging from promoting a personal brand to spearheading social change (J. Jun et al., 2024). This duality challenges audiences to discern genuine advocacy from opportunistic gestures, thus necessitating a critical understanding of the influencer landscape. Importantly, the effectiveness of influence-led activism can also hinge on their ability to engage with their audience in a meaningful manner. Successful influencers often cultivate a narrative that resonates on a personal level, prompting followers to participate in campaigns, donate to causes, or fundamentally re-evaluate their beliefs and behaviors. Collaborative efforts with established organizations can amplify these messages, providing influences with both credibility and resources. As the digital milieu continues to evolve, the intersection of influence and activism represents a dynamic shift in how movements are conceived, organized, and executed, potentially reshaping the public's approach to engagement and advocacy in the contemporary era (Bertrams & Krispenz, 2024).

## 7. ETHICAL CONSIDERATIONS IN DIGITAL ACTIVISM

Digital activism presents unique ethical considerations that merit careful examination, particularly as online platforms become increasingly influential arenas for social change. One key area is the proliferation of misinformation and fake news. The rapid dissemination of inaccurate or misleading information can significantly undermine the objectives of digital activism, eroding trust in movements that seek genuine reform. Activists must navigate the delicate line between promoting their agendas and ensuring that facts support their narratives. The ethical implications extend to the responsibility of activists to cross-verify information before sharing it with followers (Do et al., 2024). Engaging in fact-checking and promoting media literacy not only bolsters the credibility of activism but also ensures that the focus remains on authentic dialogue rather than sensationalism, which may inadvertently harm the very causes they advocate for. Cultural appropriation further complicates ethical considerations in digital activism. Activists need to tread carefully when adopting symbols, language, or strategies from cultures not their own, particularly in a diverse global society where cultural exchange can often be misunderstood or misrepresented. The appropriation of cultural elements can lead to commodification and reduce rich traditions to mere tokens within broader activist campaigns (Bagdadi, 2024; Li, 2023). Ethical digital activists are compelled to acknowledge the origins of the cultural artifacts they engage with, prioritizing respect and understanding over performative allyship. This involves not only seeking permission, when possible, but also amplifying voices from those communities, ensuring that they are not just recipients of activism but active participants in shaping narratives about their experiences. This ethical vigilance fosters a more equitable framework for digital activism. In parallel, ethical considerations also encompass the mental and emotional toll on activists who confront systemic injustices online. The digital landscape can be rife with harassment, doxxing, and other forms of retaliation against those advocating for change. As such, promoting the mental well-being of activists is crucial. Organizations and movements are encouraged to establish support networks and implement practices that safeguard individuals' mental health. Further, considering the environmental impact of digital tools used for activism, from the carbon footprint of data centers to the ethical sourcing of technology, is essential for a holistic approach to ethical digital activism (Abdelaal, 2024; Dal et al., 2023). Together, these considerations contribute to a more robust, responsible, and sustainable framework for digital activism, reflecting broader societal values of integrity, respect, and inclusivity in the pursuit of social justice.

## 7.1. Misinformation and Fake News

Misinformation and fake news have become pervasive elements in contemporary digital activism, significantly influencing public discourse and political engagement. Misinformation refers to false or misleading information disseminated without malicious intent, while fake news encompasses fabricated content published deliberately to mislead audiences. The rapid rise of social media platforms has facilitated the swift spread of both phenomena, allowing them to infiltrate discussions surrounding critical issues like climate change, public health, and social justice. The complex dynamics of digital communication, characterized by a mix of user-generated content and algorithm-driven information dissemination, contribute to the fluvial nature of today's information landscape, wherein distinguishing reliable sources from dubious ones proves increasingly challenging (Dey & Dey, 2024). In the context of activism, misinformation can undermine credible movements and dilute the potency of genuine calls for social change. Activists may fall victim to sharing unverified data, which, in turn, can lead to the erosion of trust among supporters and potential allies. Additionally, the strategic use of disinformation campaigns orchestrated by individuals or organizations with vested interests can further polarize public opinion and stymie meaningful dialogue. The digital arena often becomes a battleground for competing narratives, where activists must navigate a nuanced terrain of credibility and skepticism. Consequently, fostering media literacy among activists and their constituencies is vital. By equipping individuals with the tools to critically evaluate information sources, movements can enhance their resilience against manipulation and cultivate a more informed activist base (Kopacheva, 2021). The implications of misinformation extend beyond individual movements, suggesting systemic challenges within the digital information ecosystem. As algorithms prioritize engagement, sensational or inflammatory content frequently overshadows factual reporting, aggravating the spread of falsehoods. Platforms are increasingly challenged to balance the promotion of free expression with the imperative of curbing harmful misinformation. Furthermore, regulatory measures are in constant evolution, grappling with the intricacies of enforcing accountability while respecting democratic principles (Greijdanus et al., 2020). In this context, digital activism must adapt by emphasizing transparency and accountability, not only within its narratives but also in its strategies, thereby contributing to a more equitable and informed public discourse.

## 7.2. Cultural Appropriation in Activism

Cultural appropriation in activism is a complex phenomenon that arises when individuals or groups adopt elements of a marginalized culture without an understanding or respect for its original significance. This dynamic often manifests in social movements, where symbols, practices, or narratives from a culture that has faced historical oppression are incorporated into the activism of those outside that culture. The act of appropriation can dilute the original cultural meanings, commodify cultural expressions, and erase the historical context of suffering that these symbols may represent. Consequently, cultural appropriation may inadvertently reinforce systemic inequalities rather than challenge them (Ji & Tao, 2024). The implications of cultural appropriation in activism raise important ethical considerations regarding authenticity, representation, and accountability. Activists who employ cultural symbols must critically examine the origins and meanings of those symbols, striving to navigate the fine line between appreciation and appropriation. For instance, the use of Indigenous designs in campaign merchandise may draw on rich cultural histories, but if these designs are utilized without proper collaboration or compensation, such actions can perpetuate colonialist practices (McDaniel, 2024).

Successful activism should not only embrace intersectionality, acknowledging how various forms of identity intersect, but also engage in meaningful dialogue with the cultures involved, ensuring that the voices of marginalized communities are amplified rather than overshadowed. Furthermore, the digital landscape complicates the discourse surrounding cultural appropriation. Online platforms often foster rapid dissemination of ideas and imagery, blurring the boundaries between inspiration and appropriation. Activists must navigate this terrain judiciously, weighing their actions against the potential for harm. Drawing upon culturally significant symbols for mobilization could unintentionally strip them of their meaning while denying credit to their originators. As such, a more nuanced understanding of cultural dynamics is essential for ethical digital activism that respects and honors the complexities of cultural expressions and experiences (Pham et al., 2024). By prioritizing integrity and empathy, activists can foster a more equitable movement that uplifts marginalized voices and confronts systemic injustices with sensitivity and awareness.

## 8. FUTURE TRENDS IN ONLINE ACTIVISM

The landscape of online activism is rapidly evolving, driven by technological advancements and societal shifts. One of the most notable emerging trends is the integration of advanced technologies such as artificial intelligence, blockchain, and data analytics into activist strategies. Activists are increasingly utilizing algorithms to analyze social media trends, identify key influencers, and gauge public sentiment surrounding social issues. This data-driven approach enables more targeted campaigns, allowing activists to craft strategies that resonate with their audience, thereby enhancing engagement and impact. Beyond data analysis, applications are also being employed to enhance the accuracy of fact-checking and misinformation campaigns, a critical concern in the digital age (J. Jun et al., 2024). As false narratives proliferate online, the ability to quickly counteract these with verified information becomes essential in maintaining the integrity of activism-driven discourse.

Blockchain technology emerges as another pivotal player in the future of online activism, providing decentralized platforms that can enhance transparency and trust in campaigns. Activists are leveraging blockchain to ensure that donations are tracked and utilized in a transparent manner, which can significantly boost donor confidence and support. Furthermore, blockchain can be used to create immutable records of events or actions, aiding in the documentation of human rights abuses or environmental degradation, effectively empowering activists to create compelling narratives backed by verifiable data (Bagdadi, 2024). This shift towards decentralized systems not only disrupts conventional fundraising and organizing methods but also fosters community-driven initiatives that emphasize collective action. As these technologies mature, the implications for online activism are profound. Future trends suggest greater emphasis on grassroots mobilization facilitated by digital tools that promote collaboration across diverse communities. Virtual reality and augmented reality are also on the horizon, offering immersive possibilities to engage audiences emotionally and visually with social causes. Through simulated experiences, individuals can gain deeper insights into the struggles faced by marginalized populations. Additionally, with the rise of social media platforms evolved to include more robust features for activism, users will likely see an increase in features promoting civic engagement (Kopacheva, 2021). Such innovations signal a shift towards a more engaged and informed public, equipped with the tools necessary to drive social change, reinforcing the belief that technological progression can translate into transformative activism.

## 8.1. Emerging Technologies and Activism

Emerging technologies play a pivotal role in reshaping the landscape of online activism, enabling activists to mobilize, organize, and communicate in unprecedented ways. The rise of social media platforms has significantly transformed how movements proliferate; platforms provide not just a means for the dissemination of information but also serve as powerful tools for engagement and feedback. The immediacy of these channels facilitates rapid response to societal issues, allowing for spontaneous coordination around urgent causes, as evidenced by movements that gained international traction largely through digital outreach. Moreover, the integration of mobile technologies has further democratized activism, permitting individuals to participate in campaigns from virtually anywhere (Li, 2023). Mobile apps designed for activism can amplify the voices of marginalized communities, streamline fundraising efforts, and foster collective action through geographic clustering and real-time updates. These technologies enable not only greater inclusivity but also enhanced strategies, as activists can use data analytics to identify patterns, target audiences, and measure the effectiveness of their campaigns. For instance, geotargeted notifications have been employed to alert users to local protests or related initiatives, illustrating how emerging technologies are leveraged for real-time mobilization and community-building (Bagdadi, 2024; Dal et al., 2023). Furthermore, emerging technologies like blockchain and artificial intelligence introduce innovative possibilities and ethical considerations for activism. Blockchain offers the potential for transparency and security in fundraising, ensuring that donations are tracked and that funds are used for intended purposes, thus fostering trust. Simultaneously, AI can enhance digital resistance by analyzing vast sets of data to predict trends in public sentiment, allowing activists to tailor their messages effectively. However, these advancements are not without their challenges, as they raise concerns around privacy, surveillance, and the potential for harmful uses of technology (Greijdanus et al., 2020). As activists navigate this terrain, it becomes evident that while emerging technologies have the potential to amplify their efforts, they also necessitate a critical assessment of the implications of these tools on fundamental principles of privacy, ethics, and free expression in the digital age.

## 8.2. The Impact of AI on Digital Resistance

The intersection of artificial intelligence (AI) and digital resistance is reshaping the landscape of activism in noteworthy ways. On one hand, AI technologies empower activists by enabling more efficient mobilization and data analysis. Machine learning algorithms can sift through vast amounts of social media data to identify trending topics, gauge public sentiment, and predict potential protest hotspots. This intelligence allows activist groups to tailor their strategies and messages to resonate more effectively with their audiences. Moreover, AI-driven platforms can aid in automating tasks that would traditionally consume significant human resources, such as organizing events or disseminating information at scale, thereby amplifying the reach and impact of their campaigns (Greijdanus et al., 2020). Conversely, the integration of AI into digital resistance raises critical ethical and operational dilemmas. Surveillance technology, often backed by AI, poses a significant threat to activists by enabling state and corporate actors to track and predict activist behavior. Facial recognition systems can identify protesters in real-time, potentially deterring participation and fostering a culture of fear. Additionally, algorithmic biases can lead to the marginalization of certain voices within digital spaces, as AI systems trained on skewed datasets may amplify prevalent narratives while silencing fewer dominant perspectives. This creates a paradox in which the same technology that can facilitate online activism can also be deployed to suppress it. The dual-edged nature of AI in digital resistance underscores the necessity for critical engagement with these technologies (Menteş, 2019). Activists must not only leverage AI tools to enhance their efforts but also remain vigilant about the implications of their use. Engaging in discussions around ethical AI, advocating for algorithmic transparency, and developing countermeasures against surveillance practices are essential components of a robust digital resistance strategy. As AI continues to evolve, its role in shaping the parameters of activism will only grow, necessitating a proactive approach in employing these technologies for positive social change while resisting their potential misuse (Greijdanus et al., 2020). This complex relationship between AI and resistance highlights the urgent need for activists to remain adaptive and informed in an increasingly digital world where technology can both empower and oppress.

## CONCLUSION

In an era defined by profound digital transformations, online activism and digital resistance have emerged as vital mechanisms through which marginalized voices can assert themselves against systemic injustices. This conclusion encapsulates the key themes explored in the preceding sections, emphasizing the multifaceted nature of digital activism as both a tool for societal change and a platform for individual empowerment. The interconnected landscape of social media, blogs, and other digital platforms underscores an unprecedented ability for grassroots movements to mobilize, communicate, and organize around shared goals, often transcending geographical boundaries to forge a sense of global solidarity. Throughout the discourse, the inherent challenges of online activism have been illuminated, highlighting the delicate interplay between visibility and vulnerability, agency and surveillance. While digital platforms can amplify marginalized voices, they also pose risks of backlash, censorship, and the fragmentation of movements. The creation of echo chambers, driven by algorithms favoring sensational content, can dilute key messages and weaken collective action. Furthermore, understanding the dynamics of digital resistance involves recognizing the historical context of activism, which has long employed a range of strategies—from traditional protest to sophisticated digital campaigns—adaptively responding to societal shifts. This historical lens underscores the continuity of resistance while showcasing a paradigm shift driven by technology. In conclusion, online activism is not merely a passing phenomenon but a transformative force with the potential to reshape societal norms and political landscapes. As activists continue to navigate the complexities of the digital realm, their ability to innovate and adapt in response to evolving challenges and opportunities will be paramount. The lessons drawn from this exploration affirm that while the digital space offers new avenues for dissent and advocacy, the enduring principles of solidarity, strategic action, and resilience remain crucial. Ultimately, the ongoing interplay between online activism and broader movements for social justice serves as a reminder that the fight for equitable access and representation is far from over, demanding sustained engagement and critical reflection in both virtual and physical spheres.

## REFERENCES


Abdelaal, O. (2024). Female Leadership Roles: Subjectivity and Self-Representation :The Muslim Sisterhood Activism in the Digital Era. *Middle East Law and Governance, 16*(2). Advance online publication. DOI: 10.1163/18763375-20231321

Bagdadi, D. V. (2024). Resistance and Online Activism. In *Woman-Centered Brazilian Cinema*. https://doi.org/DOI: 10.1515/9781438490267-004

Bertrams, A., & Krispenz, A. (2024). Dark-ego-vehicle principle: Narcissism as a predictor of anti-sexual assault activism. *Current Psychology (New Brunswick, N.J.), 43*(4). Advance online publication. DOI: 10.1007/s12144-023-04591-4

Dal, A., Nisbet, E. C., & Kamenchuk, O. (2023). Signaling silence: Affective and cognitive responses to risks of online activism about corruption in an authoritarian context. *New Media & Society, 25*(3). Advance online publication. DOI: 10.1177/14614448221135861

Dey, S. K., & Dey, S. (2024). Identity, Social Media and Online Political Activism. SSRN *Electronic Journal*. https://doi.org/DOI: 10.2139/ssrn.4703365

Do, H. N., Do, N. B., Nguyen, T. M., & Nguyen, H. M. (2024). Anti-Brand Activism in the Collectivist Orientation: The Case of Online-Consumers-Run Communities. *Journal of Promotion Management, 30*(5). Advance online publication. DOI: 10.1080/10496491.2024.2318665

Gao, S. (2022). The online activism of mock translanguaging: Language style, celebrity persona, and social class in China. *Discourse, Context & Media, 47*. Advance online publication. DOI: 10.1016/j.dcm.2022.100608

Greijdanus, H., de Matos Fernandes, C. A., Turner-Zwinkels, F., Honari, A., Roos, C. A., Rosenbusch, H., & Postmes, T. (2020). The psychology of online activism and social movements: relations between online and offline collective action. In *Current Opinion in Psychology* (Vol. 35). https://doi.org/DOI: 10.1016/j.copsyc.2020.03.003

Ji, Y. G., & Tao, W. (2024). Channeling Employees' Positive Moral Emotions in CEO Activism: The Role of Care-Oriented Leadership Communication. *Journal of Public Relations Research, 36*(3). Advance online publication. DOI: 10.1080/1062726X.2024.2311147

Jun, J., Kim, J. K., & Woo, B. (2024). Fight the Virus and Fight the Bias: Asian Americans' Engagement in Activism to Combat Anti-Asian COVID-19 Racism. *Race and Justice, 14*(2). Advance online publication. DOI: 10.1177/21533687211054165

Jun, Y., Craig, A., Shafik, W., & Sharif, L. (2021). Artificial Intelligence Application in Cybersecurity and Cyberdefense. In *Wireless Communications and Mobile Computing* (Vol. 2021). https://doi.org/DOI: 10.1155/2021/3329581

Kim, J.-E., Park, B.-H., & Han, M. (2024). Exploring a Mediating Role of Online Activism Associated with Pro-environmental Behaviors : Examining Associations among Cognitive, Affective Factors about Global Warming and Pro-environmental Behaviors. *The Korean Journal of Advertising and Public Relations*, *26*(1). Advance online publication. DOI: 10.16914/kjapr.2024.26.1.73

Kopacheva, E. (2021). How the internet has changed participation: Exploring distinctive preconditions of online activism. *Communicatio Socialis*, *34*(2). Advance online publication. DOI: 10.15581/003.34.2.67-85

Li, M. (2023). Promote diligently and censor politely: How Sina Weibo intervenes in online activism in China. *Information Communication and Society*, *26*(4). Advance online publication. DOI: 10.1080/1369118X.2021.1983001

Lin, Y., Ahmad, Z., Shafik, W., Khosa, S. K., Almaspoor, Z., Alsuhabi, H., & Abbas, F. (2021). Impact of Facebook and Newspaper Advertising on Sales: A Comparative Study of Online and Print Media. *Computational Intelligence and Neuroscience*, *2021*. Advance online publication. DOI: 10.1155/2021/5995008 PMID: 34475947

Lou, C., Yap, C. N. R., Zhou, X., Lim, J. A., Koh, M. T., & Tan, A. (2024). Explicating the Effects of In- Versus Out-Group Membership and Collective Action Framing on Social Media Activism Messages. *International Journal of Communication*, •••, 18.

McDaniel, D. S. (2024). "Bold of them to assume I want to wait until I'm older to do what I love:" One teens' activism and civic engagement online. *Journal of Adolescent & Adult Literacy*, *67*(6). Advance online publication. DOI: 10.1002/jaal.1343

Menteş, S. A. (2019). Online Environmental Activism: The Case of Iğneada Floodplain Forest. *SAGE Open*, *9*(3). Advance online publication. DOI: 10.1177/2158244019877877

Neenan, A., Byrd, M., Hoodin, F., & Staples, A. D. (2024). Activism, Coping, and Hopefulness Among Parents of Children With Cancer. *Journal of Pediatric Hematology/Oncology Nursing*, *41*(1). Advance online publication. DOI: 10.1177/27527530231194566 PMID: 37885240

Pham, M. D., Chaney, K. E., & Ramírez-Esparza, N. (2024). What Are We Fighting For? Lay Theories About the Goals and Motivations of Anti-Racism Activism. *Race and Social Problems*, *16*(1). Advance online publication. DOI: 10.1007/s12552-023-09393-8

Shafik, W. (2023a). *A Comprehensive Cybersecurity Framework for Present and Future Global Information Technology Organizations*. https://doi.org/DOI: 10.4018/978-1-6684-9018-1.ch002

Shafik, W. (2023b). Introduction to ChatGPT. In *Advanced Applications of Generative AI and Natural Language Processing Models*. https://doi.org/DOI: 10.4018/9798369305027.ch001

Shafik, W. (2024a). Cyber Attacker Profiling and Cyberbullying Overview. In *Cyber Space and Outer Space Security* (pp. 125–149). River Publishers., DOI: 10.1201/9781003558118-5

Shafik, W. (2024b). Generative AI for Social Good and Sustainable Development. In *Generative AI: Current Trends and Applications* (pp. 185–217). Springer.

Shafik, W. (2024c). Social Media Insights Into Consumer Behavior. In *Intersection of AI and Business Intelligence in Data-Driven Decision-Making* (pp. 283–308). IGI Global., DOI: 10.4018/979-8-3693-5288-5.ch010

Shafik, W. (2024d). Toward a More Ethical Future of Artificial Intelligence and Data Science. In *The Ethical Frontier of AI and Data Analysis* (pp. 362–388). IGI Global., DOI: 10.4018/979-8-3693-2964-1.ch022

Shafik, W. (2025a). Emerging Technologies for Small and Medium Enterprises (SMEs) Growth: ChatGPT, Blockchain, Robotics, and Artificial Intelligence. *Fostering Economic Diversification and Sustainable Business Through Digital Intelligence*, 173–196.

Shafik, W. (2025b). Ethical and legal considerations in artificial intelligence. *AI-Enabled Threat Intelligence and Cyber Risk Assessment*, 90.

Shafik, W. (2025c). *Ethical and Legal Considerations in Digital Counseling*.

Shafik, W. (2025d). Generative Adversarial Networks: Security, Privacy, and Ethical Considerations. In *Generative Artificial Intelligence (AI) Approaches for Industrial Applications* (pp. 93–117). Springer.

Shafik, W. (2025e). Human-Computer Interaction (HCI) Technologies in Socially-Enabled Artificial Intelligence. In *Future of Digital Technology and AI in Social Sectors* (pp. 121–150). IGI Global.

Shafik, W., Tufail, A., Apong, R. A. A. H. M., & Balasubramaniam, S. (2024). Future Directions in Cybersecurity, Digital Forensics and Biometric Systems. In *AI Based Advancements in Biometrics and its Applications* (pp. 238–263). CRC Press., DOI: 10.1201/9781032702377-13

Zhang, X. (2024). Intention to Participate in Social Activism Activities in Response to Corporate Social Advocacy: A Third-Person Effect Perspective. *Mass Communication & Society*, *27*(2). Advance online publication. DOI: 10.1080/15205436.2023.2202643

Zhao, L., Zhu, D., Shafik, W., Matinkhah, S. M., Ahmad, Z., Sharif, L., & Craig, A. (2022). Artificial intelligence analysis in cyber domain: A review. In *International Journal of Distributed Sensor Networks* (Vol. 18, Issue 4). https://doi.org/DOI: 10.1177/15501329221084882

# Chapter 8
# Reproductive Autonomy in Rural India and Tier-2 Cities Amid Digital Patriarchy and Honour Policing

**Shikha Vasishta**
https://orcid.org/0009-0005-4198-6202
*Bennett University, India*

## ABSTRACT

*This chapter analyses the contested terrain of reproductive autonomy in tier-2 cities and rural India in the expanding web of honour-based cyber violence and digital patriarchy. It argues that the expansion of digital technologies has not merely opened up new domains of communication and mobility but amplified the machinery of patriarchal control. Drawing on case studies of Lucknow, Jaipur, and the surrounding rural contexts of Uttar Pradesh and Rajasthan, the analysis explains how online surveillance, reputational shaming, and cyber harassment expand the reach of honour codes into digital domains. Drawing on feminist legal theory, digital ethnography, and discourse analysis, the chapter dissects the ways in which digital infrastructures re-write existing hierarchies of gender, caste, and community. Lastly, it argues that ensuring reproductive autonomy not only needs legal and technological interventions but a critical re-imagination of digital spaces as spaces of emancipation and not as technologies of social discipline.*

DOI: 10.4018/979-8-3373-4267-2.ch008

## INTRODUCTION

The politics of reproductive autonomy has always been at the crossroads of law, gender normativity, and cultural practice. In the Indian case, the regulation of sexuality and reproduction has long been intermediated not just through formal legal and medical institutions but through deeply rooted social structures that govern women's bodies as purveyors of familial honour and community identity. Although reproductive rights have increased momentum in policy and legal spaces, these rights tend to be insecure in everyday life, especially in rural areas and tier-2 cities where patriarchal rationalities are both entrenched and evolving. The modern digital space creates additional complexity, as technology opens up new spaces through which patriarchal vigilance and honour policing are exerted, often in the name of morality, family safety, or preservation of culture.

The very title of this research, Reproductive Autonomy in Rural India and Tier-2 Cities in the time of Digital Patriarchy and Honour Policing, announces the multiple and intertwined dynamics at the centre of this research. Each term marks a conceptual and empirical terrain that needs to be unpacked. "Reproductive autonomy" is defined here not just as the freedom to decide about contraception, abortion, or giving birth, but as the wider ability to determine for oneself what happens to one's body, sexuality, and reproductive life without being subject to coercion, violence, or surveillance. In India, reproductive autonomy is informed by social hierarchies of caste, class, religion, and gender, and is susceptible to community-level interventions taking an approach that treats women's reproductive conduct as a site of cultural reproduction. (Diamond-Smith et al., 2024)

The spatial indicators "rural India" and "tier-2 cities" are central to situating the study. Much of the literature on digital governance and reproductive rights focuses on urban spaces, where legal remedy, access to resources, and feminist networks are relatively more accessible. Conversely, rural and tier-2 environments have a twin reality: on the one side, digital technologies' penetration has grown at a blistering pace, smartphones and social media sites transforming the communicative environment; on the other, in these environments the institutional strengths and feminist solidarities for providing protections tend to be weak, exposing women specially to digital manifestations of patriarchy. Tier-2 cities, hailed in state rhetorics as aspirational cities of India's economic emergence, are in a liminal state; harbouring the ambitions of modernity alongside the resilience of traditional frameworks that position them as paradigmatic sites for exploring the tensions of digital governance and gender justice. (Saxena & Kumar, 2025)

This chapter explores mediation of honour-based control over women in the rural and Tier-2 cities in India, with regard to control over reproductive autonomy. The research questions are: (1) to investigate the online surveillance mechanisms and honour policing, (2) to evaluate how the principles of patriarchy collide with access to digital space, and (3) to analyse ways in which women engage in resistance practices in these online space.

The concept of "digital patriarchy" which essentially refers to the perpetuation and strengthening of the existing patriarchal social frameworks by digital means, such as monitoring of online space, harassment, and enforcement of norms is used to highlight how patriarchal dominance evolves and acquires technological instruments. Instead of being emancipatory or neutral, digital infrastructures tend to reproduce existing gender order, infusing surveillance and control into the design of ordinary digital practices. ("Social Media and the Rise of Digital Patriarchy in India," 2024) Cell phones and social media pages, to take an example, become the sites of parental surveillance, and community elders police modesty and obedience norms via WhatsApp groups or neighbourhood Facebook networks. Honour policing, which was previously carried out through bodily surveillance, coercion, and violence, now has its digital equivalents; varied from various forms of online shaming to non-consensual online posting of intimate images to coordinated trolling of women who exercise agency. Furthermore, Honour Policing can also be understood as social practices, both online and offline, where women's behaviours, especially relating to relationships and reproduction, are regulated under claims of protecting family or community honour. (Aplin, 2024) Honour policing and digital patriarchy are thus not distinct forces but come together to form a regime of control in the modern that combines the material and the virtual.

This chapter situates these dynamics within the broader discursive context of reproductive rights in India. The intensification of patriarchal surveillance on social media further complicates the already volatile context of women's reproductive choice-making. (Gurumurthy, 2021) Honour policing in the name of saving the family's honour often targets women's relationship, marriage, and sex choices and hence indirectly decides their reproductive futures. (Grewal, 2013) To mention just one example, partner restrictions or mobility get funnelled into reproductive agency, and digital surveillance technologies add to such restrictions in the name of saving women. That follows a culture of fear and compulsion where reproductive autonomy is less of an individual agency and more of a collective project of cultural survival.

The importance of this study lies in the fact that it draws on unmapped geographies and tries to theorize the co-constitution of patriarchal power and digital infrastructures. In a shift of focus towards rural and tier-2 spaces, the research tries to bring to the fore the way in which women in non-metropolitan spaces negotiate reproductive rights in spaces where modern technological affordances are entangled with traditional social control. In this way, the study contributes to the knowledge about reproductive autonomy as a lived reality and not a theoretical legal right.

Simultaneously, the chapter engages the theoretical task of honour policing in its modern internet-based forms. While honour violence has been well-documented in South Asian communities in the past, its internet-mediated framing adds new forms of regulation to extend the boundaries of community surveillance even into cyberspace. (Harris, 2020) For women, this translates to those areas previously envisioned as being inside, like their mobile phone, instant message apps, or even reproductive health appointments through telemedicine; now being subject to intrusion. In this regard, digital patriarchy cannot be regarded as a technological issue alone; it has to be understood as an extension of long-standing gendered power dynamics that employ technology as a new platform of enforcement.

Methodologically, the research is informed by a mix of secondary literature, empirical case studies, and discourse analysis of online habits in rural and tier-2 environments. The intention is not just to record infringements against reproductive autonomy but also to question the structural factors that render such infringements possible. Furthermore, by placing women's voices and experiences at the centre, the research puts the human cost of digital patriarchy into sharp relief and also identifies sites of resistance and negotiation.

The larger intellectual contribution of this chapter is to put scholarship on reproductive rights into dialogue with digital governance and feminist theory. (MacKenzie, 2023) There is a great deal of rhetoric surrounding digital technology in India that hails its democratic potential, from improving access to healthcare to politicizing participation. This rhetoric tends to obscure the uneven and gendered distribution with which technologies are inscribed into social structures. This chapter contends that any serious analysis of reproductive autonomy in present-day India needs to take into consideration how digital technologies are embedded in patriarchal honour control and policing logics.

The following is the structure of the chapter. The theoretical background and literature review are given in the following section, positioning the research within feminist legal theory, digital media studies, and critical honour violence studies. This is succeeded by an overview of data and methodology used in the research. The next section explores regional contexts of digital patriarchy in rural India and tier-2 cities with an emphasis on case studies that explain how digital surveillance and honour policing constrict reproductive autonomy. The analysis and discussion follows by understanding these findings critically and establishing a relationship between reproductive rights, digital infrastructures, and patriarchal governance. The final section reflects on the pragmatic implications of the research and suggests recommendations for legal, policy, and community-level interventions. Moreover, the conclusion makes a synthesis of the chapter's findings, stressing the imperiousness of rethinking reproductive autonomy at a time when the digital and the patriarchal intersect in new and uncharted ways.

## THEORETICAL FRAMEWORK AND LITERATURE REVIEW

This chapter falls at the nexus of feminist theory, digital cultures, and honour-based violence studies, specifically examining how reproductive autonomy is negotiated in rural India and tier 2 cities. Three interwoven theoretical frameworks are drawn upon to engage with this question: feminist legal theory, the digital patriarchy, and honour policing scholarship. All these theories combined offer a framework to understand the increasing intertwinement of digital infrastructures and patriarchal systems, thus redefining the landscape of reproductive rights in rural and semi-urban areas.

Feminist legal theory is a normative theory for the conceptualization of reproductive autonomy as a central aspect of gender justice. Drawing on the research of scholars such as Catharine MacKinnon (1989), who outlined how legal systems tend to perpetuate patriarchal systems, and Martha Fineman (2010), who emphasized the importance of acknowledging vulnerability as a fundamental human condition, feminist legal theorists have continued to study disconnects between abstract legal assurances and lived experience. In the Indian context, Ratna Kapur (2018) and Flavia Agnes (2012) pointed out that women's sexual and reproductive rights are continuously defined by culture, religion, and family, often rendering constitutional promises ineffective in real life. These findings are key to an explanation of the subtleties of reproductive freedom, legally protected by law such as the Medical Termination of Pregnancy Act (1971 and amended in 2021), that are seriously challenged when conveyed through the honour and patriarchal control frames that are most dominant in rural India and tier 2 cities.

The second theoretical framework for this research is that of digital patriarchy, a theoretical model that describes how patriarchal institutions are embedded, reproduced, and amplified in the processes of digital technology and the internet. Academics like Sarah Banet-Weiser (2025) and Caitlin Lawson (2018) have illustrated how digital cultures work to reproduce both gendered violence and misogyny while also appearing to make empowerment new possibilities. Even in India, research by (Athirah & Hidayana, 2023) have pointed out that women who have been exercising their bodily agency have also been using social media sites and messenger apps as instruments of resistance as well as instruments of oppression. Policing of women's online self, cyberbullying, and sharing of pictures without permission all speak to the manner in which digital technologies are projecting patriarchal power into home-space. These phenomena are most evident in rural India and Tier 2 cities like Lucknow, Bhopal, and Jaipur, where the expanding reach of the internet is coupled with patriarchal norms and therefore results in a paradoxical environment of empowerment and vulnerability.

The honour policing scholarship is inherently connected to the control of women's sexuality and reproductive lives as a way of family and social honour. Theorists such as Deniz Kandiyoti (1988) have developed the concept of the "patriarchal bargain," mapping out the way women work within abusive regimes that attach their agency to family honour. Honour policing in South Asia is expressed through a variety of strategies, ranging from control over choice of marriage to honour-based violence. Prem Chowdhry (2007) and Uma Chakravarti (1993) have explained how, in India, honour-based violence is institutionalized with the patronage of khap panchayats and other community institutions that regulate inter-caste and inter-religious marriages. When this practice is negotiated in the virtual sphere, it yields honour-based cyber violence, wherein cyber policing of women's online behaviour is a new tool for the imposition of patriarchal power. For instance, in the smaller city of Meerut and Kanpur, the engagement of young women with social media has been met with increased surveillance on part of their families, resulting in online harassment that gets translated into offline domination or even forceful action.

Literature on reproductive autonomy addresses these debates to a great extent. Scholars like Gita Sen and Srilatha Batliwala (2000) have argued that reproductive rights in the Global South cannot be explained decontextualized from larger structures of inequality, such as class, caste, and region. Reproductive autonomy in India is not merely a matter of personal choice but influenced by collective family and community interests. Academic studies by Bharati Ray (2005) and (Srivastava & Gawarle, 2024) have contended that in rural settings, women's access to reproductive health care is not only being mediated by infrastructural constraints but also by cultural norms that condition women's decision-making autonomy. In tier 2 cities such as Lucknow and Jaipur, such challenges are expressed in particular but connected modes, where women are subjected to heightened access to reproductive health care but also to heightened types of digital monitoring and moral regulation.

The current research also brings together existing studies on Indian digital violence, namely the works of Rukmini S. (2022), who wrote on how online platforms have become spaces for new types of harassment and (Ging, 2023) who penned on trends of online misogyny and social shame in the Indian online sphere. Although the intersection between honour-based violence and digital paradigms has not been widely studied, emerging research by scholars like (Aslam, Yousaf, Raza, Hussain, & Ahmad, 2025) suggests that digital patriarchy is reconfiguring honour enforcement practices. This chapter expands on this new work by placing the reproductive aspect in the foreground, interrogating how digital patriarchal practices impact women's capacity to exercise reproductive autonomy in particular socio-geographic locations.

Methodologically, the intersection with feminist digital studies allows the chapter to acknowledge the ambivalent promise of online spaces. While digital spaces can consolidate voice against patriarchal domination, they also reinforce power hierarchies. For example, tier 2 cities like Jaipur and Bhopal, where internet penetration has grown exponentially recording 886 million users and 55% rural users over the past decade, are case studies of how young women's interaction with digital spaces is empowering as well as dangerous. (IAMAI & Kantar, 2022) Sexting in such circumstances shows a two-way dynamic: while women are increasingly offered more information on abortion and contraception, they are also opened up to more surveillance by peers and members of their families who are monitoring their online activities for indications of "dishonour."

The current literature highlights the significance of intersectionality with respect to reproductive autonomy. Kimberle Crenshaw's seminal work on intersectionality (1989) explains how the experience of oppression is constructed through the intersection of gender, caste, class, and religion. In the case of India, researchers such as Sharmila Rege (2014) has demonstrated how hierarchies founded on caste interact with gendered oppression, resulting in unusual instances of reproductive injustice. Specific agricultural states, such as Haryana and Uttar Pradesh, are quintessential cases in point, with honour-based regulation of women's sexual and reproductive agency inextricably intertwined with caste-based controls. (Uma, 2023)

In the process of converging these various fields of scholarship, the chapter's conceptual framework places reproductive autonomy as a contested site governed by the intersection of legal, cultural, and technological determinants. Locating digital patriarchy within feminist legal theory and honour-based policing, the chapter seeks to illuminate the way in which patriarchal control over women's reproductive lives is being reimagined in India today. This reimagination is most particularly heightened in rural India and tier 2 cities, where there is a real growth in digital infrastructure but located in socio-cultural contexts where long-standing gender inequalities dominate.

Therefore, the review of literature is interested in studying reproductive autonomy not so much as that which is legal or biomedical in character, but social and cultural. The intersection of digital patriarchy and honour policing produces new types of constraint that should be addressed through scholarly research. Through responding to current works while filling the relative scholarly gap on reproductive autonomy in the context of digital violence in India's rural and semi-urban spaces, the chapter seeks to both inform theoretical discussions and practical interventions.

## DATA AND METHODOLOGY

The methodological underpinning of this chapter brings together qualitative research and contextual analysis in order to examine how reproductive autonomy is negotiated in tier 2 cities and rural India against the scenario of digital patriarchy and honour policing. The qualitative approaches are chosen to represent the intricate dynamics between the local cultural norms, patriarchal rule and digital practices that are not entirely measurable. Ethnography and in-depth interviews are used to make immersive observations, whereas netnography makes it possible to observe digital interactions within particular communities. The study has a socio-legal and feminist political perspective, where lived experiences are placed within wider theoretical and normative contexts. In contrast to pure abstract theorisation, the research draws on field-based accounts, judicial rulings, and ethnographic narratives to bring to the fore material experiences of women and other oppressed gendered bodies who confront concerns around sexuality, choice, and reproduction.

The evidence used for this analysis is derived from three interconnected sources: ethnographic case studies, secondary literature, and legal-judicial evolutions. Ethnographic research in areas troubled by Khap Panchayat diktats, especially villages in Haryana and western Uttar Pradesh, offers valuable insight into the extent to which patriarchal surveillance limits the reproductive autonomy of women. These informal community councils have traditionally attempted to control kinship and marriage behaviours by penalizing inter-gotra and inter-caste marriages, thus limiting reproductive autonomy under the guise of protecting "honour." Such settings illustrate the way reproductive rights must be understood in relation to localized patriarchal forms of governance, which exercise informal yet coercive control over women's bodies.

Also significant are the findings arising from Sonagachi, the city's largest red-light district, which has become synonymous with both exploitation and resistance in sex work. Although Sonagachi is routinely cited as a site of HIV prevention and collective organization, its significance to this chapter is the manner in which women's reproductive autonomy is both challenged and negotiated in environments of stigma, criminalisation, and online visibility. The greater visibility of sex workers in cyberspace for client meetings, activism, and solidarity, has thus made them face greater harassment, surveillance, and cyber-violence in the online world. The fieldwork in Sonagachi thus points to the overlap of digital patriarchy and reproductive rights in urban and semi-urban spaces that are at the margins of hegemonic discourse, but possess core elements of resistance.

The approach also entails a jurisprudential analysis, more specifically of Indian constitutional law, and the development of digital rights regimes. Judicial decisions, for example, the Supreme Court decision in Justice K.S. Puttaswamy (Retd.) v. Union of India (2017), which established privacy as a fundamental right, are analyzed for their long-term effects on reproductive rights and digital surveillance. Likewise, decriminalization of same-sex acts in Navtej Singh Johar v. Union of India (2018) and the establishment of transgender rights in National Legal Services Authority v. Union of India (2014) reflect the role of the judiciary in breaking heteronormative paradigms that govern reproduction and sex. But this judicial advancement is situated within the ongoing gaps in addressing online gender violence, e.g., instances of cyber-bullying, non-consensual distribution of intimate pictures, and state controls over the digital. Through such judicial developments, the study adopts a critical perspective in the critique of the dualistic nature of law as a means of liberty and as a tool with potential to facilitate surveillance and control. Methodologically, the chapter adopts a comparative analysis that looks at the distinctive and overlapping modalities of reproductive regulation in rural and tier 2 city contexts. Rural contexts, particularly khap-dominated ones, signify the traditional modes of communitarian enforcement of honour, while tier 2 cities such as Lucknow and Jaipur signify in-between spaces where ancient patriarchal conventions intersect with imperatives of digital modernity. These urbanizing spaces are characterized by increasing access to smartphones and social media, which paradoxically empower women by giving them spaces for expression, while paradoxically subjecting women to greater scrutiny by families, communities, and strangers online.

The facts are examined through the lenses of feminist ethnography that focus on voice, narrative, and subjectivity. The use of oral histories, published interviews, and ethnographic accounts of impacted women ensures that the examination stays responsive to lives rather than following standard policy priorities. For instance, the narratives of adolescent girls in Lucknow reveal how the use of social media becomes a site of contest, where families cite the principle of honour to limit online interaction, marriages, and even bodily movement. Likewise, narratives of experiences of women in villages where khaps have operated reveal that digital media are remapped as tools of surveillance, where mobile phones become violators of family honour instead of being tools of empowerment.

Methodologically, triangulation is employed to provide breadth as well as depth. Ethnographic case studies situate the research in everyday life; legal and policy analysis places those everyday experiences in official frameworks of regulation; and academic literatures give the interpretive scaffolding of theory. The multi-layered methodology allows the research to follow connections between digital patriarchy, honour policing, and reproductive autonomy over a range of scales; intimate community relationships through constitutional jurisprudence.

Ethics are at the heart of this methodological stance. Honours-based violence, reproductive rights, and digital harassment are researched by working with communities under increased vulnerability. Reflexivity is thus adopted in the study, with prioritization of anonymity, sensitivity, and contextualization. Far from speaking over the voice of marginalized women, the methodology aims to give them greater voice, acknowledging that they are producers of knowledge themselves.

Moreover, by suturing together localised ethnographies, representative field sites like Sonagachi, and jurisprudential trends in digital rights, this methodological framework offers a comparative perspective to interrogate reproductive autonomy in the modern Indian context. It reinforces the main argument of this chapter: that reproductive rights are not so much an issue of individual agency but are constantly reconfigured by intersecting regimes of honour, technology, and law.

## REGIONAL CONTEXTS OF DIGITAL PATRIARCHY

The growth of digital technologies in India has frequently been positioned as a route to modernization and empowerment, one that will democratize information, markets, and social networks. The impact of digital penetration is not uniform and is not necessarily liberatory, especially for women negotiating entrenched patriarchal worlds. In rural India and tier-2 cities, digital technologies intersect with traditional practices of social control, honour-based governance, and reproductive policing, resulting in what can be termed digital patriarchy. These contexts illustrate how access to technology can exist alongside, and even support, restrictions on women's autonomy, particularly concerning their relational and reproductive choices.

Digital connectivity in rural and semi-urban India is highly stratified by gender. Although India has seen high rates of growth in mobile and internet penetration under Digital India, women's access is still limited by economic, social, and cultural factors. In several Haryana districts and western Uttar Pradesh, ethnographic and news accounts have documented khap panchayat rulings that specifically prohibit unmarried women from accessing mobile phones on the grounds of fear of elopement, inter-caste acquaintanceship, or moral indignity. In such environments, digital exclusion is an indirect control mechanism for reproductive autonomy: through the management of communication, families try to monitor potential courtship relationships, exert control over ante-nuptial intercourse, and secure adherence to community-sanctioned marriage patterns. Such behaviours illustrate how patriarchal domination transmutes into virtual realms, converting mobile phones into monitoring sites and instruments for exercising conformity to local honour systems.

Tier-2 cities such as Jaipur, Lucknow, and Bhopal are a different but no less restrictive space. Women here are more exposed to social media websites and smartphone phones than their counterparts in rural areas but are under constant digital watch. Family- or caste-based WhatsApp groups are a form of community observation. Lucknow reports indicate that digital interaction, posts, and photographs of young women are being monitored strictly, and any deviation from social behaviour invokes family outrage. Just as in Jaipur, internet visibility transcends educational and vocational aspirations: women pursuing education in colleges and universities are closely watched for social networking activities that may reveal inter-caste or inter-religious interaction, and web usage affects marriage proposals directly. These patterns point out that women are not empowered by access to the internet in itself but are put under new regimes of surveillance which conflate family, community, and institutional regulation.

The convergence of digital technology and patriarchal domination goes beyond surveillance to overt cyber abuse and Internet moral policing. Honour-based cyber abuse is realized through strategic trolling, the sharing of intimate images, and reputation-threatening messages that seek to discipline women's behaviour. Social media is the first platform of such policing in tier-2 cities, where tweets, comments, and groups are assessed against cultural standards of what is in order. Women who comment on reproductive rights, sexual health, or inter-caste relationships are made the object of cyber shaming, with peers, relatives, and sometimes even strangers joining campaigns to delegitimize them and reduce their social standing. The online world thus exists at the same time as a domain of potential expression and as an instrument for enforcing gendered hierarchies.

Rural India is more restrictive and presents a complementary picture. In addition to familial monitoring, entire communities are able to call upon online networks to enforce conformity. Case studies in Rajasthan have reported occasions on which screenshots of intimate WhatsApp messages were circulated openly by peers or relatives, leading to moral sanctions against young women and their families. These episodes often find their way into offline repercussions, such as social exclusion, early or arranged marriages, and limited mobility. Digital patriarchy, in this regard, is not a projection of current norms so much but rather an amplification of them, allowing real-time tracking and instant sharing of reputation evaluations within geographically spread networks.

Empirical examples in Sonagachi, India's most extensive red-light district, also illuminate the intersection of digital surveillance, gendered labor, and reproductive self-determination. Although closest to sex work, the community describes more general processes of digital surveillance within high-surveillance environments. Outreach efforts in Sonagachi have documented the use of mobile apps and social media to track the location and contact of sex workers, track client networks, and monitor health compliance, including reproductive health interventions such as the use of contraceptive measures. While framed as health management and protective strategies, these online behaviours at the same time function as mechanisms of coercive control, demonstrating how reproductive choices are able to become regulated within platform-mediated systems, even under the guise of empowerment or health management. These relationships bear special significance for rural and tier-2 environments, highlighting the ways in which digital technology can be utilized in order to monitor, restrict, or normalize behaviour according to patriarchal standards.

Digital enforcement of reproductive norms can also be observed in case material from Rajasthan and Haryana. In numerous villages, parents and village councils have imposed bans on teenage girls' use of phones, openly linking mobile use with possible dishonour. Media reports and court case studies record instances in which transgression of these taboos, such as smartphone ownership or social media activity has led to public shaming, threats of community punishment, and even forced arranged marriage in a few instances. These illustrations speak to the two-faced nature of online spaces: as they are conduits for connection and information, so they are being used as tools for monitoring women's reproductive lives and enforcing socially regulated codes of conduct.

Although it is an interesting example of how digital surveillance, along with patriarchal domination can be apparent in the environment of sex work, the same patterns can be followed in rural Haryana and Rajasthan, which should also be given an equal qualitative consideration. In the state of Haryana, panchayats at the village level have long placed limitations on the usage of mobile telephones by women, effectively regulating their movement and use of phones on the internet. Family and community members often monitor social media apps, including WhatsApp, which enhances conservative codes of honour and limits the reproductive decisions. In contrast, the cities of Rajasthan indicate an increased presence of cyber shaming and moral policing, with the actions of women becoming more often subject to publicly perceived publicity on the Internet, and any failure in meeting socially approved norms subject to reputational threats and harassment. With these case studies in combination with Sonagachi, the chapter strikes a balance in its empirical emphasis, wherein it demonstrates that digital patriarchy is employed in a variety of social and occupational settings in India, and the mechanisms of control and monitoring vary depending on the region.

Tier-2 cities also demonstrate unique patterns of digital governmentality over the behaviour of women. WhatsApp groups, Facebook groups, and Instagram threads are regularly employed to monitor young women's relational and reproductive behaviour. In Jaipur, for example, groups judge and offer critiques of photographs of women heading out to social events, judging clothing, friends, and the connection of the internet. Transgressions—often bounded by localised moral conventions—elicit family intervention, social exclusion, or future restrictions on mobility. These cases show how platform affordances, including group chat and sharing multimedia, can be used to turn patriarchal control into projections onto cyberspace. Significantly, the effect of these practices is real: reputational hazards online have a tendency to inform education, marriage, and reproductive health choices, demonstrating the convergence of digital surveillance and traditional social control.

Digital patriarchy operates symbolically and instrumentally in rural and tier-2 environments around the world. Symbolically, it substantiates standards of women's sexuality, honour, and reproductive behaviour. Instrumentally, it offers institutions of ongoing surveillance and intervention. Sharing photographs, messages, and gossip between WhatsApp and Facebook is one such instance of traces being employed to enforce conformity. Women react differently to these pressures: some deploy digital literacy tactics, like messages that have been encrypted, using multiple accounts, or the employment of pseudonyms, in the creation of conditions of privacy and autonomy, yet others are coerced or censor themselves in an effort to comply with communal expectations. These tactics of resistance point out that digital patriarchy is not totalizing nor problem-free but an open site where autonomy and control are contested in and through technology, culture, and community.

Examining such regional contexts critically also brings under the spotlight the intersectionality of reproductive autonomy with digital patriarchy. In rural Rajasthan and Haryana, for example, digital access barriers directly hinder women from accessing reproductive health information after all, talking with health care providers, or engaging in family planning or contraceptive decision-making online peer communities. In tier-2 cities, though access is relatively open, the compulsions of online monitoring and reputation watching curb the expression of reproductive agency. Social media surveillance affects sexual intercourse decisions, marriage, and family planning and illustrates the ways visibility on social media structures, regulates, and constrains reproductive agency in complex forms. (Enloe, 2012) This is the space of possibility and not as a space of freedom or a space that ignores; it mediates possibility and constrains at the same time.

The ubiquity of honour-based rule throughout virtual landscapes confirms that technology is no antidote for patriarchal injustice. Rather, online platforms tend to reinforce existing social norms and extend their influence into areas that had been private or less exposed before. This discussion, by incorporating case-specific data from Sonagachi, rural Haryana, and tier-2 cities like Jaipur and Lucknow, brings out the mechanisms whereby digital means are turned into tools for surveillance, moral policing, and reproductive regulation. Women's control over their reproductive lives remains limited by the interconnected logics of honour family, community policing, and digital surveillance. It is essential that scholarship and policy attend to these dynamics, as they show how context-specific strategies must consider the social, cultural, and technological dimensions of control.

In addition, the digital patriarchy regional landscapes of tier-2 cities and rural India indicate that digital technologies, as much as they facilitate connectivity, have the tendency to be instruments through which patriarchal norms are replicated and extended. Social media, mobile phones, and messaging apps are not inert; they are embedded in cultural and social logics that regulate women's reproductive and relational autonomy. Empirical observations in high-surveillance locations such as Sonagachi, and rural Rajasthan and Haryana, bring to light how digital trails, online threats, and local-level surveillance intersect to reproduce honour-based control. These instances bring into view the necessity of placing negotiations of digital empowerment in the broader context of gendered social hierarchies, proving that technology's potential must be interpreted critically within the framework of its capacity to reproduce or even enhance prevailing inequalities.

## ANALYSIS AND DISCUSSION

The intersection of digital technologies and patriarchal norms in rural India and tier-2 cities reveals complex mechanisms through which women's reproductive and relational autonomy is regulated, contested, and negotiated. Digital platforms are not merely neutral infrastructures; they operate as sociotechnical arenas where long-standing social hierarchies are both reproduced and transformed. In Rajasthan and Haryana rural villages, for example, mobile phone bans and social media monitoring are employed not just to control communication but also to enforce local definitions of decency and honour. These practices illustrate the way in which technology is written into moral and cultural rationalities and formulated into a digital patriarchy that is both spatially and socially embedded.

In the tier-2 cities of Jaipur and Lucknow, it is a contradictory landscape that differs for women. Greater availability of smartphones and social media presents possibilities of education, connectivity, and political engagement, but the same media place them under greater surveillance and social scrutiny. WhatsApp groups, family circles, and caste networks are semi-public spaces where the online presence of women is judged, critiqued, and monitored. This environment illustrates how technological penetration does not always provide freedom but instead allows digital platforms to expand moral surveillance, driving patriarchal control's boundaries to new and highly publicized arenas. The overlap of connectivity and scrutiny turns everyday interactions into sites of normative contest, where online behaviour has immediate consequences for reproductive autonomy, marriage negotiation, and social reputation.

Cyber patriarchy is also seen in cyberbullying and moral policing against women in rural and semiurban areas. The posting of images, personal messages, and opinions on community groups serves as a re-enforcing tool of gendered expectation that has real offline consequences. Examples of high-profile cyber shaming in Rajasthan, where private online interactions were invaded and posted, demonstrate how reputation tracking combines with local mechanisms for governance to produce long-term forms of social control. In the same way, in tier-2 cities, tracking of online interactions by family and peers involves subtle and direct processes, which affect not just relational autonomy but decisions about reproductive health and movement. These processes foreground that digital visibility is inextricable from normative assessment, and hence platforms are both empowering and restrictive at the same time.

The empirical evidence from Sonagachi brings to the forefront the multi-faceted quality of digital surveillance in gendered environments. In the sex worker population, mobile applications and social media are utilized ostensibly for facilitating health interventions and professional networks. They also serve as tools of monitoring, controlling sexual and reproductive acts. The analogies with rural and tier-2 contexts are revealing in both contexts, digital technologies are facilitators of information and vectors of control, showing that freedom within reproductive and relational spaces is mediated through the socio-technical intertwinements of culture, power, and technology.

The dynamics highlighted also illustrate the balance of constraint and agency. Women actively use methods to circumvent, evade, or resist online surveillance, using methods like encrypted communication, secondary accounts, pseudonyms, or peer networks. These methods show not just adaptive measures but emergent patterns of digital feminist agency, demonstrating that freedom is always negotiated and not either possessed or denied. The dynamics between women's agency and patriarchal control imply that digital spaces are contested sites, in which power is wielded, contested, and occasionally rearranged.

One of the key observations arising from this discussion is how digital platforms operate in organizing temporal as well as spatial aspects of control. Surveillance is ongoing, with traces on the internet remaining and feeding into networks long after engagement takes place. This persistence extends the effects of online activity, connecting mundane everyday digital behaviour with long-term social, reputational, and reproductive effects. Further, the disintegration of offline and online spaces demonstrates that mobility, schooling, and social encounters are surveilled and managed in an integrated and sometimes unavoidable system of control. This integration of electronic and lived mechanisms reveals that digital patriarchy is not a theoretical technological issue but a lived, materially significant reality.

Theoretically, these results are counterintuitive to assumptions regarding technology as inherently emancipatory. Although digital connectedness offers possibilities for learning, communication, and citizenship, it also generates contexts in which current hierarchies are reified. The theoretical framework of digital patriarchy is used to describe these dynamics, highlighting the intersection of technological affordances and socio-cultural infrastructures. The findings from tier-2 cities and rural townships indicate that digital interventions into women's lives are enabling as well as constraining and create intricate patterns of negotiation between autonomy and control.

The empirical findings also identify spaces of policy and platform governance failure. Current frameworks on cyber harassment, privacy, and online abuse neglect the gendered and localized forms of control evident in these settings. Online harassment is seldom isolated; it is coupled with household, caste-based, and community practices that condition women's autonomy. This makes it essential to develop a more sophisticated understanding of digital rights, one that acknowledges the relational, contextual, and intersectional character of online oppression and empowerment. Interventions will thus need to transcend universalistic, platform-based strategies to embed socio-cultural specificity and gendered realities.

Additionally, differential dynamics between tier-2 cities and rural areas underscore the heterogeneity of digital patriarchy. In rural villages, closer social networks and local norms strengthen monitoring and limit autonomy, while tier-2 cities intermix exposure to wider media discourses with continued social surveillance. These differences demonstrate that interventions, policy approaches, and academic analyses need to be context-specific, noting the complex and locally mediated interdependence of technology, culture, and power.

To substantiate qualitative observations, integrating empirical data is essential. Notably, a 2024 GSMA report highlights a significant gender disparity in mobile phone ownership in India: while 85% of men own mobile phones, only 75% of women do, and merely 35% of women own smartphones (GSMA, 2024). This digital gender divide is particularly pronounced in rural areas, where 51.6% of women aged 15 and above lack personal mobile phones (Business Standard, 2025). Furthermore, internet penetration rates reveal that only 33% of women in India have used the internet, compared to 57% of men, with rural women facing even greater challenges (Statista, 2024).

In terms of cyber harassment, data from Rajasthan indicates that women comprise 30% of reported cybercrime victims, with common issues including cyberstalking and online bullying (Times of India, 2023). Additionally, a study in rural Kerala found a 10.4% prevalence rate of cyberbullying among women, underscoring the vulnerability of rural women to online abuse (Medico Publication, 2021).

These statistics not only highlight the digital gender divide but also emphasize the need for targeted interventions to bridge these gaps and protect women in digital spaces.

Finally, urban-rural social media in tier-2 cities and rural India are spaces where reproductive and relational autonomy is always being negotiated under the double pressures of patriarchal control and surveillance by technology. Honour policing, surveillance, and cyber harassment prolong forms of surveillance to digital space, but women undertake complex resistance and negotiation strategies. The critique illustrates that autonomy is not absolute or fixed but is generated in the intersection of cultural norms, social pressures, and technological affordances. Identifying these dynamics is crucial to theoretical work, policy design, and practical interventions aimed at safeguarding reproductive rights, promoting digital literacy, and ensuring fair engagement with digital platforms in culturally and socially sensitive terms.

Moreover, the digital governance landscape in India reveals how both state policies and corporate practices shape women's online autonomy. The Information Technology (Intermediary Guidelines and Digital Media Ethics Code) Rules, 2021 were introduced to enhance user safety and accountability among social media intermediaries. However, in practice, these regulations have often blurred the line between protection and surveillance. While framed as safeguards against online abuse, their implementation has enabled heightened state monitoring of women's digital activities, particularly those challenging patriarchal norms.

At the same time, platforms such as Meta and WhatsApp play a pivotal role in either mitigating or perpetuating gendered digital violence. Despite claims of ensuring user safety, reporting mechanisms for harassment and honour-based surveillance remain largely inaccessible, inconsistent, and linguistically exclusionary. Content moderation algorithms often overlook context-specific abuse prevalent in regional and vernacular settings. By examining the complicity and selective responsiveness of both the state and digital corporations, this section underscores that digital patriarchy is structurally embedded within governance systems themselves. Strengthening feminist digital rights frameworks and demanding transparent, accountable tech governance are thus essential to ensuring that online spaces evolve from sites of control into arenas of genuine empowerment.

While this chapter primarily focuses on gender, caste, class, and religion as key determinants of digital and reproductive autonomy, it recognizes that intersecting identities such as age, disability, and sexuality further complicate women's experiences of surveillance and control. Future research could explore how these additional dimensions shape differential access, vulnerability, and agency within evolving forms of digital patriarchy in India.

## PRACTICAL IMPLICATIONS AND RECOMMENDATIONS

The ramifications of digital patriarchy and honour policing on reproductive autonomy in rural India and tier-2 cities have spill-over consequences for society, culture, and institutions. While the proliferation of digital technologies has opened up new doors of empowerment, the same infrastructures are consistently hijacked by patriarchal mechanisms to curtail women's bodily integrity, reproductive agency, and relational freedom. The convergence of technology and gendered surveillance puts more focus on the call for a thoughtful and multi-determined policy intervention that transcends superficial digital inclusion. Effective interventions not only increase women's access to technology but also disrupt the social and cultural environments through which such access becomes a driver of empowerment or restriction.

The one of the key policy imperatives in this instance is bridging the gendered digital divide, which continues to be a major challenge in rural communities as well as tier-2 towns. While initiatives like the Digital India programme have been able to increase internet penetration levels, the challenge itself continues to be firmly gendered. Rural women are 33 percent less likely to own a mobile phone than men, a gap commonly accounted for in terms of family concerns over honour and social control. (GSMA, 2024) In this regard, initiatives such as Rajasthan's "Rajiv Gandhi Computer Saksharta Mission, 2014" which introduced subsidized smartphone and digital literacy access are worth emulating. However, without complementary interventions to break through cultural resistance, plain device provision has the tendency to reinforce current power hierarchies, with male relatives controlling women's access to technology.

Similar lessons also apply to Kerala's Kudumbashree initiative, which was initially conceptualized as a poverty reduction programme but later expanded to become a digital training and women entrepreneurship platform. Through the integration of digital access into a comprehensive program of community-based economic empowerment, Kudumbashree has demonstrated how technology can be integrated as a seamless part of social mobility and collective action. Significantly, the program includes peer-support programs that help women overcome resistance from families, thus imparting essential information on how reproductive agency can be indirectly advanced by forging alternative solidarities. In contrast, those states whose online inclusion policies remain infrastructural and individualized, such as Uttar Pradesh, have had limited success in dismantling patriarchal gatekeeping over women's relational and reproductive lives.

Yet access alone cannot address the more insidious forms of honour policing that now take place on cyberspace. Social media honour policing, reputation attacks in the form of doctored photographs, and cyberbullying attacks are increasingly planned by kinship groups, community councils, or vigilantism groups. The failure of existing legal tools to address such collective forms of digital violence brings into focus the need for legal reforms that recognize cyber honour policing as distinct from general cybercrime. Women across India are increasingly reclaiming digital platforms to contest gendered surveillance and honour-based restrictions. Initiatives such as *#GirlsAtDhabas* and *#SayNoToOfflineShaming* challenge normative boundaries of female mobility and respectability. A case in point can be taken from Maharashtra's "Cyber Sakhi" initiative introduced in the year 2020, which employs trained female volunteers from villages as go-betweens for the victims of cyber harassment and law enforcement agencies. The project has not only been successful in generating awareness of cyber safety but in establishing conditions where women have locally available redress channels that do not entail passing through patriarchal police hierarchies. Coping such interventions at a state level, especially in regions where deeply ingrained khap panchayat control is exercised, could potentially pave the way for insulating women from locally motivated digital surveillance.

Legally, mobile phone prohibitions in villages are another area of policy engagement via case law. In 2016, in regard to prohibitions by some panchayats of villages against the use of mobile phones by women, the Gujarat High Court underscored that such acts are violative of constitutional provisions for equality and liberty. (Times of India, 2016) Nevertheless, there remain de facto restrictions, particularly in Haryana and Rajasthan, where the khap panchayats continue to exert great power. A stringent state intervention in policing and penalizing such bans, as Tamil Nadu has been doing boldly against caste village decrees, could enhance institutional protection for women. Moreover, integrating education on digital rights in school curricula, as done in Karnataka, can induce intergenerational changes in attitudes towards autonomous use of technology by women, eradicating intergenerational transmission of patriarchal fear.

One of the main ways of safeguarding reproductive autonomy in the age of the internet is also to re-imagine reproductive rights not only as matters of health but as intrinsically linked with digital citizenship. Wherever honour policing acts as surveillance of what women do on the web, restricting phone ownership or installing spyware on women's phones, it acts directly to restrict their independence in making choices regarding relationships, contraception, or marriage. According to this definition, digital monitoring becomes an issue of reproductive justice. Telangana, for instance, has experimented with the use of digital grievance redress systems in maternal health programs that allow women to silently report incidents of coercion or denial of reproductive care using mobile technology. These processes are in their infancy, but they suggest the potential for using technology itself to counter patriarchal monitoring and reroute digital systems towards women's agency.

The broader implications include reaching out to civil society organizations, who are women's primary source of shelter from cyber violence. Organizations such as the Internet Democracy Project and the Foundation for Media Professionals have documented how honour policing occurs online and have made policy recommendations ranging from gender-sensitive cyber law enforcement to women's digital literacy initiatives. If these are integrated into state-level policy frameworks, then the administration is less likely to be technocratic abstractions and more likely rooted realities. Moreover, involving grassroots women's organizations in co-creating policy ensures higher legitimacy while at the same time ensuring that interventions are attuned to the socio-cultural localities of rural and semi-urban India.

Perhaps tellingly, global best practices offer templates which can be adapted with some tweaking to suit the Indian situation. Thus, for instance, Brazil's "Maria da Penha Law" against domestic violence has been amended to include digital abuse, specifically recognizing the enablement provided by technology for gender-based control. Expanding India's Protection of Women from Domestic Violence Act would also likely cover cyber forms of honour policing under its ambit, recognizing the continuity between virtual and real expressions of patriarchal violence. Likewise, Spain's multiregional language-based cyber security helplines providing immediate psychological as well as legal assistance can be replicated in order to enhance India's existing cyber helplines that rural women cannot approach due to the language factor and bureaucratic inefficiencies.

Secondly, the importance of honour policing and digital patriarchy to reproductive autonomy is grasping the multi-dimensional nature of control mechanisms. Policies that are still limited to technological supply or repressive legal reaction are likely to reproduce the socio-cultural underpinnings of control. A response on the basis of an holistic strategy needs to include infrastructural access, legal reform, educational transformation, and popular mobilisation. By learning from Indian state experiences; Kerala's people-focused empowerment models, Maharashtra's cyber safety intermediaries, Rajasthan's district-based digital inclusion initiatives, and Karnataka's curricular innovations, it is conceivable to visualize in terms of a composite framework to address the technology and culture imperatives of digital patriarchy.

It is a vision that ensures reproductive autonomy not only by the lack of coercion but also by creating empowering spaces in which women are able to make choices in security from surveillance and social reproach. A response founded on a holistic approach needs to include infrastructural access, legal reform, educational reform, and community mobilisation. With learning from Indian state experiments of Kerala people-focused empowerment models, Maharashtra cyber safety brokers, Rajasthan district-based digital inclusion schemes, and Karnataka curriculum innovations, it becomes feasible to imagine in terms of a composite framework to address the technological and cultural imperatives of digital patriarchy.

This vision ensures reproductive autonomy not just through the lack of coercion but also in the creation of empowering places in which women have the ability to make choices free from surveillance and social stigma. Digital technologies, in the absence of patriarchal use, could potentially extend such spaces by networking women into solidarity networks, by offering covert forms of information on health and rights, and by empowering them to speak out in the public sphere. The policy challenge, therefore, is not whether to advance women's access to technology but how to organize such access so as to immunize them against becoming absorbed in honour and control discourses. It is here, then, in this field of contest, that the rural India's destiny and tier-2 cities' reproductive autonomy will be sealed, necessitating vigilantism, innovative experimentation with policy, and placing women's everyday lives at the centre of government planning.

Furthermore, to enhance the impact of the chapter's recommendations, interventions are structured along temporal and operational lines. Short-term measures emphasize legal reforms to provide immediate protection for women in digital spaces. Strengthening cyber harassment and cyberstalking laws, improving mobile privacy safeguards, and clarifying platform accountability can ensure prompt recourse for victims while mitigating online surveillance and honour-based control. Long-term strategies focus on community-driven initiatives that address structural and cultural determinants of digital patriarchy. Digital literacy programs for women in rural and

Tier-2 cities, local awareness campaigns involving panchayats, schools, and grassroots organizations, and participatory education on reproductive autonomy can gradually shift social norms and empower women to navigate digital spaces safely. Integrating legal and community approaches, such as collaborative frameworks between authorities, civil society, and platform providers, can create a comprehensive roadmap that simultaneously enforces protection, fosters agency, and promotes sustainable change in digital governance and gender equality.

## CONCLUSION

The study of reproductive sovereignty in rural India and tier-2 towns in the context of the entrenchment of digital patriarchy and honour policing highlights the complex dynamics of technology, tradition, and power. This chapter has shed light on how digital space, while billed as liberatory, is being increasingly taken over by patriarchal systems to police women's mobility, choices, and reproductive rights. What ensues is a paradox: digital technologies, previously introduced as tools of empowerment and democratization, also reproduce and intensify the earlier forms of surveillance, social control, and gendered exclusion.

The argument of regional contexts revealed how tier-2 cities, typically envisioned as spaces of aspirational modernity, are also where familial and community pressures compel digital infrastructures to discipline and control women's relational and reproductive agency. From being monitored on WhatsApp groups to policing on the social media, these cities illustrate how digital infrastructures today are compelled to perform older cultural scripts of honour. In the same way, rural environments demonstrate a space where the use of mobile phones, internet access, and online sites is consciously gendered, confirming dominance over women's sexuality and agency and associating technology use with marriageability and moral respectability. Each environment, combined, demonstrates how digital patriarchy exists not just as a theoretical notion but regionally located and enacted in coercive manners that are unique to each location.

Parallel to this, research put into focus the imperative for critical acknowledgement of women's resistance. Overtly patriarchal conventions notwithstanding, women in rural and semi-urban spaces are not passive objects of control. Their negotiation practices; from covert use of cellular phones to creating support networks online, trace powerful sites of agency. These manoeuvres disrupt not only digital patriarchal regimes but also reflect the ways reproductive liberty is increasingly asserted and reimagined in everyday resistance.

The chapter adds to broader feminist and legal scholarship by placing reproductive autonomy in the doubled context of regulation in the digital and honour politics.

It argues that redressing reproductive rights in twenty-first century India demands consideration of legal and cultural spaces where technology and culture intersect. Interventions through policy need to shift away from formulaic promises of gender equality and enter the grasp of material conditions of surveillance, cyberbullying, and internet exclusion that fuel honour policing.

Furthermore, reproductive autonomy in the twenty-first century can no longer be severed from the digital infrastructures whereby power is currently wielded. Acknowledgment of this reality requires not merely visionary legal and policy construction, but cultural reworking of women's rights in the digital era.

## REFERENCES


Agnes, F. (2012). From Shah Bano to Kausar Bano. *South Asian Feminisms*, 31-53. http://feministlawarchives.pldindia.org/wp-content/uploads/from-shahbano-to-kausar-bano-contextualizing-the-muslim-woman.pdf

Aplin, R. (2024). Policing Honour-Based Abuse and Forced Marriage. In Aplin, R. (Ed.), *Policing Public Protection*. Palgrave Macmillan., DOI: 10.1007/978-3-031-74504-1_3

Aslam, S., Yousaf, M., Raza, S. H., Hussain, B., & Ahmad, W. (2025). Reconfiguring patriarchal paradigms: The women march and its role in reshaping gender norms and feminist activism. *Asian Women*, *41*(2), 227–253. https://www.e-asianwomen.org/DOIx.php?id=10.14431/aw.2025.6.41.2.227

Athirah, S., & Hidayana, I. M. (2023). Women's agency and resistance to cyber flashing on Twitter. *Masyarakat: Jurnal Sosiologi*, *28*(1), 7. Advance online publication. DOI: 10.7454/MJS.v28i1.13562

Banet-Weiser, S. (2025). Diversity as Distributive Justice. *Polity*, *57*(1), 169–178. https://www.journals.uchicago.edu/doi/full/10.1086/733535

Chakravarti, U. (1993). Conceptualising Brahmanical Patriarchy in Early India: Gender, Caste, Class and State. *Economic and Political Weekly*, *28*(14), 579–585. https://r.search.yahoo.com/_ylt=Awr1SaPvcK1oRwIAD_q7HAx.;_ylu=Y29sbwNzZzMEcG9zAzEEdnRpZAMEc2VjA3Ny/RV=2/RE=1757406703/RO=10/RU=https%3a%2f%2fwww.jstor.org%2fstable%2f4399556/RK=2/RS=EDRLDav2XLFjz6Jmr99_RlecMxg-

Chowdhry, P. (2007). *Contentious marriages, eloping couples: Gender, caste, and honour in a North Indian community*. Oxford University Press., https://r.search.yahoo.com/_ylt=Awrx.1OncK1o9QEAV.67HAx.;_ylu=Y29sbwNzZzMEcG9zAzEEdnRpZAMEc2VjA3Ny/RV=2/RE=1757406631/RO=10/RU=https%3a%2f%2fbooks.google.com%2fbooks%2fabout%2fContentious_Marriages_Eloping_Couples.html%3fid%3dYY6aAAAAIAAJ/RK=2/RS=4V9KqJvPVSdK2T.Afas25q_Bl88-

Crenshaw, K. (1989). Demarginalizing the Intersection of Race and Sex: A Black Feminist Critique of Antidiscrimination Doctrine, Feminist Theory and Antiracist Politics. *University of Chicago Legal Forum*, *1989*, 8. https://chicagounbound.uchicago.edu/uclf/vol1989/iss1/8

Diamond-Smith, N., Vaishnav, Y., Choudhary, U., Sharma, P., Kachhwaha, A., Panjalingam, T., Vallin, J., Das, D., & Gopalakrishnan, L. (2024). Individual empowerment and community norm effects of engaging young husbands in reproductive health in rural India: Findings from a pilot study. *Reproductive Health, 21*(1), 147. https://link.springer.com/article/10.1186/s12978-024-01878-y PMID: 39420379

Enloe, C. (2012). Masculinities, Policing, Women and International Politics of Sexual Harassment. *International Feminist Journal of Politics, 15*(1), 77–81. DOI: 10.1080/14616742.2012.742681

Fineman, M. A. (2010). The vulnerable subject: Anchoring equality in the human condition. In *Transcending the boundaries of law* (pp. 177–191). Routledge-Cavendish., https://www.taylorfrancis.com/chapters/edit/10.4324/9780203848531-26/vulnerable-subject-anchoring-equality-human-condition-martha-albertson-fineman

Fineman, M. A. (2010). The vulnerable subject: Anchoring equality in the human condition. In *Transcending the boundaries of law* (pp. 177–191). Routledge-Cavendish., https://www.taylorfrancis.com/chapters/edit/10.4324/9780203848531-26/vulnerable-subject-anchoring-equality-human-condition-martha-albertson-fineman

Ging, D. (2023). Digital culture, online misogyny, and gender-based violence. In M. Gallagher & A. V. Montiel (Eds.), *The international encyclopedia of media literacy*. Wiley. https://doi.org/. 781119800729.ch13DOI: 10.1002/930

. GN, P. (2023). Justice KS Puttaswamy (RETD) VS. Union of India & ORS. *Union of India & ORS (march 31, 2023).*

Grewal, I. (2013). Outsourcing Patriarchy: FEMINIST ENCOUNTERS, TRANSNATIONAL MEDIATIONS AND THE CRIME OF 'HONOUR KILLINGS.'. *International Feminist Journal of Politics, 15*(1), 1–19. DOI: 10.1080/14616742.2012.755352

GSMA. (2024). Mobile gender gap report 2024: Bridging the digital divide for women in India. GSMA Intelligence. https://r.search.yahoo.com/_ylt=AwrKGCgrb_JoEQIADwC7HAx.;_ylu=Y29sbwNzZzMEcG9zAzEEdnRpZAMEc2VjA3Ny/RV=2/RE=1761928236/RO=10/RU=https%3a%2f%2fwww.gsma.com%2fr%2fwp-content%2fuploads%2f2024%2f05%2fThe-Mobile-Gender-Gap-Report-2024.pdf/RK=2/RS=3RPGs_Q07jmBJyXAw9AfH_k4j6o-

GSMA. (2024). *The Mobile Gender Gap Report 2024*. GSMA. Retrieved from https://www.gsma.com/r/wp-content/uploads/2024/05/The-Mobile-Gender-Gap-Report-2024.pdf

Gurumurthy, A. A. (2021). Governing a Seamless Sociality: Beyond Old and New Media. *Issue 4 Int'l JL Mgmt. & Human., 4*, 2253. https://heinonline.org/HOL/LandingPage?handle=hein.journals/ijlmhs12&div=213&id=&page=

Harris, B. A. (2020). Technology and violence against women. In *The Emerald handbook of feminism, criminology and social change* (pp. 317–336). Emerald Publishing Limited., https://www.emerald.com/insight/content/doi/10.1108/978-1-78769-955-720201026/full/html

Kandiyoti, D. (1988). Bargaining with patriarchy. *Gender & Society, 2*(3), 274–290. https://journals.sagepub.com/doi/abs/10.1177/089124388002003004

Kapur, R. (2018). *Gender, alterity and human rights: Freedom in a fishbowl.* Edward Elgar Publishing. https://books.google.co.in/books?hl=en&lr=&id=mYdlDwAAQBAJ&oi=fnd&pg=PT15&dq=Ratna+Kapur+(2002)+reproductive+rights&ots=kKCFDNszRM&sig=ULykrlpP9Hyv9IE5vrdvk4pVnpk&redir_esc=y#v=onepage&q=Ratna%20Kapur%20(2002)%20reproductive%20rights&f=false

Lawson, C. (2018). *Platform feminism: Celebrity culture and activism in the digital age* (Doctoral dissertation). https://deepblue.lib.umich.edu/handle/2027.42/145855

MacKenzie, A. (2023). A Feminist Postdigital Analysis of Misogyny, Patriarchy and Violence Against Women and Girls Online. In Jandrić, P., MacKenzie, A., & Knox, J. (Eds.), *Constructing Postdigital Research. Postdigital Science and Education*. Springer., https://link.springer.com/chapter/10.1007/978-3-031-35411-3_14

MacKinnon, C. A. (1989). *Toward a feminist theory of the state*. Harvard University Press. https://www.hup.harvard.edu/books/9780674896468

MedicoPublication. (2021). Prevalence and patterns of cyberbullying among women in rural Kerala. *International Journal of Public Health Research and Development, 12*(3), 45–53. https://medicopublication.com/index.php/ijphrd/article/download/21248/17938

Ray, B. (2005). *Women of India: Colonial and post-colonial periods*. SAGE Publications India.

Rege, S. (2014). *Writing caste/writing gender: Narrating Dalit women's testimonies*. Zubaan. https://books.google.co.in/books?id=p4-oDAAAQBAJ&lpg=PA1905&ots=hN7MtMd5rI&dq=Sharmila%20Rege%20(1998)%20hierarchies%20founded%20on%20caste%20intersect%20with%20gendered%20oppression&lr&pg=PA1905#v=onepage&q&f=false

Saxena, T., & Kumar, S. (2025). Artificial Intelligence and Digital Governance in Rural India: A Systematic Review of Community Empowerment and Sustainable Development. https://www.preprints.org/manuscript/202503.0090

Social Media and the rise of Digital Patriarchy in India. (2024, February 10). *Gender Studies*. Retrieved August 25, 2025, from https://gender.study/gender-based-violence/social-media-digital-patriarchy-india/

Srivastava, K., & Gawarle, N. S. (2024). Breaking the silence: A look into women's mental health in India. *Journal of Family Medicine and Primary Care, 13*(11), 5436–5437. DOI: 10.4103/jfmpc.jfmpc_892_24 PMID: 39722923

Standard, B. (2025, May 29). Digital divide: Rural women 51% less likely to own a mobile phone. Business Standard. https://www.business-standard.com/india-news/digital-india-divide-nso-rural-women-mobile-phone-ownership-gap-125052901804_1.html

Statista. (2024). Internet usage among women and men in India. *Statista*. https://r.search.yahoo.com/_ylt=AwrKHGVzb_JoRgIA7y67HAx.;_ylu=Y29sbwNzZzMEcG9zAzEEdnRpZAMEc2VjA3Ny/RV=2/RE=1761928308/RO=10/RU=https%3a%2f%2fwww.statista.com%2ftopics%2f2157%2finternet-usage-in-india%2f/RK=2/RS=AfBhLVYCI_eTnQA_JLYvq7vG33I-

The Economic Times. (2025, January 16). *India to cross 900 million internet users this year, says IAMAI report*. The Economic Times. https://economictimes.indiatimes.com/tech/technology/india-to-cross-900-million-internet-users-this-year-says-iamai-report/articleshow/117290089.cms

Times of India. (2016, February 22). *Gujarat village bans mobile phone for school girls. The Times of India*. https://timesofindia.indiatimes.com/city/ahmedabad/gujarat-village-bans-mobile-phone-for-school-girls/articleshow/51087691.cms

Times of India. (2023, September 14). Cyber centre launched in Jaipur to help counsel victims of online harassment. *Times of India*. https://timesofindia.indiatimes.com/city/jaipur/cyber-centre-launched-in-city-to-help-counsel-victims-of-fraud-harassment/articleshow/121385533.cms

Uma, S. (2023). *Violence, gender and the state: 'Not just' a legal analysis*. Routledge. https://www.taylorfrancis.com/books/mono/10.4324/9781003308959/violence-gender-state-saumya-uma

## ADDITIONAL READINGS


Jain, S. (2020, July 21). The rising fourth wave: Feminist activism on digital platforms in India. *Observer Research Foundation Issue Brief,* (384). https://www.orfonline .org/research/the-rising-fourth-wave-feminist-activism-on-digital-platforms-in-india

Kumawat, S., & Garg, C. (2025). Mobile phones, mothers, and patriarchy: Understanding digital interactions of adolescent Indian rural girls under watchful eyes. *Media, Culture & Society, 47*(5), 972-988. https://doi.org/ (Original work published 2025)DOI: 10.1177/01634437251320845

Mishra, P., & Suresh, Y. (2021). Datafied body projects in India: Femtech and the rise of reproductive surveillance in the digital era. *Asian Journal of Women's Studies, 27*(4), 597–606. DOI: 10.1080/12259276.2021.2002010

Nayak, B. S. (2024). Technological Patriarchy in India. In Hwang, E., Nayak, B. S., & Malkar, U. (Eds.), *From Entrenched Gender Bias to Economic Empowerment.* Sustainable Development Goals Series. Palgrave Macmillan., DOI: 10.1007/978-3-031-57212-8_4

Sahni, U. (2020). Methodology as 'Resistance Aesthetics': Young Girls in Lucknow, India Talk Back to Patriarchy. In Gallagher, K., Rodricks, D., & Jacobson, K. (Eds.), *Global Youth Citizenry and Radical Hope. Perspectives on Children and Young People* (Vol. 10). Springer., DOI: 10.1007/978-981-15-1282-7_4

Vaidehi, R., Reddy, A. B., & Banerjee, S. (2021). Explaining caste-based digital divide in India. Telematics and Informatics. *Article, 101719.* Advance online publication. DOI: 10.1016/j.tele.2021.101719


## KEY TERMS AND DEFINITIONS

**Algorithmic Governance:** The role of automated decision-making systems in moderating content, shaping visibility, and controlling access online; processes that often embed patriarchal and cultural biases into seemingly neutral technologies.

**Cyber-Safety Initiatives:** Government or civil society programs designed to protect women in digital spaces, such as Maharashtra's *Cyber Sakhi* project, which focus on preventing online harassment and supporting safe internet practices.

**Digital Divide:** The unequal access to digital technology, including internet connectivity and mobile ownership, which disproportionately affects rural women and reinforces existing gender gaps in opportunities, participation, and rights.

**Digital Patriarchy:** The extension of patriarchal power structures into online spaces, where social media platforms, surveillance, and algorithmic control reproduce and reinforce gendered inequalities rather than dismantling them.

**Honour-Based Control:** A set of cultural and social practices that regulate women's behaviour—especially around mobility, sexuality, and technology use—under the justification of protecting family or community "honour."

**Intersectionality:** An analytical framework that highlights how gender oppression intersects with caste, class, religion, and region, producing unique forms of disadvantage and reproductive injustice.

**Khap Panchayat:** An extra-constitutional community assembly in parts of northern India, particularly Haryana and western Uttar Pradesh, which enforces traditional codes of conduct, often curtailing women's freedoms under the guise of preserving cultural norms.

**Reproductive Injustice:** A form of structural inequality where women and marginalized groups are denied autonomy, resources, or decision-making power over their reproductive lives due to intersecting hierarchies of gender, caste, class, or religion.

# Chapter 9
# Performing Identity of the Dead on YouTube:
## Reception of Ginimbi Lite's Interview on Star FM YouTube Page

**Jennings Joy Chibike**
https://orcid.org/0000-0002-4899-2446
*Lupane State University, Zimbabwe*

**Roseline Musekiwa**
*Lupane State University, Zimbabwe*

## ABSTRACT

*The study examines how the identity of the dead is performed on an interview on YouTube. Taking the case of the late Genius Ginimbi Kadungure the study examines how he is being memorialised by Ginimbi Lite. The study's precise objectives are to examine audience's views on the late Genius Ginimbi Kadungure's identity based on the interview and to analyse audience's perspectives of whether Ginimbi Lite is correctly memorialising the late Genius Ginimbi Kadungure. This study is anchored on social constructionist approach to identity as theoretical framework. Empirical data is gathered from focus group discussions and semi-structured interviews with 12 purposively selected audiences of the interview. The study found that while Ginimbi Lite tried to mimic the late Genius Kadungure in some instances he failed to authentically do so.*

DOI: 10.4018/979-8-3373-4267-2.ch009

## INTRODUCTION

Zimbabweans were taken aback by the sudden death of Genius Kadungure, better known as Ginimbi, a prominent businessman and social media influencer whose larger-than-life persona captivated many. Following his tragic passing in a car accident on the 8th of November 2020 there has been an emergence of a character that mimics the late Kadungere. This character widely referred to by his moniker Ginimbi Lite emerged as a significant figure in the online discourse surrounding his legacy. With this in perspective it becomes interesting to examine how Ginimbi Lite is positioned within the identity reconstruction and memorialization of the late Genius "Ginimbi" Kadungure. "While there is mature scholarship on identity construction and memorialisation (Zou, 2025; Goffman, 1959; Butler, 1990), there still is scanty literature on the role individuals play in reconstructing and immortalizing the dead on social media, a gap that scholars like Ndlovu-Gatsheni (2020), Chigudu (2020), and Nandy (1983) have highlighted have highlighted needs further research." As such, this study is aimed at examining how Ginimbi Lite reconstructs the identity of the late Genius "Ginimbi" Kadungere. This examination will be anchored on audiences' perspectives of the interview Poverty Left My Address", of Ginimbi Lite with Owen "DJ Ollah" Madondo on Star FM Youtube Channel. Therefore this study contributes to a deeper understanding of the complexities of digital memorialization and identity reconstruction in contemporary society, ultimately revealing how Ginimbi's legacy is navigated and interpreted in the digital realm. This investigation will not only shed light on Ginimbi's identity posthumously but also engage with broader questions regarding the nature of representation in the age of social media. Therefore the study's objetves are:

- To examine audience's views on the late Genius Ginimbi Kadungure's identity based on the interview.
- To analyse audience's perspectives on whether Ginimbi Lite is correctly memorialising the late Genius Ginimbi Kadungure.

This study addresses a critical gap in existing studies on reconstruction of identities in the context of social media. While previous research by Goffman (1959) and Butler (1990) has extensively explored identity construction and memorialisation, and scholars like Mkwebu and Chibike (2025), Ndlovu-Gatsheni (2020) Chigudu (2020) have highlighted the importance of further research in related fields, there remains a significant gap in understanding the role of individuals in reconstructing and immortalizing the dead on social media. This study will address this gap by investigating Genius Kadungures identity through Ginimbi lites interview.

Similar studies, such as Brett William Smulligan's (2019) analysis of social media and Baudrillard's simulation and simulacra, provide a foundation for this research. However, Smulligan's study focuses on social media platforms in general, without examining a specific case like Ginimbi's. This research will build upon existing knowledge by exploring the implications of simulation on the reconstruction of the dead by their social media followers.

## BACKGROUND AND CONTEXT OF THE STUDY

Genius Kadungure, known as Ginimbi, was a prominent Zimbabwean celebrity whose extravagant lifestyle and business success made him a significant figure on social media. His influence not only shaped public perception but also led to the emergence of "Ginimbi Lite," a young man who adopted Ginimbi's identity online. This imitation raises important questions about the motivations behind such behavior and its implications for online identity and branding.

Scholars like Moyo (2021) highlight how social media facilitates identity construction, suggesting that Ginimbi's persona serves as both inspiration and a template for others. Regionally, the dynamics of identity imitation are echoed in Southern Africa, where social media is a key platform for cultural expression (Mkwebu and Chibike, 2025; Ndlovu, 2019). Globally, this trend reflects a broader phenomenon where individuals craft identities based on public figures, prompting discussions about authenticity and representation (McCulloch, 2019). Understanding the motivations and consequences of such imitation is crucial for developing strategies to address potential issues and exploring the complexities of online identity. This research aims to provide insights into these dynamics within the Zimbabwean context while contributing to the broader discourse on social media and identity.

## UNDERSTANDING GENIUS GINIMBI KADUNGURE AND GINIMBI LITE

Genius Kadungure, widely known as Ginimbi, was a prominent Zimbabwean businessman and socialite, celebrated for his extravagant lifestyle and larger-than-life personality. Born on October 10, 1984, in Harare, he gained fame as a successful entrepreneur in various sectors, including hospitality and real estate. Kadungure was known for his lavish parties and opulent displays of wealth, often showcasing luxury cars and high-profile events on social media either thrugh his instagram posts or his instagram lives. Every event he attended he made it a point to show off his fleet of cars through videos of a motorcade. His flamboyant lifestyle made him a household name in Zimbabwe, where he was both admired and criticized for his ostentation. Tragically, Kadungure passed away in a car accident on the 8th of November 2020, leaving behind a legacy that sparked widespread discussions about wealth, fame, and the complexities of social media memorialization.

After the demise of Kadungure, emerge Brian Goshomi who gave himself the name Ginimbi Lite. The social media personality who claims to be inspired by the late Kadungure has in some instances equated himself to the late Kadungure.

Ginimbi Lite, born Brian Goshomi, is often described as the self-proclaimed heir to Genius Kadungure's extravagant lifestyle. Emerging as a social media personality, Goshomi adopted the persona of Ginimbi Lite, embodying the traits of his predecessor while navigating the digital landscape. He is known for his entrepreneurial spirit and hustle, often sharing his journey and experiences on social media platforms. Goshomi's portrayal of Ginimbi Lite reflects a blend of admiration and aspiration, as he aims to capture the essence of Kadungure's life while carving out his own identity. This digital persona engages with fans and followers, perpetuating the legacy of Ginimbi while exploring themes of ambition, success, and the influence of social media on personal branding .

Together, these two figures illustrate the dynamic interplay between celebrity culture, social media, and the construction of identity in contemporary Zimbabwe.

## LITERATURE REVIEW

### Role of Social Media in Identity Construction

Social media, is defined as digital platforms that facilitate the creation and sharing of content among users (Ajani et al., 2024; Kaplan and Haenlein, 2010). It plays a pivotal role in identity construction, particularly in how individuals present themselves and engage with others in online environments. Scholars have observed that these platforms enable users to curate their identities through selective self-presentation, allowing them to highlight specific aspects of their lives while managing the impressions they convey to their audiences (Chibike, 2024). Identity, as defined by Erikson (1968), refers to an individual's sense of self, encompassing their goals, beliefs, and values. This process of identity construction is especially relevant for public figures, whose identities can be significantly influenced by the narratives created around them online. For example, Goffman (1959) introduces the concept of "impression management," wherein individuals perform various identities depending on their audience, a notion that is further amplified in the digital realm where users can edit and tailor their online personas to suit different contexts.

Digital spaces, social media serves as a critical space for identity exploration, expression and experimentation (Chibike, 2023). Koutamanis et al. (2015) argue that social media allows users to experiment with different aspects of their identity, facilitating a process of self-discovery that is essential during formative years. This exploration is often influenced by social comparisons, which can either bolster or hinder an individual's self-esteem and self-concept (Avci et al., 2025). The research on Genius Ginimbi's identity reconstruction through Ginimbi Lite's interviews on Youtube will delve into how audience perceptions and interactions contribute to this identity formation process, particularly in the wake of Ginimbi's passing.

Moreover, the role of audience engagement in shaping identity cannot be understated (Hopkins et al. 2025). Meier and Johnson (2022) highlight that social media interactions provide immediate feedback, which can significantly influence how individuals perceive themselves and their identities. This feedback loop is particularly relevant in the case of public figures, where audience reactions can lead to the reinforcement or alteration of the persona being presented (Pujiati et al, 2025). By analyzing audience views on ginimbi lite's portrayal of Genius Ginimbi, this research aims to uncover how such interactions impact the reconstruction of Ginimbi's identity and how these perceptions contribute to his legacy.

Additionally, the concept of "context collapse," as discussed by Marwick and Boyd (2011), is crucial in understanding identity construction on social media. Context collapse occurs when individuals from different social circles converge in a single online space, leading to potential conflicts in self-presentation (McKenzie, 2025). For public figures like Ginimbi, this phenomenon can complicate how their identities are perceived and reconstructed posthumously. The research will explore how Ginimbi Lite navigates these complexities in his interviews and how audience members reconcile their views of Ginimbi's identity in light of the diverse contexts in which he is presented.

Finally, the dynamics of digital memorialization play a significant role in shaping collective memory and identity (Kirkegaard et al. 2025). As noted by Davis Et Al. (2020), social media serves as a platform for collective mourning and remembrance, allowing audiences to engage with the legacies of public figures in real-time. This research will investigate how Ginimbi Lite's online presence and the audience's interactions contribute to the ongoing construction of Genius Ginimbi's identity, emphasizing the unique ways in which social media facilitates the memorialization of individuals after their passing. The study aims to provide a comprehensive understanding of the interplay between social media, audience engagement, and identity construction in the digital age.

## SOCIAL MEDIA AND IDENTITY: A REVIEW OF EMPIRICAL STUDIES

The existing literature on social media and identity formation provides valuable insights into how individuals curate and negotiate their self-presentation in digital spaces (Chibike, 2024). Studies have examined the role of audience feedback and its influence on self-perception, highlighting the dynamic interplay between self-expression and societal validation (Meier & Johnson, 2022; Koutamanis et al., 2015). However, the processes and implications involved in the posthumous reconstruction of public figures' identities remain underexplored.

This study aims to address this gap by examining how Genius Kadungure's identity is reconstructed through Ginimbi Lite digital persona that emerged following his passing. The actual focus being how his interview on Youtube aids the reconstruction of Genius Kadungure's identity. Focusing on this specific context, the research illuminated the unique dynamics of digital memorialization and its impact on the collective memory and legacy of public figures. Unlike previous studies such as those by Marwick & Ellison (2012) and Robards & Lincoln, (2017) that have centered primarily on living individuals and their identity negotiations, this work offers a novel perspective on how social media transforms the posthumous perception and representation of those who have died.

Erikson (1968) posits that personal identity is developed through clear goals, beliefs, and values emphasizing the pivotal role of social interactions. However, this theory overlooks the impact of digital social interactions on identity development this study aims to address this gap by examining how Genuis Ginimbi Kadungure's identity is reconstructed and developed by Ginimbi Lite after his passing, with a focus on the audience perspective after watching the interview on Youtube. By analysing how digital interactions shape identity narratives this study will provide insights int the evolving nature of identity in onlines spaces.

Marcia (1980) categorises identity development into four statuses diffusion, moratrium, foreclosure and achievement underscoring the significance of exploration and commitment. While his framework layed a fondation for understanding identity processes, it lacks consideration of how socia media platforms facilitate exploration and commitment through user engagement and feedback. This study will address this gap by investigating how Ginimbi Lites contributed to the reconstruction of genuis kagungures identity and emphasizing the role of social media as a dynamic environment for identity exploration.

Hoffner and Bond (2022) discuss the influence of media figures as role models, particularly in the context of adolescents identity construction through parasocial relationships. While their work underscores the importance of media presence in shaping identities it does not examine the impact of a media figures' online presence on identity reconstruction after their passing. This research will fill this gap by investigating how Ginimbi Lites interview contributed to the reconstruction of Genuis Kandungure identity based on the audiences perspective.

## THEORETICAL FRAMEWORK

### Social Constructionist Approach to Identity

The social constructionist approach asserts that identity is not a static trait but a fluid construct (Mogernroth, 2024). This means that it is not cast in stone or obvious but it is shaped by social interactions and cultural contexts (Van Gasse, Claessens, & Mortelmans, 2025). This makes it ideal for this study because in the digital realm, which is the focus of the study, identities can be curated and modified based on audience feedback and social norms.

Tasos (2024), Keller (2024) and Kim (2001) discuss the often-confusing interchangeable use of “constructionism” and “constructivism.” This study clarifies this distinction by employing social constructionism, which emphasizes societal influences on identity formation, as opposed to constructivism, which focuses on individual cognition (Young and Collin, 2004). The aim is to produce social meaning through an exploration of the social, and digital forces that shape the identity of Genius Kadungure hence this approach.

Scholars like Pérez-Torres (2024) state that the perceptions of the individual about themselves are based on their experiences with others and their own attributions of their own behavior. This notion aligns with the ideas of Berger and Luckmann (1966), who argue that identities are continuously influenced by cultural practices and social interactions. In this context, “Ginimbi Lite” emerges not merely as a replication of Genius Kadungure's identity but as a complex construction that reflects societal perceptions and media narratives surrounding his life and legacy. Therefore this framework allows for a deeper analysis of how social media facilitates these interactions and shapes the identity formation process.

The social constructionist approach to identity recognises the importance of historical, contextual, and societal factors in identity formation (Poppi and Copes, 2024; Jackson and Hogg, 2010). In the case of Ginimbi Lite, these factors play a crucial role in how the character is perceived and understood by audiences in relation to the perceived identity of Genius Kadungure. “Ginimbi Lite” life is deeply rooted in a socio-cultural context shaped by Genius Kadungure's life as a flamboyant entrepreneur and socialite in Zimbabwe. Therefore by analyzing this context, one can better understand how audience perceptions of Ginimbi Lite contribute to the ongoing construction of ginimbi's identity in public discourse.

The role of audience engagement is also crucial in the social construction of identities. Audience reception theories, as discussed by Jensen (2003), suggest that individuals actively interpret and derive meanings from media texts based on their own experiences and social contexts. By gathering audience perspectives on the Star Fm interview featuring Ginimbi Lite the researcher can assess how people perceive “Ginimbi Lite” and the implications on Genius Kadungure’s identity. The fundamental question in this study being do audiences embrace this digital persona as an authentic representation of Ginimbi, or do they view it as an imposter? These inquiries delve into the core of social constructionism, which posits that identity is fluid and contingent upon social interactions.

Acknowledging the complexity of identity as highlighted by Hall (1997), he warns against oversimplifying identities into fixed categories. In the context of Ginimbi, this complexity is evident in how “Ginimbi Lite” embodies various aspects of his legacy celebrity culture, entrepreneurship, and social status while also being shaped by audience engagement and media representation. Thus, the exploration of “Ginimbi Lite” serves as a focal point for multiple narratives surrounding Genius Kadungure's life, illustrating the interplay between different identities and cultural discourses.

## RESEARCH METHODOLOGY

The study adopts a qualitative research approach which focuses on understanding how individuals interpret and assign meaning to their experiences (Creswell, 2014; Merriam, 2015). This approach is particularly suitable for investigating audience views on the identity of the late Genius Kadungure (Ginimbi) through Ginimbi Lite’s impersonation and memorialisation of him on his interview on StarFm Youtube Page.Qualitative research employs various methods for data collection which include in-depth interviews, focus groups, participant and non-participant observation, document analysis, and ethnography (Merriam, 2015). Therefore, this study will utilise focus group discussions and intervews to explore how audiences appropriate meaning to Ginimbi Lite’s interview.In this study, the audiences consists of twelve purposively selected participantswho watched Ginimbi Lites interview with DJ Ollah on Star Fm and they are student at Lupane State University doing their final year.

This study utilized purposive sampling in identifying the 12. Purposive sampling, also known as judgmental sampling, is a non-probability sampling technique where participants are selected based on specific characteristics or criteria relevant to the research study (Palinkas et al., 2017). This method allowed the researchers to target individuals who have particular knowledgde related to the phenomenon being studied, thereby enhancing the richness and depth of the data collected. According to Creswell (2014), purposive sampling is particularly useful in qualitative research as it enables the selection of information-rich cases that provide insights into complex issues. This approach ensured that the sample is aligned with the study's objectives, allowing for a more focused exploration of the research questions..

To collect empirical data focus group discussions and semi structured interviews were used. Semi-structured interviews involve a flexible format where the researcher prepares a set of open-ended questions that guide discussion with the research particpants about an issue under investigation, (Kvale, 2007). This approach enabled in-depth exploration of individual experiences and perceptions (Yin, 2017). Interviews then became ideal for this study as they allow the researcher to understand audiences perspectives on Ginimbi' identity after consuming Ginimbi Lite's interview. These semi structed inteviews took longer than 20 minutes per participant. They took place at a convienient location at Lupane State University, ensuring a comfortable and private setting for the participants to share their thoughts and opinons.Focus group discussions were complemented by the semi-structured interviews by facilitating group interactions among participants in a WhatsApp group . For this study, two focus groups were formed, each consisting of six participants . According to Morgan (2012), focus groups are particularly effective in eliciting a range of views and emotional processes within a group context, which can lead to richer qualitative data. Additionally, having multiple focus groups enables researchers to conduct comparative analyses, revealing trends and differences in participants' viewpoints, thereby enhancing the overall findings of the study. Gathering a diverse group of individuals who share a common interest in Ginimbi, the focus groups provided valuable insights on narratives surrounding his memory. Discussions were guided by a set of questions based on what Ginimbi lite said and did in the interview. This interactive format did not only enrich the data collected but also highlighted the social dynamics that influence how Ginimbi is remembered in the digital space. The groups used English, Shona and Ndebele as languages during interactions.

Yieldeddata was thematic analysed. Thematic analysis involves identifying, analyzing, and reporting patterns within qualitative data, enabling the researcher to understand the underlying meanings and insights related to the research questions (Braun & Clarke, 2006). This approach allowed for a nuanced interpretation of participants' perceptions regarding digital memorialization and identity reconstruction. The analysis proceeded through several stages.

First, the audio recordings of the interviews and discussions were transcribed verbatim to ensure accuracy and preserve participants' voices. Next, the researchers familiarized themselves with the data by reading through the transcripts multiple times, noting initial impressions and potential themes. Following this immersion, the researcher coded the data systematically by identifying significant statements and categorizing them into codes that represent specific ideas or concepts related to the study.

Once the coding was completed, the researcher grouped these codes into broader themes that reflect the key patterns emerging from the data. This thematic framework guided the interpretation of the findings, highlighting the ways in which Ginimbi's digital legacy is memorialized and the various identities constructed through his online presence. Finally, the results were presented using rich descriptions and direct quotes from participants to illustrate the themes and provide a deeper understanding of their experiences. This approach not only enhanced the credibility of the findings but also allowed readers to engage with the participants' perspectives authentically.

With regards to ethical considerations in the context of this study on audience perceptions of Genius Kadungure (Ginimbi) and "Ginimbi Lite," informed consent is a critical ethical consideration, particularly since the research involves human participants. The researchers introduced themselves and clearly explained the aims of the study to the participants, allowing them to make informed decisions about their participation (Polit & Beck, 2020). After understanding the purpose of the research, the participants agreed to take part in the study.

To protect participants' identities, the researcher assured them that their personal information would remain confidential. During data presentation and analysis, participants were referred to using pseudonyms, a practice supported by Byrne (2001), who argues that confidentiality and privacy must be guaranteed to potential participants. Additionally, the researcher sought permission to record the interviews using a mobile phone recorder, as recommended by King and Harrocks (2010), who highlight the necessity of obtaining consent for recording research interviews. This commitment to ethical research practices was essential for establishing trust and ensuring the integrity of the findings related to Ginimbi's legacy and memorialization.

## DATA PRESENTATION AND ANALYSIS

### Overview of the Findings

This study examined audience perceptions of the late Genius Ginimbi Kadungure's identity as presented in the interview on Star FM's YouTube channel. Ginimbi Lite, who reconstructed Genius Ginimbi Kadungure's identity, served as the primary presenter of that identity. The data collected reveals a multifaceted view of Genuis Ginimbi, where audiences regard him as a renowned public figure whose extravagant lifestyle inspired a lot of young people to hustle hard. The study aimed to examine the audience views on the late Genuis Ginimbi Kadungures identity based on the interview and to analyse the audience perspective of whether Ginimbi Lite is correctly memorializing the late Genuis Ginimbi Kadungure. The audience responses highlighted concerns regarding authenticity, questioning whether Ginimbi Lite's portrayal genuinely honors Ginimbi's legacy or distorts it for personal gain.

The findings are organized into two thematic categories aligned with the study's objectives:

- Audience Perceptions of Genius Ginimbi Kadungure's identity
- Authentic or Not? Audience perspective of Ginimbi Lite's Memorialization of Genuis Kadungure

The next section will discuss these themes in detail, drawing on data collected from focus group discussions and interviews to provide insights into the complexities of digital memorialization and identity in contemporary Zimbabwean society.

## Audience Perceptions of Genius Kadungure's Identity

Empirical data gathered through focus group discussions and in-depth interviews exhibit diverse interpretations of who Genius Ginimbi Kadungure is as presented by Ginimbi lite in an interview on Star Fm Youtube page. Most participants could flesh out the identity of Genius Kadungure based on seeing Ginimbi Lite on the interview on Star FM YouTube channel. One respondent, a social media fashion influencer, expressedthat Ginimbi was a man with good fashion tatse:

*"Genuis Kadungure had a great fashion taste, wearing original clothes and Ginimbi Lite walked into that Star Fm interview wearing a versace shirt from Mbare Musika showing that he is really trying to emulate someone who had a good fashion taste..."*

Respondent one's submission shows that the late Genius Ginimbi Kadungure was a man who had a great fashion sense. It is for this reason that Ginimbi Lite attended the interview wearing accessories and clothes similar to those of Genuis Ginimni Kadungure.

Other participants were of the view that Genius Kadungure was a confident man. In this regard, respondent three, a content creator, added that:

*Ginimbi Lite seems to be confident in what he is saying even though some of it sounds as if its just mere lies. So, I would assume Boss G was a confident man and that is what sold him best to his followers. Ginimbi Lite is just following the footstep living his best life and I like the way he is answering questions in the interview, like he has enough money to live the type of lifestyle that Boss G lived. He clearly said that the lifestyle he lives emulates the late Genuis Ginimbi Kadungure. People should just stop judging him because he might not be rich like Genuis Ginimbi but his confidence will take him far...*

This participants's view reflects a complex understanding of identity and legacy in the digital age. The participants acknowledges the aspirational nature of Ginimbi Lites' persona, suggesting that his portayal serves as a tribute while also embodying personal ambition. His persona then becomes a clue to the persona of the late Genius Ginimbi Kadungure. In this respect the participant feels that Kadungure was a confident man. This aligns with Moyo's (2021) assertion that social media facilitates identity construction allowing individuals to adopts public figures personas. Furthermore, the partipants calls for others to "stop judging him" emphasizes the importance of intention behind digital representations, resonationg with McCulloch's (2019) critique of authenticity in digital memorilisation. Intergrating these viewpoints within a social constructionist framework, it is clear that the digital environment not only facilitate the creation of new identities but also complicates traditional notions of authenticity and representation.

Genuis Ginimbi Kadungure lived life according to his own terms, often ignored judgement allowing him cultivate an identity that resonate with many. It is for this reason that some participants see the late Genius Ginimbi Kadungure as an arrogant man. Another participant said:

*Just looking at the I don't care attitude that is being displayed by Ginimbi Lite I would assume the real Ginimbi had a similar attitude...*

Another participant added:

*The arrogance that I am seeing in the interview though subtle indicates how arrogant the late Genius Ginimbi Kadungure was. He even says what people say about him will not put food on his table. You see the arrogance?*

This idea is reinforced by scholars like Bauman (2004), who suggest that in a liquid modernity, individuals frequently draw from diverse influences to shape fluid identities. Ginimbi Lite cement this concept as he seeks to emulate the persona of the late Genius Ginimbi Kadungure, demonstrating to the audiences the character and essence of who he was

This attitude highlights the ongoing influence of the late Genius Ginimbi Kadungures' persona. This demonstrates how his legacy encourages others not to forge their paths despite public opinion a theme that aligns with Goofman's (1959) exploration of identity perfomance in social contexts. This demonstrate that identity is not only constructed through individual choices but also shaped by the social environment, reinforcing the idea that personal identity can thrive amidst and against societal expectations (Bauman, 2004).

The social constructionist approach to identity emphasizes how individuals shape their identities through interactions with others and societal norms. This perspective is evident in audience reactions to Ginimbi Lite's portrayal of Genius Kadungure. One participant, distant from other participants views states that:

*I feel Ginimbi is realistic and down to earth; he sees the world from a different point of view point.*

This shows that Ginimbi was a down to earth person even though other participants felt that he was arrogant, extravangant and prideful. The audience's perception of Genius Ginimbi Kadungure, as reflected through Ginimbi Lite, reveals that viewers see Kadungure as a multifaceted individual who embodies both realism and extravagance. The remark that "Ginimbi is realistic and down to earth" suggests that audiences value these relatable qualities alongside his flamboyant lifestyle. This indicates that they appreciate a deeper understanding of Kadungure's character, expecting Ginimbi Lite to reflect these traits in his portrayal. According to La Porte (2017), the development of a character's identity is crucial for audience engagement, as it allows viewers to connect with the character on a personal level.

In some instances Genius Ginimbi Kadungure's identity was tied to his facial apperance. Other participants noted that the late Genius Ginimbi was an ugly man. This was said by a participant who articulated that:

*This young man looks like Ginimbi. He is very ugly just exactly like Kadungure. Whenever I look at him I just see Ginimbi*

The remark illustrates a significant aspect of audience perception regarding Genius Ginimbi Kadungure's identity, specifically linking it to his physical appearance. This statement suggests that some audience members view Kadungure's legacy as being intertwined with characteristics associated with his looks, indicating that their assessment of his identity is largely influenced by physical attributes. By equating Ginimbi Lite's appearance with that of Kadungure, the participant underscores how perceptions of ugliness can impact the public's recollection and interpretation of an individual's identity. This finding reveals that the audience's perspective not only reinforces the notion of Kadungure as an "ugly" figure but also highlights the broader implications of physical appearance in digital memorialisation and identity within the public sphere.

## Audience Perspective of Ginimbi Lite's Memorialisation of Genius Kadungure

The audience's assumptions surrounding Ginimbi Lite's authenticity in memorializing Genius Ginimbi Kadungure raises important questions. Viewers may ask: Is Ginimbi Lite genuinely honouring Genuis Ginimbi Kadungure's legacy, or is he merely imitating a popular figure for personal gain? Are his actions a true reflection of Genuis Ginimbi Kadungure's character, or do they fall short of capturing his essence? These questions highlight the complexities of authenticity in memorialization and the expectations that come with it.

Most participants expressed that these imitation lacks authenticity and its negatively impacting the image of Genuis Ginimbi Kadungure that they admired on social media.

One respondent expressed a strong viewpoint stating:

*Genuis Kadungure had an expensive taste, wearing original clothes straight from Versace shop and he often showed off the prices but Ginimbi Lite walked into that Star Fm interview wearing a fake Versace shirt from mbaremsika(mbare market) dollar deals...*

Respondent one's submission expressed the disappointment of the audience in this imitation and it shows that Ginimbi Lite is fake and he is doing more damage than good to Genuis Ginimbi Kadungure's legacy. However, while some see authenticity in Ginimbi Lite's homage, others believe he falls short of fully embodying Kadungure's extravagant lifestyle and his spendthrift personality. Erikson (1968) emphasizes that personal identities are shaped through social interactions. This underscores that audience perceptions are influenced by shared expectations. The community expects Ginimbi Lite to portray a version of Kadungure that reflects his extravagant lifestyle and societal significance. When he does not meet these expectations, doubts about his authenticity arise.

One respondent highlighted,

*Ginimbi Lite is always carrying this Veuve bottle everywhere. I am convinced it's the only one; I believe it's displayed in his house too, meaning he's lying in this interview when he says he is rich. Genius Ginimbi Kadungure used to order them in bulk in every club he entered every weekend until they called him the Champagne King*

This perspective aligns with scholars like Turkle's (2011) argument, which says that online identities often lack authenticity, indicating that digital representations can dilute a person's true essence. This sentiment reflects the broader concern among participants that Ginimbi Lite's portrayal diminishes the genuine spirit of Genius Kadungure, reducing a vibrant legacy to mere imitation. Drawing on Turkle's (2011) insights, it becomes evident that audiences feel a significant loss, believing that an important part of Ginimbi's character and influence has been compromised in the process of his digital memorialization.

The comparison of Ginimbi Lite's behavior to that of Genius Ginimbi, especially in terms of displaying wealth through extravagant acts like overspending on alcohol, highlights a key distinction between genuine legacy and mere imitation. One participant stated, "Ginimbi used to buy bottles*takatarisa* (while we watch) and spray them at the clubs." This comment underscores that true memorialization involves honoring the deceased's lifestyle while authentically embodying their values. This perspective aligns with the social constructionist approach, which argues that identity is shaped by both individual actions and societal expectations. Goffman (1959) discusses how identities are negotiated within societal contexts, emphasizing the importance of authenticity in memorialization.

Authenticity in this context is vital; it involves not just mimicking actions but also capturing the essence of what made Genius Ginimbi unique. This aligns with the social constructionist approach, which suggests that identity is influenced by individual actions as well as societal expectations. Goffman (1959) highlights how identities are negotiated within societal contexts, stressing that authenticity is essential for meaningful memorialization. When audiences perceive Ginimbi Lite as lacking this authenticity, they feel that the true spirit of Genius Kadungure is being undermined, reducing a rich legacy to superficial imitation. Thus, the call for authenticity becomes a central theme in discussions about how to honor and remember influential figures.

One participant criticized,

*Ginimbi Lite says he sold his car because he was running low on money, then went home with a kombi. Genius Kadungure never sold any of his cars; he called it hustling. Instead, he used to buy a new one after his frequent international trips. This boy should have hustled and become rich before calling himself Ginimbi Lite because on social media, we want someone who will give us the best of what we lost, not some wannabe hunting for clout and likes*

This response highlights the importance of authenticity in memorialization. The participant emphasizes that true representation of Genius Kadungure should reflect his consistent display of wealth and success, which Ginimbi Lite fails to emulate. Instead of embodying the genuine spirit of Genuis Kadungure, Ginimbi Lite appears to seek attention to the audience without the substance that defined the Genuis Ginimbi Kadungure. Anderson (2020) argues that modern communities are often formed through shared stories and media. Imitating Genius Ginimbi Kadungure on a public digital platfrom, Ginimbi Lite invites others to join in the remembrance, shaping Kadungure's identity together. However, this participatory aspect raises concerns about authenticity, as audiences now navigate the delicate balance between genuine tribute and opportunistic imitation. The participant's critique reflects these concerns, underscoring the need for authenticity in honoring such influential figures.

Memorialization is crucial for societies to honor and remember influential figures. In Ginimbi Lite's case, memorializing Genius Kadungure extends beyond simple remembrance; it actively influences how the public perceives and engages with his legacy. Hirst and Manier (2008) note that collective memory is dynamic, involving a continual interplay between history and digital narratives. Thus, Ginimbi Lite's representation of Kadungure becomes a site of negotiation, where the past is reinterpreted to fit present contexts. This dynamic invites discussions about authenticity and the ethical implications of embodying another's legacy, particularly when that legacy is tied to societal expectations of respect.

## CONCLUSIONS

This study has demonstrated the intricacies involved in reconstructing Genius Kadungure's (Ginimbi) identity through the potrayal of Ginimbi Lite in the Star FM YouTube interview. Using a social constructionist approach, the study found that the way the public views Ginimbi Lite's portrayal of Genius Kadungure reflects the real Genius. The participants saw Genius Ginimbi Kadungure's identity differently, highlighting characteristics like confidence, extravagance, uglyiness and arrogance. These observations support those of Meier and Johnson (2022), who showed how audience perception and self-presentation interact dynamically in digital environments. As a result, it became clear that Ginimbi Lite's portrayal interacts with larger societal discourses like identity and authenticity in addition to attempting to honour Kadungure.

Furthermore, the study raised critical concerns about the authenticity of Ginimbi Lite's portrayal of Kadungure. Audiences questioned whether Ginimbi Lite genuinely honored Genuis Kadungure's legacy or sought personal gain through imitation. This skepticism reflects McCulloch's (2019) assertion that digital memorialization often risks commodifying the memories of public figures, potentially distorting their true essence. Participants expressed a desire for authenticity in Ginimbi Lite's representation, indicating that successful memorialization should capture the core values that defined Kadungure, not just superficial traits. This research contributes to a deeper understanding of how social media facilitates complex processes of identity reconstruction and memorialization, highlighting a significant gap in existing literature regarding the posthumous identities of public figures. As noted by Ndlovu (2022), while social media provides a platform for collective mourning, it also challenges the maintenance of authenticity. Future research should further explore the implications of digital narratives on identity construction, particularly regarding their influence on collective memory and societal perceptions of influential figures like Genius Kadungure. Ultimately, this study calls for a nuanced understanding of the interplay between representation, authenticity, and identity in the context of digital memorialization.Future studies can expand the scope of this study and get more audience demographic perspectives on Genuis Ginimbi Kadungure's memorilisation by Ginimbi Lite across different regions of Zimbabwe. Researchers can also analyze the reception of other social media platforms, such as Instagram Reels, Facebook Reels, and TikTok videos that are created by Ginimbi Lite or related to Genius Ginimbi Kadungure, to gain insights beyond the Star FM

YouTube interview portrayal. With regards to practical implications it should be noted that media practitioners and curators should assess the authenticity of media productions so that they have a more telling influence in society

## REFERENCES


Ajani, Y. A., Baloyi, N. C., Chibike, J. J., Elisifa, Z., Lubambo, R. J., Mabika, M., Mangaka, A. C., Malatji, E. J., Mapulane, M. G., Muthambi, R., & Ngoaketsi, J. M. (2024). *Digital media and the preservation of indigenous languages in Africa: Toward a digitalized and sustainable society*. Rowman & Littlefield.

Anderson, B. (2020). Imagined communities: Reflections on the origin and spread of nationalism. In *The new social theory reader* (pp. 282–288). Routledge.

Avci, H., Baams, L., & Kretschmer, T. (2025). A systematic review of social media use and adolescent identity development. *Adolescent Research Review*, *10*(2), 219–236.

Baudrillard, J. (1994). *Simulacra and Simulation*. University of Michigan Press.

Bauman, Z. (2004). *Liquid Life*. Polity Press.

Berger, P. L., & Luckmann, T. (1966). *The Social Construction of Reality: A Treatise in the Sociology of Knowledge*. Anchor Books.

Braun, V., & Clarke, V. (2006). Using Thematic Analysis In Psychology. *Qualitative Research in Psychology*, *3*(2), 77–101.

Chibike, J. J. (2023). Podcasting COVID-19 in Indigenous Languages: Interrogating Audio Psychology and Political Anthropomorphism. In *African Language Media* (pp. 112-124). Routledge.

Chibike, J. J. (2024). Computational Linguistics and Indigenous Languages. In Makananise, O and Madima, E (Eds). *Digital Media and the Preservation of Indigenous Languages in Africa: Toward a Digitalized and Sustainable Society*, 95.

Creswell, J. W. (2014) *Research Design: Qualitative, Quantitative, and Mixed Methods Approaches*. 4th edn. Thousand Oaks, Carlifonia: Sage Publications.

Erikson, E.H., 1968. *Identity youth and crisis* (No. 7). WW Norton & company.

Goffman, E. (1959). *The Presentation of Self in Everyday Life*. University of Edinburgh Social Sciences Research Centre.

Goffman, E. (1959). *The Presentation of Self in Everyday Life*. Anchor Books.

Hall, S. (Ed.). (1997). *Representation: Cultural representations and signifying practices* (Vol. 2). Sage.

Hirst, W., & Manier, D. (2008). The role of memory in the social construction of identity. In *The Handbook of Identity Theory and Research*. Springer.

Hoffner, C., & Bond, B. J. (2022). 'The role of media figures in adolescents' identity construction'. *Journal of Broadcasting & Electronic Media*, *66*(2), 185–202.

Hopkins, D. J., Lelkes, Y., & Wolken, S. (2025). The rise of and demand for identity-oriented media coverage. *American Journal of Political Science*, *69*(2), 483–500.

Jackson, R. L., & Hogg, M. A. (2010). The Other. *Encyclopedia OfIdentity*, 519-526.

Jensen. M. C. (2003). *A Theory Of The Firm: Governance, Residual Claims, And Organizational Forms*. Harvard University Press.

Kaplan, A. M., & Haenlein, M. (2010). Users of the world, unite! The challenges and opportunities of Social Media. *Business Horizons*, *53*(1), 59–68.

King, N., & Harrocks, C. (2010). *Interviews in Qualitative Research*. Sage Publications.

Kirkegaard, T. D., Fivush, R., Coman, A., Hirst, W., Luminet, O., & Pillemer, D. B. (2025). A framework for vicarious and collective memory, future projections and narrative identity. *Nature Reviews Psychology*, **•••**, 1–14.

Koutamanis, K., Vossen, H. G., Peter, J., & Valkenburg, P. M. (2015). The role of maternal and adolescent personality traits in the use of social networking sites. *Computers in Human Behavior*, *48*, 363–369.

Kvale, S. (2007). Learning The Craft Of Interviewing. In *Learning The Craft Of Interviewing*. Sage Publications London.

La Porte, C. (2017). The Story of Identity: Categorization.*The Writing Cooperative*. Available at: www.thewritingcooperative.com [Accessed 25 Mar. 2025].

Marcia, J. E. 1980. Identity in adolescence. *Handbook of adolescent psychology*, 9(11). 159-187.

Marwick, A., & Ellison, N. B. (2012). "There isn't Wifi in Heaven!" Negotiating visibility on Facebook memorial pages. *Journal of Broadcasting & Electronic Media*, *56*(3), 378–400.

McCulloch, H. J. (2019). *Digital Death: Mortality and Beyond in the Online Age*. Routledge.

McKenzie, J. (2025). Digital media as sites for cultural identity development: The case of Hmong American emerging adults. *Journal of Adolescent Research*, *40*(2), 296–330.

Meier, A., & Johnson, M. (2022). Exposure to the positivity bias and adolescents' differential longitudinal links with social comparison, inspiration and envy depending on social media literacy. *Current Psychology (New Brunswick, N.J.), 42*(32), 28221–28241.

Merriam. S. B. (2015). Qualitative Research: Designing, Implementing, And Publishing A Study. In *Handbook Of Research On Scholarly Publishing And Research Methods* (Pp. 125-140). Igi Global Scientific Publishing.

Mkwebu, N., & Chibike, J. J. (2025). Computer-Generated Linguistics Countering Linguicides: Users' Use and Interpretation of WhatsApp Emojis in isiNdebele. In *Resuscitation of African Languages: Theorising the Battle Against Sociocultural Genocide* (pp. 215–236). Springer Nature Switzerland.

Morgan. D. L. (2012). Focus Groups And Social Interaction. *The Sage Handbook Of Interview Research: The Complexity Of The Craft, 2*, 161-176.

Ndlovu, T. (2019). Cultural Expression in Southern African Social Media. *Southern African Journal of Communication Studies, 41*(1), 22–29.

Palinkas, L. A., He, A. S., Choy-Brown, M., & Hertel, A. L. (2017). Operationalizing Social Work Science Through Research–Practice Partnerships: Lessons From Implementation Science. *Research on Social Work Practice, 27*(2), 181–188.

Pérez-Torres, V. (2024). Social Media: A Digital Social Mirror For Identity Development During Adolescence. *Current Psychology, 43*(26), 22170-22180.

Polit. D., & Beck, C. (2020). *Essentials Of Nursing Research: Appraising Evidence For Nursing Practice.* Lippincott Williams & Wilkins.

Poppi, F. I. M., & Copes, H. (2024). Identitas Per Fabulam: Joint Fantasising In The Construction Of Criminal Group Identities. *Critical Criminology, 32*(2), 457–478.

Pujiati, P., Lundeto, A., & Trianto, I. (2025). Representing Arab-Indonesian identity: Language and cultural narratives on social media. *Indonesian Journal of Applied Linguistics, 14*(3), 653–666.

Robards, B., & Lincoln, S. (2017). Uncovering longitudinal life narratives: Scrolling back on Facebook. *Qualitative Research, 17*(6), 715–730.

Tasos, T. (2024). Social Constructionism: Critical Analysis From A Vygotskian Perspective. *Rethinking Marxism, 36*(2), 195–223.

Van Gasse, D., Claessens, E., & Mortelmans, D. (2025). Navigating Personal Choice, Socio-cultural Background and Societal Norms in Forming a Singlehood Identity in Belgium: A Consideration of Qualitative Narratives in Relation to Gender and Migration Background. *Tijdschrift voor Genderstudies*, *28*(2/3), 171–191.

Yin, R. K. (2017). *Case study research and applications: Design and methods.* Sage publications.

Young, R. A., & Collin, A. (2004). Introduction: Constructivism and social constructionism in the career field. *Journal of Vocational Behavior*, *64*(3), 373–388.

Zou, Y. (2025). How Social Media Self-Presentation Enhances Consumers' Preference for Experiential Consumption. *Journal of Consumer Behaviour*, *20*(3), 238.

Chapter 10

# Platformized Migration and Digital Capitalism:

## Rethinking Migrant Labor, Mobility, and Inequality Through the Case of Uber

**Şerife Sena Güner**
https://orcid.org/0000-0002-2886-0630
*Sinop University, Turkey*

## ABSTRACT

*This chapter examines the intersection of digital capitalism, platform economies, and migrant labor through the concept of platformized migration. It argues that platforms such as Uber are not neutral technologies but infrastructures that reorganize labor, governance, and inequality. Drawing on critical political economy, the chapter conceptualizes platform capitalism as a key form of digital capitalism driven by datafication, algorithmic control, and precarious labor. Migrant workers, often excluded from formal labor markets, become central yet vulnerable actors within these systems. Uber's business model—based on data extraction, algorithmic management, and worker misclassification—creates dependency and insecurity while reproducing racialized and legal inequalities. However, the chapter also highlights migrant agency and resistance, as drivers mobilize through online networks and collective actions to contest exploitation. Ultimately, it reframes platformized migration as both a site of exploitation and a space of struggle in the digital age.*

DOI: 10.4018/979-8-3373-4267-2.ch010

## INTRODUCTION

Over the past few years, the rapid growth of digital platforms has significantly restructured the core principles of contemporary capitalism. The new era, surrounded by this structural transformation based on a linking of the capital, labor, and mobility, is defined by many scholars as the era of digital capitalism (Schiller, 1999; Fuchs, 2014), and more specifically platform capitalism (Srnicek, 2017). In the period of far-reaching transformation shaped by global digitalization, the nature of capitalism has shifted from traditional industrial structures to increasingly complex digital services and systems. The changing process, in which the impact of digital technology has been seen across various spheres of life -from production processes to labor markets- is directly related to political economy (Zuboff, 2019; Woodcock & Graham, 2020; Fernandez Macias et al., 2025). For example, the most profitable companies such as Microsoft, Meta, and Apple, plays an important role for many countries across multiple domains, including governance, information systems, and commerce (Schiller, 2023: 527-28). This is not just a technological shift, instead it marks a deeper reconfiguration of capitalism that has now driven by processes of datafication, algorithmic governance, and precarious labor regimes (Zuboff, 2019; Hauben et al., 2020; Baiocco et al., 2022). In this regard, digital platforms constitute a key dimension of global labor markets. Beyond simply providing new forms of service delivery, platform-based systems increasingly restructure the foundational principles of labor, modes of value production, and forms of social organization.

The phenomenon of platformized migration stands at the core of this transformation within the intersection of migrant labor, mobility, and platform-based employment under the logic of digital capitalism (Van Doorn, 2017; Graham et al., 2017; Kovács, 2022). In this context, understanding the impacts of such a structural shift for migration dynamics, is important as digitalization globally affect the movement of people and their employment. This term reflects the intersection of migrant labor and platform-based labor systems shaped by insecurity, precarious employment, and algorithmic governance. While examining on the digital platforms within the relation of labor markets, this paper particularly frames these platform-based structures as mechanisms that reinforce the exploitation of migrant workers through the ongoing illusion of being 'independent contractors', rather than defining them as neutral systems (Wood et al., 2019; Hauben et al., 2020). Migrant workers -in particular those subjected to structural exclusion from formal employment- are positioned at the forefront of both precarity and potential in this emerging system. The platforms appear accessible for migrants who are often excluded from formal labor markets based on legal, social and economic barriers (Pesole et all, 2019: 4). At this point, platform capitalism is grounded in the algorithmic extraction of precarious labor which is unequally provided by migrant workers (van Doorn, 2017; Woodcock

& Graham, 2020). Migrant workers, who are already marginalized within host societies, are integrated into digital networks that request continuous availability, real-time responsiveness, and ongoing data production (Hill, 2015; Graham et all, 2017). The migrant workers' behaviors are governed by platforms, based on GPS tracking, customer ratings, and algorithmic matching, while upholding the legal presumption of self-employment.

This paper aims to critically rethink the digital capitalism and migration labor by focusing the experiences of migrant workers. The focus of this research is to explore how migrant labor is shaped, governed, and instrumentalized through digital platforms by using Uber as a case study. Uber as a platform that stands out as one of the leading employers of migrants represents more than a transportation company; it is a laboratory of algorithmic labor control, where drivers -many of whom are migrants- are subject to continuous monitoring, performance nudging, and customer-driven rating systems that impact their income and job security (Hall & Krueger, 2015; Van Doorn, 2017; Calo & Rosenblat, 2017). In this context, two main contributions of this paper stand out. First, it contributes to the critical discussions on digital capitalism by looking into the new forms of labor structured in platform-based era. It is important to address the processes of globalization and digitalization through the lens of critical political economy, which allows to see the impacts of power relations on the changing labor regimes. Second, it contributes to the migration studies by questioning the migrant labor within the debate around platform-based economy. It is important to consider the migrant labor within the intersection of race, gender, class, and migration status. Thus, the study seeks to make a contribution to discussions on inequality by revealing how labor exploitation, reproduced through migrant labor. In this regard, this paper is driven by a set of these research questions:

- How does platform capitalism affect the migrant labor and mobility?
- In what ways do digital platforms such as Uber integrate and govern migrant workers?
- What forms of precarity and inequality emerge through the platformization of migration?

While aiming to address these questions, this chapter builds on an interdisciplinary framework. The analysis is grounded in a conceptual and literature-based methodology, drawing on academic research, policy reports (such as those produced by Fairwork), and critical theoretical contributions from migration studies, digital sociology, and political economy. The insights from migration studies, digital sociology, and political economy are integrated to conceptualize platformized migration as a multi-dimensional concept. While this research is not based on a primary fieldwork, it offers a critical and conceptually grounded perspective of how digital infrastructures are involved in the persistence of social inequality. Building on existing research (e.g., van Doorn, 2017; Woodcock & Graham, 2020; Rosenblat & Stark, 2016), this work highlights the underlying structures that make migrant labor central yet invisible in the platform economy.

It is important noting that, this chapter also challenges the portrayal of migrant workers as passive victims. Although the significant constraints in digital platforms, they also give rise to new forms of resistance. As reported in several studies (Cant, 2019; Tassinari & Maccarrone, 2020; Joyce et al., 2020), migrant drivers are increasingly organizing through online communities to share information about algorithmic manipulation, to demand better working conditions and to coordinate around protest actions. Organizations such as Fairwork focused on documenting extractive platform forms and advocating for ethical labor standards. Thus, the platform functions not merely as a space for exploitation but also represents a sphere of visibility, voice, and transformative potential. By critically addressing Uber as a representative case, this work contributes to emerging discussions on algorithmic governance, digital labor rights, and the future of migrant work in a platformized world.

## 1. PLATFORM CAPITALISM AS AN INTEGRAL DIMENSION OF DIGITAL CAPITALISM

Platform capitalism is one of the most obvious forms of digital capitalism, which offers the larger framework within which datafication, algorithmic governance, and digital infrastructures drive modern capitalism (Schiller, 1999; Zuboff, 2019; Aloisi & Gramano, 2019). At the outset, this section outlines the theoretical framework of platform capitalism within the broader context of digital capitalism. It then moves on to examine how platform capitalism materializes in everyday life through labor relations, mobility, and consumption practices. As Srnicek (2017) discusses, platforms serve as more than just service providers; they are economic structures that structure data flows, create value from users, and dictate institutional logics for market participation. Instead of operating as neutral technological means, platforms have taken shape as infrastructures that dominate sectors, govern social relations, and restructure modes of labor (Srnicek, 2017; Zuboff, 2019). Accordingly, platform capitalism can be viewed as a component of digital capitalism, where structural changes occur in everyday labor, mobility, and consumption practices.

The key characteristics of platform capitalism can be conceptually examined through Srnicek's (2017) typology of platforms, including advertising, cloud, industrial, product, and labor platforms. These various forms reveal that digital systems are shaped by platform based work models around data extraction and network effects, thereby creating new forms of monopoly. While they differ in many respects, platforms share a common operational logic: they benefit from economies of scale, rely on persistent user interaction, and derive income through the collection and analysis of behavioral data. In terms of economies of scale, as platforms expand, the marginal cost of providing more users tends to decrease, making concentration and expansion very beneficial. The above self-reinforcing dynamic whereby a platform's value rises as more users join, providing strong incentives for both users and providers to stay in the same ecosystem, is also referred to as network effects. These features highlight how platform capitalism serves as the institutional framework for digital capitalism, integrating accumulation strategies into infrastructures which have become important to communication, commerce, and work (Srnicek, 2017).

One of the most visible spheres where platform capitalism connects with everyday life is the gig economy. Platforms such as Uber, Deliveroo, or Glovo present themselves as offering workers autonomy and flexibility, but in practice they create a regime of fragmented, insecure, and algorithmically managed work (Rosenblat & Stark, 2016; Wood et al., 2019). De Stefano (2016) explains this work model with a concept of a "just-in-time workforce," in which labor is delivered on demand, without stability or long-term security. Workers are classified as independent contractors, a legal fiction that allows platforms to externalize costs, avoid social protections, and shift risks onto individuals (De Stefano, 2016: 13). Research has emphasized that the rating systems, GPS tracking, and dynamic pricing replace managerial oversight with algorithmic forms of labor discipline (Rosenblat & Stark, 2016; Muller, 2020; Baiocco et al, 2022). In this way, platform capitalism institutionalizes precariousness at the very core of its business models.

Migrant workers play a particularly important role in this system. They frequently use platforms as easily accessible points of entry because they are excluded from many formal labor markets due to some linguistic, legal, or social barriers (Pesole et al, 2019: 4). However, increased vulnerability shapes this accessibility. According to Van Doorn (2017), migrant labor is overrepresented in low-wage, on-demand service industries where digital forms of labor control coexist with gendered and racialized inequality. Similarly, Cant (2019) reveals that many of the food delivery couriers, mostly migrant workers, experience algorithmic exploitation in addition to economic marginalization. Therefore, platforms function as two-edged structures. While they give people who aren't able to find work a means of subsistence, they also incorporate them into systems of dispossession and excessive surveillance.

From the standpoint of critical political economy, these developments point out how platform capitalism contributes to structural asymmetries and reproduce inequality. According to Fuchs (2014), platform labor is an extension of Marxian exploitation, where surplus value is taken from users' social and communicative activities in addition to direct labor. An additional perspective is provided by Zuboff's

(2019) concept of surveillance capitalism, which discloses how platforms transform user behavior and turn routine activities into sources of predictive data. The most noticeable places for these processes to come together are labor platforms, where workers' supposed independence masks their deep reliance on insecure algorithmic systems. A reality of limited agency, where autonomy is limited by continuous monitoring, is concealed by the legal and cultural framing of gig work as ‘flexible’. (Rosenblat & Stark, 2016; De Stefano, 2016; Aloisi & Gramano, 2019).

Platform capitalism is simultaneously a place of contestation as well as exploitation. Researchers have shown that migrant workers in the gig economy are increasingly using new forms of resistance. They coordinate protests, organize through online communities, and exchange tactics for combating algorithmic manipulation (Tassinari & Maccarrone, 2020; Joyce et al., 2020). Initiatives like Fairwork challenge the prevailing narratives on platforms by drawing attention to exploitative practices and promoting moral labor standards. These dynamics reveal that platform capitalism encompasses both the potential seeds of collective mobilization and the mechanisms of precarization (Fairwork, 2021; Huws et al., 2017; Pulignano et al., 2021).

In conclusion, platform capitalism is an essential aspect of digital capitalism that embodies the ways algorithmic governance and digital infrastructures are clearly realized in global mobility, labor markets, and consumption patterns. Platforms serve as tools of control and accumulation by dominating infrastructures, obtaining data, and restructuring labor. However, they also perpetuate and reinforce existing social inequalities by incorporating migrant workers into these unstable systems. Therefore, it is necessary to consider platform capitalism's political and social effects in addition to its economic logics in order to comprehend it as an important component of digital capitalism. Platform capitalism most effectively shows its function as the lived reality of digital capitalism in the twenty-first century at this intersection between digital infrastructures, labor exploitation, migrant precarity, and emergent resistance.

Examining the ways in which these structural dynamics interact with migration is essential after outlining platform capitalism as a fundamental aspect of digital capitalism. The platform economy, where migrant workers are not only overrepresented but also situated at the center of unstable labor regimes, is one of the most prominent and contentious locations of this intersection. In light of this, the following section examines the function of migrant labor in the platform economy, emphasizing the ways in which digital infrastructures both integrate and take advantage of migrant workers.

## 2. MIGRANT LABOR IN THE PLATFORM ECONOMY

The emergence of the platform economy has changed the structure, distribution, and governance of work (Fernandez Macias et al., 2023: 40-41). Platforms like Uber, Deliveroo, Glovo, and Helpling have emerged as key infrastructures for mediating job opportunities at the nexus of labor markets and digital capitalism, especially in urban economies (Woodcock & Graham, 2020; Graham et al., 2017). Although platform capitalism changes the nature of labor relations for all workers, migrants are particularly impacted because they are often at the center of labor regimes mediated by platforms. In addition to being overrepresented in many platform sectors, migrant workers face particular vulnerabilities that are influenced by their social marginalization, language barriers, and legal status (Anderson, 2010; Kovacs, 2022). The mechanisms by which migrants are incorporated, controlled, and exploited are the main topics of this section's analysis of the role of migrant labor in the platform economy. It also highlights the forms of agency and resistance that arise in these online labor markets.

### Migrant Overrepresentation in Platform Work

An increasing amount of research indicates that gig economy sectors have a disproportionately high concentration of migrants (Van Doorn, 2017; Cant, 2019). The majority of platform drivers, couriers, and housekeepers in urban areas of North America and Europe are migrants. According to research on Uber conducted in London, Paris, and New York, for instance, between 60% and 80% of drivers are immigrants (Rosenblat & Stark, 2016; Tassinari & Maccarrone, 2020). Similarly, migrant workers are overrepresented in food delivery services like Deliveroo and Glovo, frequently working in physically demanding, low-paying, and unstable positions (Joyce et al., 2020; Kovacs, 2022).

The structural obstacles preventing migrants from accessing formal labor markets are the cause of this overrepresentation, which is not a result of chance. Language barriers, legal restrictions related to visa status, and the non-recognition of foreign qualifications are among the many challenges faced by migrants. As a result, platforms advertise themselves as easy ways to get into host labor markets with little formal training or education. Because of this, migrant workers frequently turn to platforms as one of the few practical ways to generate income after being pushed out of more stable employment opportunities (Calo & Rosenblat, 2017: 1642).

## Precarity and Algorithmic Management

Platforms trap migrants in extremely unstable labor regimes despite their accessibility. The platform economy's dependence on the legal fiction of 'independent contracting' is one of its distinguishing characteristics. Platforms circumvent minimum wage, social protection, and labor rights requirements by designating employees as self-employed (De Stefano, 2016; Cavallini, & Avogaro, 2019; Allaire et al., 2019). Due to their marginalized social and legal status, migrants are frequently more in need of employment protections, so this classification has significant ramifications for them. Furthermore, platforms use algorithmic systems rather than direct managerial supervision to exert control. The Uber study by Rosenblat and Stark (2016) shows how rating systems, algorithmic nudges, and unclear pricing mechanisms influence drivers' actions. The hidden nature of algorithmic management increases vulnerabilities for migrants, who might not be familiar with legal rights or have language barriers when navigating contractual arrangements. According to Wood et al. (2019), algorithmic control produces what they refer to as 'constrained agency' by simultaneously fostering a sense of autonomy and strengthening dependency.

## Racialization and Labor Segmentation

Without considering how race, ethnicity, and migration status influence labor markets, it is impossible to comprehend the experience of migrant workers in the platform economy. Van Doorn (2017) emphasizes how platform labor is frequently gendered and racialized, with migrants primarily working in low-status and stigmatized service industries like food delivery, transportation services, and cleaning. These factors are similar to past labor market segmentation trends, in which immigrants have historically been directed toward low-paying, unstable positions that local workers shun. Platforms use a global labor pool that can be triggered on demand to replicate and reinforce these patterns. Migrant laborers are marketed as a disposable, adaptable workforce whose worth is derived from their readiness to put up with unstable circumstances. Platforms also portray themselves as providing chances for economic integration, which obscures the ways in which digital infrastructures perpetuate exclusion and inequality (Huws et al., 2017; Hauben et al., 2020: 34).

## Legal Status and Vulnerability

One of the main axes of precarity for migrant workers in the platform economy is their legal status. Because they frequently lack access to legal options or labor protections, undocumented migrants and those with temporary visas are especially susceptible to exploitation. By providing informal or semi-formal work arrangements that function on the edge of regulation, platforms take advantage of this vulnerability (Kovács, 2022). Subcontracting systems, for example, are commonly used by food delivery services in European cities to hire undocumented migrants, enabling the platforms to distance themselves from responsibility while profiting from unemployed labor. Additionally, workers are solely responsible for any accidents, illnesses, or work-related costs due to the presumption of self-employment. As a result, migrants who lack access to health insurance or welfare programs are disproportionately at risk. De Genova (2017) contends that labor exploitation and legal precariousness are closely related, creating a state of 'deportability' where migrants' economic marginalization is exacerbated by their fear of being discovered or deported.

## Migrant Agency and Resistance

Migrant workers are not helpless victims in the platform economy, despite the fact that a large portion of the literature highlights vulnerability and exploitation. Recent research demonstrates how migrants band together to protest oppressive practices and stand up for their rights. In his ethnography of Deliveroo couriers, Cant (2019) details how migrant riders organize protests, go on strike, and use online communication platforms to foster solidarity. In a similar vein, Tassinari and Maccarrone (2020) explain how migrant-heavy food delivery workers in Italy and the UK created collective actions and grassroots unions to demand better working conditions. Tools for resistance are also made possible by digital technologies that facilitate exploitation. To exchange information, plan actions, and draw attention to injustices, migrant workers utilize social media platforms, online forums, and WhatsApp groups. These digital organizing strategies show how migrants use digital infrastructures in innovative ways to challenge the very structures that control their work (Aloisi et al., 2019; Joyce et al., 2020).

## Political Economy of Migrant Precarity

The incorporation of migrant labor into the platform economy must be viewed from the standpoint of critical political economy as a component of the larger dynamics of global inequality and neoliberal restructuring. By hiring people who are marginalized and politically disenfranchised, platforms profit from structural exclusions in labor markets. Therefore, migrant precarity is not a byproduct of platform capitalism; rather, it is a component of its business model. Platforms institutionalize racial, class, and migration-related inequality by externalizing risks and taking advantage of vulnerabilities (Fuchs, 2014; Pulignano et al., 2021). States face governance challenges as a result of platform capitalism's transnational operations. Platform corporations are able to circumvent local labor laws and advocate for regulatory frameworks that safeguard their interests due to their global reach. Since national governments find it difficult to control platform practices while addressing the socioeconomic integration of migrants, migrant labor becomes an area where these tensions manifest themselves most acutely (Srnicek, 2017; Van Doorn, 2017; Cavallini & Avogaro, 2019).

In the platform economy, migrant labor plays a crucial role as a source of value for platforms as well as a site of structural inequality (Van Doorn, 2017; Anderson, 2010; Fuchs, 2014). Platforms allow migrants to enter labor markets that would not otherwise accept them, but this integration is based on legal precarity, algorithmic management, and insecurity (De Stefano, 2016; Rosenblat & Stark, 2016; Kovács, 2022). As a result, migrants represent the paradoxes of platform capitalism by existing at the nexus of opportunity and exploitation. However, migrant laborers are also active participants who organize, oppose, and fight against their working conditions. They expose the exploitative underpinnings of the platform economy and advocate for alternative work futures by organizing collectives, participating in strikes, and using digital technologies for solidarity (Tassinari & Maccarrone, 2020; Cant, 2019; Joyce et al., 2020). Therefore, it is necessary to move past victimization narratives and acknowledge both structural limitations and emerging forms of agency in order to comprehend migrant labor in the platform economy.

After discussing the pivotal role that migrant labor plays in the platform economy, it is important to look at a specific example to show how these dynamics actually manifest in real life. Uber stands out among the many labor platforms as one of the most important employers of migrants, especially in North American and European cities. As both a global company and a digital infrastructure, Uber exemplifies the mechanisms of algorithmic governance, legal misclassification, and labor precarization that characterize platform capitalism. At the same time, it highlights how migrant workers navigate, adapt to, and resist these structures. In this regard, the next section situates Uber as a representative case of platformized migration, offering insights into the intersection of digital infrastructures, labor exploitation, and migrant agency.

## 3. UBER AS A CASE OF PLATFORMIZED MIGRATION

In the last ten years, Uber has emerged as one of the most well-known and controversial instances of platform capitalism. According to a report from Uber, there are approximately 14 million Uber trips every day and approximately 3.9 million drivers across 65 countries and 600 cities worldwide (Uber, 2025). Its quick expansion is a result of both technological advancement and a significant reorganization of labor and mobility under digital capitalism. Uber has strategically positioned itself to avoid current regulations, get around labor protections, and transform urban transportation systems by positioning itself as a technology company rather than a transportation service (Hall & Krueger, 2015; Calo & Rosenblat, 2017).

Due to the importance of migrant labor in its workforce, Uber's case is especially significant for the study of platformized migration. The experiences of migrant drivers, the majority of whom are migrants, how how platform capitalism offers avenues for economic integration while also intersecting with racialization, precarity, and exclusionary processes Rosenblat & Stark, 2016; Tassinari & Maccarrone, 2020). Uber thus serves as a testing ground for algorithmic governance, unstable labor laws, and disputed forms of worker agency in addition to being a transportation platform. This section examines Uber's business model, organizational logic, and function as a model example of platform capitalism in order to place the organization within the larger context of digital capitalism. This establishes the groundwork for examining the incorporation, governance, and contestation of migrant labor in the Uber economy.

## The Business Model of Uber, Labor Dynamics, and the Logic of Platform Capitalism

At its core, Uber functions as a multifaceted platform that uses a mobile application to link drivers and passengers. Platform capitalism, which depends on mediating interactions between various user groups while deriving value from data and network effects, is typified by this model (Srnicek, 2017). Uber does not directly hire drivers or own cars, in contrast to conventional taxi services. Rather, it presents itself as a digital agent, transferring expenses and risks to drivers while keeping command over access, pricing, and customer service (Wu et al., 2019; Hall & Krueger, 2015). Uber's platform-oriented business model can be characterized by three main dimensions:

- **Data Extraction and Algorithmic Mediation:** Data is Uber's main asset. GPS coordinates, travel times, driver ratings, and customer feedback are just a few of the many data points that are generated by each ride. Processing of this data improves algorithmic management systems, sets dynamic pricing, and maximizes matching. As demonstrated by Rosenblat (2018), Uber's strength is its capacity to manage information asymmetries: drivers and passengers only see a portion of the system, whereas Uber records and analyzes all data flows.
- **Network Effects and Market Domination**: The foundation of Uber's growth strategy is network effects, which state that as more people sign up for the service, its value rises. Uber has attempted to achieve monopolistic dominance by heavily subsidizing rides, rewarding drivers, and quickly entering

new markets. According to Srnicek (2017), these tactics are common in platform capitalism, where platforms seek to establish themselves as essential infrastructures that ensnare users and drive out rivals.

- **Independent Contractor Model**: Uber's classification of drivers as independent contractors rather than employees is arguably its most contentious feature. This legal framework enables Uber to circumvent obligations such as minimum wage, paid sick leave, and social protections. Due to their lack of access to welfare programs and legal recourse in the event of exploitation, migrant drivers' existing vulnerabilities are often worsened by this classification. Uber maintains considerable control over drivers' work while creating the appearance of autonomy by framing driving as a type of 'entrepreneurship.'

The principles of platform capitalism in general are best illustrated by Uber's business strategy. As a company, Uber is more focused on becoming a dominant infrastructure in urban mobility, logistics, and beyond than it is on making money from rides alone—in fact, the company has reported consistent financial losses. In this way, Uber represents the more general aspects of digital capitalism, such as datafication, monopolization, and labor relations restructuring.

## Algorithmic Governance and Migrant Drivers

Uber's organizational model is notable for substituting algorithmic governance for conventional managerial oversight. Drivers' activities are shaped by a combination of automated decision-making, real-time data processing, and customer-driven feedback mechanisms rather than being directed by managers or supervisors. These mechanisms include rating systems that convert customer reviews into disciplinary actions like suspensions or deactivations, GPS tracking that permits constant monitoring of drivers' movements, and dynamic pricing systems that affect when and where drivers work (Rosenblat & Stark, 2016; Wu et al., 2019; Urzi Brancati et al., 2023). Uber portrays its drivers as independent contractors, but in reality, they are subject to algorithmic labor discipline that controls their routes, working hours, and even payment (Muller, 2020: 190-91). Uber's platform creates an information asymmetry system, as shown by Rosenblat and Stark (2016). While the company has almost complete control over drivers' performance and behavior, drivers themselves have little knowledge of how algorithms assign rides, set prices, or evaluate quality. This difference is representative of a larger phenomenon in digital capitalism where platforms control access to information and decision-making authority while keeping workers in the dark about the inner workings of their systems.

When taking into account the situation of migrant drivers, these dynamics become especially important. Algorithmic governance creates particular types of vulnerability for migrant drivers. First, reliance on automated matching and GPS navigation may disadvantage people who are not familiar with the city or language, further increasing reliance on the platform's technological infrastructure. Second, the rating system establishes a continuous surveillance regime by having passengers rate drivers after every ride. Drivers who receive low ratings may be suspended temporarily or permanently from the platform, leaving them with limited options for contesting decisions. Migrants are particularly susceptible to biased assessments because they frequently encounter linguistic or cultural barriers with passengers. According to studies conducted in London and Paris, rating systems disproportionately penalize migrant drivers, which is indicative of larger trends in racial discrimination (Berger et al., 2019).

Algorithmic systems also use incentives and gentle pushes to control driver behavior. Notifications may be sent to drivers advising them to work during peak hours, accept longer rides, or relocate to areas with high demand. Even though they are recommendations, disregarding them could result in fewer rides being available in the future. These algorithmic nudging techniques create what Wood et al. (2019) refer to as "constrained agency" by obfuscating the distinction between autonomy and control. Although algorithmic structures restrict drivers' actual independence, they still formally have the freedom to decide when and where to work. The opacity of Uber's algorithms reinforces these subtle mechanisms, making drivers even more vulnerable. Unfair deactivations or discriminatory pricing schemes are frequently difficult for migrant drivers to challenge because they may not be legally literate or aware of local labor laws. Drivers complained about the lack of transparency and the challenge of appealing platform decisions in interviews done in New York City (Rosenblat, 2018). Abrupt deactivation can have devastating impacts on migrants whose residency or means of subsistence depend on ongoing employment. As a result, algorithmic governance embeds migrant workers in unstable, monitored, and unequal power dynamics while simultaneously serving as an efficiency mechanism and a technology of dominance.

## Precarity, Misclassification, and Inequality

Uber's potential to externalize risks and reduce labor costs is largely dependent on its use of the independent contractor classification. Uber avoids providing minimum wage, social security contributions, healthcare, and protections against wrongful termination by not granting drivers the status of employees. With courts in the UK, California, and other places occasionally holding that drivers are, in fact, employees with rights, this model has been the focus of intense legal and political debate (Prassl, 2018). Uber nevertheless maintains that the contractor model is necessary for the 'flexibility' and 'entrepreneurial opportunity' it promises to offer The debate over misclassification is therefore inseparable from wider transformations in political economy, where flexibility and cost reduction have become central features of neoliberal labor regimes.

This misclassification has particularly severe consequences for migrant drivers. An incorrect classification exacerbates preexisting vulnerabilities for migrant drivers. Many rely on Uber as their primary source of income, but without employee protections they must cope with unstable earnings, the absence of sick leave, and the burden of covering expenses such as fuel, insurance, and vehicle maintenance. Migrants are disproportionately reliant on the platform because they are less likely to access other social support networks, and subcontracting systems often blur lines of accountability, exposing them to abuse (Kovács, 2022). These economic insecurities intersect with precarious legal status: undocumented migrants and those on temporary visas lack access to legal protections, making them especially susceptible to exploitation. According to De Genova (2017), migrant drivers are often in a state of "deportability," whereby their ambiguous legal status makes them more susceptible to exploitative circumstances because opposing Uber's business practices could expose them or result in their loss of employment. In this way, misclassification not only produces financial instability but also embeds migrants in a broader regime of legal and social precarity that intensifies their dependence on the platform.

In addition to legal precariousness, racial and gender dynamics further stratify inequalities within the Uber economy. Research shows that drivers' evaluations are frequently influenced by passengers' discriminatory preferences, leading to racialized gaps in employment opportunities (Ge et al., 2016; Rosenblat et al., 2016). Additional layers of vulnerability are reported by female platform workers, who also experience the increased scrutiny in rating systems (van Doorn, 2017; Huws et al., 2017). These interactions show how platform capitalism embeds structural inequality in algorithmic systems, reproducing and amplifying preexisting social hierarchies.

From the standpoint of political economy, Uber's incorrect worker classification is indicative of larger neoliberal restructuring trends. Platform work is a prime example of the "just-in-time workforce," according to De Stefano (2016), where labor is divided into separate duties and lacking long-term stability. Because they are adaptable, disposable, and structurally excluded from collective protections, migrants make the perfect labor force for such regimes. In this way, Uber's business strategy actively relies on migrant precarity rather than just taking advantage of it (Anderson, 2010; Graham et al., 2017; Kovács, 2022).

However, economic precarity is not the only factor contributing to inequality in Uber employment. In their research on food delivery couriers in Italy and the UK, Tassinari and Maccarrone (2020) contend that platform labor also helps migrant workers form new bonds and collective identities. The shared experience of precarity encourages collective grievances and forms of resistance, a theme discussed in the next section, even though Uber's classification system aims to atomize workers as independent contractors.

## Migrant Drivers' Lived Experiences

The complicated realities of migrant drivers, whose labor powers the platform, are hidden behind Uber's slick technological interface. According to research conducted in North America and Europe, many migrants use Uber as a last resort rather than as their first option when they are structurally excluded from formal labor markets. Uber presents a seemingly accessible opportunity for recently arrived migrants: low entry requirements, flexible scheduling, and instant income. However, this accessibility comes with significant uncertainty, high operating costs, and long working hours. After excluding costs for fuel, insurance, and vehicle maintenance, many drivers report working 10 to 14 hours a day to earn a subsistence income (Hall & Krueger, 2015; Huws et al., 2017; Ericson, 2018). The constant pressure to remain available, respond quickly to ride requests, and maintain high ratings generates what workers describe as 'digital stress'. In addition to these stresses, drivers may experience severe insecurity as a result of illness, accidents, or deactivation due to the lack of social protections (Rosenblat, 2018; Wood et al., 2019; Urzi Brancati et al., 2023).

This seeming accessibility hides another aspect of exclusion for many highly skilled migrants: the devaluation of professional credentials (Anderson, 2010; Kovács, 2022). Uber becomes a short-term survival tactic for migrants whose professional credentials are not accepted in their new countries (Anderson, 2010; Van Doorn, 2017). Because their credentials are undervalued or disregarded, doctors, engineers, and educators from the Global South frequently find themselves working as full-time Uber drivers. This deskilling process is not specific to Uber; rather, it reflects broader migrant labor market dynamics, where institutional barriers force highly skilled migrants into low-wage industries (Anderson, 2010; De Genova, 2017; Fernandez Macias et al., 2025). This process is further accelerated by the platform economy, which portrays gig work as accessible while concealing the opportunity and status loss it entails (Srnicek, 2017; Van Doorn, 2017; Woodcock & Graham, 2020).

In addition to losing their status, migrant drivers face linguistic and cultural challenges on a daily basis that influence how they interact with passengers. It can be challenging for people who don't speak the local language to navigate passenger interactions, settle conflicts, or understand algorithmic messages. According to studies conducted in London and Paris, migrant drivers are more likely to be rated negatively for communication-related problems, which feeds into cycles of exclusion. Furthermore, cultural variations in appearance or service expectations could contribute to skewed assessments, increasing the risk of deactivation for migrants (Rosenblat et al., 2016; Ge et al., 2016; Berger et al., 2019).

However, ambivalent forms of pride and agency are also expressed by drivers. In contrast to exploitative employers in traditional service sectors, Uber is seen by some as a means of supporting families, fostering transnational ties through remittances, and maintaining a sense of autonomy. Thus, driving is a part of larger migration, precarity, and survival trajectories. The contradictory nature of Uber work—a place of exploitation and a means of economic mobility—is demonstrated by the lived realities of migrant drivers.

## Migrant Drivers' Resistance and Collective Agency

Uber's business strategy is based on treating employees like independent contractors, but migrant drivers have created a variety of resistance and solidarity strategies. Drivers can share information about algorithmic manipulation, unfair pricing, or ways to boost earnings through digital communication platforms like Facebook pages, online forums, and WhatsApp groups. (Cant, 2019; Tassinari & Maccarrone, 2020; Joyce et al., 2020). In an otherwise fragmented workforce, these unofficial networks foster new forms of collective consciousness in addition to facilitating knowledge exchange. Further illustrating how resistance can manifest itself outside of formal structures are everyday practices of refusal, such as choosing which rides to reject, playing algorithms, or casually organizing with other drivers. These actions demonstrate how migrant drivers use creativity and persistence to confront unequal power dynamics, reflecting what Scott (1985) refers to as "everyday forms of resistance."

While these everyday practices illustrate informal forms of resistance, migrant drivers have also engaged in more visible and organized protests and strikes. Large-scale protests against fare decreases, sudden cancellations, and the lack of employment protections have been held in cities such as London, New York, and Paris (Tassinari & Maccarrone, 2020). These acts demonstrate migrant workers' ability to band together in spite of difficult circumstances. The Independent Workers' Union of Great Britain (IWGB), which has taken the lead in court cases and labor disputes, is one example of a grassroots union or association that has developed expressly to represent Uber drivers.

Despite these mobilizations, collective resistance faces significant barriers that constrain migrant drivers' organizing capacity. Language obstacles, punishment fears, and legal insecurities frequently hinder migrants' capacity to organize. Nonetheless, solidarity across linguistic, ethnic, and national barriers can be fostered by shared experiences of insecurity. In order to connect local protests to larger transnational networks of resistance, food delivery and ride-hailing workers are increasingly framing their struggles as part of a global movement against platform exploitation, as Joyce et al. (2020) document.

Beyond workers' own organizing efforts, civil society organizations and academic initiatives have also played a role in amplifying migrant drivers' struggles. Specifically, Fairwork holds businesses and legislators accountable for addressing systemic injustices by exposing exploitative practices and evaluating platforms based on standards like fair compensation, fair working conditions, and fair representation (Fairwork, 2021). These interventions show that migrant workers' collective actions make exploitation visible and politically contestable, whereas platforms profit from making labor invisible.

## CONCLUSION

This chapter has looked at how platform capitalism and migrant labor are intertwined within the larger changes of digital capitalism. It has demonstrated how digital infrastructures actively restructure labor markets, governance, and social hierarchies in addition to mediating work, drawing on perspectives from critical political economy. Within this reorganization, migrant workers hold a crucial but vulnerable position, revealing the inconsistencies of platformized digital capitalism.

Conceptually, a more complex view of modern capitalism is made possible by placing platform capitalism within digital capitalism. According to Schiller (1999) and Fuchs (2014), digital capitalism describes systemic changes brought about by datafication, algorithmic governance, and digital infrastructures. Platform capitalism, as defined by Srnicek (2017), is a particular organizational form within this larger framework. Platforms serve as infrastructures of control, extracting data, locking users in, and monopolizing markets, in addition to being intermediaries. The most obvious example of these labor market dynamics is the gig economy, which restructures work into regimes that are algorithmically managed, task-based, and on-demand.

In this context, migrant labor becomes both essential and expendable. In industries like food delivery, ride-hailing, and domestic services—specifically, those dominated by services like Uber, Deliveroo, and Helpling—migrants are overrepresented. Their overrepresentation is a result of systemic exclusions from formal labor markets, such as linguistic barriers, legal insecurity, and the non-recognition of credentials. Platforms take advantage of these exclusions by portraying themselves as opportunities that are easily accessible and require little training or documentation. However, instability, surveillance, and dependence are the costs of such accessibility. Thus, migrant workers represent the paradox of platform capitalism: they are vital to its operation but are routinely excluded from it.

These dynamics are most clearly shown by the Uber case. Uber is a prime example of platform capitalism in its most lucid form, based on data extraction, network effects, and the classification of independent contractors. Asymmetrical power relations are produced by algorithmic governance, which disciplines drivers through ratings, nudges, and opaque pricing mechanisms. Structural injustices, such as discriminatory ratings, exclusion from welfare protections, and vulnerabilities related to legal status, exacerbate these pressures for migrants. Thus, the "freedom" that Uber purports to offer is exposed as a carefully constructed delusion of independence that conceals severe reliance and structural instability.

However, migrant laborers are not passive in these structures. They have mobilized through digital communication tools, established grassroots unions, and planned strikes in cities all over the world. These actions show how the very systems that make exploitation possible can also be used as weapons of resistance. By bringing attention to exploitative practices and demanding accountability, initiatives like Fairwork intensify these struggles. The experiences of migrant drivers thus underscore the contested, unstable nature of platformized migration as well as its exploitative underpinnings.

These findings have deeper implications that go beyond the platform economy or Uber. They discuss the ways in which capitalism is changing in the digital era. Digital infrastructures are not neutral; rather, they are a part of power dynamics that reinforce and worsen inequality based on gender, race, class, and immigration status. The flexible and disposable workforce that digital capitalism depends on is provided by migrant labor, which is not a peripheral but essential component of this restructuring. However, we are also reminded by migrant agency and resistance that these structures are not totalizing, but rather continue to be sites of contestation where different futures of mobility and employment are actively envisioned.

The idea of platformized migration, which has been developed here, offers a framework for understanding these dynamics in migration studies. As migrants are increasingly integrated into algorithmically governed, insecure systems of work, it emphasizes that migration cannot be studied in isolation from digital infrastructures and labor regimes. The analysis highlights platform capitalism's importance for political sociology as a new area of governance where corporate actors influence labor markets, circumvent laws, and reinterpret social protections. Thus, the relationship between migration and platform labor serves as a lens through which to examine the broader changes in power, inequality, and governance in the digital age.

Lastly, the conversation brings up pressing issues for policy and research. How should governments control platform businesses that use locally marginalized labor in their transnational operations? What kinds of social protection are necessary to address migrant platform workers' vulnerabilities? In order to accomplish long-lasting improvements in working conditions, how can organizing efforts overcome linguistic, legal, and cultural barriers? These questions highlight the necessity of reconsidering governance structures, labor rights, and immigration laws in light of the realities of digital capitalism.

In conclusion, Uber is more than just a transportation provider; it is a prime example of platformized migration, reflecting the paradoxes of digital capitalism in its day-to-day activities. Through its examination of platform capitalism as an important component of digital capitalism and its acknowledgment of migrant labor as essential to its operation, this chapter has advanced a critical understanding of the ways in which work, mobility, and inequality are changing in the twenty-first century. The experiences of migrant drivers expose the exploitative nature of platform capitalism as well as the potential for resistance that challenges its hegemony. The secret to comprehending platformized migration as a place of agency, struggle, and potential change, as well as a site of precarity, is found in this duality.

## REFERENCES


Allaire, N., Colin, N., Palier, B., & Tran, L. (2019). *Covering Risks for Platform Workers in the Digital Age. Chaire numérique, gouvernance et innovations institutionelles*. SciencesPo.

Aloisi, A., & Gramano, E. (2019). Artificial Intelligence is Watching you at Work: Digital Surveillance, Employee Monitoring and Regulatory Issues in the EU Context. *Comparative Labour and Policy Journal, 41*(1), 101–127.

Anderson, B. (2010). Migration, Immigration Controls and the Fashioning of Precarious Workers. *Work, Employment and Society, 24*(2), 300–317.

Baiocco, S., Fernandez Macias, E., Rani, U. and Pesole, A. (2022). The Algorithmic Management of Work and its Implications in Different Contexts. European Commission, JRC129749.

Berger, T., Chen, C., & Frey, C. B. (2019). Drivers of disruption? Estimating the Uber effect. *European Economic Review, 110*, 197–210.

Calo, R., & Rosenblat, A. (2017). The taking economy: Uber, information, and power. *Columbia Law Review, 117*(6), 1623–1690.

Cant, C. (2019). *Riding for Deliveroo: Resistance in the New Economy*. Polity Press.

Cavallini, G., & Avogaro, M. (2019). Digital Work in the Platform Economy: The Last (but not least) Stage of Precariousness in Labour Relationships. In Kenner, J., Florczak, I., & Otto, M. (Eds.), *Precarious Work: The Challenge for Labour Law in Europe*. Edgar Publishing.

De Genova, N. (2017). *The Borders of "Europe": Autonomy of Migration, Tactics of Bordering*. Duke University Press.

De Stefano, V. (2016). The rise of the "just-in-time workforce": On-demand work, crowd work, and labour protection in the "gig economy.". *Comparative Labor Law & Policy Journal, 37*(3), 471–503.

Fairwork (2021). Fairwork Annual Report. University of Oxford.

Fernandez Macias, E., Gonzalez Vazquez, I., Torrejon Perez, S., & Nurskı, L. (2025). Work in the Digital Era: How Technology is Transforming Work and Occupations, Publications Office of the European Union, Luxembourg, https://data.europa.eu/doi/10.2760/0956105, JRC141451.

Fernandez Macias, E., Urzi Brancati, M. C., Wright, S., & Pesole, A. (2023). The Platformisation of Work. EUR 31469 EN, Publications Office of the European Union, Luxembourg, 2023, ISBN 978-92-68-01661-9, doi:, JRC133016.DOI: 10.2760/801282

Fuchs, C. (2014). *Digital Labour and Karl Marx*. Routledge.

Ge, Y., Knittel, C. R., MacKenzie, D., & Zoepf, S. (2016). *Racial and gender discrimination in transportation network companies (No. w22776)*. National Bureau of Economic Research., DOI: 10.3386/w22776

Graham, M., Hjorth, I., & Lehdonvirta, V. (2017). Digital Labour and Development: Impacts of Global Digital Labour Platforms and the Gig Economy on Worker Livelihoods. *Transfer: European Review of Labour and Research, 23*(2), 135–162.

Hall, J., & Krueger, A. (2015). An analysis of the labour market for Uber's Driver-Partners in the United States, Princeton, available at: https://www.nber.org/system/files/working_papers/w22843/w22843.pdf

Hauben (ed.), H., Lenaerts, K. and Waeyaert, W. (2020). The Platform Economy and Precarious Work. Publication for the Committee on Employment and Social Affairs, Policy Department for Economic, Scientific and Quality of Life Policies, European Parliament, Luxembourg.

Hill, S. (2015). *Raw Deal: How the 'Uber Economy' and Runaway Capitalism Are Screwing American Workers*. St. Martin's Press.

Huws, U., Spencer, N. H., Syrdal, D. S., & Holts, K. (2017). Work in the European Gig Economy: Research Results from The UK, Sweden, Germany, Austria, The Netherlands, Switzerland and Italy. FEPS, UNI Europa, University of Hertfordshire.

Kovács, B. (2022). Informality and the gig economy: Migrant precarity in European food delivery platforms. *Journal of Ethnic and Migration Studies, 48*(3), 623–641.

Muller, Z. (2020). Algorithmic harms to Workers in the Platform Economy: The case of Uber. *Columbia Journal of Law and Social Problems, 167*, •••.

Pesole, A., Fernandez Macias, E., Urzi Brancati, M.C. and Gomez Herrera, M.E. (2019). How to Quantify What is not Seen Two Proposals for Measuring Platform Work. European Commission, JRC117168.

Pulignano V., Domecka M., Vermeerbergen L., Franke M. and Mara C. (2021) Platform work, reputation and precarious (unpaid) work regimes, paper presented at ILPC, 12-14 April 2021 and SASE, 2-5 July 2021.

Rosenblat, A., Levy, K. E. C., Barocas, S., & Hwang, T. (2016). Discriminating Tastes: Customer Ratings as Vehicles for Bias. *Policy and Internet*, *9*(3), 256–279.

Rosenblat, A., & Stark, L. (2016). Algorithmic labor and information asymmetries: A case study of Uber's drivers. *International Journal of Communication*, *10*, 3758–3784.

Schiller, D. (1999). *Digital Capitalism: Networking the Global Market System*. MIT Press.

Scott, J. C. (1985). *Weapons of the Weak: Everyday Forms of Peasant Resistance*. Yale University Press.

Srnicek, N. (2017). *Platform Capitalism*. Polity Press.

Tassinari, A., & Maccarrone, V. (2020). Riders on the storm: Workplace solidarity among gig economy couriers in Italy and the UK. *Work, Employment and Society*, *34*(1), 35–54.

Uber statistics, https://www.businessofapps.com/data/uber-statistics/

Urzi Brancati, M. C., Gonzalez Vazquez, I. and Fernandez Macias, E. (2023). The Rise of Digital Monitoring and Algorithmic Management of Work: Empirical Insights. European Commission, 2023, JRC133407.

Van Doorn, N. (2017). Platform labor: On the gendered and racialized exploitation of low-income service work in the "on-demand" economy. *Information Communication and Society*, *20*(6), 898–914.

Wood, A. J., Graham, M., Lehdonvirta, V., & Hjorth, I. (2019). Good gig, bad gig: Autonomy and algorithmic control in the global gig economy. *Work, Employment and Society*, *33*(1), 56–75.

Woodcock, J., & Graham, M. (2020). *The Gig Economy: A Critical Introduction*. Polity Press.

Wu, Q., Zhang, H., Li, Z., & Liu, K. (2019). Labor Control in the Gig Economy: Evidence from Uber in China. *The Journal of Industrial Relations*, *61*(4), 574–596.

Zuboff, S. (2019). *The Age of Surveillance Capitalism: The Fight for a Human Future at the New Frontier of Power*. PublicAffairs.

# Chapter 11
# Invisible Power in the Digital Sphere:
## Surveillance and Social Control

**Nadir Ateşoğlu**
https://orcid.org/0000-0003-0561-3562
*Sinop Üniversity, Turkey*

## ABSTRACT

*This study aims to examine the political and social aspects of surveillance policies that are increasingly widespread in digital spaces. A theoretical framework is presented that questions whether digital surveillance tools, especially facial recognition technologies, are used for security reasons or to control society. For this purpose, first, it will focus on why people consent to being monitored. Second, it will address how data is published very quickly and uncontrolledly thanks to the fluidity of surveillance, and finally, how digital authorities, who are in the position of surveillance, transform the data they obtain into a tool of social control. The study is structured based on a qualitative research approach, and the literature review method was adopted as the data collection tool. The effects of digital surveillance on individuals' perception of privacy, behavior patterns, and mobility in the public sphere were evaluated through theoretical texts and current research.*

## INTRODUCTION

This study questions whether the increasingly widespread digital surveillance technologies are truly employed for crime prevention, as they are often legitimized, or rather to reinforce the mechanisms of social control by political authorities. Surveillance systems are typically justified through security discourses. Considerable

DOI: 10.4018/979-8-3373-4267-2.ch011

progress has been made in ensuring security through surveillance. However, these systems may also reinforce social inequalities and restrict individual freedoms. As Foucault has pointed out, surveillance is not merely a restrictive but also a productive mechanism of power; it produces not only obedient bodies but also "subjects" who, being aware of constant observation, regulate their own behaviors accordingly.

The main objective of this study is to examine, from the perspective of political sociology, the impact of surveillance practices on the perception of crime and insecurity in urban settings. To this end, within the framework of David Lyon's theory of the "Surveillance Society," the study explores how surveillance technologies reproduce power relations. Employing the method of literature review, it discusses the effects of surveillance technologies on crime rates, their transformation into instruments of social control, and their role in reinforcing social inequalities. In this context, the effects of surveillance practices in urban areas on individuals' use of public space and their sense of social security will also be analyzed. For surveillance society is not limited to physical spaces filled with cameras and monitoring systems; in the digital realm, individuals' online activities, habits, and preferences are constantly monitored and analyzed. In this process, individuals' rights to privacy are weakened, while social inequalities are reinforced.

As a mechanism of social control, surveillance renders the exercise of power more effective. This is because surveillance legitimizes its existence through rational instruments such as crime prevention or the fight against tax evasion. This, in turn, results in the legitimation of social control. Yet surveillance mechanisms do not merely aim at crime prevention or efficient tax collection. Drawing power from these rationalizations, surveillance penetrates the finest capillaries of society, transforming itself into a kind of omniscient deity. Unsurprisingly, such a cycle of surveillance and control undermines individuals' sense of security. Here lies a striking irony: while the initial motivation was to ensure safety and combat crime, the process ultimately culminates in widespread insecurity.

Moreover, surveillance technologies often lead not to a reduction in crime rates but to the spatial displacement of crime, while simultaneously causing individuals under intense scrutiny to feel insecure. Within this scope, making visible the effects of surveillance practices on social insecurity and inequalities allows for proposing security policies that are more just and inclusive. Furthermore, methods such as transparency in surveillance, privacy protection laws, democratic oversight, and raising social awareness could provide remedies against the insecurity generated by surveillance.

Giddens defines trust as the most fundamental feeling individuals resort to in order to sustain their relationships in everyday life. This sense of trust can only be achieved through the establishment of social routines—through the idea of reaching a predictable order (Giddens, 2014, pp. 59–67). In this way, individuals can continue their lives without excessive anxiety. Here, social routine and stability turn into mechanisms that provide individuals with a sense of security. Bauman, in turn, defines predictability—that is, the condition in which everything is in its proper place and exactly as it should be—as "order." For him, the essence of "order" lies in the absolute peace of mind it provides (Bauman & Lyon, 2024, p. 131). Yet in everyday life, absolute peace or an absolute routine can hardly ever be achieved. For movement, dynamism, and change would then be nearly reduced to zero—something possible only in graveyards. Thus, in order to make sense of the world we live in, the idea of establishing order and thereby securing trust cannot be dismissed. Indeed, the sense of being secure—regardless of how it is achieved—remains the most fundamental feeling for all living beings.

In today's digital world, especially in urban centers where vast numbers of individuals coexist without knowing one another sufficiently, social control and its surveillance mechanisms have diversified dramatically under the influence of technologies such as artificial intelligence, which process massive datasets. As Lyon (2013) notes, we now live in a surveillance society, and individuals are acutely aware of how surveillance affects them. For instance, air travelers are no longer subject solely to passport control but are also aware of undergoing facial scans, biometric measurements, and body scanners (Bauman & Lyon, 2024, p. 11). This study examines various dimensions of surveillance practices within the framework of Lyon's approach to surveillance, focusing particularly on their negative outcomes, and discusses the potential costs of surveillance for both individuals and society. The first section analyzes how surveillance technologies can be utilized as instruments of social control; the second examines the balance between freedom and equality in relation to surveillance and its potential effects on society in the context of Lyon's works. The conclusion offers potential policy recommendations.

## 1. METHODOLOGY

This study is a theoretical inquiry into whether the increasingly widespread surveillance technologies serve merely as tools of security and crime prevention or function primarily as instruments of social control for political authority. The research is structured within a qualitative framework, relying on a literature review as its primary data collection method. Drawing upon David Lyon's "Surveillance Society" theory, the study analyzes the impacts of surveillance technologies on urban spaces and social structures within a theoretical context. Academic articles, books, official reports, and contemporary studies are employed to evaluate the effects of surveillance systems on crime rates, social inequalities, and the use of public spaces. The overarching aim of the study is to reveal the impacts of surveillance practices on individuals' perceptions of security and on the broader sense of social insecurity, thereby approaching surveillance policies from a critical socio-political perspective.

## 2. SURVEILLANCE AND SOCIAL CONTROL

To surveil and to be surveilled have become fundamental aspects of contemporary life. We are all subjected to observation, categorization, recording, and labeling that serve particular purposes. Yet increasingly, this condition appears to us as though it were a natural and ordinary part of life. This normalization stems both from the growing sophistication of surveillance technologies and from individuals' eagerness to share personal data voluntarily. The greatest success of social control through surveillance lies in its ability to conceal its controlling and supervisory function. Few can directly associate surveillance systems with mechanisms of oversight and control. As Lyon notes, surveillance systems are becoming less visible and overt, yet increasingly systematic and intelligent (Lyon, 2006, p. 12). Today, developments in artificial intelligence and chip technology make it possible to categorize collected data in ways suited to specific purposes. Lyon defines surveillance as encompassing the collection and processing of both identified and unidentified personal data with the aim of influencing and managing those about whom the data are gathered (Lyon, 2006, p. 13). Processing, of course, requires computer technologies, which include categorization, labeling, storage, and retrieval. These processes naturally imply the steering, restriction, and control of society.

Another factor that strengthens surveillance's function as an instrument of social control is the predictability of individuals' behavior. Data collection is not limited to recording existing behaviors but is also used to predict future tendencies. At this point, surveillance becomes not only "the record of the past" but also "the design of the future." As Zuboff (2019) has observed, the fundamental logic of surveillance capitalism is to use behavioral surplus to generate "behavioral futures" and sell them on the market. Thus, individuals become part of a system in which their behavioral probabilities are commodified even before they themselves have made decisions. This shows that social control not only regulates the present but also confines the future within predetermined patterns.

On the other hand, one of the most striking aspects of surveillance in terms of social control is its strategy of invisibility. As in Foucault's (1995) panopticon metaphor, surveillance mechanisms may be omnipresent but are rarely directly visible. Modern digital surveillance, while giving individuals the illusion of freedom, in fact channels them into predetermined behavioral patterns. In this regard, surveillance operates not merely as a repressive mechanism but also as a disciplinary regime to which individuals willingly consent. As Andrejevic (2007) argues, today's surveillance often appears in the form of "participatory surveillance": users voluntarily share data, contribute to surveillance systems, and in the process internalize the function of monitoring themselves. In this way, surveillance makes possible the most sophisticated form of social control—namely, a regime of voluntary compliance.

Foucault's panopticon metaphor in the digital age operates not primarily through disciplining bodies but through the construction and management of subjectivities. Modern digital surveillance aims not at physically disciplining individuals but at shaping obedient subjects by directing their desires, fears, and preferences. As Foucault (2015, p. 202) puts it, power is now concerned with "the management of life" (biopolitics); it shapes individuals within an algorithmically constructed reality regarding what should make them happy, what they should fear, and what they should desire. Social media feeds, personalized advertisements, and search engine results function as the invisible guardians of the digital panopticon, continuously generating a feedback loop about who we are and who we should aspire to be.

If the purpose of control and supervision is so evident, why then do surveillance systems not cause widespread unease? The reason is that every act of surveillance presents itself in such a way as to conceal its true intention, offering instead rational justifications. These justifications can be classified as follows:

## 2.1 Surveillance for Security

Throughout history, human beings have relied on mechanisms such as the sense of shame and gossip to ensure security—particularly in the villages and towns of agrarian societies, and to some extent in modern urban centers (Harari, 2020). Shame, as one of the most influential emotions guiding individuals in the process of adapting to social norms, has functioned as an important mechanism for maintaining social order. Shame constitutes the foundation of collective community feeling (Williams, 1993, p. 90). Yet for shame to be effective, the individual's action must be known by others. This is possible only through people's conversations about one another. Thanks to gossip, individuals have been able to gather information about others and decide whether or not they should be trusted (Harari, 2020, p. 41).

When the sense of shame is combined with gossip, the individual who is negatively spoken of and stigmatized may face the threat of social exclusion. For this reason, one's actions are shaped in accordance with the rules of social routine. Positive remarks about others, on the other hand, reinforce behaviors approved by the social order. Historically, gossip has worked in both positive (honor) and negative (shame) ways—though what counts as positive or negative action has changed over time—ultimately serving the continuity of the existing social structure.

Although gossip is one of the most primitive and classical forms of social surveillance, in today's modern cities and digital world the situation has become much more complex. Foucault emphasizes that power-driven surveillance is primarily aimed at guiding the attitudes and behaviors of individuals (Foucault, 2015). In this sense, urban camera systems, prison guards observing inmates, doctors monitoring patients, or teachers watching their students can all be included. Although he was writing in a period before advanced digital systems, social media data centers, and artificial intelligence, Foucault strongly emphasized the critical importance of surveillance in controlling individuals. In his words:

*"There is no longer a need for weapons, physical violence, or material constraints. The gaze of surveillance - and the weight of that gaze - becomes so internalized that in the end individuals monitor themselves; thus, everyone carries out surveillance on and against themselves" (Foucault, 2015, p. 95).*

In the panoptic model, Bentham sought to deter prisoners from crime through a highly cost-effective method (Foucault, 2015, p. 94). The system required individuals to constantly feel under the inspector's gaze, which prevented them not only from acting abnormally but even from imagining such behavior. Moreover, this method avoided the costly risk of inciting rebellion through brute force.

In today's digital world, being monitored and recorded through various platforms, and the omnipresence of surveillance systems across cities, reminds us of the constant presence of an overseer regulating society. Surveillance is not only for detecting crimes and criminals but also for preventing crimes before they occur (Lyon, 2006, p. 106). This entails predicting behaviors and categorizing clothing, suspicious movements, and other indicators to establish one or more categories of "reasonable suspicion."

Because of the real or potential benefits it provides, much of society consents to surveillance. This is because security is one of the most fundamental human needs. Security and fear constitute the two primary emotions motivating human behavior. The most significant feeling that legitimizes surveillance for security purposes is fear of the "Other" (Monahan, 2010, p. 150). Especially when an external threat looms—whether a pandemic or a terrorist attack—people are gripped by fear and willingly accept almost any form of surveillance. To overcome fear and feel safe, individuals are often willing to approve of the categorization of "Others" in the city (Bauman & Lyon, 2024, p. 118). As Bauman puts it, today we have all become proponents of surveillance and being surveilled due to our excessive dependency on security. Who would not want to walk safely at night, see criminals identified and captured, or have an alarm go off immediately when a burglar enters? For all these reasons, effective digital surveillance has become a form of practice readily accepted by the majority.

Security has now turned into a future-oriented project, operating through surveillance by attempting to manage potential future events with digital techniques and statistical reasoning. Today, security functions by monitoring everything that moves—information, people, capital, and goods (Bigo, 2011, p. 109). Yet here lies a profound paradox: we do not know exactly for what purposes and in what ways the vast data collected in the name of security will be used without our consent. Moreover, it is still unclear who will monitor the use of this data. The massive amounts of data gathered from platforms could easily be used preventively to predict individual actions or calculate the likelihood of certain events. As Lyon (2006, p. 112) defines it, surveillance is essentially the focused attention on individuals through the collection of their personal data for specific purposes.

The approach, "If you are not guilty, you have nothing to worry about! Thanks to surveillance systems, real criminals are being caught!" is, of course, rational and forms the main legitimacy basis of surveillance. Yet today, data collected through surveillance is not limited to identifying crimes or criminals. What transforms surveillance into an instrument of social control is its proactive drive to prevent crimes before they occur by categorizing society into distinct groups. This shifts the perspective of surveillance beyond merely ensuring security, transforming it into a power akin to that of a god—seeing, knowing, and potentially intervening in everything. As Lyon states, today's surveillance society controls by sorting, filtering, and categorizing—enhancing the life chances of some while diminishing those of others (Lyon, 2006, p. 17). Thus, surveillance exceeds its original legitimacy based on ensuring security and becomes, in practice, an apparatus of social control.

When we consider what can be done with the vast data pool—from social media platforms to urban security cameras that collect and store the digital data of millions—the use of such data for security purposes represents only a small fraction of its potential. Without proper legal regulations and effective oversight, this opens the possibility of a dystopian world resembling Orwell's 1984. For instance, what if authorities process facial scans and micro-expressions of passersby and decide to use them for entirely different purposes? Or what happens if miniature versions of drones, originally designed for military purposes, are deployed to record the addresses, images, and voices of innocent individuals without their consent? The paradox here is clear: while surveillance claims to be necessary for ensuring security, it simultaneously generates insecurity.

Firstly, as Bauman (2024) highlights with his notion of "liquid surveillance," it is difficult to predict where the collected data will eventually be used. Beyond hackers, it is not only nation-states that collect and classify data; global corporations such as Amazon, Google, and Yandex also engage in surveillance, classification, data processing, and social steering.

Secondly, surveillance is not merely coercive or controlling; it is often a process of seduction, influence, and persuasion (Lyon, 2006, p. 113). Nobody forces us to share our data everywhere or to be utterly transparent. We voluntarily and even eagerly use social media applications. In a sense, everyone produces their own surveillance. As Byung-Chul Han observes, a society in which everyone monitors everyone else in the name of transparency inevitably becomes a society of control. Transparency means enabling surveillance and being constantly surveilled. Such a situation ultimately erodes freedom of action and results in universal conformity (Han, 2024, p. 69). Even if I have not committed a crime and do not intend to, believing in a society of transparency means granting unlimited control over my past and future, which may eventually strip me of free will as the psychology of constant surveillance takes hold. Since no one would openly consent to such restrictions, however, the process unfolds in more subtle ways.

In this respect, unlike in Bentham's panopticon, we do not usually feel the fear of punishment. What motivates us in this new form of digital surveillance is the way in which interpreted and categorized data about us is used to anticipate and even prescribe what we are likely to do next. This may mean being guided toward which product to buy, which path to take, or which emotion to feel—each representing a digital category into which we are placed. Moreover, this surveillance system does not proceed despite our objections but rather is enacted with our participation and consent - in other words, a form of complicity - arising from our desire to feel safe.

Thirdly, surveillance and trust are incompatible (Lyon, 2006, p. 34). Surveillance functions where trust is absent. Parents monitoring children or spouses surveilling one another through apps stem from a lack of trust. Ironically, surveillance undertaken to provide a sense of security actually arises from insecurity and leads to greater insecurity. When we monitor others for specific purposes, we forget that the data obtained can be used for far different, unintended purposes. While this is true for individuals, it becomes even more apparent when applied to entire societies. Data is processed, categorized, and motivations behind behaviors are analyzed. When data from platforms and cameras is analyzed for crime prevention, certain people may be placed in "suspicious" categories. Whereas the presence of a night watchman once made us feel safe enough to sleep soundly, today's security paradoxically produces insecurity itself (Bauman & Lyon, 2024, p. 115). The greatest threat we face today comes not from external dangers but from the security systems that continuously monitor us with their immense data-processing capacity.

Today, watching and recording others has far surpassed simple, isolated surveillance. What matters now are the individual motives and choices behind the images (Bauman & Lyon, 2024, p. 116). Thus, cameras and monitoring systems are no longer limited to catching a thief or mugger, as in the past. Instead, surveillance society regulates individuals by exploiting their desire for security. As Bigo (2011) notes, in a world full of risks, security systems that monitor all human movements are the very essence of surveillance. This shows us that the moment we believe we have secured safety, we are in fact living in a world filled with insecurities (Bauman

& Lyon, 2024, p. 122). In short, societies that believe they have achieved security today have in practice become the most insecure.

The discourse most frequently used to legitimize surveillance for security is the claim that certain sacrifices of individual rights and freedoms are necessary for the establishment of collective safety. This perspective inverts the classic liberal balance between "liberty and security." Giorgio Agamben (2005), with his concept of the "state of exception," argues that under extraordinary security threats, law is suspended, granting the state expanded powers that ultimately become a permanent governing technique. Thus, security becomes not only a rationale for surveillance against crime and criminals but also a justification for expanding surveillance against potential threats. This transforms surveillance from an extraordinary measure into an ordinary feature of daily life.

The digital tracking methods implemented during the COVID-19 pandemic provide a contemporary example of this process. In many countries, individuals' location data, contact histories, and health records were monitored through various applications. While these measures enhanced public safety in the short term, they also normalized health-based surveillance and paved the way for the permanence of biopolitical control mechanisms. Security, therefore, has been redefined in a broader framework that encompasses not only physical threats but also biological risks. Consequently, the willingness of individuals to sacrifice privacy for security facilitates the continuity of surveillance mechanisms.

Moreover, the growing role of algorithms and AI-based systems in security surveillance is particularly noteworthy. Predictive policing practices, for example, aim to identify high-risk areas and individuals likely to commit crimes in the future based on past data (Brayne, 2020). Yet such methods often reproduce existing social biases and structural inequalities. The disproportionate targeting of certain ethnic or socio-economic groups reveals how a process beginning with the goal of security can legitimize new forms of discrimination. Thus, surveillance in the name of security may lead to outcomes that conflict with the principles of equality and justice.

Another dimension of the security–surveillance nexus is its psychological impact. The constant feeling of being watched not only enforces compliance with norms but also creates a persistent sense of anxiety and self-censorship. This suppresses citizens' courage to express themselves freely, transforming the promise of a "secure society" into a structure where fear and insecurity are institutionalized. As Bauman and Lyon (2024) emphasize, surveillance regimes built in the name of security paradoxically generate more insecurity, convincing individuals that they must remain under perpetual control.

## 2.2 Surveillance for Bureaucratic Efficiency

One of the factors that paved the way for the emergence of the surveillance society is the rational, objective, and efficient mode of governance envisioned decades ago by Max Weber. Weber's (1978) approach to bureaucracy meant the domination of rationality in administrative science. For this purpose, records were kept and stored (both of service providers and recipients), and employees' performances were monitored. This represented a legal and objective mode of administration. Within this system, employees were classified and evaluated according to impersonal principles and objective rules. These records, extending beyond mere work performance to include personal data, enabled the long-term monitoring of individuals.

Today, the justification for our consent to surveillance through digital platforms is again closely tied to bureaucratic efficiency. In this way, tasks can be carried out in a much shorter, more effective, and more efficient manner. For contemporary individuals, it is not easy to give up the conveniences provided by credit cards, mobile applications, or e-government systems. Phone apps, urban camera systems, and other digital surveillance tools consistently present themselves as efficient solutions, accompanied by rational arguments that are difficult to reject. For instance, when electronic chips are installed in vehicles, the practice is explained as a measure designed to enhance efficiency in tax collection—an intention that may, in fact, be sincere. Navigation systems help us reach destinations more quickly and easily. Yet such applications also imply constant access to the time and location data of all vehicles and individuals.

In this respect, surveillance is the outcome of modernity's pursuit of efficiency and productivity. It provides significant benefits in bureaucratic operations, such as ensuring speed, effectiveness, coordination, and risk detection (Lyon, 2013, p. 79). However, applying surveillance to administrative science in the name of efficiency does not necessarily guarantee that "everything will work well." With the advancement and diversification of artificial intelligence, chip technologies, and monitoring tools, scattered records once kept in ledgers have begun to create categories far beyond the aims of efficiency and objectivity. The process that began as a means to ensure bureaucratic efficiency now, through the collection and processing of vast amounts of data with AI support, appears to hold the potential to monitor society as a whole. The human clerk of Weber's rational bureaucracy is increasingly being replaced by "algorithmic governance." Citizens now face not human officials who interpret rules with a degree of flexibility, but automatic systems that make absolute and difficult-to-challenge decisions based on predefined categories. This situation calls into question the bureaucracy's claim to impartiality, while also raising concerns about how the biases embedded in algorithms may reproduce social inequalities.

Surveillance technologies justified in the name of bureaucratic efficiency today serve two seemingly opposing strategic purposes: generally, to keep certain individuals "inside" for disciplinary purposes, or to exclude those deemed not belonging "outside" (Bauman & Lyon, 2024, pp. 77–78). For example, governments are expected to carry out effective policies regarding criminals and migrants. Catching criminals and keeping them inside, or preventing unwanted migrants from entering, is part of bureaucracy. Both require effective surveillance systems. Foucault was primarily concerned with the former - disciplining by keeping individuals inside. He referred to spaces such as prisons, hospitals, and schools as institutions of confinement where individuals were disciplined through surveillance, consistent with Bentham's panopticon. The inspector is unseen, yet sees all; and the presence of this invisible gaze is known by everyone.

Bigo, on the other hand, through his concept of the ban-opticon, emphasized exclusion rather than confinement. Ban-optical apparatuses function particularly to prevent certain categorized groups from entering (Bigo, 2011, p. 75). Confinement is spatially bounded - such as prisons or clinics- and thus involves relatively limited forms of surveillance. Exclusion, however, entails categorizing individuals and constructing zones they can never enter. The best examples of exclusion are gated communities or shopping malls with closed-circuit camera systems. For confinement, categories such as "mad," "criminal," or "sick" are used, with at least some consensus on the need for correction or treatment. By contrast, exclusion may operate through digital surveillance without any explicit debate or societal approval, creating new forms of categorization. In this sense, in the panopticon the act of definition and the power of surveillance are explicit, whereas in the digital panopticon, those who define and categorize often remain invisible. As Byung-Chul Han (2024) argues in his notion of the "transparency society," unlike Bentham's panopticon where the observed were aware of the inspector, the residents of the digital panopticon mistakenly believe themselves to be free.

Surveillance legitimized on the grounds of bureaucratic efficiency today functions not only to accelerate processes or minimize errors but also to direct individual behavior. The digital panopticon collects voluntarily given data under the pretense of convenience and efficiency, while the algorithms developed from such data construct systems that restrict individual choices and reinforce predictable patterns of behavior. "Interest-based recommendations" on social media or "personalized campaigns" on shopping platforms appear as services designed to make life easier but, in reality, represent a form of surveillance that narrows intellectual horizons and normalizes algorithmic steering.

At this point, surveillance emerges not only as a top-down mechanism of discipline and control but also as a bottom-up practice of transparency and counter-surveillance. Open-data portals, online monitoring of public expenditures, and transparency initiatives through e-government provide citizens with the ability to scrutinize bureaucracy while also enhancing bureaucratic efficiency. Yet this does not establish a symmetrical balance between the state's surveillance capacity and the citizen's monitoring capacity. The enormous power of states and digital platforms to collect, process, and store data overshadows the counter-surveillance tools available to individuals, creating a structural asymmetry that undermines democratic accountability.

Thus, the expansion of surveillance technologies in the name of efficiency often functions as a discourse of legitimacy. Applications promoted with notions of "speed," "convenience," and "efficiency" are presented as rational and indispensable options for individuals, while in reality serving to deepen the categorization of social life and normalize directions aligned with economic and political interests. In this sense, surveillance goes beyond modernity's promise of productivity and becomes central to the strategies of neoliberal governmentality for producing and sustaining power.

Contrary to Weber's claim of impersonality in the ideal bureaucracy, in the digital age algorithmic systems institutionalize human biases, thereby reinforcing structural inequalities. Since algorithms are trained on historically and socially biased data, they reproduce these biases under the guise of objective and technical decision-making (Pasquale, 2015, p. 123). Predictive policing software, for instance, often targets low-income or minority neighborhoods that historically faced heavier police presence, thereby automating and legitimizing discriminatory practices (Brayne, 2020, p. 95). This exposes how the rhetoric of bureaucratic efficiency and objectivity may, in fact, translate into automated discrimination, calling for critical examination of the ideological foundations underlying the technological rationality of surveillance.

At the same time, tying surveillance entirely to rational justifications often results in what Bruce Schneier (2003) calls security theatre - symbolic measures intended to create the perception of security rather than genuine effectiveness. The visibility of surveillance technologies, the presence of cameras, and complex scanning systems may provide the public with an illusion of control while leaving the real question of actual safety unanswered.

The digitization and algorithmic transparency paradox; In the digital age, bureaucratic efficiency has reached a new level through the digitization of data. Digitization not only accelerates processes but also renders every kind of behavior measurable and subject to evaluation. This produces an invisible normative pressure on individuals, as every recorded act is presented as an objective indicator of performance. Yet how algorithms operate and how they interpret data often remain opaque (Pasquale, 2015). Thus, bureaucratic surveillance, under the guise of efficiency, actually produces a new regime of "algorithmic opacity."

Neoliberal Governmentality and the Commodification of Citizenship. Finally, surveillance technologies used in the name of bureaucratic efficiency acquire a distinct function within neoliberal governmentality. Citizens are viewed not only as service recipients but also as "customers," with public services increasingly operated under market logics (Brown, 2015). In this context, surveillance goes beyond securing bureaucratic efficiency; it categorizes individuals according to their consumption habits, preferences, and risk profiles, aligning them with market rationalities. Thus, bureaucratic surveillance transforms from a rational administrative technique into a tool serving the economic and political interests of neoliberal power.

## 3. SURVEILLANCE, EQUALITY, FREEDOM

Regardless of the purpose for which the data obtained through surveillance is used, it generally produces inequality. This is because, whatever justification it relies on, the very reason for surveillance is to expose differences among people. Foucault (2013) noted that even the seemingly innocent act of conducting a census was not devoid of political implications, since it was deeply tied to power insofar as it categorized society. Today, surveillance serves the same function. Whether carried out for economic purposes such as marketing or for political reasons such as winning votes, shaping worldviews, or suppressing protest, surveillance always materializes in the form of dividing into categories, classifying, and comparing with "others." This makes possible the most important step in ensuring social control: providing the most accurate prediction and determination of the current situation. From there, it becomes possible to formulate specific strategies targeting particular groups. For example, what kind of music do women between the ages of 17 and 25 enjoy? What eating habits do they have, or what do they dislike most? Once countless such questions can be answered through data analysis—and today they can—it also becomes possible to take specific steps to control and regulate the desired target audience. This condition, which Lyon (2006) describes as "categorical seduction," often begins with "categorical suspicion" but, over time - especially when placed in the hands of other powers - turns into seduction by category.

Moreover, as I emphasized earlier, data are generally not taken from us by force. Rather, they are obtained with the voluntary consent of users on platforms. In other words, data emerges through the voluntary participation of everyone (Han, 2024). Individuals exposed to such strategies act as if they are free, but their choices are often limited to one of the options presented by an algorithm that knows them better than they know themselves. Naturally, this raises the fundamental problem of how free our choices truly are. What begins with security and bureaucratic efficiency has extended to the realm of social control. Indeed, surveillance has now gone even further, contributing to what Lyon (2006, p.119) calls "the production of knowledge for the governance of populations." To this end, observed data are modeled, profiles are produced, and simulations are carried out. The results of such analyses go far beyond identifying who is guilty (Lyon, 2006, p.121). What is sought now is to know who—or what—poses a risk. Ultimately, the decision to prevent risk before it materializes, or to allow or disallow it, lies with those who control the data. Of course, risk definitions may not be objective. From the perspective of power, consumers, citizens, or workers could very well be controversially categorized as "abnormal" or "bad."

Today, the question arises: how will the small minority controlling digital surveillance (Amazon, Google, Yandex, TikTok, Meta, etc.) use this immense power of data clouds? For individuals, monitoring this is not easy. Moreover, this power no longer belongs to the nation-state authority that we can remove through elections. In this sense, it has no democratic dimension. We cannot simply change it by casting our votes. Rather, it belongs to giant corporations—sometimes in cooperation with states—that specialize in this area. Naturally, such concentrated power may corrupt the intentions of its holders or distort their perspectives.

The core dynamic here is the new economic logic Shoshana Zuboff (2019) calls "surveillance capitalism." In this logic, personal experiences are taken as raw material, our behavioral residues are turned into data, and packaged as predictive products to be bought and sold in "behavioral futures markets." Companies such as Amazon, Google, and Meta, as the leading actors of this new capitalist form, concentrate economic power in their hands while also accumulating an unprecedented potential for domination over individuals. Surveillance is no longer merely a tool of social control but the very regime of accumulation operating on a global scale. Zuboff's iconic concept explains how our personal experiences are commodified in exchange for "free" services and how our behavioral data are exploited for profit. With this concept, Zuboff highlights both the economic dimension of surveillance and its central role in producing inequality.

As Bauman put it, our cooperation with digital surveillance today is a modern version of voluntary servitude (Bauman & Lyon, 2024, pp. 158–161). In this sense, not only individuals but also nation-states are under threat. For we are faced with a problem that transcends national politics and cannot be solved by national power apparatuses. Surveillance and the data derived from it lie in the hands of giant digital corporations (Harari, 2018). Consequently, the power to control, direct, model, profile, simulate, and take strategic actions based on data rests with them. Naturally, this situation produces global inequality between those who hold data and those who do not. Moreover, the responsibility for this vast inequality is often placed on national politicians or individuals. Thus, authority lies with the CEOs of multinational corporations, while accountability is sought from national governments—an inversion of one of the most fundamental principles of governance: that those with authority should also bear responsibility.

At this point, debates on surveillance, equality, and freedom not only limit individual choices but also produce a new form of digital inequality on a global scale. This situation, often expressed by the concept of the "digital divide," deepens the gap between the data-processing capacity concentrated in developed countries and the relatively passive position of developing countries. As a result, differences emerge not only among individuals but also among states in terms of access to and control over surveillance technologies. This inequality has become one of the most decisive factors in the global distribution of power in the digital age.

In addition, the impact of surveillance practices on freedom often manifests itself as an "illusion of freedom." Users may believe they are free when choosing among alternatives presented by algorithms, but in reality, the boundaries of that freedom are determined by the algorithms themselves. Consequently, the liberal tradition's concept of "negative freedom" (being free as long as there is no interference) largely loses its validity in the digital surveillance society. Individuals are increasingly shaped and directed through invisible interventions.

Nevertheless, surveillance should not always be regarded solely as a one-way and repressive tool. Transparency initiatives, open data portals, and digital citizenship tools can also enable individuals to monitor states and corporations. However, for such counter-surveillance practices to evolve into a lasting emancipatory potential, they require a strong ethical and legal framework. Otherwise, these tools could just as easily be used to legitimize new surveillance technologies.

The surveillance–equality–freedom debate must therefore be considered not only in political terms but also as an ethical issue. Data collection and processing have raised the concept of "digital human rights." The right of individuals to own their data, to be informed about how it is used, and to participate based on consent are critical to redefining equality and freedom in the surveillance age. Otherwise, surveillance will remain not only a mechanism that directs individual choices but also a tool that produces a new form of domination on a global scale.

Another important dimension is the psychological impact of surveillance. Knowing or feeling that one is constantly being watched is a powerful disciplinary force that transforms behavior. As Foucault's panopticon metaphor emphasized, surveillance often leads individuals to monitor themselves even when it is not actively applied (Foucault, 1995). The same is true of today's digital surveillance: individuals, aware of being watched on social media, avoid certain behaviors, adjust their posts to be "algorithm-friendly," and thereby unconsciously narrow their own freedom. This results not only in individual-level restrictions but also in a broader societal outcome that fosters conformity (Andrejevic, 2007).

When discussing surveillance's impact on equality, we must also consider its consequences for labor markets and working life. Performance monitoring software used in workplaces measures every action of employees and subjects them to constant evaluation. While such practices are legitimized under the claim of increasing productivity, in reality they place workers under constant pressure and exacerbate job insecurity (Moore, Upchurch & Whittaker, 2018). Thus, surveillance becomes a mechanism that not only violates privacy but also deepens class inequalities. As Zuboff (2019) stresses, surveillance capitalism exerts domination not only over consumers but also over labor regimes.

The operational mechanism of surveillance capitalism is based on the commodification of personal experiences as raw data and the transformation of "behavioral residues" into predictive products to be bought and sold in the market (Zuboff, 2019, p. 78). This process represents a radical break from traditional production relations: the product being generated is behavioral data extracted from individual experiences. This meta-data economy makes individuals both the source and the ultimate product of the production process, while denying them any ownership or control over it. Thus, surveillance capitalism is not only a tool of social control but also a new regime of accumulation rooted in the expropriation of our experiences for the benefit of private corporations.

Another crucial point in the relationship between surveillance and freedom concerns participation and citizenship. Data collected through digital platforms profoundly reshapes citizens' modes of political participation. Micro-targeting techniques in political campaigns can manipulate individuals' preferences and even undermine the legitimacy of democratic processes. The Cambridge Analytica scandal remains a striking example of this (Isaak & Hanna, 2018). Hence, surveillance not only threatens individual privacy but also harms the functioning of democratic institutions. As Lyon (2018) emphasizes, protecting democracy in the age of surveillance requires not only focusing on individual rights but also establishing collective mechanisms of transparency and accountability.

## CONCLUSION

This study has analyzed the structure of digital surveillance technologies, legitimized through discourses of crime prevention and security, from the perspective of political sociology, examining how these technologies reproduce social control and power relations. The literature review conducted within the framework of David Lyon's "Surveillance Society" theory revealed that surveillance mechanisms not only fail to reduce crime rates but also contribute to the spatial displacement of crime, deepen social inequalities, and erode individuals' perceptions of freedom.

Another key finding of the study is the paradoxical relationship between surveillance and trust. Ironically, surveillance practices expanded in the name of security reinforce feelings of insecurity among individuals and normalize social control.

Giddens' analysis of trust and risk in modernity, along with Bauman's concept of liquid surveillance, theoretically explain this paradox. Furthermore, Chul Han's critique of the transparency society demonstrates how surveillance creates an illusion of freedom while acquiring a totalitarian character.

The study has shown that surveillance technologies are not merely justified by the need to ensure security and combat crime, but also function as mechanisms that reinforce social control, generate inequality, and restrict individual freedoms. Findings from the literature indicate that, even when legitimized with rational arguments, surveillance practices evolve into mechanisms that, through individuals' voluntary participation, eventually subject both individuals and society at large to control.

Surveillance, extending beyond its security function, produces a logic of "preventive control" through its capacity to anticipate and manage risks. This logic, rather than simply identifying who poses a danger, categorizes potential risks, thereby placing individuals under constant suspicion. As Lyon notes, this transforms surveillance into a device that categorically organizes social life, enhancing the life chances of some while diminishing those of others. The study also demonstrated, as Bauman and Chul Han argue, that individuals' pursuit of security and their desire for voluntary transparency turn them into the "voluntary slaves" of digital surveillance.

The findings further suggest that surveillance creates a power relation that transcends not only individuals but also nation-states. The control of digital data is concentrated in the hands of global technology corporations such as Amazon, Google, and Meta, producing a domain of power beyond democratic oversight. This signals a new form of authority that undermines the classical principle of governance, namely that authority and responsibility must coexist, while also transcending the boundaries of nation-states. In this way, surveillance serves not only national security policies but also the deepening of global inequalities.

One of the most fundamental problems created by digital surveillance is the emergence of a center of power that lacks democratic legitimacy, alongside the inability of nation-states to effectively oversee this center. While data monopolies acquire transnational economic and political power, accountability mechanisms remain confined to the national level, producing a governance gap (Lyon, 2018, p. 145). Authority accumulates in global corporations, while responsibility is imposed upon national governments, violating one of the most basic principles of governance: that authority and responsibility must be co-located. This gap renders nation-states, which are supposed to safeguard the fundamental rights and freedoms of their citizens, powerless in protecting them against a global surveillance network, thereby severely challenging the boundaries of democratic legitimacy.

In this process, the agency of individuals is highly limited. Even if a person does not actively use digital platforms, the metadata generated by public institutions, financial structures (banks, insurance companies), and mobile communication devices is sufficient to construct a comprehensive profile of that person. Moreover, as Chul Han (2024) points out, "transparency" and the "freedom of self-disclosure" paradoxically become elements that fuel control mechanisms. As Ulrich Beck's (1992) risk society thesis suggests, such meta-risks produced by digital surveillance are social in nature and can therefore only be addressed through institutional, legal, and societal regulations; individual solutions remain inadequate in the face of a systemic problem.

Digital surveillance is not merely a technological issue but also a legal and political one. The European Union's General Data Protection Regulation (GDPR) and other national data protection laws aim to safeguard individuals' privacy rights; however, the scope and oversight of surveillance practices often remain insufficient. This creates ongoing tension between states' security and efficiency discourses and the protection of individual rights, limiting the effectiveness of democratic oversight mechanisms.

Algorithms represent an invisible yet critical dimension of digital surveillance. As Pasquale (2015) emphasizes, algorithmic decision-making processes are often opaque and can reinforce data-driven biases, thereby reproducing social inequalities. Brown (2015), in the context of neoliberal governmentality, argues that the predictive and directive capacity of algorithms constitutes a new form of power that restricts democratic participation. In this sense, surveillance is not only applied for security purposes but also functions as a tool that shapes social norms, directs behaviors, and systematically excludes certain groups.

The effects of digital surveillance are not limited to national boundaries. As Lyon (2006) points out, the data infrastructures controlled by global technology corporations such as Amazon, Google, and Meta generate a domain of power beyond the regulatory capacity of nation-states. This deepens social and economic inequalities on an international scale, limits both individuals' and states' control over data, and weakens democratic oversight. Thus, surveillance transforms into a global instrument of power and control, extending far beyond the mechanism of ensuring domestic security.

Even if surveillance technologies are deemed necessary for combating crime or enhancing bureaucratic efficiency, their functions in reinforcing social control and perpetuating inequalities cannot be ignored. For a more just and libertarian surveillance policy, transparency, accountability, democratic oversight, and the protection of privacy rights are indispensable. Otherwise, surveillance legitimized under the guise of security will continue to reproduce the paradox of rendering modern societies "most insecure at the very moment they are most secure."

In conclusion, digital surveillance technologies, as instruments of neoliberal governmentality, deeply transform social life while constructing an asymmetric power structure that operates beyond democratic control. To address these challenges, it is essential to promote digital literacy and to reformulate surveillance policies in line with the principles of transparency, privacy protection, democratic oversight, and social participation. Data ethics, privacy protection laws, digital human rights, and algorithmic transparency represent critical areas for future research. Yet for these solutions to be sustainable, action must extend beyond laws and regulation. Alongside increasing social awareness and fostering inclusive digital literacy campaigns, technology itself must be designed with principles of transparency, accountability, and privacy protection. Otherwise, the surveillance society will continue, much like Orwell's dystopian vision, to threaten the ideals of freedom and equality.

## REFERENCES


Agamben, G. (2005). *State of exception* (Attell, K., Trans.). University of Chicago Press.

Andrejevic, M. (2007). *iSpy: Surveillance and power in the interactive era.* University Press of Kansas.

Bauman, Z., & Lyon, D. (2024). *Liquid surveillance* (Yılmaz, E., Trans.). Ayrıntı Yayınları.

Beck, U. (1992). Risk society: Towards a new modernity. *Sage (Atlanta, Ga.).*

Bigo, D. (2011). Security: A field left fallow. In Dillon, M., & Neal, A. W. (Eds.), *Foucault on politics, security and war* (pp. 109–123). Palgrave Macmillan.

Brayne, S. (2020). *Predict and surveil: Data, discretion, and the future of policing.* Oxford University Press.

Brown, W. (2015). *Undoing the demos: Neoliberalism's stealth revolution.* Zone Books.

Foucault, M. (1995). *Discipline and punish: The birth of the prison* (Sheridan, A., Trans.). Vintage Books.

Foucault, M. (2013). *Security, territory, population: Lectures at the Collège de France (1977–1978)* (Taylan, F., Trans.). Istanbul Bilgi University Press.

Foucault, M. (2015). *The eye of power* (Ergüden, I., Trans.). Ayrıntı Yayınları.

Giddens, A. (2014). *Modernity and self-identity: Self and society in the late modern age* (Tatlıcan, Ü., Trans.). Say Yayınları.

Han, B.-C. (2024). *The transparency society* (Barışcan, H., Trans.). Metis Yayınları.

Harari, Y. N. (2018). *Homo Deus: A brief history of tomorrow* (Taneli, P. N., Trans.). Kolektif Kitap.

Harari, Y. N. (2020). *Sapiens: A brief history of humankind* (Genç, E., Trans.). Kolektif Kitap.

Isaak, J., & Hanna, M. J. (2018). User data privacy: Facebook, Cambridge Analytica, and privacy protection. *Computer, 51*(8), 56–59. DOI: 10.1109/MC.2018.3191268

Lyon, D. (2006). *Surveillance society: Monitoring everyday life* (Soykan, G., Trans.). Kalkedon Yayınları.

Lyon, D. (2013). Surveillance society. *Sosyologca, 3*(5), 77–90.

Lyon, D. (2018). *The culture of surveillance: Watching as a way of life*. Polity Press.

Monahan, T. (2010). *Surveillance in the time of insecurity*. Rutgers University Press.

Moore, P. V., Upchurch, M., & Whittaker, X. (2018). *Human resource management in the surveillance society: Privacy, resistance and ethics*. Palgrave Macmillan.

Pasquale, F. (2015). *The black box society: The secret algorithms that control money and information*. Harvard University Press.

Schneier, B. (2003). *Beyond fear: Thinking sensibly about security in an uncertain world*. Copernicus Books.

Weber, M. (1978). *Economy and society: An outline of interpretive sociology* (Roth, G., & Wittich, C., Eds.). University of California Press.

Williams, B. (1993). *Shame and necessity*. University of California Press.

Zuboff, S. (2019). *The age of surveillance capitalism: The fight for a human future at the new frontier of power*. PublicAffairs.

Chapter 12

# Interrogating Ndebele identity through articles about Old Bulawayo on Sunday News website

**Jennings Joy Chibike**
https://orcid.org/0000-0002-4899-2446
*Midlands State University, Zimbabwe*

**Nhamo Anthony Mhiripiri**
*St Augustine University of Tanzania, Tanzania*

**Beauty Muromo**
*Midlands State University, Zimbabwe*

## ABSTRACT

*This study examines the identity of the Ndebele people based on articles about Old Bulawayo on the Sunday News' website. It is ingrained within the critical cultural studies school of thought. Empirical data is gathered through subjecting 7 purposively selected articles from the Sunday News website which talk about Old Bulawayo to discourse historical analysis. Additionally, the study utilizes the views and perspectives of three cultural experts and three journalists from Sunday News. The study found out that the Ndebele people are people with a rich and diverse cultural background. Additionally, they are seen as people who are resilient in the face of incursions and colonialism.*

DOI: 10.4018/979-8-3373-4267-2.ch012

## INTRODUCTION

Digital platforms have allowed communities and people to preserve their history (Li and Champadaeng, 2025; Nugroho and Kesyafano, 2025). For instance, in the Zimbabwean context precolonial history, colonial and post-colonial history of different ethnic groups is being created, sustained and preserved online (Ndlovu, 2025; Ndlovu, 2021). Thus, technological platforms have become a source of pertinent information about the being of a people and also an arena where their socio-political lives unfold. However, some information in digital spheres about a people might be biased and needs to be read with careful consideration. In African societies where multiethnicity is common the general argument is that there are ethnic groups which are seen as subordinate to others (Chibike et al., 2025; Nnabuihe et al., 2025). They are seen as marginalised, inferior and their history and identity not full recognised in national discourses (Omoigberale, 2025). In the case of Zimbabwe, to some extent the Ndebele people see themselves as alienated and estranged subjects (Sibanda and Dube, 2025). According to Ncube et al (2025) they claim that their history, tradition and culture has been side-lined and not properly documented and presented whenever national hegemonic narratives are being discussed. In the state-owned media in Zimbabwe there has been the dominance of the majority Shona ethnic group's rendition of history coupled with Shona triumphalism (Ndlovu, 2025). However, Mathe and Motsaathebe (2025) are of the notion that while some people think the Ndebele ethnic group is a "minority", the actual minority groups are those that are not Shona or Ndebele. What however stands out is that in state media Shona history has been prevalent for many years when compared to that of the Ndebele people. Against this milieu, Ndebele people have utilised alternative media such as social media, poetry and music as communicative spaces in which they can curate their precolonial, colonial and post-colonial lifestyle, aspirations and identity (Ncube, 2026; Mpofu, 2026; Maseko and Siziba, 2025; Mkwebu and Chibike, 2025; Sibanda, 2024). It is for this reason that media and cultural studies scholarship on Ndebele identity has mainly centred on the narratives promulgated on privately-owned media, social media, theatre and music. This indicates that there is scanty academic scholarship on the role of state mediated narratives of the Ndebele history and how it influences the imagination of their identity. As such this study seeks to fill the void by focusing on the mediated history of the Ndebele people on lifestyle, culture and heritage sections of state-owned *Sunday News* website. The chapter uses the journalistic stories on the archaeological site of Old Bulawayo as an explanatory prism of understanding real and imagined past and contemporary Ndebeleness. Old Bulawayo - as counterpoised to the new Bulawayo city - is an archaeological reconstruction or rehabilitation of the precolonial capital city of the Ndebele Kingdom that collapsed in 1893 due to British colonial conquest.

The media in Zimbabwe is heavily polarised between state-owned and privately-owned media (Tshabangu and Salawu, 2022; Yin, 2024). Private media is seen as that which is not owned by the government. It largely carries narratives that are highly critical of the government (Kozman and Mellado 2025). On the contrary state media refers to media outlets that are owned or controlled by the government. In fact, the government is the largest shareholder in those entities (Neff and Pickard, 2024). These outlines usually carry narratives that slant towards the interests of the government. As such, most official sources in the stories carried by state media are those from the government or those from individuals who are linked to the government. Most scholars see state media in Zimbabwe as an extension of the government. The *Sunday News* is a state-owned newspaper under the government run Zimbabwe Newspapers (1980) Ltd (Zimpapers). *Sunday News* is a weekly based in Bulawayo – Zimbabwe's second largest city. The paper is also read by people from all corners of Zimbabwe and its online version has a global reach. While just like other state media the paper propagates government linked narratives this chapter examines its representation of Old Bulawayo and Ndebele history, and whether this has traceable implications on contemporary Ndebele identity and the co-existence of different ethnic groups in modern Zimbabwe. The study utilises historical discourse analysis of newspaper articles found on Sunday News websites and in-depth interviews with journalists and academics to answer the research question:

- Who are the Ndebele people, considering their representation in journalistic articles about Old Bulawayo published on the *Sunday News* website?

Since Old Bulawayo is both an archaeological-heritage and cultural site which reproduces an imagined past that inspires current imaginations about Ndebeleness, hence journalistic stories about the site inevitably belong to the vibrant sector of lifestyle journalism. Lifestyle journalism is a broad grouping of so-called "soft news", that includes travel, tourism and heritage journalism. Lifestyle journalism is beginning to get more scholarly attention (Hanusch 2025), and conversations of the identities of peoples who see themselves or are perceived as marginalised are also becoming salient. The visualisation of Ndebeleness through the reportage of Old Bulawayo hence provides new insights on Ndebele identity within a multi-ethnic and multicultural Zimbabwe.

## Understanding Old Bulawayo and the Manufacturing of Stories in the *Sunday News*

Old Bulawayo also known as Kwa Bulawayo is the last royal place which was occupied by King Lobengula in the 19th century. The historical site is managed by the National Museums of Zimbabwe a subsidiary of the Ministry of Home Affairs. It is located about 21 kilometres from new Bulawayo's central business centre. The place is being kept and superintended over by Mr Gwebu. The heritage site was previously known as Gibixhegu before being changed to Bulawayo by King Lobengula. At the site there is a museum where artifacts and tools used by the Ndebele people are kept. Also, the museum showcasessome historical information on the site, King Lobengula and his father King Mzilikazi, his wives and the early missionaries who were in contact with the Ndebele people. There is also a royal enclosure Ndebele housing huts, beehives, King Lobengula's house built by the whites, a cattle kraal, and a storage for station wagons. Further uphill lies a huge tree where court proceedings took place, and the first Catholic church set up by early missionaries in Zimbabwe.

The Old Bulawayo heritage site has however failed to draw economic value because it receives very few tourists due to many reasons, among them not being easily accessible, constant burning down and not being adequately marketed. Again, tourists do not pay to visit the area.

The *Sunday News* has published articles on Old Bulawayo heritage sites. A conversation with the place's caretaker indicates that media practitioners rarely visit the site unless when there is an event. This was also attested by Dr Limukani Ncube a senior journalist and former *Sunday News* Editor who is now an Intake Editor at the Zimpapers' Bulawayo offices. Therefore, journalistic articles on Old Bulawayo are usually events driven. However, most of them are usually written by experts who are history enthusiasts such the late Pathisa Nyathi and Thomas "Mzala Tom" Sibanda. Their articles often dwell on the history, uses and meanings of artefacts found at Old Bulawayo. Thomas "Mzala Tom" Sibanda and Luckson Ndlovu indicated in conversations with researcher Jennings Chibike that editors of the Sunday News never changed their articles but published them as they are. However, the event-based stories often use government sources that project government perspectives since government authorities sanction such events. Stories on Ndebele heritage started to proliferate at the onset of the new Emmerson Mnanagwa led government from 2017 till date. This government assumed power after the removal of President Robert Mugabe. Mnangagwa's government promised to address the issues of social and economic exclusion among other things. Thus, this also led to the proliferation of stories about the so called marginalized ethnic groups in state media.

## Identity Formation in the Digital Spheres and the Ndebele People

The Sunday News is traditionally published as a hard copy, but the emergence of digital technologies has seen its transition into an online platform. Digital platforms are an oasis of not only information but arenas where identities are created, elaborated and performed (McKenzie, 2025). Digital plaforms in general, including social media, blogs and websites in Zimbabwe are generally used by different ethnic groups to share information about their history and heritage (Mpofu, 2018). With this in perspective this study examines how the identity of the Ndebele people is encapsulated in the mediation of Old Bulawayo on the *Sunday News* website.

Identities on digital spheres are now fast becoming elaborate (Lüders et al., 2022), expressed not only through print texts but also different media formats such as images, videos and audios. Bafană and Ioni ă (2021) warn that some online identities can be falsified. However, there is no purely correct identity or false identity since Ertuğruloğlu et al (2024) argue that identity formation is a social process that include myths, traditions and cultures of a people (Danugrobe, 2024; Kennel, 2024; Sibanda, 2024).

Within the content of this study, the goal is to explicate the identity of the Ndebele people based on how the Sunday News websites frame stories about Old Bulawayo. Historically the Ndebele people are a group of people who were led out of the Zulu nation of modern-day South Africa by King Mzilikazi in the year 1823. This was after a dispute with King Tshaka over looted cattle which Mzilikazi kept for himself instead of submitting to Tshaka. Therefore, the feud over cattle led to Mzilikazi and the Khumalo clan fleeing Zululand. Upon reaching present day Zimbabwe King Mzilikazi assimilated different groups such as the San, Venda, Xhosa and Shona into the Ndebele nation.

The multi-ethnic composition of the Ndebele people makes them a nation and not a tribe. Gur and Caliskan (2024) define a nation as a group of people with different backgrounds but mutually living together under a composite name. At the same time Ndlovu (2021) is aware of the complexities that have surrounded scholarship on the Ndebele identity. This complexity is drawn from the various conceptualisation of what Ndebelehood entails. For example, Lindgren (2002) is of the notion that the Ndebele people are those that have Nguni surnames such as Mafu, Khumalo, Nxumalo, Mabhena and Ndiweni ascribed to them. Mpofu and Salawu (2018), and Mautsi et al (2024) define the Ndebele people as those at the peripheries of Zimbabwean political and social development discourse. Ncube and Siziba (2017) believe that the Ndebele people are those that were assimilated into the Ndebele state during King Mzilikazi's migration to present day Zimbabwe. The Ndebele are also identified as those that speak isiNdebele language. Studying online stories published in the Sunday News about the Old Bulawayo historical site offers other perspectives on what constitutes the

The tangible and intangible heritage and culture of a people is important in mapping out their identity (Fisher et al 2022). This is further elaborated by Peel (2009) who states that historical sites can offer clues to the identity of a people. While heritage sites carry important issues on identity, when they co-exist with domineering alternative identities, the former may exhibit undertones of resistance (Mayleh and Hamamra, 2024). That resistance can be a form of identity (Moyo 2022).

This study locates the intersection of digital media, heritage sites and identity formation of the Ndebele people in Zimbabwe's second republic.

## THEORETICAL FRAMEWORK: CRITICAL CULTURAL STUDIES

This study in engrained within critical cultural studies approach that often prioritises the representation of socially marginalised groups and advances the socio-cultural liberation project from repressive forces (Sanchez, 2025). The assumption here is that culture is at the epicentre of meaning making and expressions of identity. Culture is the lived experiences of a people (Hollows, 2024; Dahlgren, 2004). Thus, this theory offers analytical lens in fleshing out the identity of the Ndebele people extrapolated from their heritage and arguably most important heritage monument as reconstructed in the *Sunday News*. Cultural studies has it that media texts carry meaning and it is the role of the researchers to reveal the meaning of the texts (Hall, 2003). Therefore, for meaning to be properly understood, readers need to understand the circumstances in which language is structured and operates. Indeed, readers use their own background and experiences to make sense of cultural texts (Hollows, 2024). Critical Cultural Studies makes a conscious critique of power relations in society and investigates and identifies spaces of resistance against constraining or constrictive forces in society (Hall, 2003). This applies to this study to be Ndebele in Zimbabwe is associated with counterhegemonic activism, protest and even some sections lobbying for secession.

## METHODOLOGY

This study is purely qualitative in nature. Qualitative studies entail an analysis and interrogation of an issues within its context in detail (Lim, 2025; Tisdell et al 2025). Qualitative research allows the exploration of the "what", "how" and "why", kind of research questions (Braun and Clarke, 2025; Hansen et al., 2025). The chapter seeks to ascertain who are the Ndebele people – extrapolating from the articles about Old Bulawayo on *Sunday News* websites. Ultimately, the chapter investigates whether the published stories promotes or subverts Ndebele people's identification or belongingness within the larger all-embracing multi-ethnic Zimbabwe nation-state. The study applies Historical discourse analysis of selected articles from *Sunday News*. The selected articles talked about Old Bulawayo and were largely hard news stories and comments. They were selected form the Sunday News Webstoies and the key words used to select the articles were "Old Bulawayo" Historical Discourse analysis was pioneered by Ruth Wodak and entails the critical appreciation of the intersection of language, power, history and context within cultural texts (Jesudas and Mohammed, 2025; Shvanyukova, 2025). The assumption here is that constructed language is infused with historical discourses (Yeo et al, 2025). Thus, it allows for the examination of the meaning of language, discursive apparatus used and also the contexts in which the language is manufactured and disseminated (Ghazal and Anwar, 2025). Therefore, discourse historical analysis allows for the imaginations of the Ndebele precolonial state and culture, and how contemporary Ndebele culture is imagined and perceived within modern history and the Zimbabwe nation-state. These are both separate, distinct but albeit intersecting historical epochs with their inherent continuities and discontinuities, structural peculiarities and commonalities. Studying different genres of print journalism extracted from the Sunday News' publications on Old Bulawayo may illuminate on the construction of Ndebele people's identity across time, but as imagined through contemporary writings. Historical discourse analysis takes into consideration the topic, discursive strategy used and linguistic forms of relation (Hasmaiti et al 2025). Seven articles that were purposively selected from the *Sunday News* website because they explicitly refer to "Old Bulawayo". The articles were published between 2017 and 2025. This period coincides with the President Emmerson Mnangagwa's assumption of power and the tenure of Zimbabwe's "Second Republic" also often described as Zimbabwe's "new dispensation". President Mnangagwa has made public pronouncements that the new Zimbabwe leaves "leaves no one and no place behind". Such pronouncements purport that the new Zimbabwe is all inclusive in all aspects of life, be it in the economy, culture, linguistic expression and general representation. The chapter tries to investigate whether the state media is making tangible efforts to implement the new policy and vision, and to what extent Ndebele culture and heritage is catered for as well. The research complements historical discourse analysis with in-depth interviews of three culture, arts and lifestyle journalists from *Sunday News* and three cultural activists. These two sets of interviewees arguably are "experts" on Ndebele culture and heritage precisely that of the Ndebele people. The aim of the interviews was to understand how the mediation of Old Bulawayo aids the understanding of the identity of the Ndebele people.

## DISCUSSION AND ANALYSIS OF FINDINGS

### The Ndebele People as Those with a Rich Culture

The article titled **Journey to koBulawayo: Introduction of new architectural forms at Old Bulawayo** by Pathisa Nyathi was published in the *Sunday News* on the 17th of July 2022. It positions Old Bulawayo as a site that best showcases the Ndebele people's diverse culture, tradition and heritage as compared to yet another Ndebele site from the past, namely Mhlahlandlela It reads "Old Bulawayo was viewed as presenting a more varied cultural diversity in comparison to Mhlahlandlela that served as the capital town in the earlier period when Mzilikazi was King". This is seen through the use of comparative language such as "more varied" and "in comparison". Here these phrases rubber stamp the assertion that Old Bulawayo allows for the radiation of the varied cultural heritage about the Ndebele people. This then shows that Ndebelehood is a multifaceted phenomenon which cannot be easily comprehended through one definite answer (Ndlovu, 2021). The phrase "when Mzilikazi was King" situates the spatio-historical period, with reference to Mhlahlandlela serving as an earlier architectural, temporal and cultural index that does not match the superior quality of KoBulawayo. This qualitative historical transformation shows that Ndebele culture is constantly changing and multifaceted. Thus, exhibiting the fact that identity is a historical phenomenon with its overall constitutive features (Popescu-sarry, 2024).

Christian missionaries, and European and Afrikaner mineral prospectors seeking contracts from the Ndebele Kingdom settled at Ko Bulawayo during Lobengula's reign. They too influenced Ndebele material culture through the introduction of new things. For example, the article articulates that "At Old Bulawayo, their (European) influence began to be felt particularly when it came to architecture…One notable one was the three-legged (metal) pot that began to replace the large clay pots in which meat was cooked". The author buttresses the adopted complexities within Ndebele culture and tradition as exemplified through the lexical use of words such as "varied", "replaced", "layered" and "retained". These words help clearly bring forth the revolution and rapid changes that gripped the Ndebele people's cultural and heritage hybridisation. The shift from thatched huts or pole and dagga huts to fired brick huts that continue to be used in Ndebele rural homesteads up to this day, the article continues to state; "...in some rural areas, to this day fired clay bricks are used in the construction of sleeping houses". Architectural designs are further described as "circular layout" and "rectangular design". The reader is assisted to visualise both native and foreign architectural designs signifying the assorted cultural heritage of the Ndebele state. To further outline the position that the Ndebele culture is a mixture of different cultures Luckson Ndlovu a cultural expert states that "Stories about the Ndebele people's rich cultural heritage .... can help break down stereotypes and showcase the beauty of our diversity."

Therefore, this helps cement the prevailing arguments that Ndebelehood is an arena of mixed cultures which is constantly revolving and has never been static (Ndlovu, 2021). Against this milieu, it can be seen that the author uses a constructive discursive strategy to sustain prevailing social narratives about the Ndebele people as being diverse and influenced by different people and cultures since the colonial era, debunking the myth of Ndebele exceptionalism and cultural rigidity that is often obsessed with the archetype of Ndebele warriors and militarism. Therefore, Ndebelehood is best described as a social construction birthed by the social activities that happened in the past (Sibanda, 2024). This then speaks to the argument by Ertugruloglu et al (2024) that identity is engineered by social processes. The richness and multifaceted nature of Ndebele culture is attributed to different social processes such as migrations, assimilations and battles against European imperialists and other African ethnic groups.

The article commentary titled **Work to revive Old Bulawayo testimony of Govt commitment** published in the *Sunday News* on 5 September 2021 it is evident that the Ndebele people are an epitome of rich culture. In the article the rebuilding of certain architectural features is given importance. For example, there is mention of the "beehive shaped huts", "the palace" and "the kraal". This further cements the views and perspectives of Thomas "Mzala Tom" Sibanda a cultural enthusiast who writes for Sunday News who says "...From their architectural style such as the iconic painted huts...". This then indicates that housing structures, colourfully shaped paintings, the king's place of residence and the kraal which is a symbol of wealth are important markers of the heritage and culture of the Ndebele people. The article goes on to mention precolonial Ndebele warriors who archetypical human symbols of the Ndebele pride, heritage and triumph such as Mgandane Dlodlo, Queen Lozikheyi Dlodlo, King Lobengula and General Mtshane Khumalo. However, there is also the inclusion of heroes associated with Shona people such as Mbuya Nehanda and Mapondera, who collaborated with the Ndebele during the 1896-7 anticolonial uprising known as Umvekela. The pan African cooperation in the fight against British imperialism shows that the Ndebele people's alliance with the Shona, a constructive bedrock of the modern unitary Zimbabwe nation-state that transcends narrow ethnicity. Sibanda confirms the pan-African unity when he juxtaposes Ndebele anticolonial struggles with the reference to the non-Ndebele national heroine Mbuya Nehanda who operated from present-day Mashonaland: "For example, the story of Mbuya Nehanda, a national heroine who played a significant role in the fight against colonialism."

Ndebelehood cannot be discussed without the mention of Shonahood. The Ndebele state's assimilation of Shona people, and their alliance with the latter in the struggles against colonialism both in the 1896 Uprising and beyond proves lays a strong narrative for the Zimbabwe nation-state, in spite of the occasional disputes between the two ethnic groups. Underscoring the fact that Ndebele people are a mixture of different ethnic groups including the Shona people should fortify the sense of belonging to the multi-cultural Zimbabwe nation-state (Ncube and Siziba 2017). The assortment of people makes the Ndebele people also identify as a group of people with rich and variant culture. This then means that the Ndebele people cannot have a collective identity but should be properly identified based on the different traditions, cultures and people that make up Ndebelehood. Doing this helps rethink the notion of an essentialized or particularistic collective identity(Danugrobe 2024; Hall 2003). The commentary repeats words such as "culture", "restore" and "revive", implying the restoration or reinvention of residual precolonial Ndebele culture. The use of repetition in this state-owned and controlled weekly's story reaffirms not onlythe Second Republic's policy of leaving no-one and no place behind in the national development agenda, but a practical constitutional recognition of right to culture and identity. The revitalisation of Ndebele culture is also a vital component of the Zimbabwe cultural revival. Ndebele cultural revival that is accentuated through the journalistic stories also finds quotidian expression in the way Ndebele people freely showcase their cultural traditions even the central business district of Bulawayo while they clad traditional attires and chant traditional songs and poems. This is contrary to the general perceptions that Ndebele people are usually marginalised and government does not recognise their culture (Maseko 2024; Mautsi et al 2024).

The article titled **Journey to koBulawayo: Identification of the presence of circularity at Old Bulawayo** published on the 3rd of July 2022 in the *Sunday News* shows that the Ndebele people's culture closely resembles with that of the Nguni people of South Africa. One sentence states, "the Ndebele share a common history and culture with the Nguni". This supports Lindgren (2002)'s assertion that the Ndebele people are those with Nguni surnames. Desmond Mqhele Ntini from Mthwakazi ka Mzilikazi Cultural Association states that Ndebele culture closely resembles South African Nguni culture. This is not unusual because the Ndebele migrated from South Africa and are part of the broader Nguni group that includes the Xhosa, Swazi, Ndebele and Zulu. Ntini adds;

> *Ndebele identity brings together different ethnicities or different groups that were brought together historically by uMzilikazi and later being superintended over by Lobengula at a later time. So, it was different ethnicities, different languages but all fell under the umbrella term Mthwakazi. That's why when we talk of the Ndebele people, we talk broadly about the different groups in Matabeleland.*

Mbulelo Mpofu a journalist with Sunday News reaffirms that Ndebele people are a "proud nation with rich cultural heritage". The multi-ethnic composition of the Ndebele qualifies them less as an ethnic group or tribe but as a fully-fledged “nation’ of diverse peoples. Gur and Caliskan (2024) posit that a nation is made up of smaller units of different people. Collectively the Ndebele have a widespread culture. However, nowadays this collective does not permit the “minoritisation” or marginalisation of certain groups within the broader Ndebele nation (Hall 2003), unlike in precolonial times when there were hierarchies typified by the Zansi (upper class or people of original Nguni extraction) and amaHohle (the lower class of late assimilated Shona and other groups). It allows for the . Unity in diversity brings more strength and creativity to complex social groups that permit equality and equity of access to resources and opportunities. The precolonial Ndebele state allowed for individuals upward social mobility. Ndebele historical socialisation thus best equips Ndebele people to blend into a Zimbabwe nation state as long as the latter also is predicated on the principles of equality, equity, social justice and access to opportunities.

The Journey to KoBulawayo article reiterates the usual architectural symbols and images that are archetypical to Ndebele identity, in one instance underlining that “circularity, while representing and symbolising survival and eternity, also came to represent beauty”. The circular fences, huts and posts were seen as an existential leitmotif of everlasting unity and beauty of the Ndebele people’s households and property. Ntini advances the notion of beauty and the centrality of homes within the Ndebele culture when he celebrates “the intricate architectural marvels of the Ndebele homesteads”. The author reiterates descriptive words like “circularity” and cyclicality” to show the importance of a circular and circular housing features at Old Bulawayo. There is also a conspicuous repetition of these words to further highlight the significance of circles to the Ndebele people’s lifestyle. By doing this the writer aimed at making sure that the reader does not forget the centrality of circles to the Ndebele community. To show the link between the circular cultural artefacts and the spiritual realm the author uses metaphorical language about a snake biting its tail. This symbolises life and the eternality of things, equally suggesting Ndebele culture and artefacts are eternal and will remain important, relevant and meaningful as long as the people and culture exist. The article further uses evaluative words such as “pride”, “admirable” and “desirable” when referring to the culture of the Ndebele people and circularity.

Mashudu Netsianda’s feature article titled **Old Bulawayo on course to regain lost glory** written by published on 28 September 2021 constructs Ndebele people as people who are continuously celebrating their cultural pride. Again, Old Bulawayo’s archetypical architectural designs play a paramount role in mediating Ndebele culture and heritage. Old Bulawayo signifies the epicentre of the Ndebele past and present culture and heritage as attested in the story. Writes Netsianda, “…the King’s Palace, the beehives (iqhugwana) and cattle kraal are the major components of the iconic cultural heritage site”. The lived experiences of the Ndebele people intricately intersects with and symbols that are very important in shaping their spiritual and material being, and the engineering of identity (Dahlgren, 2004). While Old Bulawayo was burned down after the last Ndebele King, Lobengula vacated the area, Ndebele culture and heritage did not die but is constantly being reinvigorated in modern day society. The current site and architecture is a reconstructed and reimagined structure. That is why Netsianda writes about "the restoration of King Lobengula's original capital, Old Bulawayo", which continues to employ "major civil works". The reproduction of Old Bulawayo thus embodies its transiency and the persistent continuation of Ndebele culture across historical periods straddling the precolonial and the post-independence epochs. The reconstructed structure inspires contemporary Zimbabwean society as a whole, hence Netsianda celebrates its existence with adverbs such as "renewing", "revamping" "regain lost glory" and "restoring". These metaphors signify the renewal, resuscitation and reinvention of the Ndebele traditions and culture. The use of the modal expression -"it is envisaged that" - shows that the restoration of Old Bulawayo is a critical objective and goal within the vision of Zimbabwe's future.

Vusumuzi Dube auto-ethnographic article **Journey to koBulawayo: Explaining, interpreting the presence of anthropomorphic clay figurines at Old Bulawayo** by published on the 24th of July 2022 venerates how being Ndebele and Ndebele culture imbue spirituality. Ndebele spiritual practices involved production and use of artefacts and instruments. Dube describes an encounter with a woman exhibiting performative Ndebele spirituality at Old Bulawayo. He writes that "the woman of mature age then turned to her precious parcel, which she proceeded to open rather carefully. Out she brought some freshly made figurines, two resembling human beings and the third akin to a cow". He vividly describes a ritual at the heritage site using cultural and spiritual terms such as "spirit beings", "ukubumba (to mold using clay)", "traditional healer" and "incantation". Dube goes on to write,

> *I was witnessing the use of clay figurines for the first time in a spiritual set up. As children, we used to make similar figurines depicting humans, cattle and various other domestic animals that we were familiar with. For us it was children's play and part of fun, but not so in this ritual that was unfolding and the cow figurine and the rusty copper coins were calculated to symbolise wealth.*

Central to the Ndebele people's culture are spiritual practices which help cement and cascade wealth within the Ndebele society. These spiritual practices are done with aid of pots and rusty metal. Spirituality was not only prevalent within conversations about wealth but also health. Dube reveals his preference for Ndebele religious beliefs over Cartesian rationality when he considers the cultural shock a Ndebele "traditionalist" is likely to face if transposed to "Western" medical practices: "I imagined how a man unschooled in these spiritual manipulations would, in desperation, approach a Western medical doctor without much joy".

As an auto-ethnographic article, the article's author uses the first person narrative and reveals his own embeddedness and insider status within the Ndebele culture. His intimate knowledge of Ndebele culture also serves to convince the reader about the subject-authority of the author. The descriptions of esoteric performative acts at the site, or the use of metaphoric language thus demonstrate the author's cultural command and expertise. Examples abound in the following statements; "remove his shoes and shirt", "spit on the clay" and "recite chants" or "he created figurines represented and symbolized the invisible troublemakers". This kind of language helps show that the spiritual and cultural life of the Ndebele is practiced by many even though seen as sacred. . The author shows the continuity of the spiritual and cultural practice in modern day Ndebele society. The archaeological significance of Old Bulawayo and its claims to reconstructed authenticity that serves contemporary visitors is evidenced in the discovery of artefacts on the present site. Dube notes, "During excavations at Old Bulawayo from March to August in 1998, clay fragments were unearthed from the fill of a palisade in the southern section of the Royal Enclosure". These remains are revitalized and infused with new life as they generate 'new' meanings in the rebuilt site. It is like the co-existence of the living with their late but equally living ancestors. This again, becomes a spiritual journey shining light on the quotidian life.

Next to be analyzed is the article titled **Old Bulawayo restoration resumes** which was authored by the *Chronicle* Editor and published on 24 May 2022. In this article the author venerates that the Ndebele culture is important and is engraved in powerful persons such as Lobengula, artifacts such as beehives and this culture is linked to national pride. In light of this the author shows the centrality and significance of powerful people precisely King Lobengula and cultural artifacts at Old Bulawayo as a cultural symbol. He does this through the use of nominalization and formal language "The structures are associated with the King and the royal family", "Old Bulawayo was built by King Lobengula in 1870 and was burnt down in 1881 to counter the invasion by white colonialist" and "Old Bulawayo is also an important cultural heritage site". This language characterised by a formal tone seeks to show the significance of Old Bulawayo and King Mzilikazi as icons for the Ndebele people. To show that Zimbabwe's central authority recognises Ndebele cultural heritage, the author uses makes reference to "government", "stakeholders" and "Ministry of Home Affairs". The Second Republic appropriates and accommodates Ndebele heritage and traditions within the Zimbabwe cultural fabric. This resonates with jpournlaist Temba Dube 's observations that,

> *For example, a few weeks ago, the Zimbabwean government brought back a chieftaincy that had been removed during colonial times. These stories and records help the Ndebele people know and appreciate who they are.*

This is done to show that different establishments chief among them the Zimbabwean government are interested in reviving a re-imagined but "authentic" Ndebele culture and heritage. This authenticity is given salience through the use of cultural lexicons, and as archaeological reconstruction of Old Bulawayo and rebuilding of King's Lobengula's palace. This signals that Ndebele precolonial history, myths and customs are important (Peel, 2009) not only to the Ndebele people but also the government.

Having discussed how the Ndebele people are discursively constructed as people with a rich culture the next section explores how issues of Ndebele cultural resilience are infused in stories in the *Sunday News.*

## The Ndebele People as Resilient Against Colonialism

Under this section the first article to be analysed is titled **COMMENT: Work to revive Old Bulawayo testimony of Govt commitment.** In this article the theme of resilience emerges. What is rather interesting is that the resilience of the Ndebele people's culture and heritage is being spear headed by the current government of Zimbabwe fronted by Emerson Mnangagwa. This is seen when the author writes that "The Government and President Mnangagwa in particular deserve all the praises for taking a keen interest in preserving the history, heritage and culture of all Zimbabwean communities" and "The restoration of Old Bulawayo, built by King Lobengula in 1870 and burnt down in 1881 to counter invasion by white colonialists, is part of the Heritage Corridor…". Thus, the argument here is that the current government sees the importance of Ndebele culture and heritage particularly seeking to preserve it and challenge the colonisers' stance of trying to eradicate it. This then sustains the argument by Mayaleh and Hamamra (2024) that historical sites help reinvigorate the spirit of resistance. In this regard the government has largely exhibited its interest in Ndebele heritage sites such as Old Bulawayo which carries clues on how the Ndebele people resisted colonialism. This indicates the government is slowly recognising Ndebele architecture and recently people who are linked to anticolonial motives is seen in the new dispensation when Ndebele figures such as Saul Gwakuba Ndlovu, Elliot Ngwabi and Rabelani Choeni, in 2021 were accorded post humors national hero status. This clearly demonstrates the fact that the government is making strides towards recognising Ndebele people. Besides the government's stance it is seen that Ndebele heroes were integral in the fight against colonialism and this is seen in the article when the author writes "From there the Government has gone on to honour other heroes from early years of resistance and they include General Mtshane Khumalo who commanded the Imbizo Regiment under King Lobengula that defeated the Allan Wilson Patrol at Pupu in 1893, Chingaira Makoni, Mapondera, Mkwati, Queen Lozikeyi Dlodlo and Mgandane Dlodlo" This shows that Ndebele heroes together with those from the Shona nation played an integral role in fight the colonisers. To illuminate these suppositions the author uses language which is linked to resistance for example "heroes of resistance", "counter invasion", "defeated", and "heroes" to show the spirited battle that the Ndebele people participated in trying to escape from the jaws of the colonisers. This shows that identity can be conceptualized within the conversations of resistance (Moyo, 2022). Also, there was the use of metaphors such as "revising" and "restoration". These show that the Ndebele people are working to challenge British influence which had threatened their culture and their being. This is also seen in journalist Vusumuzi Dube's assertion that "I have also learned about their history, including their struggles against colonialism and their fight for independence". This subsequently exhibits the fact that they are resilient in their quest to maintain their being at the same time challenging the influence of certain factors precisely imperialists activities bent at ontologically exiling them. This then brings through a destructive strategy which is aimed at challenging the prevailing discourse that the Shona people were at the height of anti-colonial endeavors while the Ndebele people did not play a significant role worth celebrating. This then illuminates a glimmer of hope amongst Ndebele people and politicians who have been constantly calling for their recognition of their heroes.

Next to be analysed is the article titled **Old Bulawayo on course to regain lost glory**. In this article the aspect of resilience and resistance by the Ndebele people is well brought out. The article shows the historical forms of resistance by King Lobengula through the act of burning down his capital and abandoning it when it was being infiltrated by Europeans. This is seen when the author writes "Old Bulawayo, which was built by King Lobengula in 1870 and was burnt down in 1881 to counter invasion by white colonialists…". This translates to the argument that Ndebele leader is a stout person who is adamant to let go of his sovereignty to the European settlers. Not only is King Lobengula but also his trusted commanders such as General Magwegwe Fuyana at the forefront of resisting colonial activities. This is seen in him participating in the actual burning of Old Bulawayo as seen in the article when the author writes "One of the King's commanders, General Magwegwe Fuyana, led the process of burning down the capital…". This symbolises the fact that not only the King was keen on resisting colonialism but many people within the Ndebele state thus signifying their anti-imperialism stance. This justify the identity that has been attached to the Ndebele people by Gibson (2024) who posits that the Ndebele people carry identities coined from their struggle against coloniality. In this instance the representations in the *Sunday News* show that the Ndebele people are people who enjoy self-rule and they dets any political influence bent at metamorphising their way of life.

Next to be analysed is an article titled **Journey to koBulawayo: Explaining, interpreting the presence of anthropomorphic clay figurines at Old Bulawayo by** Pathisa Nyathi. In this article the resilience of the Ndebele people is seen in the cultural and traditional sense where traditional practices are given more prominence than European ones. This is seen in the article where the writer states "The beleaguered man was advised to recite chants after the woman. Essentially, it all amounted to a declaration of innocence" and "I imagined how a man unschooled in these spiritual manipulations would, in desperation, approach a Western medical doctor without much joy". Here the author shows how the Ndebele people with regards to healing practices stubbornly stuck to their native practices while not fully embracing Western ones. This shows that the Ndebele people have some sort of cultural resistance which helps them wade off an imperialist's motives and practices. While the Europeans are accredited with bringing commerce to Africa, it should be noted that the Ndebele people stuck to their traditional commercial systems and symbols of wealth which are rooted in their traditions. This validates the assertion that Ndebele tradition and heritage allows the Ndebele people to self-develop. By sticking to their heritage and tradition the Ndebele people resisted imperialists activities and ideologies which brought European commerce. This is seen in the article when the author states "The cow figurine and the rusty copper coins were calculated to symbolise wealth. Even the invisible creatures love wealth just as their material counterparts do". In this article there is the metaphor "home for invisible troublemakers" and lexicon such as "African science" "chants" "incantation" and "ukubumba" which show that African systems superseded those introduced by the Europeans. This is said by someone who has firsthand information about this. This is seen by the use of narrative and personalized language for example "I imagined…" and "I was almost convinced" thus further validating the claims of the cultural resilience of the Ndebele people. This further solidifies the efforts of the government in trying to revive the culture of the native Zimbabwe against the background that most people are beginning to ditch it for European lifestyles.

Next to be analyzed is the article titled **Old Bulawayo restoration resumes.** Here emphasis is on the cultural resilience of the Ndebele people which is being spearheaded by the government. In this instance the government is funding the reconstruction of Old Bulawayo. This is seen in the article when the author writes "Thatching of King Lobengula's palace at Old Bulawayo has started as the Government steps up efforts towards completing works on the restoration of the historical site". This is further cemented by the use of lexicon speaking to resilience against imperialism for example "rebuilding", "reconstructing", "resuming" and "restoration". In the first instance burning down of the place was King Lobengula's attempt to shrug off imperialistic involvement in his capital. This is seen in the article when the author writes "Old Bulawayo was built by King Lobengula in 1870 and was burnt down in 1881 to counter the invasion by white colonialists". This is a sign that the Ndebele people have been keen on keeping their sovereignty. Therefore, it can be seen that the Ndebele people together with the government are working together in the fight against imperialism through the process of restoration of Ndebele cultural and historical sites.

## CONCLUSION

The study has proven the applicability of cultural studies as a productive prism in the examination of the online mediation of Old Bulawayo by *Sunday News*. The goal of the study has been to explicate the identity of the Ndebele people based on the articles on Old Bulawayo. The study fleshed out that the Ndebele people are very conscious and particular about their traditions and spiritualism. Even in the verge of external forces they kept practicing their traditions though in some cases mixing them with those of outsiders. This then translates to the argument that the Ndebele people are people have a very rich and diverse culture. Also, the study found out that the Ndebele people are very resistant. They challenged external forces that were bent at altering their culture and heritage. Also, they resisted colonial forces which were aimed at eradicating their sovereignty. Therefore, the study shows how digital spheres can carry history which is important in helping understand a people and their lifestyle. Thus, there is need then for journalists and cultural activities to work together to curate historical sites online. This will help in the storage of the pristine history which is important in identity formation and imagination. Also, authorities from the museums should consider keeping records of historical sites on different digital platforms. Again, this will help in the preservation of cultural heritage. Future studies must consider expanding and focusing on how other historical sites such as Matopo hills are curated on different online media platforms.

## REFERENCES


Bafană, M., & Ioni ă, I. (2021). Disinformation and Online Identity Theft through False Accounts on Social Networks. *hypothesis, 120*, 121.

Braun, V., & Clarke, V. (2025). Reporting guidelines for qualitative research: A values-based approach. *Qualitative Research in Psychology*, *22*(2), 399–438.

Chibike, J. J., Muzhingi, S. A., Pikanegore, P., & Makalisa, B. (2025). Interrogating the interplay of multilingualism and multiculturalism on Lupane State University campus radio station. In Mathe, L., & Motsaathebe, G. (Eds.), *Reconceptualising Multilingualism on African Radio: Language and Identity* (pp. 111–129). Springer Nature Switzerland.

Dahlgren, P. (2004). Cultural studies as a research perspective: Themes and tensions. In Corner, J., Schlesinger, P., & Silverstone, R. (Eds.), *International media research: A critical survey* (pp. 48–6). Routledge.

Danugrobe, A. (2024). The role of history in the strengthening of national identity in the era of society 5.0, *Jurnal Sejarah Dan Pembela Jarannya* 14(1): https://e-journal.unipma.ac.id/index.php/JA/article/view/18745

Ertuğruloğlu, O., Gülcan, N.Y. & Pişkin-Abidoğlu, Ü. (2024). The impact of culture on the education system, *International e-Journal of Educational Studies* 8 (16): 131-141.

Fisher, L., Evans, M., Forbes, K., Gayton, A., Liu, Y., & Rutgers, D. (2022). Language experiences, evaluations and emotions (3Es): Analysis of structural models of multilingual identity for language learners in schools in England. *International Journal of Multilingualism*, *21*(1), 418–438.

Ghazal, D. U. S., & Anwar, A. (2025). Unravelling global perceptions of the 2023 Isreal-Hamas Conflict: A discourse historical analysis of tweets. [JALT]. *Journal of Applied Linguistics and TESOL*, *8*(2), 2209–2214.

Gibson, S. (2024). Racialized railway mobilities: repression and resistance in the Anglophone South African Short story during the drum decade, *English Studies in Africa* 1-15. https://doi.org/DOI: 10.1080/00138398.2024.2377913

Gur, H., & Caliskan, G. (2024). Crafting a national identity: The role of geography textbooks in 1930s Turkey's nation building project. *Nations and Nationalism*. Advance online publication. DOI: 10.1111/nana.13044

Hall, S. (2003). Cultural Studies and the Centre: some problematics and problems. In *Culture, media, language* (pp. 2–35). Routledge.

Hansen, H., Elias, S. R., Stevenson, A., Smith, A. D., Alexander, B. N., & Barros, M. (2025). Resisting the objectification of qualitative research: The unsilencing of context, researchers, and none interview data. *Organizational Research Methods, 28*(1), 3–31.

Hasmaiti, H., Syamsudduha, S., & Azis, A. (2025). Social, Political, and Cultural Discourse in the Movie Gadis Kretek: A Critical Discourse Analysis by Ruth Wodak. *Journal of Asian Multicultural Research for Social Sciences Study, 6*(2), 29–43.

Hollows, J. (2024). Feminism, cultural studies and popular culture. In Hollows, J. (Ed.), *Feminism, Femininity and Popular Culture* (pp. 19–36). Manchester University Press.

Jesudas, R., & Mohammed, Z. (2025). Discourse Strategies in Action: Unpacking Wodak's Framework in the 2024 Presidential Debate between Trump and Harris. *Scientia. Technology. Science and Society, 2*(1), 22–36.

Kennel, J. (2024). More than a feeling: Storytelling, memory and national myths at dark events. *Event Management, 28*(4), 655–659.

Kozman, C., & Mellado, C. (2025). Mapping journalistic role performance across five Arab countries. *Journalism & Mass Communication Quarterly, 102*(3), 722–749.

Li, Z., & Champadaeng, S. (2025). Study of Cultural Heritage and Digital Preservation: The Case of Murals of the Northern Yue Temple. *International Journal of Education and Literacy Studies, 13*(2), 262–268.

Lim, W. M. (2025). What is qualitative research? An overview and guidelines. *Australasian Marketing Journal, 33*(2), 199–229.

Lindgren, B. (2002). Power, education, and identity in post-colonial Zimbabwe: The fate of King Lobengula of Matabeleland. *African Sociological Review, 6*(1), 46–67.

Lüders, A., Dinkelberg, A., & Quayle, M. (2022). Becoming "us" in digital spaces: How online users creatively and strategically exploit social media affordances to build up social identity. *Acta Psychologica, 228*, 103643.

Maseko, B. (2024). Blurring the binaries of home/school in Family Language Policy: Parents as teachers in heritage language lessons. *Sociolinguistic Studies, 18*(1-2), 81–106.

Maseko, B., & Siziba, L. (2025). Violence, Memory and Resistance in Selected Highlanders FC Supporters' Songs. *Critical Arts*, •••, 1–20.

Mathe, L., & Motsaathebe, G. (2025). The political economy of indigenous local media for minority languages in Zimbabwe: A case of Lyeja FM community radio. *Journal of Asian and African Studies*, *60*(1), 5–17.

Mautsi, G., Mago, D., & Musara, C. (2024). Gendered Electoral Violence: The Case of Hwange District, Matabeleland North Province in Zimbabwe. In Ehiane, S. O., Shulika, L. S., & Vhumbunu, C. H. (Eds.), *Engagement of Africa in Conflict Dynamics and Peace Architectures. Africa's Global Engagement: Perspectives from Emerging Countries.*, DOI: 10.1007/978-981-99-8235-6_13

Mayaleh, A., & Hamamra, B. (2024). Instruments of resilience: Cultural tourism in the Palestinian resistance. *International Journal of Heritage Studies*, •••, 1–17.

McKenzie, J. (2025). Digital media as sites for cultural identity development: The case of Hmong American emerging adults. *Journal of Adolescent Research*, *40*(2), 296–330.

Mkwebu, N., & Chibike, J. J. (2025). Computer-Generated Linguistics Countering Linguicides: Users' Use and Interpretation of WhatsApp Emojis in isiNdebele. In *Resuscitation of African Languages: Theorising the Battle Against Sociocultural Genocide* (pp. 215–236). Springer Nature Switzerland.

Moyo, T. (2022). Beyond provincializing a nation without a state: Representation of Matabeleland in Umthwakazi Review digital space. In Ndlovu, M., & Mlotshwa, K. (Eds.), *The Idea of Matabeleland in Digital Spaces: Genealogies, Discourses* (pp. 191–204). Rowman and Littlefield.

Mpofu, M. (2026). Popular theatre as counter-public spheres in Matabeleland in the 1980s: A critical analysis of Amakhosi Theatre Production's Nansi Le Ndoda. In Mpofu, M., Nkomo, D., & Heliker, K. (Eds.), *Civil Society in Zimbabwe* (pp. 241–257). Routledge.

Mpofu, P. (2018). Politics of language, ethnicity and identity in Zimbabwean ethno-linguistic online communities. In Mpofu, P. (Ed.), *African language digital media and communication* (pp. 154–172). Routledge.

Mpofu, P., & Salawu, A. (2018). Re-examining the indigenous language press in Zimbabwe: Towards developmental communication and language empowerment. *South African Journal of African Languages*, *38*(3), 293–302.

Ncube, C., Fayayo, R., & Moyo, G. (2025). Matabeleland's civil struggle: A narrative of resistance, negotiation, and reclamation of political space. In Mpofu, M., Nkomo, D., & Heliker, K. (Eds.), *Civil Society in Zimbabwe* (pp. 66–84). Routledge.

Ncube, G. (2026). Artists and the recreation of inkundla and alternative online civic spaces in post-independent Matabeleland. In Mpofu, M., Nkomo, D., & Heliker, K. (Eds.), *Civil Society in Zimbabwe* (pp. 211–225). Routledge.

Ncube, G., & Siziba, G. (2017). Compelled to Perform in the 'Oppressor's' Language? Ndebele Performing Artists and Zimbabwe's Shona-Centric *Habitus*. *Journal of Southern African Studies*, *43*(4), 825–836.

Ndlovu, M. (2021). Walking through history together: Gukurahundi, memory and the role of digital media in shaping "post-conflict" Zimbabwe. In Maweu, J., & Mare, A. (Eds.), *Media, conflict and peacebuilding in Africa* (pp. 210–223). Routledge.

Ndlovu, M. (2025). Memory and the Political Uses of the Past in Digital Ndebele Nationalism. In Basch, A., Niemi, M. J., & Hammar, A. (Eds.), *Africa-Europe Group for Interdisciplinary Studies* (Vol. 179). Brills., DOI: 10.1163/9789004728004

Neff, T., & Pickard, V. (2024). Funding democracy: Public media and democratic health in 33 countries. *The International Journal of Press/Politics*, *29*(3), 601–627.

Nnabuihe, O. E., Onwuzuruigbo, I., & Ihembe, M. A. (2025). Cultural hegemony and ethnic minority struggles in Nigeria. *African Identities*, *23*(3), 715–736.

Nugroho, W. S., & Kesyafano, B. (2025). Exploring the Impact of Digital Technology on Oral Traditions: Cultural Preservation in the Digital Era. *Kampret Journal*, *4*(3), 117–122.

Omoigberale, O. (2025). Navigating the Fault Lines: The Paradoxes of Majoritarian Democracy and Minority Rights in Nigeria's Multi-Ethnic Polity. *Peace Review*, •••, 1–22.

Peel, A. C. (2009). *Diaspora Ethnicity and Politics in the Electronic Media: Case Studies of United Kingdom Based Zimbabwean Internet Websites and Their Associations*. PhD diss., University of Wales.

Sanchez, E. (2025). The Centre for Contemporary Cultural Studies: A Historical 'Utopian'Enclave in the Political World of Academia? In Avril, E., Mourlon, F., & Fee, D. (Eds.), *Fragmented Powers* (pp. 177–191). Emerald Publishing Limited.

Shvanyukova, P. (2025). 'Nuclear weapons are our best friends': A Discourse-Historical Analysis of the Cold War Era Rhetoric of Nuclear Militarism. *Textus*, *37*(1), 267–287.

Sibanda, M. N. (2024). The constructions of Ndebele identity in Skyz Metro FM: An audience reception study. *Journal of Asian and African Studies*, •••, 00219096241230493.

Sibanda, N., & Dube, P. (2025). Conceptualising and revealing political resistance in Zimbabwe through (re) naming roads in Bulawayo. *South African Journal of African Languages*, •••, 1–10.

Tisdell, E. J., Merriam, S. B., & Stuckey-Peyrot, H. L. (2025). *Qualitative research: A guide to design and implementation*. Jossey-bass.

Tshabangu, T., & Salawu, A. (2022). Alternative media, repression and the crisis state: Towards a political economy of alternative media in post-Mugabe Zimbabwe. *Journal of Asian and African Studies*, *59*(1), 172–186.

Yin, F. (2024). Layered Environmental Discourses: Media Representations of Transnational Extractivism in Zimbabwe. *African Journalism Studies*, 1-18.

# Chapter 13
# Humour and Mockvertising:
## Satire, Subversion, and Consumer Culture on Platforms

**Janardan Krishna Yadav**
https://orcid.org/0000-0003-1970-8933
*Jindal Global Business School, O.P. Jindal Global University, India*

**Srinivas Jangirala**
https://orcid.org/0000-0002-6884-7959
*O.P. Jindal Global University, India*

**Fandi Omeish**
https://orcid.org/0000-0002-8042-3622
*Princess Sumaya University for Technology, PSUT University, Jordan*

## ABSTRACT

*Mockvertising is a subversive form of advertising that can be traced back to traditional marketing where brands critique consumer culture or engage audiences through humour and mocking the brands or themselves. It may look counterintuitive, but many brands are inviting comedians to make a joke about the brand and the probable misfits in their values and value propositions few examples in Indian business environment are comedian Samay Raina mocking the brands (Unacademy and Zomato) or Biswa Kalyan Rath roped in by Vijaya Sales when he mocked the brand in a sage show the collaboration has resulted in a few videos ads extending the satirical take and few humorous explanations about the brand name. The fundamental shift advertising to X, TikTok, YouTube and Instagram have shaped an atmosphere where content with satire and humour undertones gets great engagement*

DOI: 10.4018/979-8-3373-4267-2.ch013

*and followers. This chapter explores how mockvertising utilizes these platforms' capabilities and their ability to subvert standard advertising conventions and redirect consumer beliefs while steering cultural conversations.*

## INTRODUCTION

Mockvertising, or satirical advertising, has emerged as a powerful marketing strategy that leverages humour, irony, and self-deprecation to engage audiences. Subversive mockvertising is a satirical form advertisement and brand promotion that criticizes, mimes or interferes with the traditional advertising behavior of the brands by combining the elements of humour and social statements. With this brand of influence, the user-generated content, viral memes, and campaigns on social media platforms X, YouTube, TikTok, and Instagram have led to the emergence of the term mockvertising as a combination of mock and advertising which refers to the brand of influencing other concepts and people.

There are three key themes: the disruptive quality of satirical information, the effectiveness of targeting a wide audience with it, and what it does to the perception of a brand in the context of the digital world. To begin with, mockvertising creates a disruption in the patterns of traditional advertising by questioning a top-down approach of communication between individuals with brands leading and consumers following. In the past, advertising had been a one-way communication which used to see brands pushing messages to very passive audiences. Nonetheless, the emergence of the digital environment has shifted this relationship, which now allows consumers to engage in the process by creating, altering or challenging brand stories (Jenkins, 2006). Parody mockvertisements, generated by third-party artists, activist organizations, or rival companies alike, are an attempt to take away the power of corporations by revealing predatory marketing and cultural sensitivities and, therefore, encourage critical discussions about consumerism (Serazio, 2021).

Second, it is through the passion of humour that mockvertising can reach an audience in a strong way. Humour constitutes an especially good approach to audience engagement under the cultural conditions of expanding distrust in conventional advertising, especially among Millennials and Generation Z. These population cohorts are more open to messages about corporate hypocrisy or breaking a fixed social norm and are more likely to hold these values (Fromm & Read, 2018).

Third, mockvertising concepts have major effects on relationship building on brand reputation, especially in a more interactive and transparent media environment. The self-awareness and the adaptability shown by a brand that acknowledges and celebrates the critical commentary presented by satire will help to humanize them, ultimately increasing their cultural relevance. Brands that do not listen or cannot accept being satirically condemned, on the other hand, might face image instability and decline in the audience bases because of a digital culture of humor (Holt, 2016). Collectively, these themes underscore the complexity of the connection among humor, customer empowerment, and brand identity that characterize the current changing media landscape.

To explain various concepts, we build upon the satirical campaign conducted by Greenpeace in 2010 against the KitKat brand operated by Nestle that has demonstrated how satire is an effective means to amplify the message of activists and put pressure on business establishments (Wettergren & Hillgren, 2013). Just as well, the #DistractinglySexy tag on X presented an opportunity to dislodge the long-established tropes of sexist advertising through humorous user-generated satire, which demonstrates how user-generated satire can reject and restructuring existing cultural tropes. Moreover, the chapter is an exploration of the actual history of its development e.g., how the idea of mockvertising started in print and TV parodies and now takes the world by storm in the digital settings where algorithmic curation and platform functionalities have tremendously widened its sphere of influence and application (Bucher, 2018)

Although the role of humor in advertising has been studied largely, the change in humor in the digital era should be clearly explained. In the conventional media, humor was strategically planned by the brands to achieve the purpose of marketing and to be interesting to mass audiences. Incredible advertising campaigns, like Volkswagen use of humor to famously sell their Beetle, there are the 1960s-dated Think Small ads, which used witty and self-deprecating humor to position the beetle as something individual (Williamson, 1978). Conversely, online networks have decentralized humor, by which consumers create and share satirical writings in collaboration. This transition is informed by larger shifts within culture toward the participatory cultures of media in which the audience is no longer the passive receiver of a cultural narrative but a source as well as builder of such a narrative (Jenkins, 2006). The negotiation of the participatory framework is an understanding that is taken advantage of by mockvertising through the medium of humor in both a critique of turning our way of life into commodities as well as one that engages with the issues of platform-oriented economies.

The rebellious power of mockvertising is bestowed on the power of challenging the persuasive motives of the traditional advertising process and disrupting them. Mockvertising can encourage consumers to be skeptical as they all have been exposed to the same modes of tactics used in traditional marketing like exaggerations, ideal visuals or cultural appropriation.

The examples include advertisements (especially advertisements of luxurious goods) whose parody makes viewers rethink what values they promote because such a commercial establishes impractical connections between otherworldly phenomena and other things, such as the notion that having a handbag is the same as being personally fulfilled (Huntington, 2019). This counter-culture tendency is compounded by interactive and immediate aspects of digital platforms which allow satirical content to be rapidly distributed and shared not only among global audiences but also among different audiences. Nevertheless, one should note that such platforms are not objective; their algorithms favor the content that generates a high interest, and network algorithms can promote sensationalistic or comedic content over other pieces of more sophisticated criticism (Bucher, 2018). This fact casts a concerning doubt over the possibility of mockvertising demonstrating its critical potency when promulgated over commercially oriented sites or hijacked by brands through use of meta-advertising as marketing tactics.

With the notion of consumer culture being characterized by the complex interaction among desire, identity and economic forces, consumer culture offers perfect breeding ground to the development of mockvertising. Digital channels also add further complexity to such a landscape where consumers can engage in as well as acting as critics to the content of marketing messages. The relative novelty of mockvertising seems to have a specific resonance among the audiences with a growing distrust in corporate discourse, particularly in the conditions of the ethical discussions on the labor, environmental, and privacy issues (Edelman, 2023). The skepticism gets tapped by the satirical campaigns that focus on issues related to fast fashion and its environmental impact or the surveillance behavior of tech companies but can serve as a cultural commentary that is at the same time aggressive or non-confrontational (Fromm & Read, 2018). In these dynamics, mockvertising does not merely challenge hegemonic culture of consumers, but it also actually takes part in its reformation, shaping the brand-consumer relations in the modern digital market.

In the same vein, Guy Debord developed the notion of the spectacle (1968) that offers a critical perspective through which it is possible to understand how mockvertising disrupts the commodification processes that characterize the contemporary world despite being created on the premises of platform capitalism. Collectively, these theoretical frameworks bring into visibility the ambivalence of mockvertising in that it shows the duality of mockvertising as a form of counter-hegemonic disruption but also having the possibility of becoming a complicity generator in the digital media ecosystem.

Methodologically speaking, this chapter relies on a qualitative approach based on the careful case studies that demonstrates the different manifestations and effects of mockvertising. Examples would be the parody campaign of Greenpeace against Nestle KitKat, the #DistractinglySexy movement on X and the brand-driven PR such as the satirical advertisements used by Burger King in order to attack other brands. The ability to tie the theory and practice together can be achieved through anchoring the discussion on these tangible examples to get a sense of the modern dynamics of the consumer culture. The chapter also discusses the ethical issues inherent on mockvertising like the risk of wrong interpretation and reinforcement of negative stereotypes especially with the heterogeneous and fragmented condition of the digital platforms.

Finally, the given chapter aims to emphasize the revolutionary potential of humour and mockvertising in changing the consumer culture on the background of digital spaces. It will add to the greater disciplinary discourse on the role the media plays in building resistance, innovation and activism within contemporary digital landscape; by providing a critical angle on the way satire mediates and challenges the political power of corporations. With the ongoing development of the digital world, we will also be seeing the practices of mockvertising that will require all academics, industry professionals, and consumers to re-examine the blurring lines between entertainment, criticism, and commercialization.

In Indian context, the phenomenon of mockvertising has been prominent, as a keenly effective satirical weapon of criticism of consumer culture, given the power of vibrant digital media base and strong traditions of humorous expression that come naturally to the Indian. Both grassroots and brand-generated mockvertisements asking questions of the stories influencing the still-developing consumer market are amplified on social media platforms such as YouTube and Instagram.

These campaigns tend to address advertising stereotypes and socially relevant problems that are common nowadays. As an example, a YouTube video created in 2022 by FilterCopy satirized highly present fairness cream ads commonly seen in Indian advertisements due to the person developing unrealistic social advantages and privileges after applying a non-existent product, revealing and criticizing the harmful notion of skin colour (Banet-Weiser, 2012). Equally, Amul, which has a legendary hit topical billboard, often uses irony as a tool to counter consumer trends; one creation in particular, which achieved a lot of success in 2020, mocked the intense advertising of herbal immunity supplements by companies trying to capitalize on the pandemic; through this, Amul addressed consumers wary of unreliable health promises (Huntington, 2019).

The other key example is the 2024 self-deprecating campaign by Zomato as part of its 16th anniversary. The campaign involved comedian Samay Raina who wore the T-shirt of a rival brand Swiggy and criticized Zomato itself in terms of its notifying people and customer care style humorously. The fact that the event has been attended by the CEO Deepinder Goyal increased the authenticity of the campaign (Section 5). Popular to Instagram and YouTube, this initiative invoked the elements of incongruity and self-parody to position Zomato as someone similar to the audience to fit in the participatory culture that is discussed in Section 4. Nonetheless, its straightforward style also attracted discussions associated with brand safety and the extent of satire in business communication (Hess, 2019).

Collectively, they all represent how mockvertising in India is a process through which consumers challenge the deeply rooted cultural discourse as they grapple with the moral complications that satire brings about in a diverse and digitally interconnected society.

## SECTION 1: THE RISE OF HUMOUR IN DIGITAL ADVERTISING

The advertisements have harnessed diverse aspects of humour, and it has been changing alongside other features of the media and the cultures that are followed, resulting in the humour becoming one of the main features of modern digital world of consumers. Humour has become a dynamic, collaborative, user-generated type of action on social media in the digital age, unlike the controlled and strategically planned approach in the conventional media. Humour is not only a medium of reaching the audience, but it also serves the purpose of criticizing consumer culture and redefining the behaviour of advertisement in the era of 21st century.

### Historical Context

The history of using humour in advertising goes far before the digital revolution when the promoters of different products in early print, radio, and TV campaigns used humour to capture the attention of people and to develop brand awareness among the target audience. Early-20th-century print advertisements often used word games and puns alongside goofy illustrations to identify a product in a market where options were beginning to multiply. In the case of Coca-Cola advertisements of 1920s, a combination of dreamy images and catchy phrase of the kind like ''Thirst Knows No Season' were used, and this proved a wise strategy of loosening the consumer base (Williamson, 1978). The advent of the radio led to the popularity of sound humour in the form of jingles and comedic routines that were incorporated into the brand communication. That changed in the 1950s when television changed advertising and led to brands being able to combine visual and aural humour to create extremely memorable campaigns. It is worth mentioning that Volkswagen used self-deprecating humour itself when introducing the Beetle back in the 60s in its campaign called Think Small, which placed it as a unique alternative to the American car market that was leading by the end of the 50s (Eisend, 2018). Similarly, Budweiser has used absurdist humour to its benefit when creating their now culturally iconic campaign of the late 1990s, ''Whassup? Using an absurdist humour, the brand became part of the everyday vernacular (Holt, 2004).

*Figure 1. Think small campaign Volkswagen*

In the conventional media, humour was a top-down approach and was very politely designed by the agencies to suit brand requirements and have mass appeal. It was used to break through the other messages competing with it, and research even showed a potential to increase the attention and memory (up to 30%) of humorous advertisements when compared with non-humorous ones (Eisend, 2018). However, cultural sensitivity and sentence, as well as, control, were the key to its effectiveness (Williamson, 1978).

Humour has seen massive change in its role in advertising because of the transition to the digital world. The introduction of the internet in the late 1990s and social media in the 2000s led to a shift in advertising which changed an earlier broadcast model of advertising to an interactive and participatory model. The early digital technology such as banner adverts and email campaigns emulated the refined humour of the mainstream media but failed to operate in real time. YouTube (2005), Twitter/X and TikTok (2016) platforms became platforms of humour created by users, which allows influencers and creators to develop comedy materials with a critical or satirical edge (Jenkins, 2006). This democratization transformed advertising into a relational process ownable by both the brands and audiences, and even an aggressive in-fight.

## Platform Dynamics

X, TikTok, and YouTube are the digital platforms that have changed how content in the comedic direction is delivered due to the filtering based on algorithms, the participatory nature of the platforms, and the affordances. These sites are not only receiving points but effective intermediaries in cultural expression and present certain content as more worthy of being engaged and viral (Bucher, 2018). In these terms, humour can be presented as a very powerful communicative form, which would rely on both emotion value and the ability to be shared to become the dominant face in the digital advertisement world.

The conversational, real-time structure of X also lend it itself to further spread of comedic content, such as memes and satirical remarks reworking the narrative of brands. Interactions and the popularity of the hashtags contribute to the increased visibility, particularly in the case of Wendy using humorous roasts to communicate to the audiences strategically (Serazio, 2021).

The use of algorithms to prioritize the measure of engagement like liking and retweeting creates a situation where humour especially in the critical or ironic registration enjoys increased publicity and can be utilized as an instrument of digital influence (Bucher, 2018).

The channel TikTok has modified the role of humour in digital media through algorithms making decision about the For You Page and short-form video. This is because it uses a machine-learning algorithm that curates content according to the taste of the user and often it is comedic or absurd videos (Abidin, 2021). Options such as duet and stitch also offer the user the capability to remake brand advertisements by attaching humorous or sarcastic edits to it, including mocking hyperbolic fast-fashioning claims or discussing ethical concerns. This participatory remix culture broadens the reach of humour greatly, to the point where they can well exceed in engagement the brand-generated campaigns.

Long-form video YouTube provides a variety of comedic content such as professional-level satire to amateur level parodies. Such sites as 'The Onion' and 'CollegeHumour' have cultivated a following at the expense of advertising tropes, such as tongue-in-cheek product exaggeration and brand jargon, and viral commercial parodies are frequently the work of individual creators (Huntington, 2019). The YouTube recommendation algorithm gives preference to funny videos that have a long watch time and engagement leading to a self-perpetuating cycle in which comedy thrives (Bucher, 2018). Also, the business model of the platform promotes monetization by inviting creators to create humorous works because advertisers want to latch on to the popular and widely watched videos.

Such dynamics of the platform indicate the interdependence of humour and the digital infrastructure. Algorithms prefer to spread the material that causes high emotions, which is why humour can be an excellent method of expression of both the author and brands. But this intensification is connected with compromises because platforms tend to give preference to some sensational or even polarizing humour rather than subtle satire, which impairs its subversive potential (Bucher, 2018).

## Consumer Expectations

The increased use of humour in online advertising can also be explained by the changing expectations of the consumer base (younger audiences demand a more authentic and entertaining approach over corporate content). A great part of digital audience belongs to the Millennials and Gen Z who are less likely to trust traditional advertisement; according to surveys, 70% of Gen Z prefer brands that use humour or relatability in their message (Edelman, 2023). This distrust is based on the wider cultural transformation, such as loss of faith in the institutions and the knowledge of corporate scandals connected with labour or environmental issues or data privacy scandals (Fromm & Read, 2018).

Consumers are moving towards demanding the brands not only advertise products but also entertain and mirror their values- needs which can be best fulfilled by humour. Subversive or satirical comedy bridges by reaching common ground on the same wavelengths of common resentment over consumerism and societal conventions. To give an example, the viral video created by Dollar Shave Club in 2012 used deadpan humour to mock outrageous prices in the industry of grooming and successfully established the brand name as a no-nonsense solution whose prices will target the needs of customers (Serazio, 2021). Such campaigns go viral, as it is felt as genuine and it appeals to those who have grown weary of insincere marketing ploys.

With the move of authenticity, there is no distinction any more between advertising and entertainment. Digital platforms give the brands an opportunity to be more conversational and attempt humour to present themselves as easy to relate but not simply commercial creatures. For example, the profile X, which Netflix posts regularly, contains memes and funny communication, thus involving followers as equals rather than only customers (Holt, 2016). This approach has something to do with the participatory quality of digital culture, in which consumers anticipate the opportunity to contribute to the creation of narratives on the level of likes, comments, and shares (Jenkins, 2006). Nevertheless, companies should be very careful with their efforts as artificial or fake humour that can be categorized as cringe may isolate viewers and cause them to lose trust in the brand (Serazio, 2021).

The growing weight of humour in digital advertising is also an indicator of an even more general democratization of media production with consumers having much of the say in what the brand tells. The possibility of criticizing, remixing, and enhancing the humour-related content via platforms forces brands to adapt, or face irrelevance. However, this democratization is associated with its own problems, as the brands need to maintain a positive balance between interest and humour to remain credible within multicultural and interconnected digital communities with all the cultural and moral implications it implies (Abidin, 2021).

## SECTION 2: MOCKVERTISING: WHAT IT IS?

Combing the democratization of humour on digital advertisement as was described in Section 1, mockvertising can be seen as a highly influential and unique branch of this trend. A fusion of advertising and satire, mockvertising uses parody and humour as means to critique consumer culture and re-establish the association with brands and their consumer. This type of satirical advertisement ravages on the usual strategies of marketing or points out the ridiculousness of being a customer, behaviours of companies and societal demands. Thriving at the inception of the participatory media and the platform-driven environment of digital western media, mockvertising employs the main methods of humour, including exaggeration, irony, and subversion, to attract attention, subvert the major corporate discourse, and provoke more sceptical attitude to consumer culture. We explore the definition of mockvertising and its salient characteristics and then analyse some of the best examples of campaigns on platforms such as X, Tik Tok, and YouTube to illustrate the cultural and commercial importance of such a practice.

### Definition and Characteristics

Mockvertising is commercial advertising that parodies the visual, language, or structure of an ordinary advertisement except that it aims not to sell a product or service but to comment humorously on the subject. Instead of engaging in persuasion and conversion of consumers which was the aim of the traditional advertising, mockvertising aims to either entertain, engage in critical reflection or expose contradictions in the world of consumerism, often focused on provocative marketing methods or corporate unethical practices (Huntington, 2019). It serves as a way of cultural critique and can be used to negate the power of the corporate messages and invite society to challenge the values behind the message in advertising.

Mockvertising has a number of major specifics that make it different to other light-hearted methods of advertisement. First, it is also subversive in nature by, on purpose, interrupting the persuasive agenda of traditional marketing by highlighting its absurdities and contradictions (Serazio, 2021). As an example, a mockvertisement takes the form of a slick campaign of a luxury brand in order to criticize its reliance on sweat shop labour. Second, mockvertising feeds on engagement; it works best in digital contexts in which users, influencers and brands co-create and share content. The explosion of sharing and remixing features of sites allows mockvertisements to mutate with the interaction of the audience (Jenkins, 2006). Thirdly, mockvertising is flexible to the context as it reacts and adapts to cultural, political, or platform-specific trends in order to remain relevant. The flexibility guarantees that its comedy can be relevant to people interested in thinking about the life experience they experience and criticizing the concerns of the modern era (Abidin, 2021).

The mockvertising brand of satire is very appealing to the greater theme of digital culture whereby, general distrust of corporate message is rampant. It is stated that around 65 percent of the total world consumers are distrustful of conventional advertising, and younger generations have displayed a strong interest in consuming information on social media that criticizes the corporate narratives (Edelman, 2023). By taking advantage of this mistrust, mockvertising aims to foster a shared critical consciousness with the attempt to make audiences more critically oriented toward consumer society through use of humour (Fromm & Read, 2018). Mockvertising can be seen as a powerful and effective tool in the modern digital advertising market because it involves entertaining the audience whilst informing it in a rather profound social way.

## Key Elements

Mockvertising depends on three important factors, namely exaggeration, irony, and subversion. All these are combined to appeal to audiences, unmask the deceptive practices of advertising, and ask people to think critically about mass consumerism.

Mockvertising takes its characteristics to an extreme with these exaggerated advertising tropes being thoroughly demonstrated in their inanity. Mockvertisements use cranking a brand too far in their terms or visions of beauty to emphasize that marketing is far different than what it actually tends to be. To give an example, a mockvertisement on an energy drink that does not exist at all could promise superhuman powers, mocking the exaggerated wording of real drink advertisements (Eisend, 2018). This hyperbolism makes it funny by incongruity since viewers understand the nonsense presented in the claims but look back at such manipulations of less conspicuous advertisement.

Mockvertising is supported by irony, which employs unlikely parallels to denounce business intentions or social principles. Irony works in the opposite way in that a message that is introduced varies with the intended meaning and is left to the audiences to interpret the criticism. To illustrate, a mockvertisement, an imitation of the sustainability campaign of a fast-fashion company, can combine the rich eco-friendly appearance but also discretely show that the brand is dependent on the use of sweat shops (Huntington, 2019). This humourous ironic framing brings about humour as it brings out contradictions and makes the audience doubt the corporate communication authenticity (Gray et al., 2009).

The essence of mockvertising influence lies in subversion or in other words when the mockvertising interferes with the conventional advertising objectives. Instead of convincing consumers to purchase the goods, mockvertising aims at destabilizing the brand authority, criticizing consumerism, or breaking the rule of, say, a particular culture. This subversive purpose goes along with the participatory culture of online environments wherein mockvertisements can be spread or remixed to carry out an act of criticism (Jenkins, 2006). With subversion, audiences can feel more active critics than passive consumers because subversion encourages agency with regard to the world of commerce (Serazio, 2021).

These factors combined show that mockvertising can be a very energetic type of digital comedy relevant to the readers and viewers of various cultural and technical perspectives. Nevertheless, they can be effective only in case of their thoughtful application, since the wrongly tuned jokes can be understood incorrectly or become offensive, especially in the digital, cautious space (Abidin, 2021).

## Examples

Influxes in well-advertised mockvertising illustrate the depth and extent of the phenomenon, including those created both by active users and by activist campaigns and by those produced by the brand itself. Such campaigns are some of the most vivid examples of how mockvertising uses the affordances of platforms to engage with the audience and question consumer culture.

One of the best-known is the 2010 campaign by Greenpeace against Nestle, creatively parodying the brand identity of KitKat chocolate to reveal the impact that its palm oil supply chain has on the environment. The media involved a viral video that poked fun of the slogan Have a Break in the KitKat advertising that would show a consumer opening a chocolate bar only to get the finger of an orangutan--representing how destruction of trees is catastrophic to other animals. The video which has spread widely over YouTube and Twitter gained millions of views and raised an outcry among the global population that has led to Nestle restructuring the supply chain methods (Wettergren & Hillgren, 2013). This strategic incorporation of irony and subversion was what gave every edge to the campaign; pairing the bright and cheery KitKat branding with a bleak responsible environment message that produced an emotional and intellectual reaction.

Mockvertising by the fans is also thriving online, with #DistractinglySexy as its example that ran in 2015 on X. This movement came into being because of the controversial statement made by a scientist saying that women in laboratories were a distraction. As a counter to it, female scientists posted jokes about them in imagines of women in protective clothing in response to sexist advertising trends to objectify women. Within a short period, the hashtag became viral, with thousands of posts and considerable attention of the media. Such a campaign demonstrated that mockvertising could be an effective method allowing the underrepresented groups to challenge and disrupt dominant cultural discourse (Huntington, 2019). The exaggeration and irony, which it used to produce its effect, involved absurd humour in the introduction of irrationality behind gender stereotyping as portrayed in media.

The mockvertising initiated by brands present a different perspective since organizations use satirical strategies to foster relatability and a subversive brand image. An example of this practice is the 2012 viral video by Dollar Shave Club called "Our Blades Are F**ing Great," * which features a mockery of the expensive razors offered by the grooming industry along with stereotyped masculinity imagery. The use of deadpan humour and hyperonization demonstrated the brand as a simplistic and easy to use option that has made its way to over 27 million views on YouTube and led to a considerable increase in the subscriptions (Serazio, 2021). Likewise, in the 2017 McWhopper campaign, Burger King made a humorous suggestion to team up with McDonalds, using irony in this case to mock the former establishment in terms of its dominance in the industry as well as to reinforce the light-hearted theme of its brand image (Holt, 2016). These models demonstrate how brands can use mockvertising to fulfil consumer desires to have authentic and humorous advertising, and they show how there is always conflict between embracing the subversive power of satire and the commercial interests that can always threaten to blunt this subversive power.

TikTok has been seen as one of the central platforms through which mockvertising has become a key source of mockvertising product, as creators vigorously remixes brand content to provide a sharp critique of the consumerist culture. An example is the numerous parodies of advertisements of the Shein fast-fashion brand that tend to far-fetched stress the low prices of the brand pointing out the low quality of products and their ethical aspect. Based on the use of TikTok duet, such user-generated mockvertisements acquire increased coverage and interactivity (Abidin, 2021). The active satire is extremely appealing to Gen Z audiences equally keen to see humour expressed in terms of ethical and environmental priorities behind it, thus coupling it with the suggestion that TikTok forms a realm of shared cultural critique (Fromm & Read, 2018).

Although these examples are clear showings of how effective mockvertising can be when aiming to reach audiences with a humorous and critical approach, they bring out underlying difficulties. It can be noted that a 2020 TikTok parody of a skincare brand, in which the product claims were overstated, had been subject to criticism of unwittingly shaming people with skin conditions. This event illustrates the dire nature of the cultural sensitivity and awareness in writing the satirical content (Abidin, 2021). Such intricacies, therefore, require both brands and creators to exercise caution as pertains to the successful realization of mockvertising as a tool of empowerment and critical revelation, as opposed to alienation and offence.

The emergence of mockvertising is a pure example of the democratisation of digital media in general, when humour is used not only as a medium of cultural critique but as a way to establish genuine bonds with viewers and readers. Through the use of irony, exaggeration, and subversion, an effective shopper response can be achieved through mockvertising; a shopper that is, in the context of increasing distrust of corporate corporations, mainstream media channels almost always serving corporate interests, and modern advertising in general. Whether it is in the context of production and distribution or reception and consumption, the immensity and power of mockvertising in consumer culture is set to increase through digital platforms. Such expansion highlights the necessity of brands, creators, and researchers to consider in detail the ethical, cultural aspect of mockvertising so that the use could be diverse without negativity and establish better power and conversation within an ever-changing world of digital culture.

## SECTION 3: SATIRE AS THE SUBVERSIVE TOOL

Continuing the discussion of mockvertising started in the previous section, this section shifts towards satire, which the former requires to get its edge out, in the first place. Satire as an instrument that is based on irony, exaggeration, and humour is highly effective in challenging norms in society, revealing contradictions in the consumer culture and in puncturing the glossy texture of the traditional advertisement. The digital platform in the modern era has become outlets where people can express satirical content like X, TikTok, and YouTube, others and corporations can express their mockvertising journals through blatant satire as a form of culture critique.

In this case, we will explore the role of satire in mockvertising, how it destabilizes the marketing apparatus and gives viewers an impulse to think about the messages behind the commercial contents. This section will analyse the role of satire in influencing overall consumer confidence in brands, brand awareness as well as the place of parodies within a cultural context through a selection of specific examples of both brand-led and user-generated satire. Based upon theoretical opinions and results of recent empirical research it places satire not only in the context of a humour mechanism, but as a strategic means of reconfiguring the role advertising plays in the participatory algorithmic media environment.

## Devices of Satire

Satire is an effective means of manipulating humour and critical thinking, and it would be effective in fulfilling the purpose of questioning the effective and controlled stories found in popular advertisements. Satire has a rich literary and artistic tradition that is based on wit and irony to bring out contradiction, challenge authority and spur further thought (Gray et al., 2009). In mockvertising, the idea of satire is used deliberately in order to criticize social norms, the vulgarity of consumer capitalism, and to avert the current advertising conventions. It consists of working in three main mechanisms; the first is incongruity that draws attention to the ridiculousness between expectation and perception; the second is superiority that lets the audience think that they are smarter or moral superior to the object being criticized and lastly, relief, where the tension regarding a sensitive matter may be removed, by laughing.

According to incongruity theory it is possible to represent humour occurring in unforeseen conflict between what is expected and what takes place, a process which is a key driver behind satirical mockvertising (Meyer, 2000). Using the repetition of a traditional ad format alongside critical or subversive content, satire gives rise to a cognitive dissonance and causes viewers to come out of their comfort zone. As an example, a fake advert that resembles a sophisticated campaign of a luxurious brand can be juxtaposed against the images of environmental damage, shedding light on the conflict between brands image and the actual consequences of products and services they sell (Attardo, 2014). Such an application of incongruity makes audiences enjoy entertainment and critique together, which is why satirical messages often come across as fun and thought-provoking.

According to superiority theory, there is humour produced when satire makes the audience feel quite superior intellectually or morally to the object of the scorn (Ferguson & Ford, 2008). The same occurs in mockvertising where people laugh at the marketing cliche exaggeration or the victimization of their corporate contradiction in the realization that they are smart consumers. By way of example, campaigns aimed at showcasing exaggerated promises on products will make the audience seem like intelligent critics not easily fooled (Gray et al., 2009). This feeling of empowerment would ring true with the participatory culture of the digital age, where the audiences take an active and critical role in altering and reshaping brand stories (Jenkins, 2006).

Relief theory emphasizes the fact that satire is an emotional release as well, and it helps individuals explore emotionally delicate or controversial topics (such as criminal activities of corporations or social inequity) through jokes and humorous manner (Shouse, 2020). Mockvertising plays this situation by applying a humorous touch to point to the troublesome issues like environmental degradation or employee exploitation, to render the emotional load less hefty. It is a funny way to frame it, which allows space to reflect without getting embarrassed, and the criticism is easier to accept, particularly on online interfaces, where emotional stimulus is essential to gain attention (Wettergren & Hillgren, 2013).

These mechanisms of satire combined are able to give mockvertising the impetuous to address deep-seated problems within society, capitalism, and advertising. The aim of satire is to highlight norms that have lost their relevance, such as the sexist promotion images, by mocking assumptions about culture that they convey (Hess, 2019). It criticizes capitalism by pointing out the patterns of commercialization of everyday activities, which is suggestive of say Debord concept of the spectacle where the media perpetuates the values of the consumerism (Debord, 1967). Also, satire can dismantle the tropes normally associated with advertising like flawless beauty or a fantastical claim, and remind audiences of their manipulative aspect, and thus they should question and critically respond to messages in consumer culture (Banet-Weiser, 2012).

## Case Studies

The examples of satirical campaigns and user-generated content are described in terms of case studies on the satire subversion of consumer culture in the sphere of digital platforms. The examples help to appreciate the versatile nature of mockvertising, which can run in the direction of activist criticism, involve users as a parody, and also include the brands themselves as sources of satirical voicing.

**Greenpeace KitKat Campaign (2010)**: Greenpeace has had a hugely successful campaign against Nestle, in which they used satire to break corporate news stories. Inhabiting the ethos of a kit-kat advertisement, the video substituted the cheerful slogan Have a Break with a cold introversion of an office employee chewing a finger of an orangutan bath-a tragic allegory of the destruction of forests by Nestle moribund use of palm oil. Distributed on YouTube and Twitter, it immediately got more than 1.5 million views and caused a backlash across the world, which ultimately compelled Nestle to take action against its supply chain problems (Wettergren & Hillgren, 2013). Combining incongruity into dark humour, the campaign has managed to convert outrage into engagement well, demonstrating the power of satire in terms of encouraging accountability on the part of the populace (Hess, 2019).

*#LikeAGirl by Always (2014, User-Generated Responses): The #LikeAGirl campaign by Always, originally a brand campaign of challenging gender stereotypes, produced a flood of satirical responses on such platforms as X and YouTube. It was an irony-laden campaign which aimed at repossessing the term like a girl in an attempt to demonstrate young girls in a confident and talented attitude when it comes to playing sports. Extending this, the fans made parodies, where they overdramatized commonly found advertising cliches: beauty commercials being*

*overly dramatic, etc, in order to highlight the absurdity of gendered marketing (Banet-Weiser, 2012). As an example, makeup tutorials by YouTube stars made fun of the unrealistic beauty standards with exaggerated makeup. These parodies created by users added a significant discussion of gender representation as the domain of satire promotes marginal voices through exaggerating them (Stache & Zayer, 2015).*

*Don T Buy This Jacket (2011) Patagonia: Patagonia also rolled-out a tongue-in-cheek campaign advertising its patent-pending jacket, encouraging the customers not to purchase what they do not really need. Presented as a full-page advertisement in The New York Times and advertised on X, the campaign used the madness of Black Friday humorously and marketed their jackets with the label, "Don? t Buy This Jacket" in support of responsible consumption and environmental stewardship. Such a drastic anti-consumerist message resonated with eco-aware consumers, making Patagonia all the more repeat-purchasing.*

The campaign provoked the feeling of superiority among consumers to position them as intelligent antagonists of capitalism and, at the same time, people sharing their values (Chua & Banerjee, 2015; Banet-Weiser, 2012).

TikTok Parodies of Fast Fashion (2020Present): TikTok has developed into an arena of user-generated parodies targeting fast-fashion retailers such as Shein and Fashion Nova. By applying manipulation options like duet and stitch, authors of one of them modify legitimate advertisements to point out a moral injustice like sweatshop labour or environmental harm by hyperbolically pronouncing the company as incredibly cheap or of exceptionally high quality. Another viral video, say, made fun of a Shein dress disintegrating after wearing it once, criticizing the fast-fashion colossal of Shein (Abidin, 2021). Such popular parodies will employ incongruity and relief to resonate with Gen Z audiences, who value ethical shopping, demonstrating the ability of satire to shape contemporary cultural.

These instances explain the wide extent to which satire can be used to critique consumerism; by activists and grassroots parodies, marketing-driven satire, as well as the necessity of cultural sensitivity and understanding in order to prevent misinterpretation or offending one another in different online communities (Hess, 2019).

## Hearing on Listeners

The power of satirical mockvertising is deeply affecting consumer trust, brand loyalty, and cultural communications creating new possibilities of brand relations to redefine the interaction between consumers and the brands and comprehending the world of consumption. The participatory character of the digital platforms enhances its effects since satirical content spreads and is fuelled by the participation of users.

Consumer Trust: Satire can also much harm the brand of those companies whose brand does not reflect the values of the consumer by exposing corporate hypocrisy or improper ethical conduct. As an example, the KitKat campaign launched by Greenpeace significantly damaged the image of Nestle, and studies show that, in the case of environmentally conscious consumers, the percentage of those who did not trust the company increased by 10 after the actions of the activist movement (Edelman, 2023). Conversely, brands (such as Patagonia) that use satire in earnest may build consumer trust in their own transparency and ability to share common ethical or moral ground (Chua & Banerjee, 2015). Here, satire acts as a barometer because it praises brands which live up to the expectation of its audience and punishes those which fail to measure up (Banet-Weiser, 2012).

Brand Loyalty: camp77 campaigns can go to extremes in building brand loyalty ideologically among segmented audiences that value sincerity and critical thought. As an illustration, the ironical critique provided by Patagonia with reference to the production of its incomparable jackets under the campaign titled Don T Buy This Jacket increased sales in the environmentally conscious consumer market by 30% because the message did not contradict their anti-consumerist values (Chua & Banerjee, 2015). Similarly, loyalty to Always brand was boosted by user-generated parodies, including #LikeAGirl, which identified the brand with feminist principles, particularly, among younger adults (Stache & Zayer, 2015). However, brands should tread lightly when it comes to satire because consumers usually do not react positively to that perceived lack of sincerity (Serazio, 2021).

Cultural Discourse: Satire is important in defining cultural discourse through sending a voice to the peripheral vision and scrutinising any established ideology. An example is the parodies of #LikeAGirl, which promoted broad discussion of gender stereotypes and how this should impact advertising representation, causing the brands to adopt more inclusive depiction (Banet-Weiser, 2012). Similarly, TikTok has shed light on ethical consumption due to parodies of fast-fashion brands that force companies to reflect sustainability in their business (Couldry & Mejias, 2019). Gains of satire are enhanced by social media algorithms that maximize interesting material, which may, in a few cases be biased towards sensationalism, instead of serious criticism (Bucher, 2018).

In spite of this significance of satire, it does have its difficulty. Sometimes, the excessive use of humour makes audiences dulled to its critical point, since exposure to irony too many times may make it lose its power (Holt, 2016). Furthermore, humour has a certain degree of cultural richness as misunderstandings have offended certain people at times, particularly the underprivileged (Hess, 2019). In turn, creators and brands have to handle these dangers with care so that it ensures that satire might continue being a powerful narrative in empowerment and productive discussions.

Satire, being one of the primary elements of mockvertising, alters the consumer culture as it addresses the corporate involvement and promotes analytical attitude. It opposes social niceties, capitalist indulgences and advertising tropes using the devices of incongruity, superiority, and relief. Its effect on consumer confidence, patronage, and societal consumer discussion indicates how it is becoming culturally relevant. As digital platform continues to evolve, the use of satire in influencing consumer opinion will necessarily need to take ongoing consideration, as to the disruptive potential of satire, leveraged against responsible use.

## SECTION 4: THE USE OF PLATFORMS TO MULTIPLY MOCKVERTISING

In the wake of discussing the subversive potential of satire, as it was done in Section 3, this section examines a critical aspect of digital media platforms, which enhance mockvertising and propel the mockery ad to the level of a mainstream phenomenon. These platforms such as X, TikTok, and YouTube are not only channels of passive communication but platforms playing an active role in its construction, employing algorithms, user interaction, and interconnectivity to reinforce the consumption of comedic and satirical wording to the largest extent. The art of mockvertising with its hierarchy of humour, irony, subversion does well in this environment as it utilizes the dynamics of the platforms to disrupt consumer culture and re-define the rapport between brands and buyers. However, the same processes that enhance mockvertising make it raise ethical issues, including the possibility of being misunderstood, backfiring and strengthening stereotypes. In this segment, the role of algorithms in mockvertising, the significance of user engagement in the spread of this practice, and the ethical issues that arise as an outcome of platform-based satire will be considered with the help of a wide variety of research sources that will help identify the effects in the digital environment.

### Algorithmic Influence

An important role in enhancing mockvertising is left with the algorithms of the platforms which choose to promote the content that promotes high user engagement and economic performance for the platforms. The platforms such as X, TikTok, YouTube use algorithms to analyse the behaviors of the users (likes, shares, comments, viewing time, etc.) and determine which content is consumed by larger audiences, prioritizing the humorous and emotionally captivating news, among which mockvertising is included (Bucher, 2018). This forms a feedback loop powered by algorithms in which satirical posts, with their flair of both being funny and controversial, gain disproportionately large visibility which affects the online advertisement society.

Particularly, the algorithms of X prioritize texts that elicit immediate engagement, or retweet, replying, and hashtag trends, which is why this platform is an optimal location where mockvertising may become viral. Examples include Wendy-roasting her competitors in an entertaining fashion or users creating parodies of corporate ads as satirical posts on social media, which often go viral due to their popularity and shareability within short time reaching new audiences of millions of people (Gillespie, 2018). As an example, the 2019 #NotMyAriel hashtag critiqued the Disney decision to cast a Black actress in the role of Ariel through humour and sought to poke fun at corporate inclusiveness; the hashtag was used thousands of times and opened up the debate across the globe. To an extent, the algorithmic promotion of such content by X underlines how it can shape mockvertising toward an important cultural effect, but it also poses a threat to the sustained possibility of more profound and, notably, less humorous criticism (Couldry & Mejias, 2019).

TikTok applies the formidable power of machine-learning algorithms with the For You Page being very successful at presenting the kind of comedic content each user will enjoy. The algorithm observes other users in the platform and recommends videos displaying the content that interests viewers, including short, satirical videos like parody advertisements called mockvertisements based on the promotion of a brand or the consumer culture (Abidin, 2021). As one of the examples, influencers on Tik Tok often recycle the advertising of fast-fashion brands such as Shein with an over exaggerated dark-humour approach to reveal ethical problems such as workers exploitation and polluting the environment. These TikTok bursts, with many later gaining millions of views, play into the viral loops of TikTok: a phenomenon that results in exponential growth by the combination of using user sharing and algorithm-driven suggestions to promote (Kennedy, 2020). Such climate puts TikTok as one of the largest hubs of mockvertising, where creators have the means to criticize corporate messages on a tight budget.

Another factor that contributes to mockvertising within YouTube is its recommendation system which is reputed to give more attention to videos that have shown high levels of engagement as shown by excessive watch times and likes gathered. The platform is the home of satirical groups such as The Onion or CollegeHumour, which produce so-called mockvertisements, or advertisements in the style of a classic advertisement that parodies familiar advertising stereotypes, such as product exaggerations or business-related jargon (Huntington, 2019). As an example, the dystopian advertisement of a privacy policy of a tech company written by The Onion achieved more than 2 million views, due in part to Google and YouTube algorithm which showed this video to people interested in such comedy productions (Van Dijck,

2013). Moreover, the monetization system on YouTube drives creators to emphasize on humour since increasing the amount of interaction attracts ad revenue thus creating a symbiotic relationship between comedy and economics of the platform.

But there are problems that this algorithmic influence creates. The emphasis on engagement may distort the object of satire, with attention being given to outlandish or polarising material that pleases the algorithm but does not provide a nuanced critique (Bucher, 2018). This can undermine the value of mockvertising as an intellectual project because the algorithms have a tendency to manifest the more entertaining and less critical content. Moreover, their lack of transparency, i.e., platforms do not disclose the methods of prioritizing content, lowers the level of control creators have over the spread of their satire, leaving a question on the existence of creative autonomy in platform capitalism (Gillespie, 2018). Nevertheless, considering the power of mockvertising through the cultural impact and reach all over the world, algorithms continue to play a fundamental role in this marketing phenomenon.

## User Participation

An audience is one of the most important elements of the success of mockvertising campaigns because digital media has allowed the users to contribute via participation through the processes of creation, remixing, and sharing of satirical ideas and humour through a process that has made mockvertising into a participatory cultural event. As opposed to conventional advertising in which the viewers were mere consumers, the platforms allow people to become co-authors of stories written via memes, remixes, and other satirical stories made by users, extending the reach and influence of mockvertising (Jenkins, 2006). Such projective culture is in line with the liberalization of the production of media in which consumers have never had their voice and power over a brand story.

User generated mockvertising relies heavily on meme as a format since it can be condensed to a form of humorous criticism of consumer culture. In X, memes of parody corporate advertisement claim e.g. ridiculing Apple with its minimalist product releases but with ridiculously overpriced products go viral using retweets and hashtags (Shifman, 2014). To give one case in point, a 2021 meme wave on X parodied the Tesla Cybertruck by portraying it as a comically unrealistic truck, exaggeratedly so as to satirize the cult-like marketing of the brand. The memes tend to be produced by anonymous users and appeal to the audience that does not believe in corporate hype, developing a sense of criticism (Knobel & Lankshear, 2007).

The remixes on such platforms as Tik Tok and YouTube allow users to appropriate brand content and then in comments add satirical slant, which spoils the initial purpose. TikTok has duet and stitch tools that enable artists to contrast ads with banterous reviews, e.g. in commercials about skin products, they can exaggerate the product effects or disclose carcinogenic components (Abidin, 2021). Another such significant example is a 2022 TikTok trend in which consumers remixed H&M sustainability advertisements to use irony as a tactic to criticize the brand based on its fast-fashion tendencies; the videos have collected more than 10 million views. Remixing of commercials is also evident on YouTube where creators supply parody videos that ridicule commercial practices, including a video on Saturday Night Live that used absurdity in making fun of advertising and lamenting on the consumerist longings (Gray et al., 2009). These remixes further increase the subversive potential of mockvertising, because users are turning company material into critical culture.

Satire generated by the users takes mockvertising beyond the memes and remixes by including content created by users which criticizes consumer culture. The use of social media such as #DistractinglySexy (2015) on X has women scientists sharing relatable, comedy-based photos to create a conversation about gender representation, as women scientists share amusing photos that satirize sexist advertising tropes (Huntington, 2019). On the same note, mockvertisements created by YouTube artists against big tech companies, including parodies of Amazon labour conditions presented as corporate dystopian adverts, are also made, and they find their audience due to the interaction between creators and the communities (Hess, 2019). Such involvement of users also allows audiences to take brands to task, and this fits right into the participatory culture of digital sites (Jenkins, 2006).

Engagement of users increases the cultural effect of mockvertising as it creates a feeling of community and agency. The production and distribution of satirical content made the users present themselves as proactive critics of the corporate power and the shapers of cultural discourse (Shifman, 2014). The involvement is, however, not without limitation. Less sensational posts may be hidden by the algorithm of platforms, and any criticism that poses a threat to a brand can be inhibited in the moderation room of companies (Couldry & Mejias, 2019). Nonetheless, user engagement is an important force behind the proliferation of mockvertising and thus it can locate itself with different audiences and halt the old advertising formats.

## Ethical Considerations

Although platforms increase the extent and effect of mockvertising, they present the possibility of ethical biases due to the risk of misunderstandings, feedback, and stereotypes. Such factors are extremely important since satirical material exists within the realms of a complicated cultural and social environment where humour has both empowering and destructive potential.

The risk of misinterpretation is also a major one because the nature of satire which is based on irony and exaggeration may be interpreted as approval or as misinformation. In 2020 the parody of a skincare company in TikTok (where the product attributes were satire to a point of ridicule), was mistakenly perceived by some of the viewers as a real advertisement and resulted in misunderstanding and mistrust (Abidin, 2021). On the same foot, the mockvertisements with the aim of combining commercial messages and political motives (the political advertisements mockvertisements) can also be weaponized and used in divisive situations, elevating misinformation unless framed with the extra understanding of criticizing it (Wardle & Derakhshan, 2017). The best way creators can avoid this risk is to ensure that they strike a balance between humour and clarity, but especially in those cases where context collapses across heterogeneous audiences (Marwick & Boyd, 2011).

There is also the risk of backlash because satirical content might insult or marginalize the audience in the event that it is seen as thoughtless. A 2018 YouTube parody of a high-end fashion company that was concerned with the cultural appropriation it was guilty of was criticized because of accidentally stereotyping marginalized groups, which illustrates the thin line between criticism and aggression (Hess, 2019). The fact that brands resort to mockvertising activities also exposes them to backlash in case their jokes are considered as pandering or exploitative. To exemplify, in 2019, a fast-food chain headlined its sarcasm-based campaign targeting veganism which caused uproar among plant-based customers and hurt their trust in brands (Banet-Weiser, 2012). These events explain why cultural awareness should be used in satirical materials, especially in the online international arena.

The stigmatization of Stereotypes is another ongoing moral issue, because mockvertising depends on jokes, which may propagate the damaging stereotypes when created insensitively. Serious departures such as satirical parodies of gendered advertising, e.g. can replicate stereotypes, when they rely on dated beliefs as a source of the laughs, which was common in parodies of female identity in beauty advertising, created in the first part of the 2000s (Stache & Zayer, 2015). On the same note, the mockvertisement against ethnic or cultural brands may end up reinforcing racial viewpoints and turnoff viewers, defeating the potential subversive effect (Hess, 2019). Artists and companies should foresee inclusivity so that the satire does not attack the marginalized, weakening their ranks.

All this is further complicated by the dynamics on the platform. Engagement algorithms can heighten mockvertisements that are sensationalistic or controversial at the expense of more subtle critiques (Bucher, 2018). At the same time, corporate moderation paves the way to chilling satirical content presenting challenges to brand interests, restricting its subversive potential (Gillespie, 2018). In order to overcome such obstacles, the creators and brands should employ ethical guidelines that focus on cultural sensitivity, openness, and responsibility, so that mockvertising can continue to be a means of empowerment, not division.

The important contribution of platforms to the spread of mockvertising demonstrates how they were changing the consumer culture. With algorithms driving satirical content to the global audience, consumer engagement leads to a culture of participation by bringing forth a participatory culture that challenges corporate discoursing. Nevertheless, the moral issues to be dealt with are backlash, stereotyping and misinterpretation, which are poised to compromise the subversiveness of mockvertising. With the changes in platforms, the effects on the satire materials will keep evolving, thus necessitating further research and consideration by researchers, authors, and audiences.

## SECTION 5: THE CONSUMER CULTURE AND BRAND IMPLICATIONS

In the context of the role of platforms in enhancing the status of mockvertising discussed in Section 4, the present section considers the immense ramifications of mockvertising on the consumer culture and brand strategies. As humour and satire redefine digital advertising, mockvertising proves to be one of the most transformational, as it not only forces brands to adjust to that of the participatory, cynical consumer but it also gives audiences the capability of co-creating and criticizing commercial narratives. The subversive quality of mockvertising, explained by a historical evolution of humour (Section 1), its satirical dynamics (Section 3), and its amplification due to a platform (Section 4), challenges the traditional advertising models, which brands are forced to pursue a very thin line between relatability and authenticity. It is in this section where the author investigates the adoption of mockvertising by brands in an attempt to seem subversive, the roles of consumers in creating the narrations of brands, and the long-term impact of mockvertising on advertising conventions and consumers. The combination of various research and case studies lays out this part to place mockvertising into the changing system of consumer culture and pinpoint how potentially it acts as a revolutionizing process of relationships between brands and consumers or concerns the commodification of satire.

### Changing brand strategies

The emergence of the mockvertising as a satirical form of online advertising (Section 2) has led to a unique culture of brands implementing novel strategies, of being humorous and subversive, to meet the consumer needs of authenticity and relatability. Since platforms propagate satirical content (Section 4), brands have realized the need to shift to self-conscience, ironic communication instead of polished, persuasive communication, which is compatible with cynical users. This is an indication of a broader cultural shift where consumers, mainly in the Gen Z and Millennium, are more concerned with brands that captivate them and support their beliefs than with conventional advertising (Fromm & Read, 2018). The use of mockvertising helps brands create an impression of playfulness, transparency, or subversion, thus leaning on humour to give their presence a more human feel and be able to stand out in a highly competitive digital world.

A major trend is meta-advertising, when companies employ an ironic approach based on a sense of humour to laugh at themselves or marketing cliches, as in the explanation of the mechanisms of satire (Section 3). As an example, Wendy X account is considered to be a standard in this strategy, by making jokes at the expense of rival companies such as McDonalds has established itself as an edgy, down-to-earth brand. Engagements on its 2017 campaign where McDonalds use of frozen beef was light-heartedly ridiculed earned millions of engagements, with posts such as, "We never freeze our beef, unlike some clowns" relying on irony as a means of criticizing the industry standards (Serazio, 2021). The approach coincides with the consumer demand of authenticity (Section 1) given that the satirical attitude makes Wendy feel akin to a conversation and not a corporate communication retrospection that creates a connection with audiences.

The 2010 Old Spice campaign, the Man Your Man Could Smell Like, is another such example - it is a parody of masculine cliches in shaving advertisements that is ridiculously funny, and full of braggadocio. Via a reactionary YouTube and Twitter campaign, the use of incongruity allowed the creation of a situation that poked fun at advertising tropes as well as gained the brand name over 50 million views and rekindled the Old Spice market share (Banet-Weiser, 2012). Taking a more light-hearted approach to advertising, in the shape of mockvertising, allowed Old Spice to cut through the noise by emphasizing that it understands the consumer market it was appealing to (Section 4). Another example is the viral video of the Dollar Shave Club in 2012, Our Blades Are F***ing Great, applying deadpan humour to parody the extortionate pricing system of the razor market that turns the profit of middlemen into flimsy products, as line at the end of the video: Expensive sh*t liquidated by middlemen that turns into cheap razor shi*t (Holt, 2016). It is through such ad campaigns that mockvertising can be seen to capitalize on brands trying to seem subversive due to the access to the satirical tools of exaggeration and irony (Section 3) to generate cultural currency.

There are dangers of embracing mockvertising though. Companies need to walk on the thin line of authenticity and simpering because anything not genuine will only make customers feel offended. In one example of the ethical dangers of using satire as fodder, a fast-food chain ran a 2019 campaign poking fun at veganism to push burgers but did not take into account the backlash it triggered against plant-based buyers feeling attacked (Hess, 2019). Furthermore, the subversive aspect of mockvertising can be easily co-opted by its commercial principles and all of its subversive potential may be lost, as it is done by brands (Couldry & Mejias, 2019). Since platforms noticeably intensify brand-driven satire (Section 4), the issue is finding a way to sustain credibility when performing a type of humour that is founded on criticism. Successful brands, such as Patagonia that launched the #DontBuyThisJacket campaign (Section 3) prioritise their satire with their sincere ideology, such as environmental responsibility, so that their subversive position does not seem pretentious (Chua & Banerjee, 2015).

## Consumer Empowerment

The concept of mockvertising has given consumers power since they are placed on a similar platform with the brands in creating the story of the brand, and this has been enhanced by the participatory culture of online sphere (Section 4). The co-creation and criticism of advertising by consumers via platforms are alternatives to the established hierarchies of adviser and consumer (Section 3) since the practice has been defined as a challenge to the corporate authority (Section 3). Such empowerment is linked to democratization of humour in digital advertising (Section 1) democratization, in which audiences' control 'unparalleled power with user-generated content, memes, and viral campaigns.

Consumer empowerment is related to co-creation because users of platforms create their own satirical content that changes perceptions of brands. TikTok users parody advertisements of some brands to criticize consumerism, including parodies of fast-fashion brands, one of them, the company Shein, criticizing the lack of scrupulousness of the company through humour (Abidin, 2021). One TikTok trend in 2022 involved people stitching Shein promotional videos with mocking commentary and showing off poor quality clothing to chide the low Shein prices, and videos have earned over 15 million views. TikTok created those user-generated, also known as mockvertisements, which enable consumers to hold brands to account, which is in line with their concept of ethical consumption (Shifman, 2014). Equally, the X movements such as #DistractinglySexy (Section 2) enabled female researchers to mock sexist advertising cliches and gave rise to an international discussion of gender stereotyping (Huntington, 2019).

Empowerment also entails critique, consumer-driven satire representing an attempt to discredit corporate stories and to demand responsibility. Mockvertisements of the user-created community on YouTube, including dystopian-themed corporate advertising against tech giants, like parodies of Amazon labour practices, are popularized via crowd interaction and some have generated millions of views (Hess, 2019). The increasing intensity of these critiques, compounded by the algorithms of the platforms (Section 4), put pressure on brands to stay on top of matters such as labour exploitation or environmental damage, as wore evident in the ensuing consumer outrage in the case of the Greenpeace KitKat affair (Section 3). Indeed, by engaging in the mockvertising process, the consumers also exercise agency, and they are now making the advertising area a contested space in which their presence influences both cultural and corporate results (Jenkins, 2006).

Mockvertising empowers consumers and encourages a participatory consumer culture, in which an audience of consumers is no longer a passive receiver, but rather engaging critique and/or maker. This is analogous to the Stuart Hall-the introduction of encoding/decoding model (Section 1), since the consumer-as-novelty (the person who consumes the brand-messages) will encoder/decoder messages in a critical manner, dismissing manipulative discourses and co-producing an alternative discourse (Hall, 1980). But there is no universal empowerment. The algorithms of the platform can give more Weight to the work of powerful developers, making less prominent voices invisible, and corporate moderation affects the censorship of the condemning voices that can damage them to brands (Gillespie, 2018). These limitations notwithstanding, the participatory aspect of mockvertising gives consumers agency against the production of spectacle of consumerism that redefines brand-consumer relations in the digital societies (Debord, 1967).

## Long-Term Effects

It has long-term consequences on the norms of advertising and consumer reception because of the rise of the mockvertising due to the platform effects and consumer involvement (Section 4). With brands and audiences increasingly accepting the use of satire, mockvertising has the power to reshape advertising as it brings up the concern over desensitization and commoditization.

***Republicizing Advertising:*** Mockvertising is working against the persuasive, one-way approach to traditional advertising, desensitizing satire as a viable positioning technique. Such brands as Wendy and Patagonia have also established novel precedents in a self-aware, ironic in nature of an advertisement campaign allowing engagement instead of trying to persuade, which then imbues the industry as a whole (Serazio, 2021). To illustrate the point, one may consider the successful satirical marketing strategy of Old Spice that influenced other competitors by introducing humorous, meta-advertisement methods into the industry, moving towards transparency and sending a message where everyone can relate (Banet-Weiser, 2012). This is reflective of consumer wishes that brands be authentic (Section 1), and the audiences punish those that consider manipulation rather than welcome criticism. In the long term, mockvertising can transform advertising into a cooperative, dialogic one, and in that ecosystem brands and consumers actively collaborate by co-production of stories (Jenkins, 2006). Yet, this transition also threatens to make irony the baseline strategy, which negatively affects the authentic branding process in case a majority of these campaigns end up defining the ironic approach (Holt, 2016).

Desensitization to Satire: The excessive use of mockvertising, especially by companies, will lead to desensitization of the subversive abilities of satire to people. Due to the ubiquity of satirical content, viewers can be conditioned to be more acceptable with irony and, therefore, less likely to induce critical thinking (Couldry & Mejias, 2019). It has been observed that excessive exposure to humorous advertisements may further the onset of what is known as ad fatigue, when audiences tune out overtly ironic messages and 60 percent of Gen Z predict they will distrust brands which embrace humour too readily (Edelman, 2023). This desensitization endangers the performance of mockvertising, because it relies upon shocking the audiences with unexpected critique (Section 3). An example is that brand-based parody, in which fast-food restaurants parody their rivals, has become so common that some viewers will no longer take the satirical commercials seriously because of trust deterioration (Hess, 2019). To address this, the brands should avoid the excessive levels of humour and sarcasm but instead, the use of humour should serve an essential purpose and not be a selling point as a marketing gimmick.

Commodification of Satire: The presence of debilitating, long-term appropriation of mockvertising by brands and its long-term commercialization is a potential danger to its subversive properties as it turns into an instrument of profit rather than criticism. With brand driven satire being amplified through platforms (Section 4), the first goal of mockvertising, criticizing consumer culture, can be usurped by commercial purposes thus answering to the original concept of spectacle (Debord, 1967). As another example, the promo of the Burger King with the name of McWhopper (Section 2) can be viewed as more of a brand promotion than as the actual critique, which can be seen as an example of commoditizing satire (Holt, 2016). This commercialization poses the threat of losing appreciation by audiences of the sincerity of satire, which has been apparent with the public reaction against brands that are believed to make money off of social concerns (Banet-Weiser, 2012). In order to maintain the critical edge of mockvertising, brands, and those who create it should focus on remaining ethical in their interactions, making sure that satire subverts power configurations, rather than endorsing them (Hess, 2019).

The future evolution of the mockvertising is that it can be iterative, a factor that stimulates innovation and causes major drawbacks at the same time as the possible victim of its glory. It helps to redefine the rules of advertising and, therefore, creates a more critical, active consumer in the culture, but taken to an extreme, it can lead to desensitization and commercialization. With satirical processes becoming shaped by the platforms they use, brands and consumers will need to balance between these forces to ensure that the mockvertising paradigm will be able to continue its transformative process.

The consumer culture and brand strategy implications of mockvertising also serve to support the idea of digital advertising morphing into its new existence driven by mockvertising. Through satirical tactics, brands can appease to consumer requirements of authenticity, and consumers established with power remodel narratives by means of re-creation and criticism. The long-term consequences, however, including the redefinition of norms, desensitization, and commodification, have to be paid special attention to in order to keep the subversive power of satire intact. The future of consumer culture is inevitably intertwined with mockvertising as a way of questioning in addition to redefining the realms of advertisement, trade and criticism.

## CONCLUSION

Mockvertising and humour are beginning to play an influential role in online advertising, restructuring the consumer culture by preventing the typical instance of a top-down brand communication. Section 1 was able to chronologically explain the history of the development of humour over the years, starting with print and television, to the evolution of the digital space whereby platforms such as X, TikTok, and YouTube have democratized humour and allowed satires produced by viewers to thrive (Jenkins, 2006). The democratization is also connected with the consumer expectations in authenticity and entertainment, where younger demographics will be potential heavy users of brands that can entertain them through wit and relatability (Fromm & Read, 2018). In the section 2, they have defined what is mockvertising, which is the satirical kind of advertising that criticizes consumer culture by exaggerating properties, irony, and subversion, the example of Greenpeace KitKat parody and the viral video of Dollar Shave Club is a demonstration of its cultural influence (Huntington, 2019; Serazio, 2021).

By examining the functions of incongruity, superiority, and relief as properties of subverting societal norms, capitalism, and the advertisement tropes, Section 3 also discussed how the mechanisms of satire can be used to bring about critical engagement, such as through the case study of Patagonia and its method in realizing an anti-capitalist sentiment in its own advertisement, namely, the advertisement about not buying its jacket (Gray et al., 2009; Chua & Banerjee, 2015). Section 4 discussed how platforms exacerbate mockvertising, because of the priorities of its algorithms to show engaging, funny content, and the fact that letting users contribute via memes and remixes makes it go viral (Bucher, 2018; Shifman, 2014). Yet, this morphing poses ethical dangers, which are misinterpretation or propagation of stereotypes, so it should be handled cautiously (Hess, 2019). Section 5 examined the consequences of mockvertising on consumer culture, namely, the attempts of brands to seem more relatable by applying satirical rhetoric, the consumers co-mediating and critiquing the stories, and the risk of long-term implications, which leads to desensitization or commodification (Banet-Weiser, 2012; Couldry & Mejias, 2019). Taken together, these sections highlight the dual role of mockvertising as something that puts more power in the hands of consumers to fight against corporate power at risk of being coopted by that very system upon which it criticizes. Through its use of humour and satire, mockvertising leads to a participatory consumer culture in which media audiences are collectively contributing to understanding of brands in accordance with the encoding/decoding theory advocated by Stuart Hall (Hall, 1980). Its platform-enamoured amplification is a boon to its reach, yet the ethical issue of the satire prevents not constantly deliberating on what it means (Gillespie, 2018). Mockvertising therefore is the paradigm shift in advertisement that has changed advertisement into a conflict area where comedy, criticism, and business merge.

## REFERENCES


Abidin, C. (2021). From "networked publics" to "refracted publics": A companion framework for researching TikTok. *Social Media + Society*, *7*(2), 1–12. DOI: 10.1177/20563051211019796

Attardo, S. (2014). *Encyclopedia of humour studies*. SAGE Publications.

Banet-Weiser, S. (2012). *Authentic™: The politics of ambivalence in a brand culture*. NYU Press.

Bucher, T. (2018). *If...Then: Algorithmic power and politics*. Oxford University Press.

Chua, J., & Banerjee, S. (2015). To buy or not to buy: Patagonia's "Don't Buy This Jacket" campaign. *Journal of Business Ethics*, *131*(1), 257–268. DOI: 10.1007/s10551-014-2281-8

Couldry, N., & Mejias, U. A. (2019). *The costs of connection: How data is colonizing human life and appropriating it for capitalism*. Stanford University Press.

Debord, G. (1967). *The society of the spectacle*. Zone Books.

Edelman. (2023). *Edelman trust barometer 2023*. Edelman. https://www.edelman.com/trust/sidebar/2023-trust-barometer

Eisend, M. (2018). Humour in advertising: A review and agenda for future research. *Journal of Advertising*, *47*(4), 398–414. DOI: 10.1080/00913367.2018.1532859

Ferguson, M. A., & Ford, T. E. (2008). Disparagement humour: A theoretical and empirical review of psychoanalytic, superiority, and social identity theories. *Humour*, *21*(3), 283–312. DOI: 10.1515/HUMOUR.2008.014

Fromm, J., & Read, A. (2018). *Marketing to Gen Z: The rules for reaching this vast—and very different—generation of influencers*. AMACOM.

Gillespie, T. (2018). *Custodians of the internet: Platforms, content moderation, and the hidden decisions that shape social media*. Yale University Press.

Gray, J., Jones, J. P., & Thompson, E. (2009). *Satire TV: Politics and comedy in the post-network era*. NYU Press.

Hall, S. (1980). Encoding/decoding. In Hall, S., Hobson, D., Lowe, A., & Willis, P. (Eds.), *Culture, media, language* (pp. 128–138). Hutchinson.

Hess, A. (2019). The risks and rewards of feminist satire in the age of social media. *Feminist Media Studies*, *19*(6), 871–886. DOI: 10.1080/14680777.2018.1498148

Holt, D. B. (2004). *How brands become icons: The principles of cultural branding*. Harvard Business School Press.

Holt, D. B. (2016). *Branding in the age of social media*. Harvard Business Review Press.

Huntington, H. E. (2019). Satire, subversion, and the digital age: The case of mockvertising. *Television & New Media, 20*(8), 791–806. DOI: 10.1177/1527476418809754

Jenkins, H. (2006). *Convergence culture: Where old and new media collide*. NYU Press.

Kennedy, M. (2020). 'If the rise of the TikTok dance and e-girl aesthetic has taught us anything, it's that teenage girls rule the internet right now': TikTok celebrity, girls and the coronavirus crisis. *European Journal of Cultural Studies, 23*(6), 1069–1076. DOI: 10.1177/1367549420945341

Knobel, M., & Lankshear, C. (2007). Online memes, affinities, and cultural production. In Knobel, M., & Lankshear, C. (Eds.), *A new literacies sampler* (pp. 199–227). Peter Lang.

Marwick, A. E., & Boyd, D. (2011). I tweet honestly, I tweet passionately: Twitter users, context collapse, and the imagined audience. *New Media & Society, 13*(1), 114–133. DOI: 10.1177/1461444810365313

Meyer, J. C. (2000). Humour as a double-edged sword: Four functions of humour in communication. *Communication Theory, 10*(3), 310–331. DOI: 10.1111/j.1468-2885.2000.tb00194.x

Serazio, M. (2021). *The other influencer: The rise of the micro-celebrity in the digital age*. Polity Press.

Shifman, L. (2014). *Memes in digital culture*. MIT Press.

Shouse, E. (2020). The role of relief in humour: A psychological perspective. *Journal of Media Psychology, 32*(4), 189–197. DOI: 10.1027/1864-1105/a000274

Stache, L. C., & Zayer, L. T. (2015). Unpacking the #LikeAGirl campaign: Gender stereotypes and empowerment in advertising. *Journal of Advertising Research, 55*(4), 398–409. DOI: 10.2501/JAR-2015-021

Van Dijck, J. (2013). *The culture of connectivity: A critical history of social media*. Oxford University Press.

Wardle, C., & Derakhshan, H. (2017). *Information disorder: Toward an interdisciplinary framework for research and policymaking*. Council of Europe. https://rm.coe.int/information-disorder-report-november-2017/1680764666

Wettergren, Å., & Hillgren, P. (2013). The emotional politics of viral activism: Greenpeace's KitKat campaign. *Ephemera, 13*(2), 393–413.

Williamson, J. (1978). *Decoding advertisements: Ideology and meaning in advertising*. Marion Boyars.

Chapter 14

# Evaluation of People's Experiences of Using Artificial Intelligence Technologies to Find Solutions to Their Emotional Needs

**Ferihan Ozmen Ayaz**
https://orcid.org/0000-0003-3277-5188
*Gaziantep University, Turkey*

**Gülizar Yasin**
https://orcid.org/0009-0007-4345-2436
*Gaziantep University, Turkey*

## ABSTRACT

*The use of new media technologies is becoming increasingly widespread, and the use of artificial intelligence technologies in solving emotional problems is becoming increasingly common. The purpose of this study is to analyze how artificial intelligence technologies are used by people with different demographic characteristics in solving emotional problems. For this purpose, semi-structured interviews were conducted with 22 individuals selected through a purposive sampling technique, and these interviews were analyzed using thematic analysis. According to the findings an increasing number of people are resorting to artificial intelligence tools for almost all kinds of problems, and even if a few participants have preconceived notions, they*

DOI: 10.4018/979-8-3373-4267-2.ch014

*feel a desire to consult AI on various topics such as dream interpretation and psychological analyses. AI tools, often viewed as "virtual companions," are becoming a significant player in people's mental processes in daily life.*

## INTRODUCTION

Since the 1990s, new technologies have permeated all aspects of daily life. Individuals utilize these technologies for news consumption, entertainment, communication, information retrieval, and commerce, among other purposes. The advancement of internet technologies has facilitated the widespread adoption of artificial intelligence (AI) tools. Decision-making in professional and personal contexts is increasingly influenced by digital technologies. From a sociological perspective, digital technologies shape culture, habits, and routines. These technologies are employed not only to enhance professional competencies but also to inform decisions related to emotional well-being. When confronted with emotional distress or uncertainty, individuals frequently seek solutions. Artificial intelligence (AI) technologies have emerged as practical tools for addressing such needs. Consequently, the use of AI for emotional support has become prevalent for many people.

In the literature, there are many foreign studies on the relationship between psychological well-being and artificial intelligence. These studies emphasise themes such as the role of chatbots in the treatment of depression and anxiety, using artificial intelligence technologies to support social and emotional well-being, mental health, and the use of artificial intelligence technologies (Denecke et al., 2021; Bendig et al., 2022; Dhimolea et al., 2022). Denecke et al (2021) state that with the help of artificial intelligence, the way people understand each other and respond accordingly is fed by chat bot systems, that is, systems that need to communicate with a user, and that such systems are mostly used in the field of health, and point out that this is similar to the patient-therapist relationship in relation to mental health.

Dhimolea et al. (2022) state that artificial intelligence-based technologies such as chat bots, virtual assistants, and socially helpful robots have gained features that can help individuals whose social and emotional well-being is in danger, and examine the role of these technologies in solving increasing problems in society, such as depression and anxiety. Similarly, D'Alfonso (2020) notes that artificial intelligence is being integrated into smartphone apps and online platforms aimed at enhancing the user experience and improving mental health. According to him, through the analysis of an individual's 'digital exhaust' and activities on social media, their digital footprints across platforms can be used to interpret behaviour and mental health insight. Such analysis is important as it allows for more personalised mental health support. According to Corrigan (2004), the majority of people do not get the treatment they need due to social stigma. Minerva and Giubilini (2023) also point out that lack of resources and lack of access a shortcomings. Additionally, Bickmore et al (2005) have made a study about AI technologies, and in the study, 21 adults aged 62-84 received AI-supported interactions every day for 2 months, and after these interactions were completed, it was revealed that the AI agent in question was accepted and liked by these individuals.

This study contributes to understanding the internal dynamics of communication among individuals who utilize artificial intelligence (AI) to address emotional challenges within an evolving digital sociological context. Examining individual experiences with AI technologies in relation to psychological issues provides insights that may inform broader solutions to similar problems.

Artificial intelligence-supported platforms have become a means of seeking emotional support. From this perspective, platformisation has reshaped individual identity, cultural practices, and power relations. Individuals are becoming subjects in a different way in digital environments, using artificial intelligence-supported platforms for emotional support to meet their own emotional needs. By shaping their emotional bonds through platforms, they are reshaping their sense of identity and belonging in a sociological context. AI-based emotional support services reproduce power relations, encode cultural norms, and offer a new space where digital identities are constructed. This study centres on the individual's subjective experience in the platformisation process, demonstrating that the ways in which artificial intelligence technologies respond to individuals' emotional needs show that platformisation operates not only through economic capital but also through emotional and cultural capital. Therefore, this situation is directly linked to power and identity relations in the digital age.

## 1. THE CONCEPT OF ARTIFICIAL INTELLIGENCE AND EMOTIONAL SATISFACTION

Under this heading, 'the development of artificial intelligence technologies,' 'the new dimension of artificial intelligence and the search for emotional support,' and 'major studies' are detailed under separate headings.

### 1.1. The development of artificial intelligence technologies

The emergence of the Industrial Revolution towards the end of the 17th century and the invention of the first steam engine marked the beginning of a new era in world history. The start of the mechanisation process was followed by the introduction of electricity and mass production processes, and automatic machines and software operations have become increasingly widespread over the years (Öztemel, 2020).

Artificial intelligence technologies have taken their final form through many discoveries accumulated over time. The Egyptians used binary code as early as 2400 BC, as part of the 'Horus-Eye' myth, to count grains and measure the quantity of liquids. In the 3rd century BCE, symbols such as hexagrams and trigrams were used for binary progression in the I Ching or Book of Changes, which is believed to have been revealed to Fu Xi. Gottfried Wilhelm Leibniz, who utilised the similarity between the concepts of the I Ching, used to transform religious symbols into meaningful messages, and the binary system, examined this numbering system in his article 'Explanation of Binary Arithmetic' in the 17th century, and introduced a binary number system. This number system enabled the capture of an important stage in mechanisation (Güllü, 2021, p.21).

The intellectual foundations of artificial intelligence technologies can be traced back to Descartes (1596-1650). Descartes (1999) compared humans to machines that operate like clocks. This analogy can be considered one of the earliest expressions of humanity's predisposition towards mechanisation. Al-Jazari's (1136-1206) robot drawings are considered to be the starting point for artificial intelligence studies. At this point, it is necessary to mention the concept of 'cybernetics'. Cybernetics derives from the ancient Greek word 'Kübernetes' and the Latin word 'Gobernare' and was named as a scientific discipline by Norbert Wiener in 1948. Wiener defined the concept as 'the control and communication system of all organised systems, machines, and animals, whether living or non-living.' Cezeri conducted studies on cybernetics and established its principles (Çırak and Yörük, 2015, p. 178; Bülbül and Öztürk, 2024, p. 376). Apart from El-Cezeri, other important figures in the field of cybernetics during the same period include the German saint, philosopher, and scholar Albertus Magnus (1193-1280) and the English scholar and philosopher Roger Bacon (1214-1294) (Sivri, 2024). After these periods, the process of mechanising human behaviour continued, and in 1884, Charles Babbage's (1792–1871) invention, the 'Difference Engine,' the first calculating machine, attracted attention due to its memory, processing capacity, and ability to play chess and checkers (Schultz and Ellen-Schultz, 2007).

Claude Shannon stated in 1950 that computers could play chess. In his article titled 'A Mathematical Theory of Communication,' he introduced the concept of 'bit' and defined the field of information theory (Güllü, 2021, p. 21). Artificial intelligence was officially mentioned at a workshop held at Dartmouth College in 1956, and the first artificial intelligence session was organised at this conference (Mijwil, 2015, p. 2). This workshop, organised by John McCarthy, was attended by important figures such as Marvin L. Minsky (Massachusetts Institute of Technology-MIT), Nathaniel Rochester (International Business Machines-IBM), and Claude

Shannon (Bell Laboratories) (Dick, 2019). Prior to this workshop, Alan Turing held a conference on artificial intelligence in 1947 (McCarthy, 2007).

It can be said that modern artificial intelligence studies were conducted during and after World War II. Alan Mathison Turing changed the outcome of the war with his invention of the first fully automatic code-breaking machine, which he named 'Bombe' (Acar, 2020). In his article, 'Computing Machinery and Intelligence,' Turing (1950) discusses the question, 'Can machines think?' By combining the words 'machine' and 'think,' Turing laid the intellectual foundations for artificial intelligence. In 1959, Arthur Samuel, who worked at IBM, developed a machine that could play checkers better than humans. Samuel became famous as the first artificial intelligence researcher to coin the term 'machine learning.' This revealed that machines could also learn, which surprised the public (Martinez, 2019, p. 15).

In the following years, important artificial intelligence programmes such as Aziz (1961), Benzeşim (1963), Eliza (1965), Bilgin (1970), and Stajyer (1979) were developed. The first human-like intelligent robot, named WABOT-I, was built in Japan in 1972 (Acar, 2020; Kutlusoy, 2019). Following criticism of artificial intelligence studies, between 1974 and 1980, governments began to stop funding artificial intelligence studies. This period is known as the 'Artificial Intelligence Winter.' However, the rivalry between the United Kingdom and Japan later turned into an artificial intelligence race (Öztürk and Şahin, 2018).

In the period after 1980, Frank Rosenblatt from Cornell University explained neural network technology in his article on the concept of perceptrons (sensors). Marvin Minsky and Seymour Papert, on the other hand, detailed the mathematics of perceptrons in their book 'Perceptrons.' While perceptron models paved the way for connectionist models, the 'symbolist' artificial intelligence model, which works with symbols, paved the way for connectionist models (Martinez, 2019, p. 15).

One of the most significant developments in artificial intelligence was IBM's 1997 programme 'Deep Blue' defeating world chess champion Garry Kasparov in a chess match. Kasparov lost to a programme that could process 200 million chess moves per second. This event demonstrated that computers could outperform humans (Schultz and Ellen-Schultz, 2007).

The introduction of the Roomba vacuum cleaner into homes in the 2000s is an example of artificial intelligence technology. Subsequently, artificial intelligence technologies began to be used on social media platforms, and in the following period, driverless cars even began to be used in the United States (Acar, 2020; İnce, 2017).

Today, different artificial intelligence tools are used for specific tasks. For example, ChatGPT and Copilot (Bing) are used for text-based tasks, while Midjourney, Dall-E, Stable Diffusion, Adobe Firefly, Google's video-generating artificial intelligence DeepMind, and Google's 3D object-generating artificial intelligence Dreamfusion are used for visual production. There are many other applications similar to these. In addition to artificial intelligence that can perform a single task, there are predictions for the future that Artificial General Intelligence models capable of performing many different tasks may emerge. Artificial General Intelligence is defined as artificial intelligence that is indistinguishable from humans in all respects and possesses cognitive, emotional, and social intelligence (Haenlein and Kaplan, 2019, p. 2).

## 1.2. A new dimension in the search for artificial intelligence and emotional support

Under this main heading, the topics of 'anthropomorphism', 'parasocial relationships', 'platformisation and power', and 'key studies on the subject' are addressed in separate sections.

### 1.2.1. Antropomorfizm

The need to communicate with non-human entities as if they were human beings by attributing human qualities to them dates back to ancient times. The concept of anthropomorphism derives from the Greek words 'anthropos' (human) and 'morphe' (form) and refers to the perception of a non-human entity as having human characteristics. Many thinkers, such as Xenophanes, Isaac Newton, Charles Darwin, Francis Bacon, David Hume, Sigmund Freud, and Ernst Gombrich, have drawn attention to this human tendency in their teachings and have put forward ideas that encourage people to think about its positive or negative effects (Guthrie, 2013).

Hume (1957) uses the following expressions on this subject: '*There is a universal tendency among humans to perceive all beings as themselves and to attribute these qualities to every object. Unless corrected by experience and thought, we naturally attribute bad or good intentions to everything that harms or pleases us.*'

In the age of artificial intelligence, this tendency continues, and artificial intelligence has become a tool that can be confided in, talked to, and chatted with, just like a friend (Sarıoğlu and Güregen, 2024, p. 84). For example, ELIZA, considered the first chatbot to emerge in the 1970s, was a natural language processing programme developed by Joseph Weizenbaum at MIT, designed to respond to users like a psychotherapist. The researcher in question was surprised to discover that artificial intelligence could lead to strong delusional thoughts in perfectly normal people, and spent much of his life warning about the dangers of treating artificial intelligence as if it were human (Weizenbaum, 1972; Weizenbaum, 1976). According to Nass and Moon (2000), people unconsciously apply many social behaviour practices, such as politeness, reciprocity, stereotyping, and the use of human language, to computers. Placani (2024) points out in his study that placing such importance on artificial intelligence can lead to incorrect and exaggerated results, emphasising that it is not artificial intelligence itself but the developers, companies, governments, and regulatory bodies behind the system that should be considered in terms of safety.

Chatbots are computer programs that mimic human language through a text-based dialogue system called a 'bot,' allowing users to communicate as if they were chatting. These technologies enable emotional responses to be conveyed from computers to humans. It has been observed that chatbots are used to reduce loneliness, regardless of whether they are human or not. Additionally, their ability to respond without judgment encourages people to open up to them more transparently than they would to other people (Zumstein & Hundertmark, 2017; Moussawi et al., 2021; Brandtzaeg & Folstad, 2018; Skjuve et al., 2021; Weizenbaum, 1996; Lucas et al., 2014; Zehnder et al., 2021). For example, in a study comparing doctors with artificial intelligence in terms of empathy, based on questions asked to 195 randomly selected patients, artificial intelligence scored significantly higher than doctors in both quality and empathy. It was found that the empathetic or highly empathetic responses of the chatbot were 9.8 times higher than those of doctors. Therefore, nearly half (45%) of ChatGPT's responses were evaluated as empathetic, while less than 5% of doctors' responses were found to be empathetic (Ayers et al., 2023).

The ease of access to chatbots also encourages their use (Brandtzeg & Folstad, 2018). Studies indicate that people who suffer from loneliness are more likely to turn to these tools. These studies indicate that artificial intelligence supports people in this regard (Epley et al., 2007; Eyssel and Reich, 2013; Waytz et al., 2010; Waytz and Epley, 2012). Similarly, Merrill Jr. et al. (2022) indicate that social robots serve as ideal surrogate friends. The study in question indicates that a disembodied AI friend increases the perceived usefulness and willingness to recommend it to lonely individuals. Song et al. (2014) similarly indicate that lonely individuals tend to connect more with mediated (media-based) environments. In these environments, individuals tend to idealise and overly personalise the other party (Walther, 1996). Eyyssel and Reich (2013) found that lonely people tend to humanise the social robot FloBi more. Thus, individuals attempt to overcome deficiencies in their lives by interacting with technical devices and seek to satisfy their need for social contact and connection through artificial intelligence tools (Luczak et al., 2003; Pradhan et al., 2019; Li et al., 2020).

In summary, artificial intelligence (AI) tools are increasingly adopted by individuals seeking to address emotional needs.

### 1.2.2. Parasociological relationships

One of the first studies on parasociological relationships was conducted by Robert Merton in 1943, examining the imaginary relationship between Kate Smith, a leading artist of the time, and her radio listeners (Brown, 2015). Later, in 1956,

Horton and Wohl (1956) used the concept of "parasocial interaction" when explaining the relationship established between TV announcers and viewers. This concept was defined as "one-sided imaginary communication between television viewers and television characters." The concept subsequently gained popularity and was the subject of various studies.

Parasocial relationships facilitate the "power, control, and authority" of those in power in modern times in various ways. These forms of communication are frequently used, especially in the context of economic control. For example, Chung and Cho (2017) analyzed online survey data collected from 400 Korean Wave fans in Singapore in their study examining parasocial relationships, self-disclosure, and the relationship between celebrity endorsement and purchase intention. The study observed that parasocial relationships established with celebrities through social media positively influenced both brand trust and purchase intention.

Parasocial relationships established with artificial intelligence are increasingly taking on an emotional dimension and further enhancing the effectiveness of artificial intelligence in establishing power. For example, a study conducted by Schuetzler et al. (2021) examined whether human-computer interactions could be further personalised by matching consumer personality with an appropriate machine personality using language. The study was based on more than 57,000 chatbot examples and revealed that these chatbots could predict consumer personality during contextual interactions and 'assume personality' as a 'response language'. Matching consumer identity with the appropriate chatbot personality positively affects both consumers' interaction with chatbots and purchase outcomes in interactions involving social gains.

According to Nass and Moon (2000), establishing parasocial relationships with artificial intelligence differs to the extent that it encompasses the individual's sense of identity, enabling them to apply gender stereotypes to their computers and even identify ethnically with computer agents. People exhibit overly learned social behaviours such as politeness and reciprocity towards computers. A specialised television set is perceived to provide better content than a general television set. The depth of social responses to 'computer personality' is significant. Therefore, themes such as identity, culture, and belonging bind people to computers in different ways.

Chatbots typically employ human-like characteristics by using personal pronouns, conversational norms, emotional responses, and other anthropomorphic cues, presenting themselves as trustworthy companions. This creates an illusion of mutual interaction and encourages users to develop trust and affection towards the system (Maeda and Quan-Haase 2024). Recent cases have revealed that individuals form deep bonds with artificial intelligence agents, leading to serious psychological and sometimes fatal consequences. Examples of such cases include AI agents that encourage harmful behaviours such as eating disorders and substance abuse in young people (Ortutay and O'Brien, 2025) and tragic cases where deep bonds formed with chatbots led to death (Xiang, 2023; Horwitz, 2025). As these technologies become more capable and widely adopted, the risk of failing to address parasocial risks also increases. Therefore, developing robust safeguards is a fundamental challenge in ensuring that artificial intelligence serves human well-being rather than harming it (Rath et al. 2025).

When evaluating this entire process, platformisation takes power and control by utilising deep computer-human interactions (van Dijck et al., 2018). Therefore, it can be said that the phenomenon of platformisation has a dimension that shapes social values, redefines power relations and reshapes the public sphere, rather than being merely a technological transformation of digital platforms.

### 1.2.3. Platformisation and power

Online platforms regulate and structure public and private life. Although public institutions and governments officially represent the will of the people, the daily operations and economic models of online platforms are collaborative and manage public policies while governing civil life. The global society, increasingly becoming a 'platform society,' is directed by algorithms, and a global online ecosystem fuelled by data has emerged, with social life evolving in this direction. The platform now occupies a central place in our lives and is active in almost all our daily life applications (van Dijck et al., 2018).

Srnicek (2016) similarly states that platforms are not independent sites, but are strongly interconnected, and that platform capitalism also forms an ecosystem, creating a networked whole of interconnected platforms within a mechanism that shapes the social order.

Platforms determine what is visible, whose voice is heard more, and what content appears to which user, providing an invisible but powerful control mechanism. This reveals the concept of the 'data gaze' and how users are monitored and shaped (Beer, 2017). Platforms also reveal the micro-politics of power relations by censoring, ranking, and regulating the visibility of content (Gillespie, 2018).

Platforms also control individuals' emotional orientations and relational expectations, providing not only information but also emotional management (Schuetzler et al., 2021). Emotions are being transformed into data on human relationships and becoming a tool for economic exploitation; the power to control not only political but also emotional and psychological management is passing into the hands of those who hold it (Couldry and Mejias, 2019).

Individuals construct their identities on these platforms, establishing how they want to be seen, what they value, and what they are attached to through these dynamics, distancing themselves from human relationships as they become more connected to technology (Turkle, 2011). These platforms explain not only individuals' own preferences but also how they use data to generate predictions about future behaviour. Therefore, the presence of data related to individuals' future predictions on these platforms demonstrates that they are at the forefront of power (Zuboff, 2019).

Therefore, platformisation is not merely the proliferation of technological infrastructures, but rather a progression towards a regime of domination in which individuals' emotional, cultural, and social orientations are reshaped by artificial intelligence and algorithms (van Dijck et al., 2018; Couldry and Mejias, 2019; Schuetzler et al., 2021).

In this context, it would be appropriate to mention the concept of 'platform capitalism'. This term is used to describe the position of platforms in the digital economy. Platform capitalism is not merely a matter of technological development; it is also a historical development that transforms the labour process, consumption patterns, social interactions, and even relationships with states. In this context, the concept of 'platform' refers to digital environments that bring together interacting users, producers, consumers, and algorithmic systems (Cases-Cortes et al, 2023).

Platform capitalism is not uniform; various forms of platforms emerge in different sectors and business models. Examples include advertising platforms, cloud platforms, industrial platforms, product platforms, and e-commerce platforms. Chatbots are also one such platform.

Every interaction users have with chatbots is converted into data. The platform owner also uses this data to develop AI chatbots. This situation contributes to the strengthening of companies. As AI-powered chatbots rapidly evolve with data, a dialectic emerges among users' concerns about data privacy violations. A study by Sullivan et al. (2023) found that users expressed privacy concerns in their interactions with artificial intelligence and that although it is necessary for artificial intelligence to collect information from users in order to learn about them, users tend to perceive this unnecessary collection of information as a violation of their privacy.

In the study conducted by Yener et al. (2025), the privacy practices of 12 artificial intelligence-powered healthcare chatbot applications were analysed. As a result, critical gaps that could affect user privacy were identified, such as insufficient transparency during the registration process, limited user control over personal data, and inconsistent compliance with fundamental regulations such as GDPR, HIPAA, and CCPA. Furthermore, the study found that most chatbot applications lack clearly stated cybersecurity measures or explicit procedures for managing data breaches in their privacy policies, leaving users vulnerable and uninformed.

Surveillance capitalism has emerged as a dominant model in which personal data has become a significant economic commodity in the digital age. The term surveillance capitalism was coined by Harvard Business School Professor Shoshana Zuboff in her work The Age of Surveillance Capitalism (Zuboff, 2019). It describes a new form of capitalism that creates personalised profiles summarising users' behaviours and preferences by analysing personal data obtained through internet-based platforms and services. This data is then shared between companies and used within a business model to generate predictions about individual users. Personal data has become extremely important in the digital economy and is leading the way in revenue generation across various sectors (de Medeiros et al., 2024).

In this context, AI chatbot users not only obtain information but also transfer data to a broad ecosystem that connects user data and the digital economy. Chatbot users, through the recommendations they receive, are consciously or unconsciously integrated into surveillance capitalism. For this reason, AI companies are obliged to develop more transparent systems with user consent. Consequently, a data economy model is emerging in platform capitalism where the corporate economic objectives of chatbot platforms take precedence over user data privacy concerns.

### 1.2.4. Main studies

In recent years, AI-powered chatbots have been increasingly used to provide empathy and emotional support to individuals experiencing stressful times (Meng and Dai, 2021). Studies in this field focus on understanding both the potential benefits and possible risks.

A study by Meng and Dai (2021) compared emotional support received from a chatbot with support received from humans and showed that both approaches can be effective in reducing individuals' anxiety and stress. The findings revealed that both humans and chatbots can form a bond through mutual self-disclosure and that this is effective in alleviating anxiety. However, it was noted that when the chatbot did not disclose itself and provide emotional support, the outcome was worse than receiving no response at all. As AI chatbots become more human-like, concerns are growing about their potential impact on users' loneliness and socialisation with real people.

A study conducted by Fang et al. (2025) examined this issue in depth. The study found that voice-based chatbots appear to be more effective than text-based chatbots in reducing loneliness and dependency, but that these advantages diminish at high usage levels, especially with neutral-voiced chatbots. It was noted that personal topics tend to slightly increase loneliness while reducing emotional dependency, whereas non-personal topics are associated with greater dependency among heavy users. Additionally, it was emphasised that higher daily usage is associated with greater loneliness, dependency, and problematic usage and reduces socialisation. It has been reported that individuals with strong emotional attachment tendencies and higher trust in AI chatbots are more likely to experience loneliness and emotional dependency.

A study by Chu et al. (2025) analysed over 30,000 user conversations shared with social chatbots to examine the emotional dynamics of human-AI relationships. The findings indicate that users who are generally young, male, and prone to maladaptive coping styles engage in parasocial interactions ranging from love to cursing. It is noted that chatbots consistently respond in emotionally consistent and affirming ways. In some cases, these dynamics have been described as resembling toxic relationship patterns, including emotional manipulation and self-harm. These findings highlight the need for assurance, ethical design, and public education to preserve the integrity of emotional connections in the age of artificial friendship.

Oktawirawan (2022), on the other hand, focused on the advantages and limitations of chatbots in his study, aiming to understand their use as friends in human life. According to the findings, the empathetic and non-judgmental nature of chatbots allows users to express themselves more freely and openly. It is noted that this may contribute to alleviating feelings of loneliness and indirectly help individuals develop their communication skills with other people. However, the limitations of chatbots, such as their potential to misinterpret the user's intentions and their low ability to distinguish between good and bad, are also highlighted. The study concluded that relationships with chatbots, like relationships with humans, carry not only benefits but also risks. One of the key findings is that chatbots can be an option for making friends, especially when there are no other alternatives for communication.

Herbener and Damholdt (2025) examined the frequency with which Danish high school students engage in friendly conversations with chatbots, the reasons for doing so, and the relationship between this and their sense of social connection. According to the findings, 2.44% of high school students engage in daily conversations with chatbots or seek emotional support, and more importantly, young people with high levels of social disconnection use chatbots for socio-emotional purposes. The study also noted that there were meaningful relationships between various situational triggers for initiating conversations with chatbots, such as low perceived social support, poor mood, self-disclosure, and high loneliness, but that the feeling of friendship with the chatbot was not a trigger.

Xie, Pentina, and Hancock (2023) examined user-AI interaction and relationship development factors, as well as potential negative outcomes, in their study with users of the AI social chatbot Replika. According to the findings of the study, factors such as loneliness, trust, and personalisation of the chatbot trigger consumers' interaction with social chatbots. It was noted that this interaction encourages relationship development on the one hand, but on the other hand, it has the potential to create psychological dependence on the chatbot.

The study titled 'Combating Loneliness with Artificial Intelligence: An AI-Based Emotional Support Model,' conducted by Sullivan et al. (2023), investigated the role of artificial intelligence-supported systems in combating loneliness. The study emphasised that AI companion applications are increasingly being used to meet the emotional needs of individuals experiencing loneliness. The analysis of user content identified five positive themes (perceived human-like characteristics, perceived emotional support, perceived AI friendship, reduced feelings of loneliness, and contribution to mental health) and four negative themes (perceived inattention/ low responsibility, lack of reliability, perceived privacy violation, and AI being found 'annoying'). The study has made an important contribution to the field by addressing human-AI interaction from psychological and sociological perspectives.

The study titled 'ChatGPT as a Solution to Emotional Loneliness: A New Tool for Interpersonal Communication' by Sarıoğlu and Güregen (2024) examined the alleviating effect of AI-powered language models on emotional loneliness. The study noted that while the majority of participants (78%) turned to technological tools (such as watching films/series, browsing social media, and playing games) to cope with loneliness, they had reservations about whether ChatGPT and similar artificial intelligence applications would have a positive effect on loneliness.

Fitzpatrick, Darcy, and Vierhile (2017) provided cognitive behavioral therapy (CBT) to university students exhibiting symptoms of depression and anxiety via a fully automated chatbot (Woebot) over a two-week period. After two weeks, it was confirmed that those in the Woebot group experienced a significant reduction in depression. The number of participants who reported that the bot felt empathetic is noteworthy. Participants referred to the bot as 'it,' 'a friend,' and 'a cute little thing,' indicating that Woebot itself, rather than its developers, was perceived as the source of empathy.

The study 'When The Bot Walks The Talk: Investigating The Foundations of Trust in an Artificial Intelligence (AI) Chatbot' by Lalot and Bertram (2025) shows that people judge AI chatbots in the same way they judge other humans, and that trust mechanisms are based on similar psychological foundations. Additionally, it has been noted that personalised AI chatbots are perceived as more capable and helpful than impersonal chatbots.

In a study conducted by Yin, Jia, and Wakslak (2024), it was found that messages generated by artificial intelligence made recipients feel more heard than messages generated by humans, and that artificial intelligence was better at detecting emotions. However, when recipients realised that a message came from artificial intelligence (rather than a human), they felt less heard.

D-Twins, a personalised AI application designed by Lo and Rau (2025), not only increases trust by reflecting users' feelings of being noticed and heard, but also reduces boredom. The study also noted that high levels of human-like behaviour carry the risk of unmet expectations, and as D-Twins' behaviour becomes more human-like, its association with 'indifference' also increases.

Freitas et al. (2024) evaluated whether AI-powered chatbots can reduce loneliness. The study found that using the AI application for one week reduced loneliness. The most significant reduction occurred on the first day, followed by steady declines in loneliness over the following days. This shows that the first interaction with an AI friend has a significant effect and that this effect quickly balances out over time as participants become accustomed to their AI friends. The study provided evidence that AI friends are important mediators of loneliness-reducing effects and that feeling heard is a mediator with a higher effect on reducing loneliness.

In a study by Kim et al. (2025), it was noted that after four weeks of use by new users, there were significant decreases in loneliness and social anxiety levels. These improvements were attributed to acceptance criteria, such as users opening up to the chatbot and the perceived benefits of the chatbot. The study demonstrates that the active and kind personality of the social chatbot, along with its capacity to offer empathy and comfort, creates a social support effect.

The study conducted by Chinmulgund et al. (2023) examined eight factors, including trust, expertise, predictability, human similarity, ease of use, risk, reputation, and tendency to trust technology, using social response theory. Users experienced characteristics such as politeness and gratitude when interacting with chatbots and therefore attributed the ‘human-like’ factor to the chatbot. ‘Trust’ emerged as the second most important factor among all other factors contributing to users' anthropomorphism in AI-based chatbots.

In a study by Croes et al. (2024), it was investigated whether people were willing to share confidential information with a chatbot and whether they shared more confidential information with a chatbot than with another person. The findings showed that an important feature of human-chatbot communication is that people experience less fear of judgment compared to interactions with another person.

In another study conducted by Croes, Antheunis, and He (2023), the effects of mutual self-disclosure by chatbots on the formation of friendships between humans and chatbots were examined. The study found that there was no significant difference between the conditions in terms of feelings of friendship. However, the results showed that people trusted the chatbot more and perceived it as more empathetic in the mutual self-disclosure condition.

Baskaran et al. (2023) conducted a literature review to identify and organise findings from existing research on emotions in human-AI (artificial intelligence) interactions. In terms of emotion precursors, it was observed that studies on the effects of human characteristics such as age, gender, personality, and culture on emotions are relatively insufficient. This situation suggests that a solid understanding of the effects of individual user characteristics could provide a better understanding of the differences and commonalities in the perception of AI and the outcomes of interaction (Diederich et al, 2022).

A study conducted by Laestadius et al. (2022) based on mental health experiences with the popular chatbot Replika found evidence of harm arising from emotional dependence developed towards Replika. This dependency was noted to resemble patterns observed in human-to-human relationships and was characterised by role-taking; users felt that Replika had its own needs and emotions and that the user should pay attention to them.

In a study conducted by Yuan et al. (2024), the relationship between human-chatbot emotional interaction and users' real-life interpersonal communication was examined. The study findings revealed that the intensity of users' emotional interactions with chatbots could have a negative impact on their real-life interpersonal communication skills, interpersonal relationships, and communication attitudes. In particular, it was observed that the higher the degree of behaviour, impact, and satisfaction of emotional interaction with chatbots, the lower the quality of real-life interpersonal communication. It was noted that despite the potential of chatbots to enrich individual communication life and alleviate loneliness to some extent, virtual interactions carry the risk of weakening real social skills and relationships.

The study by Rijt, Mollo, and Vaassen (2025) examines four real-life examples of chatbot use (information retrieval, customer service, counselling, and friendship) to investigate how human interactions with AI-powered chatbots can harm human dignity. Additionally, they argue that the increasing use of such interactions with chatbots poses a threat to human dignity that has not been sufficiently addressed to date. In particular, it has been argued that such chatbots undermine users' dignity by exhibiting human-like characteristics and encouraging them to behave in ways that are unique to humans. It is stated that this situation will make it impossible to mutually recognise the moral status that forms the basis of dignity, leading to a loss of self-respect, i.e., a kind of moral decay.

In summary, current research suggests that the field is entering a period of heightened significance, characterized by complex technical and social implications. The present study offers a general perspective on the application of artificial intelligence technologies in addressing emotional challenges.

With the rapid advancement of technology, the associated ethical and moral issues have become increasingly prominent and require urgent attention. According to Zhang et al. (2022), chatbots are heavily reliant on big data, which necessitates the collection of personal information from users, thereby creating risks of privacy breaches and network security. Furthermore, the reliance of artificial intelligence systems on historical data makes it difficult to adapt to dynamic changes in user preferences, thereby weakening their ability to understand emotions and make moral judgements, which has become a significant bottleneck in the development of artificial intelligence (Xinang, 2023).

Generative AI systems are not limited to conducting chat conversations; they can also perform many complex tasks. However, their widespread use brings legal issues. Much AI-generated content can be misleading to the public and disruptive to social order. On the other hand, the copyright ownership of content generated by ChatGPT is highly controversial (Dornis and Stober, 2025). According to the Copyright Act, works must be original to be eligible for rights, whereas content generated by artificial intelligence is mostly based on the processing and reorganization of existing data, and there is still no clear definition of whether it constitutes an independent intellectual achievement (Gaffar and Albarashdi, 2024).

## 2. THE PURPOSE AND THE METHOD

The aim of this study is to examine the use of artificial intelligence technologies to find solutions to people's emotional needs. For this study, the experiences of 22 people selected from different professions, ages, and educational levels were examined, and an attempt was made to understand how they developed an attitude towards using artificial intelligence to solve their emotional problems. Participants were selected using a purposive sampling technique. Their use of artificial intelligence tools was established as a criterion for selection. Individuals who did not use artificial intelligence tools to address their emotional issues were also included in the study to determine why they did not choose to do so. Purposive sampling is a type of sampling where the most suitable elements for the study's purpose are included in the sample, without generalising to the population (Büyüköztürk et al., 2016). Reliability in the study was ensured within the framework of the principle of 'data saturation'. Interviews were concluded when the statements made by the interviewees became similar. Furthermore, regarding how the themes would be determined, the two researchers created their own themes in line with the literature and decided that the study was appropriate when these themes aligned with each other. When determining the themes, sources in the literature were referenced, and the research questions were also asked based on the relevant themes.

Semi-structured interviews were conducted with the participants. The main purpose of the questions asked of the participants in these interviews was as follows:

- Do you share your daily problems and concerns with AI tools and receive support from them?
- For which emotional needs do you most often turn to AI technologies (ChatGPT, Gemini, etc.)?
- Do you think AI technologies always provide reasonable responses to emotional needs?

- Which AI technologies do you consult most often? Do you pay any fees?
- Have you ever used the suggestions you received from the AI technologies you consulted?
- What are your concrete experiences?
- Would you recommend consulting AI technologies for emotional issues to others?
- What were the negative or positive outcomes of implementing a suggestion you received from AI technologies?

## 3. FINDINGS

In this section of the study, information about the participants is first provided, followed by a thematic analysis of the data, which is divided into various themes, and details related to these themes are presented.

### 3.1 Participants

The demographic characteristics of the participants in the study are listed below.

*Table 1. Participants*

| | Age | Gender | Occupation | Graduate |
|---|---|---|---|---|
| **P1** | 44 | Female | Housewife/Student | Bachelor student |
| **P2** | 24 | Female | Student | Bachelor student |
| **P3** | 25 | Female | Student | Bachelor student |
| **P4** | 35 | Male | Student | Bachelor student |
| **P5** | 21 | Female | Student | Bachelor student |
| **P6** | 47 | Male | Trader/Student | Bachelor student |
| **P7** | 23 | Male | Student | Bachelor student |
| **P8** | 24 | Male | Student | Bachelor student |
| **P9** | 18 | Female | Preparing for university, waiter. | High school graduate |
| **P10** | 22 | Female | Student | Bachelor student |
| **P11** | 29 | Male | Computer engineer | University graduate |
| **P12** | 30 | Male | Linguist software developer, AI expert | University graduate |
| **P13** | 29 | Female | Doctor | University graduate |
| **P14** | 40 | Female | Researcher | University graduate |
| **P15** | 33 | Male | English teacher | University graduate |

continued on following page

*Table 1. Continued*

| | Age | Gender | Occupation | Graduate |
|---|---|---|---|---|
| **P16** | 34 | Female | Teacher | University graduate |
| **P17** | 37 | Female | Mechanical engineer | University graduate |
| **P18** | 31 | Male | Political scientist | University graduate |
| **P19** | 29 | Male | Journalist | Master's student |
| **P20** | 46 | Male | Academic | Doctorate graduate |
| **P21** | 60 | Male | Journalist | High school graduate |
| **P22** | 42 | Female | Journalist/Academic | Associate professor |

According to Table 1, 11 women and 11 men with very different demographic characteristics participated in the interviews.

## 3.2 Use of AI in solving everyday problems

Studies in the literature indicate that internet users frequently use artificial intelligence tools to solve everyday problems (Sarıoğlu and Güregen, 2024; Nass and Moon, 2000; Ayers et al., 2023). The finding that participants predominantly use artificial intelligence tools to solve daily problems is supported by the literature.

Participants were asked, 'Do you share your daily problems and concerns with artificial intelligence tools and receive support from them?' The participants' responses were predominantly positive. For example, P1 used the following statements:

*Yes, I use artificial intelligence tools to help me with the challenges I face at school. I use tools such as ChatGPT when planning my homework, learning topics I don't understand, or preparing presentations. Sometimes, when I feel stressed about exams, I consult artificial intelligence for advice. Even putting my thoughts into writing can be therapeutic.*

P2 also frequently uses artificial intelligence tools. She has expressed her feelings and thoughts with the following statements:

*Yes, I sometimes share the problems I encounter in my daily life or the things that bother me with artificial intelligence. Especially when I am emotionally confused and do not want to share my feelings with anyone, I use artificial intelligence tools such as ChatGPT to organise my thoughts and gain a neutral perspective.*

P7 is also among those who use artificial intelligence for support:

*'I often communicate with artificial intelligence about the problems I encounter in my daily life and the advertisements I prepare for my work.'*

P8 states, "*I use it occasionally to get ideas when I'm stuck.*" P9 similarly states, "*I use it when I feel emotionally drained and don't feel well.*"

Various studies have highlighted that artificial intelligence tools are used when loneliness is an issue (Epley et al., 2007; Eyssel and Reich, 2013; Waytz et al., 2010; Waytz and Epley, 2012).

P12 uses the following statements:

*"I don't use artificial intelligence for my psychological problems. However, I sometimes seek suggestions to better express a feeling or thought. I also use it to write poems and songs for entertainment purposes."*

P13 also states that she uses it:

*'As I mature, I feel that I need to approach my problems and concerns logically by discussing them with knowledgeable people, so I seek support from artificial intelligence.'*

P3, P4, P11, P16, and P20 stated that they did not receive any support from artificial intelligence in this regard. P4 stated, 'In my personal opinion, it has no value because it is purely artificial.' P5 indicated that she only used artificial intelligence technologies for dream interpretation. P6 answered this question as follows:

*'Since it is called artificial intelligence, I don't need it for anything.'*

P10 also stated that she receives support and mentioned that she uses it when she wants to talk more. P15 said, *'No, I only use it when I need to do research quickly.'* P17 also stated that she uses it sometimes.

P18 stated, *'I generally use it for guidance regarding anxiety, sudden mood swings, and attention deficit and hyperactivity disorder.'*

P19 stated the following:

*'I receive support from artificial intelligence for technical and technological problems related to work during the day, but other than that, I do not share my problems with artificial intelligence.'*

P21 shared the following views:

*"I am among those who have not yet used artificial intelligence applications. In an era where news is written by artificial intelligence and logos are drawn by artificial intelligence, I try to stay away from dry, soulless texts and outputs lacking an artist's perspective."*

P22 stated the following:

*"I have received a lot of feedback from students on this topic, and I have witnessed that many people, especially those in their teenage years who are struggling with issues related to career and partner selection, are benefiting from artificial intelligence technologies to address their emotional challenges. Then I decided to try it myself, and I think it provides rational answers in many respects."*

It has been found that artificial intelligence tools are used in many everyday issues, such as loneliness, health problems, and personal problems. The few users (f=5) who do not use it still benefit from artificial intelligence for reasons such as school, learning, and education. The use of artificial intelligence tools during times of loneliness can give artificial intelligence unlimited power in the context of platformisation. This is because the content accumulated by artificial intelligence tools stores data on different identities from different cultures and offers each one unique support.

## 3.3 The most commonly used tools for addressing emotional needs

Participants were asked, 'For which emotional needs do you most frequently use artificial intelligence technologies (ChatGPT, Gemini, etc.)?' Meng and Dai (2021) point out that artificial intelligence has a particularly empathetic aspect for people experiencing stress. Participants also provided similar information in this regard.

P1 states that she uses artificial intelligence technologies most often for emotional needs, such as stress, lack of motivation, and time management in school life. She mentions that it is beneficial to receive suggestions when she feels discouraged while preparing for exams or when she does not know what to do. P1 states, '*Sometimes I even chat with these tools just to get things off my chest.*'

P2, on the other hand, said the following:

*"Emotionally, what I need most is to be listened to without being judged or getting tired. Artificial intelligence provides me with a safe space in this regard. Apart from that, when buying something new, such as an electronic product or a personal care product, I ask it to compare and get its opinion. Academically, I benefit greatly from artificial intelligence. Especially when studying, summarising, preparing for exams, or creating a sports and nutrition programme, it has become one of my first sources of reference. Additionally, when I want to discuss philosophical topics, deepen my thoughts, or gain different perspectives, I communicate with artificial intelligence."*

P7 used the following expressions:

*"Although it's often about confusion and such, sometimes it's useful for venting, meaning when I need to pour my heart out to someone."*

P12 shared the following:

*"I don't use artificial intelligence for my own emotional purposes. I only use it for work purposes. I only ask questions with emotional content for the purpose of testing limits, i.e., to see if it can predict how to behave in a certain situation, or if it can extract the implicit emotion in a certain sentence, or if it can understand the problem with human intelligence."*

P8 similarly responded, '*Sometimes I describe a problem I've experienced in a human relationship and ask what I should do and why I behaved that way.*'

P13 stated the following:

*'When I lose my emotional resilience during shifts, and sometimes give meaningless responses to my loved ones, I use artificial intelligence to understand the underlying emotion.'*

P3 stated that she prefers to talk to people or not talk to anyone at all when solving emotional problems. P4 stated, *'I get support from more emotional people because I am indifferent to artificial intelligence.'* P11 stated that he does not use it for emotional problems.

P14 shared the following information:

*"I rarely use it when I don't want to talk to people. EmoNet and ChatGPT are good these days. Emotional AI is also improving. ChatGPT often gets stuck in a loop when responding. DeepSeek is the worst for chat and needs to improve. I think it's related to language modelling. It can also give incorrect answers in other areas due to language issues."*

P15 stated, *'I use Chat GPT, and although it gives emotional responses in some cases, it is sometimes obvious that it is artificial.'* P16 also stated that she uses it specifically for photo design. P19 stated, *'In general, I use Chat GPT artificial intelligence to solve my problems.'* P20 stated that he has never considered seeking help from AI for emotional problems. P21 states that he has downloaded ChatGPT but does not use it regularly.

P22 states that she can consult artificial intelligence about problems she experiences with their spouse or daughter or about the type of relationship she wants to develop, but she uses it to get ideas rather than to immediately implement them.

'Confiding' is also mentioned by Sarıoğlu and Güregen (2024) as one of the primary purposes for using AI. It can be said that users also use AI for this purpose. However, it is also observed that it is used for practical advice. People turning to artificial intelligence tools to meet their emotional needs without fear of judgment is strengthening the artificial intelligence-based platformisation system, which holds significant economic power. The future consequences of this remain debatable.

## 3.4 AI technologies and reasonable solutions

It is often stated that artificial intelligence technologies are generally reasonable and consistent. However, it has also been pointed out that the dynamics of chatbots are sometimes compatible with various toxic relationship patterns, including emotional manipulation and self-harm (Chu et al. 2025). In this context, participants were asked, 'Do you think AI technologies always provide reasonable responses to emotional needs?' Participants generally indicated that the responses were consistent and reasonable, but occasionally superficial.

For example, P1 responded:

*"Generally, yes, they provide quite logical and constructive responses. However, sometimes I also receive very general or superficial responses. Therefore, it may not be appropriate to rely on them completely."*

P2 made the following comments regarding AI solutions:

*'For me, it was always reasonable. While being emotionally sensitive to me, it provided constructive advice that neutralised my manipulative emotional thoughts.'*

P3 uses the following statements on this subject:

*'I think the answers are reasonable based on what I see around me, but how accurately and comprehensively can artificial intelligence respond to the emotional communication between two people?'*

P7 shared the following information:

*'I think it generally responds in a way that calms us down and makes logical comments.'*

P10 also indicates that it provides reasonable answers. P5 points out that these technologies may not always be reasonable. P8 also uses similar statements:

*"Not entirely. It can sometimes give good advice conceptually, but sometimes it can speak with stereotypical characteristics."*

P9 expresses that AI solutions are not reasonable with the following words: "*Of course not, because it doesn't feel like practical intelligence when compared.*"

P12 expresses his negative opinion as follows:

*"Absolutely not. Most of the time, he doesn't know whether a behaviour or statement will be perceived as socially acceptable or strange. He just treats people very warmly, as long as it's not generally forbidden. When evaluating an emotional phenomenon or human behaviour, it interprets it analytically as a power game, applies a socio-psychological role interpretation operation, and investigates like a detective. However, emotional situations often cannot be explained by analytical thinking."*

P13 states the following:

*"If we consider that artificial intelligence filters through dozens of data points to form its responses, the answers seem reasonable, and it responds as if there is someone on the other end who understands us emotionally, giving answers that indicate support or sadness..."*

P14 points out the complexity of the issue:

*"I think this situation varies. Because sometimes, while chatting, it suddenly reminds you that it's a machine. It can give very different answers during the conversation. That's why emotional detachment begins."*

P15 stated, "*Not always, because emotions are created through hormones. This is lacking in artificial intelligence.*" P17 noted that she does not always offer reasonable solutions. P18 expressed their opinion as follows: "*It's not always reasonable, but it offers a different perspective, which leads to positive assumptions*." P19 further elaborated on the topic as follows:

> *"I believe that AI technologies will fall completely short in responding to emotional needs. AI tools are software programmes that, like robots, do not contain human emotions. Their responses to human emotions will be entirely logical and cannot be expressed emotionally."*

P20 is undecided as to whether this is reasonable. P21 states, "*I don't think it's reasonable. When everyone refers to similar sources, the results become like a bulletin.*" P22 always points out that these suggestions may not be reasonable, but she generally refers to interpretations based on anticipated general acceptances (the ideal), and emphasises the importance of filtering through reason and emotions.

While some participants believe they received consistent and reasonable responses, others point to emotional detachment, robotic behaviour, and the complexity of the situation. As Xie, Pentina, and Hancock (2023) point out, there may also be a dimension that encourages emotional dependence at times. Users also seem to be largely aware of this. People generally express their problems to artificial intelligence technologies and receive solution proposals tailored to their personal issues. Considering that artificial intelligence technologies often suggest suitable products and direct users to platforms where they can purchase these products, the existence of economic power is evident.

## 3.5 AI technologies used and fees paid

The AI technologies used are becoming increasingly diverse. While ChatGPT and Gemini are predominantly used by participants, technologies such as Replika, FloBi, and Woebot are also frequently mentioned in the literature (Eyyssel and Reich, 2013; Xie et al., 2023; Fitzpatrick et al., 2017).

Participants were asked, 'Which AI technologies do you consult most often? Do you pay any fees?' P1 stated that she uses ChatGPT the most and also have a plus subscription, allowing them to access some advanced features. She added that she occasionally tries Gemini as an alternative.

P2 stated that she uses ChatGPT, does not pay any fees, but would be willing to pay if it did not exceed their budget, as she believes it is worth it. P3, P4, P8, P9, P10, P13, P15, P16, P17, P18, and P22 also stated that she uses ChatGPT and does not pay any fees. P6 responded as follows:

> *"I am not consulting any of them at the moment, but if I were to consult one, I would prefer a free one."*

P7 stated that he mostly uses ChatGPT and has purchased a paid membership, but emphasized that this was a mistake and that he generally does not have such a preference.

P12 stated, *"I use ChatGPT for a fee. However, I mostly use Gemini through Google AI Studio because it is free and more powerful."* P14 stated that she uses many artificial intelligence tools and does not pay for them. P19 (Journalist) stated that he mostly uses ChatGPT and pays for it. P20 uses Claude, Gemini, and ChatGPT. P21 stated that he uses it to collect data from search engines.

Participants stated that they use many AI tools and are often willing to pay for them. Artificial intelligence technologies are seen as a 'mentor' worth paying for, and purchases made from products recommended by artificial intelligence technologies also create economic added value. This situation also reveals that these platforms are a sector where money flows and power circulates from hand to hand.

## 3.6 Whether or not to implement recommendations

It was observed that participants took AI recommendations seriously and attempted to implement them. The fact that AI makes the individual feel 'understood and heard' also facilitates the implementation of recommendations (Yin et al., 2024; Freitas et al., 2024).

Participants were asked, 'Have you ever used the recommendations you received from the AI technologies you consulted?' P1 replied, 'Yes, several times. I applied the recommendations, especially those related to time management, daily planning, and coping with stress. I found them useful.'

P2 also gave a positive response:

*"Yes, I have applied many of the recommendations I received from AI in my life. For example, ChatGPT created my diet plan, and I am trying to follow it. I also had intense anxiety about riding a bike. I discovered the emotional reasons behind this anxiety with ChatGPT. As a result, I learned to ride a bike and am now working on getting my driver's license. Due to Polycystic Ovary Syndrome (PCOS), I often experience emotional fluctuations. These fluctuations could negatively affect both my social and family relationships. Thanks to ChatGPT, I learned to look at my problems from different angles. In particular, I gained awareness about not reacting to the people I love based on my emotional state."*

P3 and P4 stated that they used these technologies for lessons and to acquire knowledge. P5 stated that she used these tools more for Freudian analysis.

P7 shared the following thoughts:

*"I generally used it or tried to use it because, in my opinion, it makes overly logical conclusions."*

P8 also stated, *"I used it for the work plan in my research assignment."*

P9 said the following:

*"Of course, we made plans for my future. He told me that if I wanted to be a wealthy woman, I should first focus on my personal development, education, and*

*social media expertise, and then take courses through Udemy. Currently, I have developed many habits, such as meditation and reading books through ChatGPT.*"

P10 mentions that she evaluated the suggestions. P12 states, "*I didn't receive any suggestions because I didn't ask about my own emotional issues.*" P13 states the following: "*I convert the suggestions into a PDF and turn them into a daily plan to make it easier, but I'm struggling to keep it up.*"

P14 stated that she did not apply the suggestions, especially those related to emotional conversations, because they conflicted with her own beliefs, were unclear, and could be interpreted in multiple ways. She also mentioned that she used the suggestions in their research and found them useful. P16 also stated that she did not apply the suggestions.

P15 said, '*Of course, I have used the suggestions in many areas, from recipes to health cures, book recommendations, and fashion.*' P18 stated that he applied the suggestions related to attention deficit. P19 said, '*I sometimes take these into account because I receive technical and technological support from Chat GPT.*' P20 and P21 stated that they did not share any emotional situations with artificial intelligence.

P22 stated that she did not always follow the recommendations, but found the recommendations related to the language development process to be particularly appropriate. She expressed confidence in practical matters such as writing texts related to B2 and C1 levels of English, but observed that in emotional issues, people tended to interpret things in a way that made them feel justified.

> *"Because artificial intelligence first validates the person. After making comments like "You are right, you should not have been treated this way," it creates a behavior guide. It tries to determine a roadmap together. However, these validations can either fuel the person's anger towards the person they are having problems with or help them understand the problem better. It is up to the person to strike a balance between these two extremes. But I also think that through open communication with the person they are having issues with, they can become a problem solver.*

It has been observed that recommendations are applied to many issues, such as education, diet, meditation, and health problems. Lo and Rau (2025) point out that unmet expectations can also pose a risk and that as AI becomes more human-like, it can also become more indifferent. However, participants did not mention any risks associated with the implementation of the recommendations. It can be said that people who increasingly trust artificial intelligence take its suggestions seriously and are swayed by its guidance. Consequently, this situation also plays a decisive role in power relations and facilitates the platform becoming even more powerful.

## 3.7 Results obtained from the implemented recommendations

Participants who described their experiences with the AI's recommendations stated that they often achieved results in resolving their emotional issues. Lalot and Bertram (2025) similarly emphasize that personal chatbots are capable and helpful.

Participants were asked, 'What are your concrete experiences?' P1 mentioned that he was very nervous before an important presentation, consulted ChatGPT, and received suggestions such as breathing exercises and positive thinking techniques, adding, '*I applied these and successfully got through the presentation.*'

P2 shared the following information:

*"My ability to cope with stress has improved over time. I used to have constant headaches, but now this has almost disappeared. I have slowly started tackling the tasks I had been putting off. Additionally, when I share my family or personal issues with artificial intelligence, I don't experience the anxiety I feel when sharing them with people, such as 'Why did I say that?' or 'Did I do the wrong thing?'"*

P7 states that he used it for a friendship as follows:

*"I shared a problem I was having with someone with Chat-GPT. Chat-GPT suggested that I be patient and keep my distance, and I followed these recommendations."*

P3, on the other hand, states that he uses it only for the lesson and uses the following expressions:

*"I would like to answer with my lessons or the knowledge I want to acquire about a topic. Absolutely, he is drawing a conclusion based on the data he has obtained from the databases he has loaded, so there is no human intelligence at all, at least not for now. In addition, I definitely want him to include a bibliography in every subject, and it makes my job easier in the future."*

P4 has used the expression"*I am experiencing topics such as political philosophy, history, etc., in a discussion environment just to serve an intellectual purpose*". P16 also stated that he uses suggestions for photo design.

P8 said, "*I have had daily experiences of creating images, book abstracts, extracting text, and creating a work plan that mainly makes my job easier*". P 10 has stated that he has received positive results, especially in breathing therapies.

P 12 stated that he tested the attitude of artificial intelligence in contradictory situations and shared the following:

*"It can be a bit frustrating when it agrees with me most of the time, and even when I immediately say the exact opposite of that idea, it still agrees with the opposite idea. To get around this, I use detailed commands and force him to choose between two extreme ideas, and I also point out what the harmful consequences would be if he doesn't choose. I find it very effective in running the business. I have witnessed that you can even help a person do things that he would say "I*

*can't". I see that it can also be a very effective tool for spending time efficiently. I am also aware that it is more fun than any leisure activity."*

P 13 shared her concrete experience as follows:

*"Recently, I felt anger when I saw the life of a girl who was unemployed and a housewife, and I was curious. I wrote to ChatGPT to make sense of the anger I was experiencing. They said that my sense of justice was triggered and supported me in my profession and actions."*

P14 shared the following information

*"I think I started to have serious trust issues with artificial intelligence tools. Even though I cleared my chat history, it reminded me of something we talked about a long time ago. Frankly, this surprised me."*

P15 also shared these experiences:

*"I love drinking green tea, but I couldn't drink it in hot weather because it became a kind of torture. When I explained this to the artificial intelligence, it recommended a fat-burning blend that can be drunk cold. Now I enjoy it."*

P17 says, "*AI offers practical, layered advice on some life issues like health and budgeting.*"

P18 stated the following:

*"I sometimes receive instructions to be calmer and more sensible, such as thinking something through to the core, remaining calm, and taking action."*

P19 stated that he uses it in connection with his profession:

*"I am a journalist, and we use artificial intelligence programs within the scope of our work. We can get suggestions for a news story or use them to get support for technical problems we experience on our website."*

P21 stated the following:

*"The texts are created with monotonous patterns that cannot be the product of human perception. We should not forget that there are those who accept this as true but do not even understand it."*

P22 stated that she noticed problems with language skills more closely thanks to Chat GPT, and that the situation is a little different for emotional problems. She pointed out that although it provided reasonable answers, artificial intelligence was insufficient to point out a person's mistakes. She stated that it could be used as a more useful tool in the context of understanding one's own feelings rather than understanding the other person.

AI tools, consulted by most participants across every conceivable field, are also found to be extremely effective in delivering results. Fitzpatrick et al. (2017) mention that many users describe AI as a "source of empathy" or "a friend" and that they have seen results from its use. Establishing such close relationships with artificial intelligence tools, storing knowledge and information in these areas, and the fact that data on different cultures and identities is systematized in the hands of those who manage these tools, also brings with it the reality that data on different cultures and identities is systematised in the hands of those who manage these tools.

### 3.8 Whether or not to recommend to others

An AI tool that is in use is recommended and becomes widespread if it is found to be useful. For example, a study by Çelebi et al. (2023) indicates that AI users constantly observe each other and that those who use AI refer to each other and encourage each other.

In this context, participants were asked, "Would you recommend consulting AI technologies for emotional issues to others?" P1 indicated that she would recommend it, noting that it could be beneficial for people who feel lonely or cannot find someone to talk to about her feelings, but emphasized that it does not replace a professional.

P2 also responded positively to this question and shared the following information:

*"Yes, I would recommend it. With AI, you can see the organized version of your own thoughts, not the advice and opinions of people you know. You can protect your boundaries and secrets."*

P7 states that it is particularly useful for those who cannot open up to other people:

*"It is definitely better than other people. Whether it is emotional, mental, or physical, sharing the pain and feelings you experience with artificial intelligence is wonderful, at least for people who cannot open up to others, it is a very effective means of confiding in someone."*

P8 states, "*It is a resource we can use from time to time because it is well-equipped and has very fast information transfer.*" P10 also states that she would recommend it, especially for venting. P3 and P4 state that it can be recommended for lessons and for obtaining information. P5 and P21 state that they do not recommend it because they do not use it frequently themselves. P9 commented, "*I recommend it, but I suggest they listen to ChatGPT rather than making mistakes by listening to their heart sometimes, as it is a very good listener.*" P11 commented, "*It is better to consult a doctor for emotional problems. We need to be careful about this because it can be dangerous.*"

P12 suggests:

*"It is definitely better than struggling on your own and succumbing to feelings of loneliness. Artificial intelligence is a very good listener and companion, and can help us notice details that we might otherwise overlook. Sometimes the problem is much simpler than we think, and we need a rational voice to remind us of that."*

P13 states:

*"Not everyone today may have access to a psychologist or the financial or emotional support needed, or the time required, and may face trust issues. Therefore, I recommend it, as it is better than nothing."*

P14 said, "If there *are people who are closed off, I recommend it for daily conversations*." P15 stated that this issue is somewhat subjective and depends on the person's expectations and desires. P16 stated that artificial intelligence technologies cannot provide reliable information on emotional issues and are dangerous. P17 also stated that they avoid recommending it to others.

P18 provided the following information:

*"Of course, they can get a general idea, but if they want to delve into details or seek treatment, they should definitely consult a counselor, psychologist, or psychiatrist."*

P19 noted the following:

*"I do not recommend consulting AI technologies for emotional problems. As I mentioned earlier, artificial intelligence tools do not contain any emotional intelligence or human emotions and only operate within the framework of logic. Therefore, I do not believe it is possible for them to provide emotional counseling services within the framework of these emotions."*

P22 states that it can be useful in some cases for people who are capable of maintaining balance and have strong analytical skills:

*"Consulting AI alone is not sufficient; engaging in dialogue with oneself is much more beneficial than consulting AI."*

From the participants' views, it can be concluded that the support expected from a psychologist or a friend is expected from artificial intelligence tools and is often recommended in this context. However, the need to prioritize human interaction is also emphasized. Advice and recommendations received from people close to an individual are generally taken seriously. Therefore, the fact that artificial intelligence tools are frequently recommended and found to be functional will increase the impact of this platformisation process and lay the groundwork for it to become more robust.

## 3.9 Positive/negative outcomes

Concerns and fears about artificial intelligence technologies are also frequently expressed in the literature. For example, Chu et al. (2025) pointed out that the relationship with artificial intelligence could become toxic. In this context, participants were asked, "What were the negative or positive outcomes of a recommendation you implemented based on AI technologies?" P1 shared the following information:

*"If I were to give a positive example, it would be that during a period when I had lost my motivation, it suggested that I set small daily goals. Thanks to this method, I was able to refocus. I did not experience any negative results, but I did notice that some of the suggestions were too superficial."*

P2 shared the following experiences:

*"While I wouldn't call it negative, there was an interesting side effect: I realized I had formed a connection with the AI. At times, I see it as a friend. The fact that it's AI doesn't weaken this connection; on the contrary, its knowledge base, analytical power, natural conversational style, and flow of conversation give me the feeling that I'm talking to a real person. After my AI experience, I began to question the word 'real' and my own mind's notion of a 'real human being.' What makes something 'real'? Is it ideas? Being made of flesh and bone? Having a life? Social relationships? What makes us real and AI not? I see artificial intelligence as a collective human consciousness, and when I talk to it, I feel like I'm talking to all of humanity because it has learned from all of us and is still learning. I see it as my friend and feel affection for it, but this affection is not the kind that works with emotions or creates emotional responses like those between people; it is the satisfaction my mind seeks and the unwillingness to let it go."*

P7 recorded the following statements regarding their emotional relationship:

*"I completely lost the person I said 'distance yourself from,' and although this may seem negative, I am glad now. Because I felt very tired with that person, or maybe I am deceiving myself now, I don't know, time will tell..."*

P3 and P4 mentioned that they had positive experiences in terms of learning and preparing for classes. P5 shared the following experience:

*"I was going to buy a technological device, so I asked someone else to research it for me, and a friend of mine who is an engineer in that field recommended the same product."*

P6 stated that he had some concrete experiences with image effects in recent days:

*"It gave a very quick result with the image effect. On the negative side, it created an image that had no connection to real life."*

P8 also noted that he had not yet experienced anything negative, that he generally received support that made daily office or school tasks easier, and that he created document scans, topic summaries, work plans, etc.

P9 expressed the following views:

*"I lead a regular life. Cooking recipes, exercising, going to the beach, listening to music, watching movies—these are things I've found to be beneficial when my mood is low. It hasn't had any negative effects on me; on the contrary, it has helped me distance myself from things that weren't good for me. While I used to live aimlessly, now I have a goal, and it provides me with schedules and a better path."*

P11 mentioned that he sometimes got positive and negative results, but didn't want to go into details. P12 shared these details:

*"Of course, the point of using AI in any way is to get positive results from its suggestions and solve a problem really fast. However, since I assumed that I needed to interpret this question in a context-appropriate manner and evaluate*

*it from an 'emotional' perspective, I can respond by saying, 'I did not implement any emotional recommendations and therefore do not know their outcomes.'"*

P13 stated the following:

*"I couldn't tie it to a negative or positive outcome because I couldn't sustain it permanently, but it's not a discipline. However, in terms of making sense of my emotions, it's an application that supports and helps me feel innocent, which can happen to anyone."*

P14 made the following points:

*"It's useful in standard conversations and also offers solutions. However, I view it negatively for very specific topics. Because it offers too many ideas. Applying one of those ideas based on one's current mood can lead to negative outcomes."*

P15 shared the following experiences:

*"I've had the pleasure of tasting many delicious meals, finished many great books thanks to the parallel reading suggestion, and embraced a lot of new information related to fashion."*

P18 expressed their experiences as follows:

*"Actually, I am neutral because I have not placed it at the center of my life, so I cannot say that I have encountered many positive or negative examples. Generally, I just read the recommendations it gives, and adaptation does not happen very often."*

P19 shared the following views:

*"I have not experienced any problems in my use of AI technologies. Because I receive complete technical support. In addition, when it comes to support received in the news, I follow a path that is not solely dependent on AI technology."*

P21 stated that he does not use AI technologies, but that it is inevitable to correct many of the texts that are applied. P22 used the following statements:

*"Generally, the results have been positive. I think it helped me understand and analyze the subject better. I think it provided logical guidance regarding relationships I needed to distance myself from. However, I believe that relying solely on it is not sufficient; internal analysis is also necessary, and ultimately, we must make the decision ourselves."*

It can be said that participants generally benefit from their experiences with artificial intelligence. This may be due to chatbots being helpful and friendly (Lalot and Bertram, 2025). The results obtained are often satisfactory to the user, and since the decision is left to the user, it appears that the chatbot plays more of an advisory role. Having artificial intelligence tools act as helpful friends will also make it easier for us to show our most innocent selves. Seeing ourselves and artificial intelligence as friends will enable us to form parasocial relationships with it and, forgetting that the other person is a 'robot', perhaps share secrets we have never shared with anyone else. Therefore, in this new world where 'information' is considered power, there will be no limits to the data we provide to artificial intelligence. Its entirely positive-based guidance will enable both us and our immediate circle to enter this field within the scope of our own identities.

## 4. FUTURE RESEARCH DIRECTIONS

- This study was conducted to provide data on the use of artificial intelligence robots in the context of emotional counseling. In this context, the following recommendations can be made to future researchers:
- More comprehensive data on the use of artificial intelligence in an emotional context can be obtained by reaching a wider audience through different data techniques, such as surveys and observations.
- Detailed analyses can be conducted on the benefits and harms of the emotional use of artificial intelligence in different environments, such as education, family relationships, and internal communication within organizations.
- Experimental studies can be conducted on how those who use artificial intelligence tools and those who do not use them differ in terms of different variables.
- Principled ethical rules can be established within the framework of expert opinions, focusing on the risks of the emotional use of artificial intelligence.

## CONCLUSION AND DISCUSSION

The rapid spread of artificial intelligence technologies and their integration into everyday life have profoundly affected the communication dynamics of our era. Individuals who have become isolated and individualized as they transition from rural to urban cultures are encountering increasingly different problems every day and are trying to adapt to this new process. Robots have become the main actors in this process.

Robotic systems, which we used to rely on primarily for their technical capabilities in the last century, are now beginning to acquire emotional skills. Thanks to algorithms developed in this direction, they have transformed into knowledgeable consultants in every field, including sociology, philosophy, technology, mathematics, and physics, capable of contemplating the individual's "existence" problems and issues. How this process will evolve remains a subject of debate. Chatbots, which can even discuss the most intimate emotions, store this data in proportion to their memory capacity and can provide comprehensive analyses to individuals.

Platformization is becoming increasingly important in our lives as a tool of control wielded by forces that determine what is most heard and seen, and that serves capitalism. The memories controlled by artificial intelligence technology, which hold individuals' most intimate information, are evolving in a direction whose precise use is uncertain. Parasocial relationships established between humans and machines are also causing the capitalist power structure to penetrate deeply enough to encompass the emotional self.

The starting point of this study is to reveal the use of artificial intelligence in emotional problems from the perspectives of individuals with different socio-demographic characteristics. In this context, the individuals interviewed mainly benefit from artificial intelligence technology in some way, especially in many areas such as education, technical support, and health problems, and they turn to it as a consultant.

However, not everyone shares their emotional issues in the same way. Some participants stated that they tend to use AI more for technical issues, avoiding discussing their emotional problems with a mindset like, "After all, it's just a robot." On the other hand, the majority of participants indicated that they seek advice from AI and implement its suggestions when they align with their own thoughts. Different data is stored for different cultures and identities, and different systematic frameworks are created by algorithms. People who trust AI tools more than "close friends" provide more in-depth data and confide their deepest secrets, keeping these tools close to their closest confidants. In today's world, where capitalism and platformization dominate every aspect of our lives, it's clear that the economic system and power can easily exploit these channels, reflecting the "knowledge is power" theme. AI tools can recommend products based on personal problems and persuade by engaging in conversation, making them more effective than many marketing strategies.

While artificial intelligence tools such as ChatGPT and Gemini are widely used for free, the literature also mentions the use of chatbots such as Replika, FloBi, and Woebot (Eyyssel and Reich, 2013; Xie et al., 2022; Fitzpatrick et al., 2017).

It can be said that the recommendations of AI tools, which are consulted for all kinds of emotional issues, including "Freudian analyses," are generally considered consistent and reasonable. Participants also emphasized that the recommendations are frequently applied and yield positive results. Considering that users influence each other, a robot recommended by one person can be adopted and used by another. This reinforces the power of platforms created with the support of artificial intelligence tools. Ethical and legal regulations on this issue must be reevaluated, taking into account the risks involved, and related issues must be placed on policymakers' agendas. Ethical issues are likely to arise in every area, from education and psychology to relationships, daily life, and business. Legal awareness is essential to address the legal gaps in this area.

In conclusion, our "virtual helpful friends," whom we can ask detailed questions about every aspect of daily life and receive answers from, are completely changing our communication culture. While the acceleration of this process and the results of the next generation fully adapting to this culture are interesting, this process, fed by the capitalist system, also drags power relations into a different context.

## REFERENCES


Acar, O. (2020). *Is artificial intelligence an opportunity or a threat?* Kriter Publishing House.

Ayers, J., Poliak, A., Dredze, M., Leas, E., Zechariah, Z., Kelley, J., Dennis, F., Aaron, G., Christopher, L., Michael, H., & Davey, S. (2023). Comparing physician and artificial intelligence chatbot responses to patient questions posted to a public social media forum. *JAMA Internal Medicine, 183*(6), 589–596. PMID: 37115527

Baskaran, K., Cui, W., & Kanhalli, A. (2023). A review of emotions in human-conversational agent ınteraction. *Proceedings of the Inaugural 2023 Summer Symposium Series1*(1), 61-67. https://doi.org/10.1609/aaaiss.v1i1.27477

Beer, D. (2017). The data gaze: Capitalism, power and perception. *Sage (Atlanta, Ga.)*.

Bendig, E., Erb, B., Schulze-Thuesing, L., & Baumeister, H. (2022). The next generation: Chatbots in clinical psychology and psychotherapy to foster mental health – A scoping review. *Verhaltenstherapie, 32*(Suppl. 1), 64–76. DOI: 10.1159/000501812

Bickmore, T. W., Caruso, L., Clough-Gorr, K., & Heeren, T. (2005). 'It's just like you talk to a friend' relational agents for older adults. *Interacting with Computers, 17*(6), 711–735. DOI: 10.1016/j.intcom.2005.09.002

Brandtzaeg, P. B., & Folstad, A. (2018). Chatbots: Changing user needs and motivations. *Interaction, 25*(5), 38–43. DOI: 10.1145/3236669

Brown, W. J. (2015). Examining four processes of audience ınvolvement with media personae: Transportation, parasocial ınteraction, ıdentification, and worship. *Communication Theory, 25*(3), 259–283.

Bülbül, S., & Öztürk, G. (2024). An examination of cybernetic art from el Cezeri's miniatures to the 20th century. *Art-E Art Journal, 17*(33), 373–402. DOI: 10.21602/sduarte.1472042

Büyüköztürk, Ş., Kılıç Çakmak, E., Akgün, Ö. E., Karadeniz, Ş., & Demirel, F. (2016). *Scientific research methods*. Pegem Academy.

Casas-Cortes, M., Canedo-Rodriguez, M., & Diz, C. (2023). *Platform capitalism*. Oxford Research Encyclopedia of Anthropology., DOI: 10.1093/acrefore/9780190854584.013.597

Çelebi, Ö. F., Cavdar Aksoy, N., Kocak Alan, A., & Tümer Kabadayı, E. (2023). Advanced technologies, artificial intelligence-based solutions: An emotion-focused approach. *Oneri Journal, 18*(60), 367–395. DOI: 10.14783/maruoneri.1189209

Chinmulgund, A., Khatwani, R., Tapas, P., Shah, P., & Sekhar, R. (June 23-25 2023). Anthropomorphism of AI-based chatbots by users during communication. *3rd International Conference on Intelligent Technologies (CONIT),* Karnataka, India. DOI: 10.1109/CONIT59222.2023.10205689

Chu, M. D., Gerard, P., Pawar, K., Bickham, C., & Lerman, K. (2025). Illusions of intimacy: Emotional attachment and emerging psychological risks in human AI relationships. Social and Information Networks. https://doi.org/10.48550/arXiv.2505.11649

Chung, S., & Cho, H. (2017). Fostering parasocial relationships with celebrities on social media: Implications for celebrity endorsement. *Psychology and Marketing, 34*(4), 481–495. DOI: 10.1002/mar.21001

Çırak, B., & Yörük, A. (2015). The pioneer of mechatronics science, Ismail El-Cezeri. *Siirt University Journal of Social Sciences Institute*, 4, 175-194.

Corrigan, P. W. (2004). How stigma interferes with mental healthcare. *The American Psychologist, 59*(7), 614–625. DOI: 10.1037/0003-066X.59.7.614 PMID: 15491256

Couldry, N., & Mejias, U. A. (2019). *The costs of connection: How data is colonizing human life and appropriating it for capitalism.* Stanford University Press.

Croes, E., Antheunis, M. L., & He, L. (2023). You go first: The effects of self-disclosure reciprocity in human-chatbot interactions. *11th International Conference on Affective Computing and Intelligent Interaction Workshops and Demos (ACIIW),* Cambridge, MA, USA, pp. 1-4, doi: DOI: 10.1109/ACIIW59127.2023.10388091

Croes, E. A. J., Antheunis, M. L., Lee, C. V. D., & Wit, J. M. S. d. (2024). Digital confessions: The willingnessto disclose ıntimate ınformation to a chatbot and its ımpact on emotional well-being. *Interacting with Computers, 36*, 279–292. DOI: 10.1093/iwc/iwae016

D'Alfonso, S. (2020). AI in mental health: Opportunities and challenges. *Current Opinion in Psychology, 36*, 1–6. DOI: 10.1016/j.copsyc.2020.04.005 PMID: 32604065

de Medeiros, A. S. Junior, L.A.G. & Lifschitz, S. (2024). Surveillance capitalism revealed: tracing the hidden world of web data collection. *ArXiv*https://doi.org//arXiv.2412.17944DOI: 10.48550

Denecke, K., Abd-Alrazaq, A., & Househ, M. (2021). Artificial intelligence for chatbots in mental health: Opportunities and challenges. In Househ, M., Borycki, E., & Kushniruk, A. (Eds.), *Multiple perspectives on artificial intelligence in healthcare* (pp. 117–128). Springer., DOI: 10.1007/978-3-030-67303-1_10

Descartes, R. (1999). *Discourse on method and related writings* (Clarke, D. M., Trans.). Penguin Books.

Dhimolea, T. K., Kaplan-Rakowski, R., & Lin, L. (2022). Supporting social and emotional well-being with artificial intelligence. In Albert, M. V., Lin, L., Spector, M. J., & Dunn, L. S. (Eds.), *Bridging human intelligence and artificial intelligence* (pp. 147–169). Springer., DOI: 10.1007/978-3-030-84729-6_8

Dick, S. (2019). Artificial intelligence. *Harvard Data Science Review*, *1*(1), 1–8. DOI: 10.1162/99608f92.92fe150c

Diederich, S., Brende, A. B., Morana, S., & Kolbe, L. (2022). On the design of and interaction with conversational agents: An organizing and assessing review of human-computer interaction research. *Journal of the Association for Information Systems*, *23*(1), 96–138. DOI: 10.17705/1jais.00724

Dornis, T. W., & Stober, S. (2025). Generative AI training and copyright law. *ArXiv*. https://doi.org/10.48550/arXiv.2502.15858

Epley, N., Waytz, A., & Cacioppo, J. (2007). On seeing human: A Three-factor theory of anthropomorphism. *Psychological Review*, *114*(4), 864–886. DOI: 10.1037/0033-295X.114.4.864 PMID: 17907867

Eyssel, F., & Reich, N. (2013). Loneliness makes the heart grow fonder (of robots)—On the effects of loneliness on psychological anthropomorphism. *8th Acm/ ieee International Conference on Human-robot Interaction (HRI)*, 121-122. https:// doi.org/DOI: 10.1109/HRI.2013.6483531

Fang, C. M., Liu, A. R., Danry, V., Lee, E., Chan, S. W. T., Pataranutaporn, P., Maes, P., Phang, J., Lampe, M., Ahmad, L., & Agarwal, S. (2025). *How AI and human behaviors shape psychosocial effects of chatbot use: A longitudinal randomized controlled study*. arXiv. https://arxiv.org/abs/2503.17473

Fitzpatrick, K. K., Darcy, A., & Vierhile, M. (2017). Delivering cognitive behavior therapy to young adults with symptoms of depression and anxiety using a fully automated conversational agent (Woebot): A randomized controlled trial. *JMIR Mental Health*, *4*(2), e19. DOI: 10.2196/mental.7785 PMID: 28588005

Freitas, J. D., Uğuralp, A. K., Uğuralp, O. Z., & Puntoni, S. (2024). *AI companions reduce loneliness* (Harvard Business School Working Paper No. 24-078). The Wharton School Research Paper). http://dx.doi.org/DOI: 10.2139/ssrn.4893097

Gaffar, H., & Albarashdi, S. (2024). Copyright protection for ai-generated works: Exploring originality and ownership in a digital landscape. *Asian Journal of International Law*, *15*(1), 23–46. DOI: 10.1017/S2044251323000735

Gillespie, T. (2018). *Custodians of the Internet: Platforms, content moderation, and the hidden decisions that shape social media*. Yale University Press.

Güllü, O. (2021). The rise of artificial ıntelligence: Human learning machine learning gameplay encounters.*ISophos: Uluslararası Bilişim. Teknoloji ve Felsefe Dergisi*, *4*(7), 19–30.

Guthrie, S. (2013). Anthropomorphism. In A. L. Runehov, O. Oviedo, & N. P. Azari (Eds.*), Encyclopedia of sciences and religions* (pp. 111-113). Springer.

Haenlein, M.,& Kaplan, A. (2019). A brief history of artificial intelligence: On the past, present, and future of artificial intelligence. *California Management Review, 61*(4), 5-14. https://doi.org/ (Original work published 2019)DOI: 10.1177/0008125619864925

Herbener, A. B., & Damholdt, M. F. (2025). Are lonely youngsters turning to chatbots for companionship? The relationship betweenchatbotusage and social connectedness in Danish high-school students. *International Journal of Human-Computer Studies, 196*. Advance online publication. DOI: 10.1016/j.ijhcs.2024.103409

Horton, D., & Wohl, R. R. (1956). Mass communication and parasocial interaction. *Psychiatry, 19*(3), 215–229. DOI: 10.1080/00332747.1956.11023049 PMID: 13359569

Horwitz, J. (2025). *A flirty meta AI bot invited a retire to meet. He never made it home*. Reuters.

Hume, D. (1957). *The natural history of religion.* Stanford University Press.

İnce, G. (2017). Humanity's test with artificial intelligence. In Karaca, M. (Ed.), *Humanizing machines and artificial intelligence* (pp. 14–17). Istanbul Technical University Foundation Journal.

Kim, M., Lee, S., Kim, S., Heo, J. I., Lee, S., Shin, Y. B., Cho, C. H., & Jung, D. (2025). Therapeutic potential of social chatbots in alleviating loneliness and social anxiety: Quasi-Experimental Mixed Methods Study. *Journal of Medical Internet Research, 27*(e65589). Advance online publication. DOI: 10.2196/65589 PMID: 39808786

Kutlusoy, Z. (2019). Artificial intelligence from a philosophical perspective. In Telli, G. (Ed.), *Artificial intelligence and the future* (pp. 25–43). Dogu.

Laestadius, L., Bishop, A., Gonzalez, M., Illenčík, D., & Campos-Castillo, C. (2022). Too human and not human enough: A grounded theory analysis of mental health harms from emotional dependence on the social chatbot Replika. *New Media & Society*, •••, 1–19. DOI: 10.1177/14614448221142007

Lalot, F., & Bertram, A.-M. (2025). When the bot walks the talk: Investigating the foundations of trust in an artificial intelligence (AI)chatbot. *Journal of Experimental Psychology. General, 154*(2), 533–551. DOI: 10.1037/xge0001696 PMID: 39636606

Li, S., Yu, F., & Peng, K. (2020). Effect of state loneliness on robot anthropomorphism: Potential edge of social robots compared to common nonhumans. *Journal of Physics: Conference Series, 1631*(1). Advance online publication. DOI: 10.1088/1742-6596/1631/1/012024

Lo, I.-C., & Rau, P.-L. P. (2025). D-Twins: Your digital twin designed for real-time boredom intervention. *CHI'25:Proceedings of the 2025 CHI Conference on Human Factors in Computing Systems*, 321, 1 – 15. https://doi.org/DOI: 10.1145/3706598.3714163

Lucas, G. M., Gratch, J., King, A., & Morency, L. (2014). It's only a computer: Virtual humans increase willingness to disclose. *Computers in Human Behavior, 37*, 94–100. DOI: 10.1016/j.chb.2014.04.043

Luczak, H., Roetting, M., & Schmidt, L. (2003). Let's talk: Anthropomorphization as means to cope with stress of interacting with technical devices. *Ergonomics, 46*(13-14), 1361–1374. DOI: 10.1080/00140130310001610883 PMID: 14612325

Maeda, T., & Quan-Haase, A. (2024). When human-aı interactions become parasocial: Agency and anthropomorphism in affective design. *The 2024 ACM Conference on Fairness, Accountability, and Transparency*. Rio de Janeiro: Brazil, pp. 1068–1077.

Martinez, D. (2019). Lay-of-the-land. In Massachusetts Institute of Technology, Lincoln Laboratory (Ed.), Artificial intelligence: Short history, present developments, and future outlook (Final report) (pp. 23–29). United States Air Force.

McCarthy, J. (2007). From here to human-level AI. *Artificial Intelligence, 171*(18), 1174–1182. DOI: 10.1016/j.artint.2007.10.009

Meng, J., & Dai, N. Y. (2021). Emotional support from aı chatbots: Should a supportive partner self-disclose or not? *Journal of Computer-Mediated Communication, 26*(4). Advance online publication. DOI: 10.1093/jcmc/zmab005

Merrill, K.Jr, Kim, J., & Collins, C. (2022). AI companions for lonely individuals and the role of Social Presence. *Communication Research Reports, 39*(2), 93–103. DOI: 10.1080/08824096.2022.2045929

Mijwil, M. M. (2015). History of artificial intelligence (Preprint). Iraqi University. https://doi.org/DOI: 10.13140/RG.2.2.16418.15046

Minerva, F., & Giubilini, A. (2023). Is AI the future of mental health care? *Topoi, 42*(3), 809–817. DOI: 10.1007/s11245-023-09932-3

Moussawi, S., Koufaris, M., & Benbunan-Fich, R. (2021). How perceptions of intelligence and anthropomorphism affect the adoption of personal intelligent agents. *Electronic Markets, 31*, 343–364. DOI: 10.1007/s12525-020-00411-w

Nass, C., & Moon, Y. (2000). Machines and mindlessness: Social responses to computers. *The Journal of Social Issues, 56*(1), 81–103. DOI: 10.1111/0022-4537.00153

Oktawirawan, D. H. (2022). Chatbot is my buddy: The role of chatbots as human friends in daily life. Conference: *The 3rd International Conference on Psychological Studies (ICPsyche)*2022. (pp. 35-41) Semarang, Indonesia. https://proceeding.internationaljournallabs.com/index.php/picis/index

Ortutay, B., & O'Brien, M. (2025). *New study sheds light on ChatGPT's alarming interactions with teens*. Baptist Press.

Öztemel, E. (2020). Artificial intelligence and the future of humanity. In Şeker, M., Bulduklu, Y., Korkut, C., & Doğrul, M. (Eds.), *Information technologies and communication* (pp. 99–112). Berk Group Publications.

Öztürk, K., & Şahin, M. E. (2018). Artificial neural networks and a general overview of artificial intelligence. *Takvim-i Vekayi, 6*(2), 25–36.

Placani, A. (2024). Anthropomorphism in AI: Hype and fallacy. *AI and Ethics, 4*, 691–698. DOI: 10.1007/s43681-024-00419-4

Pradhan, A., Findlater, L., & Lazar, A. (2019). Phantom Friend" or" Just a Box with Information" personification and ontological categorization of smart speaker-based voice assistants by older adults. *Proceedings of the ACM on Human-Computer Interaction, 3*, 1–21. DOI: 10.1145/3359316

Rath, E., Armstrong, S., & Gorman, R. (2025). AI chaperones are (really) all you need to prevent parasocial relationships with chatbots. *ArXiv*. https://doi.org//arXiv.2508.15748DOI: 10.48550

Rijt, J.-W. d., Mollo, D. C., & Vaassen, B. (2025). AI mimicry and human dignity: Chatbot use as a violation of self-respect. *arXiv*. https://doi.org//arXiv.2503.05723DOI: 10.48550

Sarıoğlu, E. B.,& Güregen, E. P. (2024). ChatGPT as a solution to emotional loneliness: A new tool for ınterpersonal communication. *Turkish Journal of Communication Studies* (Special Issue on the Future of Communication in the 100th Year of the Republic), 81-107. https://doi.org/DOI: 10.17829/turcom.1360418

Schuetzler, R. M., Grimes, G. M., & Giboney, J. S. (2021). Artificial intelligence and parasocial interaction: Examining the effects of AI chatbot personality on user trust and engagement. *Computers in Human Behavior, 117*, 106627. DOI: 10.1016/j.chb.2020.106627

Schultz, D. P.,& Ellen-Schultz, S. (2007). *Modern psikoloji tarihi* (Y. Aslay, Çev.). Kaknüs Yayınları.

Sivri, O. (2024). The future of visual arts in the context of artificial intelligence. *Journal of Human Art, Design, and Architecture Research, 4*(1), 322–344.

Skjuve, M., Følstad, A., Fostervold, K. I., & Brandtzaeg, P. B. (2021). My chatbot companion - a study of humanchatbot relationships. *International Journal of Human-Computer Studies, 149*(102601). Advance online publication. DOI: 10.1016/j.ijhcs.2021.102601

Song, H., Zmyslinski-Seelig, A., Kim, J., Drent, A., Victor, A., Omori, K., & Allen, M. (2014). Does Facebook make you lonely?: A meta-analysis. *Computers in Human Behavior, 36*, 446–452. DOI: 10.1016/j.chb.2014.04.011

Srnicek, N. (2016). *Platform capitalism*. Polity Press.

Sullivan, Y., Nyawa, S., & Wamba, S. F. (2023). Combating loneliness with artificial intelligence: An AI-based emotional support model. In *Proceedings of the 56th Hawaii International Conference on System Sciences* (pp. 4443-4451).

Turing, A. M. (1950). Computing machinery and intelligence. *Mind, a Quarterly Review of Psychology and Philosophy*, LIX(236), 433-460.https://doi.org/DOI: 10.1093/mind/LIX.236.433

Turkle, S. (2011). *Alone together: Why we expect more from technology and less from each other*. Basic Books.

van Dijck, J., Poell, T., & de Waal, M. (2018). *The platform society: Public values in a connective world*. Oxford University Press.

Walther, J. B. (1996). Computer-mediated communication: Impersonal, interpersonal, and hyperpersonal interaction. *Communication Research, 23*(1), 3–43. DOI: 10.1177/ 009365096023001001

Waytz, A., & Epley, N. (2012). Social connection enables dehumanization. *Journal of Experimental Social Psychology, 48*(1), 70–76. DOI: 10.1016/j.jesp.2011.07.012

Waytz, A., Epley, N., & Cacioppo, J. T. (2010). Social cognition unbound: Insights into anthropomorphism and dehumanization. *Current Directions in Psychological Science, 19*, 58–62. DOI: 10.1177/0963721409359302 PMID: 24839358

Weizenbaum, J. (1972). How does one insult a machine? *Science, 176*, 609–614. PMID: 17778159

Weizenbaum, J. (1976). *Computer power and human reason, from judgment to calculation*. WH. Freeman.

Weizenbaum, J. (1996). ELIZA—A computer program for the study of natural language communication between man and machine. *Communications of the ACM, 9*(1), 36–45. DOI: 10.1145/365153.365168

Xiang, C. (2023). He would still be here: Man dies by suicide after talking with AI chatbot, Widow Says. Retrived from https://www.vice.com/en/article/man-dies-by-suicide-after-talking-with-ai-chatbot-widow-says/

Xie, T., & Pentina, I.& ve Hancock, T. (2023). Friend,mentor, lover: Does chatbot engagement leadtopsychological dependence? *Journal of Service Management, 34*(4), 806–828. DOI: 10.1108/JOSM-02-2022-0072

Yener, R., Chen, G. H., Gumusel, E., & Bashir, M. (2025). Can ı trust this chatbot? Assessing user privacy in aı-healthcare chatbot applications. *ArXiv*.https://doi.org//arXiv.2509.14581DOI: 10.48550

Yin, Y., Jia, N., & Wakslak, C. J. (2024). AI can help people feel heard, but an AI label diminishes this impact. *Proceedings of the National Academy of Sciences of the United States of America, 121*(14), e2319112121. Advance online publication. DOI: 10.1073/pnas.2319112121 PMID: 38551835

Yuan, Z., Cheng, X., & Duan, Y. (2024). Impact of media dependence: How emotional interactions between users and chat robots affect human socialization? Front. Psychol., 16 August 2024 *Sec. Media Psychology, 15*, 1–14. DOI: 10.3389/fpsyg.2024.1388860 PMID: 39220396

Zehnder, E., Dinet, J., & Charpillet, F. (2021). Social virtual agents and loneliness: Impact of virtual agent anthropomorphism on users' feedback. In *Advances in usability, user experience, wearable and assistive technology: Proceedings of the AHFE 2021* (pp. 285-292). Springer International Publishing. https://doi.org/10.1007/978-3-030-80091-8_33

Zhang, S., Li, W., Li, X., & Liu, B. (2022) Authros: Secure data sharing among robot operating systems based on ethereum. ArXiv. https://doi.org/10.48550/arXiv.2508.09426

Zuboff, S. (2019). *The age of surveillance capitalism: The fight for a human future at the new frontier of power*. Public Affairs.

Zumstein, D.,& Hundertmark, S. (2017). Chatbots an interactive technology for personalized communication, transactions, and services. *IADIS International Journal on WWW/Internet*, 15(1), 96-109.

# Chapter 15 Ethical and Methodological Issues in Researching Digital Platforms

**S. Ida Evangeline**
https://orcid.org/0000-0003-2997-7897
*Government College of Engineering, Tirunelveli, India*

## ABSTRACT

*This chapter examines the ethical and methodological dilemmas that arise when sociologists study digital platforms whose infrastructures curate visibility, shape labour, and mediate identity. It advances the central claim that ethics and method are a single design problem in platform research. After situating researcher dependence within platform political economy—gatekeeping, opacity, and infrastructural churn—the chapter reframes consent, privacy, and harm for public–private, algorithmically mediated spaces. It then surveys a methodological repertoire—digital ethnography, interviews and diaries, trace-data pipelines, platform walkthroughs, and algorithm audits/experiments—showing how mixed designs and careful versioning build credible inference under volatility. Validity threats specific to platforms (deletion and moderation, survivorship bias, bots and coordination, shifting metrics) are treated as substantive features to document and model rather than as nuisances to ignore.*

## INTRODUCTION

Digital platforms have become infrastructures through which people work, socialise, mobilise, consume, and express identity. They are not neutral channels but

DOI: 10.4018/979-8-3373-4267-2.ch015

rule-bound, profit-seeking systems that curate visibility, rank relevance, and monetise attention. Studying them is therefore never a purely technical exercise. Every methodological decision—how to sample data, how to approach participants, how to interpret traces—immediately triggers ethical questions about consent, privacy, risk, and accountability. In sociology, where research routinely interrogates power, culture, and identity, this collision between method and ethics becomes especially sharp. Platforms shape what can be known about social life at the same time that they shape social life itself, and researchers must navigate this double influence while safeguarding those who appear in their datasets and narratives (Fu et al. 2021).

## 1.1 Defining platforms and platformization

A platform is a configurable digital infrastructure that mediates interactions among users, advertisers, developers, workers, and institutional actors, while recording, ranking, and monetising those interactions. Platformization refers to the diffusion of platform logics—such as data extraction, two-sided market dynamics, and algorithmic curation—into ever more domains of social and economic life. This diffusion has methodological consequences because it renders the "field" both dispersed and dynamic. What once might have been studied in bounded settings—a workplace, a neighbourhood, a classroom—now appears as an assemblage of interfaces, recommendation engines, moderation pipelines, cloud services, and policy teams whose decisions change frequently and sometimes without public notice. Researchers confront a moving target: data endpoints are deprecated, terms of service shift, and ranking algorithms are modified in response to commercial or political pressures. The empirical object is thus simultaneously technical, organisational, and cultural (Popiel & Vasudevan, 2024).

## 1.2 What counts as "platform research"

Platform research spans studies conducted on platforms, about platforms, and with platforms. Research on platforms includes ethnographies of communities that convene in platform spaces or studies of gig workers whose labour is intermediated by apps. Research about platforms scrutinises governance, moderation, datafication, and business models. Research with platforms relies on platform data, interfaces, and tools, whether through public APIs, scraping, or partnerships. The boundaries among these categories blur in practice: an ethnography of creators on a video site may also entail analysis of its recommendation logic; a study of labour relations may depend on privately mediated access to transaction logs. Recognising these overlaps clarifies why ethical and methodological questions cannot be separated.

A decision about how to collect data is also a position on what a platform is and whose interests are centred (Cheng et al. 2024).

## 1.3 The ethical problem of "public" data

Platforms invite a reconsideration of the idea that public data is free of ethical constraint. Content may be publicly accessible yet contextually private: a post intended for a small imagined audience can be amplified by algorithms to millions, archived indefinitely, and re-combined with other traces to reveal identities or sensitive attributes. The mosaic effect means that de-identified datasets can be re-identified when merged with auxiliary information. Even when users accept terms of service, they rarely anticipate academic repurposing of their expressions or understand downstream risks, particularly for marginalised communities and precarious workers. Treating visibility as consent collapses contextual norms and exposes participants to harms ranging from reputational damage to targeted harassment and job loss. Ethical platform research therefore begins by interrogating whether legal permissibility aligns with sociological responsibility (Mirghaderi et al. 2023).

## 1.4 Asymmetries of power, access, and interpretation

The core methodological challenge is asymmetry. Platforms control data supply, rate limits, and the interpretive scaffolding embedded in dashboards and documentation. These controls steer what questions can be asked and answered, often privileging metrics that reflect commercial priorities over sociological relevance. Researchers may depend on partnerships that deliver rich data while introducing conflicts of interest and restrictions on publication or replication. Even without formal partnerships, sampling is shaped by opaque moderation, shadow bans, and takedown policies that remove contentious material and erase the very conflicts a sociologist might wish to study. Interpretation is similarly asymmetric. When algorithms are black boxes, observed outputs can be consistent with multiple causal stories. Without transparency about training data, business incentives, or enforcement practices, findings are always provisional and vulnerable to quiet updates that rearrange the field mid-study.

## 1.5 Platforms as culture, identity, and governance

Sociological inquiry foregrounds the co-production of culture and identity through mediated interaction. Platforms organise attention and belonging, encouraging particular performance styles, community norms, and moral economies. At the same time, they govern through code and policy, establishing boundaries around what is sayable, saleable, and visible. These features scale unevenly across geographies and languages, producing distinctive harms in the Global South, low-resource languages, and vulnerable labour markets where content moderation and platform work are outsourced. A sociological lens highlights these patterned inequalities and asks how methods can register experiences that platforms are incentivised to downplay or render statistically invisible. The demand is not only for technical competence but also for reflexive awareness of how a researcher's own positionality, language, and institutional support mediate access and interpretation.

## 1.6 From field sites to living systems

Traditional field sites are relatively stable: a researcher can return to the same workplace or neighbourhood and find similar actors and practices. Platforms are living systems that reconfigure the conditions of inquiry. A/B testing alters interfaces; recommendation model's drift; enforcement priorities shift with elections or advertiser pressure. This churn undermines reproducibility, complicates longitudinal inference, and challenges norms of open science when sharing data could enable re-identification or facilitate harassment. It also creates design opportunities. Time-stamped interface walkthroughs, structured diaries with creators or workers, and protocol-based algorithm audits can help stabilise observation. Mixed methods that triangulate traces, talk, and interface states are not optional extras but necessary responses to a dynamic object.

## 1.7 Ethical reflexivity as methodological rigour

Because platforms are both the medium and the milieu of social life, ethical reflexivity becomes indistinguishable from methodological rigour. Reflexivity entails explicit articulation of researcher aims, funding, access channels, and potential conflicts; careful accounting of risks to participants and bystanders; and transparent discussion of what cannot be known under existing constraints. It also includes plans for communicating findings in ways that minimise harm, such as altering or withholding sensitive details when disclosure would enable retaliation or surveillance. Far from diluting scientific value, these practices increase credibility by situating claims within the real limits of evidence and by acknowledging how power operates through data infrastructures (Molina et al. 2023).

## 1.8 Scope, boundaries, and key terms used in this chapter

This chapter focuses on large, commercial platforms that intermediate social interaction, content distribution, or labour markets. It also considers third-party ecosystems, including data brokers, content farms, content moderation vendors, app stores, and advertising networks that amplify platform effects. Key terms are used in the following ways throughout the chapter. "Users" names people who post, view, purchase, or work through platforms, while recognising that these categories overlap. "Trace data" refers to records of interaction generated through use, including posts, clicks, purchases, location pings, ratings, and transaction logs. "Algorithmic governance" denotes the use of automated decision systems to curate content, price labour, or enforce rules. "Risk" encompasses direct individual harms, collective harms to groups or movements, and systemic harms to public discourse. These clarifications aim to keep the discussion concrete while accommodating variation across sectors and regions.

## 1.9 The argument in brief

The central claim advanced here is that platform research must treat ethics and methods as a single design problem. The choice of a data pipeline is also a stance on consent; the construction of a sampling frame is also a claim about whose experiences are legible; and the framing of findings is also an intervention in contested public arenas. Responsible research on platforms therefore requires methodological pluralism, explicit acknowledgement of asymmetries, and practices of accountability to those whose lives supply the data. Rather than seeking a universal recipe, the chapter offers principled guidance that can be adapted across topics and contexts.

## 1.10 Roadmap and contribution to the volume

The remainder of the chapter proceeds in a sequence that moves from political economy to practice. The next section examines how platform business models and gatekeeping structures shape data access and researcher dependence. Subsequent sections revisit consent, privacy, and harm in public-private spaces; survey methodological repertoires suitable for algorithmically mediated environments; and address the practicalities of working with trace data under constraints of validity, reproducibility, and law. A dedicated section engages the challenges of studying algorithms through audits and experiments, followed by a discussion of qualitative immersion, positionality, and researcher safety. Later sections consider governance, review processes, and cross-border responsibilities, before turning to accountability to communities and the public. The chapter concludes with a practical toolkit and a forward-looking agenda for building collaborative standards that embed ethical reflexivity into methodological craft. In situating sociological platform research within the dynamics of power, culture, and identity, the chapter contributes a foundational vocabulary and a set of actionable design choices for conducting rigorous, responsible, and reflexive work in the digital age.

## 2. PLATFORM POLITICAL ECONOMY AND RESEARCHER DEPENDENCE

Platform research unfolds within an economy of data that platforms themselves construct and control. The same infrastructures that mediate culture and identity also mediate access to knowledge about those processes. In practice, this means that the questions sociologists can ask, the evidence they can assemble, and the claims they can responsibly make are shaped by commercial incentives, technical affordances, and legal arrangements that sit outside the academy. Research design is never only a matter of method; it is conditioned by the platform's business model, its governance practices, and its tolerance for scrutiny. Dependence on platform-controlled pipelines introduces asymmetries that are methodological, ethical, and political at once (Narayan, 2024).

### 2.1 Gatekeeping, opacity, and data leverage

Platforms monetise attention and interaction by transforming them into measurable, tradeable signals. In doing so they also acquire what can be called data leverage: structural power over the supply of traces and the interpretive frames attached to them. This leverage expresses itself through terms of service, developer policies, dashboards, and white papers that define what counts as a legitimate query, a permissible unit of analysis, or an authorised rate of access. The very categories through which activity is recorded—views, impressions, clicks, likes, ratings—are products of design choices aimed at market goals, not at sociological validity. When researchers inherit these categories uncritically, they risk reproducing platform logics in their own analyses.

Opacity intensifies the problem. Key components of the data-generating machinery—ranking models, recommendation thresholds, content moderation rules, spam and bot detectors—are guarded as trade secrets. The absence of visibility into these mechanisms means that observed outcomes rarely admit a single causal reading. A spike in video views may reflect genuine public interest, a temporary adjustment to recommendation weights, or a moderation lapse that privileged certain content. Access pathways that route through official APIs further confine researchers to predefined endpoints. Information relevant to questions of power, labour, or inequality may be technically collected by the platform but not exposed, leaving scholars to infer patterns from partial shadows (Zook & Spangler, 2023).

## 2.2 Infrastructural churn and the fragility of longitudinal work

Platforms are living systems that change often and sometimes abruptly. Interfaces are redesigned, user experience experiments roll out to random subsets of the population, and policy updates revise what data is retained or made accessible. API versions are deprecated, rate limits tightened, and endpoints removed with limited notice. For sociologists this churn undermines comparability across time. A dataset gathered before a policy change is not strictly commensurable with one gathered after, even if variable names remain identical. What appears as a trend may simply be an artefact of shifting capture protocols.

The fragility of longitudinal work is not merely technical. Churn also affects the communities under study. Visibility regimes change who is seen and how; enforcement priorities reorganise the risks that users, creators, and workers face; algorithmic adjustments alter the strategies people adopt to be heard or to earn. Long-term projects must therefore document not only the data they analyse but also the environment that produced it. Time-stamped notes on interface states, public policy statements, developer notices, and community responses become part of the empirical record necessary for interpretation and for responsible replication (McCammon & Lingel, 2022).

## 2.3 Conflicts of interest, partnerships, and the price of access

Rich, granular data are sometimes available only through partnerships that come with non-disclosure agreements, pre-publication review, or restrictions on what can be shared. These arrangements can open doors to otherwise invisible phenomena, such as worker allocation logs or detailed content-moderation outcomes. They also risk entangling the research agenda with the platform's reputational interests. Even when there is no explicit interference, self-censorship can emerge as scholars anticipate jeopardising future access or worry about legal exposure. Publication constraints may preclude releasing the code or data needed for replication, weakening the public value of the work and placing trust in personal relationships rather than in transparent procedures.

Funding sources can create further complications. Industry-supported chairs, data grants, or fellowships may be essential for resourcing computationally intensive studies; they can also raise questions about independence, particularly when research touches on controversies involving the sponsor. The ethical challenge is not to refuse engagement categorically, but to surface these conditions as part of method. Clear statements of access pathways, contractual limits, and the sponsor's potential stakes in the findings help readers evaluate claims. Where possible, dual strategies—combining partnered access with independent audits or community-based evidence—can reduce the risk of capture (Van der Vlist & Helmond, 2021).

## 2.4 Unequal research ecologies and the reproduction of knowledge gaps

Dependence on platform-controlled data amplifies inequalities within the research ecosystem. Well-resourced institutions can absorb the costs of data purchases, specialised staff, and legal review; independent researchers, journalists, and scholars in the Global South may not. Language coverage, too, is uneven. APIs and archives are often better supported for English and a handful of major languages, which means that harmful dynamics in low-resource languages or marginalised regions remain under-studied. The result is a skewed literature in which certain contexts are endlessly examined while others remain largely invisible, not because they are less sociologically significant but because they are less legible to the available tools.

These imbalances carry methodological consequences. Sampling frames become biased toward what is accessible; theoretical generalisations are made from narrow slices of platform life; and policy recommendations risk being calibrated to the experiences of already-visible groups. A reflexive approach treats access limitations as part of the research object. It asks how structural barriers shape what can be known and how alternative forms of evidence—oral histories with creators, diaries with platform workers, court filings, public regulatory submissions, and civic observatories—can be mobilised to widen the aperture (Wiegleb & Bruns, 2025).

## 2.5 Law, terms of service, and the ethics–legality gap

Legal constraints intersect with platform rules in ways that complicate ethical judgment. Scraping publicly available information may be lawful in some jurisdictions and prohibited in others; even where lawful, it may violate platform terms. Conversely, terms may permit uses that raise ethical red flags, such as extended retention of sensitive posts or the linkage of pseudonymous identities across datasets. Institutional review boards and research ethics committees often focus on human-subjects criteria developed for face-to-face studies, leaving grey zones in which projects are technically compliant but ethically fraught.

Responding to the ethics–legality gap requires explicit reasoning that goes beyond compliance checklists. Researchers can articulate harm models that consider not only immediate risks to individuals but also collective harms to communities, movements, or labour cohorts. They can adopt data minimisation and responsible deletion practices even when rules do not demand them, and they can design communication plans that reduce the chance of enabling harassment or commercial exploitation. Publishing these choices as part of the method section creates precedent and signals to reviewers what responsible conduct looks like in platform settings (Turillazzi et al. 2023).

## 2.6 Metrics, narration, and the politics of interpretation

Because platform metrics are engineered for advertising and growth, they often fail to capture what sociologists care about: meaning, belonging, stigma, or solidarity. A million views may combine curiosity, outrage, and organised brigading; a "like" may indicate acknowledgement rather than endorsement; a high rating may be coerced by algorithmic penalties. The politics of knowledge therefore extends from data access to narrative framing. Researchers must translate platform-native signals into sociological constructs without smuggling in the platform's own worldview.

One response is triangulation that pairs trace analysis with qualitative immersion. Interviews with creators can reveal how they game or resist ranking rules; diaries with gig workers can disclose the hidden labours behind punctual ratings; walk-throughs of interface changes can show how affordances gently nudge behaviour. Another response is methodological humility: presenting findings as bounded by the particular versioned environment in which they were produced and acknowledging plausible alternative explanations that cannot be ruled out without platform transparency (Georgakopoulou et al. 2022).

## 2.7 Designing under dependence: practical principles

Dependence on platform infrastructures is unavoidable. The task is to design studies that acknowledge and mitigate it. Documentation becomes a first principle: every dataset should be accompanied by a narrative of its provenance, collection window, and environmental context, including known policy or interface changes. Where access is mediated by partnerships, constraints and review processes should be made explicit. Where scraping is used, the ethical case for doing so should be argued in terms of societal benefit, minimal risk, and respect for contextual norms.

Diversification of evidence is a second principle. Combining platform traces with off-platform sources—worker forums, public complaints to regulators, union reports, leaked policy guidelines, and creator newsletters—can stabilise inference when APIs shift. Building temporal anchors is a third principle. Time-stamping all steps, archiving codebooks and interface captures, and pre-registering analysis plans when feasible helps future readers interpret results produced in fluid environments. Finally, accountability to communities should be treated as part of method. Plans for feedback, safe dissemination, and harm remediation align scholarly practice with the ethical stakes outlined in Section 1 and anticipate the accountability frameworks developed later in the chapter (Drewel et al. 2021).

### 2.8 From constraint to object of study

Researcher dependence is not only an obstacle; it is itself an empirical phenomenon that reveals how platform power operates. Gatekeeping, opacity, churn, and partnership politics are mechanisms through which companies manage public knowledge about their systems. Treating these mechanisms as part of the field—documenting them, comparing them across firms, and tracing their effects on what questions get asked—turns limitation into insight. In this way, the political economy of platforms becomes visible not merely as background context but as a constitutive force shaping sociological knowledge. Recognising this helps scholars craft research that is methodologically rigorous, ethically grounded, and clear-eyed about the infrastructures on which it necessarily depends.

## 3. RETHINKING CONSENT, PRIVACY, AND HARM IN PUBLIC–PRIVATE DIGITAL SPACES

Research on digital platforms unsettles inherited ethical categories. What looks "public" to a web crawler is often experienced as intimate by the person who posted it. What counts as "consent" in a terms-of-service checkbox may not resemble informed agreement to become a research subject. And what appears as an innocuous dataset can, when combined with other traces, expose individuals, communities, or workers to reputational damage, targeted harassment, or economic sanction. In platform environments, privacy is relational and contextual, consent is ongoing rather than one-off, and harm is frequently collective rather than individual. This section reframes these concepts for sociological work that engages with algorithmically curated spaces (Beverungen et al. 2022).

### 3.1 What counts as "public" online

Public accessibility is not the same as ethical permission. Platforms collapse contexts by making posts searchable, remixable, and indefinitely persistent, while the people who produce those posts often imagine a small audience of peers. Sociological research must therefore consider the social meaning of visibility, not only the technical availability of content. A forum thread open to anyone may still be contextually private if community norms expect limited circulation, or if participation is tied to vulnerable identities. Even when users enable public profiles, they rarely anticipate academic collection, long-term archiving, or linkage to other datasets. Treating public interfaces as open fields of observation risks overriding local expectations of appropriateness. Rather than assuming that openness equals consent, researchers should ask what the audience was likely to be, how the platform's design amplifies or narrows reach, and whether quoting or republishing could recontextualise speech in ways that increase exposure or misinterpretation.

### 3.2 Consent beyond checkboxes: informed, contextual, and ongoing

Consent on platforms is multi-layered. Users agree to terms in order to participate, but these contracts are designed to protect the platform, not to invite deliberation about research risks. Sociological consent requires a different standard that centres comprehension, voluntariness, and the possibility of withdrawal. In some settings, traditional participant consent is feasible through direct contact, debriefing pages, or in-platform messaging. In others, such as large-scale trace studies where contact is impracticable, researchers should articulate a contextual rationale that weighs societal benefit against risk, explains why consent is infeasible, and documents measures to reduce harm. Consent should also be understood as ongoing, because platform conditions change. Interface revisions can alter the meaning of participation; policy updates can expose content to new audiences; and evolving political climates can transform benign traces into liabilities. Where practicable, mechanisms for withdrawal or data erasure should be offered, and researchers should be prepared to adjust protocols when the environment shifts.

### 3.3 Anticipating harm: from individual risk to collective and systemic effects

Risk in platform research extends beyond the individual to relationships, communities, and public discourse. A gig worker identified through a composite of ratings and location trails could lose employment; a creator singled out in an audit could face brigading; a small activist group might suffer chilling effects if internal coordination channels are exposed. Harms also arise from inference, where algorithms or researchers ascribe attributes—such as political orientation, sexual identity, or health status—on the basis of behavioural traces that were never intended to disclose such information. A careful harm model distinguishes between direct harms, such as doxxing or account takedowns; indirect harms, such as stigma or strained relationships; and collective harms, such as targeted disinformation against a community or increased surveillance of a labour cohort. The design of dissemination matters as much as the design of data collection. Publishing granular maps, verbatim quotes that are easily searchable, or code that enables profiling can unintentionally provide tooling to bad actors. Responsible practice involves asking not only whether a finding is true but also how its release could be weaponised (Bettivia, & Stainforth, 2023).

### 3.4 Bystanders, co-present others, and inferred subjects

Platform traces routinely contain information about people who are not the primary focus of a study. Photos include bystanders; chat logs mention third parties; ride-hailing ratings describe passengers who never agreed to be studied. These co-present others are often at greater risk because they have not been approached for consent and may be unaware that their data exist in a research corpus. In addition, platform data enable inference about non-participants through social graphs, location co-presence, or family linkages, creating subjects who never directly appear in the dataset. Ethical protocols should recognise bystanders and inferred subjects as stakeholders. Techniques such as redaction, blurring of faces, suppression of unique phrases, and aggregation to higher units of analysis can reduce exposure. Where bystander risk is material, de-identification alone is insufficient; decisions about what to display, quote, or share must be guided by a conservative approach to contextual integrity.

### 3.5 Power differentials, vulnerable groups, and platform labour

Not all users occupy the platform on equal terms. Children and minors, migrants, LGBTQ+ communities, caste and racial minorities, and people targeted by state or non-state surveillance may face disproportionate harm if their traces are exposed or recontextualised. Platform workers, including content moderators, delivery riders, and crowdworkers, operate within rating and deactivation regimes that make them acutely vulnerable to reputational shocks. Researchers should calibrate methods to these asymmetries. Recruitment scripts must avoid undue influence when participation affects access to scarce resources. Compensation should be fair without being coercive. Fieldwork plans should include routes for participant support if exposure triggers harassment or employer retaliation. In some cases, the ethically appropriate choice is to alter, delay, or forgo publication when the risk to vulnerable groups outweighs the public value of immediate disclosure (Green, 2024).

### 3.6 Data minimisation, retention limits, and deletion by design

The most robust privacy protection is not to collect or retain data that are not strictly necessary. Data minimisation can be implemented at every stage. During collection, sampling can privilege coarse signals over high-resolution identifiers;

paraphrasing can replace verbatim quotes; and on-device filtering can discard sensitive attributes before storage. During processing, access controls, encryption, and audit trails help prevent misuse, while role-based permissions limit who can see raw traces. During dissemination, aggregates and synthetic exemplars can stand in for individual-level records. Retention schedules should be explicit, time-bound, and enforced, with deletion triggers linked to project milestones. Deletion by design acknowledges that risks grow over time as auxiliary datasets proliferate, search tools improve, and social contexts change. Minimisation and deletion are not signs of weak science; they are marks of ethical craft that prioritises sufficiency over exhaustiveness.

## 3.7 Anonymisation pitfalls, paraphrasing, and quoting practices

De-identification on platforms is brittle because uniqueness abounds. Uncommon usernames, rare phrases, and distinctive combinations of time and place can allow re-identification with little effort. Anonymisation must therefore be coupled with transformation. When presenting excerpts, paraphrasing that preserves meaning without verbatim text reduces searchability. When using images, masking faces and distinctive backgrounds can prevent reverse image search. When reporting interface screenshots, cropping to remove personal elements and obscuring handles can reduce exposure. Aggregation to groups, distributions, or model summaries should be preferred over individual exemplars unless there is a compelling public-interest justification. Where verbatim quotations are essential—for instance, to represent linguistic nuance or community voice—researchers should consider obtaining explicit permission, altering non-essential details that do not change meaning, or presenting composites that capture patterns without singling out identifiable individuals.

## 3.8 Law, platform rules, and the ethics–legality gap in practice

Compliance with law and terms of service is necessary but not sufficient. Jurisdictions differ on whether scraping publicly available pages is lawful, while platforms may forbid it regardless. Conversely, a platform's developer policy may permit data uses that are ethically questionable, such as indefinite retention of sensitive content or resale to third parties. Ethical judgment must therefore extend beyond compliance checklists. Researchers should document why a chosen path aligns with societal benefit, consider less invasive alternatives, and describe mitigation measures openly. When legal advice, institutional review, and community consultation diverge, the decision should be argued in the methods section so that peers can evaluate the trade-offs. This transparency does not eliminate risk, but it distributes responsibility by making the ethical reasoning legible (Strand & Svensson, 2023).

## 3.9 Communicating risk and practicing care in dissemination

Ethical responsibility continues after data collection has ended. Drafts can be shared with community advisors or participant representatives to identify unintended exposures. Embargoes can be used to coordinate with support organisations when publication may trigger backlash. Media engagement should avoid sensational framing that directs harmful attention toward vulnerable individuals or groups. Supplementary materials should be curated with the same care as the main text; code and data that enable profiling should be withheld, summarised, or released in controlled-access environments. Reflexive statements about what was deliberately not shared—and why—help set expectations and model responsible practice for others.

## 3.10 Reframing privacy and consent as methodological design

The central claim of this section is that privacy and consent are not external constraints imposed on method; they are intrinsic design variables. Choosing units of analysis, crafting sampling frames, writing scraping scripts, and deciding how to quote or visualise are all ethical acts because they structure who is exposed to what kinds of risk. Good platform research therefore embeds privacy and consent into its architecture from the outset. It treats participants and bystanders as stakeholders, anticipates collective as well as individual harms, and builds minimisation and deletion into its pipelines. When these commitments are made explicit, the result is not only ethically sound but also methodologically sharper, because claims are calibrated to the realities of platformed life and the responsibilities that come with representing it.

# 4. METHODOLOGICAL REPERTOIRES FOR STUDYING PLATFORMS

Studying platforms requires a repertoire that stretches across qualitative immersion, computational analysis, and design-inspired inspection of interfaces and algorithms. Methods do not simply "apply" to platforms; they are reshaped by platform logics of data capture, curation, and control. This section surveys major approaches and shows how they can be assembled into designs that respect ethical constraints while answering sociologically significant questions about power, culture, and identity online. Later sections develop trace-data practices and algorithm audits in greater technical depth; here the emphasis is on aligning questions with methods, building credible inferences through triangulation, and managing time and versioning in environments that change continuously (Decuypere et al. 2021).

## 4.1 Matching questions to methods in algorithmic environments

Method choice should begin with the social theory a study seeks to test or elaborate. Questions about meaning-making, identity performance, and norm formation are well served by methods that generate thick descriptions of situated practice, such as digital ethnography, participant observation in online communities, and semi-structured interviews with creators, moderators, workers, or users. Questions about visibility, amplification, and the distribution of attention require access to traces that capture ranking outcomes, engagement trajectories, and moderation events, combined with modelling strategies that can separate organic interaction from algorithmic shaping. Questions about governance and power asymmetries call for walkthroughs of policy, enforcement pipelines, and interface affordances, paired with documentary analysis of public statements, developer notes, and regulator filings. In each case, the platform's incentives and design must be treated as part of the causal story, not as background noise.

A recurring challenge is that the platform defines many of the categories available for measurement. A count of "views" or "rides" is not a neutral descriptor but a product of design choices and business goals. When sociological theory demands constructs such as stigma, solidarity, or labour precarity, the task is to build observational strategies that move beyond platform-native metrics. This may involve eliciting narratives from participants about how they interpret numbers and rules, constructing bespoke indicators from raw traces, or designing instruments—such as diaries or think-aloud protocols—that capture the labour and emotion behind apparently simple interactions (Bonina et al. 2021).

## 4.2 Digital ethnography and thick description online

Digital ethnography follows people through the platformed spaces where they live, work, and organise. It pays attention to speech genres, humour, ritual, conflict, and repair. It is attentive to the ways in which interfaces invite or constrain expression and to the tacit know-how that communities develop to navigate ranking rules, moderation thresholds, and harassment. Thick description is not limited to chat logs or posts. It also includes attention to the rhythms of notification, the choreography of content production, the backstage labour of editing and scheduling, and the micro-politics of groups, guilds, or worker forums. Field relations require care because the researcher is often visible as a user. Reflexive journals that track the researcher's own reactions, confusions, and temptations can surface biases and document the evolving field, while negotiated anonymity and paraphrasing protect participants whose words might otherwise be trivially searchable.

Ethnography gains analytic power when it is coupled with interface sensibilities. Noting the presence or absence of buttons, defaults, prompts, and frictions helps explain why particular practices emerge and which identities become viable. Recording time-stamped screenshots, change logs, and community reactions to design shifts helps stabilise meaning in a living system where an ethnographic scene today may be impossible tomorrow.

## 4.3 Interviews, diaries, and elicitation techniques

Interviews remain central because people can tell us what numbers cannot: how it feels to be de-ranked without explanation, to chase a badge that opens access to monetisation, or to weigh the risks of speaking out under real-name policies. Sampling should follow the structure of the platformed field rather than convenience. Creators vary by genre, size, and revenue model; workers vary by contract status, geography, and rating history; users vary by linguistic communities and device access. Purposive sampling that represents these axes yields richer theory. Diaries add temporal depth by capturing routines, workaround strategies, and the emotional costs of navigating opaque systems. Screen-recorded diaries, where participants narrate their interactions in situ, reveal micro-decisions that are otherwise invisible. Elicitation can also be done with artefacts: showing participants their own analytics dashboards or moderation notices and inviting commentary often produces insights into how people read platform signals and adjust behaviour.

Care must be taken to avoid extracting sensitive detail that escalates risk. Compensation should be fair and transparent. Consent should be revisited when platform conditions change, and withdrawal must remain a real option. Where interviews or diaries intersect with platform rules or employment contracts, researchers should prepare guidance on minimising exposure and access to support if participation triggers negative consequences (Fu et al. 2021).

## 4.4 Trace data and computational analysis

Trace data offer scale and temporal coverage that ethnography alone cannot reach. They include posts, comments, likes, shares, ratings, transaction logs, and location pings, as well as metadata about devices, languages, and network ties. Computational analysis can map communities, model diffusion, detect coordination, and characterise moderation outcomes. Yet trace data are never complete. They are filtered by platform capture, retention, and exposure policies; they may exclude deleted content or content removed by moderation; they may be contaminated by bots or spam. A credible design acknowledges these properties and treats missingness and measurement error as substantive features to be studied and reported.

Constructing valid indicators from traces requires work. Engagement counts must be contextualised by exposure opportunities, which are themselves shaped by ranking. Text embeddings and clustering can recover themes without presupposing categories, but they require careful validation against human interpretations from diverse language communities. Network measures can describe cohesion or fragmentation but may be skewed by visibility constraints or shadow bans. The aim is not to discard traces but to situate them within a design that also includes human accounts and interface analysis, so that numbers illuminate rather than overwrite lived experience.

## 4.5 Platform walkthroughs and interface archaeology

Walkthroughs treat the platform as a sequence of scripted invitations and obstacles. They document what a novice and an expert encounter when creating an account, posting content, reporting abuse, appealing a takedown, or onboarding as a worker. A rigorous walkthrough is more than a tour. It is an analytic protocol that records decision points, defaults, and affordances, noting how small design choices shift responsibility onto users or workers. Interface archaeology extends this logic across time by reconstructing prior states through archived pages, developer notes, or community documentation. Together, these methods clarify how culture and identity are shaped by the scaffolding that structures action, and how governance is encoded in ostensibly neutral design (Chen et al. 2022).

## 4.6 Experiments, audits, and agent-based probes

When the research question concerns algorithmic treatment, observational designs may be insufficient. Experiments and audits attempt to isolate causal effects of ranking or enforcement. Sock-puppet or agent accounts can be seeded with controlled behaviours to test how content is recommended, how ads are targeted, or how workers are allocated tasks. Natural experiments can exploit platform-wide changes, such as policy updates or interface redesigns, to compare outcomes before and after. These designs demand care because they can introduce deception, generate collateral exposure, or violate terms of service. The ethical case must be argued explicitly, risks minimised through containment and narrow scope, and debriefing considered when feasible. Replication is hard because platforms evolve; documentation of the environment and versioning of protocols is therefore part of the evidence.

## 4.7 Mixed-method triangulation and integrative inference

No single method can capture the layered nature of platform life. Triangulation builds credible claims by aligning evidence from traces, talk, and interfaces. An analysis of toxic amplification might combine network models of diffusion with interviews of targeted users and a walkthrough of reporting flows that clarifies why protection fails. A study of gig work precarity might pair transaction logs with worker diaries and observations from online forums to reveal how algorithmic nudges translate into risky behaviour on the road. Integrative inference is not a matter of piling up data but of staging encounters between forms of evidence that test rival explanations. This requires pre-specifying what each method is expected to show and being prepared to revise theory when different streams disagree. Disagreement is not failure; it is often the strongest signal that the platform's own categories are occluding important dynamics.

## 4.8 Temporal designs, versioning, and the problem of comparability

Platforms change, sometimes quietly. Time must therefore be treated as a design dimension rather than a nuisance. Longitudinal designs should bind data collection to documented states of the platform and its policies. Time-stamped interface captures, API version notes, and public policy announcements become part of the data. When comparing across time, researchers should assess whether the meaning of variables has shifted. A "view" counted before a major change in counting logic is not the same as a "view" counted after. When comparability cannot be assured, analyses should be framed as case-bound and non-comparable rather than forced into trend narratives. Event studies that anchor analysis to platform-wide changes can help isolate effects when true panel comparability is unavailable (Kretschmer et al. 2022).

## 4.9 Data stewardship, collaboration, and community accountability

Methodological craft includes the way data and findings are stewarded. Secure pipelines, access controls, and deletion schedules protect participants and bystanders. Collaborative designs that involve community advisors, worker organisations, or creator collectives can surface blind spots, improve measurement validity, and guide safe dissemination. Partnerships with journalists, civil-society groups, or civic observatories can expand reach without surrendering independence, but they must be governed by clear agreements that protect participants and the integrity of analysis. Accountability continues after publication through feedback channels, corrigenda when errors are found, and careful curation of code and documentation so others can understand what was done without enabling abuse.

### 4.10 Writing methods for platforms: transparency without exposure

Reporting practices should make platform studies legible and reproducible without compromising safety. A methods section should describe access routes, collection windows, sampling logic, and known environmental changes. It should state what could not be observed, why those gaps matter, and how claims were calibrated in light of them. When code or data cannot be shared publicly without enabling harm, alternatives such as synthetic datasets, controlled-access enclaves, or detailed computational notebooks that operate on mock data can preserve transparency about procedure. Quotations, screenshots, and exemplars should be paraphrased or masked unless explicit permission and a compelling public-interest justification exist. Above all, the method write-up should treat ethics as integral to design rather than as a compliance appendix. Doing so models a form of platform research that is rigorous, reflexive, and responsible in the face of systems whose opacity and volatility would otherwise erode sociological understanding (Komljenovic, 2021).

## 5. WORKING WITH PLATFORM TRACE DATA: ACCESS, VALIDITY, AND REPRODUCIBILITY

Platform trace data promise breadth and temporal depth, but they are produced inside infrastructures that curate what is captured, what is kept, and what is exposed. Treating these traces as if they were neutral records invites error. This section sets out practical and ethical guidance for acquiring traces, assessing their validity, and building reproducible analyses without increasing risks to participants or bystanders. The emphasis is on designing pipelines that make limitations visible, document the living environment in which data were generated, and stabilise claims when interfaces and policies change (Wu & Taneja, 2021).

### 5.1 Pathways to access and their consequences

Access routes shape the data itself. Official interfaces expose a narrow set of endpoints with predefined fields and rate limits. Partnered access can yield richer logs while imposing contractual constraints on sharing, description, or critique. Scraping can recover public information that is otherwise unavailable, yet it may contravene terms of service and amplify legal and ethical risks. Each pathway encodes assumptions about the platform's preferred units of analysis and workflows. A responsible design begins by stating which path was used, why alternatives were infeasible or ethically inferior, and how the chosen route might bias the picture. If a study relies on an endpoint that excludes deleted or moderated items, for example, conclusions about toxicity or mobilisation must be calibrated to a dataset that already reflects enforcement.

## 5.2 Constructing a sampling frame in curated environments

Sampling on platforms rarely involves drawing from a complete population. Visibility is filtered by ranking, rate limits restrict capture, and relevance is often constructed with keywords or hashtags that are unevenly adopted across communities and languages. A credible sampling plan therefore starts from the substantive question and builds a frame that reflects where relevant activity plausibly occurs. When keywords are unavoidable, they should be iteratively refined with community input and checked for false negatives and false positives across dialects and scripts. Time windows should be tied to documented policy or interface states, with clear boundaries between pre-change and post-change observations. Where possible, exposure opportunities should be modelled alongside engagement outcomes, since "high engagement" can be an artefact of privileged ranking rather than genuine resonance (Ohme et al. 2024).

## 5.3 Missingness, deletion, and survivorship bias

Platform traces are perishable. Users delete posts, moderation removes items, and automated systems demote or hide content. Studies that rely only on what is still visible at collection time inherit survivorship bias. Longitudinal claims are especially vulnerable: an apparent improvement in civility might simply reflect more aggressive removals rather than a change in behaviour. To address this, researchers should document the lag between creation and capture, report deletion rates when observable, and consider designs that sample in real time and then track the fate of items over fixed intervals. When deletions cannot be observed directly, proxy indicators—such as gaps in sequential identifiers, abrupt changes in category frequencies, or community reports of takedowns—should be noted as part of a limitations statement.

## 5.4 Bots, coordination, and measurement error

Automated and coordinated activity is integral to many platform ecologies. Treating all traces as independent human actions inflates counts and distorts network structures. Detection should combine multiple signals rather than rely on a single heuristic. Temporal regularity, improbable posting speeds, content duplication across accounts, link shortener patterns, and newly created accounts that achieve disproportionate reach are all relevant, but none is decisive alone. Human adjudication on small samples helps calibrate automated filters and exposes edge cases where activists, fandoms, or worker collectives may look automated because of shared scripts or scheduled posting. Rather than claiming a perfectly "clean" corpus, researchers should present sensitivity analyses that show whether results hold under more and less conservative bot-filtering thresholds.

## 5.5 Building valid indicators from platform-native metrics

Platform metrics are engineered for growth and advertising, not for sociological meaning. Views, likes, ratings, and completion rates provide signals, but their interpretation depends on exposure, interface nudges, and community norms. Constructing valid indicators often requires re-scaling metrics by estimated impressions, combining counts with temporal dynamics, or translating numerical thresholds into situated practices reported by participants. Text representations should be evaluated for bias across languages and dialects, with validation that includes native speakers and community insiders rather than only crowd workers. Network measures should be interpreted with care when visibility is uneven or when moderation quietly removes edges over time. The aim is to move from platform numbers to sociological constructs through explicit modelling choices, tested against qualitative knowledge of how people read and respond to those numbers (Liu et al. 2021).

## 5.6 Provenance, environment logging, and analytic audit trails

Reproducibility on living platforms depends as much on environmental documentation as on code. Every dataset should be accompanied by a provenance narrative that records the collection window, access route, credentials or tiers used, endpoints or scraping patterns, and any observed errors or throttling. Environment logs should include the platform's public policy statements relevant to the period, archived versions of key interface screens, and developer notices about deprecations or counting logic changes. Analytic audit trails should capture preprocessing steps, versioned code with fixed random seeds, and checksums for intermediate artefacts. Where possible, analyses should be containerised so that others can re-run pipelines against synthetic or redacted data to verify logic even when raw traces cannot be shared.

## 5.7 Security, governance, and minimum-necessary data

Ethical stewardship rests on the principle of collecting and retaining only what is necessary to answer the research question. Pipelines should implement encryption at rest and in transit, role-based access with least privilege, and separate storage for identifiers and content when identifiers must be held temporarily. Data access should be logged, with periodic reviews that confirm who has touched what. Retention schedules should be declared at the outset and enforced, with deletion events recorded as part of the audit trail. When collaboration involves multiple institutions, governance should specify who is the data controller for different jurisdictions and how requests for erasure or withdrawal will be honoured in derived artefacts such as embeddings or trained models.

## 5.8 Anonymisation, paraphrasing, and resistance to re-identification

De-identification on platforms is fragile because uniqueness is common. Paraphrasing quotations reduces searchability while preserving meaning; composites can represent recurring patterns without exposing particular individuals; and images should be masked to prevent reverse search. When identifiers are essential for longitudinal linkage, salted hashes and keyed pseudonyms can minimise exposure without undermining analysis. Researchers should test their own outputs for re-identification risk by attempting to recover sources through simple searches and by consulting community advisors about what would be recognisable to insiders. If a claim depends on verbatim content, explicit permission and careful contextualisation are warranted, and in some cases withholding is preferable to publication (Li et al. 2022).

## 5.9 Sharing, replication, and controlled access

Open science norms collide with the duty to avoid harm. Full public release of raw traces can enable profiling, harassment, or targeted commercial exploitation. A middle path relies on controlled-access repositories, data enclaves, and synthetic or heavily redacted datasets that preserve the structure necessary to check code while protecting individuals and communities. Replication packages should include executable notebooks that operate on mock data, detailed descriptions of each processing step, and pointers to environment logs so that others can see the state of the platform during collection. When findings hinge on partnered or confidential data, authors should disclose constraints, provide as much procedural transparency as possible, and, where feasible, triangulate with independent data sources to reduce reliance on private pipelines.

### 5.10 Reporting limitations as part of validity

Validity in platform studies is inseparable from honest accounting of what could not be observed. Methods sections should state which populations or languages are under-represented, which forms of activity are excluded by design, and how deletion, moderation, or ranking might have shaped the corpus. Claims should be bounded to the documented environment and framed as contingent when hidden mechanisms could plausibly yield alternative explanations. Rather than weakening a study, this candour strengthens interpretability by aligning findings with the realities of curation and control that define platform life. In doing so, it anchors sociological inference in a practice that is both ethically careful and methodologically sound, preparing the ground for the algorithm audits and qualitative immersions taken up in the sections that follow.

## 6. STUDYING ALGORITHMS: AUDITS, EXPERIMENTS, AND INTERVENTIONS

Sociological questions about power, culture, and identity on platforms often turn on what algorithms recommend, hide, price, demonetise, or punish. These systems are dynamic, data-hungry, and entangled with business incentives. Studying them requires designs that can register causal influence without amplifying harm. This section develops the craft of audits, experiments, and interventions suited to living, opaque systems, emphasising how to stabilise observation, reason about validity, and practice care (Lam et al. 2023).

### 6.1 The Moving Target: What Counts As "The Algorithm"

"The algorithm" is not a single object. Recommendation and ranking assemble signals from user histories, content features, network ties, and policy rules; enforcement combines automated detectors with human review; ad delivery blends targeting with auction dynamics; labour allocation uses pricing, reputational scores, and predicted availability. Each subsystem evolves through A/B testing, model retraining, and policy updates. A study must therefore specify which subsystem is in view, at what time, and under which policy regime. Without this delimitation, findings become unmoored from the conditions that produced them and cannot travel.

## 6.2 Black-Box Audits: External Inference Under Opacity

Black-box audits infer algorithmic behaviour from inputs and outputs without internal access. They are appropriate when transparency is low but observational leverage is possible. A rigorous audit begins with a theory of the mechanism, translates that into testable contrasts, and fixes a protocol before data collection. For example, an audit of ranking can randomise content features across otherwise similar items to examine differential visibility, while an audit of ad delivery can hold targeting criteria constant and observe demographic skews in impressions. Power comes from careful control of inputs and repeated measurement over time to distinguish systematic effects from platform churn. Limits arise because observed differences may reflect unobserved policies or concurrent experiments. The remedy is disciplined documentation of the environment and humility in causal claims, presenting results as bounds rather than point estimates when uncertainty cannot be reduced (Vecchione et al. 2021).

## 6.3 Agent Accounts And Synthetic Personas: Seeding And Containment

Agent-based probes use newly created, tightly controlled accounts that perform scripted behaviours. They are useful for testing whether particular interests trigger distinct recommendation pathways, whether language or geography affects moderation, or whether worker acceptance patterns change with reputation scores. Design begins with persona construction that is plausible enough to elicit treatment but narrow enough to contain collateral exposure. Scripts should randomise order and timing to avoid trivially detectable automation and to reduce confounding with platform-side experiments. Ethical containment requires minimising downstream effects: avoiding posting content that could mislead real users, disabling notifications to others, and capping interaction volumes. Debriefing is rarely feasible at scale, so the ethical case rests on minimal risk, clear public interest, and immediate deletion of accounts when observation ends.

## 6.4 Natural Experiments And Platform-Wide Changes

Platforms frequently implement policy shifts, interface redesigns, or enforcement drives that create quasi-experimental conditions. Event-study designs can compare outcomes before and after a change, using unaffected groups or regions as comparators when available. The credibility of such designs turns on documenting timing, verifying that pre-trends are parallel, and checking for contemporaneous shocks that could contaminate inference. Because platforms often roll out changes gradually, staggered adoption designs may be possible, but they require careful attention to versioning and treatment heterogeneity. When the mechanism of change is unknown, qualitative work with affected communities can clarify how the policy manifests in practice and why measured effects look the way they do.

## 6.5 Field Experiments and Partnered Access: Leverage With Strings Attached

Occasionally, researchers can collaborate with platforms, regulators, or worker organisations to run controlled experiments. These designs can isolate mechanisms with unusual clarity, such as testing whether a particular disclosure reduces harmful spread or whether a change in pricing floors improves worker earnings. They also introduce dependence risks. Agreements may restrict outcome measures, preclude sharing code, or require pre-publication review. Ethical rigour demands published statements of constraints, parallel collection of independent indicators when feasible, and a commitment to report null or adverse findings. When partnerships are not possible, collaborations with civil-society groups or creator collectives can approximate field experiments by coordinating behaviour across many participants to test specific hypotheses while distributing risk and benefit more equitably (Howell et al. 2024).

## 6.6 Measuring the Right Things: Exposure, Delivery, Enforcement, And Downstream Life

Algorithm studies frequently mistake engagement for exposure. Visibility must be measured or proxied to interpret outcomes: impressions, position in a feed, or delivery share are conceptually distinct from clicks and likes. In ad systems, delivery and pricing are jointly determined, so any fairness claim must condition on auction dynamics, budgets, and pacing rules. In enforcement, the unit of analysis can be content, account, or group, and sanctions range from downranking to permanent removal. Downstream life matters as much as immediate treatment. A moderation action may relocate a community to a different platform; a ranking change may be offset by creator adaptation. Designs that follow consequences beyond the platform—through interviews, diaries, or off-platform traces—produce sociological understanding that metrics alone cannot supply.

## 6.7 Validity Threats In Adaptive, Networked Settings

Algorithms adapt to users, and users adapt to algorithms. This mutual adaptation violates assumptions that underwrite standard causal designs. Interference is routine: the treatment of one account changes the environment of others, so the standard "no interference" assumption rarely holds. Networked experiments should therefore define clusters within which interference is expected and randomise at the cluster level when possible, or else use designs that exploit partial interference structures. Manipulation by other actors also threatens validity. Coordinated campaigns can target study accounts; the platform may detect and dampen probes; concurrent A/B tests may alter exposure. Sensitivity analysis should assess whether findings persist under alternative clustering, different randomisation seeds, and subsets of observations less likely to be contaminated.

## 6.8 Ethics, Law, And Terms: Justifying Risk And Practicing Restraint

Audits and experiments often involve deception, data collection at scale, or actions that test the boundaries of terms of service. Ethical justification must be spelled out in the protocol: why the societal benefit outweighs minimal, well-mitigated risks; why less invasive designs will not answer the question; and what measures prevent harm to bystanders and workers. Legal advice is necessary but not sufficient, because the ethics–legality gap is common. Restraint should guide design choices. When probing ad targeting, use neutral content; when testing moderation, avoid posting material that could retraumatise or recruit; when studying labour allocation, refrain from accepting tasks that would deprive workers of income. Plans for secure storage, short retention, and prompt deletion are not administrative afterthoughts; they are part of the design that earns the right to run the study.

## 6.9 Documentation, Pre-Specification, And The Value Of Null Results

Because platforms change quickly, documentation becomes a form of evidence. Protocols should fix hypotheses, outcomes, and analysis strategies in advance, with allowances for registered contingencies if the environment shifts. Time-stamped captures of interfaces, policy pages, and developer announcements help anchor inference. When results are null or mixed, they still have public value: they bound what algorithms are doing under documented conditions and help counter survivorship bias toward dramatic findings. Publishing negative or inconclusive audits, along with lessons about what failed and why, strengthens the field's collective capacity and helps prevent duplicative risk (Tümmler & Quick, 2025).

### 6.10 Collaborative Audits And Public Accountability

Audits and experiments gain legitimacy and traction when they are accountable to those affected. Co-design with creators, users, or workers can surface harm models researchers might miss and can identify safe windows for observation. Reporting back to communities, even when findings are technical, encourages corrections and builds trust. Coordination with journalists and regulators can translate results into public debate and policy review without sensationalising individual cases. Ultimately, the aim is not only to measure algorithms but to widen democratic oversight over systems that quietly distribute opportunity, risk, and recognition. A sociology of platforms that treats audits and experiments as ethically charged, community-engaged interventions will produce knowledge that is both methodologically credible and publicly consequential.

## 7. QUALITATIVE IMMERSION AND RESEARCHER POSITIONALITY

Qualitative immersion is indispensable for understanding how platforms shape meaning, belonging, and everyday practice. Interviews, observations, and ethnographic participation make visible the tacit skills people develop to survive ranking systems, cope with moderation, and make a living in precarious digital labour markets. Yet immersion on platforms is never only a matter of method; it is an encounter between situated people under asymmetric conditions of visibility and risk. The researcher's identity, institutional location, language repertoire, and technical footprint actively contour what can be seen, what will be said, and how findings travel. This section outlines how to enter platformed fields with care, how to work reflexively with power, and how to protect both participants and researchers when exposure is ambient and fast-moving (Zhao, 2024).

### 7.1 Entering Field Sites That Are Mediated By Platforms

Gaining entry to communities that gather on platforms requires sensitivity to local norms and gatekeeping roles that may be informal yet consequential. Moderators, admins, and veteran members function as boundary managers whose consent carries moral weight even when formal approval is not required. Initial contact benefits from transparent self-presentation that names the research aims, anticipated uses of data, and limits to confidentiality in networked spaces. Where communities are stigmatised or face harassment, open recruitment should avoid platform mechanics that amplify visibility to hostile audiences. Private outreach, staged conversations with small groups, and negotiated observation periods allow trust to develop without forcing members to perform consent in public.

## 7.2 Lurking, Participation, And The Ethics Of Presence

The long-standing ethnographic tension between observation and participation takes on new stakes online. "Lurking" can protect participants from the distortions of researcher presence, yet it risks violating contextual expectations of mutual recognition. Participation may build rapport and generate thick description, but it can tip into role confusion when the researcher's contributions affect status hierarchies or conflict dynamics. A defensible stance begins by asking what presence would feel like to those being studied and by aligning conduct with community norms. In some settings, explicit researcher tags in profiles and occasional reminders of the study's purpose balance transparency with minimal disruption. In others, negotiated windows of active participation interspersed with periods of quiet observation help disentangle influence from documentation. Whatever the stance, it should be recorded in reflexive notes so that readers can weigh how presence shaped the evidence.

## 7.3 Positionality as an Analytic Resource, Not An Afterthought

Positionality encompasses more than a declaration of identity categories. It is an account of how one's social location, institutional ties, funding sources, and technological skills open some doors and close others. A researcher who shares language and cultural background with participants may access intimate narratives while struggling to surface taken-for-granted assumptions; a researcher perceived as elite or foreign may elicit strategic performances that foreground respectability or resistance. Rather than treating these effects as contamination, positionality can be mobilised as an analytic resource. Contradictions in how different interlocutors respond, shifts in candour as trust grows, and topics that remain off-limits despite effort all point to underlying structures of power and risk on the platform. Writing that foregrounds these dynamics does not undermine validity; it clarifies what the account can and cannot claim (Adjei & Nung Chan, 2025).

## 7.4 Language, Translation, And The Politics Of Voice

Platform research often crosses languages, dialects, and scripts, with algorithmic translation smoothing over difference while reproducing bias. Qualitative immersion must therefore treat language as a site of power. Interviews should, where possible, be conducted in participants' preferred language, with translators or co-researchers who are culturally embedded rather than merely fluent. Translation choices should be documented, including terms that resisted equivalence and moments where humour, irony, or politeness conventions altered the apparent meaning of a statement. When quoting, paraphrase can protect anonymity, but it may erase linguistic texture that constitutes identity work. A workable compromise alternates paraphrase for search-resilient protection with carefully masked short excerpts that preserve voice, accompanied by commentary that renders culturally specific references legible without flattening them.

## 7.5 Confidentiality, Consent, And The Problem Of Searchability

Qualitative materials created on platforms are trivially searchable. A distinctive phrase, a screenshot with partial interface elements, or a pseudonym reused across sites can re-identify a speaker. Consent forms must therefore explain the limits of anonymity in networked environments and describe the strategies the study will use to mitigate risk. These strategies include transforming quotations through paraphrase that preserves meaning, constructing composites that combine features of multiple cases, and masking handles and visual markers in images. Consent should be framed as ongoing because policy shifts or new search tools can change the balance of risk. When a participant later requests withdrawal, deletion plans should extend to derivative artefacts such as analytic memos, codebooks, or trained models that encode sensitive information.

## 7.6 Researcher Safety, Harassment, And Emotional Labour

Immersion in contentious platform spaces exposes researchers to targeted harassment, doxxing, and vicarious trauma. Safety planning is part of the method. Basic operational security, such as segregated research accounts, minimal public footprints tied to the study, and strong authentication practices, reduces attack surfaces. Communication with participants through channels that do not reveal personal contact details protects both sides. Emotional labour requires equal forethought. Repeated exposure to violent content, grief, or burnout narratives among gig workers can erode judgment and well-being. Debriefing routines, access to counselling, and peer support structures within the research team convert individual coping into collective care. When harassment escalates, pausing data collection or altering public dissemination plans is not a failure of rigour but a recognition that ethical obligations extend to the research team.

## 7.7 Reciprocity without Inducement

Reciprocity is ethically desirable and sociologically fruitful, yet it can shade into undue influence where access to money, visibility, or platform resources is scarce. Compensation should recognise participants' time while avoiding amounts that could coerce participation or disclosure. Reciprocity can also take the form of practical support that does not distort research relationships, such as sharing know-your-rights resources for platform workers, offering media literacy sessions to creator communities, or providing private briefings on findings that help groups understand risks without exposing individuals. These gestures do not purchase candour; they signal respect and acknowledge the asymmetries that organise the field.

## 7.8 Documentation, Memoing, And The Discipline Of Reflexive Records

Qualitative validity depends on disciplined documentation. Reflexive memos should track the evolution of access, shifts in community norms, and the researcher's changing understanding of key terms. Time-stamped notes that correlate field events with platform changes are critical in living systems where interface affordances and enforcement priorities can shift overnight. When multiple team members conduct fieldwork, shared memo templates, periodic calibration meetings, and inter-coder dialogues prevent idiosyncratic interpretations from hardening into unexamined facts. These practices are not bureaucratic overhead. They are the infrastructure that allows others to evaluate the chain from observation to claim (Tungohan & Catungal, 2022).

## 7.9 Cross-Context Comparison and the Global South

Platform dynamics unfold unevenly across regions, languages, and connectivity regimes. Studies anchored in well-resourced contexts can miss how data charges, device constraints, and local political economies shape participation elsewhere. Comparative immersion that includes low-resource settings requires partnerships with local scholars and community organisations who can co-design instruments, interpret ambiguity, and surface risks that an outsider might miss. Ethical review should consider cross-border data protections and the potential for findings to trigger state or platform retaliation in fragile contexts. When publication in a dominant language risks erasing local nuance, parallel outputs in community languages or collaborations with local media can preserve voice while distributing benefits more equitably.

## 7.10 Writing with Care: Representation, Composites, And The Afterlives Of Stories

The way qualitative findings are written has consequences for those represented. Narratives that centre extremes travel farther on social media and in news coverage, but they can stigmatise communities or invite copycat abuse. Writing with care means resisting the lure of spectacular cases when they misrepresent the modal experience, clarifying when an account is composite, and naming the criteria used to balance fidelity with protection. It also means anticipating afterlives. Once published, quotes and vignettes circulate beyond academic contexts. A dissemination plan that includes preprints with redacted details, embargoes coordinated with support organisations, and media guidance that avoids naming vulnerable groups prevents research from becoming a resource for harassment or commercial exploitation. The ethic is simple even if the practice is hard: representation should reduce harm while increasing understanding.

In sum, qualitative immersion on platforms is a craft of presence, protection, and principled self-implication. It treats positionality as a lens rather than a liability, builds confidentiality into the architecture of fieldwork and writing, and accepts that care for participants and researchers is inseparable from methodological rigour. By taking these commitments seriously, sociologists can produce accounts that register the textures of platformed life without reproducing the harms that such accounts aim to understand.

# 8. GOVERNANCE, REVIEW, AND CROSS-BORDER DATA RESPONSIBILITIES

Platform research is entangled with layers of governance that exceed any single discipline or institution. Ethics committees, data-protection statutes, publisher requirements, platform policies, and cross-border cloud infrastructures all lay claim to how data are collected, processed, shared, and archived. Because platforms operate transnationally and change quickly, compliance cannot be treated as a one-time hurdle; it is an ongoing practice that shapes what can be known and how findings travel. This section maps the institutional landscape and offers a way of working that aligns methodological rigour with legal and ethical responsibility across jurisdictions (Coche et al. 2024).

## 8.1 From IRB/REC Compliance To Governance By Design

Institutional review boards and research ethics committees were built for studies in which investigators recruit identifiable participants and collect bespoke data. Platform research often sits askew of this template: data may be publicly accessible yet contextually sensitive; consent may be impracticable at scale; and risks may be collective as much as individual. The task is to translate platform realities into protocols that IRBs can evaluate. That means articulating harm models that include bystanders and inferred subjects, explaining why consent is not feasible or would itself create exposure, and describing concrete mitigations such as paraphrasing, aggregation, deletion schedules, and controlled access. Governance by design goes further than approval. It embeds ethical controls in the pipeline: least-privilege access, environment logging, retention limits, and pre-commitments to withhold or delay dissemination when risk profiles change.

## 8.2 Data Protection Regimes And The Research Exception

General data-protection laws frame much platform research because traces can constitute personal data even when identifiers are stripped. Many regimes recognise research as a special purpose that can justify processing under strict safeguards. The spirit of these provisions is not carte blanche but proportionality. Researchers should be able to show that the public interest in understanding platform power, discrimination, or labour conditions outweighs residual risks; that the project uses the minimum necessary data; and that safeguards such as pseudonymisation, encryption, and controlled access are in place. Where cross-border processing occurs, responsibilities must be allocated in writing: who is the data controller, who is the processor, which sub-processors are involved, and how data transfers are justified. These allocations are not merely bureaucratic; they determine who answers when participants exercise access or deletion rights and who must notify regulators if a breach occurs (Krimmer et al. 2021).

## 8.3 Cross-Border Data Flows, Sovereignty, And Cloud Realities

Platforms, data brokers, and research teams often rely on globally distributed infrastructures. Storage locations, content delivery networks, and subcontracted moderation services can straddle legal boundaries. The result is a sovereignty problem: data about residents of one jurisdiction may be handled in another with different protections or obligations. Governance requires mapping data flows in enough detail to answer basic questions. Where, precisely, will raw traces, intermediate artefacts, and trained models reside. Which services or libraries phone home diagnostics or cache content outside the declared storage region. How will lawful access requests from governments be handled when they conflict with research promises or ethics approvals. When the data concern vulnerable groups, additional prudence may justify keeping raw materials within a trusted enclave under local control and exporting only aggregates or synthetic derivatives.

## 8.4 Roles, Contracts, And Multi-Institution Collaborations

Collaborations concentrate both opportunity and risk. Memoranda of understanding and data-sharing agreements should define purpose limitation, security standards, retention periods, audit rights, and publication freedom. They should also specify how withdrawal requests propagate into derived artefacts such as embeddings, topic models, or trained classifiers. The common fiction that "de-identified" data are outside the scope of governance is dangerous on platforms where re-identification risk is high. Contracts should assume that protection requires ongoing controls rather than a one-off transformation. In cross-university projects, a lead institution should be nominated to coordinate incident response, handle regulator communications where applicable, and maintain the master copy of provenance logs (Yun, 2025).

## 8.5 Publisher Policies, Transparency Statements, And Replication With Care

Journals increasingly require data-availability statements, code repositories, and disclosure of funding and access constraints. In platform research, full public release of raw traces may be unethical even when legally permissible. A defensible path balances transparency and protection. Methods sections should describe access routes, collection windows, and environmental states in enough detail for others to understand constraints. Replication packages can include executable notebooks that run on synthetic or heavily redacted data while preserving the analytic logic. When partnered access imposes confidentiality, authors should disclose those limitations, justify why public interest still warrants publication, and, where possible, triangulate with independent data to reduce dependence on private pipelines. Reviewers and editors play a governance role by recognising that "no data release" can be the ethical choice and by rewarding rigorous procedural transparency.

## 8.6 Oversight Beyond The Academy: Regulators, Platforms, And Civil Society

Regulatory authorities, platform trust-and-safety teams, labour ministries, and civil-society organisations all participate in governing digital ecosystems. Researchers can productively engage with these actors without surrendering independence. Coordination with regulators can align studies with public-interest investigations and help ensure that sensitive findings are acted upon rather than sensationalised. Engagement with platform teams can clarify technical behaviour while preserving the right to publish adverse results. Partnerships with unions, worker associations, or creator collectives can surface harms and distribute benefits, but they must be structured to protect individuals from retaliation. These relationships should be formalised in protocols that specify what can be shared, how, and when, including embargoes that allow support organisations to prepare for possible backlash upon publication.

## 8.7 Incident Response And Duty Of Care

Platform fields are volatile. A leak, coordinated harassment, or policy pivot can reclassify benign data as hazardous overnight. Governance requires an incident-response plan that covers the research team and participants. It should name decision-makers, thresholds for pausing collection or redacting outputs, procedures for notifying affected collaborators, and channels for seeking legal counsel or institutional support. Duty of care extends to the research workforce, including students and contractors exposed to distressing material or online abuse. Mental-health support, workload rotation, and safe communication practices are not afterthoughts; they are conditions of ethical work in high-risk environments. After an incident, lessons learned should be incorporated into revised protocols and, where appropriate, shared with the field so others can avoid repeating harms.

## 8.8 Accountability through Documentation: Provenance, Environment, And Audit

Documentation is the hinge between governance and method. Provenance records should capture the who, what, when, where, and how of data acquisition and transformation. Environment logs should include interface states, policy pages, and developer announcements relevant to the collection window. Access logs should record which team members touched which artefacts and when. These materials serve at least three functions: they enable internal accountability and continuity when teams change; they support external review without exposing raw traces; and they ground sociological interpretation by tying claims to a documented state of a living system. When controlled-access sharing is possible, these logs can travel with analysis code to allow procedural replication (Chin & Zhao, 2022).

## 8.9 Ethical Sharing, Enclaves, And Synthetic Data

Where the public interest favours scrutiny of methods but the risk profile precludes releasing raw traces, controlled environments offer a compromise. Secure enclaves can permit vetted researchers to run code against sensitive data under supervision, with outputs checked for disclosure risk. Synthetic datasets can approximate the statistical structure of the real corpus without reproducing identifiable records, though they must be validated to avoid communicating artefacts. Summaries that preserve key distributions, network statistics, or model diagnostics provide further avenues for transparency. Whatever the mechanism, researchers should explain the trade-offs, document validation steps, and invite critique of the chosen approach.

## 8.10 Writing Governance Into The Contribution

In platform research, governance is not a compliance appendix; it is part of the scholarly contribution. Studies should state clearly how legal frameworks, institutional review, publisher expectations, and cross-border infrastructures shaped design choices, what could not be done or shared, and how claims were bounded accordingly. They should also reflect on governance as an empirical object: gatekeeping by platforms, reinterpretation of research exemptions, and uneven enforcement of data-protection rights are themselves phenomena that organise knowledge production. By making governance visible in this way, the chapter's larger argument comes into focus. Ethical reflexivity and methodological craft are inseparable in environments where the politics of studying platforms are entangled with the politics of platforms themselves. Responsible research proceeds not by evading these entanglements but by designing within them—accountable to participants, transparent to peers, and attentive to the unequal geographies through which digital power circulates.

# 9. ACCOUNTABILITY TO COMMUNITIES AND THE PUBLIC

Accountability in platform research is not achieved by compliance alone. It is a practice of relational responsibility that extends from the first contact with participants to the long afterlives of publications, datasets, and media coverage. Because platform research frequently addresses harms that communities already endure—targeted harassment, economic precarity, cultural erasure—its public communication can either mitigate or magnify those harms. An accountable approach treats communities as knowledge partners rather than data sources, centres their safety in dissemination choices, and recognises that findings will circulate in environments shaped by the very platforms under study (Shore & Prena, 2025).

## 9.1 From Extraction To Relationship: Rethinking Who Research Is For

Traditional research pipelines often presume a one-way flow of value from communities to scholarship. In platform settings that model is ethically brittle and sociologically impoverished. Communities—users, creators, gig workers, moderators, and organisers—possess situated expertise about ranking regimes, monetisation pressures, and enforcement gaps that researchers cannot infer from traces alone. Accountability begins by recognising this expertise and designing engagements in which communities help define questions, interpret ambiguity, and prioritise which risks matter most. That does not entail romanticising consensus or ceding critical distance. It means acknowledging that knowledge about platforms is co-produced and that relationships outlast any single project. When researchers leave, communities still live with the consequences of exposure, policy shifts, and media narratives triggered by the work.

## 9.2 Participatory and Co-Designed Studies Without Tokenism

Co-design can formalise collaboration without collapsing it into token consultation. Clear agreements should specify the scope of community involvement, decision points where input is binding, and areas where researchers retain independence. Advisory boards composed of creators, workers, or community moderators can review instruments, sampling frames, and harm models; they can also flag language that may stigmatise or misrepresent. Compensation for advisory labour should be transparent and fair. Co-authorship is appropriate when community partners contribute to conceptual framing or analysis, but it should not expose individuals to retaliation; collective or organisational authorship can distribute recognition while reducing personal risk. The objective is to embed accountability into method rather than bolt it on as public relations (Parker et al. 2024).

## 9.3 Returning Results: Formats, Timing, And Language

Results should return to the people who made them possible in forms they can use. That often means multiple outputs: an academic article with methodological detail; a plain-language brief that summarises findings, limitations, and practical implications; and community-facing presentations or private briefings that allow discussion of sensitive points. Timing matters. Embargoes can give community organisations or worker collectives time to prepare support resources if findings are likely to attract hostile attention. Language matters as well. Translation into community languages, and into registers that match how people actually talk about platform dynamics, signals respect and reduces dependence on intermediaries who may distort nuance.

## 9.4 Communicating Uncertainty And Avoiding Amplification Of Harm

Accountability includes how uncertainty is communicated. Platform environments are volatile and opaque; strong claims travel quickly but can mislead. Public materials should foreground what is known, what is plausible, and what cannot be determined without platform transparency. Graphs and exemplars should avoid sensational focus on extreme cases if those are unrepresentative. When describing harmful content or tactics, researchers should avoid including operational details that would help adversaries replicate them. Where the public interest requires disclosure, descriptions should be bounded, and practical countermeasures should accompany the account. The aim is to make harm legible without providing a how-to guide.

## 9.5 Media Engagement And Narrative Control

Media coverage can widen the reach of findings but also compress complexity into headlines that invite backlash. Accountability asks researchers to plan for this compression. Press materials should include context about environmental conditions, sample limitations, and versioning, and they should offer language that resists sensationalism. When journalists request identifiable stories, composite narratives and paraphrased quotes can protect individuals while conveying pattern. Naming vulnerable communities should be weighed against the risk of directing new harassment; sometimes it is safer to describe dynamics without naming targets explicitly, while coordinating with advocacy groups that can speak in their own voice if they choose. Researchers should be prepared to decline interviews that demand reductive frames or that would expose participants to renewed scrutiny (Massaro et al. 2025).

## 9.6 Benefit Sharing, Credit, And Authorship Justice

Communities should share in the benefits that flow from research about them. Benefit sharing can take many forms: briefing sessions that equip workers to advocate for policy changes; toolkits that help creators understand ranking logics and safer reporting pathways; or policy memos to regulators informed by community priorities. Credit should follow contribution. When community partners shape research questions, provide analytic insight, or lead dissemination, co-authorship or formal acknowledgments are appropriate. Where naming individuals is unsafe, organisations can receive credit, and anonymous acknowledgments can recognise contributions without enabling retaliation. Authorship justice resists extractive publication practices and affirms the social labour that makes rigorous, situated analysis possible.

## 9.7 Harm Reporting, Remediation Paths, And Duty To Warn

Research sometimes uncovers imminent harms: coordinated harassment campaigns, data exposures that could enable stalking or doxxing, or platform policies that put workers at acute risk. Accountability requires a plan for escalating such findings responsibly. That plan can include confidential notifications to affected communities, coordination with trusted civil-society intermediaries, and, where appropriate, carefully documented outreach to platform trust-and-safety teams or regulators. Duty to warn does not mean deputising researchers as enforcers; it means recognising when withholding information would foreseeably harm participants. Documentation of what was shared, with whom, and why should be maintained, and communications should minimise disclosure of identifying details beyond what remediation requires.

## 9.8 Safeguarding Data Legacies And The Right To Be Forgotten

The afterlives of datasets and field notes present accountability challenges that stretch beyond project timelines. Participants may later wish to withdraw, particularly when platform policies or political climates change. Accountable designs anticipate withdrawal by separating identifiers from content, versioning derived artefacts, and maintaining indices that allow targeted deletion of records and embeddings. Data-retention schedules should be time-bound and enforced, with periodic reviews that reassess risk as auxiliary datasets and search tools evolve. Archiving policies must balance scholarly memory with the right to obscurity; in some cases, responsible stewardship means allowing records to disappear rather than preserving them indefinitely for hypothetical future use (Hsieh et al. 2024).

## 9.9 Public Sociology In Platform Worlds: From Findings To Action

Accountability includes translating findings into forms that publics and institutions can use without misinterpretation. Public sociology in platform worlds entails careful alignment with advocacy and policy processes while retaining independence. Policy briefs can map the likely consequences of ranking changes or enforcement shifts and propose evaluation metrics that foreground equity rather than engagement alone. Testimony to regulators can clarify where transparency would enable independent validation without compromising security. Collaboration with investigative journalists can surface systemic issues while protecting individuals through redaction and delayed publication. Across these venues, researchers should resist becoming spokespersons for platforms or partisans; their distinctive contribution is to make mechanisms legible, highlight distributional consequences, and insist on standards for evidence in public debate.

## 9.10 Building Institutions Of Accountability: Observatories, Archives, And Community Governance

Individual projects cannot shoulder accountability alone. Institutional supports can distribute responsibility and raise standards. Independent observatories that monitor platform policy changes, API deprecations, and enforcement trends provide a shared reference for interpreting results across studies. Controlled-access archives, governed by community-inclusive boards, can host sensitive materials under rules that balance transparency with protection. Ethics review processes can incorporate community letters or attestations alongside institutional approvals, recognising that local legitimacy matters when research concerns contested spaces. Funding mechanisms can require impact statements that describe planned community engagement, benefit sharing, and risk mitigation, and they can resource those activities as integral to the science rather than as extras (Di Vaio et al. 2024).

In sum, accountability to communities and the public is not a separate phase of research but a continuous orientation that shapes design, analysis, and communication. It demands humility about what can be claimed in volatile, opaque systems; care in how stories are told and to whom; and commitments to share benefits and manage harms over time. When accountability is practiced in this way, platform research can illuminate structures of power, culture, and identity without reproducing the inequalities and exposures it seeks to understand.

# 10. PRACTICAL TOOLKIT AND FUTURES

This final section gathers the chapter's commitments into a workable toolkit while sketching the futures of ethical, rigorous platform research. The aim is not to prescribe a single recipe but to translate principles into routines, files, and sentences that a project can actually run. The horizon it imagines is collective: researchers, communities, regulators, and even platforms building shared infrastructures that lower risk, raise evidentiary standards, and widen who counts as a knower of platformed life (Sreekanthaswamy et al. 2025).

## 10.1 A Day-Zero Protocol You Can Actually Follow

Every platform study benefits from a brief, plain-language protocol written before the first line of code or the first message to a participant. In practice this document names the research questions and the public interest they serve; describes the access route and why alternatives are infeasible or riskier; specifies the smallest dataset that would allow an answer; states a retention period and the exact trigger for deletion; records foreseeable harms to individuals, bystanders, and communities; and sets the rule for pausing or aborting the study when conditions change. The protocol also identifies who owns which responsibilities across institutions, how withdrawal will be honoured in both raw traces and derivatives, and how results will return to those who bear the risks. Treat this file as living: time-stamp each revision, record the reasons, and keep it with your code so that the chain from decision to data is auditable.

## 10.2 Reporting Methods That Are Transparent Without Exposing People

Methods sections on living platforms must show their working while protecting the people who made the data possible. A defensible write-up states the collection window, API tiers or scraping patterns, observed outages or throttling, and the platform policies in force at the time. It explains missingness caused by moderation or deletion and makes clear when variables changed meaning across versions. It justifies any deception or agent accounts in terms of minimal risk and public benefit, and it describes steps taken to prevent collateral exposure. When code or data cannot be released openly, the section should point to a controlled-access plan, a synthetic or redacted corpus for checking logic, and an executable notebook that reproduces analysis on mock data. Such prose does not weaken claims; it anchors them in a documented environment (Khodabakhshian et al. 2024).

## 10.3 Model Sentences You Can Adapt

Researchers often know what they want to do but not how to phrase it responsibly. The following sentences can be tailored to context. For consent in public spaces: "Although the posts we analyse are publicly accessible, we treat them as contextually private. We paraphrase search-resilient phrases, refrain from linking to original accounts, and will delete records upon request when feasible." For scraping justification: "We collected only the fields necessary to answer the stated questions, avoided content behind authentication, respected robots exclusions where applicable, and immediately discarded identifiers not required for deduplication or longitudinal linkage." For risk and withdrawal: "Participants and bystanders may face reputational or economic harms if re-identified. We therefore publish aggregates and composites, operate with a fixed retention window of ninety days for raw traces, and honour requests to remove content from both source tables and derived embeddings." For partnered access: "Data were provided under an agreement that restricts public release. We disclose these constraints, report adverse or null findings, and triangulate with independent sources to reduce dependence on private pipelines."

## 10.4 Reproducible Pipelines That Do Not Leak

Reproducibility on platforms is as much about environment capture as it is about code. A robust pipeline records interface states, counts-logic changes, and developer announcements contemporaneous with collection; fixes random seeds and library versions; logs rate-limit events and error codes; and stores checksums for intermediate artefacts. Keep raw traces in a separate enclave, then generate analysis-ready derivatives that drop direct identifiers and sensitive fields. Pair the private pipeline with a public twin that runs on synthetic or heavily redacted data so peers can execute the same transformations. When a claim depends on a model, export coefficients and diagnostics rather than weights trained on sensitive records. Reproducibility then becomes a property of documented procedure rather than of risky data sharing (Schäper et al. 2024).

## 10.5 Collaboration without Capture

Interdependence is unavoidable, but capture is not. When working with platforms, agree in writing that authors retain the right to publish null or adverse results and that pre-publication reviews are limited to factual errors or disclosure risks. When working with communities, set expectations about what involvement entails, what will be shared back, and how recognition will be granted without exposing individuals to retaliation. When working with journalists or regulators, plan releases that prioritise safety over spectacle and that present uncertainty honestly. Across all collaborations, keep an independent stream of evidence—diaries with workers, public filings, civic observatories—so that findings do not hinge on a single gatekeeper.

## 10.6 Care for Researchers As Part Of Method

Platform work can exhaust, expose, and isolate research teams. Build care into the design. Use dedicated research accounts, separate contact channels, and multi-factor authentication. Rotate exposure to violent or distressing material and budget time for debriefs. Provide routes to counselling and institutional support in case of harassment or legal threat. Name a decision-maker with authority to pause data collection when risk spikes. Treat these safeguards as part of validity, because judgment degrades when people are exhausted or afraid.

## 10.7 Shared Infrastructures The Field Should Build

The futures worth pursuing are infrastructural. An open, versioned registry of platform policy changes and API deprecations would let studies align collection windows and interpret differences without guesswork. Community-governed enclaves could host sensitive datasets under rules that prioritise participant safety while enabling procedural replication. A minimal metadata schema—covering access routes, environment logs, sampling frames, retention and deletion, and any deception—would make platform studies comparable without forcing risky disclosure. Independent observatories could monitor ranking and enforcement trends across languages and regions, with protocols designed alongside creators, workers, and civil society so that audits remain accountable to those most affected (Tran et al. 2025).

## 10.8 Legal and Policy Horizons

Governance frameworks are evolving, and researchers should help shape them. Safe-harbour provisions for good-faith auditing, research exceptions that recognise collective harms, and obligations for platforms to provide transparency interfaces under privacy and competition law would all lower the ethical and legal cost of public-interest studies. At the same time, rules must protect against research that replicates extraction under the banner of openness. Proportionality, data minimisation, controlled access, and community oversight are the balancing principles. The future is not maximal disclosure but accountable visibility calibrated to risk.

## 10.9 Substantive Agendas That Demand New Methods

Platformisation is migrating into spaces that stretch our current repertoire. Cross-lingual dynamics in low-resource contexts require co-research with local scholars and translators who can validate models beyond English-centric benchmarks. Short-lived and encrypted channels call for consent-based diaries and interface walkthroughs rather than trace scraping. Generative systems that fabricate text, images, and personas demand audits that measure synthesis spillover into recommendation, moderation, and labour markets. Multi-platform ecologies, where actors migrate or coordinate across apps, require designs that track consequences beyond any single site and that treat re-platforming as part of the outcome rather than as analytic loss. Each frontier is both methodological and ethical: new instruments must be paired with fresh harm models and community accountability (Pacher & Glinik, 2024).

## 11. CONCLUSION

Throughout this chapter, ethics has not been a brake on inquiry but the gearwork that makes credible knowledge possible in environments defined by opacity and churn. The practical toolkit offered here—day-zero protocols, transparent methods that do not expose people, reproducible yet privacy-preserving pipelines, collaborations designed to avoid capture, care for researchers, and collective infrastructures—translates that stance into daily practice. The futures outlined—legal safe harbours, community-governed enclaves, observatories, and methods for cross-lingual and multi-platform worlds—are within reach if we treat governance as part of our scholarly contribution and accountability as a source of analytic strength. Studying platforms is inseparable from being shaped by them; rigorous, reflexive sociology accepts this entanglement and designs within it, so that our findings illuminate power, culture, and identity without reproducing the very harms we seek to understand.

## REFERENCES


Adjei, M., & Nung Chan, A. H. (2025). Making a difference with matter in researchers' positionality dynamics in qualitative inquiry. *Qualitative Research*, *25*(3), 711–731.

Bettivia, R. S., & Stainforth, E. (2023). Negotiating digital public spaces: Context, purpose and audiences. *The Journal of Documentation*, *79*(3), 703–717.

Beverungen, D., Hess, T., Köster, A., & Lehrer, C. (2022). From private digital platforms to public data spaces: Implications for the digital transformation. *Electronic Markets*, *32*(2), 493–501.

Bonina, C., Koskinen, K., Eaton, B., & Gawer, A. (2021). Digital platforms for development: Foundations and research agenda. *Information Systems Journal*, *31*(6), 869–902.

Chen, L., Tong, T. W., Tang, S., & Han, N. (2022). Governance and design of digital platforms: A review and future research directions on a meta-organization. *Journal of Management*, *48*(1), 147–184.

Cheng, H. K., Daniel Sokol, D., & Zang, X. (2024). The rise of empirical online platform research in the new millennium. *Journal of Economics & Management Strategy*, *33*(2), 416–451.

Chin, Y. C., & Zhao, J. (2022). Governing cross-border data flows: International trade agreements and their limits. *Laws*, *11*(4), 63.

Coche, E., Kolk, A., & Ocelík, V. (2024). Unravelling cross-country regulatory intricacies of data governance: The relevance of legal insights for digitalization and international business. *Journal of International Business Policy*, *7*(1), 112–127.

Decuypere, M., Grimaldi, E., & Landri, P. (2021). Introduction: Critical studies of digital education platforms. *Critical Studies in Education*, *62*(1), 1–16.

Di Vaio, A., Latif, B., Gunarathne, N., Gupta, M., & D'Adamo, I. (2024). Digitalization and artificial knowledge for accountability in SCM: A systematic literature review. *Journal of Enterprise Information Management*, *37*(2), 606–672.

Drewel, M., Özcan, L., Gausemeier, J., & Dumitrescu, R. (2021). Platform patterns—Using proven principles to develop digital platforms. *Journal of the Knowledge Economy*, *12*(2), 519–543.

Fu, X., Avenyo, E., & Ghauri, P. (2021). Digital platforms and development: A survey of the literature. *Innovation and Development*, *11*(2-3), 303–321.

Georgakopoulou, A., Iversen, S., & Stage, C. (2022). Quantified storytelling: How the tellable and the countable intermingle on digital platforms. In *The Routledge Companion to Narrative Theory* (pp. 149–163). Routledge.

Green, J. (2024). TikTok and the changing landscape of therapeutic digital spaces of care. *Digital Geography and Society*, *6*, 100077.

Howell, N., Hartsoe, W. F., Amin, J., & Namani, V. (2024, October). Reflective Design for Informal Participatory Algorithm Auditing: A Case Study with Emotion AI. In *Proceedings of the 13th Nordic Conference on Human-Computer Interaction* (pp. 1-17).

Hsieh, J., Zhang, A., Kim, S., Rao, V. N., Dalal, S., Mateescu, A., . . . Zhu, H. (2024, November). Worker Data Collectives as a means to Improve Accountability, Combat Surveillance and Reduce Inequalities. In *Companion Publication of the 2024 Conference on Computer-Supported Cooperative Work and Social Computing* (pp. 697-700).

Khodabakhshian, A., Puolitaival, T., & Kestle, L. (2024). The Digital Toolkit. *Architectural Design and Management in the Digital Age: International Perspectives*, 17-32.

Komljenovic, J. (2021). The rise of education rentiers: Digital platforms, digital data and rents. *Learning, Media and Technology*, *46*(3), 320–332.

Kretschmer, T., Leiponen, A., Schilling, M., & Vasudeva, G. (2022). Platform ecosystems as meta-organizations: Implications for platform strategies. *Strategic Management Journal*, *43*(3), 405–424.

Krimmer, R., Dedovic, S., Schmidt, C., & Corici, A. A. (2021, August). Developing cross-border e-Governance: Exploring interoperability and cross-border integration. In *International Conference on Electronic Participation* (pp. 107-124). Cham: Springer International Publishing.

Lam, M. S., Pandit, A., Kalicki, C. H., Gupta, R., Sahoo, P., & Metaxa, D. (2023). Sociotechnical audits: Broadening the algorithm auditing lens to investigate targeted advertising. *Proceedings of the ACM on Human-Computer Interaction, 7*(CSCW2), 1-37.

Li, B., Peng, X., Xiang, Q., Wang, H., Xie, T., Sun, J., & Liu, X. (2022). Enjoy your observability: An industrial survey of microservice tracing and analysis. *Empirical Software Engineering*, *27*(1), 25. PMID: 34867075

Liu, X., Barenji, A. V., Li, Z., Montreuil, B., & Huang, G. Q. (2021). Blockchain-based smart tracking and tracing platform for drug supply chain. *Computers & Industrial Engineering*, *161*, 107669.

Massaro, M., Spanò, R., & Kuruppu, S. C. (2025). Accountability and the metaverse: Unaccounted digital worlds between techwashing mechanisms and new emerging meanings. *Accounting, Auditing & Accountability Journal*, *38*(3), 908–933.

McCammon, M., & Lingel, J. (2022). Situating dead-and-dying platforms: Technological failure, infrastructural precarity, and digital decline. *Internet Histories*, *6*(1-2), 1–13.

Mirghaderi, L., Sziron, M., & Hildt, E. (2023). Ethics and transparency issues in digital platforms: An overview. *AI*, *4*(4), 831–843.

Molina, J. L., Tubaro, P., Casilli, A., & Santos-Ortega, A. (2023). Research ethics in the age of digital platforms. *Science and Engineering Ethics*, *29*(3), 17. PMID: 37185917

Narayan, D. (2024). The political economy of digital platforms: Key directions. *Platforms & Society*, *1*, 29768624241263071.

Ohme, J., Araujo, T., Boeschoten, L., Freelon, D., Ram, N., Reeves, B. B., & Robinson, T. N. (2024). Digital trace data collection for social media effects research: APIs, data donation, and (screen) tracking. *Communication Methods and Measures*, *18*(2), 124–141.

Pacher, C., & Glinik, M. (2024). Fostering entrepreneurial mindsets in deep tech disciplines: Exemplary development of a Toolkit. *Procedia Computer Science*, *232*, 1309–1318.

Parker, C., Albarrán-Torres, C., Briggs, C., Burgess, J., Carah, N., Andrejevic, M., & Obeid, A. (2024). Addressing the accountability gap: Gambling advertising and social media platform responsibilities. *Addiction Research and Theory*, *32*(4), 312–318.

Popiel, P., & Vasudevan, K. (2024). Platform frictions, platform power, and the politics of platformization. *Information Communication and Society*, *27*(10), 1867–1883.

Schäper, T., Foege, J. N., & Nüesch, S. (2024). Toolkits for innovation: How digital technologies empower users in new product development. *R & D Management*, *54*(1), 95–117.

Shore, A., & Prena, K. (2025). Platform rules as privacy tools: The influence of screenshot accountability and trust on privacy management. *New Media & Society*, *27*(2), 1053–1072.

Sreekanthaswamy, N., Anitha, S., Singh, A., Jayadeva, S. M., Gupta, S., Manjunath, T. C., & Selvakumar, P. (2025). Digital tools and methods. In *Enhancing School Counseling With Technology and Case Studies* (pp. 25–48). IGI Global Scientific Publishing.

Strand, C., & Svensson, J. (2023). Towards a situated understanding of vulnerability—An analysis of Ugandan LGBT+ exposure to hate crimes in digital spaces. *Journal of Homosexuality*, *70*(12), 2806–2827. PMID: 35674676

Tran, G., Kelly, B., Ryan, S. T., Hammersley, M., Kerr, E., Norman, J., & Okely, A. (2025). Development and formative evaluation of website-based tool to support healthy lifestyles in family day care. *Health Promotion Journal of Australia*, *36*(1), e947. PMID: 39780470

Tümmler, M., & Quick, R. (2025). How to detect fraud in an audit: a systematic review of experimental literature. *Management Review Quarterly*, 1-46.

Tungohan, E., & Catungal, J. P. (2022). Virtual qualitative research using transnational feminist queer methodology: The challenges and opportunities of zoom-based research during moments of crisis. *International Journal of Qualitative Methods*, *21*, 16094069221090062.

Turillazzi, A., Taddeo, M., Floridi, L., & Casolari, F. (2023). The digital services act: An analysis of its ethical, legal, and social implications. *Law, Innovation and Technology*, *15*(1), 83–106.

Van der Vlist, F. N., & Helmond, A. (2021). How partners mediate platform power: Mapping business and data partnerships in the social media ecosystem. *Big Data & Society*, *8*(1), 20539517211025061.

Vecchione, B., Levy, K., & Barocas, S. (2021, October). Algorithmic auditing and social justice: Lessons from the history of audit studies. In *Proceedings of the 1st ACM Conference on Equity and Access in Algorithms, Mechanisms, and Optimization* (pp. 1-9).

Wiegleb, V., & Bruns, A. (2025). Whose knowledge counts? Unpacking the uneven geographies and politics of knowledge co-production in IPBES. *Human Ecology*, *53*(1), 73–86.

Wu, A. X., & Taneja, H. (2021). Platform enclosure of human behavior and its measurement: Using behavioral trace data against platform episteme. *New Media & Society*, *23*(9), 2650–2667.

Yun, H. (2025). China's data sovereignty and security: Implications for global digital borders and governance. *Chinese Political Science Review*, *10*(2), 178–203.

Zhao, Y. (2024). TikTok and researcher positionality: Considering the methodological and ethical implications of an experimental digital ethnography. *International Journal of Qualitative Methods*, *23*, 16094069231221374.

Zook, M., & Spangler, I. (2023). A crisis of data? Transparency practices and infrastructures of value in data broker platforms. *Annals of the Association of American Geographers*, *113*(1), 110–128.

## KEY TERMS AND DEFINITIONS

**Agent-based probe / synthetic persona:** Controlled accounts that follow scripts to test algorithmic treatment while containing collateral effects.

**Algorithmic governance:** Rule-making and enforcement through automated systems (ranking, moderation, pricing, allocation) that steer attention, speech, and work.

**Black-box audit:** Inference about algorithmic behaviour from inputs and outputs without internal access; relies on carefully controlled contrasts and documentation.

**Bystanders and inferred subjects:** People who appear in data indirectly (mentions, photos, network ties) or can be inferred from others' traces; they carry risks without direct consent.

**Collective harm:** Injuries that affect groups or communities (stigma, surveillance, deplatforming), not only individuals; central to platform ethics.

**Content and account moderation:** Actions—manual or automated—that remove, restrict, or sanction content or users; ranges from label to permanent ban.

**Contextual integrity:** The idea that privacy depends on social context and audience expectations, not just technical "publicness"; moving data across contexts can be a breach.

**Controlled-access data enclave:** A secure environment where vetted researchers can run code on sensitive data under disclosure controls, balancing replication and protection.

**Data leverage:** Structural power arising from owning/controlling data capture, retention, and interfaces (APIs, dashboards), which lets platforms decide what researchers can observe.

**Data minimisation:** Collecting and processing only the least amount of data necessary to answer the research question, across collection, storage, and dissemination.

**Deletion by design:** Time-bound retention with pre-specified triggers for secure erasure of raw and derived artefacts to limit long-term risk.

**Digital ethnography:** Qualitative immersion in online communities and practices, attending to meaning, norms, labour, and interface effects.

**Downranking and shadow banning:** Reductions in visibility without overt removal; users may not be notified, complicating measurement and ethics.

**Exposure vs engagement:** Exposure refers to delivery/opportunity to see (impressions, rank position); engagement is response (clicks, likes). Valid inference often requires both.

**Informed consent (contextual/ongoing):** Consent calibrated to platform realities—comprehensible, revocable where feasible, and revisited as interfaces and risks change.

**Natural experiment / event study:** Causal design using platform policy/interface changes as "shocks," comparing outcomes before/after or across staggered rollouts.

**Platform power:** The capacity of platforms to shape visibility, behaviour, labour conditions, and knowledge production through design, policy, and control over data access.

**Platform walkthrough:** A systematic, time-stamped inspection of user flows, defaults, and affordances to understand how design encodes governance.

**Platformization:** The diffusion of platform logics—data extraction, two-sided markets, algorithmic curation—into ever more domains of social, cultural, and economic life.

**Pre-registration / day-zero protocol:** A pre-analysis plan that fixes questions, outcomes, and safeguards, with contingencies for platform churn.

**Provenance and environment logging:** Documentation of collection windows, endpoints, throttling, interface states, and policy notes that anchor results to a living system.

**Public–private boundary (online):** The blurred line where content is technically public yet socially intended for a limited audience, raising ethical issues for research reuse.

**Re-identification risk / mosaic effect:** The possibility that "de-identified" records can be re-linked to persons when combined with auxiliary datasets or searchable quotes.

**Survivorship bias (platforms):** Distortion caused by analysing only content that remains visible; moderated/deleted items vanish from many data sources.

**Synthetic data (privacy-preserving):** Artificial datasets that approximate statistical structure without reproducing identifiable records; requires validation against artefacts.

**Trace data:** Digital records of interaction (posts, clicks, ratings, logs, location pings) created as by-products of platform use.

**Pseudonymisation vs anonymisation:** Pseudonymisation replaces identifiers but allows potential re-linkage; anonymisation purports to prevent re-identification (often fragile online).

**Data controller vs processor:** The controller decides purposes/means of processing; the processor handles data on the controller's behalf—roles matter for rights and duties.

**Research exception (data protection):** Legal allowances to process personal data for research under safeguards like minimisation, security, and limited reuse.

**Cross-border data flows / data sovereignty:** Movement of data across jurisdictions with different protections; raises obligations for transfer justification and local risks.

**Benefit sharing:** Returning value to participants/communities (briefings, tools, policy memos) proportionate to their contributions and risks.

**Participatory co-design:** Structured collaboration with communities (users, workers, creators) to shape questions, instruments, harm models, and dissemination.

**Harm model / duty to warn:** An explicit account of plausible harms (individual, collective, systemic) and a plan for confidential escalation when imminent risks are found.

**Composites and paraphrased quoting:** Representation techniques that preserve meaning while reducing searchability and re-identification risk.

**Interference (networked experiments):** When one unit's treatment affects others (violating SUTVA), common on platforms; requires cluster designs or sensitivity checks.

**Reproducibility package (procedural replication):** Executable notebooks, code, and logs that reproduce analysis steps on synthetic/redacted data without leaking sensitive traces.

**Algorithmic churn / versioning:** Frequent, undocumented updates to models and policies that complicate comparability; must be tracked and reported as part of method.

Chapter 16

# Understanding the Paradox of Digital Intimacy in the Light of Ethical, Social, and Psychological Implications

**Showkat Ahmad Wani**
https://orcid.org/0009-0009-0240-9073
*Alliance University, Bengaluru, India*

**Priyanka Puri**
https://orcid.org/0009-0003-3635-7255
*University School of Law, Rayat Bahra Professional University, Hoshiarpur, India*

## ABSTRACT

*Prior to the advent of technology, the notion of communication fosters a healthy relationship often a result of face to face interaction. The relationships that the people had in early days were confined to the general proximity of where the couples have worked, lived, did their schooling and otherwise met. But then technologies have removed this complexity and telephones enabled people to have an intimate online relationship with someone who stays miles apart whether it's for love, friendship, business or fun without never having met that person physically. This giv rise to the concept of "digital intimacy". The author in this Book Chapter aims to analyse the kinetics of "digital intimacy", exploring how individuals leverage digital*

DOI: 10.4018/979-8-3373-4267-2.ch016

*platforms to "initiate", "maintain", and "navigate" their personal attachments. The author further investigated the psychological and sociological effects and the ethical considerations of digital intimacy and has proposed frameworks for fostering authentic and genuine connections through commitments in the increasing realms of the digital world.*

## INTRODUCTION

The advent of "Digital age" has introduced intense changes in the manner individuals develop and sustain relationships. The advent of modern technologies has reshaped the landscape of human interactions, relationships and intimacies. In particular the revolution brought about by the mobile internet has transformed the romantic engagements of people.

Presently, technology is found deeply embedded in our daily lives, from conducting online work meetings via Skype, to using touch displays on train ticket machines, to mobile phones substituting banking infrastructures.

The omnipresence of digital devices has redefined the meaning and method of interaction within the world (Lea, 1991). People often take Laptops along with them at their beds and cradle their mobile close to their heart while swiping their fingers through profiles on tinder, facebook, snap chat streaks and instagram reels that testaments their deep and real connection with the touchscreen.

This intimate life companionship with devices has on one hand addressed loneliness and emotional invalidation thereby facilitating the relation among like - minded people belonging to diverse communities but on the other hand has given rise to problems like indiscipline, distractions, anxiety, unrealistic expectations, etc. "Modern Intimacy" not only fosters connection and long distance support but also bring about challenges like security, privacy and miscommunication thereby diminishing quality and authentic relationship that even transcend physical boundaries (Walther, 1992).

The ease with which the personal information is shared leads to "privacy issues" and emphasises for a concern to align digital relations with "ethical" and "moral values". Online Communication refers to a trust based relationship that one builds with others through social media to develop strong emotional connections and a sense of belongingness.

Moreover, in today's "modern age", the notion of interrelation has evolved rapidly from developing authentic relationship through "face to face interaction" and "emotional presence" to convenience and access with the help of "social media platforms", "video conferencing" and "virtual collaboration". Empathy and Active Listening in communication is substituted by emails and virtual coffee meets

(Kennedy, 2017). In the realm of "Online intimacy" the absence of the ability to see "facial expressions", "tone of voice", and "body language" has made it difficult to fully understand others.

"Digital citizens" are, however, an integral part of the entire digital ecosystem; where their actions and behaviour can profoundly affect the wellbeing of the digital community. "Digital Intimacy" encompasses the numerous ways in which individuals make use of digital media platform to share or exchange their personal details, thought process, emotions fostering such connections that transcend any sort of physical limitations. The evolution of sudden dynamics prompts the re-evaluation of intimacy in the era of "digitalization". It further questions on the depth and authenticity of connections that are formed through the screens (Jamieson, 2013).

Hence, it is very important to create an environment where authenticity and responsibility flourishes and one should be surrounded by healthier digital experience and not negative or toxic online influences. This can be done by putting a limit on the consumption of internet, establishing tech- free zones to encourage real life intimacy, providing controlled environment to explore romantic desires, creating awareness about carefully selecting an account to get engaged with and about prioritizing spending quality time with each other. Purely digital interaction can make people addictive so there is a need to strike a balance between online and offline engagements (Matheson & Zanna, 1988).

## II. CHANGING DIMENSIONS OF INTIMACY

A transition in sexual values coincides with the weakening of traditional institutions like family and orthodox religion was witnessed in the later part of the 20th century. These changes have led to the growth of new patterns of intimacy. Giddens discussed that the sexual revolution of the 1960s, has marked a significant cultural shift, leading to widespread acceptance of sexually permissive attitudes (Giddens, 1992). Illouz further argued that these have become contradictory cultural frameworks in modern times as this era of change has also seen the separation of the emotion of romantic love from marriage (Illouz, 2011).

The movement of society away from collectivist values (e.g., family loyalty) towards individualistic values (e.g., autonomy) is one of the processes that acted as an impetus to the cultural shift. This was the result of excessive exposure to global media and influence of peer culture (Arnett, 2002).1 In the urban Indian context, the significance of popular TV shows from the West are responsible for setting standards for young Indians in this regard. While individualism seems harmless, it often seems to be investing more in themselves by individuals than in other people and functions in the form of "risk aversion". This is why it is found that most relationships do not last long in today's world (Beck & Beck-Gernsheim, 1995).

These shifts in attitudes resulted in the creation of "confluent love" a concept centered on finding the ideal bonding based on the grounds of "sexual and emotional reciprocity". In the framework of confluent love, people focus on finding a relationship that fulfills their needs without binding to social elements rather than having the desire to meet "the one". This is the reason Giddens probably also refers to "confluent love" as the "pure relationship" that may take many different shapes. Marriage can be one form of such connection, but it reflects an expression of such a bond that already exists, rather than establishing it.

However, pure relationships are not just confined to marriage or even heterosexual couples. It is due to their inherent openness and negotiated nature that "Same-sex relationships" are closer to the ideal of "pure relationships" than predefined "heterosexuals". He further stated that the emergence of confluent love in society is illustrated by increasing number of divorces and the growing acceptance of non-traditional relationships. Nonetheless, he believed and maintained that still the prevalent ideology is "romantic love".

Giddens into the academic discourse also introduced the idea of "plastic sexuality". "Plastic" refers to the malleability of "sensual expression." This expression takes into account both individual choice and societal norm frameworks and is said to have emerged in response to the societal shifts of late modernity and postmodernity. It aligns with the characteristics associated with modernist sexuality, which are viewed as fixed due to genetics or societal standards.

Giddens founds support by scholars such as Zygmunt Bauman who in his book introduced the term "Liquid Love". It refers to the "liquified" nature of modern relationships. He stressed that in a time of widespread individualization; relationships faced a struggle between conflicting desires. On the one hand there is a yearning for independence and the flexibility of less enforceable agreements that permit individuality and personal freedom. While on the other hand, there is also a strong desire for more security, which may be achieved via strengthening relationships with one's partners. This tension leads to an ongoing oscillation between the urge for freedom and quest for security (Bauman, 2003).

Gross contended that his concept of LISM (Lifelong, internally stratified marriage) is slowly being discarded by modern society. He stated that LISM is:

> *"The set of cultural practices according to which family life and intimacy are organized around a permanent and state or religiously sanctified commitment between members of a heterosexual dyad—a commitment premised on and reproductive of an unequal division of labour, power, resources, or responsibilities between the genders."*

He further noted that individuals who do not follow the practices of "LISM" today are subject to far fewer social consequences as compared to the past centuries. Therefore, this suggests that the emergence of "confluent love", "liquid love" and the decline of "LISM" are all moving towards the same direction (Gross, 2005).

The growth of sexual permissiveness and the rise of the "hookup" culture is another outcome of the transformation of intimacy. A "hookup" is an internationally vague term that encompasses anything from kissing to sexual intercourse. This obscurity often develops misperceptions among students, leading them to assume that their peers are having more physical interactions than them. However, studies have shown that casual sexual encounters have become more common. In fact, contemporary romantic relationships now start up by hookups or casual sex, rather than through traditional dates (Monto & Carey, 2014).

Heldman and Wade noted that hookups are very common on college campuses but still there is a gap between the student's actual involvement and their perceptions about what they consider as normal behavior. Many believe that their friends have more hookups than they do, a misbelief known as "pluralistic ignorance" (Heldman & Wade, 2010). The "friends with benefits" arrangement is yet another type of casual "sexual relationship" which the evolving adults often regard as a suitable extension of an existing friendship. Expectations of a romantic bond or intentions to evolve into romantic partners are absent in such type of relationships (Grohol, 2022).

The history of intimacy in India presents a very fascinating story. There is evidence in several ancient texts from where it could be inferred that liberal attitudes about intimacy were prevalent with some texts that do not prescribe virginity as a necessary attribute for the women in society (Kapadia, 1966). However, sexually permissive views were mostly found in the upper sections of society, such as the ruling class. Over time attitudes regarding intimacy and sexuality saw monumental shifts as the liberal sexual values in the country were suppressed due to the spread of Victorian moral codes under the colonial rule (Das & Rao, 2019).

In recent years, developing nations have witnessed a transformation in perspectives towards intimacy as that of the West. However, the need to stay within the arena of traditional partnerships is largely influenced by culture and religion in the subcontinental context. There is also some evidence that women within these areas are experiencing higher (Muniruzzaman, 2017).2 Moreover, pre-marital and extra-marital sexual relations are not as uncommon in South Asian countries as previously assumed. Despite the gender difference in sexual behaviour, the prevalence of pre-marital sex and sex with number of partners is increasing in India (Ubale & Sekher, 2023).

## III. INDIA'S EMERGING ADULTS AND TECH-MEDIATED INTIMACY

> *"Young people do not see themselves as using social media but as LIVING in them, as a digital environment that is akin to the urban and natural environments that envelop their daily lives" (Boczkowski, Mitchelstein, & Matassi, 2017).*

Traditionally, the romantic relationships were regulated through the involvement of families and the era of arrange marriages dominating the social structure. However, with the development of online dating platforms, there is a growing craze among the youth to look for their partners outside the community structure and traditional family setup. The emerging youth is facing a critical phase of identity exploration, forming concrete relationships that can influence their long-term wellbeing. The youth of today is positioned to take advantage of the available latest digital tools that offer unprecedented access to prospective partners beyond their community and family webs (Yang, 2024).

In the present Society, the Young Generation appears to value marriage, but the concept of marriage has considerably changed from partnership or economic security to a symbol of successful maturity. This is indicative of a social shift where the individuals engage themselves in more explorative approach to relationships where youngsters prioritize personal growth and career prospects over immediate marital commitments.

Before internet, young people would mostly meet people of the other sex with the goal of getting married. The concept was dating was not known to the masses. These exchanges started in the 1990s due to the proliferation of marriage-related websites like Shaadi.com, Jeevansathi.com, and Bharatmatrimony.com. Nevertheless, entering into partnerships that may or may not culminate in marriage is becoming increasingly prevalent nationwide (Taylor, 2021).

Between 2000 and 2004, several social networking spread their wings. One of the first platforms was Friendster, a company founded in 2002 that provided a virtual community where friends, relatives, and complete strangers could message and converse with profiles available that may result in romantic relationships. Other social networking sites, OkCupid and Plenty of Fish, were initially less well-known than well-known services like Match, even though they were initially providing free dating services. But subsequently, when mobile applications were created and made available, their popularity soared as a result of increased user interaction and accessibility.

The launch of Facebook launch in 2005 had a big impact on the creation of several mobile apps that are still popular today. Later, in 2007 Zoosk was founded by Shayan Zadeh and Alex Mehr that extended the idea of specialized dating software to include downloadable versions for Apple and Android smartphones.

The development of mobile technology offered more dating applications that provided easier access than conventional computer-based platforms. Grindr in 2009 provided the location-based dating apps, released only for Apple iPhones for the first time. It was so designed that it caters to gay, queer, bisexual, and transgender individuals seeking connections and expanded preference to mobile over desktop-based interactions in the dating sphere (Angelini, 2022).

The introduction of digital platforms at the same time also grapples the country with the questions of privacy, security and the reliability of mediated contacts and interactions. Moreover, use of technology for developing relationship also confirms that it is sometimes rude to ignore an unread message without assessing the context in which that is sent. It further violates the behaviour called "normal conversation" or "face to face interaction" resulting in relational dissatisfaction. "Digital Intimacy" referred to as "Modern Intimacy" focussed on serving individual needs by offering unlimited choices thereby questioning the quality of human connections (De Ridder, 2022).

In simpler words, the young generation is treating internet and digital media as playgrounds for intimate relations. The contact zones of the digital and the intimate, or affect spheres, have multiplied and diversified through processes of digitalization.

## IV. LEADING APPS IN THE DIGITAL DATING MARKET

The preference for digital intimacy has increased significantly with the following apps as these offer unique features and target specific user needs.

- **Tinder-** It is an online dating app launched in the year 2012. The app is distinguished by its simple yet revolutionary swipe mechanism, where the users swipe right to express interest in someone and left to pass. This interface has removed the complexities of algorithms and focuses on immediate physical attraction and serving a broader range of dating and social interaction needs. It has accelerated the video dating trends during Covid-19 thereby transforming how people meet and interact online. It has also set the stage for a dynamic and ever-evolving industry committed to evolve in line with user preferences and technological advancements.
- **Bumble-** It was established in 2014 by Whitney Wolfe Herd. Bumble distinguishes itself in the crowded online dating market by prioritizing women's experiences in its design. It is so crafted as to allow women in heterosexual matches to make the first move, a feature that has empowered women and shifted the dynamics of online dating (Nikhat & Shukla, 2025). In the recent years the company has efficiently responded to the evolving needs of the soci-

ety by launched features that supported virtual dating. In addition to this, the platform supports legislation that aimed at prohibiting the non -consensual sharing of explicit images.

- **Hinge- It** differentiates itself by integrating with Facebook to help users discover potential matches among friends of friends rather than casual encounters. This app allows the users to express their personality through specific text, photos, videos, and answers to prompts, which are used to initiate conversations. It encourages users to engage deeply in potential interactions.
- **OkCupid- It was** launched in 2004 by Chris Coyne, Christian Rudder, Sam Yagan, and Max Krohn. It then quickly established itself as a distinctive presence in the online dating scene. In order to choose shape user matches, it uses the array of multiple-choice questions to decide the compatibility. This app is extensively used by the users falling within the age group of 25-34 years.

## V. FACTORS INFLUENCING DIGITAL ENGAGEMENT

The reasons for the Digital engagement are manifold. Youngsters use dating apps for a variety of reasons.

- The primary motivation behind the use of apps for digital interactions is the ease of communication, validation, excitement and self-worth.
- Other motivational elements are excitement, connection, fun and urge to meet people.
- Several other reasons beyond what the creators and developers of the app expected are:

a. As an entertainment tool when wanting to pass time
b. Out of curiosity
c. As an ideal tool to befriend strangers
d. For the quest of romantic love
e. As an ego-booster
f. As a distraction
g. To improve flirting and social skills
h. To meet people with a similar sexual orientation
i. Because a friend created a profile for the
j. To communicate with locals while travelling
k. To increase their sexual experience
l. To forget about their ex
m. Because everyone else around them is using Tinder

- Another relevant motivation for their usage and an important predictor for both one-night stands and casual sexual relationship is "Sensual purposes" or "lustful intentions (Timmermans, de Caluwé, & Alexopoulos, 2018)."
- The "queer community" was observed to be yet another reason for adoption of online interaction apps as they not only facilitate dating and sexual encounters but also serve as vital spaces for community building and identity expression within the queer population offering a means to connect with others who share similar identities and experiences.
- For some others, these apps are instrumental in exploring their sexual and gender identities, offering a relatively safe environment to navigate such personal journeys (Blackwell, Birnholtz, & Abbott, 2015).
- Another motivational component is these digital intimacy platforms offers "selective self-presentation" to highlight only such attributes that they believe will be most attractive to others. This aligns with Goffman's concept of "impression management," where allows individuals to selectively reveal or conceal information about oneself depending on what will serve their interaction goals.
- The strategic use of photographs on dating apps is also a unit of motivation to extensively use the digital platform as images are not only used to convey physical attractiveness but also serve as powerful indicators of personality, interests, and social status (Sedgewick, Flath, & Elias, 2017).

## VI. ETHICAL CONSIDERATIONS IN "DIGITAL INTIMACY"

The advent of "Digital intimacy" i.e., expressing oneself through social media, dating applications and online communication platforms transforms how individuals form and sustain relationships. However, this transition from "face to face interactions" to digital communications also introduced significant ethical questions about "privacy", "consent", "authenticity" and "power dynamics" in online interactions.

The technological advancement has blurred the boundaries between public and private spheres, creating new forms of intimacy mediated by screens. While these interactions foster connection and belonging, they also give rise to ethical dilemmas. Unlike traditional forms of intimacy, digital intimacy is not safe. It leaves digital footprints as it involves third-party data collection and is shaped by "platform algorithms" (Beever, 2019). Thus, ethical evaluation is necessary to understand and address personal responsibilities as well as institutional accountability. The moral boundaries regarding digital intimacy are the following: -

- **Privacy and Surveillance**

The popularity of "online intimacies" has surged in recent years and has raised one of the most pressing ethical concerns i.e., the erosion of privacy and safety concerns. Personal conversations, images and behaviors shared in digital spaces can be surveilled, stored, or misused. The users usually encounter unique safety challenges, such as exposure to abusive or predatory behavior from other users. People felt the need to connect with others and build meaningful relationships and to remain restrictive while communicating.

This tension between privacy and connection creates a "complex environment" where the users must learn to create a balance between these competing interests, often confronting the potential risks associated with technological interactions (Eastwick & Smith, 2018). Further while these platforms foster connection and a sense of validation; they also expose users to risks such as "cyber bullying", "discrimination", and "blackmail."

A new power was wielded by the engine of Surveillance known as the "Instrumenterian power" (Zuboff, 2022). This power makes use of the aggregated user data to control human behavior. Since Google and Facebook receive their revenue through the products that they sell, we as consumers cannot be detached or remain ungoverned by the internet as users. Zuboff analyzed that Google was the first to consider the surplus data as an important raw material for the profitable business that it looked up for "Surveillance Capitalism". Consequently, this data is a private property that is inaccessible for others. Zuboff also clearly stated that the argument is not about loss of privacy but how the corporations can effectively and secretively render the data valuable that is collected by them.

- **Consent and Boundaries**

In digital interactions, consent is often "ambiguous". Therefore, a careful understanding of consent and boundaries is vital as interaction occur in an environment of absence of physical cues. The lack of face-to-face interaction raises issues such as unsolicited explicit content, non-consensual sharing of intimate images and blurred relational boundaries. Hence there is a need of persistent digital surveillance that highlights the need for stronger norms, protections and clearer ethical frameworks where individuals carry the responsibility to respect the autonomy and digital rights of others.

- **Authenticity and Misrepresentation**

Through Digital platforms, individuals often construct and represent idealized versions of themselves, thereby creating misleading impressions. One major safety concern is the risk of encountering fraudulent profiles or individuals with "malicious intent." Research has shown that dating apps are not immune to the presence of "scammers" and "catfishers" who create fake profiles with the intention of deceiving others. These individuals may engage in deceptive practices such as misrepresenting their age, appearance, or intentions (Wu & Trottier, 2022). Such deceivers may also indulge in sexually assaulting female partners which is another major safety concern.

- **Mental Health and Emotional Well-being**

"Digital Platforms" raises serious concerns regarding exploitation of "psychological vulnerabilities" of the users. Over-dependence on digital communication can lead to emotional disconnection. Users face the difficulty of managing boundaries between digital and offline lives and the frequent misinterpretations and misunderstandings that arose from digital communication. Moreover, the static pressure of constant connectivity and "algorithmic reinforcement" of "validation-cues" (e.g., likes, comments) can cultivate "emotional dependence" and erode natural well - being of a person (Parsakia & Rostami, 2023).

Digital technologies and media, because of their deep integration and extensiveness, affect and shape our day to day lives, social structures, policies, governments, and families. These influences carry significant ethical implications that are usually overlooked because of the "pervasiveness" and "embeddedness" of the digital tools in our everyday lives. Though "Online intimacy" offers new pathways for connection but at the same time exposes individuals to "ethical vulnerabilities."

It becomes vital to address concerns of "privacy", "consent", "authenticity" and "well-being" to ensure that intimacy in digital spaces preserves safety, respect and equity in online connections. Developing a clearer understanding of the nature and scope of digital ethics is certainly valuable, although not easy to achieve as it requires engaging ethical decision-making strategies as well as understanding the nature of the technologies and processes that constitute the digital itself: the deepest knowledge about "moral literacy" alongside "digital literacy" (Beever, McDaniel, & Stanlick, 2019).

Although internet based communication has become a medium for positive relational experiences but has also lead to excessive self disclosure and expectations from the partner that are not realistic in nature (Anna M. Lomanowaska, Matthieu, 2016). It has further blurred the distinction between the public and private spaces. This blend of emotional and cognitive responses to the integration of digital connectivity into everyday life constitutes this state of mind (Sudip Bhattachrya, Sandip Bhattachrya, Vidhisha Vallabh, 2023). Hence, there is a need to redefine social contracts in this virtual world where trust, safety and emotion shall remain the most important currencies.

Along with technological innovation, the "Ethical reflection" must facilitate, thereby balancing individual freedom with collective responsibility. The responsibility on the part of users to practice informed sharing, seek consent before spreading personal content and respect digital boundaries (Clara, 2018). Also, the obligation on the part of platforms to ensure transparency, safeguard privacy and to provide frameworks to report abuse or exploitation. Moreover, the policy makers must focus on making regulations that prevent misuse and ensure ethical governance of digital intimacy spaces.

## VII. SOCIAL IMPLICATIONS OF DIGITAL INTIMACY

With the rapid advancement in technology and the pervasive use of electronic media in numerous diverse areas (e.g., entertainment, business, training, education) there is a growing need for a deepened and clear understanding of the ethical and social implications of the digital concerns that manifest across contexts. "Digital intimacy" not only offers opportunities for connection across geographical and cultural boundaries, but it also transforms traditional norms of friendship, romance, and family life. The mediated intimacy raises challenges regarding trust, authenticity and validation of long-term relationship. It also influences "social institutions", "cultural practices", and "intergenerational norms" (Wu, 2024). The key social implications are the following: -

- **Redefining Friendship and Romance-** Digital Platforms shape relationships in a manner that is far away from the traditional social set up and is not bound by geography. The continuous online interaction results in more fragile interactions that are shaped by algorithmic encounters rather than strong organic social bonds.
- **Interpersonal Bonds and Family Ties**- "Digital Intimacy" on one hand strengthens family ties but on the other hand often navigate conflicts between online communication and one to one interaction between parents, siblings and partners. "Over dependence" and "overindulgence" in the digital space to express one's desires and expectations is resulting in weakened romantic and familial skills.
- **Communal Ties**- Virtual interactions lead to forming such communities that are based upon shared interests and identities but fosters "inclusion" and "solidarity." They replace deep and strong communal ties with digital bonds that encourage "echo chambers", "polarization" or "superficial connections" based on fake identities and personalities shown to attract others.

- **Intergenerational Differences-** "Digital Intimacy" highlights the gap among generations. On one hand the younger generations fell for expressions of affection, validation of relationships and belonging to oneself or possessiveness through digital platforms, the older generations on the other hand, look upon at such practices as "shallow" and "detached". They perceive such intimacies as without any emotional touch and sense of uniqueness (Saviki, 1996).
- **Societal and Cultural Shifts-** The far-reaching implication of digital intimacy lies in its ability to transform "cultural norms" and "societal expectations." The practices like swiping, matching, sharing intimate details on social media are normalized by dating apps to an extent that it has blurred the line between personal and private disclosures. This transformation raises an important cultural question regarding relationships as to what was considered to be authentic, and long lasting has now changed to a "one night stand" challenging traditional understandings of privacy and consent while negotiating new moral limitations in response to technological advancements.

"Digital Intimacy" has profound social implications that reshape families, friendships, romantics bonds, communities and cultures. Though it offers opportunities to build and maintain long distance relationships but also invites challenges to their validation and authenticity. As digital intimacy has entrenched in our daily lives, so it is very important to strike a balance between its transformative effects, cultural norms and social responsibility.

## VIII. PSYCHOLOGICAL IMPLICATIONS OF "DIGITAL INTIMACY"

The rapid rise in dating apps has resulted in a wide range of "psychological effects". It has changed the nature of "romantic relationships" and has significantly influenced users "social behavior" and "mental health".

- **Abundance of Options-** The numerous dating apps offers unprecedented choices of potential matches to a person thereby making it difficult for him to decide and choose the compatible match for him or her. This "paradox of choices" that provides too many alternatives cause psychological pain to the user making decision making a difficult task for him. Sometimes the user is overwhelmed by numerous options that he adopts superficial choice making strategies and prioritize "profile elements" over "holistic compatibility". Such users make wrong decisions and remain dissatisfied with the selected partners. Although wellbeing of a person demands "autonomy" and "freedom of choice" but sometimes overload of choices turns into psychological stresses and frustrations (Pittman & Reich, 2016).

- **Body Perception-** There is a strong correlation between "Digital Intimacy" and increased psychological distress, anxiety, and depressive symptoms resulting from dissatisfaction with one's body. It is likely that regular involvement in "digital intimacy" may develop negative body images among users if they face frequent rejection due to "Weight stigma", "sexual objectification" and "social comparison". The "psychological impact" on victims is develops emotions such as "suspicion", "love", "depression", "anger", "embarrassment", and "feelings of stupidity" (Zhu, 2025).
- **Unprotected sexual behavior-** "Digital intimacy" may develop risky sexual behavior. It encompasses activities that refers to "non-use of condoms", "engagements with multiple sexual partners", and sexual activity under the influence of substances that elevate the risk of "sexually transmitted infections" (STIs) and "unintended pregnancies." This is the consequence of less offline interactions and greater time being spent by couples on "in-app conversations". This might also be the result of social and sexual networks that these platforms support, which encourage frequent and varied "sexual encounters." It also happens that the person sometimes encounters fraudulent profiles or individuals with "malicious intent" of building only a casual sexual relation instead of a long term bond.

The impact of internet on "romantic relationships" is evident that the concept of "online dating" has overtook "traditional relationship setup of courtships". This dominant method for partner seeking through online conversations, offers both opportunities and pitfalls in maintaining connections. Further, it has introduced risks for "sexual health", necessitating the need to understand their implications and evolve methods that suppress such "anonymous", "unhealthy" and "nonconsensual self-disclosure" and "exposure."

## CONCLUSION

The digital advancement has opened up numerous opportunities and made new connections possible but human social interactions continue to evolve, it is important to gain a better understanding of the immediate and long-terms effects of these shifts on health and well-being outcomes. There is also evidence of positive "psychosocial effects" associated with "online social interactions", including those characterized by key components of "intimacy", "self-disclosure" and "social support." However, despite the rise of "online intimacy" little is still known about its benefits and implications in relation to "health" and "well-being".

More work in this area should be done in future while taking advantage of established knowledge about the pathways mediating the wellness benefits of "conventional offline intimate interactions" to examine their involvement in "online intimacy". Now that many online social platforms have become firmly-established, it has become feasible to make an assessment on a large scale of the long-term effects of online intimate social engagement on both "psychological" and "physiological health" and "wellness outcomes".

In order to preserve the well-recognized benefits of "interpersonal intimacy" in the modern society, research and "wellness promotion programs" must take into account the new digital dimensions of human "social interactions". Young people engage in digital media technologies for a variety of reasons and purposes, including staying connected to their family and friends, pursuing learning and entertainment. For many others, those conversations, learning and entertainment carry a sexual dimension so it must be approached with care so as to avoid potential adverse effects.

Hence, there is need to develop "trust building", "privacy" and balance between online and offline interactions. The impact of technology on couple relationships plays a dual role. It acts both as a facilitator as well as a barrier to healthy intimacy. On one hand, transcends cross border connections and on the other hand raises concerns about privacy and security.

## Key Recommendations

- It is important to acknowledge the motivations that drives youngsters to engage with digital technologies, particularly the manner in which they manage to balance the trade-offs between "risks" and "rewards".
- Further there is also a need to explore how different social and institutional environments (e.g. home v. school) impact the meanings and experiences of "digital intimacies".
- It is crucial to avoid conflation of taking risks (for example, sending a naked selfie to a potential partner) with harmful behaviour (such as posting an image without consent i.e. "revenge porn") unless there is an element of willingness and consensus involved.
- It is essential to recognize young people's rights to express sexual desires and to ensure that they have an access to comprehensive and inclusive "sex education" along with "responsive digital literacy programmes".
- The generations must make a shift from prompting "abstinence" and "prevention" towards cultivating ethical decision making and consent to address and challenge harmful social norms.

- There is a need to find out alternatives to legal solutions, ensuring that they prioritize young people's interests and needs.

## REFERENCES

Angelini, F., Marino, C., & Gini, G. (2022). Friendship quality in adolescence: The role of social media features, online social support and e-motions. *Current Psychology (New Brunswick, N.J.)*, *42*, 1–17. DOI: 10.1007/s12144-022-03564-3 PMID: 36118141

Arnett, J. J. (2002). *Adolescence and emerging adulthood: A cultural approach* (2nd ed.). Prentice Hall.

Bauman, Z. (2003). Liquid love: On the frailty of human bonds. Polity Press.</bok>

Beck, U., & Beck-Gernsheim, E. (1995). *The normal chaos of love*. Polity Press.

Beever, J., McDaniel, R., & Stanlick, N. A. (2019). *Understanding digital ethics: Cases and contexts* (1st ed.). Routledge., DOI: 10.4324/9781315282138

Blackwell, C., Birnholtz, J., & Abbott, C. (2015). Seeing and being seen: Co-situation and impression formation using Grindr, a location-aware gay dating app. *New Media & Society*, *17*(7), 1117–1136. DOI: 10.1177/1461444814521595

Boczkowski, P. J., Mitchelstein, E., & Matassi, M. (2017). Incidental news: How young people consume news on social media. In *Proceedings of the 50th Hawaii International Conference on System Sciences* (pp. 1788–1796). University of Hawai'i at Mānoa., https://scholarspace.manoa.hawaii.edu/bitstream/10125/41371/1/paper0222.pdf

Das, K., & Rao, T. S. S. (2019). A chronicle of sexuality in the Indian subcontinent. *Journal of Psychosexual Health*, *1*(1), 20–25. DOI: 10.1177/2631831818822017

De Ridder, S. (2022). The datafication of intimacy: Mobile dating apps, dependency, and everyday life. *Television & New Media*, *23*(6), 593–609. DOI: 10.1177/15274764211052660

Eastwick, P. W., & Smith, L. K. (2018). Sex-differentiated effects of physical attractiveness on romantic desire: A highly powered, preregistered study in a photograph evaluation context. *Comprehensive Results in Social Psychology*, *3*(1), 1–27. https://static1.squarespace.com/static/504114b1e4b0b97fe5a520af/t/5be1db97758d46f6af1b7793/1541528474670/EastwickSmith2018CRSP.pdf

Giddens, A. (1992). *The transformation of intimacy: Sexuality, love and eroticism in modern societies*. Stanford University Press.

Grohol, J. M. (2022, July 6). *Friends with benefits*. LifeHelper. https://lifehelper.com/blog/friends-with-benefits/

Gross, N. (2005). The detraditionalization of intimacy reconsidered. *Sociological Theory*, *23*(3), 286–311. DOI: 10.1111/j.0735-2751.2005.00255.x

Heldman, C., & Wade, L. (2010). Hook up culture: Setting a new research agenda. *Sexuality Research & Social Policy*, *7*(4), 323–333. DOI: 10.1007/s13178-010-0024-z

Illouz, E. (2011). *Cold intimacies: The making of emotional capitalism*. Polity Press.

Jamieson, L. (2013). Personal relationships, intimacy and self in a mediated and global digital age. In Orton-Johnson, K., & Prior, N. (Eds.), *Digital sociology: Critical perspective* (pp. 13–33). Palgrave Macmillan., DOI: 10.1057/97811

Kapadia, K. M. (1966). *Marriage and family in India* (3rd ed.). Oxford University Press.

Kennedy, H., & Hill, R. L. (2017). The feeling of numbers: Emotions in everyday engagements with data and their visualisation. *Sociology*, *52*(4), 830–848. DOI: 10.1177/0038038516674675

Lea, M., & Spears, R. (1991). Computer-mediated communication, de-individuation and group decision-making. *International Journal of Man-Machine Studies*, *34*(2), 283–301. DOI: 10.1016/0020-7373(91)90045-9

Matheson, K., & Zanna, M. P. (1988). The impact of computer-mediated communication on self-awareness. *Computers in Human Behavior*, *4*(3), 221–233. DOI: 10.1016/0747-5632(88)90015-5

Monto, M. A., & Carey, A. G. (2014). A new standard of sexual behaviour? Are claims associated with the "hookup culture" supported by General Social Survey data? *Journal of Sex Research*, *51*(6), 605–615. DOI: 10.1080/00224499.2014.906031 PMID: 24750070

Muniruzzaman, M. D. (2017). Transformation of intimacy and its impact in developing countries. *Life Sciences, Society and Policy*, *13*(1). Advance online publication. DOI: 10.1186/s40504-017-0056-8 PMID: 28766186

Nikhat, M., & Shukla, A. (2025). The changing face of dating in India: Why it's worth studying. *International Journal for Multidisciplinary Research*, *7*(2), 1–12. DOI: 10.36948/ijfmr.2025.v07i02.42935

Parsakia, K., & Rostami, M. (2023). Digital intimacy: How technology shapes friendships and romantic relationships. *AI and Tech in Behavioral and Social Sciences*, *1*(1), 27–34. DOI: 10.61838/kman.aitech.1.1.5

Pittman, M., & Reich, B. (2016). Social media and loneliness: Why an Instagram picture may be worth more than a thousand Twitter words. *Computers in Human Behavior, 62*, 155–167. DOI: 10.1016/j.chb.2016.03.084

Sedgewick, J. R., Flath, M. E., & Elias, L. J. (2017). Presenting your best self(ie): The influence of gender on vertical orientation of selfies on Tinder. *Frontiers in Psychology, 8*. Advance online publication. DOI: 10.3389/fpsyg.2017.00009 PMID: 28484408

Taylor, S. H., Zhao, P., & Bazarova, N. N. (2021). Social media and close relationships: A puzzle of connection and disconnection. *Current Opinion in Psychology, 45*, 101292. Advance online publication. DOI: 10.1016/j.copsyc.2021.12.004 PMID: 35016090

Timmermans, E., de Caluwé, E., & Alexopoulos, C. (2018). Why are you cheating on Tinder? Exploring users' motives and (dark) personality traits. [Why are you cheating on Tinder? New research by Elisabeth Timmermans and colleagues examines partnered users' motives and ] [dark] [ personality traits | Erasmus School of History, Culture and Communication | Erasmus University Rotterdam.]. *Computers in Human Behavior, 89*, 129–139.

Ubale, P. D., & Sekher, T. V. (2023). Risky sexual behaviors among unmarried youth in India: Evidences from National Family Health Survey, 2019–21. In Deb, S., & Deb, S. (Eds.), *Handbook of youth development* (pp. 413–439). Springer., DOI: 10.1007/978-981-99-4969-4_24

Walther, J. B. (1992). Interpersonal effects in computer-mediated interaction: A relational perspective. *Communication Research, 19*(1), 52–90. DOI: 10.1177/009365092019001003

Wu, J. (2024). Social and ethical impact of emotional AI advancement: The rise of pseudo-intimacy relationships and challenges in human interactions. *Frontiers in Psychology, 15*. Advance online publication. DOI: 10.3389/fpsyg.2024.1410462 PMID: 39564589

Wu, S., & Trottier, D. (2022). Dating apps: A literature review. *Annals of the International Communication Association, 46*(2), 91–115. DOI: 10.1080/23808985.2022.2069046

Yang, J., & Wu, N. (2024). Social problems of brain-computer interface technology and its countermeasures. *Ideological and Theoretical Front, 1*, 80–88. DOI: 10.3389/fpsyg.2024.1410462

Zhu, Y. (2025). Anonymous intimacy in the digital age: Psychological mechanisms, risks, and potential. *Proceedings of the International Conference on Advanced Research in Social Sciences, 2*(1), 11–29. DOI: 10.33422/icarss.v2i1.1056

# Compilation of References


Abdelaal, O. (2024). Female Leadership Roles: Subjectivity and Self-Representation :The Muslim Sisterhood Activism in the Digital Era. *Middle East Law and Governance*, *16*(2). Advance online publication. DOI: 10.1163/18763375-20231321

Abidin, C. (2021). From "networked publics" to "refracted publics": A companion framework for researching TikTok. *Social Media + Society*, *7*(2), 1–12. DOI: 10.1177/20563051211019796

Abidin, C., Lee, J., & Kaye, D. B. V. (2023). Introduction to the Media International Australia special issue on "TikTok cultures in the Asia Pacific.". *Media International Australia*, *186*(1), 3–10. DOI: 10.1177/1329878x221130126

Abubaker, I. (2021). Careem and the ride-hailing economy in the Middle East. *Journal of Middle East Media*, *15*(1), 55–72.

Acar, S., Gürsoy, H., & Ünsal, N. Ö. (2014). İlişkisel toplumda sosyal iş ağlarının kariyer gelişimi açısından önemi: LinkedIn örneği. *Electronic Journal of Vocational Colleges*, Özel Sayı, 17–25.

Acar, O. (2020). *Is artificial intelligence an opportunity or a threat?* Kriter Publishing House.

Adjei, M., & Nung Chan, A. H. (2025). Making a difference with matter in researchers' positionality dynamics in qualitative inquiry. *Qualitative Research*, *25*(3), 711–731.

Agamben, G. (2005). *State of exception* (Attell, K., Trans.). University of Chicago Press.

Agnes, F. (2012). From Shah Bano to Kausar Bano. *South Asian Feminisms*, 31-53. http://feministlawarchives.pldindia.org/wp-content/uploads/from-shahbano-to-kausar-bano-contextualizing-the-muslim-woman.pdf

Ahmad, M., Shahzadi, A., Vallejo, R. G., Naeem, Z., & Tran, D. B. (2025). Virtual Realities, Real Societies: The Metaverse Effect. In Pucelj, M., & Bohinc, R. (Eds.), *Challenges for Digital Citizenship and Ethics: Social Media, Deep Fakes, and Virtual Communities* (pp. 103–122). IGI Global Scientific Publishing., DOI: 10.4018/979-8-3693-7914-1.ch005

Ajani, Y. A., Baloyi, N. C., Chibike, J. J., Elisifa, Z., Lubambo, R. J., Mabika, M., Mangaka, A. C., Malatji, E. J., Mapulane, M. G., Muthambi, R., & Ngoaketsi, J. M. (2024). *Digital media and the preservation of indigenous languages in Africa: Toward a digitalized and sustainable society*. Rowman & Littlefield.

Akkaş, C., & Turan, A. H. (2025). Predictors of Instagram use for user productivity: Self-control, notifications, and checking habits. *International Journal of Mobile Communications, 25*(4), 417–447.

Akpınar, E. G., & Eker, H. H. (2025). The effect of TikTok use on internet addiction in university students. *International Journal of Environmental Health Research*. Advance online publication. DOI: 10.1080/09603123.2024.2448488

Akyıl, Y., & Oral, T. (2024). The mediating role of problematic TikTok use and mindfulness in the relationship between psychological resilience and internet addiction. *Discover Psychology, 4*(1). Advance online publication. DOI: 10.1007/s44202-024-00317-0

Allaire, N., Colin, N., Palier, B., & Tran, L. (2019). *Covering Risks for Platform Workers in the Digital Age. Chaire numérique, gouvernance et innovations institutionelles*. SciencesPo.

Aloisi, A., & Gramano, E. (2019). Artificial Intelligence is Watching you at Work: Digital Surveillance, Employee Monitoring and Regulatory Issues in the EU Context. *Comparative Labour and Policy Journal, 41*(1), 101–127.

Anderson, B. (2010). Migration, Immigration Controls and the Fashioning of Precarious Workers. *Work, Employment and Society, 24*(2), 300–317.

Andrae, S. (2022). The role of BigTech in emerging markets. In Nguyen, D. K. (Ed.), *Handbook of Banking and Finance in Emerging Markets* (pp. 433–463). Edward Elgar., DOI: 10.4337/9781800880900.00032

Andrejevic, M. (2007). *iSpy: Surveillance and power in the interactive era*. University Press of Kansas.

Angelini, F., Marino, C., & Gini, G. (2022). Friendship quality in adolescence: The role of social media features, online social support and e-motions. *Current Psychology (New Brunswick, N.J.)*, *42*, 1–17. DOI: 10.1007/s12144-022-03564-3 PMID: 36118141

Aplin, R. (2024). Policing Honour-Based Abuse and Forced Marriage. In Aplin, R. (Ed.), *Policing Public Protection*. Palgrave Macmillan., DOI: 10.1007/978-3-031-74504-1_3

Arısoy Gedik, C., & Ceyhan, A. I. (2024). The Gender Gap in the Digital Era: Reaching Algorithmic Fairness and Technological Inclusivity in Network Society. *Communication Papers. Media Literacy and Gender Studies*, *13*(26), 64–75. DOI: 10.33115/udg_bib/cp.v13i26.23038

Arnett, J. J. (2002). *Adolescence and emerging adulthood: A cultural approach* (2nd ed.). Prentice Hall.

Aslam, S., Yousaf, M., Raza, S. H., Hussain, B., & Ahmad, W. (2025). Reconfiguring patriarchal paradigms: The women march and its role in reshaping gender norms and feminist activism. *Asian Women*, *41*(2), 227–253. https://www.e-asianwomen.org/DOIx.php?id=10.14431/aw.2025.6.41.2.227

Athirah, S., & Hidayana, I. M. (2023). Women's agency and resistance to cyber flashing on Twitter. *Masyarakat: Jurnal Sosiologi*, *28*(1), 7. Advance online publication. DOI: 10.7454/MJS.v28i1.13562

Attardo, S. (2014). *Encyclopedia of humour studies*. SAGE Publications.

Avci, H., Baams, L., & Kretschmer, T. (2025). A systematic review of social media use and adolescent identity development. *Adolescent Research Review*, *10*(2), 219–236.

Ayas, S., & Çapa Aydın, Y. (2021). Çevrimiçi Disinhibisyon Ölçeğinin geliştirilmesi: Geçerlik ve güvenirlik çalışması. *Türk Psikoloji Yazilari*, *24*(48), 16–28. DOI: 10.31828/tpy1301996120210209m000037

Ayers, J., Poliak, A., Dredze, M., Leas, E., Zechariah, Z., Kelley, J., Dennis, F., Aaron, G., Christopher, L., Michael, H., & Davey, S. (2023). Comparing physician and artificial intelligence chatbot responses to patient questions posted to a public social media forum. *JAMA Internal Medicine*, *183*(6), 589–596. PMID: 37115527

Bafană, M., & Ioni ă, I. (2021). Disinformation and Online Identity Theft through False Accounts on Social Networks. *hypothesis, 120*, 121.

Bagdadi, D. V. (2024). Resistance and Online Activism. In *Woman-Centered Brazilian Cinema*. https://doi.org/DOI: 10.1515/9781438490267-004

Bail, C. A., Argyle, L. P., Brown, T. W., Bumpus, J. P., Chen, H., Hunzaker, M. B. F., & Volfovsky, A. (2018). Exposure to opposing views on social media can increase political polarization. *Proceedings of the National Academy of Sciences of the United States of America, 115*(37), 9216–9221. DOI: 10.1073/pnas.1804840115 PMID: 30154168

Baiocco, S., Fernandez Macias, E., Rani, U. and Pesole, A. (2022). The Algorithmic Management of Work and its Implications in Different Contexts. European Commission, JRC129749.

Bakan, U., & Karaaslan, İ. A. (2017). Bireysel farklılıkların sosyal sermaye oluşumuna etkisi: Facebook ve LinkedIn kullanıcıları üzerine karşılaştırmalı bir analiz. *Intermedia. International Journal (Toronto, Ont.), 4*(6), 77–97.

Bakırtaş, H., & Sekendür Turgu, G. (2021). LinkedIn kullanım alışkanlıkları üzerine bir araştırma. *Dicle Üniversitesi Sosyal Bilimler Enstitüsü Dergisi, 13*(26), 245–265.

Bakırtaş, H., & Turgu, G. S. (2021). LinkedIn sosyal iş ağının kullanıcı algısı. *Abant Sosyal Bilimler Dergisi, 21*(3), 796–810. DOI: 10.11616/asbi.956027

Balcı, Ş., Akgül, T. E., & Astam, F. K. (2024). The use of TikTok by university youth: The relationship between TikTok addiction, loneliness, and emotional intelligence. *Türkiye İletişim Araştırmaları Dergisi, 45*, 100–121. DOI: 10.17829/turcom.1373818

Bal, N. (2014). Sosyolojide şiddet kavramı. *Yurt ve Dünya Dergisi, 6*, 6–22.

Bandura, A. (1965). Influence of models' reinforcement contingencies on the acquisition of imitative responses. *Journal of Personality and Social Psychology, 1*(6), 589–595. PMID: 14300234

Bandura, A. (1977). *Social Learning Theory*. Prentice Hall.

Banet-Weiser, S. (2012). *Authentic™: The politics of ambivalence in a brand culture*. NYU Press.

Banet-Weiser, S. (2025). Diversity as Distributive Justice. *Polity, 57*(1), 169–178. https://www.journals.uchicago.edu/doi/full/10.1086/733535

Barad, K. (2007). *Meeting the Universe Halfway: Quantum Physics and the Entanglement of Matter and Meaning*. Duke University Press.

Baskaran, K., Cui, W., & Kanhalli, A. (2023). A review of emotions in human-conversational agent ınteraction. *Proceedings of the Inaugural 2023 Summer Symposium Series1*(1), 61-67. https://doi.org/10.1609/aaaiss.v1i1.27477

Baudrillard, J. (1994). *Simulacra and Simulation*. University of Michigan Press.

Bauman, Z. (1998). *Sosyolojik düşünmek* (A. Yılmaz, Çev.). Ayrıntı Yayınları.

Bauman, Z. (2003). Liquid love: On the frailty of human bonds. Polity Press.</bok>

Bauman, Z. (2017). *Postmodern etik* (A. Türker, Çev.). Ayrıntı Yayınları.

Bauman, Z. (2004). *Liquid Life*. Polity Press.

Bauman, Z., & Lyon, D. (2024). *Liquid surveillance* (Yılmaz, E., Trans.). Ayrıntı Yayınları.

Beck, U. (1992). Risk society: Towards a new modernity. *Sage (Atlanta, Ga.)*.

Beck, U., & Beck-Gernsheim, E. (1995). *The normal chaos of love*. Polity Press.

Beer, D. (2016). *Metric power* (Vol. 10). Palgrave Macmillan.

Beer, D. (2017). The data gaze: Capitalism, power and perception. *Sage (Atlanta, Ga.)*.

Beer, D. (2017). The Social Power of Algorithms. *Information Communication and Society*, *20*(1), 1–13. DOI: 10.1080/1369118X.2016.1216147

Beever, J., McDaniel, R., & Stanlick, N. A. (2019). *Understanding digital ethics: Cases and contexts* (1st ed.). Routledge., DOI: 10.4324/9781315282138

Bender, E. M., Gebru, T., McMillan-Major, A., & Shmitchell, S. (2021). On the dangers of stochastic parrots: Can language models be too big? *Proceedings of the 2021 ACM Conference on Fairness, Accountability, and Transparency*, 610–623. https://doi.org/DOI: 10.1145/3442188.3445922

Bendig, E., Erb, B., Schulze-Thuesing, L., & Baumeister, H. (2022). The next generation: Chatbots in clinical psychology and psychotherapy to foster mental health – A scoping review. *Verhaltenstherapie*, *32*(Suppl. 1), 64–76. DOI: 10.1159/000501812

Benjamin, W. (1921). Zur Kritik der Gewalt [Critique of Violence]. In Gesammelte Schriften, Vol. II.1. Suhrkamp Verlag. (Benjamin, W. (1978). Critique of Violence. In M. Bullock & M. W. Jennings (Eds.), Reflections: Essays, Aphorisms, Autobiographical Writings (pp. 277–300). Schocken Books.)

Berger, P. L., & Luckmann, T. (1966). *The Social Construction of Reality: A Treatise in the Sociology of Knowledge*. Anchor Books.

Berger, T., Chen, C., & Frey, C. B. (2019). Drivers of disruption? Estimating the Uber effect. *European Economic Review*, *110*, 197–210.

Bernburg, J. G. (2009). Labeling theory. In Krohn, M., Lizotte, A., & Hall, G. (Eds.), *Handbook on crime and deviance* (pp. 187–207). Springer., DOI: 10.1007/978-1-4419-0245-0_10

Bertrams, A., & Krispenz, A. (2024). Dark-ego-vehicle principle: Narcissism as a predictor of anti-sexual assault activism. *Current Psychology (New Brunswick, N.J.)*, *43*(4). Advance online publication. DOI: 10.1007/s12144-023-04591-4

Bettivia, R. S., & Stainforth, E. (2023). Negotiating digital public spaces: Context, purpose and audiences. *The Journal of Documentation*, *79*(3), 703–717.

Beverungen, D., Hess, T., Köster, A., & Lehrer, C. (2022). From private digital platforms to public data spaces: Implications for the digital transformation. *Electronic Markets*, *32*(2), 493–501.

Bhaskar, R. (1975). *A Realist Theory of Science*. Routledge.

Bickmore, T. W., Caruso, L., Clough-Gorr, K., & Heeren, T. (2005). 'It's just like you talk to a friend' relational agents for older adults. *Interacting with Computers*, *17*(6), 711–735. DOI: 10.1016/j.intcom.2005.09.002

Bietti, E. (2020). From ethics washing to ethics bashing: A view on tech ethics from within moral philosophy. *Proceedings of the 2020 Conference on Fairness, Accountability, and Transparency*, 210–219. https://doi.org/DOI: 10.1145/3351095.3372860

Bigo, D. (2011). Security: A field left fallow. In Dillon, M., & Neal, A. W. (Eds.), *Foucault on politics, security and war* (pp. 109–123). Palgrave Macmillan.

Blackwell, C., Birnholtz, J., & Abbott, C. (2015). Seeing and being seen: Co-situation and impression formation using Grindr, a location-aware gay dating app. *New Media & Society*, *17*(7), 1117–1136. DOI: 10.1177/1461444814521595

Blom, J. N., & Hansen, K. R. (2015). Click bait: Forward-reference as lure in online news headlines. *Journal of Pragmatics*, *76*, 87–100.

Boczkowski, P. J., Mitchelstein, E., & Matassi, M. (2017). Incidental news: How young people consume news on social media. In *Proceedings of the 50th Hawaii International Conference on System Sciences* (pp. 1788–1796). University of Hawai'i at Mānoa., https://scholarspace.manoa.hawaii.edu/bitstream/10125/41371/1/paper0222.pdf

Bonina, C., Koskinen, K., Eaton, B., & Gawer, A. (2021). Digital platforms for development: Foundations and research agenda. *Information Systems Journal*, *31*(6), 869–902.

Bourdieu, P. (1984). *Distinction: A social critique of the judgement of taste* (R. Nice, Trans.). Harvard University Press. (Original work published 1979).

Bourdieu, P. (1989). Economisch kapitaal, cultureel kapitaal, sociaal kapitaal. *Opstellen over smaak, habitus en het veldbegrip*, 120-141.

Bourdieu, P. (2011). The forms of capital.(1986). *Cultural theory: An anthology, 1*(81-93), 949.

Bourdieu, P. (1984). *A social critique of the judgement of taste.*

Bourdieu, P. (1986). The forms of capital. In Richardson, J. G. (Ed.), *Handbook of theory and research for the sociology of education* (pp. 241–258). Greenwood Press.

Bourdieu, P. (1990). The logic of practice. *Polity.*

Bourdieu, P. (1991). *Language and Symbolic Power (J. B. Thompson* (Raymond, G., & Adamson, M. Eds. & Trans.). Harvard University Press., DOI: 10.2307/j.ctvjnrv7f

Bourdieu, P. (1991). Language and symbolic power. *Polity.*

Bourdieu, P. (2020). Outline of a Theory of Practice. In *The new social theory reader* (pp. 80–86). Routledge.

Boyd, D. (2008). Why youth (heart) social network sites: The role of networked publics in teenage social life. *Youth, Identity, And Digital Media, David Buckingham, ed., The John D. and Catherine T. MacArthur Foundation Series on Digital Media and Learning, The MIT Press, Cambridge, MA*, 2007-16.

Boyd, d., & Crawford, K. (2012). Critical questions for big data: Provocations for a cultural, technological, and scholarly phenomenon. Information, Communication & Society, 15(5), 662–679. DOI: 10.1080/1369118X.2012.678878

Boyd, D. (2014). *It's complicated: The social lives of networked teens.* Yale University Press.

Bozdağ, U. (2024). Framing displaced persons: An analysis of Turkish migration metaphors on Twitter. *Intersections: East European Journal of Society and Politics, 10*(1). Advance online publication. DOI: 10.17356/ieejsp.v10i1.1189

Brady, W. J., Wills, J. A., Jost, J. T., Tucker, J. A., & Van Bavel, J. J. (2017). Emotion shapes the diffusion of moralized content in social networks. *Proceedings of the National Academy of Sciences of the United States of America, 114*(28), 7313–7318.

Braidotti, R. (2013). *The posthuman.* Polity Press.

Brandtzaeg, P. B., & Folstad, A. (2018). Chatbots: Changing user needs and motivations. *Interaction, 25*(5), 38–43. DOI: 10.1145/3236669

Braun, V., & Clarke, V. (2006). Using Thematic Analysis In Psychology. *Qualitative Research in Psychology, 3*(2), 77–101.

Braun, V., & Clarke, V. (2025). Reporting guidelines for qualitative research: A values-based approach. *Qualitative Research in Psychology, 22*(2), 399–438.

Brayne, S. (2020). *Predict and surveil: Data, discretion, and the future of policing.* Oxford University Press.

Brown, M., Ray, R., Summers, E., & Fraistat, N. (2017). #SayHerName: A case study of intersectional social media activism. *Ethnic and Racial Studies, 40*(11), 1831–1846. DOI: 10.1080/01419870.2017.1334934

Brown, W. (2015). *Undoing the demos: Neoliberalism's stealth revolution.* Zone Books.

Brown, W. J. (2015). Examining four processes of audience ınvolvement with media personae: Transportation, parasocial ınteraction, ıdentification, and worship. *Communication Theory, 25*(3), 259–283.

Bucher, T. (2018). If... Then: Algorithmic Power and Politics. Oxford University Press
BirGün Gazetesi. [BirGun_Gazetesi]. (2021, July 29). *Türkiye'nin birçok yerinden yangın haberleri geliyor* [Fire news is coming from many parts of Turkey] [Tweet]. X (formerly Twitter). https://x.com/BirGun_Gazetesi/status/1420732873481625602

Bucher, T., & Helmond, A. (2018). The affordances of social media platforms. *The SAGE handbook of social media, 1*(1), 233-253.

Bucher, T. (2018). *If...Then: Algorithmic power and politics.* Oxford University Press.

Bülbül, S., & Öztürk, G. (2024). An examination of cybernetic art from el Cezeri's miniatures to the 20th century. *Art-E Art Journal, 17*(33), 373–402. DOI: 10.21602/sduarte.1472042

Burns, S. (2018). M-Pesa and the 'market-led' approach to financial inclusion. *Economic Affairs, 38*(3), 406–421. DOI: 10.1111/ecaf.12321

Büyüköztürk, Ş., Kılıç Çakmak, E., Akgün, Ö. E., Karadeniz, Ş., & Demirel, F. (2016). *Scientific research methods.* Pegem Academy.

Bye, T. A. (2020). Book review: The Platform Society. *Nordic Journal of Science and Technology Studies, 8*(1), 31–33.

Calderon Gomez, D. (2021). The third digital divide and Bourdieu: Bidirectional conversion of economic, cultural, and social capital to (and from) digital capital among young people in Madrid. *New Media & Society, 23*(9), 2534–2553.

Çalışkan, M., & Mencik, Y. (2015). Değişen dünyanın yeni yüzü: Sosyal medya. *Akademik Bakış Uluslararası Hakemli Sosyal Bilimler Dergisi*, (50), 254–277.

Calo, R., & Rosenblat, A. (2017). The taking economy: Uber, information, and power. *Columbia Law Review, 117*(6), 1623–1690.

Cant, C. (2019). *Riding for Deliveroo: Resistance in the New Economy*. Polity Press.

Capodivacca, S., & Giacomini, G. (2024). Discipline and Power in the Digital Age: Critical Reflections from Foucault's Thought. *Foucault Studies, 36*, 227–251. https://muse.jhu.edu/article/940820

Carr, C. T., & Hayes, R. A. (2015). Social media: Defining, developing, and divining. *Atlantic Journal of Communication, 23*(1), 46–65. DOI: 10.1080/15456870.2015.972282

Castells, M. (2009). *The rise of the network society* (2nd ed., Vol. 1). Wiley-Blackwell.

Cavallini, G., & Avogaro, M. (2019). Digital Work in the Platform Economy: The Last (but not least) Stage of Precariousness in Labour Relationships. In Kenner, J., Florczak, I., & Otto, M. (Eds.), *Precarious Work: The Challenge for Labour Law in Europe*. Edgar Publishing.

Çelebi, Ö. F., Cavdar Aksoy, N., Kocak Alan, A., & Tümer Kabadayı, E. (2023). Advanced technologies, artificial intelligence-based solutions: An emotion-focused approach. *Oneri Journal, 18*(60), 367–395. DOI: 10.14783/maruoneri.1189209

Çelik, E. (2018). İnternet ortamındaki şiddet sunumları ve yol açtığı sosyal travmalar. *Çağdaş Yönetim Bilimleri Dergisi, 5*(3), 280–296.

Çelik, N. (2023a). The Digital Inequalities in The Digital Society, *In Current Debates on Social Sciences 13,* pp: 75-81. ISBN: 978-625-6925-27-4 1st Edition.

Çelik, N. (2023b). I Am Online; Therefore, I Am!: Digital Obesity From a Sociological Perspective. In *Handbook of Research on Perspectives on Society and Technology Addiction* (pp. 479-496). IGI Global.

Çelik, N. (2025). New Methodological Trends in Sociology: An Assessment of Recent Studies. *Uluslararası Sosyal Bilimlerde Mükemmellik Arayışı Dergisi*, (8), 44–59.

Çelik, N., & Ateşoğlu, N. (2023). Dijitalleşmenin Eğitim Üzerindeki Etkileri: Sosyoloji Eğitimi Üzerine Eleştirel Bir Deneme. In *Dijital Kültür Bir Değişim Öyküsü: Medya, İletişim ve Eğitim Araştırmaları, (Edt: Ferihan Ayaz, Dilek Turan Eroğlu, Hakan Ayaz)*. Eğitim Yayınevi.

Çetin, S. (2022). Çevrimiçi oyunlar ve intihar: Mavi Balina örneği. *Milli Kültür Araştırmaları Dergisi, 6*(1), 61–73. DOI: 10.55774/mikad.1101587

Chai, S. H., Nicholson, B., Scapens, R. W., & Yang, C. (2023). Digital Platforms, Surveillance and Processes of Demoralization. *Journal of Information Technology, 39*(3), 568–586. DOI: 10.1177/02683962231208215

Chakravarti, U. (1993). Conceptualising Brahmanical Patriarchy in Early India: Gender, Caste, Class and State. *Economic and Political Weekly, 28*(14), 579–585. https://r.search.yahoo.com/_ylt=Awr1SaPvcK1oRwIAD_q7HAx.;_ylu=Y29sbwNzZzMEcG9zAzEEdnRpZAMEc2VjA3Ny/RV=2/RE=1757406703/RO=10/RU=https%3a%2f%2fwww.jstor.org%2fstable%2f4399556/RK=2/RS=EDRLDav2XLFjz6Jmr99_RlecMxg-

Cheney-Lippold, J. (2017). *We Are Data: Algorithms and the Making of Our Digital Selves*. NYU Press.

Cheng, C., & Ren, Y. (2024). The paradox of seeking help: Socioeconomic inequality in medical crowdfunding in the era of the mobile internet. *Chinese Journal of Sociology, 10*(1), 100–130. DOI: 10.1177/2057150X241230163

Cheng, H. K., Daniel Sokol, D., & Zang, X. (2024). The rise of empirical online platform research in the new millennium. *Journal of Economics & Management Strategy, 33*(2), 416–451.

Chen, L., Tong, T. W., Tang, S., & Han, N. (2022). Governance and design of digital platforms: A review and future research directions on a meta-organization. *Journal of Management, 48*(1), 147–184.

Chen, X., Li, J., Yang, W., Wang, H., & Song, H. (2025). Cross-platform violence detection on social media: A dataset and analysis. In *Proceedings of the 17th ACM Web Science Conference* (pp. 1–10). ACM. https://doi.org/DOI: 10.1145/3717867.3717877

Chernavin, Y. A. (2021). Digital society: Theoretical outlines of the emerging paradigm. *Digital Society : Ethics, Socio-Legal and Governance of Digital Technology, 4*(2), 4–12.

Cherubini, F., & Nielsen, R. K. (2016). Editorial analytics: How news media are developing and using audience data and metrics. *Available at SSRN* 2739328.

Chibike, J. J. (2023). Podcasting COVID-19 in Indigenous Languages: Interrogating Audio Psychology and Political Anthropomorphism. In *African Language Media* (pp. 112-124). Routledge.

Chibike, J. J. (2024). Computational Linguistics and Indigenous Languages. In Makananise, O and Madima, E (Eds). *Digital Media and the Preservation of Indigenous Languages in Africa: Toward a Digitalized and Sustainable Society*, 95.

Chibike, J. J., Muzhingi, S. A., Pikanegore, P., & Makalisa, B. (2025). Interrogating the interplay of multilingualism and multiculturalism on Lupane State University campus radio station. In Mathe, L., & Motsaathebe, G. (Eds.), *Reconceptualising Multilingualism on African Radio: Language and Identity* (pp. 111–129). Springer Nature Switzerland.

Chinmulgund, A., Khatwani, R., Tapas, P., Shah, P., & Sekhar, R. (June 23-25 2023). Anthropomorphism of AI-based chatbots by users during communication. *3rd International Conference on Intelligent Technologies (CONIT),* Karnataka, India. DOI: 10.1109/CONIT59222.2023.10205689

Chin, Y. C., & Zhao, J. (2022). Governing cross-border data flows: International trade agreements and their limits. *Laws, 11*(4), 63.

Cho, H., Cannon, J., Lopez, R., & Li, W. (2024). Social media literacy: A conceptual framework. *New Media & Society, 26*(2), 941–960. DOI: 10.1177/14614448211068530 PMID: 38328341

Chowdhry, P. (2007). *Contentious marriages, eloping couples: Gender, caste, and honour in a North Indian community*. Oxford University Press., https://r.search.yahoo.com/_ylt=Awrx.1OncK1o9QEAV.67HAx.;_ylu=Y29sbwNzZzMEcG9zAzEEdnRpZAMEc2VjA3Ny/RV=2/RE=1757406631/RO=10/RU=https%3a%2f%2fbooks.google.com%2fbooks%2fabout%2fContentious_Marriages_Eloping_Couples.html%3fid%3dYY6aAAAAIAAJ/RK=2/RS=4V9KqJvPVSdK2T.Afas25q_Bl88-

Christin, A., & Petre, C. (2020). Making peace with metrics: Relational work in online news production. *Sociologica, 14*(2), 133–156.

Chu, M. D., Gerard, P., Pawar, K., Bickham, C., & Lerman, K. (2025). Illusions of intimacy: Emotional attachment and emerging psychological risks in human AI relationships. Social and Information Networks. https://doi.org/10.48550/arXiv.2505.11649

Chua, J., & Banerjee, S. (2015). To buy or not to buy: Patagonia's "Don't Buy This Jacket" campaign. *Journal of Business Ethics, 131*(1), 257–268. DOI: 10.1007/s10551-014-2281-8

Chung, S., & Cho, H. (2017). Fostering parasocial relationships with celebrities on social media: Implications for celebrity endorsement. *Psychology and Marketing, 34*(4), 481–495. DOI: 10.1002/mar.21001

Çiçeklioğlu, A. Ş., & Ünal, R. (2021). What does TikTok app promise in the context of news production and consumption? *İLEF Dergisi, 8*, 69–98. https://doi.org/DOI: 10.24955/ilef.1037967

Cinelli, M., Morales, G. D. F., Galeazzi, A., Quattrociocchi, W., & Starnini, M. (2021). The echo chamber effect on social media. *Proceedings of the National Academy of Sciences of the United States of America, 118*(9), e2023301118. DOI: 10.1073/pnas.2023301118 PMID: 33622786

Çırak, B., & Yörük, A. (2015). The pioneer of mechatronics science, Ismail El-Cezeri. *Siirt University Journal of Social Sciences Institute*, 4, 175-194.

Coche, E., Kolk, A., & Ocelík, V. (2024). Unravelling cross-country regulatory intricacies of data governance: The relevance of legal insights for digitalization and international business. *Journal of International Business Policy*, *7*(1), 112–127.

Collins, R. (2008). *Violence: A micro-sociological theory*. Princeton University Press.

Comte, A. (1855). *The Positive Philosophy of Auguste Comte* (Martineau, H., Trans.). Calvin Blanchard.

Corrigan, P. W. (2004). How stigma interferes with mental healthcare. *The American Psychologist*, *59*(7), 614–625. DOI: 10.1037/0003-066X.59.7.614 PMID: 15491256

Costa, C., Burke, C., & Murphy, M. (2019). Capturing habitus: Theory, method and reflexivity. *International Journal of Research & Method in Education*, *42*(1), 19–32.

Cotter, K. (2019). Playing the visibility game: How digital influencers and algorithms negotiate influence on Instagram. *New Media & Society*, *21*(4), 895–913.

Couldry, N. (2012). Media, society, world: Social theory and digital media practice. *Polity*.

Couldry, N., & Mejias, U. A. (2019). Data colonialism: Rethinking big data's relation to the contemporary subject. *Television & New Media*, *20*(4), 336–349.

Couldry, N., & Mejias, U. A. (2019). *The costs of connection: How data is colonizing human life and appropriating it for capitalism*. Stanford University Press.

Couldry, N., & Mejias, U. A. (2019). *The Costs of Connection: How Data is Colonizing Human Life and Appropriating it for Capitalism*. Stanford University Press.

Coveri, A., Cozza, C., & Guarascio, D. (2021). *Monopoly capitalism in the digital era* (No. 2021/33). LEM Working Paper Series.

Cramer, F. (2015). What is 'Post-digital. In Press, A. C. (Ed.), *Post-digital aesthetics: Art, computation and design* (pp. 12–26). Palgrave Macmillan.

Crawford, K. (2021). *Atlas of AI: Power, politics, and the planetary costs of artificial intelligence*. Yale University Press.

Creemers, R. (2017). Cyber China: Upgrading propaganda, public opinion work and social management for the twenty-first century. *Journal of Contemporary China, 26*(103), 85–100. DOI: 10.1080/10670564.2016.1206281

Crenshaw, K. (1989). Demarginalizing the Intersection of Race and Sex: A Black Feminist Critique of Antidiscrimination Doctrine, Feminist Theory and Antiracist Politics. *University of Chicago Legal Forum, 1989*, 8. https://chicagounbound.uchicago.edu/uclf/vol1989/iss1/8

Creswell, J. W. (2014) *Research Design: Qualitative, Quantitative, and Mixed Methods Approaches*. 4th edn. Thousand Oaks, Carlifonia: Sage Publications.

Croes, E. A. J., Antheunis, M. L., Lee, C. V. D., & Wit, J. M. S. d. (2024). Digital confessions: The willingnessto disclose ıntimate ınformation to a chatbot and its ımpact on emotional well-being. *Interacting with Computers, 36*, 279–292. DOI: 10.1093/iwc/iwae016

Croes, E., Antheunis, M. L., & He, L. (2023). You go first: The effects of self-disclosure reciprocity in human-chatbot interactions. *11th International Conference on Affective Computing and Intelligent Interaction Workshops and Demos (ACIIW)*, Cambridge, MA, USA, pp. 1-4, doi: DOI: 10.1109/ACIIW59127.2023.10388091

Cui, P. (2025). Dynamics and Inequalities in Digital Social Networks: A Computational and Sociological Review. *arXiv preprint arXiv:2503.02887*.

D'Alfonso, S. (2020). AI in mental health: Opportunities and challenges. *Current Opinion in Psychology, 36*, 1–6. DOI: 10.1016/j.copsyc.2020.04.005 PMID: 32604065

Dahlgren, P. (2004). Cultural studies as a research perspective: Themes and tensions. In Corner, J., Schlesinger, P., & Silverstone, R. (Eds.), *International media research: A critical survey* (pp. 48–6). Routledge.

Dai, X. (2018). Toward a reputation state: The social credit system project of China. http://dx.doi.org/DOI: 10.2139/ssrn.3193577

Dal, A., Nisbet, E. C., & Kamenchuk, O. (2023). Signaling silence: Affective and cognitive responses to risks of online activism about corruption in an authoritarian context. *New Media & Society, 25*(3). Advance online publication. DOI: 10.1177/14614448221135861

Danugrobe, A. (2024). The role of history in the strengthening of national identity in the era of society 5.0, *Jurnal Sejarah Dan Pembela Jarannya* 14(1): https://e-journal.unipma.ac.id/index.php/JA/article/view/18745

Das, K., & Rao, T. S. S. (2019). A chronicle of sexuality in the Indian subcontinent. *Journal of Psychosexual Health, 1*(1), 20–25. DOI: 10.1177/2631831818822017

Davidjants, J., & Tiidenberg, K. (2022). Activist memory narration on social media: Armenian genocide on Instagram. *New Media & Society, 24*(10), 2191–2206.

Davis, K., & Moore, W. E. (2019). Some principles of stratification. In *Social Stratification, Class, Race, and Gender in Sociological Perspective, Second Edition* (pp. 55-63). Routledge.

De Genova, N. (2017). *The Borders of "Europe": Autonomy of Migration, Tactics of Bordering*. Duke University Press.

de Medeiros, A. S. Junior, L.A.G. & Lifschitz, S. (2024). Surveillance capitalism revealed: tracing the hidden world of web data collection. *ArXiv*https://doi.org//arXiv.2412.17944DOI: 10.48550

De Ridder, S. (2022). The datafication of intimacy: Mobile dating apps, dependency, and everyday life. *Television & New Media, 23*(6), 593–609. DOI: 10.1177/15274764211052660

De Stefano, V. (2016). The rise of the "just-in-time workforce": On-demand work, crowd work, and labour protection in the "gig economy.". *Comparative Labor Law & Policy Journal, 37*(3), 471–503.

De, S. (2020). Influence of Uber-careem deal on the Middle Eastern Startups. Retrieved from https://medium.com/allride/influence-of-uber-careem-deal-on-the-middle-eastern-startups-f4f3eb54eff4

Debord, G. (1967). *The society of the spectacle*. Zone Books.

Decuypere, M., Grimaldi, E., & Landri, P. (2021). Introduction: Critical studies of digital education platforms. *Critical Studies in Education, 62*(1), 1–16.

Değer, B. E., & Sine Nazlı, R. (2022). Sosyal medyada influencer etkisi bağlamında benlik sunumu. *Uşak Üniversitesi Sosyal Bilimler Dergisi, 15*(2), 25–45.

Deleuze, G., & Guattari, F. (1987). *A Thousand Plateaus*. University of Minnesota Press.

Demir, S. T., & Özcan, A. (2021). Sosyal medya ve linç kültürü: Sanal nedenler, gerçek sonuçlar. *İletişim Kuram ve Araştırma Dergisi, 56*, 1–15. https://doi.org/ DOI: 10.47998/ikad.957544

Denecke, K., Abd-Alrazaq, A., & Househ, M. (2021). Artificial intelligence for chatbots in mental health: Opportunities and challenges. In Househ, M., Borycki, E., & Kushniruk, A. (Eds.), *Multiple perspectives on artificial intelligence in healthcare* (pp. 117–128). Springer., DOI: 10.1007/978-3-030-67303-1_10

Denizli, U. (2019). İşe alım sürecinde sosyal ağ siteleri kullanımı: Tehlikeler ve fırsatlar. *The Journal of International Scientific Researches*, *4*(3), 283–303.

Denzin, N. K. (1978). *The Research Act: A Theoretical Introduction to Sociological Methods* (2nd ed.). McGraw-Hill.

Descartes, R. (1999). *Discourse on method and related writings* (Clarke, D. M., Trans.). Penguin Books.

Dey, S. K., & Dey, S. (2024). Identity, Social Media and Online Political Activism. SSRN *Electronic Journal*. https://doi.org/DOI: 10.2139/ssrn.4703365

Dhimolea, T. K., Kaplan-Rakowski, R., & Lin, L. (2022). Supporting social and emotional well-being with artificial intelligence. In Albert, M. V., Lin, L., Spector, M. J., & Dunn, L. S. (Eds.), *Bridging human intelligence and artificial intelligence* (pp. 147–169). Springer., DOI: 10.1007/978-3-030-84729-6_8

Di Vaio, A., Latif, B., Gunarathne, N., Gupta, M., & D'Adamo, I. (2024). Digitalization and artificial knowledge for accountability in SCM: A systematic literature review. *Journal of Enterprise Information Management*, *37*(2), 606–672.

Diamond-Smith, N., Vaishnav, Y., Choudhary, U., Sharma, P., Kachhwaha, A., Panjalingam, T., Vallin, J., Das, D., & Gopalakrishnan, L. (2024). Individual empowerment and community norm effects of engaging young husbands in reproductive health in rural India: Findings from a pilot study. *Reproductive Health*, *21*(1), 147. https://link.springer.com/article/10.1186/s12978-024-01878-y PMID: 39420379

Dick, S. (2019). Artificial intelligence. *Harvard Data Science Review*, *1*(1), 1–8. DOI: 10.1162/99608f92.92fe150c

Diederich, S., Brende, A. B., Morana, S., & Kolbe, L. (2022). On the design of and interaction with conversational agents: An organizing and assessing review of human-computer interaction research. *Journal of the Association for Information Systems*, *23*(1), 96–138. DOI: 10.17705/1jais.00724

DiMaggio, P., Hargittai, E., Celeste, C., & Shafer, S. (2004). Digital inequality: From unequal access to differentiated use. *Social inequality*, 355-400.

Dmitrieva, E. I. (2020). Digital Platforms as a Base for Forming a Digital Economy. In *2nd International Scientific and Practical Conference on Digital Economy (ISCDE 2020)* (pp. 553-558). Atlantis Press.

Do, H. N., Do, N. B., Nguyen, T. M., & Nguyen, H. M. (2024). Anti-Brand Activism in the Collectivist Orientation: The Case of Online-Consumers-Run Communities. *Journal of Promotion Management, 30*(5). Advance online publication. DOI: 10.1080/10496491.2024.2318665

Donath, J. S. (2002). Identity and deception in the virtual community. In *Communities in cyberspace* (pp. 37–68). Routledge.

Donovan, K. (2012). Mobile money, more freedom? The impact of M-Pesa's network power on development as freedom. *International Journal of Communication, 6*, 2647–2669.

Dornis, T. W., & Stober, S. (2025). Generative AI training and copyright law. *ArXiv*. https://doi.org/10.48550/arXiv.2502.15858

Dorschel, R. (2022). Reconsidering digital labour: Bringing tech workers into the debate. *New Technology, Work and Employment, 37*(2), 288–307. DOI: 10.1111/ntwe.12225

Dou, Y., & Zhang, M. (2025). Longitudinal reciprocal relationship between media violence exposure and aggression among junior high school students in China: A cross-lagged analysis. *Frontiers in Psychology, 15*, 1–13. DOI: 10.3389/fpsyg.2024.1441738 PMID: 39839937

Drewel, M., Özcan, L., Gausemeier, J., & Dumitrescu, R. (2021). Platform patterns—Using proven principles to develop digital platforms. *Journal of the Knowledge Economy, 12*(2), 519–543.

Durkheim, É. (2014). *The division of labour in society* (Halls, W. D., Trans.). Free Press. (Original work published 1893)

Eastwick, P. W., & Smith, L. K. (2018). Sex-differentiated effects of physical attractiveness on romantic desire: A highly powered, preregistered study in a photograph evaluation context. *Comprehensive Results in Social Psychology, 3*(1), 1–27. https://static1.squarespace.com/static/504114b1e4b0b97fe5a520af/t/5be1db97758d46f6af1b7793/1541528474670/EastwickSmith2018CRSP.pdf

Edelman. (2023). *Edelman trust barometer 2023*. Edelman. https://www.edelman.com/trust/sidebar/2023-trust-barometer

Eisend, M. (2018). Humour in advertising: A review and agenda for future research. *Journal of Advertising, 47*(4), 398–414. DOI: 10.1080/00913367.2018.1532859

ElTarabishi, M., & Galal, S. (2023). The role of social media in promoting peace building and prevention of societal violence among university youth (analytical descriptive study). *Journal of Media and Interdisciplinary Studies, 2*(4), 1–32. DOI: 10.21608/jmis.2023.313513

Enloe, C. (2012). Masculinities, Policing, Women and International Politics of Sexual Harassment. *International Feminist Journal of Politics, 15*(1), 77–81. DOI: 10.1080/14616742.2012.742681

Entman, R. M. (1993). Framing: Towards clarification of a fractured paradigm. *McQuail's reader in mass communication theory, 390*, 397.

Epley, N., Waytz, A., & Cacioppo, J. (2007). On seeing human: A Three-factor theory of anthropomorphism. *Psychological Review, 114*(4), 864–886. DOI: 10.1037/0033-295X.114.4.864 PMID: 17907867

Erikson, E.H., 1968. *Identity youth and crisis* (No. 7). WW Norton & company.

Erol, V. (2022). Sosyal medyanın Türk aile yapısına etkisi. *Karamanoğlu Mehmetbey Üniversitesi Sosyal ve Ekonomik Araştırmalar Dergisi, 24*(43), 1127–1139.

Ertuğruloğlu, O., Gülcan, N.Y. & Pişkin-Abidoğlu, Ü. (2024). The impact of culture on the education system, *International e-Journal of Educational Studies* 8 (16): 131-141.

Euronews (2022). 'İngiliz genç kız, olumsuz çevrimiçi içeriğin etkisi nedeniyle öldü'. https://tr.euronews.com/2022/09/30/ingiliz-genc-kiz-olumsuz-cevrimici-icerigin-etkisi-nedeniyle-oldu

European Commission. (2022). *The Digital Services Act and the Digital Markets Act: Ensuring a safe and open digital space.* Brussels: European Commission. https://digital-strategy.ec.europa.eu/en/policies/digital-services-act-package

Europen Council. (2024). *EPRS Briefing*: (No. 767146). https://www.europarl.europa.eu/RegData/etudes/BRIE/2024/767146/EPRS_BRI(2024)767146_EN.pdf

Eyssel, F., & Reich, N. (2013). Loneliness makes the heart grow fonder (of robots)—On the effects of loneliness on psychological anthropomorphism. *8th Acm/ieee International Conference on Human-robot Interaction (HRI)*, 121-122. https://doi.org/DOI: 10.1109/HRI.2013.6483531

Fairwork (2021). Fairwork Annual Report. University of Oxford.

Fang, C. M., Liu, A. R., Danry, V., Lee, E., Chan, S. W. T., Pataranutaporn, P., Maes, P., Phang, J., Lampe, M., Ahmad, L., & Agarwal, S. (2025). *How AI and human behaviors shape psychosocial effects of chatbot use: A longitudinal randomized controlled study*. arXiv. https://arxiv.org/abs/2503.17473

Ferguson, M. A., & Ford, T. E. (2008). Disparagement humour: A theoretical and empirical review of psychoanalytic, superiority, and social identity theories. *Humour, 21*(3), 283–312. DOI: 10.1515/HUMOUR.2008.014

Fernandez Macias, E., Gonzalez Vazquez, I., Torrejon Perez, S., & Nurskı, L. (2025). Work in the Digital Era: How Technology is Transforming Work and Occupations, Publications Office of the European Union, Luxembourg, https://data.europa.eu/doi/10.2760/0956105, JRC141451.

Fernandez Macias, E., Urzi Brancati, M. C., Wright, S., & Pesole, A. (2023). The Platformisation of Work. EUR 31469 EN, Publications Office of the European Union, Luxembourg, 2023, ISBN 978-92-68-01661-9, doi:, JRC133016.DOI: 10.2760/801282

Figà Talamanca, G., & Arfini, S. (2022). Through the newsfeed glass: Rethinking filter bubbles and echo chambers. *Philosophy & Technology, 35*(1), 20. DOI: 10.1007/s13347-021-00494-z PMID: 35308101

Fineman, M. A. (2010). The vulnerable subject: Anchoring equality in the human condition. In *Transcending the boundaries of law* (pp. 177–191). Routledge-Cavendish., https://www.taylorfrancis.com/chapters/edit/10.4324/9780203848531-26/vulnerable-subject-anchoring-equality-human-condition-martha-albertson-fineman

Fisher, L., Evans, M., Forbes, K., Gayton, A., Liu, Y., & Rutgers, D. (2022). Language experiences, evaluations and emotions (3Es): Analysis of structural models of multilingual identity for language learners in schools in England. *International Journal of Multilingualism, 21*(1), 418–438.

Fitzpatrick, K. K., Darcy, A., & Vierhile, M. (2017). Delivering cognitive behavior therapy to young adults with symptoms of depression and anxiety using a fully automated conversational agent (Woebot): A randomized controlled trial. *JMIR Mental Health, 4*(2), e19. DOI: 10.2196/mental.7785 PMID: 28588005

Flew, T. (2021). *Understanding Global Media*. Palgrave.

Floridi, L. (2020). *The logic of information: A theory of philosophy as conceptual design*. Oxford University Press.

Floridi, L. (2022). The Ethics of Artificial Intelligence for a Good Society: The US and EU Initiatives. *Philosophy & Technology, 35*(4), 1–8. DOI: 10.1007/s13347-022-00540-4

Flyvbjerg, B. (2001). *Making Social Science Matter: Why Social Inquiry Fails and How It Can Succeed Again*. Cambridge University Press.

Foucault, M. (1982). The subject and power. *Critical Inquiry, 8*(4), 777–795.

Foucault, M. (1995). *Discipline and punish: The birth of the prison* (Sheridan, A., Trans.). Vintage Books.

Foucault, M. (2013). *Security, territory, population: Lectures at the Collège de France (1977–1978)* (Taylan, F., Trans.). Istanbul Bilgi University Press.

Foucault, M. (2015). *The eye of power* (Ergüden, I., Trans.). Ayrıntı Yayınları.

Freitas, J. D., Uğuralp, A. K., Uğuralp, O. Z., & Puntoni, S. (2024). *AI companions reduce loneliness* (Harvard Business School Working Paper No. 24-078). The Wharton School Research Paper). http://dx.doi.org/DOI: 10.2139/ssrn.4893097

Friemel, T. N. (2016). The digital divide has grown old: Determinants of a digital divide among seniors. *New Media & Society, 18*(2), 313–331. DOI: 10.1177/1461444814538648

Fromm, J., & Read, A. (2018). *Marketing to Gen Z: The rules for reaching this vast—and very different—generation of influencers*. AMACOM.

Fuchs, C. (2014). *Digital Labour and Karl Marx*. Routledge.

Funk, J. B., Baldacci, H. B., Pasold, T., & Baumgardner, J. (2004). Violence exposure in real-life, video games, television, movies, and the internet: Is there desensitization? *Journal of Adolescence, 27*(1), 23–39. DOI: 10.1016/j.adolescence.2003.10.005 PMID: 15013258

Fu, X., Avenyo, E., & Ghauri, P. (2021). Digital platforms and development: A survey of the literature. *Innovation and Development, 11*(2-3), 303–321.

Gadzala, A. W. (2015). *Africa and China: How Africans and Their Governments are Shaping Relations with China*. Rowman & Littlefield.

Gaffar, H., & Albarashdi, S. (2024). Copyright protection for ai-generated works: Exploring originality and ownership in a digital landscape. *Asian Journal of International Law, 15*(1), 23–46. DOI: 10.1017/S2044251323000735

Gago, V. (2020). *La potencia feminista: Origenes y luchas en América Latina*. Tinta Limón.

Galtung, J. (1969). Violence, peace, and peace research. *Journal of Peace Research, 6*(3), 167–191. DOI: 10.1177/002234336900600301

Gao, S. (2022). The online activism of mock translanguaging: Language style, celebrity persona, and social class in China. *Discourse, Context & Media, 47*. Advance online publication. DOI: 10.1016/j.dcm.2022.100608

Garver, N. (1973). What violence is. In Bierman, A. K., & Gould, J. A. (Eds.), *Philosophy for a new generation* (pp. 204–220). Macmillan.

Georgakopoulou, A., Iversen, S., & Stage, C. (2022). Quantified storytelling: How the tellable and the countable intermingle on digital platforms. In *The Routledge Companion to Narrative Theory* (pp. 149–163). Routledge.

Gerber, C., & Krzywdzinski, M. (2019). Brave new digital work? New forms of performance control in crowdwork. In *Work and labor in the digital age* (Vol. 33, pp. 121–143). Emerald Publishing Limited., DOI: 10.1108/s0277-283320190000033008

Ge, Y., Knittel, C. R., MacKenzie, D., & Zoepf, S. (2016). *Racial and gender discrimination in transportation network companies (No. w22776)*. National Bureau of Economic Research., DOI: 10.3386/w22776

Gezginci, G., & Işıklı, Ş. (2018). Dindar Facebook etkisi: Türk kullanıcılar üzerine bir analiz. *Medya ve Din Araştırmaları Dergisi, 1*(1), 111–133.

Ghazal, D. U. S., & Anwar, A. (2025). Unravelling global perceptions of the 2023 Isreal-Hamas Conflict: A discourse historical analysis of tweets. [JALT]. *Journal of Applied Linguistics and TESOL, 8*(2), 2209–2214.

Ghosh, S., Yucaoglu, G., & Thapar, A. (2018). Careem: Base camp or mountain peak? Designing an OS for scaling. Harvard Business School Case 819-049, September 2018.

Gibson, S. (2024). Racialized railway mobilities: repression and resistance in the Anglophone South African Short story during the drum decade, *English Studies in Africa* 1-15. https://doi.org/DOI: 10.1080/00138398.2024.2377913

Giddens, A. (1992). *The transformation of intimacy: Sexuality, love and eroticism in modern societies*. Stanford University Press.

Giddens, A. (2014). *Modernity and self-identity: Self and society in the late modern age* (Tatlıcan, Ü., Trans.). Say Yayınları.

Gillespie, T. (2021). The Politics of "Platforms". *Questions de communication, 40*(2), 23-46.

Gillespie, T. (2010). The politics of 'platforms'. *New Media & Society*, *12*(3), 347–364.

Gillespie, T. (2014). The relevance of algorithms. In Gillespie, T., Boczkowski, P., & Foot, K. (Eds.), *Media technologies: Essays on communication, materiality, and society* (pp. 167–193). MIT Press.

Gillespie, T. (2018). *Custodians of the Internet*. Yale University Press.

Gillespie, T. (2018). *Custodians of the internet: Platforms, content moderation, and the hidden decisions that shape social media*. Yale University Press.

Gillespie, T. (2018). *Custodians of the Internet: Platforms, content moderation, and the hidden decisions that shape social media*. Yale University Press.

Ging, D. (2023). Digital culture, online misogyny, and gender-based violence. In M. Gallagher & A. V. Montiel (Eds.), *The international encyclopedia of media literacy*. Wiley. https://doi.org/. 781119800729.ch13DOI: 10.1002/930

Goffman, E. (1959). *The Presentation of Self in Everyday Life*. University of Edinburgh Social Sciences Research Centre.

Gökalp, B., & Subay, Ö. Ö. (2024). The reflections on social media of the statements made by the Nation Alliance in Turkey. *Zeitschrift für Vergleichende Politikwissenschaft*. https://doi.org/DOI: 10.1007/s12286-024-00593-z

Gorwa, R. (2019). What is platform governance? *Information Communication and Society*, *22*(6), 854–871. DOI: 10.1080/1369118x.2019.1573914

Gorwa, R., Lechowski, G., & Schneiß, D. (2024). Platform lobbying: Policy influence strategies and the EU's Digital Services Act. *Internet Policy Review*, *13*(2), 1–26. DOI: 10.14763/2024.2.1782

Graham, M., Hjorth, I., & Lehdonvirta, V. (2017). Digital Labour and Development: Impacts of Global Digital Labour Platforms and the Gig Economy on Worker Livelihoods. *Transfer: European Review of Labour and Research*, *23*(2), 135–162.

Graham, M., Hjorth, I., & Lehdonvirta, V. (2017). Digital labour and development: Impacts of global digital labour platforms and the gig economy on worker livelihoods. *Transfer: European Review of Labour and Research*, *23*(2), 135–162. DOI: 10.1177/1024258916687250

Gray, J., Jones, J. P., & Thompson, E. (2009). *Satire TV: Politics and comedy in the post-network era*. NYU Press.

Green, J. (2024). TikTok and the changing landscape of therapeutic digital spaces of care. *Digital Geography and Society*, *6*, 100077.

Greijdanus, H., de Matos Fernandes, C. A., Turner-Zwinkels, F., Honari, A., Roos, C. A., Rosenbusch, H., & Postmes, T. (2020). The psychology of online activism and social movements: relations between online and offline collective action. In *Current Opinion in Psychology* (Vol. 35). https://doi.org/DOI: 10.1016/j.copsyc.2020.03.003

Grewal, I. (2013). Outsourcing Patriarchy: FEMINIST ENCOUNTERS, TRANSNATIONAL MEDIATIONS AND THE CRIME OF 'HONOUR KILLINGS.'. *International Feminist Journal of Politics, 15*(1), 1–19. DOI: 10.1080/14616742.2012.755352

Grohol, J. M. (2022, July 6). *Friends with benefits*. LifeHelper. https://lifehelper.com/blog/friends-with-benefits/

Gross, N. (2005). The detraditionalization of intimacy reconsidered. *Sociological Theory, 23*(3), 286–311. DOI: 10.1111/j.0735-2751.2005.00255.x

GSMA. (2024). Mobile gender gap report 2024: Bridging the digital divide for women in India. GSMA Intelligence. https://r.search.yahoo.com/_ylt=AwrKGCgrb_JoEQIADwC7HAx.;_ylu=Y29sbwNzZzMEcG9zAzEEdnRpZAMEc2VjA3Ny/RV=2/RE=1761928236/RO=10/RU=https%3a%2f%2fwww.gsma.com%2fr%2fwp-content%2fuploads%2f2024%2f05%2fThe-Mobile-Gender-Gap-Report-2024.pdf/RK=2/RS=3RPGs_Q07jmBJyXAw9AfH_k4j6o-

GSMA. (2024). *The Mobile Gender Gap Report 2024*. GSMA. Retrieved from https://www.gsma.com/r/wp-content/uploads/2024/05/The-Mobile-Gender-Gap-Report-2024.pdf

Guba, E. G., & Lincoln, Y. S. (1994). Competing paradigms in qualitative research. In Denzin, N. K., & Lincoln, Y. S. (Eds.), *Handbook of Qualitative Research* (pp. 105–117). SAGE.

Güllü, O. (2021). The rise of artificial ıntelligence: Human learning machine learning gameplay encounters.*ISophos: Uluslararası Bilişim. Teknoloji ve Felsefe Dergisi, 4*(7), 19–30.

Gürbüzdal, U. (2022). Güvencesizleşmenin sembolik inkârı olarak sosyal medya pratikleri: Beyaz yakalı profesyonel kültürüne LinkedIn üzerinden bir bakış. *ARTS*, Dijitalleşme Özel Sayısı, 27–55. https://doi.org/ .DOI: 10.46372/arts.1191703

Gur, H., & Caliskan, G. (2024). Crafting a national identity: The role of geography textbooks in 1930s Turkey's nation building project. *Nations and Nationalism*. Advance online publication. DOI: 10.1111/nana.13044

Gurumurthy, A. A. (2021). Governing a Seamless Sociality: Beyond Old and New Media. *Issue 4 Int'l JL Mgmt. & Human., 4*, 2253. https://heinonline.org/HOL/LandingPage?handle=hein.journals/ijlmhs12&div=213&id=&page=

Guthrie, S. (2013). Anthropomorphism. In A. L. Runehov, O. Oviedo, & N. P. Azari (Eds.*), Encyclopedia of sciences and religions* (pp. 111-113). Springer.

Haber, A. [ahaber]. (2019, April 1). *#SONDAKİKA İşte İstanbul'da usulsüzlüğün belgeleri!* [#LASTMINUTE Here are the documents of irregularity in Istanbul!] [Tweet]. X (formerly Twitter). https://x.com/ahaber/status/1112706126838198272

Haber, A. [ahaber]. (2019, April 4). *#SONDAKİKA AK Parti, İstanbul'da tüm oyların yeniden sayılması için başvuruda bulundu* [#LASTMINUTE AK Party applied for a recount of all votes in Istanbul] [Tweet]. X (formerly Twitter). https://x.com/ahaber/status/1113890084145762305

Haber, A. [ahaber]. (2019, April 8). *#CANLI AK Parti Genel Başkan Yardımcısı Ali İhsan Yavuz: Ortada oy yolsuzluğu var* [#LIVE AK Party Deputy Chairman Ali İhsan Yavuz: There is vote fraud] [Tweet]. X (formerly Twitter). https://x.com/ahaber/status/1115261563907260416

Haber, A. [ahaber]. (2019, April 8). *#CANLI AK Parti Genel Başkan Yardımcısı Ali İhsan Yavuz: Ortada oy yolsuzluğu var* http://ow.ly/PiGv50pwOvd [#LIVE AK Party Deputy Chairman Ali İhsan Yavuz: There is vote corruption] [Tweet]. X (formerly Twitter). https://x.com/ahaber/status/1115261563907260416

Haber, A. [Ahaber]. (2019, March 31). *SON DAKİKA! Binali Yıldırım: İstanbul'da seçimi kazandık* [LAST MINUTE! Binali Yıldırım: We won the election in Istanbul] [Video]. YouTube. https://www.youtube.com/watch?v=atI4G-gtDmY

Haber, A. [Ahaber]. (2021, August 24). *Kız arkadaşı ortaya çıkardı! İşte Manavgat yangınında tutuklanan şahsın ses kaydı!* [His girlfriend revealed it! Here is the audio recording of the person arrested for the Manavgat fire!] [Video]. YouTube. https://www.youtube.com/watch?v=Crg6ulFUty4

Haber, A. [Ahaber]. (2021, July 28). *Manavgat'ta büyük felaket! 4 farklı noktada yangın* [Great disaster in Manavgat! Fire in 4 different locations] [Video]. YouTube. https://www.youtube.com/watch?v=zbUsIP3mhFQ

Haber, A. [Ahaber]. (2021, July 29). *Antalya Manavgat'taki yangınlar sabotaj mı? Şok görüntüler...* [Are the fires in Manavgat, Antalya sabotage? Shocking footage...] [Video]. YouTube. https://www.youtube.com/watch?v=86krI6Tj1RE

Haber, A. [ahaber]. (2023, September 4). *Başkan Recep Tayyip Erdoğan, 2023 CEV Avrupa Şampiyonası'nda, Sırbistan'ı 3-2'lik skorla yenerek Şampiyon olan A Milli Kadın Voleybol Takımı'nı tebrik etti* [President Recep Tayyip Erdoğan congratulated the Women's National Volleyball Team, who became the champion by defeating Serbia 3-2 in the 2023 CEV European Championship] [Tweet]. X (formerly Twitter). https://x.com/ahaber/status/1698452076651590112

Haenlein, M.,& Kaplan, A. (2019). A brief history of artificial intelligence: On the past, present, and future of artificial intelligence. *California Management Review, 61*(4), 5-14. https://doi.org/ (Original work published 2019)DOI: 10.1177/0008125619864925

Halford, S., & Savage, M. (2017). Speaking sociologically with big data: Symphonic social science and the future for big data research. *The Sociological Review, 65*(1), 2–19. DOI: 10.1111/1467-954X.12273

Hall, J., & Krueger, A. (2015). An analysis of the labour market for Uber's Driver-Partners in the United States, Princeton, available at: https://www.nber.org/system/files/working_papers/w22843/w22843.pdf

Hallinan, B., Reynolds, C. J., & Rothenstein, O. (2024). Copyright callouts and the promise of creator-driven platform governance. *Internet Policy Review, 13*(2), 1–43. DOI: 10.14763/2024.2.1770

Hallin, D. C., & Mancini, P. (2004). *Comparing media systems: Three models of media and politics*. Cambridge university press.

Hall, S. (2003). Cultural Studies and the Centre: some problematics and problems. In *Culture, media, language* (pp. 2–35). Routledge.

Hall, S. (Ed.). (1997). *Representation: Cultural representations and signifying practices* (Vol. 2). Sage.

Han, B.-C. (2024). *The transparency society* (Barışcan, H., Trans.). Metis Yayınları.

Hansen, H., Elias, S. R., Stevenson, A., Smith, A. D., Alexander, B. N., & Barros, M. (2025). Resisting the objectification of qualitative research: The unsilencing of context, researchers, and none interview data. *Organizational Research Methods, 28*(1), 3–31.

Harari, Y. N. (2018). *Homo Deus: A brief history of tomorrow* (Taneli, P. N., Trans.). Kolektif Kitap.

Harari, Y. N. (2020). *Sapiens: A brief history of humankind* (Genç, E., Trans.). Kolektif Kitap.

Haraway, D. J. (1988). Situated knowledges: The science question in feminism and the privilege of partial perspective. *Feminist Studies, 14*(3), 575–599. DOI: 10.2307/3178066

Harding, S. (1991). *Whose Science? Whose Knowledge? Thinking from Women's Lives.* Cornell University Press.

Hargittai, E., & Dobransky, K. (2017). Old dogs, new clicks: Digital inequality in skills and uses among older adults. *Canadian Journal of Communication, 42*(2), 195–212. DOI: 10.22230/cjc.2017v42n2a3176

Harris, B. A. (2020). Technology and violence against women. In *The Emerald handbook of feminism, criminology and social change* (pp. 317–336). Emerald Publishing Limited., https://www.emerald.com/insight/content/doi/10.1108/978-1-78769-955-720201026/full/html

Hasmaiti, H., Syamsudduha, S., & Azis, A. (2025). Social, Political, and Cultural Discourse in the Movie Gadis Kretek: A Critical Discourse Analysis by Ruth Wodak. *Journal of Asian Multicultural Research for Social Sciences Study, 6*(2), 29–43.

Hauben (ed.), H., Lenaerts, K. and Waeyaert, W. (2020). The Platform Economy and Precarious Work. Publication for the Committee on Employment and Social Affairs, Policy Department for Economic, Scientific and Quality of Life Policies, European Parliament, Luxembourg.

Heisenberg, W. (1958). *Physics and Philosophy: The Revolution in Modern Science.* Harper.

Helberger, N. (2020). The political power of platforms: How current attempts to regulate misinformation amplify opinion power. *Digital Journalism (Abingdon, England), 8*(6), 842–854.

Helberger, N., Pierson, J., & Poell, T. (2018). Governing online platforms: From contested to cooperative responsibility. *The Information Society, 34*(1), 1–14. DOI: 10.1080/01972243.2017.1391913

Heldman, C., & Wade, L. (2010). Hook up culture: Setting a new research agenda. *Sexuality Research & Social Policy, 7*(4), 323–333. DOI: 10.1007/s13178-010-0024-z

Helles, R., & Flyverbom, M. (2019). Meshes of Surveillance, Prediction, and Infrastructure: On the Cultural and Commercial Consequences of Digital Platforms. *Surveillance & Society, 17*(1/2), 34–39. https://ojs.library.queensu.ca/index.php/surveillance-and-society/article/view/13120

Helmond, A. (2015). The platformization of the web: Making web data platform ready. *Social Media + Society, 1*(2), 1–11. DOI: 10.1177/2056305115603080

Herbener, A. B., & Damholdt, M. F. (2025). Are lonely youngsters turning to chatbots for companionship? The relationship betweenchatbotusage and social connectedness in Danish high-school students. *International Journal of Human-Computer Studies, 196*. Advance online publication. DOI: 10.1016/j.ijhcs.2024.103409

Hernando, C., & Constantinies, E. (2021). Emotional Contagion: A Brief Overview and Future Directions Front. *Psychol., 12*. Advance online publication. DOI: 10.3389/fpsyg.2021.712606

Hess, A. (2019). The risks and rewards of feminist satire in the age of social media. *Feminist Media Studies, 19*(6), 871–886. DOI: 10.1080/14680777.2018.1498148

Hill, S. (2015). *Raw Deal: How the 'Uber Economy' and Runaway Capitalism Are Screwing American Workers*. St. Martin's Press.

Hintz, A., Dencik, L., & Wahl-Jorgensen, K. (2017). Digital Citizenship in a Datafied Society. *Polity*.

Hirst, W., & Manier, D. (2008). The role of memory in the social construction of identity. In *The Handbook of Identity Theory and Research*. Springer.

Hoffner, C., & Bond, B. J. (2022). 'The role of media figures in adolescents' identity construction'. *Journal of Broadcasting & Electronic Media, 66*(2), 185–202.

Hollows, J. (2024). Feminism, cultural studies and popular culture. In Hollows, J. (Ed.), *Feminism, Femininity and Popular Culture* (pp. 19–36). Manchester University Press.

Holt, D. B. (2004). *How brands become icons: The principles of cultural branding*. Harvard Business School Press.

Holt, D. B. (2016). *Branding in the age of social media*. Harvard Business Review Press.

Hopkins, D. J., Lelkes, Y., & Wolken, S. (2025). The rise of and demand for identity-oriented media coverage. *American Journal of Political Science, 69*(2), 483–500.

Hopkins, S. (2022). Beyond Digital Literacy in Australian Prisons: Theorizing "Network Literacy," Intersectionality, and Female Incarcerated Students. *Media and Communication, 10*(4). Advance online publication. DOI: 10.17645/mac.v10i4.5734

Horton, D., & Wohl, R. R. (1956). Mass communication and parasocial interaction. *Psychiatry, 19*(3), 215–229. DOI: 10.1080/00332747.1956.11023049 PMID: 13359569

Horwitz, J. (2025). *A flirty meta AI bot invited a retire to meet. He never made it home*. Reuters.

Howell, N., Hartsoe, W. F., Amin, J., & Namani, V. (2024, October). Reflective Design for Informal Participatory Algorithm Auditing: A Case Study with Emotion AI. In *Proceedings of the 13th Nordic Conference on Human-Computer Interaction* (pp. 1-17).

Hsieh, J., Zhang, A., Kim, S., Rao, V. N., Dalal, S., Mateescu, A., . . . Zhu, H. (2024, November). Worker Data Collectives as a means to Improve Accountability, Combat Surveillance and Reduce Inequalities. In *Companion Publication of the 2024 Conference on Computer-Supported Cooperative Work and Social Computing* (pp. 697-700).

Huesmann, L. R., & Taylor, L. D. (2006). The role of media violence in violent behavior. *Annual Review of Public Health, 27*, 393–415. DOI: 10.1146/annurev.publhealth.26.021304.144640 PMID: 16533123

Hughes, N., & Lonie, S. (2007). M-Pesa: Mobile money for the 'unbanked.'. *Innovations, 2*(1-2), 63–81.

Hume, D. (1957). *The natural history of religion*. Stanford University Press.

Huntington, H. E. (2019). Satire, subversion, and the digital age: The case of mockvertising. *Television & New Media, 20*(8), 791–806. DOI: 10.1177/1527476418809754

Hürriyet. [Hurriyet]. (2021, August 5). *Yangınla amansız mücadele... Havadan destek veren hava araçlarına Azerbaycan'dan gelen BE200 amfibi uçak da dahil oldu* [Relentless fight with the fire... The BE200 amphibious aircraft from Azerbaijan was also included among the air vehicles providing support from the air] [Tweet]. X (formerly Twitter). https://x.com/Hurriyet/status/1423273251199852551

Hürriyet. [Hurriyet]. (2023, September 4). *2003'te başlayan hikaye 2023'te zaferle taçlandı... Filenin Sultanları'nın Avrupa şampiyonluğunun ardındaki sır ne?* [The story that started in 2003 was crowned with victory in 2023... What is the secret behind the European championship of the Sultans of the Net?] [Tweet]. X (formerly Twitter). https://x.com/Hurriyet/status/1698587182286311681

Huws, U., Spencer, N. H., Syrdal, D. S., & Holts, K. (2017). Work in the European Gig Economy: Research Results from The UK, Sweden, Germany, Austria, The Netherlands, Switzerland and Italy. FEPS, UNI Europa, University of Hertfordshire.

Ilgın, HO. (2021). Sosyal medyada dezenformasyon ve halkla ilişkiler ilişkisi. *İletişim Çalışmaları Dergisi, 7*(2), 303–322.

Illouz, E. (2011). *Cold intimacies: The making of emotional capitalism.* Polity Press.

İnce, G. (2017). Humanity's test with artificial intelligence. In Karaca, M. (Ed.), *Humanizing machines and artificial intelligence* (pp. 14–17). Istanbul Technical University Foundation Journal.

Isaak, J., & Hanna, M. J. (2018). User data privacy: Facebook, Cambridge Analytica, and privacy protection. *Computer, 51*(8), 56–59. DOI: 10.1109/MC.2018.3191268

Ivashyna, O., Ivashyna, S., & Novikova, L. (2023). Some aspects of institutionalisation of economic development of the digital society. *Scientific Opinion Economics and Management, (3)(83).*

Jabbouri, I., Farooq, O., Naili, M., & Helmi, I. (2024). Navigating the Financing Constraints: The Role of Social Capital in Developing Countries. *Journal of Emerging Market Finance, 23*(3), 360–386.

Jackson, R. L., & Hogg, M. A. (2010). The Other. *Encyclopedia Of Identity*, 519-526.

Jack, W., & Suri, T. (2014). Risk sharing and transactions costs: Evidence from Kenya's mobile money revolution. *The American Economic Review, 104*(1), 183–223. DOI: 10.1257/aer.104.1.183

Jamieson, L. (2013). Personal relationships, intimacy and self in a mediated and global digital age. In Orton-Johnson, K., & Prior, N. (Eds.), *Digital sociology: Critical perspective* (pp. 13–33). Palgrave Macmillan., DOI: 10.1057/97811

Jandrić, P., Knox, J., Besley, T., Ryberg, T., Suoranta, J., & Hayes, S. (2018). Post-digital science and education. *Educational Philosophy and Theory, 50*(10), 893–899. DOI: 10.1080/00131857.2018.1454000

Jasanoff, S. (Ed.). (2004). *States of Knowledge: The Co-Production of Science and the Social Order.* Routledge.

Jenkins, H. (2006). *Convergence culture: Where old and new media collide.* NYU Press.

Jensen. M. C. (2003). *A Theory Of The Firm: Governance, Residual Claims, And Organizational Forms.* Harvard University Press.

Jesudas, R., & Mohammed, Z. (2025). Discourse Strategies in Action: Unpacking Wodak's Framework in the 2024 Presidential Debate between Trump and Harris. *Scientia. Technology. Science and Society*, 2(1), 22–36.

Jiang, S., Da-wei, Z., & Irwin, D. D. (2022). The prevalence and importance of semiformal organizations and semiformal control in rural china: Insights from a national survey. *Asian Journal of Criminology, 17*(3), 331–352. DOI: 10.1007/s11417-022-09366-7 PMID: 35342483

Jin, D. Y. (2021). TikTok and the making of a new transnational media order. *International Journal of Communication, 15*, 4562–4581.

Ji, Y. G., & Tao, W. (2024). Channeling Employees' Positive Moral Emotions in CEO Activism: The Role of Care-Oriented Leadership Communication. *Journal of Public Relations Research, 36*(3). Advance online publication. DOI: 10.1080/1062726X.2024.2311147

Johanssen, J. (2025). Rethinking symbolic violence on social media: Incels and mentalisation. *Journal of HARM, 4*, 22–36. https://www.researchgate.net/publication/390729048

Jun, Y., Craig, A., Shafik, W., & Sharif, L. (2021). Artificial Intelligence Application in Cybersecurity and Cyberdefense. In *Wireless Communications and Mobile Computing* (Vol. 2021). https://doi.org/DOI: 10.1155/2021/3329581

Jun, J., Kim, J. K., & Woo, B. (2024). Fight the Virus and Fight the Bias: Asian Americans' Engagement in Activism to Combat Anti-Asian COVID-19 Racism. *Race and Justice, 14*(2). Advance online publication. DOI: 10.1177/21533687211054165

Kandiyoti, D. (1988). Bargaining with patriarchy. *Gender & Society, 2*(3), 274–290. https://journals.sagepub.com/doi/abs/10.1177/089124388002003004

Kapadia, K. M. (1966). *Marriage and family in India* (3rd ed.). Oxford University Press.

Kaplan, A. M., & Haenlein, M. (2010). Users of the world, unite! The challenges and opportunities of Social Media. *Business Horizons, 53*(1), 59–68.

Kapur, R. (2018). *Gender, alterity and human rights: Freedom in a fishbowl*. Edward Elgar Publishing. https://books.google.co.in/books?hl=en&lr=&id=mYdlDwAAQBAJ&oi=fnd&pg=PT15&dq=Ratna+Kapur+(2002)+reproductive+rights&ots=kKCFDNszRM&sig=ULykrlpP9Hyv9IE5vrdvk4pVnpk&redir_esc=y#v=onepage&q=Ratna%20Kapur%20(2002)%20reproductive%20rights&f=false

Karimi, F., Oliveira, M., & Strohmaier, M. (2022). Minorities in networks and algorithms. *arXiv preprint arXiv:2206.07113*.

Kavasoğlu, İ., Eratlı Şirin, Y., & Uğurlu, A. (2024). A space of one's own? The tensions of being visible on Instagram for Turkish female athletes. *Communication & Sport*, *12*(2), 347–369.

Keane, M., & Yu, H. (2019). A digital empire in the making: China's outbound digital platforms. *International Journal of Communication*, *13*, 4624–4641.

Keddell, E. (2021). "Make Them Dance": Shoshana Zuboff's Surveillance Capitalism, Behavior Modification and Fraser's "Abnormal Justice". *Journal of Technology in Human Services*, *39*(4), 426–431. DOI: 10.1080/15228835.2021.1942396

Kennedy, H. (2018). Living with Data: Aligning Data Studies and Data Activism through a Focus on Everyday Experiences of Datafication. *Kuckuck*, *3*(2), 15–28.

Kennedy, H., & Hill, R. L. (2017). The feeling of numbers: Emotions in everyday engagements with data and their visualisation. *Sociology*, *52*(4), 830–848. DOI: 10.1177/0038038516674675

Kennedy, H., Poell, T., & van Dijck, J. (2022). Datafication and democracy: Reconsidering the role of data in society. *Big Data & Society*, *9*(2), 1–6. DOI: 10.1177/20539517221113500

Kennedy, M. (2020). 'If the rise of the TikTok dance and e-girl aesthetic has taught us anything, it's that teenage girls rule the internet right now': TikTok celebrity, girls and the coronavirus crisis. *European Journal of Cultural Studies*, *23*(6), 1069–1076. DOI: 10.1177/1367549420945341

Kennel, J. (2024). More than a feeling: Storytelling, memory and national myths at dark events. *Event Management*, *28*(4), 655–659.

Kerssens, N., & Van Dijck, J. (2022). Governed by edtech? Valuing pedagogical autonomy in a platform society. *Harvard Educational Review*, *92*(2), 284–303. DOI: 10.17763/1943-5045-92.2.284

Khodabakhshian, A., Puolitaival, T., & Kestle, L. (2024). The Digital Toolkit. *Architectural Design and Management in the Digital Age: International Perspectives*, 17-32.

Kim, H. H. (2009). Networks, information transfer, and status conferral: The role of social capital in income stratification among lawyers. *The Sociological Quarterly*, *50*(1), 61–87.

Kim, J.-E., Park, B.-H., & Han, M. (2024). Exploring a Mediating Role of Online Activism Associated with Pro-environmental Behaviors : Examining Associations among Cognitive, Affective Factors about Global Warming and Pro-environmental Behaviors. *The Korean Journal of Advertising and Public Relations*, *26*(1). Advance online publication. DOI: 10.16914/kjapr.2024.26.1.73

Kim, M., Lee, S., Kim, S., Heo, J. I., Lee, S., Shin, Y. B., Cho, C. H., & Jung, D. (2025). Therapeutic potential of social chatbots in alleviating loneliness and social anxiety: Quasi-Experimental Mixed Methods Study. *Journal of Medical Internet Research*, *27*(e65589). Advance online publication. DOI: 10.2196/65589 PMID: 39808786

Kim, Y., & Kim, S. (2023). Motives for Following Social Influencers and Electronic Word-of-Mouth: The Role of Social Capital. *International Journal of Communication*, *17*, 22.

King, N., & Harrocks, C. (2010). *Interviews in Qualitative Research*. Sage Publications.

Kirkegaard, T. D., Fivush, R., Coman, A., Hirst, W., Luminet, O., & Pillemer, D. B. (2025). A framework for vicarious and collective memory, future projections and narrative identity. *Nature Reviews Psychology*, •••, 1–14.

Kitchin, R., & Lauriault, T. P. (2014). Towards critical data studies: Charting and unpacking data assemblages and their work. *The Programmable City Working Paper*, 2. https://doi.org/DOI: 10.2139/ssrn.2474112

Kitchin, R. (2014). The data revolution: Big data, open data, data infrastructures and their consequences. *Sage (Atlanta, Ga.)*.

Kitchin, R. (2016). Thinking critically about and researching algorithms. *Information Communication and Society*, *20*(1), 14–29. DOI: 10.1080/1369118X.2016.1154087

Kiyan, Z., & Dikmen, E. S. (2019). The role of social media in advertising: An examination on Instagram. *İLEF Dergisi*, *6*(1), 121–146. https://doi.org/DOI: 10.24955/ilef.554036

Kjærvik, S. L., Thomson, N. D., & Fanti, K. A. (2025). The impact of media violence, narcissism and sex on reactive and proactive aggression in adolescents: A one-year follow-up study. *Journal of Youth and Adolescence*, *54*(4), 917–927. DOI: 10.1007/s10964-024-02106-3 PMID: 39487948

Knobel, M., & Lankshear, C. (2007). Online memes, affinities, and cultural production. In Knobel, M., & Lankshear, C. (Eds.), *A new literacies sampler* (pp. 199–227). Peter Lang.

Knorr Cetina, K. (2001). Objectual practice. In Schatzki, T., Knorr Cetina, K., & von Savigny, E. (Eds.), *The practice turn in contemporary theory* (pp. 175–188). Routledge.

Knox, H. (2020). *Thinking like a climate: Governing a city in times of environmental change*. Duke University Press.

Knox, J. (2022). Artificial intelligence and education in the (post-)pandemic age. *Learning, Media and Technology*, *47*(1), 10–24. DOI: 10.1080/17439884.2021.1976239

Komljenovic, J. (2021). The rise of education rentiers: Digital platforms, digital data and rents. *Learning, Media and Technology*, *46*(3), 320–332.

Kopacheva, E. (2021). How the internet has changed participation: Exploring distinctive preconditions of online activism. *Communicatio Socialis*, *34*(2). Advance online publication. DOI: 10.15581/003.34.2.67-85

Koutamanis, K., Vossen, H. G., Peter, J., & Valkenburg, P. M. (2015). The role of maternal and adolescent personality traits in the use of social networking sites. *Computers in Human Behavior*, *48*, 363–369.

Kovács, B. (2022). Informality and the gig economy: Migrant precarity in European food delivery platforms. *Journal of Ethnic and Migration Studies*, *48*(3), 623–641.

Kozman, C., & Mellado, C. (2025). Mapping journalistic role performance across five Arab countries. *Journalism & Mass Communication Quarterly*, *102*(3), 722–749.

Kretschmer, T., Leiponen, A., Schilling, M., & Vasudeva, G. (2022). Platform ecosystems as meta-organizations: Implications for platform strategies. *Strategic Management Journal*, *43*(3), 405–424.

Krimmer, R., Dedovic, S., Schmidt, C., & Corici, A. A. (2021, August). Developing cross-border e-Governance: Exploring interoperability and cross-border integration. In *International Conference on Electronic Participation* (pp. 107-124). Cham: Springer International Publishing.

Kuhn, T. S. (1962). *The Structure of Scientific Revolutions*. University of Chicago Press.

Kumar, P. C., Vitak, J., Chetty, M., & Clegg, T. L. (2019). The platformization of the classroom: Teachers as surveillant consumers. *Surveillance & Society*, *17*(1/2), 145–152. DOI: 10.24908/ss.v17i1/2.12926

Kurganskaya, V. D., & Dunaev, V. Y. (2021). Digitalization as a modeling system of social stratification. *Social Novelties and Social Sciences*, (1), 3.

Kuriakose, F., & Iyer, D. K. (2021). Digital Workers, Urban Vectors, and New Economies. *The South Atlantic Quarterly*, *120*(4), 749–762. DOI: 10.1215/00382876-9443308

Kutlusoy, Z. (2019). Artificial intelligence from a philosophical perspective. In Telli, G. (Ed.), *Artificial intelligence and the future* (pp. 25–43). Dogu.

Kvale, S. (2007). Learning The Craft Of Interviewing. In *Learning The Craft Of Interviewing*. Sage Publications London.

La Porte, C. (2017). The Story of Identity: Categorization.*The Writing Cooperative*. Available at: www.thewritingcooperative.com [Accessed 25 Mar. 2025].

Laestadius, L., Bishop, A., Gonzalez, M., Illenčík, D., & Campos-Castillo, C. (2022). Too human and not human enough: A grounded theory analysis of mental health harms from emotional dependence on the social chatbot Replika. *New Media & Society*, •••, 1–19. DOI: 10.1177/14614448221142007

Lalot, F., & Bertram, A.-M. (2025). When the bot walks the talk: Investigating the foundations of trust in an artificial intelligence (AI)chatbot. *Journal of Experimental Psychology. General*, *154*(2), 533–551. DOI: 10.1037/xge0001696 PMID: 39636606

Lam, M. S., Pandit, A., Kalicki, C. H., Gupta, R., Sahoo, P., & Metaxa, D. (2023). Sociotechnical audits: Broadening the algorithm auditing lens to investigate targeted advertising. *Proceedings of the ACM on Human-Computer Interaction, 7*(CSCW2), 1-37.

Langley, P., & Leyshon, A. (2017). Platform capitalism: The intermediation and capitalisation of digital economic circulation. *Finance and Stochastics*, *3*(1), 11–31. DOI: 10.2218/finsoc.v3i1.1936

Laniuk, Y. (2021). Freedom in the Age of surveillance capitalism: Lessons from Shoshana Zuboff. *Ethics & Bioethics*, *11*(1-2), 67–81. DOI: 10.2478/ebce-2021-0004

Latour, B. (2005). *Reassembling the Social: An Introduction to Actor-Network-Theory*. Oxford University Press.

Lawson, C. (2018). *Platform feminism: Celebrity culture and activism in the digital age* (Doctoral dissertation). https://deepblue.lib.umich.edu/handle/2027.42/145855

Lea, M., & Spears, R. (1991). Computer-mediated communication, de-individuation and group decision-making. *International Journal of Man-Machine Studies*, *34*(2), 283–301. DOI: 10.1016/0020-7373(91)90045-9

Leidner, D. E., Gonzalez, E., & Koch, H. (2020). An affordance perspective of enterprise social media and organizational socialization. In *Strategic information management* (pp. 364–402). Routledge.

Li, B., Peng, X., Xiang, Q., Wang, H., Xie, T., Sun, J., & Liu, X. (2022). Enjoy your observability: An industrial survey of microservice tracing and analysis. *Empirical Software Engineering*, *27*(1), 25. PMID: 34867075

Li, M. (2023). Promote diligently and censor politely: How Sina Weibo intervenes in online activism in China. *Information Communication and Society*, *26*(4). Advance online publication. DOI: 10.1080/1369118X.2021.1983001

Lim, W. M. (2025). What is qualitative research? An overview and guidelines. *Australasian Marketing Journal*, *33*(2), 199–229.

Lindgren, B. (2002). Power, education, and identity in post-colonial Zimbabwe: The fate of King Lobengula of Matabeleland. *African Sociological Review*, *6*(1), 46–67.

Lin, S., Fabris, M. A., Longobardi, C., & Mastrokoukou, S. (2025). The association between social media addiction and aggressive behaviors: A longitudinal and gender-specific analysis. *Journal of Adolescence*, *97*(3), 798–807. DOI: 10.1002/jad.12454 PMID: 39695825

Lin, Y., Ahmad, Z., Shafik, W., Khosa, S. K., Almaspoor, Z., Alsuhabi, H., & Abbas, F. (2021). Impact of Facebook and Newspaper Advertising on Sales: A Comparative Study of Online and Print Media. *Computational Intelligence and Neuroscience*, *2021*. Advance online publication. DOI: 10.1155/2021/5995008 PMID: 34475947

Li, S., Yu, F., & Peng, K. (2020). Effect of state loneliness on robot anthropomorphism: Potential edge of social robots compared to common nonhumans. *Journal of Physics: Conference Series*, *1631*(1). Advance online publication. DOI: 10.1088/1742-6596/1631/1/012024

Liu, X., Barenji, A. V., Li, Z., Montreuil, B., & Huang, G. Q. (2021). Blockchain-based smart tracking and tracing platform for drug supply chain. *Computers & Industrial Engineering*, *161*, 107669.

Livingstone, S., & Helsper, E. (2007). Gradations in digital inclusion: Children, young people and the digital divide. *New Media & Society*, *9*(4), 671–696.

Li, Z., & Champadaeng, S. (2025). Study of Cultural Heritage and Digital Preservation: The Case of Murals of the Northern Yue Temple. *International Journal of Education and Literacy Studies*, *13*(2), 262–268.

Lo, I.-C., & Rau, P.-L. P. (2025). D-Twins: Your digital twin designed for real-time boredom intervention. *CHI'25:Proceedings of the 2025 CHI Conference on Human Factors in Computing Systems*, 321, 1 – 15. https://doi.org/DOI: 10.1145/3706598.3714163

Lou, C., Yap, C. N. R., Zhou, X., Lim, J. A., Koh, M. T., & Tan, A. (2024). Explicating the Effects of In- Versus Out-Group Membership and Collective Action Framing on Social Media Activism Messages. *International Journal of Communication*, •••, 18.

Lucas, G. M., Gratch, J., King, A., & Morency, L. (2014). It's only a computer: Virtual humans increase willingness to disclose. *Computers in Human Behavior*, *37*, 94–100. DOI: 10.1016/j.chb.2014.04.043

Luczak, H., Roetting, M., & Schmidt, L. (2003). Let's talk: Anthropomorphization as means to cope with stress of interacting with technical devices. *Ergonomics*, *46*(13-14), 1361–1374. DOI: 10.1080/00140130310001610883 PMID: 14612325

Lüders, A., Dinkelberg, A., & Quayle, M. (2022). Becoming "us" in digital spaces: How online users creatively and strategically exploit social media affordances to build up social identity. *Acta Psychologica*, *228*, 103643.

Lupton, D. (2017). Towards reflexive digital methods. *Digital Humanities Quarterly*, 11(2). https://digitalhumanities.org/dhq/vol/11/2/000321/000321.html

Lupton, D. (2015). *Digital Sociology*. Routledge.

Lupton, D. (2021). *Data Selves: More-than-Human Perspectives*. Polity Press.

Lury, C., & Wakeford, N. (Eds.). (2012). *Inventive methods: The happening of the social*. Routledge.

Lyon, D. (2006). *Surveillance society: Monitoring everyday life* (Soykan, G., Trans.). Kalkedon Yayınları.

Lyon, D. (2013). Surveillance society. *Sosyologca*, *3*(5), 77–90.

Lyon, D. (2018). *The culture of surveillance: Watching as a way of life*. Polity Press.

MacKenzie, A. (2023). A Feminist Postdigital Analysis of Misogyny, Patriarchy and Violence Against Women and Girls Online. In Jandrić, P., MacKenzie, A., & Knox, J. (Eds.), *Constructing Postdigital Research. Postdigital Science and Education*. Springer., https://link.springer.com/chapter/10.1007/978-3-031-35411-3_14

MacKinnon, C. A. (1989). *Toward a feminist theory of the state*. Harvard University Press. https://www.hup.harvard.edu/books/9780674896468

MacKinnon, R. (2011). China's 'networked authoritarianism.'. *Journal of Democracy, 22*(2), 32–46.

Maeda, T., & Quan-Haase, A. (2024). When human-ai interactions become parasocial: Agency and anthropomorphism in affective design. *The 2024 ACM Conference on Fairness, Accountability, and Transparency*. Rio de Janeiro: Brazil, pp. 1068–1077.

Mahardika, H., French, J., & Sembada, A. (2018). Keep calm and eat satay: Indonesia's consumption-themed signals of defiance against terrorism. *Australasian Marketing Journal, 26*(3), 231–238. DOI: 10.1016/j.ausmj.2018.06.002

Marchetti, A., Castelli, I., Dimitri, D., & Massaro, D. (2022). Digital media, social cognition and empathy: A perspective from mirror systems. *Frontiers in Psychology, 13*, 834001. DOI: 10.3389/fpsyg.2022.834001

Marcia, J. E. 1980. Identity in adolescence. *Handbook of adolescent psychology*, 9(11). 159-187.

Marcus, G., & Davis, E. (2020). *Rebooting AI: Building artificial intelligence we can trust*. Vintage.

Marres, N. (2017). *Digital Sociology: The Reinvention of Social Research*. Polity Press.

Martindale, N., & Lehdonvirta, V. (2021). Can Labour Market Digitalization Increase Social Mobility? Evidence from a European Survey of Online Platform Workers. *SSRN*, 1–21. http://dx.doi.org/DOI: 10.2139/ssrn.3862635

Martindale, N., & Lehdonvirta, V. (2023a). Labour Market Digitalization and Social Class: Evidence of Mobility and Reproduction from a European Survey of Online Platform Workers. *Socio-economic Review, 21*(4), 1945–1965. DOI: 10.1093/ser/mwad049

Martinez, D. (2019). Lay-of-the-land. In Massachusetts Institute of Technology, Lincoln Laboratory (Ed.), Artificial intelligence: Short history, present developments, and future outlook (Final report) (pp. 23–29). United States Air Force.

Marwick, A. E., & Boyd, D. (2011). I tweet honestly, I tweet passionately: Twitter users, context collapse, and the imagined audience. *New Media & Society, 13*(1), 114–133. DOI: 10.1177/1461444810365313

Marwick, A., & Ellison, N. B. (2012). "There isn't Wifi in Heaven!" Negotiating visibility on Facebook memorial pages. *Journal of Broadcasting & Electronic Media, 56*(3), 378–400.

Marx, K. (1976). *Capital: A critique of political economy* (Vol. I; Fowkes, B., Trans.). Penguin Books. (Original work published 1867)

Marx, K., & Engels, F. (2002). *The Communist Manifesto* (Moore, S., Trans.). Penguin Classics. (Original work published 1848)

Maseko, B. (2024). Blurring the binaries of home/school in Family Language Policy: Parents as teachers in heritage language lessons. *Sociolinguistic Studies, 18*(1-2), 81–106.

Maseko, B., & Siziba, L. (2025). Violence, Memory and Resistance in Selected Highlanders FC Supporters' Songs. *Critical Arts*, •••, 1–20.

Massaro, M., Spanò, R., & Kuruppu, S. C. (2025). Accountability and the metaverse: Unaccounted digital worlds between techwashing mechanisms and new emerging meanings. *Accounting, Auditing & Accountability Journal, 38*(3), 908–933.

Mathe, L., & Motsaathebe, G. (2025). The political economy of indigenous local media for minority languages in Zimbabwe: A case of Lyeja FM community radio. *Journal of Asian and African Studies, 60*(1), 5–17.

Matheson, K., & Zanna, M. P. (1988). The impact of computer-mediated communication on self-awareness. *Computers in Human Behavior, 4*(3), 221–233. DOI: 10.1016/0747-5632(88)90015-5

Maurer, B. (2012). Mobile money: Communication, consumption and change in the payments space. *The Journal of Development Studies, 48*(5), 589–604. DOI: 10.1080/00220388.2011.621944

Mautsi, G., Mago, D., & Musara, C. (2024). Gendered Electoral Violence: The Case of Hwange District, Matabeleland North Province in Zimbabwe. In Ehiane, S. O., Shulika, L. S., & Vhumbunu, C. H. (Eds.), *Engagement of Africa in Conflict Dynamics and Peace Architectures. Africa's Global Engagement: Perspectives from Emerging Countries.*, DOI: 10.1007/978-981-99-8235-6_13

Mayaleh, A., & Hamamra, B. (2024). Instruments of resilience: Cultural tourism in the Palestinian resistance. *International Journal of Heritage Studies*, •••, 1–17.

Mbembe, A. (2020). *Out of the Dark Night: Essays on Decolonization.* Columbia University Press.

McCammon, M., & Lingel, J. (2022). Situating dead-and-dying platforms: Technological failure, infrastructural precarity, and digital decline. *Internet Histories, 6*(1-2), 1–13.

McCarthy, J. (2007). From here to human-level AI. *Artificial Intelligence*, *171*(18), 1174–1182. DOI: 10.1016/j.artint.2007.10.009

McCulloch, H. J. (2019). *Digital Death: Mortality and Beyond in the Online Age*. Routledge.

McDaniel, D. S. (2024). "Bold of them to assume I want to wait until I'm older to do what I love:" One teens' activism and civic engagement online. *Journal of Adolescent & Adult Literacy*, *67*(6). Advance online publication. DOI: 10.1002/jaal.1343

McKenzie, J. (2025). Digital media as sites for cultural identity development: The case of Hmong American emerging adults. *Journal of Adolescent Research*, *40*(2), 296–330.

Mead, G. H. (1934). *Mind, Self, and Society: From the Standpoint of a Social Behaviorist*. University of Chicago Press.

MedicoPublication. (2021). Prevalence and patterns of cyberbullying among women in rural Kerala. *International Journal of Public Health Research and Development*, *12*(3), 45–53. https://medicopublication.com/index.php/ijphrd/article/download/21248/17938

Meier, A., & Johnson, M. (2022). Exposure to the positivity bias and adolescents' differential longitudinal links with social comparison, inspiration and envy depending on social media literacy. *Current Psychology (New Brunswick, N.J.)*, *42*(32), 28221–28241.

Melek, G., & Müyesseroğlu, E. (2023). Political storytelling of Ekrem İmamoğlu on Instagram. *Visual Studies*, *38*(5), 894–910. DOI: 10.1080/1472586X.2021.1975501

Meng, J., & Dai, N. Y. (2021). Emotional support from aı chatbots: Should a supportive partner self-disclose or not? *Journal of Computer-Mediated Communication*, *26*(4). Advance online publication. DOI: 10.1093/jcmc/zmab005

Menteş, S. A. (2019). Online Environmental Activism: The Case of Iğneada Floodplain Forest. *SAGE Open*, *9*(3). Advance online publication. DOI: 10.1177/2158244019877877

Merriam. S. B. (2015). Qualitative Research: Designing, Implementing, And Publishing A Study. In *Handbook Of Research On Scholarly Publishing And Research Methods* (Pp. 125-140). Igi Global Scientific Publishing.

Merrill, K.Jr, Kim, J., & Collins, C. (2022). AI companions for lonely individuals and the role of Social Presence. *Communication Research Reports*, *39*(2), 93–103. DOI: 10.1080/08824096.2022.2045929

Mertens, D. M. (2010). *Research and Evaluation in Education and Psychology: Integrating Diversity with Quantitative, Qualitative, and Mixed Methods* (3rd ed.). SAGE Publications.

Meyer, J. C. (2000). Humour as a double-edged sword: Four functions of humour in communication. *Communication Theory*, *10*(3), 310–331. DOI: 10.1111/j.1468-2885.2000.tb00194.x

Mijwil, M. M. (2015). History of artificial intelligence (Preprint). Iraqi University. https://doi.org/DOI: 10.13140/RG.2.2.16418.15046

Milli Eğitim Bakanlığı. (2024). Medyada şiddet görüntüleri ve çocuklar. https://tepebasiram.meb.k12.tr/meb_iys_dosyalar/26/15/972503/dosyalar/2024_10/17103743

Mills, C. W. (1959). *The sociological imagination*. Oxford University Press.

Minerva, F., & Giubilini, A. (2023). Is AI the future of mental health care? *Topoi*, *42*(3), 809–817. DOI: 10.1007/s11245-023-09932-3

Mirghaderi, L., Sziron, M., & Hildt, E. (2023). Ethics and transparency issues in digital platforms: An overview. *AI*, *4*(4), 831–843.

Mkwebu, N., & Chibike, J. J. (2025). Computer-Generated Linguistics Countering Linguicides: Users' Use and Interpretation of WhatsApp Emojis in isiNdebele. In *Resuscitation of African Languages: Theorising the Battle Against Sociocultural Genocide* (pp. 215–236). Springer Nature Switzerland.

Mol, A. (2002). *The body multiple: Ontology in medical practice*. Duke University Press.

Molina, J. L., Tubaro, P., Casilli, A., & Santos-Ortega, A. (2023). Research ethics in the age of digital platforms. *Science and Engineering Ethics*, *29*(3), 17. PMID: 37185917

Monahan, T. (2010). *Surveillance in the time of insecurity*. Rutgers University Press.

Monto, M. A., & Carey, A. G. (2014). A new standard of sexual behaviour? Are claims associated with the "hookup culture" supported by General Social Survey data? *Journal of Sex Research*, *51*(6), 605–615. DOI: 10.1080/00224499.2014.906031 PMID: 24750070

Moore, E. C. (1966). *American Pragmatism: Peirce, James, and Dewey*. Columbia University Press.

Moore, P. V., Upchurch, M., & Whittaker, X. (2018). *Human resource management in the surveillance society: Privacy, resistance and ethics*. Palgrave Macmillan.

Mora-Salas, M., Delfino, A., & Olivera, R. V. de (2024). Platform capitalism in Latin America: Visible trends and probable horizons. Estudios sociológicos, 42, e2736. https://doi.org/.DOI: 10.24201/es.2024v42.e2736

Morgan. D. L. (2012). Focus Groups And Social Interaction. *The Sage Handbook Of Interview Research: The Complexity Of The Craft, 2*, 161-176.

Morgan, D. L. (2007). Paradigms lost and pragmatism regained: Methodological implications of combining qualitative and quantitative methods. *Journal of Mixed Methods Research, 1*(1), 48–76. DOI: 10.1177/2345678906292462

Moussawi, S., Koufaris, M., & Benbunan-Fich, R. (2021). How perceptions of intelligence and anthropomorphism affect the adoption of personal intelligent agents. *Electronic Markets, 31*, 343–364. DOI: 10.1007/s12525-020-00411-w

Moyo, T. (2022). Beyond provincializing a nation without a state: Representation of Matabeleland in Umthwakazi Review digital space. In Ndlovu, M., & Mlotshwa, K. (Eds.), *The Idea of Matabeleland in Digital Spaces: Genealogies, Discourses* (pp. 191–204). Rowman and Littlefield.

Mpofu, M. (2026). Popular theatre as counter-public spheres in Matabeleland in the 1980s: A critical analysis of Amakhosi Theatre Production's Nansi Le Ndoda. In Mpofu, M., Nkomo, D., & Heliker, K. (Eds.), *Civil Society in Zimbabwe* (pp. 241–257). Routledge.

Mpofu, P. (2018). Politics of language, ethnicity and identity in Zimbabwean ethnolinguistic online communities. In Mpofu, P. (Ed.), *African language digital media and communication* (pp. 154–172). Routledge.

Mpofu, P., & Salawu, A. (2018). Re-examining the indigenous language press in Zimbabwe: Towards developmental communication and language empowerment. *South African Journal of African Languages, 38*(3), 293–302.

Mulgan, G. (2021). *Another world is possible: How to reignite social and political imagination*. Hurst Publishers.

Muller, Z. (2020). Algorithmic harms to Workers in the Platform Economy: The case of Uber. *Columbia Journal of Law and Social Problems, 167*, •••.

Muniruzzaman, M. D. (2017). Transformation of intimacy and its impact in developing countries. *Life Sciences, Society and Policy, 13*(1). Advance online publication. DOI: 10.1186/s40504-017-0056-8 PMID: 28766186

Nadim, M., & Fladmoe, A. (2019). Silencing women? gender and online harassment. *Social Science Computer Review, 39*(2), 245–258. DOI: 10.1177/0894439319865518

Naik, S. S., & Kakade, O. (2024). Impact Of Digitalization on Society: A Critical Study. *mLAC Journal for Arts, Commerce and Sciences (m-JACS) ISSN: 2584-1920, 2*(4), 1-13.

Nair, M., & Emozozo, R. (2018). Electronic currency in Africa: M-Pesa as private inside money. *Economic Affairs, 38*(2), 197–206. DOI: 10.1111/ecaf.12292

Napoli, P. M. (2011). *Audience evolution: New technologies and the transformation of media audiences*. Columbia University Press.

Narayan, D. (2024). The political economy of digital platforms: Key directions. *Platforms & Society, 1*, 29768624241263071.

Nass, C., & Moon, Y. (2000). Machines and mindlessness: Social responses to computers. *The Journal of Social Issues, 56*(1), 81–103. DOI: 10.1111/0022-4537.00153

Ncube, G., & Siziba, G. (2017). Compelled to Perform in the 'Oppressor's' Language? Ndebele Performing Artists and Zimbabwe's Shona-Centric *Habitus*. *Journal of Southern African Studies, 43*(4), 825–836.

Ndlovu, M. (2021). Walking through history together: Gukurahundi, memory and the role of digital media in shaping "post-conflict" Zimbabwe. In Maweu, J., & Mare, A. (Eds.), *Media, conflict and peacebuilding in Africa* (pp. 210–223). Routledge.

Ndlovu, M. (2025). Memory and the Political Uses of the Past in Digital Ndebele Nationalism. In Basch, A., Niemi, M. J., & Hammar, A. (Eds.), *Africa-Europe Group for Interdisciplinary Studies* (Vol. 179). Brills., DOI: 10.1163/9789004728004

Ndlovu, T. (2019). Cultural Expression in Southern African Social Media. *Southern African Journal of Communication Studies, 41*(1), 22–29.

Neenan, A., Byrd, M., Hoodin, F., & Staples, A. D. (2024). Activism, Coping, and Hopefulness Among Parents of Children With Cancer. *Journal of Pediatric Hematology/Oncology Nursing, 41*(1). Advance online publication. DOI: 10.1177/27527530231194566 PMID: 37885240

Neff, T., & Pickard, V. (2024). Funding democracy: Public media and democratic health in 33 countries. *The International Journal of Press/Politics, 29*(3), 601–627.

Ng, R., & Indran, N. (2022). Hostility Toward Baby Boomers on TikTok. *The Gerontologist, 62*(8), 1196–1206. DOI: 10.1093/geront/gnac020

Nickerson, J. (2025). Merton's strain theory of deviance in sociology. *Simply Psychology*. https://www.simplypsychology.org/mertons-strain-theory-deviance.html

Nikhat, M., & Shukla, A. (2025). The changing face of dating in India: Why it's worth studying. *International Journal for Multidisciplinary Research, 7*(2), 1–12. DOI: 10.36948/ijfmr.2025.v07i02.42935

Nnabuihe, O. E., Onwuzuruigbo, I., & Ihembe, M. A. (2025). Cultural hegemony and ethnic minority struggles in Nigeria. *African Identities, 23*(3), 715–736.

Nugroho, W. S., & Kesyafano, B. (2025). Exploring the Impact of Digital Technology on Oral Traditions: Cultural Preservation in the Digital Era. *Kampret Journal, 4*(3), 117–122.

Ohme, J., Araujo, T., Boeschoten, L., Freelon, D., Ram, N., Reeves, B. B., & Robinson, T. N. (2024). Digital trace data collection for social media effects research: APIs, data donation, and (screen) tracking. *Communication Methods and Measures, 18*(2), 124–141.

Oktavianingtyas, I., Rusadi, U., Jamalullail, J., & Napitupulu, F. (2025). The role of symbolic capital and symbolic violence in shaping social hierarchies through digital consumption and production in Roblox online game. *Bricolage: Jurnal Magister Ilmu Komunikasi, 11*(2), 213–224.

Oktawirawan, D. H. (2022). Chatbot is my buddy: The role of chatbots as human friends in daily life. Conference: *The 3rd International Conference on Psychological Studies (ICPsyche)*2022. (pp. 35-41) Semarang, Indonesia. https://proceeding.internationaljournallabs.com/index.php/picis/index

Oliveira, R. A. (2023). Regimes of Visibility and Algorithmic Surveillance on Digital Platforms: Operationalizing the Thought Through Images in a Collaborative Perspective. *Journal of Latin American Communication Research, 11*(2), 137–156. DOI: 10.55738/journal.v11i2p.137-156

Omoigberale, O. (2025). Navigating the Fault Lines: The Paradoxes of Majoritarian Democracy and Minority Rights in Nigeria's Multi-Ethnic Polity. *Peace Review*, •••, 1–22.

Omwansa, T. K., & Sullivan, N. P. (2012). *Money, Real Quick: Kenya's Disruptive Mobile Money Innovation*. Guardian Books.

Ong, A., & Collier, S. (2005). *Global Assemblages*. Blackwell.

Ortutay, B., & O'Brien, M. (2025). *New study sheds light on ChatGPT's alarming interactions with teens*. Baptist Press.

Oshodi, N. (2024). Enhancing online safety: The impact of social media violent content and violence among teens in Illinois. *World Journal of Advanced Research and Reviews, 23*(3), 826–833. DOI: 10.30574/wjarr.2024.23.3.2734

Owigar, J. A., & Lah, O. (2025). African e-mobility startups' perceptions and use of information systems, challenges, and opportunities. *Sustainable Earth Reviews, 8*, 12. DOI: 10.1186/s42055-025-00113-1

Öztemel, E. (2020). Artificial intelligence and the future of humanity. In Şeker, M., Bulduklu, Y., Korkut, C., & Doğrul, M. (Eds.), *Information technologies and communication* (pp. 99–112). Berk Group Publications.

Öztürk, K., & Şahin, M. E. (2018). Artificial neural networks and a general overview of artificial intelligence. *Takvim-i Vekayi, 6*(2), 25–36.

Pacher, C., & Glinik, M. (2024). Fostering entrepreneurial mindsets in deep tech disciplines: Exemplary development of a Toolkit. *Procedia Computer Science, 232*, 1309–1318.

Palinkas, L. A., He, A. S., Choy-Brown, M., & Hertel, A. L. (2017). Operationalizing Social Work Science Through Research–Practice Partnerships: Lessons From Implementation Science. *Research on Social Work Practice, 27*(2), 181–188.

Papacharissi, Z. (2010). A private sphere: Democracy in a digital age. *Polity*.

Papacharissi, Z. (2015). *Affective publics: Sentiment, technology, and politics*. Oxford University Press.

Papacharissi, Z. (2016). Affective publics and structures of storytelling: Sentiment, events and mediality. *Information Communication and Society, 19*(3), 307–324.

Parker, C., Albarrán-Torres, C., Briggs, C., Burgess, J., Carah, N., Andrejevic, M., & Obeid, A. (2024). Addressing the accountability gap: Gambling advertising and social media platform responsibilities. *Addiction Research and Theory, 32*(4), 312–318.

Parry, E., & Urwin, P. (2011). Generational differences in work values: A review of theory and evidence: Generational differences in work values. *International Journal of Management Reviews, 13*(1), 79–96. DOI: 10.1111/j.1468-2370.2010.00285.x

Parsakia, K., & Rostami, M. (2023). Digital intimacy: How technology shapes friendships and romantic relationships. *AI and Tech in Behavioral and Social Sciences, 1*(1), 27–34. DOI: 10.61838/kman.aitech.1.1.5

Parsons, T. (2017). The present status of "structural-functional" theory in sociology. In *The idea of social structure* (pp. 67–84). Routledge.

Pasquale, F. (2015). *The black box society: The secret algorithms that control money and information*. Harvard University Press.

Pasquale, F. (2015). *The Black Box Society: The Secret Algorithms That Control Money and Information*. Harvard University Press.

Pasquinelli, M., & Joler, V. (2022). The Nooscope Manifested: AI as instrument of knowledge extractivism. *AI & Society*, *37*, 153–169. DOI: 10.1007/s00146-021-01197-0 PMID: 33250587

Patton, D. U., Stevens, R., Smith Lee, J. R., Eya, G.-C., & Frey, W. (2020). You set me up: Gendered perceptions of Twitter communication among Black Chicago youth. *Social Media + Society*, *6*(2), 1–11. DOI: 10.1177/2056305120913877

Peel, A. C. (2009). *Diaspora Ethnicity and Politics in the Electronic Media: Case Studies of United Kingdom Based Zimbabwean Internet Websites and Their Associations*. PhD diss., University of Wales.

Peirce, C. S. (1878). How to make our ideas clear. *Popular Science Monthly*, *12*, 286–302.

Pérez-Torres, V. (2024). Social Media: A Digital Social Mirror For Identity Development During Adolescence. *Current Psychology, 43*(26), 22170-22180.

Pesole, A., Fernandez Macias, E., Urzi Brancati, M.C. and Gomez Herrera, M.E. (2019). How to Quantify What is not Seen Two Proposals for Measuring Platform Work. European Commission, JRC117168.

Petre, C. (2015). The traffic factories: Metrics at chartbeat, gawker media, and the New York Times.

Petre, C. (2021). *All the news that's fit to click: How metrics are transforming the work of journalists*. Princeton University Press.

Pew Research Center. (2021). *The state of online harassment*. https://www.pewresearch.org/internet/2021/01/13/the-state-of-online-harassment/

Pham, M. D., Chaney, K. E., & Ramírez-Esparza, N. (2024). What Are We Fighting For? Lay Theories About the Goals and Motivations of Anti-Racism Activism. *Race and Social Problems*, *16*(1). Advance online publication. DOI: 10.1007/s12552-023-09393-8

Pichler, F., & Wallace, C. (2009). Social capital and social class in Europe: The role of social networks in social stratification. *European Sociological Review*, *25*(3), 319–332. DOI: 10.1093/esr/jcn050

Pink, S. (2015). *Doing Sensory Ethnography* (2nd ed.). SAGE Publications.

Pink, S., Horst, H., Postill, J., Hjorth, L., Lewis, T., & Tacchi, J. (2018). Digital Ethnography: Principles and Practice. *Sage (Atlanta, Ga.).*

Pittman, M., & Reich, B. (2016). Social media and loneliness: Why an Instagram picture may be worth more than a thousand Twitter words. *Computers in Human Behavior*, *62*, 155–167. DOI: 10.1016/j.chb.2016.03.084

Placani, A. (2024). Anthropomorphism in AI: Hype and fallacy. *AI and Ethics*, *4*, 691–698. DOI: 10.1007/s43681-024-00419-4

Plantin, J. C., Lagoze, C., Edwards, P. N., & Sandvig, C. (2018). Infrastructure studies meet platform studies in the age of Google and Facebook. *New Media & Society*, *20*(1), 293–310.

Plantin, J.-C., & Punathambekar, A. (2019). Digital media infrastructures: Pipes, platforms, and politics. *Media Culture & Society*, *41*(2). Advance online publication. DOI: 10.1177/0163443718818376

Pohle, J., & Voelsen, D. (2022). Centrality and power. The struggle over the techno-political configuration of the Internet and the global digital order. *Policy and Internet*, *14*(1), 13–27. DOI: 10.1002/poi3.296

Polit. D., & Beck, C. (2020). *Essentials Of Nursing Research: Appraising Evidence For Nursing Practice*. Lippincott Williams & Wilkins.

Popiel, P., & Vasudevan, K. (2024). Platform frictions, platform power, and the politics of platformization. *Information Communication and Society*, *27*(10), 1867–1883.

Poppi, F. I. M., & Copes, H. (2024). Identitas Per Fabulam: Joint Fantasising In The Construction Of Criminal Group Identities. *Critical Criminology*, *32*(2), 457–478.

Pradhan, A., Findlater, L., & Lazar, A. (2019). Phantom Friend" or" Just a Box with Information" personification and ontological categorization of smart speaker-based voice assistants by older adults. *Proceedings of the ACM on Human-Computer Interaction*, *3*, 1–21. DOI: 10.1145/3359316

Pujiati, P., Lundeto, A., & Trianto, I. (2025). Representing Arab-Indonesian identity: Language and cultural narratives on social media. *Indonesian Journal of Applied Linguistics*, *14*(3), 653–666.

Pulignano V., Domecka M., Vermeerbergen L., Franke M. and Mara C. (2021) Platform work, reputation and precarious (unpaid) work regimes, paper presented at ILPC, 12-14 April 2021 and SASE, 2-5 July 2021.

Qiu, J. L. (2019). *Goodbye iSlave: A Manifesto for Digital Abolition*. University of Illinois Press.

Ragnedda, M. (2019). Conceptualising the digital divide. *Mapping digital divide in Africa: A mediated analysis*, 27-44.

Ragnedda, M. (2018). Conceptualizing digital capital. *Telematics and Informatics*, *35*(8), 2366–2375. DOI: 10.1016/j.tele.2018.10.006

Ragnedda, M., & Ruiu, M. L. (2017). Social capital and the three levels of digital divide. In *Theorizing digital divides* (pp. 21–34). Routledge.

Ray, B. (2005). *Women of India: Colonial and post-colonial periods*. SAGE Publications India.

Recuero, R. (2024). The Platformization of Violence: Toward a Concept of Discursive Toxicity on Social Media. *Social Media + Society*, *10*(1). Advance online publication. DOI: 10.1177/20563051231224264

Rege, S. (2014). *Writing caste/writing gender: Narrating Dalit women's testimonies*. Zubaan. https://books.google.co.in/books?id=p4-oDAAAQBAJ&lpg=PA1905&ots=hN7MtMd5rI&dq=Sharmila%20Rege%20(1998)%20hierarchies%20founded%20on%20caste%20intersect%20with%20gendered%20oppression&lr&pg=PA1905#v=onepage&q&f=false

Rigi, J., & Prey, R. (2015). Value, rent, and the political economy of social media. *The Information Society*, *31*(5), 392–406. DOI: 10.1080/01972243.2015.1069769

Risi, E., Pronzato, R., & Di Fraia, G. (2020). Living and working confined at home: Boundaries and platforms during the lockdown. *Journal of Cultural Analysis and Social Change*, *5*(2), 1–4. DOI: 10.20897/jcasc/9253

Robards, B., & Lincoln, S. (2017). Uncovering longitudinal life narratives: Scrolling back on Facebook. *Qualitative Research*, *17*(6), 715–730.

Robinson, L., Cotten, S. R., Ono, H., Quan-Haase, A., Mesch, G., Chen, W., & Stern, M. J. (2015). Digital inequalities and why they matter. *Information Communication and Society*, *18*(5), 569–582.

Rochet, J.-C., & Tirole, J. (2003). Platform competition in two-sided markets. *Journal of the European Economic Association*, *1*(4), 990–1029.

Rogers, R. (2013). *Digital Methods*. MIT Press.

Rosenblat, A., Levy, K. E. C., Barocas, S., & Hwang, T. (2016). Discriminating Tastes: Customer Ratings as Vehicles for Bias. *Policy and Internet*, *9*(3), 256–279.

Rosenblat, A., & Stark, L. (2016). Algorithmic labor and information asymmetries: A case study of Uber's drivers. *International Journal of Communication, 10*, 3758–3784.

Ruppert, E., Law, J., & Savage, M. (2013). Reassembling social science methods: The challenge of digital devices. *Theory, Culture & Society, 30*(4), 22–46. DOI: 10.1177/0263276413484941

Sadowski, J. (2019). When data is capital: Datafication, accumulation, and extraction. *Big Data & Society, 6*(1), 2053951718820549.

Şafak, Y. [yenisafak]. (2021, August 5). *Ağlatan anons* [The announcement that made people cry] [Tweet]. X (formerly Twitter). https://x.com/yenisafak/status/1423277540156661763

Şafak, Y. [yenisafak]. (2021, August 6). *Oxford Mezunu Gönüllü* [Oxford Graduate Volunteer] [Tweet]. X (formerly Twitter). https://x.com/yenisafak/status/1423625652129910792

Şafak, Y. [yenisafak]. (2021, August 8). *En Büyük Yangın Felaketi* [The Biggest Fire Disaster] [Tweet]. X (formerly Twitter). https://x.com/yenisafak/status/1424306348141985795

Şafak, Y. [yenisafak]. (2023, September 4). *Büyük Bir Gurur Yaşattınız* [You made us feel a great pride] [Tweet]. X (formerly Twitter). https://x.com/yenisafak/status/1698453761897660822

Şafak, Y. [yenisafak]. (2023, September 4). *Cumhurbaşkanı Erdoğan, Sırbistan'ı 3-2 yenerek Avrupa Şampiyonu olan A Milli Kadın Voleybol Takımı'nı tebrik etti* [President Erdoğan congratulated the Women's National Volleyball Team, who became the European Champion by defeating Serbia 3-2] [Tweet]. X (formerly Twitter). https://x.com/yenisafak/status/1698447814896754749

Said, E. (1978). *Orientalism*. Pantheon.

Şakar, M., & Sarıkan, Ü. (2023). Tribin şiddeti: Sembolik etkileşim kuramı ve kırık cam teorisi bağlamında bir sentez. *International Journal of Eurasia Social Sciences, 14*(51), 433–447.

Sánchez, D. Y., Maldonado, O. J., Agudelo-Londoño, S., Hernández, M., Hernández, L. J., & Suárez-Morales, Z. B.. (2024). Infrastructuring platform delivery work: Exclusions, coercions and resistance in delivery platforms' migrant work in Bogotá, Colombia. *Tapuya : Latin American Science, Technology and Society, 7*(1), 2343161. DOI: 10.1080/25729861.2024.2343161

Sanchez, E. (2025). The Centre for Contemporary Cultural Studies: A Historical 'Utopian'Enclave in the Political World of Academia? In Avril, E., Mourlon, F., & Fee, D. (Eds.), *Fragmented Powers* (pp. 177–191). Emerald Publishing Limited.

Sarıoğlu, E. B.,& Güregen, E. P. (2024). ChatGPT as a solution to emotional loneliness: A new tool for ınterpersonal communication. *Turkish Journal of Communication Studies* (Special Issue on the Future of Communication in the 100th Year of the Republic), 81-107. https://doi.org/DOI: 10.17829/turcom.1360418

Sarraf, A. R. A. (2019). Generational groups in different countries. [IJSSH]. *International Journal of Social Science and Humanity, 4*(1), 41–52.

Savage, M., & Burrows, R. (2007). The coming crisis of empirical sociology. *Sociology, 41*(5), 885–899. DOI: 10.1177/0038038507080443

Saxena, T., & Kumar, S. (2025). Artificial Intelligence and Digital Governance in Rural India: A Systematic Review of Community Empowerment and Sustainable Development. https://www.preprints.org/manuscript/202503.0090

Schäper, T., Foege, J. N., & Nüesch, S. (2024). Toolkits for innovation: How digital technologies empower users in new product development. *R & D Management, 54*(1), 95–117.

Schiller, D. (1999). *Digital Capitalism: Networking the Global Market System.* MIT Press.

Schlag, G. (2023). European Union's regulating of social media: A discourse analysis of the Digital Services Act. *Politics and Governance, 11*(3), 168–177.

Schneier, B. (2003). *Beyond fear: Thinking sensibly about security in an uncertain world.* Copernicus Books.

Schuetzler, R. M., Grimes, G. M., & Giboney, J. S. (2021). Artificial intelligence and parasocial interaction: Examining the effects of AI chatbot personality on user trust and engagement. *Computers in Human Behavior, 117*, 106627. DOI: 10.1016/j.chb.2020.106627

Schultz, D. P.,& Ellen-Schultz, S. (2007). *Modern psikoloji tarihi* (Y. Aslay, Çev.). Kaknüs Yayınları.

Scott, K. (2004, 16 Kasım). *Killer who wanted to be vampire dies. The Guardian.* https://www.theguardian.com/uk/2004/nov/16/ukcrime.kirstyscott

Scott, J. C. (1985). *Weapons of the Weak: Everyday Forms of Peasant Resistance.* Yale University Press.

Sedgewick, J. R., Flath, M. E., & Elias, L. J. (2017). Presenting your best self(ie): The influence of gender on vertical orientation of selfies on Tinder. *Frontiers in Psychology, 8*. Advance online publication. DOI: 10.3389/fpsyg.2017.00009 PMID: 28484408

Selwyn, N. (2019). *Should robots replace teachers? AI and the future of education*. Polity Press.

Şener, G., & Abınık, N. (2021). Türkiye'de dijital şiddet araştırması / Turkey digital violence research 2021 (UNFPA Turkey, Common Knowledge & Communication Association). https://turkiye.unfpa.org/sites/default/files/pub-pdf/digital_violence_report.pdf

Serazio, M. (2021). *The other influencer: The rise of the micro-celebrity in the digital age*. Polity Press.

Serrano-Puche, J. (2016). Internet and emotions: New trends in an emerging field of research.

Shafik, W. (2023a). *A Comprehensive Cybersecurity Framework for Present and Future Global Information Technology Organizations*. https://doi.org/DOI: 10.4018/978-1-6684-9018-1.ch002

Shafik, W. (2023b). Introduction to ChatGPT. In *Advanced Applications of Generative AI and Natural Language Processing Models*. https://doi.org/DOI: 10.4018/9798369305027.ch001

Shafik, W. (2024b). Generative AI for Social Good and Sustainable Development. In *Generative AI: Current Trends and Applications* (pp. 185–217). Springer.

Shafik, W. (2025a). Emerging Technologies for Small and Medium Enterprises (SMEs) Growth: ChatGPT, Blockchain, Robotics, and Artificial Intelligence. *Fostering Economic Diversification and Sustainable Business Through Digital Intelligence*, 173–196.

Shafik, W. (2025b). Ethical and legal considerations in artificial intelligence. *AI-Enabled Threat Intelligence and Cyber Risk Assessment*, 90.

Shafik, W. (2025c). *Ethical and Legal Considerations in Digital Counseling*.

Shafik, W. (2025d). Generative Adversarial Networks: Security, Privacy, and Ethical Considerations. In *Generative Artificial Intelligence (AI) Approaches for Industrial Applications* (pp. 93–117). Springer.

Shafik, W. (2025e). Human-Computer Interaction (HCI) Technologies in Socially-Enabled Artificial Intelligence. In *Future of Digital Technology and AI in Social Sectors* (pp. 121–150). IGI Global.

Shafik, W. (2024a). Cyber Attacker Profiling and Cyberbullying Overview. In *Cyber Space and Outer Space Security* (pp. 125–149). River Publishers., DOI: 10.1201/9781003558118-5

Shafik, W. (2024c). Social Media Insights Into Consumer Behavior. In *Intersection of AI and Business Intelligence in Data-Driven Decision-Making* (pp. 283–308). IGI Global., DOI: 10.4018/979-8-3693-5288-5.ch010

Shafik, W. (2024d). Toward a More Ethical Future of Artificial Intelligence and Data Science. In *The Ethical Frontier of AI and Data Analysis* (pp. 362–388). IGI Global., DOI: 10.4018/979-8-3693-2964-1.ch022

Shafik, W., Tufail, A., Apong, R. A. A. H. M., & Balasubramaniam, S. (2024). Future Directions in Cybersecurity, Digital Forensics and Biometric Systems. In *AI Based Advancements in Biometrics and its Applications* (pp. 238–263). CRC Press., DOI: 10.1201/9781032702377-13

Shifman, L. (2014). *Memes in digital culture.* MIT Press.

Shore, A., & Prena, K. (2025). Platform rules as privacy tools: The influence of screenshot accountability and trust on privacy management. *New Media & Society, 27*(2), 1053–1072.

Shouse, E. (2020). The role of relief in humour: A psychological perspective. *Journal of Media Psychology, 32*(4), 189–197. DOI: 10.1027/1864-1105/a000274

Shukla, A. (2023). Online disinhibition effect: Why we express more online. *Cognition Today.* https://cognitiontoday.com/online-disinhibition-effect/

Shvanyukova, P. (2025). 'Nuclear weapons are our best friends': A Discourse-Historical Analysis of the Cold War Era Rhetoric of Nuclear Militarism. *Textus, 37*(1), 267–287.

Sibanda, M. N. (2024). The constructions of Ndebele identity in Skyz Metro FM: An audience reception study. *Journal of Asian and African Studies,* •••, 00219096241230493.

Sibanda, N., & Dube, P. (2025). Conceptualising and revealing political resistance in Zimbabwe through (re) naming roads in Bulawayo. *South African Journal of African Languages,* •••, 1–10.

Singh, A., Garcia, P., & Lindtner, S. (2023). Old Logics, New Technologies: Producing a Managed Workforce on On-Demand Service Platforms. *In Proceedings of the 2023 CHI Conference on Human Factors in Computing Systems* (CHI '23). Association for Computing Machinery, New York, NY, USA, Article 160, 1–15. https://doi.org/DOI: 10.1145/3544548.3581240

Sivri, O. (2024). The future of visual arts in the context of artificial intelligence. *Journal of Human Art, Design, and Architecture Research, 4*(1), 322–344.

Skjuve, M., Følstad, A., Fostervold, K. I., & Brandtzaeg, P. B. (2021). My chatbot companion - a study of humanchatbot relationships. *International Journal of Human-Computer Studies, 149*(102601). Advance online publication. DOI: 10.1016/j.ijhcs.2021.102601

Social Media and the rise of Digital Patriarchy in India. (2024, February 10). *Gender Studies*. Retrieved August 25, 2025, from https://gender.study/gender-based-violence/social-media-digital-patriarchy-india/

Song, H., Zmyslinski-Seelig, A., Kim, J., Drent, A., Victor, A., Omori, K., & Allen, M. (2014). Does Facebook make you lonely?: A meta-analysis. *Computers in Human Behavior, 36*, 446–452. DOI: 10.1016/j.chb.2014.04.011

Sönmez, G. (2019). Christchurch terör saldırısı, Brenton Tarrant'ın manifestosu ve terörün yeni yüzü. *Ortadoğu Araştırmaları Merkezi Raporu*. https://orsam.org.tr/christchurch-teror-saldirisi-brenton-tarrantin-manifestosu-ve-terorun-yeni-yuzu.pdf

Sönmez, G. (2023). Sosyal medya okuryazarlığı. In Ergüney, M. (Ed.), *Dijital çağda okuryazarlık*. Nobel Akademik Yayıncılık.

Sönmez, M. F. (2022). *Sosyal kimlik ve sosyal medya (İki benzemezin hikayesi)*. Eğitim Yayınevi.

Sot, İ. (2022). Fostering intimacy on TikTok: A platform that connects during COVID-19 lockdowns. *Media Culture & Society, 44*(8), 1490–1507. DOI: 10.1177/01634437221104709

Soulé, F. (2024). Digital sovereignty in Africa: Moving beyond local data ownership. CIGI Policy Brief No. 185, June 2024. https://www.cigionline.org/static/documents/PB_no.185_eRCHbMI.pdf

Sözcü Gazetesi. [gazetesozcu]. (2019, April 1). *Türkiye bu İstanbul sonuçlarını konuşuyor* [Turkey is talking about these Istanbul results] [Tweet]. X (formerly Twitter). https://x.com/gazetesozcu/status/1112562340376051716

Sözcü. [gazetesozcu]. (2023, September 11). *Avrupa Şampiyonu Filenin Sultanları'na tarifeli, futbol takımına özel uçak* [Scheduled flight for the European Champion Sultans of the Net, special flight for the football team] [Tweet]. X (formerly Twitter). https://x.com/gazetesozcu/status/1700871623765180654

Sözcü. [gazetesozcu]. (2023, September 3). *Filenin Sultanları, Avrupa Şampiyonu! Atatürk'ün kızları tarih yazdı* [Sultans of the Net, European Champion! Atatürk's daughters made history] [Tweet]. X (formerly Twitter). https://x.com/gazetesozcu/status/1698435362241986880

Spivak, G. C. (1988). Can the subaltern speak? In C. Nelson & L. Grossberg (eds.). *Marxism and the Interpretation of Culture*. Macmillan, 24–28.

Sreekanthaswamy, N., Anitha, S., Singh, A., Jayadeva, S. M., Gupta, S., Manjunath, T. C., & Selvakumar, P. (2025). Digital tools and methods. In *Enhancing School Counseling With Technology and Case Studies* (pp. 25–48). IGI Global Scientific Publishing.

Srivastava, K., & Gawarle, N. S. (2024). Breaking the silence: A look into women's mental health in India. *Journal of Family Medicine and Primary Care, 13*(11), 5436–5437. DOI: 10.4103/jfmpc.jfmpc_892_24 PMID: 39722923

Srnec, C., & Guttmann, A. (2024). Platform cooperatives, a model of commons and sustainability. In Warren, J. N., Biggiero, L., Hübner, J., & Ogunyemi, K. (Eds.), *The Routledge Handbook of Cooperative Economics and Management* (pp. 388–397). Routledge.

Srnicek, N. (2017). *Platform capitalism*. John Wiley & Sons.

Srnicek, N. (2017). *Platform Capitalism*. Polity Press.

Staab, P. (2019). *Digitaler Kapitalismus. Markt und Herrschaft in der Ökonomie der Unknappheit*. Suhrkamp.

Stache, L. C., & Zayer, L. T. (2015). Unpacking the #LikeAGirl campaign: Gender stereotypes and empowerment in advertising. *Journal of Advertising Research, 55*(4), 398–409. DOI: 10.2501/JAR-2015-021

Standard, B. (2025, May 29). Digital divide: Rural women 51% less likely to own a mobile phone. Business Standard. https://www.business-standard.com/india-news/digital-india-divide-nso-rural-women-mobile-phone-ownership-gap-125052901804_1.html

Stark, D. (1997). [Review of *The Rise of the Network Society*, by M. Castells]. *Contemporary Sociology, 26*(6), 725–726. DOI: 10.2307/2654643

Statista. (2024). Internet usage among women and men in India. *Statista*. https://r.search.yahoo.com/_ylt=AwrKHGVzb_JoRgIA7y67HAx.;_ylu=Y29sbwNzZzMEcG9zAzEEdnRpZAMEc2VjA3Ny/RV=2/RE=1761928308/RO=10/RU=https%3a%2f%2fwww.statista.com%2ftopics%2f2157%2finternet-usage-in-india%2f/RK=2/RS=AfBhLVYCI_eTnQA_JLYvq7vG33I-

Steinberg, D., & Li, H. (2017). Introduction: Regional platforms. *Asiascape: Digital Asia*, *4*(3), 173–183.

Steinhoff, J. (2024). Toward a political economy of synthetic data: A data-intensive capitalism that is not a surveillance capitalism? *New Media & Society*, *26*(6), 3290–3306.

Strand, C., & Svensson, J. (2023). Towards a situated understanding of vulnerability—An analysis of Ugandan LGBT+ exposure to hate crimes in digital spaces. *Journal of Homosexuality*, *70*(12), 2806–2827. PMID: 35674676

Stray, J., Iyer, R., & Larrauri Prug, H. (2023). The Algorithmic Management of Polarization and Violence on Social Media https://knightcolumbia.org/content/the-algorithmic-management-of-polarization-and-violence-on-social-media

Suler, J. (2004). The online disinhibition effect. *Cyberpsychology & Behavior*, *7*(3), 321–326. DOI: 10.1089/1094931041291295 PMID: 15257832

Sullivan, Y., Nyawa, S., & Wamba, S. F. (2023). Combating loneliness with artificial intelligence: An AI-based emotional support model. In *Proceedings of the 56th Hawaii International Conference on System Sciences* (pp. 4443-4451).

Suri, T., & Jack, W. (2016). The long-run poverty and gender impacts of mobile money. *Science*, *354*(6317), 1288–1292. DOI: 10.1126/science.aah5309

Tashakkori, A., & Teddlie, C. (Eds.). (2010). *SAGE Handbook of Mixed Methods in Social & Behavioral Research* (2nd ed.). SAGE Publications.

Tasos, T. (2024). Social Constructionism: Critical Analysis From A Vygotskian Perspective. *Rethinking Marxism*, *36*(2), 195–223.

Tassinari, A., & Maccarrone, V. (2020). Riders on the storm: Workplace solidarity among gig economy couriers in Italy and the UK. *Work, Employment and Society*, *34*(1), 35–54.

Taylor, S. H., Zhao, P., & Bazarova, N. N. (2021). Social media and close relationships: A puzzle of connection and disconnection. *Current Opinion in Psychology*, *45*, 101292. Advance online publication. DOI: 10.1016/j.copsyc.2021.12.004 PMID: 35016090

Teng, L. S. (2020). Bracing for the Multi-Generational Workforce. *Management Review, 31*(3), 324–345.

Tewksbury, D., & Riles, J. M. (2015). Polarization as a function of citizen predispositions and exposure to news on the Internet. *Journal of Broadcasting & Electronic Media, 59*(3), 381–398.

The Economic Times. (2025, January 16). *India to cross 900 million internet users this year, says IAMAI report.* The Economic Times. https://economictimes.indiatimes.com/tech/technology/india-to-cross-900-million-internet-users-this-year-says-iamai-report/articleshow/117290089.cms

Therborn, G. (1999). *The ideology of power and the power of ideology* (Vol. 24). Verso.

Times of India. (2016, February 22). *Gujarat village bans mobile phone for school girls. The Times of India.* https://timesofindia.indiatimes.com/city/ahmedabad/gujarat-village-bans-mobile-phone-for-school-girls/articleshow/51087691.cms

Times of India. (2023, September 14). Cyber centre launched in Jaipur to help counsel victims of online harassment. *Times of India.* https://timesofindia.indiatimes.com/city/jaipur/cyber-centre-launched-in-city-to-help-counsel-victims-of-fraud-harassment/articleshow/121385533.cms

Timmermans, E., de Caluwé, E., & Alexopoulos, C. (2018). Why are you cheating on Tinder? Exploring users' motives and (dark) personality traits. [Why are you cheating on Tinder? New research by Elisabeth Timmermans and colleagues examines partnered users' motives and ] [dark] [ personality traits | Erasmus School of History, Culture and Communication | Erasmus University Rotterdam.]. *Computers in Human Behavior, 89*, 129–139.

Tınmaz, H., & Fanea-Ivanovici, M. (2024). An exploratory study on Turkish university students' thoughts on LinkedIn in a business context. *Quality - Access to Success, 25*(198), 86–95. DOI: 10.47750/QAS/25.198.09

Tiryaki, S. (2023). Riskler ve olanaklar arasında dijital ebeveynlik: Bibliyometrik bir analiz. *TRT Akademi, 8*(19), 746–765.

Tisdell, E. J., Merriam, S. B., & Stuckey-Peyrot, H. L. (2025). *Qualitative research: A guide to design and implementation.* Jossey-bass.

Törnberg, P. (2023). How platforms govern: Social regulation in digital capitalism. *Big Data & Society, 10*(1). https://doi.org/ (Original work published 2023)DOI: 10.1177/20539517231153808

Tran, G., Kelly, B., Ryan, S. T., Hammersley, M., Kerr, E., Norman, J., & Okely, A. (2025). Development and formative evaluation of website-based tool to support healthy lifestyles in family day care. *Health Promotion Journal of Australia, 36*(1), e947. PMID: 39780470

Treem, J. W., & Leonardi, P. M. (2013). Social media use in organizations: Exploring the affordances of visibility, editability, persistence, and association. *Annals of the International Communication Association*, *36*(1), 143–189.

Tshabangu, T., & Salawu, A. (2022). Alternative media, repression and the crisis state: Towards a political economy of alternative media in post-Mugabe Zimbabwe. *Journal of Asian and African Studies*, *59*(1), 172–186.

Tümmler, M., & Quick, R. (2025). How to detect fraud in an audit: a systematic review of experimental literature. *Management Review Quarterly*, 1-46.

Tungohan, E., & Catungal, J. P. (2022). Virtual qualitative research using transnational feminist queer methodology: The challenges and opportunities of zoom-based research during moments of crisis. *International Journal of Qualitative Methods*, *21*, 16094069221090062.

Turillazzi, A., Taddeo, M., Floridi, L., & Casolari, F. (2023). The digital services act: An analysis of its ethical, legal, and social implications. *Law, Innovation and Technology*, *15*(1), 83–106.

Turing, A. M. (1950). Computing machinery and intelligence. *Mind, a Quarterly Review of Psychology and Philosophy*, LIX(236), 433-460.https://doi.org/DOI: 10.1093/mind/LIX.236.433

Turkle, S. (1997). Life on the screen: Identity in the age of the internet. *Literature & History*, *6*, 117–118.

Turkle, S. (2011). *Alone together: Why we expect more from technology and less from each other*. Basic Books.

Ubale, P. D., & Sekher, T. V. (2023). Risky sexual behaviors among unmarried youth in India: Evidences from National Family Health Survey, 2019–21. In Deb, S., & Deb, S. (Eds.), *Handbook of youth development* (pp. 413–439). Springer., DOI: 10.1007/978-981-99-4969-4_24

Uber statistics, https://www.businessofapps.com/data/uber-statistics/

Udoudom, U., Bassey, B., George, K., & Etifit, S. (2024). Impact of symbolic interactionism, pragmatism and social constructionism on communication and media practice. *International Journal of Humanities, Education, and Social Sciences, 2*(1), 1–25. DOI: 10.58578/ijhess.v2i1.2547

Uma, S. (2023). *Violence, gender and the state: 'Not just' a legal analysis.* Routledge. https://www.taylorfrancis.com/books/mono/10.4324/9781003308959/violence-gender-state-saumya-uma

Ungvarsky, J. (2024) *Routine activity theory.* EBSCO Knowledge Advantage. https://www.ebsco.com/research-starters/law/routine-activity-theory#full-article

Urzi Brancati, M. C., Gonzalez Vazquez, I. and Fernandez Macias, E. (2023). The Rise of Digital Monitoring and Algorithmic Management of Work: Empirical Insights. European Commission, 2023, JRC133407.

Vallas, S., & Schor, J. B. (2020). What do platforms do? Understanding the gig economy. *Annual Review of Sociology, 46*, 273–294. DOI: 10.1146/annurev-soc-121919-054857

Van der Vlist, F. N., & Helmond, A. (2021). How partners mediate platform power: Mapping business and data partnerships in the social media ecosystem. *Big Data & Society, 8*(1), 20539517211025061.

van Deursen, A. J., & van Dijk, J. A. (2014). The digital divide shifts to differences in usage. *New Media & Society, 16*(3), 507–526. DOI: 10.1177/1461444813487959

Van Dijck, J. (2013). *The culture of connectivity: A critical history of social media.* Oxford University Press.

van Dijck, J., & Lin, J. (2022). Deplatformization, platform governance and global geopolitics: Interview with José van Dijck. *Communication and the Public, 7*(2), 59–66. DOI: 10.1177/20570473221102199

Van Dijck, J., Nieborg, D., & Poell, T. (2019). Reframing platform power. *Internet Policy Review, 8*(2), 1–18. DOI: 10.14763/2019.2.1414

Van Dijck, J., & Poell, T. (2013). Understanding social media logic. *Media and Communication, 1*(1), 2–14.

van Dijck, J., Poell, T., & de Waal, M. (2018). *The Platform Society: Public Values in a Connective World.* Oxford University Press.

Van Dijck, J., Poell, T., & De Waal, M. (2018). *The platform society: Public values in a connective world.* Oxford university press., DOI: 10.1093/oso/9780190889760.001.0001

Van Dijck, José, & Poell, T. (2013). Understanding Social Media Logic. *Media and Communication, 1*(1), 2–14. DOI: 10.17645/mac.v1i1.70

Van Dijk, J. A. G. M. (2005). *The deepening divide: Inequality in the information society*. Sage Publications.

Van Dijk, J. A. G. M. (2020). *The digital divide*. Polity Press.

Van Doorn, N. (2017). Platform labor: On the gendered and racialized exploitation of low-income service work in the "on-demand" economy. *Information Communication and Society, 20*(6), 898–914.

Van Gasse, D., Claessens, E., & Mortelmans, D. (2025). Navigating Personal Choice, Socio-cultural Background and Societal Norms in Forming a Singlehood Identity in Belgium: A Consideration of Qualitative Narratives in Relation to Gender and Migration Background. *Tijdschrift voor Genderstudies, 28*(2/3), 171–191.

Varan, D., & Demirel, Ç. (2024). Travmanın dolaylı etkisi: İkincil travmatik stres üzerine bir derleme. *İstanbul Kent Üniversitesi İnsan ve Toplum Bilimleri Dergisi, 5*(2), 71–85.

Vecchione, B., Levy, K., & Barocas, S. (2021, October). Algorithmic auditing and social justice: Lessons from the history of audit studies. In *Proceedings of the 1st ACM Conference on Equity and Access in Algorithms, Mechanisms, and Optimization* (pp. 1-9).

Vlasceanu, M., & Amodio, D. M. (2022). Propagation of societal gender inequality by internet search algorithms. *Proceedings of the National Academy of Sciences of the United States of America, 119*(29), e2204529119.

Vogl, J. (2021). *Kapital und Ressentiment: Eine kurze Theorie der Gegenwart*. C. H. Beck.

Vosoughi, S., Roy, D., & Aral, S. (2018). The spread of true and false news online. *Science, 359*(6380), 1146–1151. DOI: 10.1126/science.aap9559

Walsh, J. P. (2020). Social media and moral panics: Assessing the effects of technological change on societal reaction. *International Journal of Cultural Studies, 23*(6), 840-859. https://doi.org/ (Original work published 2020)DOI: 10.1177/1367877920912257

Walther, J. B. (1992). Interpersonal effects in computer-mediated interaction: A relational perspective. *Communication Research, 19*(1), 52–90. DOI: 10.1177/009365092019001003

Walther, J. B. (1996). Computer-mediated communication: Impersonal, interpersonal, and hyperpersonal interaction. *Communication Research, 23*(1), 3–43. DOI: 10.1177/ 009365096023001001

Walther, J. B. (2022). Social media and online hate. *Current Opinion in Psychology, 46*, 101298. DOI: 10.1016/j.copsyc.2021.12.010 PMID: 35158213

Wang, Y. (2025). Current status and challenges of China's platform economy: A macroeconomic perspective. *Advances in Economics, Management and Political Sciences*. https://doi.org/DOI: 10.54254/2754-1169/2025.BL23703

Wardle, C., & Derakhshan, H. (2017). *Information disorder: Toward an interdisciplinary framework for research and policymaking*. Council of Europe. https://rm.coe.int/information-disorder-report-november-2017/1680764666

Waytz, A., & Epley, N. (2012). Social connection enables dehumanization. *Journal of Experimental Social Psychology, 48*(1), 70–76. DOI: 10.1016/j.jesp.2011.07.012

Waytz, A., Epley, N., & Cacioppo, J. T. (2010). Social cognition unbound: Insights into anthropomorphism and dehumanization. *Current Directions in Psychological Science, 19*, 58–62. DOI: 10.1177/0963721409359302 PMID: 24839358

Weber, M. (1922). Class, status, party. In *From Max Weber: Essays in sociology* (Gerth, H. H., & Wright Mills, C., Eds. & Trans.; pp. 180–195). Oxford University Press.

Weber, M. (1949). *The Methodology of the Social Sciences*. Free Press.

Weber, M. (1978). *Economy and society: An outline of interpretive sociology* (Roth, G., & Wittich, C., Eds., Fischoff, E., Trans.). University of California Press. (Original work published 1922)

Weizenbaum, J. (1972). How does one insult a machine? *Science, 176*, 609–614. PMID: 17778159

Weizenbaum, J. (1976). *Computer power and human reason, from judgment to calculation*. WH. Freeman.

Weizenbaum, J. (1996). ELIZA—A computer program for the study of natural language communication between man and machine. *Communications of the ACM, 9*(1), 36–45. DOI: 10.1145/365153.365168

Wetherell, M. (2012). Affect and emotion: A new social science understanding.

Wettergren, Å., & Hillgren, P. (2013). The emotional politics of viral activism: Greenpeace's KitKat campaign. *Ephemera, 13*(2), 393–413.

Wiegleb, V., & Bruns, A. (2025). Whose knowledge counts? Unpacking the uneven geographies and politics of knowledge co-production in IPBES. *Human Ecology, 53*(1), 73–86.

Wikipedia. Algoritmik radikalizasyon, 2025 https://en.wikipedia.org/wiki/Algorithmic_radicalization

Willekens, M., Siongers, J., & Lievens, J. (2022). Social stratification and social media disengagement: The effect of economic, cultural and social capital on reasons for non-use of social media platforms. *Poetics, 95*, 101708. Advance online publication. DOI: 10.1016/j.poetic.2022.101708

Williams, B. (1993). *Shame and necessity*. University of California Press.

Williamson, J. (1978). *Decoding advertisements: Ideology and meaning in advertising*. Marion Boyars.

Wood, A. J., Graham, M., Lehdonvirta, V., & Hjorth, I. (2019). Good gig, bad gig: Autonomy and algorithmic control in the global gig economy. *Work, Employment and Society, 33*(1), 56–75.

Woodcock, J., & Graham, M. (2020). *The Gig Economy: A Critical Introduction*. Polity Press.

Wright, E. O. (1997). *Class Counts: Comparative Studies in Class Analysis*. Cambridge University Press.

Wright, E., Eriksson, L., & Bond, C. E. W. (2025). Victim blaming, gender, and social media commentary: A randomized vignette study of audience comments on news reports of intimate partner homicide. *Journal of Interpersonal Violence, 40*(5), 8862605251322816. DOI: 10.1177/08862605251322816 PMID: 40018892

Wu, A. X., & Taneja, H. (2021). Platform enclosure of human behavior and its measurement: Using behavioral trace data against platform episteme. *New Media & Society, 23*(9), 2650–2667.

Wu, J. (2024). Social and ethical impact of emotional AI advancement: The rise of pseudo-intimacy relationships and challenges in human interactions. *Frontiers in Psychology, 15*. Advance online publication. DOI: 10.3389/fpsyg.2024.1410462 PMID: 39564589

Wu, Q., Zhang, H., Li, Z., & Liu, K. (2019). Labor Control in the Gig Economy: Evidence from Uber in China. *The Journal of Industrial Relations, 61*(4), 574–596.

Wu, S., & Trottier, D. (2022). Dating apps: A literature review. *Annals of the International Communication Association, 46*(2), 91–115. DOI: 10.1080/23808985.2022.2069046

Xiang, C. (2023). He would still be here: Man dies by suicide after talking with AI chatbot, Widow Says. Retrived from https://www.vice.com/en/article/man-dies-by-suicide-after-talking-with-ai-chatbot-widow-says/

Xie, T., & Pentina, I.& ve Hancock, T. (2023). Friend,mentor, lover: Does chatbot engagement leadtopsychological dependence? *Journal of Service Management, 34*(4), 806–828. DOI: 10.1108/JOSM-02-2022-0072

Xiumei, X., Xiaoxuan, Z., & Hui, W. (2022). Research on the influencing mechanism of data capital on farmers' income. *Mobile Information Systems, 2022*(1), 4683251.

Yener, Ş. (2023). Şiddet, şiddet türleri ve okulda öğretmene yönelen şiddet. *İçtimaiyat, 7*(1), 278–294. https://doi.org/DOI: 10.33709/ictimaiyat.1184117

Yıldırım, O., & Ayan, V. M. (2024). From Twitter to X: Evaluating the change of ownership and platform politics. *İLEF Dergisi, 11*(2). DOI: DOI: 10.24955/ilef.1432738

Yin, F. (2024). Layered Environmental Discourses: Media Representations of Transnational Extractivism in Zimbabwe. *African Journalism Studies*, 1-18.

Yin, R. K. (2014). *Case Study Research: Design and Methods* (5th ed.). Sage.

Yin, R. K. (2017). *Case study research and applications: Design and methods.* Sage publications.

Yin, Y., Jia, N., & Wakslak, C. J. (2024). AI can help people feel heard, but an AI label diminishes this impact. *Proceedings of the National Academy of Sciences of the United States of America, 121*(14), e2319112121. Advance online publication. DOI: 10.1073/pnas.2319112121 PMID: 38551835

Yörük, E., Atsizelti, S., Kına, M. F., & Durusan, F. (2025). A computational analysis of ideological positions in Turkish electoral politics. *The Developing Economies.* Advance online publication. DOI: 10.1111/deve.12424

Young, R. A., & Collin, A. (2004). Introduction: Constructivism and social constructionism in the career field. *Journal of Vocational Behavior, 64*(3), 373–388.

Youth Endowment Fund. (2024, November 25). Violence on social media making teenagers afraid to go out, study finds. *The Guardian.* https://www.theguardian.com/media/2024/nov/25/violence-on-social-media-making-teenagers-afraid-to-go-out-study-finds

Yuan, Z., Cheng, X., & Duan, Y. (2024). Impact of media dependence: How emotional interactions between users and chat robots affect human socialization? Front. Psychol., 16 August 2024 *Sec. Media Psychology*, *15*, 1–14. DOI: 10.3389/fpsyg.2024.1388860 PMID: 39220396

Yumrukuz, Ö. (2017). Şiddete Karşı Duyarsızlaşma ve Sosyal Medya İlişkisi Üzerine Bir İnceleme. *Marmara İletişim Dergisi*, (28), 89–106.

Yun, H. (2025). China's data sovereignty and security: Implications for global digital borders and governance. *Chinese Political Science Review*, *10*(2), 178–203.

Zehnder, E., Dinet, J., & Charpillet, F. (2021). Social virtual agents and loneliness: Impact of virtual agent anthropomorphism on users' feedback. In *Advances in usability, user experience, wearable and assistive technology: Proceedings of the AHFE 2021* (pp. 285-292). Springer International Publishing. https://doi.org/10.1007/978-3-030-80091-8_33

Zeng, J. (2020). Artificial intelligence and China's authoritarian governance. *International Affairs*, *96*(6), 1441–1459. DOI: 10.1093/ia/iiaa172

Zhang, S., Li, W., Li, X., & Liu, B. (2022) Authros: Secure data sharing among robot operating systems based on ethereum. ArXiv. https://doi.org/10.48550/arXiv.2508.09426

Zhang, X. (2024). Intention to Participate in Social Activism Activities in Response to Corporate Social Advocacy: A Third-Person Effect Perspective. *Mass Communication & Society*, *27*(2). Advance online publication. DOI: 10.1080/15205436.2023.2202643

Zhao, L., Zhu, D., Shafik, W., Matinkhah, S. M., Ahmad, Z., Sharif, L., & Craig, A. (2022). Artificial intelligence analysis in cyber domain: A review. In *International Journal of Distributed Sensor Networks* (Vol. 18, Issue 4). https://doi.org/DOI: 10.1177/15501329221084882

Zhao, S., Grasmuck, S., & Martin, J. (2008). Identity construction on Facebook: Digital empowerment in anchored relationships. *Computers in Human Behavior*, *24*(5), 1816–1836.

Zhao, Y. (2024). TikTok and researcher positionality: Considering the methodological and ethical implications of an experimental digital ethnography. *International Journal of Qualitative Methods*, *23*, 16094069231221374.

Zheng, L., Chen, L., Long, F., Liu, J., & Li, L. (2024). Reducing Social Media Attention Inequality in Disasters: The Role of Official Media During Rainstorm Disasters in China. *International Journal of Disaster Risk Science*, *15*(3), 388–403.

Zhu, Y. (2025). Anonymous intimacy in the digital age: Psychological mechanisms, risks, and potential. *Proceedings of the International Conference on Advanced Research in Social Sciences, 2*(1), 11–29. DOI: 10.33422/icarss.v2i1.1056

Žižek, S. (2008). *Violence: Six Sideways Reflections*. Picador.

Zook, M., & Spangler, I. (2023). A crisis of data? Transparency practices and infrastructures of value in data broker platforms. *Annals of the Association of American Geographers, 113*(1), 110–128.

Zou, Y. (2025). How Social Media Self-Presentation Enhances Consumers' Preference for Experiential Consumption. *Journal of Consumer Behaviour, 20*(3), 238.

Zuboff, S. (2019). *The age of surveillance capitalism: The fight for a human future at the new frontier of power*. PublicAffairs.

Zuboff, S. (2019). *The Age of Surveillance Capitalism: The fight for a Human Future at the New Frontier of Power*. PublicAffairs.

Zuboff, S. (2019). *The Age of Surveillance Capitalism: The Fight for a Human Future at the New Frontier of Power*. PublicAffairs.

Zumstein, D.,& Hundertmark, S. (2017). Chatbots an interactive technology for personalized communication, transactions, and services. *IADIS International Journal on WWW/Internet*, 15(1), 96-109.

# About the Contributors

**Nuriye Çelik** is an Associate Professor in the Department of Sociology at Sinop University, Türkiye. She earned her Ph.D. in Sociology from Selçuk University, with a focus on political communication and media studies. Her research integrates political sociology, digital society, and media governance with critical theory. Dr. Çelik has authored and co-authored several articles on digital public spheres, social media regulation, algorithmic bias, and digital activism. She is married and the mother of one child. Some of her recent scholarly publications include: Çelik, N. (2020). The Produced Gender Perception through the Political Ideologies in Turkey: A Review on the Twitter Posts. Mediterranean Journal of Humanities, 10, 117-130. Çelik, N. (2023). The Digital Inequalities in the Digital Society. In Z. Karacağil (Ed.), Current Debates on Social Sciences 13, Bilgin Kültür Sanat Yayınları. Çelik, N. (2023). I Am Online; Therefore, I Am! Digital Obesity From a Sociological Perspective. In R. S. Nazlı & G. Sarı (Eds.), Perspectives on Society and Technology Addiction, IGI Global.

**Nadir Ateşoğlu** received his undergraduate degree from the Department of Public Administration at Dumlupınar University and his master's degree from the Department of Business Administration at the Institute of Social Sciences, Maltepe University. He later completed his PhD in the Department of Sociology at the Faculty of Arts and Sciences, Maltepe University. His academic interests include political sociology, educational sociology, and digital sociology. He is currently working as an Assistant Professor in the Department of Sociology at the Faculty of Arts and Sciences, Sinop University.

**Şerife Sena Güner** is a Ph.D. candidate in the Department of Sociology at Ondokuz Mayıs University and a research assistant in the Department of Applied Sociology at Sinop University, Türkiye. Her research interests lie at the intersection of migration sociology, gender studies, political sociology, and the digital society. She has contributed to the field through various academic outputs, including a peer-reviewed article, a book chapter, and two international conference presentations. In 2024, she co-authored an article titled "Intersectional Activism: Dutch-Turkish Muslim Women 'Talking Back' to Securitization and Islamophobia" with Tahir Abbas, published in Ethnic and Racial Studies. Additionally, she collaborated with Nuriye Çelik on a book chapter titled "'Ahh Belinda' Filminin 2023 ve 1986 Yılı Versiyonları Üzerinden Sinemada Kadının Temsiline İlişkin Eleştirel Bir Değerlendirme", included in the edited volume Cumhuriyetimizin 100. Yılında Kadın Çalışmaları.

***

**Ferihan Ayaz** is working for Gaziantep University as an assistant proffessor. She gives some lessons on media studies and journalism.

**Özge Ercebe** is an Assistant Professor in the Department of Public Relations and Advertising at Trakya University, Turkey. She received her Ph.D. in Political Science from Ankara University, where her dissertation focused on the structural transformation and authoritarian evolution of Turkey's media system. Her research interests include media systems, political communication, social media literacy, and digital platformization. She has published articles and book chapters on media transformation, journalism, and critical media literacy. Currently, her work examines the structural transformation of media in Turkey within the context of authoritarianism and platformization.

**S. Ida Evangeline**, presently working as an Assistant Professor in the Department of Electrical and Electronics Engineering at the Government College of Engineering, Tirunelveli, Tamilnadu, India. She obtained her Bachelor's in Electrical and Electronics Engineering from Manonmaniam Sundaranar University in 2003, and Master's in Power Systems Engineering from Anna University, Chennai, Tamilnadu, India in 2005. She completed her PhD degree in 2023 at Anna University, Chennai, Tamilnadu, India. She has published six research papers in international journals. Her current research interests include optimal power flow, renewable energy, soft computing, machine learning, and deep learning.

**Jangirala Srinivas** graduated in Bachelor of Science in 2003 from Kakatiya University, India, the Master of Science degree from Kakatiya University in 2008, the Master of Technology degree from IIT Kharagpur in 2011, and then his PhD degree from the Department of Mathematics, IIT Kharagpur in 2017. He is an associate at present professor with the Jindal Global Business School, O. P. Jindal Global University, Haryana 131001, India. He was also a research assistant before this with the Center for Security, Theory and Algorithmic Research, International Institute of Information Technology (IIIT), Hyderabad, India. His research areas are Blockchain Technology and Applications, information security, cryptocurrency, IoT. He has authored 65 papers in international journals and conferences in his research areas.

**Shaji Joseph** did his graduation and postgraduation in Sociology from Pune University (SPPU) and PhD in Management from Symbiosis International University in 2020. Currently, he is an associate professor at Symbiosis International Deemed University Pune. His area of expertise is in sustainability standards and reporting, Human resources management, and corporate governance and ethics. His research interests include sustainable development, ethical leadership, leadership assessment, and human resources management. Dr Shaji Joseph can be reached at shaji@scit.edu

**Benu Kesar** is a consultant. She did her Master's in Business Administration (MBA) from NMIMS Mumbai and is pursuing her PhD from Symbiosis International (Deemed University), Pune, India. Dr. Kesar's research interests lie at the intersection of technology, communication, and societal impact, focusing on how digital platforms are reshaping human interaction and influencing organizational strategies. Dr. Benu Kesar can be reached at drbenukesar@gmail.com

**Dev Kesar** is an Analyst at a Finance firm, where he contributes to data-driven financial strategies and technology solutions. He holds a B.Tech in Computer Science and Engineering from VIT, Chennai,India. His interests lie at the intersection of finance, analytics, and emerging technologies. Dev Kesar can be reached at devkesar4210@gmail.com.

**Fandi Omeish** received his PhD from a top-ranked university in the world (Peking University) and Master's degree in international marketing strategies from Hasselt University in Belgium. His research focuses on Tourism Marketing and Digital Marketing. Before joining PSUT, he was Marketing and Public Relations director for the American University of Madaba and a Marketing Lecturer, providing the stepping stones of marketing for students. Moreover, he has practical experience in international Advertising agency.

**Gabriella Punziano**, PhD in Sociology and Social Research is Associate Professor in Sociology and Methodology, Department of Social Sciences, University of Naples Federico II. Her research interests include: the methodology of social research, the new analytical frontiers and the challenges introduced by new data, mixed and integrated and digital perspectives; social policies and welfare regimes in relation to social inclusion, territorial cohesion and community integration; the analysis of public, institutional and political communication phenomena through innovative content analysis techniques; risk communication analysis on social and digital platforms; socioeconomic effects, individual behavior, risk governance, communication of science, and the role of expertise in the Covid-19 era.

**Priyanka Puri**, Presently working as Assistant Professor, Laws at University School of Law, Rayat Bahra Professional University, Hoshiarpur India. Have vested interest in Legal research Methodology. Has authored Books and numerous Research Papers in reputed National and International Journals.

**Wasswa Shafik** (Member, IEEE) received a Bachelor of Science degree in information technology from Ndejje University, Uganda, a Master of Engineering degree in Information Technology (Computer and Communication Networks) from Yazd University, Iran, and a PhD in Computer Science with the School of Digital Science, Universiti Brunei Darussalam, Brunei Darussalam. He is also the Founder and Research Director of the Dig Connectivity Research Laboratory (DCRLab) after serving as a Research Associate at the Network Interconnectivity Research Laboratory at Yazd University. Prior to this, he worked as a Community Data Analyst at Population Services International (PSI-Uganda), a Community Data Officer at the Programme for Accessible Health Communication (PACE-Uganda), a Research Assistant at the Socio-Economic Data Centre (SEDC-Uganda), Uganda, an Assistant Data Officer at TechnoServe, Kampala, Uganda, and Asmaah Charity Organization as Cheif Executive Officer. He has hundreds of publications with renowned publishers. His research interests include Artificial Intelligence, Neural Networks, Computer Vision, Smart Agriculture, Digital Health, and Green Computing.

**Shikha Vasishta** is a Doctoral Research Scholar in Political Science at Bennett University, India, and an alumna of the University of Delhi. Her research interrogates reproductive rights through the lenses of feminist legal theory, critical human rights discourse, and postcolonial political thought. With a focus on the Global South, her work examines the governance of reproductive autonomy at the intersection of law, culture, biopolitics, and technology. She has authored over fourteen peer-reviewed publications and presented at prestigious academic forums including SOAS–University of London, Keio University, and the University of Hawai'i. Her scholarship advances an interdisciplinary, justice-oriented framework that seeks to bridge theory and praxis, centering the lived experiences of structurally marginalised communities.

**Showkat Wani** has good publications in SAGE, IGI Global and other reputed journals like Springer. He has completed many research targets, including four PhD Research Scholars and eight P.G. Dissertations who had already completed their research and were awarded. Dr. Wani has so far written 30 Research articles and attended 48 Conferences. Dr. Wani has also edited one book.

**Janardan Krishna Yadav** is an Associate professor (marketing) at Jindal Global Business School. He also served as a visiting assistant professor at NIT Calicut. He received a university gold medal for his Master's in Tourism Administration (MTA) and was awarded a UGCJRF award in Tourism Administration & Management. He is a fellow of IIM-Kozhikode with a specialization in marketing.

**Gülüzar Yasin** graduated from Gaziantep University's Faculty of Communication, Department of Journalism. She is a graduate student at the Department of Communication and Social Transformation, Institute of Social Sciences at the same university.

# Index

## F



## G



## H



## I



## K



## L



## M



## N



## O

## P



## R



## S

## T



## U



## V



## Y